CONTENTS

Preface   ix

About the Contributors   xii

Part 1   PAUL F. LAZARSFELD: WORK-STYLE AND THOUGHT-STYLE

   1. **PFL: Hedgehog or Fox?**   3
     Marie Jahoda

   2. **The Vienna Years**   10
     Hans Zeisel

   3. **Recollections of PFL**   16
     Bernard Bailyn

   4. **Remembering Paul Lazarsfeld**   19
     Robert K. Merton

   5. **Organizational Innovation for Social Science Research and Training**   23
     Charles Y. Glock

   6. **The Evolution of a Thesis: Utilization of Social Research as a Sociological Problem**   37
     Ann K. Pasanella

Part 2   QUANTITATIVE METHODS AND REASONING

   7. **Generating Models as a Research Strategy**   51
     Raymond Boudon

v

8. **The Meaning of Causal Ordering** 65
Herbert A. Simon

9. **Panels and Time Series Analysis: Markov Chains and Autoregressive Processes** 82
T.W. Anderson

10. **Purposive Actors and Mutual Effects** 98
James S. Coleman

11. **The Analysis of Qualitative Variables Using More Parsimonious Quasi-Independence Models, Scaling Models, and Latent Structures** 119
Leo A. Goodman

12. **The Choice Axiom After Twenty Years** 138
R. Duncan Luce

13. **Social Exchange and Choice** 158
Anthony Oberschall

14. **Vignette Analysis: Uncovering the Normative Structure of Complex Judgments** 176
Peter H. Rossi

Part 3 QUALITATIVE METHODS AND REASONING

15. **Marx's General and Middle-Range Theories of Social Conflict** 189
Lee Benson

16. **Ethical and Practical Dilemmas of Fieldwork in Academic Settings: A Personal Memoir** 210
David Riesman

17. **On Following in Someone's Footsteps: Two Examples of Lazarsfeldian Methodology** 232
Hanan C. Selvin

18. **Disposition Concepts in Behavioral Science** 245
Morris Rosenberg

Part 4 SUBSTANTIVE SOCIAL RESEARCH

19. **Immigration, Citizenship, and Social Change: Intention and Outcome in American History** 263
Sigmund Diamond

20. **The Effects of Unemployment: A Neglected Problem in Modern Social Research** 282
Herbert H. Hyman

QUALITATIVE
AND
QUANTITATIVE
SOCIAL
RESEARCH

QUALITATIVE
AND
QUANTITATIVE
SOCIAL
RESEARCH

Papers in Honor of
Paul F. Lazarsfeld

Edited by

Robert K. Merton
James S. Coleman
Peter H. Rossi

THE FREE PRESS
A Division of Macmillan Publishing Co., Inc.
NEW YORK

Collier Macmillan Publishers
LONDON

The Free Press
A Division of Macmillan Publishing Co., Inc.
866 Third Avenue, New York, N.Y. 10022

Collier Macmillan Canada, Ltd.

Library of Congress Catalog Card Number: 78-24752

Printed in the United States of America

printing number
    2 3 4 5 6 7 8 9 10

Library of Congress Cataloging in Publication Data
Main entry under title:

Qualitative and quantitative social research.

    Includes bibliographies and indexes.
    1. Sociology--Methodology--Addresses, essays,
lectures. 2. Lazarsfeld, Paul Felix.
3. Lazarsfeld, Paul Felix--Bibliography.
I. Lazarsfeld, Paul Felix. II. Merton, Robert
King,   III. Coleman, James Samuel,
        IV. Rossi, Peter Henry,
HM24.Q34   301'.01'8   78-24752
ISBN 0-02-920930-7

21. **With What Effect? The Lessons from International Communications Research**   299
    Elihu Katz

22. **The Changing Social Origins of American Academics**   319
    Seymour Martin Lipset and Everett C. Ladd, Jr.

23. **The Professional and Academic Context of Professional Schools**   339
    Peter M. Blau, Rebecca Z. Margulies, and John B. Cullen

BIBLIOGRAPHY

  The Writings of Paul F. Lazarsfeld: A Topical Bibliography   365
    Paul M. Neurath

  Publications about Paul F. Lazarsfeld: A Selected Bibliography   389
    David L. Sills

Index of Names   397

Index of Subjects   404

PREFACE

This volume was originally planned as a gift to Paul Lazarsfeld to be presented at an appropriate ceremonial occasion on or about his seventy-fifth birthday. For reasons all too familiar to those who have held similar good intentions, our timetable slipped. We then hoped to find some appropriate time during the next year, falsely secure in the misguided, though to those who knew him, understandable conviction that Paul Lazarsfeld was indestructible and that this gift could be offered at any time.

Paul Lazarsfeld's death in the fall of 1976 clearly showed how foolish we were to believe that we could amble along without concern. His death brought an end to a long and distinguished career, one that started in the old world of Vienna and ended in the new world of New York. His more than five decades of work span the period in which are found the roots of contemporary empirical social science. That empirical social research is a well-accepted field of scholarship, that applied social research is increasingly drawn upon by the public and private sectors, and that social science knowledge has come as far as it has are all developments to which Paul Lazarsfeld made strong contributions throughout his career.

Paul Lazarsfeld was both social scientist and teacher. His scholarly contributions have helped to shape the present form of social science. His intellectual presence has helped to shape the careers of many: students, colleagues, and others.

Nothing can begin to compensate for Paul Lazarsfeld's not having lived on to enjoy the celebration that would have attended the publication of this volume. We were able, however, to show him the table of contents and the list of authors while he was in the hospital a few days before the end. Despite the distress of his illness, it was clear that he was extremely pleased to learn that this volume was in the making. Especially, he was delighted to know that many of his colleagues and former students had tendered pieces of their work in his honor. It is some small solace for our heavy sorrow over Paul's not having seen this volume in its completed form that at the least he knew of its coming existence.

To assemble a memorial volume in honor of Paul Lazarsfeld was a difficult task. The principal difficulty lay in narrowing the list of contributors: his decades of scholarly work and teaching had touched so many social scientists and so profoundly affected the development of social science that this volume could easily have been several times larger. The contributors to this volume are only a small subset of all those who would have participated in this enterprise. They share one attribute in common: they are among those persons whose personal and professional lives were deeply affected by Paul Lazarsfeld.

The organization of the volume hinges on what we believe to be major themes in Paul Lazarsfeld's contributions to social science. The first section, devoted to his work-style and thought-style, celebrates his special qualities as a social scientist at work. His was not the style of the lone scholar; on the contrary, as his many co-authored works attest, he was happiest as initiator and organizer of collaborative inquiries. His charismatic presence inspired colleagues and students wherever he was. Organized social research throughout the world owes much to his having pioneered the establishing of university-based organizations for social research in the form of the Columbia University Bureau of Applied Social Research and its predecessors. The many replicas of these research organizations in this country and abroad testify further to his foresight and influence. Of the several essays providing a miscellany of recollections on such matters, three—the ones by Hans Zeisel, Bernard Bailyn, and Robert Merton—were part of a memorial service held at Columbia University.

Paul Lazarsfeld's contributions were of diverse styles and in diverse substantive domains, but, quite evidently, his most consequential work in the social sciences is methodological. Here his contributions have been many and deep. He laid out principles of sample survey analysis that still guide researchers in unraveling sample survey data. Panel design and analysis still bear the signs of his pioneering work. His models of latent structure analysis helped provide significantly new approaches to scaling procedures. These are among the methodological contributions honored in the second section of this volume.

A less widely recognized part of Paul Lazarsfeld's contributions has been to the qualitative side of social science scholarship. From the beginning, one of his deepest interests was directed to the complicated task of interweaving qualitative and quantitative analysis. Another interest lay in tracing the long history of methods of social science inquiry. This qualitative aspect of his work is celebrated in the third section of this volume.

Paul Lazarsfeld made many major contributions to our substantive understanding of contemporary society. His early work on the human consequences of unemployment and on the workings and consequences of the mass media, his pioneering studies of voting behavior, and his unprecedented study of the impact of McCarthyism on American academic life are just a few examples of these substantive contributions. The essays in the fourth section of this volume all have connections to this portion of his work.

A measure of the extraordinary scale, breadth, and depth of Paul Lazarsfeld's life work is represented by the virtually complete topical bibliography of that work prepared by Paul Neurath which appears in the final section of this volume. We all knew that he had been a prolific scientist and scholar, but not even his closest collaborators were aware of the actual extent of his contributions until this bibliography was painstakingly assembled. Instructively complementing the abundant bibliography of Paul Lazarsfeld's own writings is a compact, briefly annotated bibliography of writings about him and his work prepared by David L. Sills.

The main themes pursued by the essays in this volume reflect only a portion of Paul Lazarsfeld's contributions to social science. Other themes have had to be passed over for want of space. None of the contributions, for example, provides a portrait of Paul Lazarsfeld as teacher or as guide and consultant to other researchers and public agencies. Several substantive domains are also neglected, for example, the considerable influence of his work on research in political behavior. Paul Lazarsfeld's life was too large to fit into so small a volume.

The preparation of this volume plainly owes much to many persons. We thank Patricia Kendall Lazarsfeld for wise counsel throughout the effort; Charles E. Smith, of The Free Press, for his unflagging commitment to the idea of the book from its very beginning; Mary Wilson Miles, Thomas F. Gieryn, and Jay Schechter for monitoring the passage of the manuscript into print; many would-be contributors for their forbearance in recognizing the preclusive constraints of limited space; and, of course, the students, colleagues, and friends of Paul F. Lazarsfeld whose papers compose this book.

R. K. M.
J. S. C.
P. H. R.

ABOUT THE CONTRIBUTORS

Theodore W. Anderson was born in Minneapolis, Minnesota in 1918. After receiving the B.S. from Northwestern University and the Ph.D. in mathematics from Princeton University, he worked as a Research Associate of the Cowles Commission for Research in Economics at the University of Chicago. From 1946 to 1967, he taught mathematical statistics at Columbia University and has since served as Professor of Statistics and Economics at Stanford University. He is a member of the National Academy of Sciences and the American Academy of Arts and Sciences. His publications include *An Introduction to Multivariate Statistical Analysis* (1958) and *The Statistical Analysis of Time Series* (1971).

Bernard Bailyn, born in Hartford, Connecticut in 1922, is Winthrop Professor of History at Harvard University where he received the M.A. (1947) and the Ph.D. (1953), after studying at Williams College. He is a member of the American Philosophical Society and the Royal Historical Society and was Trevelyan Lecturer in Cambridge University (1971). His books include *Massachusetts Shipping 1697–1714* (with Lotte Lazarsfeld Bailyn, 1959), *The Ideological Origins of the American Revolution* (1967) for which he received the Pulitzer and Bancroft Prizes, and *The Ordeal of Thomas Hutchinson* (1974), awarded the National Book Award in History the following year.

Lee Benson is Professor of Historical Social Sciences at the University of Pennsylvania, having previously taught at Wayne State University. Born in New York City, he studied at Brooklyn College and went on for the M.A. at Columbia University (1948) and the Ph.D. in History at Cornell University (1952). He returned to Columbia to work with Paul Lazarsfeld at the Bureau of Applied Social Research for almost a decade. He has been a Fellow at the Center for Advanced Study in the Behavioral Sciences and President of the Social Science

History Association (1975-77). He is the author of *Concepts of Jacksonian Democracy* (1961) and *Towards the Scientific Study of History* (1972).

Peter M. Blau, Quetelet Professor of Sociology at Columbia University, was born in Vienna (1918), received the B.A. from Elmhurst College (1942) and the Ph.D. in Sociology from Columbia University (1952) where he studied with Paul Lazarsfeld. He has taught at Wayne State University, Cornell University, the University of Chicago, and was Pitt Professor at the University of Cambridge before returning to Columbia. He has been a Fellow at the Center for Advanced Study in the Behavioral Sciences and served as President of the American Sociological Association and Editor of the *American Journal of Sociology*. His books include *The Dynamics of Bureaucracy* (1955) and *Inequality and Heterogeneity: A Primitive Theory of Social Structure* (1977).

Raymond Boudon, born 1934, studied at the École Normale Supérieure, the Sorbonne, and Columbia University with Paul Lazarsfeld. He has taught at the University of Bordeaux and the Sorbonne (Université Paris V), and was also a visiting Professor at Harvard University. His books include *Education, Opportunity and Social Inequality* (1974) and *Effets pervers et ordre social* (1977).

James S. Coleman, born in Bedford, Indiana (1926), received the B.S. from Purdue University (1949) and the Ph.D. from Columbia University (1955), where he was a research associate of the Bureau of Applied Social Research. He served as the first chairman of the Department of Social Relations at The Johns Hopkins University and is now Professor of Sociology at the University of Chicago. He is a member of the National Academy of Sciences and the American Philosophical Society. His books include *Introduction to Mathematical Sociology* (1964) and the *Mathematics of Collective Action* (1973).

Sigmund Diamond was born in Baltimore, Maryland (1920). He received the B.A. from The Johns Hopkins University (1940) and the Ph.D. in History from Harvard University (1953). He worked for the Office of Facts and Figures and the Board of Economic Warfare and as International Representative of the UAW-CIO. Since 1955, he has been teaching at Columbia University where he is now Giddings Professor of Sociology and Professor of History. He is the author of *The Reputation of the American Businessman* (1955) and *The Nation Transformed: The Creation of an Industrial Society in the United States* (1963). He has been a Fellow at the Center for Advanced Study in the Behavioral Sciences, Senior Research Fellow at the Newberry Library, Fulbright Lecturer at Tel-Aviv University, and Lecturer at the Institute for Higher Studies and Social Research in Vienna.

Charles Y. Glock was born in New York City and holds the B.S. from New York University, the M.B.A. from Boston University, and the Ph.D. in Sociology from Columbia University, 1952. He has been president of the American Association for Public Opinion Research and the Society for the Scientific Study of Religion and vice-president of the American Sociological Association. He is senior editor of the recently published *The New Religious Consciousness* (1976) and co-author of *Anti-Semitism in America* (1979).

Leo A. Goodman has been the Charles L. Hutchinson Distinguished Service Professor of Statistics and Sociology at the University of Chicago since 1970. Born in New York City (1938), he received the B.A. from Syracuse University (1948) and the Ph.D. in Mathematics and Mathematical Statistics from Princeton University (1950). He is a member of the National Academy of Sciences, the American Academy of Arts and Sciences, and the American Philosophical Society and has held Guggenheim and National Science Foundation fellowships. In 1974, he received the Stouffer Award from the American Sociological Association for outstanding advances in social science methodology. His books include *Analyzing Qualitative/Categorical Data: Log-Linear Models and Latent-Structure Analysis* (1978) and *New Methods for the Analysis of Cross-Classification Tables: Goodman's Models* published by the Hungarian Academy of Sciences.

Herbert H. Hyman, born in New York City (1918), received the B.A. (1939) and Ph.D. (1942) degrees from Columbia University. Professor of Sociology at Columbia until 1969, he is now Crowell University Professor at Wesleyan University. He has been a visiting professor at the universities of California, Ankara, Catania, Oslo and Turin. A fellow of the American Academy of Arts and Sciences, he received Guggenheim and Fulbright awards and the Woodward Award of the American Association for Public Opinion Research. His books include *Political Socialization* (1959) and *Secondary Analysis of Sample Surveys* (1972).

Marie Jahoda is Senior Research Consultant, Science Policy Unit at the University of Sussex. Born in Vienna in 1907, she received the D.Phil. from the University of Vienna in 1932 and has since taught in the Department of Social Psychology at New York University, Brunel University and the University of Sussex. Her publications include *Die Arbeitslosen von Marienthal* (1933) which she wrote with Paul Lazarsfeld and Hans Zeisel, and *Freud and the Dilemmas of Psychology* (1977).

Elihu Katz is Professor of Sociology and Communication at the Hebrew University of Jerusalem and at the Annenberg School of Communication, University of Southern California. Born in New York City in 1926, he holds three Columbia degrees. He was founding director of Israel Television and first winner of *in medias res*, the international prize for communication research. He worked with Paul Lazarsfeld at the Bureau of Applied Social Research and taught at the University of Chicago. He is co-author of *The Secularization of Leisure* (with Michael Gurevitch, 1976) and *Broadcasting in the Third World* (with George Wedell *et al.*, 1977).

Everett C. Ladd, Jr. was born in Saco, Maine and received the B.A. from Bates College and the Ph.D. from Cornell University. He is presently Professor of Political Science and Director of the Social Science Data Center at the University of Connecticut, as well as Co-Executive Director of The Roper Center. Professor Ladd has held Guggenheim, Rockefeller and Ford Fellowships. Among his books are *Ideology and America: Change and Response in a City, Suburb, and a Small Town* (1969) and *Transformations of the American Party System* (1975).

Seymour Martin Lipset, born in New York City (1922), received the B.A. from The City College of New York (1943) and the Ph.D. in Sociology from Columbia (1949). He has taught at Columbia, Berkeley, and Harvard and is now at Stanford University where he is Professor of Political Science and Sociology and Senior Fellow at the Hoover Institution. Recipient of the Gunnar Myrdal Prize (1970) and the Townsend Harris Medal (1971), he is a member of the National Academy of Sciences and of the American Academy of Arts and Sciences where he has served as Vice-President. Among his publications are *Political Man* (1960) and *The First New Nation* (1963).

R. Duncan Luce was born in Scranton, Pennsylvania (1925). He received the B.S. in Aeronautical Engineering (1945) and the Ph.D. in Mathematics (1950) from the Massachusetts Institute of Technology. He taught mathematical statistics and sociology at Columbia University, was a Benjamin Franklin Professor at the University of Pennsylvania, visiting Professor at the Institute for Advanced Study, and is now Alfred North Whitehead Professor of Psychology at Harvard University. He received the Distinguished Scientific Award of the American Psychological Association and is a member of the National Academy of Sciences and the American Academy of Arts and Sciences. His books include *Games and Decisions* (with H. Raiffa, 1957), *Individual Choice Behavior* (1959) and *Foundations of Measurement* (with D. H. Krantz, P. Suppes, and A. Tversky, 1971).

Robert K. Merton, University Professor Emeritus and Special Service Professor at Columbia University, worked closely with Paul Lazarsfeld for a third of a century both in the Department of Sociology and the Bureau of Applied Social Research at Columbia. Born in Philadelphia (1910), he received the B.A. from Temple University (1931) and the Ph.D. from Harvard University (1936). He is a member of the National Academy of Sciences and a Foreign Member of the Royal Swedish Academy of Sciences. His books include *Social Theory and Social Structure* (1949) and *The Sociology of Science* (1973).

Paul Neurath is Professor of Sociology at Queens College, CUNY, having previously taught at The City College of New York. Born in Vienna in 1911, he received the Dr. Jur. from the University of Vienna in 1937 and the Ph.D. in Sociology from Columbia University (1951). He was a Fulbright Professor at the Tata Institute of Social Sciences, Bombay in 1955-57, the University of Cologne in 1959-60, and the University of Vienna, 1978-79, where he has been an Honorar Professor since 1973. He is author of *Radio Farm Forum in India* (1960); *Statistik für Sozialwissenschaftler* (1966); and "Models of the World's Problems and Problems with the World Models" in *Problems of Growth in a Finite World* (1979).

Anthony Oberschall, born in Budapest in 1936, was educated at Harvard College and at Columbia University where he studied with Paul Lazarsfeld and received the Ph.D. in 1962. He has taught at the University of California, Los Angeles, and at Yale University and is now Professor of Sociology at Vanderbilt University. He has been a Guggenheim fellow and also a visiting professor in Uganda, Zambia and Zaire. His books include *Empirical Social Research in Germany* (1965), *Social Conflict and Social Movements* (1973) and the forthcoming *African Businessmen and Social Change in Zambia* (with Andrew Beveridge).

Ann Pasanella was born in Baltimore, Maryland and received her undergraduate degree from Vassar (1951), and the M.A. (1954) and the Ph.D. (1974) from Columbia University. She worked for several years with Paul F. Lazarsfeld at the Bureau of Applied Social Research and served as Co-Director of the project on the utilization of social science. She is co-editor (with Paul Lazarsfeld and Morris Rosenberg) of *Continuities in the Language of Social Research* (1972) and co-author (with Paul Lazarsfeld and Jeffrey Reitz) of *An Introduction to Applied Sociology* (1975). She is at present a Research Associate at the Center for the Social Sciences, Columbia University.

David Riesman, born in Philadelphia, is Henry Ford II Professor of Social Sciences at Harvard University. A graduate of Harvard College and Harvard Law School, he served as Law Clerk to Justice Brandeis and taught law at the University of Buffalo and the social sciences at the University of Chicago. He received the American Academy of Arts and Letters Award and holds honorary degrees from the University of California at Berkeley and the University of Pennsylvania. Among his books are *The Lonely Crowd* (with Nathan Glazer and Reuel Denney, 1950) and *The Perpetual Dream: Reform and Experiment in the American College* (with Gerald Grant, 1978).

Morris Rosenberg, who studied and worked with Paul Lazarsfeld, is a native New Yorker, receiving the B.A. from Brooklyn College (1946) and the Ph.D. from Columbia University (1953). He has taught at Columbia University, Cornell University, Stanford University, the London School of Economics, the State University of New York at Buffalo, and is now on the faculty at the University of Maryland. He co-edited (with Paul Lazarsfeld) *The Language of Social Research* (1955) and (with Paul F. Lazarsfeld and Ann K. Pasanella) *Continuities in the Language of Social Research* (1972). His book, *The Logic of Survey Analysis* (1968) has a Foreword by his mentor, Paul Lazarsfeld.

Peter H. Rossi was born in New York City and attended The City College of New York. He received the Ph.D. from Columbia University where he was Paul Lazarsfeld's student and sometime research assistant. Rossi has been on the faculties of Harvard, Chicago, and Johns Hopkins, and is currently Professor of Sociology at the University of Massachusetts/Amherst. His recent publications include *Reforming Public Welfare* (with Katherine Lyall, 1976) and *Prison Reform and State Elites* (with Richard A. Berk, 1977). He is currently President of the American Sociological Association.

Hanan C. Selvin, born in New York City in 1921, attended Columbia University where he received the B.A. (1942) and the Ph.D. in Sociology (1956). He has taught at the University of California, Berkeley and the University of Rochester. Since 1967, he has been Professor of Sociology at the State University of New York at Stony Brook. He served as Chairman of the Section on Methodology of the American Sociological Association and was co-winner of the C. Wright Mills Award of the Society for the Study of Social Problems. He is the author of *The Effects of Leadership* (1960) and *Delinquency Research* (with Travis Hirschi, 1967).

David L. Sills, born in New York City in 1920, received the B.A. from Dartmouth College, the M.A. from Yale University, and the Ph.D. from Columbia University. After service in the 87th Mountain Infantry Regiment as a private and in the Occupation of Japan as a sociologist, he was associated with Paul Lazarsfeld first as a student and then as a colleague at the Bureau of Applied Social Research, from 1951 until 1962. He was a Fellow at the Center for Advanced Study in the Behavioral Sciences in 1967-68, and is the editor of the *International Encyclopedia of the Social Sciences* (1968). Since 1973, he has been Executive Associate at the Social Science Research Council in New York City.

Herbert A. Simon, born in 1916 in Milwaukee, Wisconsin, is Professor of Computer Science and Psychology at Carnegie-Mellon University, where he has taught since 1949. Educated at the University of Chicago (B.A., 1936; Ph.D., 1943), he is a member of the National Academy of Sciences and has received awards for distinguished research from the American Psychological Association, the Association for Computing Machinery, and the American Economic Association. In 1978, he was awarded the Alfred Nobel Memorial Prize in Economic Science. His books include *Administrative Behavior* (1945) and (with Allen Newell) *Human Problem Solving* (1972).

Hans Zeisel was born in Kaaden, Czechoslovakia and grew up in Vienna. After receiving doctorates in law and political science, he became a member of the bar. In 1938, he emigrated to the United States and embarked on a career in market research. In 1953, he joined the faculty of the University of Chicago Law

School where his principal concern has been to explore the usefulness of social science research for the law. The major yield of those years was *The American Jury* (1971) written jointly with his late friend and colleague, Harry Kalven, Jr. He is a co-author of *Die Arbeitslosen von Marienthal* (1933) and the author of *Say It With Figures* (1947), two books that grew out of his lifelong association with Paul Lazarsfeld. He is a Fellow of the American Statistical Association.

PART 1

PAUL F. LAZARSFELD:
WORK-STYLE
AND THOUGHT-STYLE

1. PFL: HEDGEHOG OR FOX?

Marie Jahoda

Isaiah Berlin's essay on Tolstoy is based on a fragmented poetic text from antiquity: the fox knows many things, but the hedgehog knows one big thing. He explains that Goethe, for example, was a fox; Dante, a hedgehog. Berlin then proceeds to diagnose Tolstoy as a fox who believed, however, that it was more respectable to be a hedgehog.[1]

PFL's contribution to the social sciences reveals a different pattern. By talents and interest he too was a fox, remained so throughout his life and never denied the respectability of being a fox. But historical accidents forced him to masquerade as a hedgehog. Being a fox at heart and acting as if he were a hedgehog enabled him to make a lasting contribution to the essential foxiness of the social sciences, taken collectively. They, as well as he, however, have paid a price for remaining true to their nature.

Berlin found it necessary to name names in order to prevent facile value judgements. So it may be appropriate to point out here that there are remarkable individual foxes as well as hedgehogs in the human sciences. Among the contributors to this volume, David Riesman as much as James Coleman qualify for foxiness *par excellence*. It is not accidental that no true hedgehogs are included, but they do exist elsewhere. C. Wright Mills was apparently one, and Piaget is perhaps the extreme living example. Freud too was a hedgehog, even though superficial judgement often misclassifies him in this respect. For the criterion for being a fox or a hedgehog is simply this: devoting one's work to the elucidation of many topics or concentrating on one. It has nothing to do with preferring one method to another. As the examples show, quantification appeals to some foxes more than to others. Hedgehogs emerge with one theory or one point of view; foxes help us to understand the variety of the world in which we live.

The evidence for my interpretation of PFL's contribution stems first of all from statements he himself has made about the nature of his work, even though

3

I shall not necessarily take them all at their face value and shall insert an occasional *"hier irrt Goethe."* Next there are available evaluations by other social scientists of his work; I shall select one which is in disagreement with my interpretation as a strong test for it. As a result it should be possible to see PFL's contribution in a somewhat different perspective. In this reappraisal I shall risk a few general remarks about the current state of affairs in the social sciences.

Nowhere does PFL's foxiness appear clearer than in what he described as his life-long "terminological embarrassment"[2] about what to call himself. The exigencies of life forced different labels on him at different stages of his career. In the days of *Marienthal* the term social psychologist seemed appropriate. It had the great advantage of referring to a then relatively undefined field and it fitted well into PFL's position at the Bühlers' Institute of Psychology at the University of Vienna. In addition, this somewhat casual identification with a discipline permitted him to formulate one of his engaging aperçus, forerunners of the later "matrix formula," from which he as much as everybody else derived such intellectual pleasure: an approaching revolution, he said, requires, above all, economists; a successful revolution, engineers; and a lost revolution, social psychologists.

In the preface to the second German edition of *Marienthal*—the first is now virtually unavailable as a result of the bookburnings episode in 1933—PFL found the label social psychology no longer to his liking. While he now defined the subject there as "the quantitative study of mass phenomena," he thought that such a definition made *Marienthal* de facto into a sociological contribution: "We were sociologists in the modern sense, but we regarded ourselves as social psychologists." In the meantime he had, of course, become Professor of Sociology at Columbia. But he wriggled under the new label too. In part this must have been due to his close contact, collaboration and friendship with some of his colleagues in the Sociology department, Robert Lynd and, particularly, Robert Merton. Their intellectual tradition was different from his. Vienna University in his student days did not even have a department of sociology. He reported in the Memoir that on entering the university he vacillated between taking a doctorate either in a combination of economics and political theory or in applied mathematics, and regarded his doctorate in the latter subject as "almost accidental." This typically foxy comment is in line with his typically foxy lifestyle in those days. He was a leader in the Austrian socialist youth movement; he devoted a large part of his time to education through voluntary lectures as well as through the organization of summer camps for deprived children; he was deeply involved in active politics and discussions of its theoretical underpinnings; and he organized an interdisciplinary seminar of the leading intellectual Young Turks of Vienna, in which, among others, Rudolf Carnap, Heinz Hartmann and Erich Voegelin participated.

In the Memoir he traced the roots of his research style to three factors: an ideological component in his identification with Austro-Marxism; an intellectual component through the influence of Karl and Charlotte Bühler who encouraged him to acquire a deeper grounding in psychology than he later credited himself with; and the "personal" equation which in his description remains admirably impersonal and consists simply of a few additional intellectual experiences. When he applied these influences to a discussion of his early work from the perspective of 1968, however, the tone changed. By tacit implication the large variety of intellectual concerns, each of which he took fully seriously in its own right, then appear as if they had been nothing but youthful hobbies, forgotten by an enforced hedgehog perspective which appears to center on methodology for its own sake, whatever the topic under discussion. *Hier irrt Goethe. Marienthal* was not just a methodological exercise, demonstrating that "one should have objective observations as well as introspective accounts" (the latter surely a psychological, not a sociological, way of collecting data), that "case studies should be . . . combined with statistical information," that historical data should be consulted and material obtained by specific questioning as much as by what has now come to be termed unobtrusive methods. True, all this is exemplified in *Marienthal*, however naive its quantification. But the interest that book aroused at the time of its first publication was not due to these innovating ideas about how to tackle a problem methodologically, but rather because it showed how a major social problem could be illuminated by social science in a manner that was beyond the power of the public debate over unemployment that raged at the time. The public debate produced arguments for two incompatible outcomes of large-scale unemployment: it would create a revolutionary atmosphere or it would create public apathy. *Marienthal* produced an answer: apathy.

The questions asked in *Marienthal* permitted PFL, as it becomes a fox, to hit several birds with one stone—an activity which he proudly continued ever since—by combining his knowledge of social, political and economic factors with his interest in research methods and his emerging professional identity as psychologist, social psychologist or sociologist. The point I wish to emphasize is that it was the content of the study as much as the methods which preoccupied him while he directed the team of investigators. The team itself drew on several disciplines; while it contained not a single sociologist, there were students of law, economics, political science, psychology and medical doctors. Virtually all of them had experienced PFL's leadership style in the youth movement and shared his social and political concerns. In that atmosphere, any formality of organization with tight budget control or strict division of labor was an unnecessary as it was unimaginable. Social research under PFL's influence became a vocation in Max Weber's sense, not an occupation. And indeed, social science as a vocation was perhaps the most significant continuity in PFL's work-style.

Marienthal is the best remembered but certainly not the only research contribution of these early days. *Jugend und Beruf,* quite different in its methodological approach, and the help PFL gave Charlotte Bühler in the development of her baby tests through his statistical expertise and by observing his baby daughter through his long time-samples are two other examples which bear testimony to his foxiness.

To keep so many irons in the fire—and to keep them hot—was, of course, to a large extent a function of the quality of PFL's mind. But not entirely. His Vienna research style was possible only because his varied interests in many areas were matched by his knowledge of the Vienna intellectual culture. It was diversified, yet concentrated and small in size, and he was thoroughly at home in it.

The transfer to the United States did not, I propose, change the character of his interests. But, as one knows from his Memoir, it took some time before he could acquire an orientation to the new culture, so different not only in the size of the intellectual community but in many other respects as well. Those with whom he began to work had by and large the professional identification of hedgehogs. Their discipline, whether it was psychology or sociology, mattered to them in a manner PFL had never experienced. In that respect, and not only by nationality, he was again a foreigner. The *Marienthal* research style could simply not be reproduced by a foreigner in a new environment; and it never was.

The only way he could become part of the American social science scene while remaining true to his own foxiness of knowledge and interests was to shape a part of this culture to suit himself. This he proceeded to do with the result that he became regarded by some who underrated his foxy substantive contributions as a methodological hedgehog.

This is not to suggest, of course, that his work history, or anybody else's for that matter, was shaped by conscious rational decisions. Historical accidents, opportunities taken and opportunities missed, influence the course of events. Only after a considerable stretch of time and perhaps only for an outside observer does a quasi-rational pattern emerge. Forced by cultural pressures to declare a special interest but eager to master the new culture in its ramifications including political behavior, the mass media and the power of advertising as he had mastered Vienna, PFL masqueraded as a hedgehog only to indulge his unaltered substantive interests with impunity. Thus his contribution has enriched many fields, not just methodology.

To regard PFL as a fox is in sharp contrast to Raymond Boudon's persuasive essay on Lazarsfeld's work.[3] Boudon's interpretation essentially classifies PFL strictly as a hedgehog. Even though he does not, of course, mention such an animal, he attributes to PFL all its essential qualities: the obsession with a strictly limited number of themes and a concern with the fundamental unity of the social sciences through the creation of a language common to all of them. There is evidence, in this long, appreciative and powerful essay, that Boudon shares Tolstoy's prejudice in favor of the hedgehog position and that he wants to set the record straight against criticism of PFL's work, such as those by C. Wright Mills, as blind empiricism.

One can share Boudon's appreciation, agree with his defence, and yet doubt his overall thesis, not just in biographical detail but with regard to the meaning of PFL's fundamental contribution to the development of the social sciences.

Boudon is right, of course, in pointing out that to regard PFL "merely" as a methodologist implies a two-fold underestimate of his contribution: first, there is nothing "mere" about methodology; second, such a description ignores several significant aspects of his work, for example his studies in the history of the social sciences, his work on decision making and action, as well as the content of the interpretations he has offered in many of his studies. Further, the achievement of a matrix formula (in PFL's colloquial language this was called a "story-line" or even a "theory" which he was usually able to produce on confronting a body of empirical data) requires a leap of imagination from the data to a meaningful context which is certainly outside the scope of a "mere" methodologist. But such leaps are not a gift of God; they are the result of prolonged and serious involvement with the phenomena of the social world viewed from a variety of conceptual perspectives; they are not the result of an obsession with a single one.

Boudon might not agree. His major emphasis is on what he regards as PFL's obsession with the unity of the social sciences, "*toujours désirée et jamais atteinte.*" It is this phrase which epitomizes the difference in Boudon's and my own view of PFL's work. I doubt that this unity is *toujours désirée*; I am not convinced that it is desirable or achievable at this state of the social sciences and I believe that if PFL had indeed had this overwhelming obsession, his contribution to the social sciences would not have been as great as it is. Nothing in his work suggests that he regarded what he was doing as the only language of the social sciences. On the contrary. Not only did he take the existence of separate conceptual languages in the various social science disciplines for granted, but he actually used them himself. To take an example from his recent book (with Jeffrey G. Reitz), *An Introduction to Applied Sociology,* he stated as a matter of course that students wishing to become policy scientists must take courses in specific disciplines, such as economics or political science or cognitive psychology. The same book provides examples of interdisciplinary research which is in essence the application of several conceptual languages, each with its appropriate range of convenience, to one and the same problem. Economists, for example, analyze the market situation, while social psychologists assess the attitudes of housewives in one study; and a political scientist studies the institutional aspects of some local social service departments, while opinion surveys gauge the complaints and satisfactions of the population in the neighborhood. However much a social phenomenon is illuminated by such a multiple perspective, the concepts and the intellectual traditions of each single discipline cannot be expressed in one common language, not even that of PFL, unless it were taken on so basic a level that it must encompass all rational discourse, including the natural sciences, literary criticism, and even reasonably intelligent conversation. Such a broad interpretation diminishes his specific contribution and seems to me not to be in the best interest of the development of the various social sciences.

For the intellectual traditions incorporated in the specific conceptual languages of each discipline are, of course, not arbitrary. They represent approaches to the acquisition of substantive knowledge by raising discipline-specific questions, consistently looking at the phenomena of the social world from a specific point of view. This consistency in question-asking permits them to invent concepts corresponding to observed regularities and to link these concepts to each other in theories. In the nineteenth century, these were largely grand theories of man and society; in the twentieth century, they have more often been theories on an intermediate level; but independent of their scope, each has made a substantive contribution because it gave access to the world from a specific point of view. Thus it was possible for Durkheim to assert that suicide was the province of sociological, not psychological, thought, despite appearances to the contrary. The reward for his consistently sociological approach was a theory which could help to explain other regularities so conceptualized. By the same token, his theoretical language cannot accommodate what psychology knows about the dynamics of depression or the meaning of unsuccessful suicide attempts. Each approach to the understanding of suicide can benefit from PFL's work, but not to the extent of unification of explanations.

Now it might be possible at this point to arrive at a compromise with Boudon's interpretation of PFL's contribution by assuming that *some degree* of unity of the social sciences is achieved by demonstrating that they can at least partially use the same language. For strategic reasons one must discard this pleasant possibility; it might encourage confusion for the sake of unity, while greater clarity can be obtained by recognizing diversity.

There are of course several efforts to combine at least two social science disciplines into a single field; the very names of psycho-history or social psychology testify to such efforts. Both have produced some fascinating studies as well as less remarkable ones. But to the extent that they arrive at explanations or use theories, neither of them has managed to go beyond the conceptual language of a single discipline. Erikson's analysis of Luther or Ghandi is pure psychology, applied to persons who happen to have played a major role in history. In no sense does Erikson "explain" the Reformation or Indian independence. Much the same is true for social psychology. A relatively short time after it became solidly established in the U.S.A., one of its leading figures, Newcomb, suggested that two types of social psychology be recognized: a sociological and a psychological one. Even though both of these strands have profited from PFL's contribution, they cannot be unified by a common explanatory language. What exists today under the label of social psychological theory—balance theory or attribution theory, for example—are simply psychological conceptions. This does not belittle the achievements in these fields; neither does the fact that PFL's language fails to arrive at a conceptual unity of the social sciences speak against him. The major price he had to pay for having nevertheless done something of importance for each discipline is that his name is not attached to any particular increase in substantive knowledge about the social world. There is no Lazarsfeld theory, at least none with a capital T.

But probably more than any other of his contemporaries he enriched various social science disciplines by codifying some of their formal properties and by developing to a high level of rigor procedures which several of them can use. Even though I am not able to follow the mathematics of latent structure analysis I take its elegance on credit, as it were, judging by the power and clarity of exposition of what is within my scope, such as "the art of asking why" or panel or secondary survey analysis. This formal language does not lead to theories, but whatever theories are available in single disciplines lend themselves to sharper testing and better formulation when they use the tool so made available to them. It is in essence a language suitable for accurate description of the social phenomena under study and it has become accepted widely because of PFL's foxiness. Psychologists, sociologists, anthropologists and political scientists could talk with him on the same level because he understood their conceptual problems, and saw the potentialities as well as the limits of his own ability to advance their knowledge of their subject in their special language.

Looking at the current state of the social sciences from my inevitably limited perspective of a psychological social psychologist, I find that the price PFL had to pay for being able to make his contribution was quite modest; indeed, I sometimes wonder whether it is a price at all or whether he perhaps foxily managed to get the best conceivable bargain. The social sciences, overimpressed by Big Brother, have perhaps tried all too hastily to skip the stage of accurate description and analysis for the sake of premature theorizing with the result that few, if any, theoretical formulations are currently available that help us toward adequate understanding, let alone prediction. The big fox, as much as we lesser foxes, can admire without envy the intellectual struggles that accompany the efforts to construct theories while remaining convinced that the theories, if and when they come, will have to use our work as a testing ground.

Notes

1. Isaiah Berlin, *The Hedgehog and the Fox: An essay on Tolstoy's view of history.* London: Weidenfeld & Nicolson, 1953.
2. Paul F. Lazarsfeld, "An Episode in the History of Social Research: A Memoir," in Donald Fleming and Bernard Bailyn, eds., *Perspectives in American History,* II, 1968, 270–337, at 281.
3. Raymond Boudon, "A propos d'un livre imaginaire," Preface to Paul F. Lazarsfeld, *Philosophie des Sciences Sociales.* Paris: Gallimard, 1970.
4. Paul F. Lazarsfeld and Jeffrey G. Reitz, with the collaboration of Ann K. Pasanella, *An Introduction to Applied Sociology.* New York: Elsevier, 1975.

2. THE VIENNA YEARS

Hans Zeisel

I saw Paul Lazarsfeld the first time in the spring of 1919, at an open-air meeting of the socialist students in Vienna at which he spoke. I do not recall what he said, I probably never heard him then because I stood too far away, but I see him clearly before me, bent forward, the cupped hand slightly raised as he would always speak when he tried to persuade.

The war, and with it the Austrian monarchy, had come to an end, but the best of its cultural heritage survived for a time. The performing arts flowered; Vienna had seven repertory theaters; the Duse came from Italy; and from Moscow came Stanislavsky, Meierhold, and Tairoff. We were surrounded by music; the opera, which Gustav Mahler had brought to new heights, was under the direction of such giants as Weingartner, Bruno Walter, and Richard Strauss. We would sing in the choral works or, as Paul did, play an instrument, the viola. Paul also had a more intimate contact with music—the regular chamber music evenings at the Jahodas.

The important intellectual and moral influences during those years between the two world wars came from several directions: there was the depth psychology, Freud and Adler; the Vienna Circle of philosophers; our becoming acquainted with empirical social research in England and the United States; then the important arrival in Vienna of Karl and Charlotte Bühler whom the University had invited to head its Psychological Institute.

Yet, the most important influence came from our close ties to a political movement that was both messianic and enormously practical, the Austrian socialist party of those years. In Paul's case this meant also the very personal influence of the physicist Friedrich Adler, the socialist antiwar hero of the day, who was largely responsible for Paul's early interest in mathematics.

There is no need here to say much about the influence of psychoanalysis

Presented at the Columbia University Memorial Service.
10

and individual psychology, which ruptured the traditional confines of psychology. We knew Alfred Adler well, although he probably knew us better. Before he turned to curing souls, he was a pediatrician; Paul and I had been his patients.

Freud remained for us, for Vienna generally, an outsider, almost a mystical figure, although on my way to school I passed his home in the Berggasse almost every day. But we all knew one or the other of Freud's disciples. Moreover, everything psychoanalysis had to say became available in print, partly in Freud's own books, partly in the *Zeitschrift für Psychoanalyse*, and partly in *Imago*, the journal dedicated to the border areas among psychoanalysis, the social sciences, and the humanities and, therefore, of particular interest to scholars working in these neighboring fields.

Two insights of depth psychology were of particular importance for our endeavors: awareness of the limits of rational actions and of the new, until then unknown, motives of human behavior.

One should mention here also Konrad Lorenz, who in those years in Altenberg on the Danube, a few miles upstream from Vienna, studied the motivations of animal behavior in its natural habitat. He too began his academic career as an assistant at the Bühler Institute.

Of the Vienna Circle of Philosophers, little is left today in Vienna. It was a memorable group of men: Schlick, Wittgenstein, Gödel, Waismann, Feigl, the socialist Otto Neurath. But in those days Carnap was the great event. His introductory lecture into philosophy was an unforgettable intellectual adventure. Students from all over the university were packing his lecture hall, having their first encounter with critical analytical philosophy that did not claim to know what is true, good, or beautiful but limited itself to the modest analysis of what was meant by statements in science, aesthetics, and ethics.

In the confines of our own endeavors, it was again the analysis of motivations and causes, the separation of what Carnap called protocol sentences (spoken or observed behavior), and their interpretation which helped us in our thinking. We found the logical analysis of language that emerged from the Vienna Circle to touch on important points Karl Bühler's psychological analysis of language.

Then there were the books from England and the United States. We read with ardor Booth's *Survey of London* and the Lynds' *Middletown*, but primarily we studied one of the first good texts of applied statistics which at that time began to appear. I might add that in those years empirical, quantitative research was at its infancy in the German-Austrian orbit; sociology was in the main still an armchair science.

Later on, while working on *Marienthal* when we studied the development of empirical social research more carefully, we were to discover that its roots were laid not only in England and America but eminently also in continental Europe, in Belgium, France, Italy, and Germany. But in those years, in the 1920s, it was primarily the American and English studies that were important to us.

On the time scale, the Bühlers were the last of the determining influences on Paul's Vienna life, but in many ways they were the most important one. The intellectual inheritance that they brought to the Institute was twofold. There was Karl Bühler's *Denkpsychologie,* his psychology of language, and the particular role he assigned to introspection in the exploration of psychological processes. And there was Charlotte Bühler's interest in the empirical study of child behavior and her theory of the developmental phases of human life and generally of early childhood.

The practical help that the Bühlers gave was decisive. It permitted Paul and his colleagues to do important scientific work as assistants at the Institute. Those were the years in which Paul wrote his first two books: the *Statistisches Praktikum für Psychologen* and *Youth and Occupation,* a study of the motivations that guided occupational choice.

Later on, the Bühlers gave crucial help in the forming of the Oesterreichische Wirtschaftspsychologische *Forschungsstelle,* which was to become the organizational center of our work. Karl Bühler became its first president.

But of all the influences on our lives one was paramount—that of the socialist party of that day. For a brief moment in history, the humanist ideals of democratic socialism attained reality in the city of Vienna and gave new dignity and pride to the working class and the intellectuals who had won it. Eventually that movement drowned in the fascist sea. Yet, while it lasted it was, in the words of Karl Polanyi, one of the high points of western civilization.

It was a political movement, moreover, that allowed us to take part, and take part Paul did. His field of operation were the *Mittelschuler* he knew so well from having been one himself for eight years and then from having taught them mathematics for some more years.

He formed the *Verein Sozialistischer Mittelschüler,* founded its monthly newspaper, organized summer camps and winter retreats during the Christmas holidays. From that lively movement emerged a new type of political cabaret which played a small role in the development of both the political and theater history of Vienna. At its first performance Paul appeared in a self-written take-off of the monologue in Offenbach's *Beautiful Helène.* Victor Gruen, who would become a distinguished American architect, was the master of ceremonies.

For all these institutions Paul provided vitality through his unique ability to invent new organizational forms and to give them reality. The memories of these years are vivid and crowded: skiing peacefully with Paul in the Alps in the afternoon sun; conversations that tried to clarify everything from personal affairs to the future of mankind; the winter recesses, with music, and poetry readings, and evening lectures by distinguished visitors. One of them, Otto Neurath, we remembered with particular fondness; a giant of a man in more than one sense, the last *polihistor* I knew. He was a member of the Vienna Circle of philosophers, but his main interest was the study of society and how to make it better. I first encountered him when I read his lectures to the Dresden workers in 1918 where he outlined how socialism could reform their lives. The concreteness and the practicality of his ideas overwhelmed me in those days. Neurath began as a physicist, his doctoral thesis was in optics, but he soon began to range widely over economics, sociology, philosophy. Out of this wide diversity developed one of his most important thoughts, the extension of cost-benefit analysis beyond the institutions of the marketplace to include the social costs and benefits, not necessarily translatable into prices. He also pioneered the idea of social indicators.

Eventually he husbanded his encyclopaedic knowledge in a theory of the unity of science. Much impressed by the idea, we formed a debating club which appropriately had as its co-presidents, Rudolf Carnap and Oskar Morgenstern. We liked the idea because it encouraged us in our efforts to disregard in our work the medieval borderlines between the academic disciplines.

Not all of Paul's socialist endeavors ended well. At one point he thought that we socialist students, especially the psychologists such as he and some of his colleagues, could help in the education of difficult children. I do not recall the exact arrangement he had made, but I remember that one afternoon we went out to one of the outlying districts and finally reached the place where these difficult youngsters resided. We had no problem finding them because they received us with a hail of stones which they mercilessly threw at us until we got the message and decided to go home.

Through an unexpected turn of events, our immersion in the socialist movement was to lead to the most important piece of work of those years. The Austrian trade unions had just rid themselves of the ten-hour working day. Stimulated by American studies, Paul thought that we should explore how the workers were using their newly won leisure time. At that time we had the privilege of occasionally talking over our plans with Otto Bauer, the scholarly, ascetic leader of the socialist party. When Paul told him of his plan, Bauer reacted angrily: What a mockery to study leisure-time activity in a country that suffered from a chronic unemployment rate of around ten percent. *That,* he said, was the leisure time to study, the social and psychological effects of lasting unemployment. And that is exactly what we did—in Marienthal.

Marienthal, however, came late in the life of the Forschungsstelle, that improbable institution that was to become the grandmother of all the later bureaus of social research, whatever their name. It came to life in 1925 and sustained itself mainly on ideas, all of them more or less Paul's, on the unabated enthusiasm of its members, and on no money worth talking about. All its studies were brilliant, late, and cost more money than we could bill our client. Salaries were paid from what was left over. The only thing we ever paid for on time was the coffee our researchers needed when they worked on their reports in a lonely corner of a coffeehouse.

The Forschungsstelle, incidentally, was also an early manifestation of Women's Lib: the great majority of its members were women, all bright, some beautiful, and all wonderfully alive.

To sell market research in those days was about as easy as selling a bicycle to somebody who had never before heard of such an allegedly practical contraption.

After the first studies were finished, life became easier. We could show that our market research not only cost money but actually brought some to our trusting clients. The ice broke when one prominent Vienna industrialist wrote to us stating that, as a result of our study, sales of the investigated product had increased by 27 percent. After a while we could point to a respectable list of products we had studied: butter and lard, coffee, milk, beer, vinegar, coat hangers, soup, malt, shoes, laundries, rayon, wool, and, last but not least, radio listening, probably the first European study of its kind and, in retrospect, an important antecedent.

Problems were tentatively solved as they arose, and thus new analytical tools became available for the next study that had not been available before. More complex problems were systematically explored, often in the form of doctoral dissertations under Paul's direction at the Psychological Institute.

All the Vienna studies were pioneer work, and they showed the distinction both by the freshness of their approach and by their defects, which were considerable by today's standards. But in those studies first appeared many of the things that later became important: First lessons in a theory of interviewing to trace specific actions rather than to inquire about general attitudes; an early insight into the limits of conscious behavior and hence the need for what today we call motivation research; supplementing questions with observations and encouragement to the respondent to range freely over motives and details, the significance of which may become clear only later, at the time of analysis; the first fourfold tables; the first talk about spurious correlations; the increased attention to quantitative methods without allowing the qualitative nuances to be lost; the first elements of a theory of action; and lastly the title of *Say It With Figures,* which was to become the expanded codification of what we had learned from Paul in the Forschungsstelle.

Working there was an investment of very long range. But that is exactly what turned out to be important. In the end, as my sister Ilse said the other day, it is to the Forschungsstelle and to Paul that we owe our existence if not more.

Paul's Vienna years were thus a curious mixture of action and contemplation. But there was never any doubt that the one was only the means toward the other. At the core of Paul's endeavors was the enormous desire to understand human motivation, to understand how individual relationships are built and destroyed, and how social structures, both present and past, grow, change, and disappear.

The other day I came across a diagram full of lines and dots and a few names which Paul had drawn once on some coffeehouse table, to make himself and me understand the complicated relationships between the Psychological Institute and the Forschungsstelle. I think it was this catholic desire to understand human relations that made him, not only a great scientist, but also such a very interesting person.

Vienna and the Forschungsstelle was the first of Paul Lazarsfeld's lives, one full of promise that he would fulfill beyond expectation in his second, his American life.

Let me close with a poem by Rilke, Paul's and our favorite poet of those years. The poem, "Autumn Day," is in its simplicity a direct descendant from Goethe, the fount of all German poetry. The translation is by Max Knight:

> LORD: Time has come. The summer was sublime.
> Upon the sun dial cast your shadow now,
> And on the meadows loose the winds. It's time.
>
> Bid latest fruits their ultimate design,
> Allow them two more days of southern sun,
> Urge them to be fulfilled at last, and run
> The final sweetness in the heavy wine.
>
> Who has no house now, he will build no more.
> Who is alone now, will be long alone,
> Will waken, read, write letters which are long,
> And walk on tree-lined pathways, back and forth,
> Unquiet, restless, when the leaves are blown.

3.   RECOLLECTIONS OF PFL

Bernard Bailyn

A visit by Paul was like some wonderfully benign hurricane. There would be premonitory squalls for days in advance. Special delivery letters would begin to arrive long before he got there; telegrams and messages would pile up, occasionally an embarrassed assistant would appear on the doorstep having got the wrong day relayed through secretaries in two universities. The day before he was due there would be a flurry of frantic, often hilarious telephone calls rescheduling the flight, but then finally he would arrive. The cab would pull up in the driveway and Paul would struggle from the door clutching a briefcase overflowing with manuscripts, books, pipes, cigars, shirts, and some miscellaneous shoes. He would half run to the house in his odd, stiff-kneed, sideways-swinging walk; call gaily to his daughter; shake hands with the male members of the family with a slight European bow, heels together; and almost invariably, as soon as he was inside the door, say, "The most *amazing* thing happened!," and out would come an extraordinary episode, told with barely suppressed laughter and high suspense—some bizarre coincidence—and the visit would be properly launched.

He loved coincidences—the strange unlikeliness of the world amused him—and because his range of experience, his knowledge, and his personal contacts were so wide, because his sense of humor was so marvelously alive and his perceptions so keen, odd coincidences happened to him all the time, and he relished telling about them.

He was a wonderful talker, intense, clever, endlessly anecdotal. But it was his sheer energy that mainly transformed our household when he visited. The intensity level simply soared. Often he arrived at the end of one of his favorite hegiras: from New York to Vienna, to keep an eye on the Ford Center there (and incidentally to enjoy once again the Edwardian elegance of the Ambassador Hotel, 500 yards from his family's old apartment in the Seilergasse); from

Presented at the Columbia University Memorial Service.

Vienna to Paris, for talks with Stoetzel, Boudon, and assorted UNESCO officials (but really to talk French, which he did with abandon—I think it was his favorite activity—and simply to be in Paris). From Paris he would have flown to Pittsburgh for two or three seminars and several conferences; then to New York to catch up on the Bureau, the Department, and several assistants; and then, finally would have come the shuttle to Boston. All this stimulated his energy rather than drained it. Five hours after his arrival—after several games of chess with one grandson, some intense conversation about music with another, a lively dinner, and some preliminary gossip—he would settle down for an evening of talk.

This was the calm eye of the storm. He would talk fascinatingly about what he had been doing since the last trip and about anything else that occurred to him; but it was no one-sided affair. "What's been happening," he would ask. One would mumble a few sentences. "No, *NO!*" he would say: "*Tell! Tell!*" And one *would* tell, at length, to the most sympathetic and intelligent listener on earth. On and on the conversation would go—with jokes, stories, plans— until he would begin to grow tired. Then he would sip drinks to keep going. He did not care much what he drank—fine French wines were the same to him as that fearful *Grappa* that ate through the varnish of our table tops—they all had alcohol, and that served to hold back fatigue. Finally, at one o'clock or so, *we* would get tired, and so, reluctantly, he would go off to bed, with his usual haul for night reading—a new manuscript or some notes of his daughter's; two or three historical journals, the more esoteric the better; a biography or memoir of some kind; and, for the ultimate moment, a good detective story.

He usually woke early and immediately attacked the newspapers. He read a newspaper as a terrier shakes a rag doll to pieces. He would tear through page after page muttering to himself, finally would land on something, and declare, "I don't understand a vord—*nossing*!" "What's the problem," one would ask innocently. "Have you read this?" "Yes." "Well, it makes no sense . . . ," and out would come some absolutely inexplicable anomaly that one had missed completely, some sheer logical or factual nonsense that he had spotted and that defied explanation.

To a son-in-law, Paul was a blessing, with his practical ideas, his devotion to his children, and his excellent, often sardonic, advice. ("The problem," he told me when I began teaching, "is not whether you can give a *good* lecture, but how many *bad* ones you can survive.") But he posed some strange problems too. For some reason that I have never understood, Paul became convinced that the Columbia University Library was an empty shell. He believed there were books in his own library, in the Bureau's library, in the Widener Library at Harvard, and in the Baker Library at Dartmouth, but not in the Butler Library. So he would phone me from New York to please get him a few books from Widener on a subject he was working on and mail them to him, quickly. He swore he would return them, and most often he did, though I do not know how he kept this lending library straight.

The Dartmouth Library was his favorite, and his summers in Hanover were, I think, some of the best times of his life. He was utterly relaxed there, ransacking the Baker Library, reading voluminously, and working hard surrounded by friends and family. To this elemental urbanite, any backyard in Hanover was a wonderful garden, and he knew how to enjoy a garden. Dressed in shorts and some splendid Hawaiian shirt, chewing innumerable cigars and pipes, sipping yet another variation of a Viennese *Gespritzter* (Burgundy and quinine water, half and half, was his favorite in Hanover), he would pace back and forth among the flower beds or sit in a lounge chair, with books, proofs, and manuscripts strewn on all sides, scribbling notes and awaiting the next in the succession of visitors who flowed through those houses.

In these summer evenings he talked most freely—about the far-distant world of Vienna, about his early days in America, about his belief that he always was and always would be an immigrant, and even, on one occasion, about the whole pattern of his current work—the range and intricate interinvolvements of all his projects. It was fabulous—like a wiring diagram: infinitely complex, utterly rational and coherent, conceptually elegant and parsimonious. The sheer protean creativity of this great man came out to me most vividly then, and along with it a sense of his superb and innocent egotism. Once, on one of those summer evenings, I found a reference to a famous Austrian unknown to me, let us say Franz Altmann, and I asked Paul if he knew who he was. "What do you *mean*, do I know who he was? Franz Altmann? Now how can you ask me a question like that? Franzl and I went to *Gymnasium* together; we were together in the Socialist youth movement; we worked together in the *Forschungsstelle*; we used to walk together along the Traunsee . . ." and so on and so on—and I never found out who Franzl was.

I'm sorry if I fail to be appropriately solemn in saying these few words about one of the great shapers of twentieth-century social science. He meant more to me, as he did to all his friends and associates, than history could possibly record, and I cannot bear to be serious. He was the most genuine human being I ever met, the most intelligent, in many ways the wisest (though not always in personal relations), and he profoundly enriched my life and the lives of all those who came within the range of his extraordinary personality. I do not want to contemplate directly the personal meaning of his loss, and I do not have his wit to do so indirectly. So let me end simply by saying that I hope there is a heaven—Paul would know how to enjoy it. I can picture him in some sunny garden, surrounded by manuscripts of infinite learning and wisdom, sipping some unbelievable variation of a Viennese *Gespritzter*, and explaining to his latest student, a somewhat bewildered and not-very-bright Angel Gabriel, the proper tactic to use in approaching the Director for an ultimate grant that would launch a universe of brilliant studies. "*Look!*," he is saying with growing impatience, "Don't be silly; there are really only the *following* four points to make:"

4.   REMEMBERING PAUL LAZARSFELD

Robert K. Merton

Paul's death is too recent, the shock and hurt still too intense, for us to accept his actually being gone, or to face its full significance. Yet in this company it will not do simply to celebrate Paul Lazarsfeld's manysided accomplishments as one of the most innovative social scientists of our time, the founder or chief architect of a half-dozen fields of social, psychological, and political inquiry. Nor will it do to rehearse the numerous, impressive, and yet altogether inadequate honors bestowed upon him over the years. The intent, rather, is to share our memories of him. And so, I shall try to tell a little—in these few moments, a very little—of what Paul meant to me, these past thirty-five years, as colleague, friend, collaborator, teacher and, I realize now, as brother. (Our University seems to foster complex, lifelong partnerships: witness only Lionel Trilling and Jacques Barzun in the humanities, and Dickinson Richards and André Cournand in the sciences.)

Since Paul was full of years when he died, it may seem strange that his friends—including the youngest amongst us cannot quite take in the fact of his death. We cannot, I suppose, because each of us came to think of Paul as someone who would just go on and on—that he would still be there, hard at work on some self-set, demanding mission, long after we ourselves had ceased to be. I, *surely*, felt this would be so. And with ample reason. For, almost to the very end, I could see Paul being his same vital, vibrant, probing and imaginative self, intent on harnessing his undiminished energies to one or another common purpose. It would wear me out merely to *observe* Paul, during the five years after his alleged semi-retirement into Emeritus rank—to observe him commuting, once or twice a week, between Fayerweather Hall, where Columbia colleagues and students alike remained beneficiaries of his great gifts, and the University of Pittsburgh where, as Distinguished Professor of Sociology, he was still engaged in shaping new generations of students, all the while pursuing his program of research.

Presented at the Columbia University Memorial Service.

Students often came to work with Paul Lazarsfeld because he was regarded the world over as the shining light in the methodology of social science. No doubt the formidable tag of "methodologist" applies, given Paul's prodigious appetite for finding out how one goes about finding out. That tag, and perhaps his having been a founder of mathematical sociology, led some to conclude that he was wholly given over to quantitative studies. Nothing, of course, could be farther from the mark. Throughout his work life, Paul took it as his "moral duty" to demonstrate the value and, in the social sciences, the frequent necessity of combining quantitative inquiry with qualitative insight. More than once, as he confronted overly-zealous sociometricians persuaded that numbers are all, Paul could be heard intoning the monitory words of St. Augustine: "So it is, O Lord my God, I measure it and know not what it is I measure."

For Paul, methodology was a means of disciplining his passion for clarity and integrity of thought. It was a matter of discovering what one truly wanted to say, of explicating the grounds that allowed it to be said responsibly and, not least, of indicating the sort of evidence that would lead one to confess having been mistaken. That commitment to scrupulous clarity found expression in the lean, direct prose that won the admiration even of Paul's most dedicated critics. And as I discovered, upon reading his early German monographs, Paul was just as clear-spoken in his native as in his adopted language, a discovery that evoked in me no little envy and naturally obliged me to accuse him of writing a most ungermanic prose.

Paul presented us with other difficulties of like kind. For another example, his complex intellectual interests had a way of transcending the familiar academic divisions into disciplines and departments. As a result, he encountered the problem of meshing his own cognitive identity with the academic identity assigned to him. Long after he found himself appointed a Professor of Sociology, he retained the stance of an amiable but perplexed traveler in the exotic land known as sociology. He was often bemused by the strange ideas he found there and not infrequently bewildered by the equally strange idiom. Countless hours of talk during the first decade or so of our collaboration were devoted to my trying to persuade Paul that he had been thinking like a sociologist right along, albeit a *sociologue malgré lui*, and not, as he assumed in light of his training, like a psychologist making use, when needed, of the knowledge and skills he had acquired in obtaining his doctorate in applied mathematics. Slowly, very slowly, Paul began to grant the subject of sociology a measure of legitimacy. By the mid-1940s, for example, he was writing me: "I remember when you sent over some of my old writings [these being *Jugend und Beruf* and *Die Arbeitslosen von Marienthal*], you pointed out to me that they were really of a sociological nature. I know that it was meant as a compliment and I will accept it as a standard classification." In due course, he stopped thinking of sociology as something of a collective obsession, peculiar to myself and a few thousand others which, as an indulgent companion, he would no longer regard as a derivative of psychology.

Paul's conversion was first publicly affirmed in the lecture inaugurating his year at the University of Oslo, a lecture which he proudly, almost gleefully reported to me was actually devoted to sociology as a discipline. Twenty years later, he elaborated this lecture into a small book, published in his beloved Paris under the engaging (but, he felt, possibly pretentious) title: *Qu'est-ce que la sociologie?*. In Paul's private idiom, that would translate roughly into the question "What on earth *is* sociology all about?" or, as his self-mocking inscription in my copy of the book put it, "All the questions you always wanted to have answered but never dared to ask."

Even after his cognitive conversion, validated in due course by his being elected President of the American Sociological Association, Paul felt uncomfortable about this ascribed identity. Being both Viennese *and* Gallic in his insistence upon achieving clarity about himself, he would protest to his friends that he was still sailing under false colors, that he was neither sociologist nor psychologist but rather something that might be called a social scientist, ready to poach on the preserves of all the social disciplines with what he described as limited mathematical skills and unlimited humanistic leanings.

It was therefore an important symbolic moment when, in the mid-1960s, he was elevated to the newly established Chair of Quetelet Professor of Social Science. Characteristically for Paul, the honor done him by this action was as nothing compared with his pleasure in the finely calibrated designation of the Chair which, thanks to the sensitivity of Jacques Barzun, then Provost of the University, coupled Paul's prime conception of himself as a maverick social scientist with the name of one of his few culture heroes—the nineteenth-century astronomer and, for Paul, a founding father of sociology, Adolphe Quetelet.

For those able to read between the lines, all this was caught up in a quiet sentence appearing in Paul's brief memoir: "I am now Professor of Social Science, which resolved for me a terminological embarrassment." From this, it will be understood when I say that Paul Lazarsfeld was at once the most embarrassable and least pretentious man I have ever known.

Of all the missions Paul set himself, none held greater meaning for him or proved to be more consequential for the rest of us than his creation, almost forty years ago, of what came to be the Bureau of Applied Social Research. The Bureau embodied his enduring conviction that such a research institution fully incorporated into the University—for him, the functional equivalent of the laboratory in other disciplines—is essential to empirical social inquiry and to apprentice training for the conduct of such inquiry, just as he knew it to be temperamentally essential to his own well-being as scholar and scientist.

It was therefore another rare occasion for Paul to be surprised by joy when the Bureau, after almost ten years of vicissitudes owing to institutional resistance and neglect, became officially adopted as "A research unit of the Graduate Faculty of Political Science of Columbia University." Nevertheless, Paul would often express concern about continuance of this Columbia tradition, periodically reverting to a secularized parable drawn from Exodus: "Now there arose a new Pharaoh over Egypt, who knew not Joseph."

Happily, this was not the fate destined for Paul's vision. When, in the difficult days of 1970, a new president came to Columbia, he knew Joseph and his abundant works, seeing to it, among other things, that the citation of the honorary degree awarded the Quetelet Professor of Social Science would include the declaration that "By founding at this University the Bureau of Applied Social Research, now recognized as the prototype for similar research centers around the world, you have enlarged the scope of sociological inquiry accessible to colleagues and students here and to unnumbered ones elsewhere."

Nor has the recognition of Joseph's legacy remained symbolic only. The concept of the Bureau has been given renewed and extended institutional reality by the creation of the Center for the Social Sciences, in direct line of continuity with what Paul liked to call "the Columbia tradition" of social research as it had evolved over a span of four decades. His University could not have provided a more fitting memorial to Paul Felix Lazarsfeld.

5. ORGANIZATIONAL INNOVATION FOR SOCIAL SCIENCE RESEARCH AND TRAINING

Charles Y. Glock

A history of survey research has yet to be written. When it is, it will identify the modern era of survey research with Paul F. Lazarsfeld and trace its origins successively, to his work in the 1920s and early 1930s in Vienna and in the 1930s and early 1940s at the University of Newark, Princeton University, and Columbia University in the United States. In a primitive form, all the ingredients of modern survey research were present by the time Lazarsfeld began his work in Vienna. Censuses in the form of population counts can be traced back to the ancient Egyptians, Greeks, Hebrews, and Romans. Probability sampling and its application to drawing samples of human populations has its own long history. And the strategy of multivariate analysis with which Lazarsfeld is so closely identified has precedents in the work of Durkheim and independently, Yule and Kendall, at the turn of the century.[1]

That Lazarsfeld should be identified as a father of modern survey research derives therefore not from his having been the inventor of its components but from his having put them together in a unique way. By combining existing methods of data collection using probability samples with existing modes of analysis and more importantly, by articulating the logic underlying these modes of analysis to greatly enlarge their applicability, Lazarsfeld produced a synthesis which has done much to make survey research the predominant method of inquiry in sociology and political science and a major research tool in the other academic social sciences and in related professional disciplines. The broader implications of Lazarsfeld's methodological contributions, as indicated in other chapters of this volume, have still not been fully comprehended, much less wholly worked out.

Lazarsfeld's methodological innovations also underlie his unique contribution to the development of university organization for social research and sociological training, and that is why I make this brief reference to them. They

23

were of a kind that made it increasingly difficult for social scientists to work alone. Not only were an armchair and a library judged insufficient for social inquiry, but, valuable as it might otherwise be, so too was field work by a lone investigator. Not that Lazarsfeld ruled these out; rather, they were simply not enough. To utilize the new methodology, with its requirements that data about relatively large numbers of people or other social units be systematically collected, codified, and analyzed, samples had to be drawn, research instruments constructed, interviewers trained and supervised, coding systems devised, and analytic strategies formulated and put to use. There emerged an increasingly apparent need for some kind of ongoing laboratory with the equipment and trained personnel to do all of this work.

Just as modern survey research created a need for organization to conduct the research, it also made necessary an organizational setting for research training. Didactic instruction could be used to educate students in the principles and logic of the new methodology, but didactic instruction was not enough to produce a professionally competent social researcher. Learning by doing became at least as important as formal instruction. This meant creating opportunities for students to obtain apprenticeship training in the actual conduct of large-scale social research, and this was beyond the capabilities of the individual instructor to provide. The needed resources could only be furnished in an organizational setting.

Lazarsfeld was sensitive, early in his career, to the need for organization both in the conduct of research involving the collection of mass data and in the training of students in procedures for collecting and analyzing such data. As Hans Zeisel has already indicated in this volume, Lazarsfeld was instrumental in organizing an independent research center (*Wirtschaftspsychologische Forschungsstelle*) in Vienna in 1927 that afforded some facilities for the collection and processing of data and that became a place where students from the University of Vienna supplemented their academic training with practical research experience.

Soon after Lazarsfeld came to the United States in 1933 as a visiting Rockefeller Foundation Fellow, the political situation in Austria deteriorated to a point that made it personally dangerous for him to return there permanently. Deciding in 1935 to stay in this country, he sought out an institutional affiliation which would allow him to continue the kind of work he had begun at the Vienna center. Having met the president of the University of Newark, Lazarsfeld worked out plans for a "Research Center of the University of Newark" which came into being in the spring of 1936. From the beginning, it was explicitly designed as an instrumentality for research *and* training. In 1937, the Newark Center evolved into the Office of Radio Research at Princeton University, and that organization transferred to Columbia in 1939, becoming the Bureau of Applied Social Research in 1944, in recognition of the widened range of subject matters on which it was then working.[2]

The Bureau of Applied Social Research and its immediate predecessors were not the first university-based organizations for social research in the United States. As early as 1924, Howard Odum had established an Institute for Social Science at the University of North Carolina.[3] And the construction of a special building for social science research at the University of Chicago created something akin to a research center; dedicated in 1929, the building became the locus for a considerable amount of social research, provided a setting for scholars from different disciplines to work together, and afforded opportunities for students to gain practical research experience.[4] These arrangements provided for field research, including observation, the use of informants, and other interviewing. They were not equipped, however, to collect large-scale data on a regular basis, nor did they typically interrelate survey data with data obtained from observation, qualitative interviews, and other methods. Their work represents the general state of social research in the United States in the late 1920s and early 1930s, aptly described by Hans Zeisel in an Appendix to *Marienthal:*[5]

American sociography has not achieved a synthesis between statistics and a full description of concrete situations. In work of impressive conceptualization—for instance, in *The Polish Peasant*—statistics are completely missing; inversely the statistical surveys are often a regrettable routine affair.

Lazarsfeld made early note of the need for integrating different methods in social research. Summarizing his Austrian experience in a paper written in 1933, he formulates the following four rules as characterizing his philosophy of research:[6]

1. For any phenomenon one should have objective observations as well as introspective reports.
2. Case studies should be properly combined with statistical information.
3. Contemporary information should be supplemented by information on earlier phases of whatever is being studied.
4. One should combine "natural" and experimental data.

This philosophy was influential in shaping the character of the research undertaken at the Vienna and American centers and in distinguishing their work from other research organizations of the time. The philosophy also informed the organization of the several centers established by Lazarsfeld. These were designed to ensure a capability for employing the full range of methods and procedures then available for social research. Thus, he tried to have people on the staff who were knowledgeable about participant observation and depth interviewing, about content analysis and the use of biographies, and, unlike the programs at other centers, about the range of techniques required for survey research—sampling, instrument construction, data collection, coding, data processing, and analysis.[7]

The research organizations pioneered by Lazarsfeld were productive of a considerable body of important substantive research; for example, *Marienthal, The Invasion from Mars, Radio and the Printed Page, The People's Choice, Mass Persuasion, Voting, Personal Influence, Union Democracy, The Student Physician,* and *The Academic Mind.*[8] The research organizations were also the source of considerable effort to advance methods of social research, as in such works as *Say It With Figures, Content Analysis in Communications Research, Survey Design and Analysis, Conflict and Mood, The Language of Social Research,* and *Mathematical Thinking in the Social Sciences.*[9] The attention to a range of substantive topics that made use of the methodological innovations helped to develop the fields of mass communications, election behavior, political sociology, the quantitative study of organizations, and socialization in professional schools. All this was geared into the graduate and postgraduate training of a large number of social researchers, including most of the contributors to this volume.[10]

All these outcomes cannot be attributed simply to the policies and organization of these centers for social research. Some would have occurred had the organizations never been invented. Lazarsfeld's capabilities in other realms would have guaranteed that. Yet, without the organizations, not nearly so much would have been achieved.

Different observers occupying different vantage points would not wholly agree, I suspect, on what contributed most to the prodigiousness of Lazarsfeld's organizational innovations. My own observations were first made during a brief period from August 1941 to January 1942, when I was a coder and then, for a short time, a Rockefeller Foundation Fellow at the Office of Radio Research. After World War II, I had a considerably longer period, from 1946–1958, of participant observation as I collaborated with Lazarsfeld on the Bureau's management. Here, then, are my observations on what proved to be the sources of strengths and limitations in the Bureau as a research organization.

Organizational Attributes

The Substantive Contributions

Among the organizational features contributing to the quality of substantive research was Lazarsfeld's success in implementing the philosophy set forth in his rules of research. From *Marienthal* on, most research monographs and articles produced by the Viennese and American centers were characterized by the artful integration of quantitative and qualitative procedures. The classical status of *Union Democracy*, for example, owes much to its effective integration of historical, observational, and questionnaire materials.[11] *Voting, The Volunteers, The Puerto Rican Journey, Why Families Move, The Student Physician,* and *The*

Passing of Traditional Society are other Bureau monographs which in effect exemplified Lazarsfeld's rules for research.[12]

Another prime ingredient in shaping the character of the Bureau's research was Lazarsfeld's emphasis upon a clear formulation of research problems. When it came to applied research, it was a governing principle that the formulations of their problems by government, labor, business, or community organizations were not to be taken at face value. This policy often resulted in major reformulations of problems and the transformation of what would otherwise have been relatively routine inquiries into sociological studies of some consequence.

Excellent cases in point are the Bureau studies published as *Personal Influence* and *Medical Innovation*.[13] The former is widely recognized as a major contribution to the understanding of opinion formation and opinion leadership; the latter for its formulations and investigation of processes governing the adoption of innovations through a study of physicians' adoption of new drugs. Yet both studies have their origins in rather trivial questions posed originally by agencies concerned with "practical problems." *Personal Influence* is the ultimate product of an inquiry by the representatives of a magazine about the possibilities of a study to help them "upgrade" the magazine's audience. *Medical Innovation* came about because the drug company that sponsored it originally wanted to find out whether or not it should continue to advertise a new drug in the *Journal of the American Medical Association*. *They Went to College, Mass Persuasion*, and *The Volunteers* are among other Bureau studies that transformed the initial queries into sociologically significant research questions.[14]

Contributing further to the substantive work of the Bureau was the continuing effort to avoid introducing organizational attributes that might inhibit organizational flexibility. For example, the Bureau never maintained a permanent interviewing staff. Lazarsfeld believed that such a commitment would heighten the necessity of accepting contracts of no research interest to keep the interviewing staff occupied. For the same reason, other organizational commitments, such as permanent sampling and coding staffs, were also avoided.

In turn, not having such organizational resources when needed was a distinct handicap. It meant designing samples and mounting interviewing staffs *de novo* for each new study or where this was not feasible, as with studies based on national samples, of having the field work done by other research organizations. It also probably meant that some interesting opportunities for research did not come the Bureau's way. But the net effect of the policy was to enlarge more than to limit the capacity to engage in cumulative research along theoretical and methodological lines being developed in the Bureau.

The policy also augmented the Bureau's capability to adopt the research design and data collection most appropriate for the problems at hand. If the ideal design called for data about a national sample of a population—as in the case of *The Academic Mind,* for example—the field work could be assigned to research organizations with nationwide interviewing staffs.[15] But, if a national or regional sample was not suitable for investigation of a particular problem, there was no tacit assumption that it should be used to utilize an available interviewer resource. All this contributed to the diverse and sometimes imaginative research designs of Bureau studies, for example, the intricate panel design of *The People's Choice*, the sociometric design of *Medical Innovation*, and the contextual design of *The Academic Mind*.

The research program of the Bureau owed much to Lazarsfeld's preference for explanatory over descriptive research. His own substantive research was virtually always addressed to the problem of trying to account for variation rather than to describing it, and this soon became a frequent Bureau pattern as well. More concretely, the research focus was not on how people will vote, or what they are going to buy, or whether they plan a residential move. Throughout, the focus was on why people vote as they do, what leads to variations in their consumption behavior, and what accounts for the decision to move or stay. At the root of his curiosity about questions of "why" rather than about questions of "what" was Lazarsfeld's abiding intellectual interest in understanding decision-making processes. All this made for an atmosphere of intellectual excitement at the Bureau which contributed to the continuing deep commitment to empirical social research.

The Methodological Contributions

Because the Bureau was largely the organizational extension of Paul Lazarsfeld's own intellectual commitments, it was inevitable that the advancement of methodology should become a major Bureau preoccupation. He made it an abiding organizational policy that every substantive project should try to make a methodological contribution as well. Beyond these, many studies were undertaken expressly for methodological reasons.

Basic to Lazarsfeld's conception of methodology was the notion of codification, the making explicit of rules governing the proper pursuit of social inquiry. The methodological innovations with which Lazarsfeld and the Bureau are most closely associated—"the art of asking why,"[16] reason analysis, the "elaboration" formula, concepts and index formation, panel analysis, mathematical applications, the algebra of dichotomous systems, the concept of property space, the focused interview—can all be identified as efforts at codification and of the uses of this orientation.

Among the organizational attributes contributing to methodological innovation were those policies of trying to have substantive research also make a methodological contribution and of having the advancement of methodology as one of the organizational goals. Probably of more importance was the sustained effort to generate and maintain interest in the exploration of methodological problems. A premium was put on attendance at formal seminars and informal discussions with everyone—faculty, staff, and students—to initiate such discussions of any topic that suited their methodological fancy and for which they could attract participants. I can recall seminars held on such diverse topics as how to sample networks, how to process and analyze sociometric data, and how to substruct a sixteen-fold table. Weekend retreats and occasionally longer conferences were held to stimulate methodological sensitivities and work. Perhaps most important of all in Lazarsfeld's scheme of things was the preparation of "training documents," which obliged those who wrote them to engage in the kind of codification that he thought essential to the entire intellectual enterprise.

Both the methodological and substantive work was greatly aided by Lazarsfeld's ability to recruit distinguished scholars to work on Bureau-defined tasks for shorter or longer periods of time, his uncanny nose for bright and talented graduate students, and the open-door policy he followed to make Bureau facilities available to members of the Columbia faculty.

Training

The ingredients which Lazarsfeld put together to make the Bureau the preeminent training institution it became can be specified to a degree; it is more difficult to convey the excitement and zest for learning which prevailed among the students who held apprenticeships at the Office of Radio Research and the subsequent Bureau. The most important ingredient, as in other effective training organizations, was Lazarsfeld's lifelong practice of involving students deeply in the process of ongoing research. Students became more nearly collaborators than research assistants on Bureau projects. Indeed, once they had learned the basics, they came to fill the role of project director with Lazarsfeld, Merton, and other faculty and staff serving as consultants. In effect, each project became a collateral seminar focused on the project's effective development with faculty and students sharing responsibility for the outcome. As a result, students acquired a taste for research and a proficiency in doing research very early in their careers. All this is reflected in research monographs that were frequently authored by a faculty member and a student or sometimes by students alone, the former being illustrated by *Union Democracy* by Seymour Martin Lipset, James S. Coleman, and Martin A. Trow and by *The Academic Mind* by Lazarsfeld and Wagner Thielens, Jr., the latter by *The Volunteers* by David Sills and *Why Families Move* by Peter Rossi.

Bureau seminars served to advance training in several ways. There was always at least one informal seminar in process at any one time and sometimes as many as four and five. These furthered training in the arts of research as did the production of "training documents" on such topics as questionnaire construction, sampling, the techniques of qualitative interviewing, classification, and the qualitative use of documentary materials. These documents, which sought to codify the procedures addressed in a "how to do it" way, were made instruments for training by having students take part in their preparation as well as through their use in formal instruction.

The doctoral dissertation was, of course, another means for research training. Students were encouraged to write their dissertations on materials generated by the Bureau projects on which they were working as research assistants. The Bureau's archives continually served for doctoral dissertations based on secondary analysis. Lazarsfeld was among the earliest advocates of establishing data archives to preserve important survey materials for future historians as well as for more contemporary use in secondary analysis.[17]

Newer Frontiers

Lazarsfeld's interest in university organization for social science research and training was not confined to his active engagement in the creation and management of the Bureau and its predecessors. The topic interested him intellectually, and, especially during, but not confined to, the latter part of his career he was actively engaged both in doing research on the organization of social research in American universities and in championing the more effective integration of organized research units into graduate social science education.

A relatively early manifestation of this interest was a memorandum addressed in 1950 to the Columbia University administration, prepared by Lazarsfeld in collaboration with Robert Merton, calling for the establishment of a "professional school for training in social research."[18] The concept for a professional school was grounded in the observation that the emergence and refinement of new methods of social inquiry in the 1930s and 1940s had not been "paralleled by the creation of places where systematic training in such skills can be acquired." "At no university," Lazarsfeld and Merton observed, "can the student find a comprehensive exposition of all of these new techniques. Even where some of them are taught, they have not been well integrated with the older and better established procedures of, say, the historian or linguist." The proposal asserted that skilled practitioners of social research were already in short supply and implied that the demand for social researchers could be expected to grow in virtually every sector of American society.

The proposed school was conceived of as affording students training in the range of skills that had come to be required of a professional in social research, among them the skills of field work, of organizing and directing a research team, and of developing policy-oriented and theory-oriented methods of research. The instructional modes proposed for the new school were "the case method of instruction, supervised participation in current research projects, internships and externships, and a cumulative series of research seminars."

The proposal lacked details on the organization of the school and the role the Bureau of Applied Social Research was to play in its structure. Presumably these details were to follow once the idea for the school was accepted in principle. The Bureau is prominently mentioned in the proposal as having demonstrated, through its work, the value of the training devices to be incorporated in the new school. The proposal conveyed the impression that the Bureau would be integrated structurally into the new school and would provide the setting in which students would be afforded practical research experience to complement formal instruction.

The prospectus did not receive a sympathetic ear from the Columbia administration. Cost was a principal obstacle. Moreover, the plan did not have the interdepartmental support which would have been necessary for it to have been accepted. Especially among some humanistically minded members of the faculty, there were doubts about intellectual style and modes of inquiry adopted by Lazarsfeld and the Bureau.

Lazarsfeld's next opportunity to advance his deep interest in organizational forms for research and training resulted from his participation in a group brought together by the Ford Foundation to plan what subsequently became the Center for Advanced Study in the Behavioral Sciences. Lazarsfeld was a strong proponent of the Center's being a place where highly promising advanced graduate students and young Ph.D.s might be given an opportunity to collaborate with senior faculty on common research problems in a setting isolated from the everyday demands of university life. In his judgment, such collaboration could enhance the work of senior faculty and afford a unique opportunity for younger people to work on advanced problems at a crucial stage in their careers.

Lazarsfeld's ideas did not win the day. As is well known, the Center was organized, not for graduate and postdoctoral training, but to facilitate advanced study and research by already established scholars.

Subsequently, Lazarsfeld's interest in organization for social science research was directed more to doing research on the topic than to articulating additional blueprints for reform, although, as will be seen, the possibilities for reform never ceased to intrigue him. In collaboration with Sydney Spivack, Lazarsfeld undertook in 1959 an extensive study of the organization of empirical research in the United States.[19] This study was followed in the 1960s by a series of studies, undertaken with Samuel Sieber, on the organization of educational research in American schools of education.[20] Also in the 1960s, Lazarsfeld returned to his earlier interests in the history and sociology of social research and, together with Merton, presented an advanced seminar on the subject. Growing out of that seminar was a series of monographs by Lazarsfeld and several of his students devoted to the interplay between organizational problems and substantive developments during the early generations of social inquiry in Europe.[21] Implicit and at times explicit in this research is Lazarsfeld's deep-seated frustration that the organizational innovations which he and others had pioneered were not more widely adopted.[22] That frustration finds fuller expression in a report entitled, *Reforming the University: The Role of the Research Center*, written by Samuel Sieber in collaboration with Lazarsfeld in 1971:[23]

> The rise of research organizations in the universities represents one of the most far-reaching innovations in higher education of the twentieth century. Insofar as these organizations are able to stem the tide of excessive differen-

tiation, few other developments have as great a potential for improving the structure and functioning of universities. And yet, precisely because of the threat posed to the traditional structure—a structure based on classroom teaching within a loose federation of departments—the organizations have been relegated to a marginal status. In effect, they have been regarded as auxiliary agents whose chief function is to backstop the activities of the teaching departments rather than being permitted to pursue a vigorous, autonomous course in achieving fundamental goals of instruction, service and research in a more *integrated* fashion than afforded by the departments. . . . If the benefits of these agencies are to be fully realized, therefore, massive overhauling of graduate studies would seem to be called for.

By 1971, Lazarsfeld's ideas about the character of the deficiencies, and the requirements for correcting them, had changed somewhat from his earlier ideas about the proposed professional school. However, he continued to call for a radical change in graduate education in the social sciences with organized research units playing the central rather than the usual peripheral role. In the new vision, as set forth in their report, Sieber and Lazarsfeld proposed that the departmental structure for social science education should not govern after the first year of a student's graduate work. In the place of departments, interdisciplinary centers would be established, each concentrated on a "problem area of concern to the future welfare of the society—education, urban affairs, international relations, the physical environment, mass communications, crime and delinquency, and so forth." Each center would operate an educational program combining instruction in the form of courses and seminars, with intensive practical training in the conduct of social research. "The work of the centers should emphasize programmatic, inter-disciplinary research rather than specialized project research. Where possible, service and development work should proceed hand in hand with research and theory construction." The integration of theory, research, administration, and teaching is given major emphasis in the report. Under this plan, centers would operate with no more university constraint and control than are exercised over academic departments. Recognizing that any general overhaul of advanced graduate education along the lines they suggest would be utopian, Sieber and Lazarsfeld call for the establishment of "experimental universities" to demonstrate the feasibility and worth of their proposals.

Impact

A judgment of Lazarsfeld's contributions to university organization for social science research and training must continue to await the future, with the character of that judgment depending greatly on whether or not his visions of possibilities are taken up. So far, the potential represented by Lazarsfeld's most recent organizational dreams remains essentially unfulfilled on the university scene. A lag between the invention and adoption of his organizational innovations has typified Lazarsfeld's career. There remains hope, consequently, that his constructive and eminently sensible more recent proposals for reforming the organization of social science research and training may still be implemented.

Although Lazarsfeld's "wildest" organizational dreams have not been realized, no one has had a greater influence in shaping the current state of organized social research and training. The kind of research organization he pioneered has been replicated with variations many times over. Among current university-based organizations with research and training capabilities akin to those Lazarsfeld pioneered at the Bureau of Applied Social Research at Columbia are the Survey Research Center of the University of Michigan; the National Opinion Research Center at the University of Chicago; the Institute for Social Science Research at the University of California, Los Angeles; the Survey Research Laboratory at the University of Illinois; the Institute for Survey Research of Temple University; the Survey Research Laboratory of the University of Wisconsin-Extension; and the Survey Research Center of the University of California, Berkeley.

Not all of these organizations have roots traceable directly to Lazarsfeld, although, well before they launched their own organizations, other pioneers had contacts with Lazarsfeld and became familiar with his organizational innovations. Rensis Likert, who established the Survey Research Center of the University of Michigan in 1946, first met Lazarsfeld at the Psychological Corporation in New York in the early 1930s. They also were in touch with each other during World War II when Likert was in charge of the Division of Program Surveys, an agency of the Department of Agriculture's Bureau of Agricultural Economics. Another pioneer, Harry Field, who founded the National Opinion Research Center in 1941, had also met Lazarsfeld in the late 1930s. They both played a role subsequently in the organization of the American Association for Public Opinion Research.

Bureau "graduates" include a good number who have established or directed other such centers of research. They include the founders of the Bureau of Social Science Research in Washington, D.C. (Robert Bower); the Survey Research Center of the University of California, Berkeley (Charles Glock); the Center for the Study of the Acts of Man, University of Pennsylvania (Samuel Klausner); the Institute for Research in Social Behavior in Berkeley, California (Dean Manheimer); and the Survey Research Centre of the Chinese University of Hong Kong (Robert Mitchell). Peter Rossi served as director of the National Opinion Research Center from 1960 to 1967, and William Nicholls has been acting director and is now executive officer of the Survey Research Center at Berkeley. In at least one instance, Lazarsfeld's organizational progeny can be traced to the third generation. Earl Babbie, a student of Charles Glock's, founded the Survey Research Laboratory of the University of Hawaii, Honolulu.

Directly and indirectly, Lazarsfeld has also influenced the course of organized social research abroad. I have already mentioned Robert Mitchell's being the first director of the Hong Kong Survey Research Centre. Lazarsfeld played an important part in the founding of the Vienna Institute for Advanced Studies in 1963 and has been a major stimulus to the lively interest in empirical social research at the University of the Sorbonne in Paris.

All in all, the Bureau, the organizations which it spawned, and university organizations for social research generally fall short of being the resources for research and especially for training envisaged in Lazarsfeld's prospectus for a professional school of social research and in his later proposals for "experimental universities." But, then, it is the greatness of the man that he did so much to bring us where we are and set the sights high enough as to keep us from complacently assuming that we have gone far enough.

Notes

1. Hanan Selvin, "Survey Analysis," in *International Encyclopaedia of the Social Sciences,* New York: Macmillan and The Free Press, 1968, Vol. 15, pp. 411–418.

2. Some historical background of the establishment and growth of the Vienna and American centers is provided in Paul F. Lazarsfeld, "An Episode in the History of Social Research: A Memoir," in Donald Fleming and Bernard Bailyn, eds., *The Intellectual Migration: Europe and America, 1930–1960,* Cambridge, Massachusetts: The Belknap Press of Harvard University Press, 1969. See also Paul F. Lazarsfeld, "Notes on the History of Quantification in Sociology— Trends, Sources, and Problems," in Henry Woolf, ed., *Quantification: A History of the Meaning of Measurement in the Natural and Social Sciences,* Indianapolis: Bobbs-Merrill, 1961.

3. Howard A. Odum, *American Sociology: The Story of American Sociology in the United States through 1950,* New York: Longmans, Green, 1951.

4. Louis Wirth, ed., *Eleven Twenty-Six: A Decade of Social Science Research.* Chicago: University of Chicago Press, 1940. See also Harry Alpert, "The Growth of Social Research in the United States," in Daniel Lerner, ed., *The Human Meaning of the Social Sciences,* New York: Meridian Books, 1959.

5. Marie Jahoda, Paul F. Lazarsfeld, and Hans Zeisel, *Marienthal: The Sociography of an Unemployed Community,* translated from the German by the authors with John Reginall and Thomas Elsaesser, Chicago, Aldine, Atherton, 1932, reprinted 1971.

6. Paul F. Lazarsfeld, "Principles of Sociography," unpublished, 1933. Also cited in Lazarsfeld, "An Episode in the History of Social Research: A Memoir," *op. cit.,* p. 282. Lazarsfeld notes that by experimental data he meant mainly questionnaires; by natural data, what are now described as "unobtrusive measures."

7. Lazarsfeld did not include a permanent interviewing staff or fully staffed sampling and coding units among necessary organizational features. I shall comment on this policy later in this chapter.

8. Jahoda, Lazarsfeld, and Zeisel, *op. cit.*; Hadley Cantril, Hazel Gaudet, and Herta Herzog, *The Invasion from Mars,* Princeton: Princeton University

Press, 1940, paperback, New York: Harper & Row, 1966; Paul F. Lazarsfeld, ed., *Radio and the Printed Page: An Introduction to the Study of Radio and Its Role in the Communication of Ideas,* New York: Duell, Sloan and Pearce, 1940; Paul F. Lazarsfeld, Bernard Berelson, and Hazel Gaudet, *The People's Choice: How the Voter Makes up His Mind in a Presidential Campaign,* 2nd ed., New York: Columbia University Press, 1948; Robert K. Merton, Marjorie Fiske, and Alberta Curtis, *Mass Persuasion: The Social Psychology of a War Bond Drive,* New York: Harper & Row, 1946, 2nd ed., 1958; Bernard Berelson, Paul F. Lazarsfeld, and William N. McPhee, *Voting: A Study of Opinion Formation in a Presidential Election,* Chicago: The University of Chicago Press, 1954; Elihu Katz and Paul F. Lazarsfeld, *Personal Influence· The Part Played by People in the Flow of Mass Communication,* New York: The Free Press, 1955; Seymour M. Lipset, James S. Coleman, and Martin A Trow, *Union Democracy: The Internal Politics of the International Typographical Union,* New York: The Free Press, 1956; Robert K. Merton, George C. Reader, and Patricia L. Kendall, eds., *The Student Physician: Introductory Studies in the Sociology of Medical Education,* Cambridge: Harvard University Press, 1958; Paul F. Lazarsfeld and Wagner Thielens, Jr., *The Academic Mind,* New York: The Free Press, 1958.

9. Hans Zeisel, *Say It With Figures,* New York: Harper & Row, 1947, rev. ed., 1957; Bernard Berelson, *Content Analysis in Communication Research,* New York: The Free Press, 1952; Herbert Hyman, *Survey Design and Analysis,* New York: The Free Press, 1955; Patricia L. Kendall, *Conflict and Mood: Factors Affecting the Stability of Response,* New York: The Free Press, 1954; Paul F. Lazarsfeld and Morris Rosenberg, eds., *The Language of Social Research: A Reader in the Methodology of Social Research,* New York: The Free Press, 1955, paperback, 1965; Paul F. Lazarsfeld, ed., *Mathematical Thinking in the Social Sciences,* New York: The Free Press, 1954.

10. I include as Bureau "graduates" both those who apprenticed at the Bureau while pursuing a Ph.D. and persons whose research training was obtained or enriched while on the Bureau's staff.

11. Lipset, Coleman, and Trow, *op. cit.*

12. Berelson, Lazarsfeld, and McPhee, *op. cit.,* David L. Sills, *The Volunteers: Means and Ends in a National Organization,* New York: The Free Press, 1957; C. Wright Mills, Clarence Senior, and Rose K. Goldsen, *The Puerto Rican Journey: New York's Newest Migrants,* New York: Harper, 1950; Peter H. Rossi, *Why Families Move: A Study in the Social Psychology of Urban Residential Mobility,* New York: The Free Press, 1955; Merton, Reader, and Kendall, *op. cit.*; Daniel Lerner, *The Passing of Traditional Society: Modernizing the Middle East,* New York: The Free Press, 1958, paperback, 1964.

13. Katz and Lazarsfeld, *op. cit.*; James S. Coleman, Elihu Katz, and Herbert Menzel, *Medical Innovation: A Diffusion Study,* Indianapolis: Bobbs-Merrill, 1966.

14. Ernest Havemann and Patricia S. West, *They Went to College: The College Graduate in America Today,* New York: Harcourt Brace, 1952; Merton, Fiske and Curtis, *op. cit.*; David Sills, *op. cit.*

15. Lazarsfeld and Thielens, *op. cit.* See the chapter in this volume by David Riesman.

16. Paul F. Lazarsfeld, "The Art of Asking Why," *National Marketing Review,* 1 (Summer 1935), 32–43.

17. Paul F. Lazarsfeld, "The Obligations of the 1950 Pollster to the 1984 Historian," *Public Opinion Quarterly,* 14 (Winter 1950-1951), 617-638.

18. The report has been published as Chapter 18, "A Professional School for Training in Social Research," in Paul F. Lazarsfeld, *Qualitative Analysis: Historical and Critical Essays,* Boston: Allyn and Bacon, 1972, pp. 361-394.

19. Paul F. Lazarsfeld, with the collaboration of Sydney S. Spivack, "Observations on the Organization of Empirical Social Research in the United States," *Information: Bulletin of the International Social Science,* No. XXIX, December 1961.

20. Paul F. Lazarsfeld and Sam D. Sieber, *Organizing Educational Research: An Exploration,* Englewood Cliffs, N.J.: Prentice-Hall, 1964; Sam D. Sieber and Paul F. Lazarsfeld, *The Organization of Educational Research,* New York: Bureau of Applied Social Research, 1966.

21. See Anthony R. Oberschall, *Empirical Research in Germany, 1843-1914,* Paris and The Hague, Mouton, 1965; Bernard Lécuyer and Anthony R. Oberschall, "The Early History of Social Research," in *International Encyclopaedia of The Social Sciences,* New York: Macmillan and The Free Press, 1968, Vol. 15, pp. 36-53; Suzanne Schad, *Empirical Social Research in Weimar Germany,* unpublished Ph.D. dissertation, Sociology Department of Columbia University, 1971; Anthony Oberschall, ed., *The Establishment of Empirical Sociology: Studies in Continuity, Discontinuity, and Institutionalization,* New York: Harper & Row, 1972. See also Lazarsfeld, "An Episode in the History of Social Research: A Memoir," *op. cit.,* and "Notes on the History of Quantification in Sociology: Trends, Sources, and Problems," *op. cit.*

22. Lazarsfeld's concern about the problem is manifested especially in his making it a principal theme in his presidential address to the American Sociological Association. See Paul F. Lazarsfeld, "The Sociology of Empirical Social Research," *American Sociological Review,* 27 (1962), 757-767.

23. Sam D. Sieber, in collaboration with Paul F. Lazarsfeld, *Reforming the University-The Role of the Research Center,* New York: Bureau of Applied Social Research, Columbia University, 1971.

6. THE EVOLUTION OF A THESIS: UTILIZATION OF SOCIAL RESEARCH AS A SOCIOLOGICAL PROBLEM

Ann K. Pasanella

"I keep a reservoir of problems in the back of my mind and wait for an occasion to attend to them," Lazarsfeld once said.[1]

How, out of the deep, did Paul Lazarsfeld's involvement with the problem of the utilization of social research emerge? The history is tangled.

Lazarsfeld had, of course, a lifelong commitment to applied research, beginning with the early days of his consumer studies in Vienna. But, by the utilization of social research as a topic, I mean something different. It is not applied research per se, but what one might call the methodology of application. (Merton's 1949 term "applied social research on applied social research"[2] comes close.) How does one set about applying social research to the formation of policy? What intellectual operations are necessarily involved? And what are the relationships between these procedures?

In large measure, this paper is the history of a research project directed by Lazarsfeld in which I was a participant. For this, memory alone does not suffice. But, fortunately, the corridors of time are lined with files. From memos and notes and progress reports and programmatic statements, I shall try to reconstruct the career of this idea of utilization.

Somewhat arbitrarily—there were already glimmerings at the Bureau of Applied Social Research—we begin in 1960 when Lazarsfeld was elected president of the American Sociological Association (hereafter ASA). Under the external pressure of needing to organize the 1962 meetings, Lazarsfeld decided that the sessions could be arranged around the theme of "the uses of sociology." The topic must have lain in that very "reservoir" of problems he has since mentioned. But why this choice? We do know that he wanted a theme similar to that of Merton's program leading to the book *Sociology Today*,[3] but Lazars-

37

feld expected more than a mere updating of it. In a set of formal instructions to the session chairmen for the annual meeting,[4] Lazarsfeld explained what he thought the program would entail: reports on empirical studies that had been applied, testimony from sociologists who had served as policy advisors, and critical assessment of modes of increasing the social utility of sociology. In his own mind, Lazarsfeld revealed, he had the picture of a "spectrum of utility"[5] leading from the expansive use of social theory to the utilization of specific research by action agencies.

This vision was never realized, and, from Lazarsfeld's point of view, the ASA program was therefore a failure. There were indeed speeches on the role of the sociologist in public affairs, the economy, the field of health care, and so on, but they were not presented with a zestful eye for practical utility. On the contrary, Lazarsfeld has maintained that, at heart, most of the speakers prided themselves on being dispassionate and aloof from everyday concerns. For them, the uses of sociology in Lazarsfeld's sense were irrelevant, with most of the speakers seeking recognition from the profession, not the policy maker.

After the convention, the ASA appointed an editorial committee (William Sewell, Harold Wilensky, and Lazarsfeld) to ready the papers for publication. This was to prove a heroic task—a fact unerringly predicted by Donald Young, then president of the Russell Sage Foundation:

> "I don't envy you your job as a member of the committee responsible for making a volume on the uses of sociology out of the Washington papers . . . ," he wrote to Sewell.[6]

As it turned out, the editorial committee concluded that the papers were unsuitable, and, under Lazarsfeld's urging, the committee decided to start anew by commissioning papers for the proposed book.

This time, Lazarsfeld armed himself with a much more specific set of instructions. He assigned five domains to the concept of "uses." The first two had been placed in his program instructions—the use of theory and the use of empirical research. The last two were new—the use of specific research procedures and the application of the sociological perspective (although he did not specify exactly how the latter differed from theory). But it was a fifth realm that was newest of all. He called it "the mutual relations of research and policy." Some years later, this would turn out to be the core of the study of "utilization," especially the problems of "translation" and "gap," as they came to be known. In a nutshell, "translation" refers to the conversion of a practical problem into a research design; "gap" is the distance between research findings and the operational advice derived from them.

Close analysis of Lazarsfeld's guide for the contributors to the planned volume reveals two conspicuous omissions. First, he made no effort to define applied research or to deal with the usual dichotomy of basic and applied research. Later, in his own introduction to the published volume, Lazarsfeld would take a halfhearted stab at distinguishing basic from applied research, but it was a curiously unconvincing effort. He explained that the two types of research were only convenient verbal categories for studies that differed in origin and ultimate destination but not in intellectual fiber.[7] He substituted the term "autonomous" research for the misleading words "basic research," and he suggested "field-induced research" as a more apt description of "applied research." Nonetheless, his self-admitted difficulty in locating appropriate verbal tags for his ideas seems to have diluted his argument. In any case, a later distinction by Cronbach and Suppes between discipline-oriented and decision-oriented research[8] fared much better and has to some extent been incorporated into the language of social science.

Second, the guide for contributors not only excluded a definition of applied research, but the authors were informed that they need not dwell on questions of ethics, as a special paper on ethics would be prepared for the volume. (Robert Angell did write that paper, "The Ethical Problems of Applied Sociology.") It is my interpretation that both strategies of omission are worth noting because they exemplified Lazarsfeld's unceasing efforts to make applied social research academically respectable. After all, why make an evaluative distinction between "basic" and "applied" research, with "basic research" the praiseworthy arm? And, again, if ethical considerations are accorded little fanfare in the case of "basic" research, why introduce them in the context of "applied" research?

A Digression on Political Style

Later in the game, however, Lazarsfeld would run headlong into the issue of ethics. A research project on "utilization" was launched at the Bureau of Applied Social Research in 1968; the date coincided with the student uprisings at Columbia, and radical students voiced loud protest over Columbia's willingness to tolerate a project on utilization that was funded by the Office of Naval Research. How could the University condone a project that must surely be designed to tell a military agency how to apply research to the running of wars? The students published a formal objection. As we shall see, the project had virtually nothing to do with weapons and war, but, nonetheless, I believe that Lazarsfeld never prepared a formal reply to the students.

This practice of not opposing was, I think, characteristic of Lazarsfeld's working style. His very talent for improvisation and compromise facilitated an acceptance of alternative positions. He would often try to reconcile different views by identifying similarities in structure. Boudon[9] brings this out well in describing Lazarsfeld's predilection for history as merely a variant of his love for methodology. The tendency toward conciliation is evidenced in many of his writings on communications and the mass media. Perhaps it is not preposterous to say that his concept of the research bureau itself represents Lazarsfeld's consolidation of the academic and practical worlds.

There are times, however, when Lazarsfeld refused to compromise. He grew convinced that policy science centers, independent of university affiliation, represented a setback for empirical research because they drained talent from the universities with no attempt to replenish it by helping to train graduate students. His writings on the policy centers are frankly critical. For example, an article in *Policy Sciences*[10] (though labeled "An Outsider's View") takes those centers to task for neglecting the academic community and the responsibility to contribute back to sociological knowledge out of empirical studies.

The Emergence of "The Uses of Sociology"

But we now must return to our chronology. It was expected that the final book, to be entitled *The Uses of Sociology*, would require about a year of preparation, but actually, it was a book-destroying cycle that was set in motion. As the authors delayed completion of their papers, the three editors found themselves involved with other professional commitments. Long periods of silence from the editors then convinced the prospective contributors that the fate of the whole enterprise was uncertain, and they, in their turn, hesitated to send essays to the editors. Finally, in March 1964, the committee dispatched a letter to all the authors reminding them that the deadline was supposed to be June 1, 1964. Along with this reminder, Lazarsfeld inserted a critique of six of the chapters already submitted. His commentary was intended as guidance for the rest of the authors. Perhaps they found it discouraging instead; the files do not disclose their reactions, but the manuscripts were not in hand by June 1. Two years later, we find an optimistic letter from Lazarsfeld to his two co-editors reporting that the book was going well and that he was writing an introduction that would steer readers with different interests directly to appropriate parts of the book. He did note that an overabundance of the papers seemed to complain about non-uses of sociology.

Three months later, Lazarsfeld apprised his collaborators that he had developed a classified inventory of all the concrete examples in the papers and that he planned to "test out" the clarity of the detailed introduction (his fifth version) in a forthcoming Columbia seminar on the uses of social theory and research. Seven months later (April 27, 1967, to be exact), Lazarsfeld was once again in despair at the way that the authors had disregarded the guide he had prepared for them. The papers were now in, but they did not contain sufficient raw material for Lazarsfeld to develop a "theory of application" (the first time this phrase was used). Lazarsfeld continued to labor over the introduction, and, in a sense, it *became* the book for him. The introduction was tripartite: a brief note on the background of the book, a conceptual scheme dealing with the interaction between client and sociologist, and an outline of the major divisions of the book itself. The greater part of the introduction was devoted to the client-sociologist encounter.

The uneasy tale of the book came to an end in 1967 when *The Uses of Sociology* was actually published. Lazarsfeld had by then adopted the position that the introduction would serve as the prelude to further work on utilization. It did.

The "Uses" Book and Utilization

Before we describe the subsequent history of the book, we must ask how it was related to the methodology of utilization. Why do we not say unequivocally that the book was directed to that subject?

The introduction describes the *users* of sociology as sociologists and clients meeting within a structured setting. The dialogues of these meetings were seen to weave back and forth across two underlying needs: How to translate a practical concern into a research problem and how to draw policy advice from research information and conceptual analysis. Essentially, this was a static scheme, arrested in time. What Lazarsfeld did in the next stage of his work was to concentrate upon *using*, not *uses*. (He tried to highlight the difference in a speech at the North Central Sociological meetings in 1970, but, from the audience's questions after the meeting, the effort was evidently a bit premature. Lazarsfeld did not have the specific examples to nail down his point.)

The Columbia Project on Utilization

Fresh from the rigors of the *Uses* book, Lazarsfeld was asked to present a paper on "Recent Trends in American Sociology" at a conference in Rome in September 1967.[11] Toward the close of a lengthy discussion of current developments in quantitative and qualitative research, Lazarsfeld inserted a brief summary of his *Uses* introduction and spoke of the need for the academic world to learn more about the operation of applying sociology. These comments struck a responsive chord in at least one member of the Rome audience, a representative of the Office of Naval Research. Dr. Bert King was sufficiently interested in the topic of the utilization of research to suggest that Lazarsfeld submit a research proposal to his office.

On December 12, 1967, the proposal was sent. It was really a letter of intent describing, in rather general terms, a plan for a series of case studies of social research. The case studies were to run along two time lines: *retrospective* interviews with research investigators and sponsors and *prospective* followups of newly completed research as it flowed to decision makers. The Office of Naval Research was itself to be one of the research sites. The content was closely geared to the decision-making process: How policy makers communicate with sociologists and how decisions are finally reached from research. The proposal was approved almost immediately. As was his wont in beginning a new program of research, Lazarsfeld promptly began to marshal a corps of assistants at the Bureau. (Lazarsfeld regarded assistants as the standard-bearers of the future—more experienced than students, less entrenched than faculty.) Jeffrey Reitz had helped Lazarsfeld to enumerate the catalog of cases for the *Uses* introduction; the rest of the group had not been involved in the previous work. Joel Brooke, Aron Halberstam, Richard Lewis, Douglas McDonald, Carol Weiss, and I comprised the cadre. Later, other staff members would be recruited on a study-by-study basis.

How does one carve out a research program in an uncharted area like the methodology of the utilization of research? It is what Lazarsfeld had called the "translation" problem, in new guise: How does one convert an abstract idea into a series of research operations that will clarify the meaning of the initial formulation? As I see it, several decisions were crucial to the form the project took.

First, came the decision to focus on the cognitive aspects of utilization as a process. Utilization would no longer be represented by a map, as in the *Uses* book. Now, utilization would become a series of steps in time. The map had been a useful conceptual device for locating the parties engaged in utilization. But the map was less helpful in directing attention to the activity of using. The map was almost like a cast of characters and properties; the new diagram was more like a flow chart. Interestingly enough, this cycle underwent several revisions. At first, it was called the PRD cycle, the progression from problem identification to research to decision making.[12] Then it became the PKD cycle where *k*nowledge, instead of *r*esearch, was the middle phase. This change was intended to reflect the fact that sometimes the sociologist taps an existing repository of knowledge rather than embarking upon a brand-new study. In all probability, this is what a scholarly consultant will do, for example.

Eventually, Lazarsfeld dropped even the PKD cycle; its last appearance was in 1973. By then, he had determined to stop short of analyzing the actions taken by the policy makers. Instead, the project would explicate the ways in which the sociologist used research to arrive at *his* recommendations for action. This was called "the road to recommendation." The PKD arc now became a cycle of seven steps advancing all the way from problem defining to recommendation, with a glimpse of implementation and assessment beyond. (Somewhere in the last year of the project, 1975, the seven steps were quietly reduced to six.)

Concentration on the cognitive aspects of the utilization process meant the relative exclusion of such issues as the funding of research, the politics of research, or the social impediments to utilization. The topic was deliberately narrowed down for two reasons: to make the scale of the work manageable and to stake out a claim for pioneer territory. Although there were a few existing Readers on applied sociology, no research group had yet labored over the intellectual implications of what it meant to apply research to concrete decisions. After the "facts" are in, what happens next? What speculations about the past and guesses about the future must be added to empirical findings?

A second critical choice made early in the project was centering the work on case studies. These were frankly exploratory soundings. At the early stages of the project, there were no working hypotheses. The case studies were intended to provide cues for conjectures about the nature of utilization.

The Case Studies

In these field studies, the unit of analysis was not the individual but the collectivity or a set of collectivities. How did the U.S. Office of Education carry out its congressional mandate to study the effects of a student loan program? And what use did Congress make of the study in drafting new legislation on financial aid? Carol Weiss was asked to take charge of this inquiry. She "trailed" the government project through the Office of Education, a contract with the College Entrance Examination Board, a subcontract to the Bureau of Applied Social Research, a set of recommendations by the Office of Education, and a series of debates on the House floor.[13]

Another type of case study examined the role of a research program within some larger organization: an educational agency, a business company, a school. What were the organizational expectations for research? How were studies planned and initiated? What offices would be involved? How were findings transmitted horizontally and vertically? What were the organizational rewards for research? The field reports (e.g., Brooke, McDonald, Pasanella, and Weinman[14]) described the topography and raised questions for further consideration.

At the same time that the case studies were underway, Reitz was culling the literature for additional specific examples of how the phases in the utilization process had been handled. Halberstam was summarizing the controversies over the sociologist's role in the utilization of research (the sociologist as social engineer or as social enlightener or as social therapist?).

The open-ended nature of the work created some anxiety for the staff. It was often difficult to tell when a case study was productive or when it was "finished." Lazarsfeld used staff meetings to encourage the field investigators to pluck "themes" from the data—theirs or their colleagues'. Most of the themes (e.g., the road to recommendation, the organizational problems of center and periphery) were embryonic, quite a distance from true theoretical concepts. What they did was to sensitize the staff to look for comparative material in other cases or in other situations within the same organizational structure. (In a memo to the staff, Lazarsfeld referred to these types of generalizing as "lateral" and "vertical" transfer, thereby exemplifying the process of constructing themes). None of the themes derived from the case studies ever approached the level of generality of Stouffer's "relative deprivation" or Merton's "locals and cosmpolitans," which had also been drawn from case analyses. But the themes were useful anchoring points for the work.

Lazarsfeld's first progress report to the ONR was a real *tour de force* in the sense that he took a disparate set of case studies still underway and imposed a logical structure upon them. According to his report, the ultimate goal of the project was to work "toward a theory of the application of sociology," and the work thus far could be arranged in two categories, one cognitive, the other organizational. Many years before, Lazarsfeld had done much the same with his project on radio research. In 1939, he took a handful of assorted papers, persuaded the *Journal of Applied Psychology* that he should be their first guest editor, and published all the papers in an organized issue of the journal.

Lazarsfeld was quite convinced of the future utility of the case studies, and there was no attempt to generate statistical information or to develop an index of utilization. (During the middle of the project, James S. Coleman was asked to look over the case materials. He developed some intriguing propositions about the social structure of the utilization enterprise[15] and did, in fact, present a few cross-tabulations of the characteristics of researchers and clients.)

Case studies could not produce data where none existed, although the studies could point out these lacunae. If the parties engaged in utilization did not keep running records of how they reached particular decisions along the way, including the alternatives they considered but discarded, the ideas that occurred to them too late, the effects that were unanticipated, then dredging up the past was difficult, to say the least. Retrospective interviews could help, but they could never replace records of the past as it unfolded. In one kind of work, in particular, the utilization of social theory, this lack of introspection was most troubling. Perhaps a different type of case study, this one with individual experts or consultants as they were called in to give advice, would have been a better technique.

On this theme of trying to understand utilization as an ongoing process in perpetual motion, we should at least mention some of the alternatives which *this* project discarded. It will come as no surprise to researchers that the several proposals and the project had somewhat different contours. Among the plans mentioned to the sponsor but never implemented were these: an inventory of other centers concerned with utilization, an attempt to see where existing pieces of empirical research *might* have been applied, and a quantitative treatment of applied-basic controversies in the social sciences as compared with those in the natural sciences.

Expansion of the Project

Though some ideas were dropped, new ingredients were added as the project gained momentum. The work was extended to researchers at other centers, particularly the University of Pittsburgh where Lazarsfeld was helping to set up a graduate program in applied sociology. Two other sponsors, the Russell Sage Foundation and the National Science Foundation, contributed funds to the project. Lazarsfeld and Martin Jaeckel initiated a study of the utilization of sociological knowledge by presidential commissions.[16] Ruth Love[17] interviewed the clients of a research retrieval center to see what questions they asked and to what situations they transferred the answers. Brooke added a quantitative element by surveying sociologists' attitudes toward the utilization of their work; his dissertation suggested that the extent of indifference to uses might have been overestimated.[18] A conference of sociologists at the Greystone Conference Center, in Riverdale, N.Y., proved to be extremely stimulating. Invited papers from James Coleman and from Jiri Nehnevajsa introduced some of the organizational aspects of utilization that were needed to complement the project's heavy emphasis on cognitive processes. Allen Barton and Burkart Holzner provided much-needed insights about the role of social theory in utilization. Norman Hummon and Patrick Doreian[19] introduced some of the formal mathematical approaches to applied research. (The papers of the conference are expected to be published soon.)

The Summing Up

In the end, how far had the project gone toward a "theory of application," a systematic analysis of the logic of using research to solve practical problems? The "final report" was a book modestly entitled *An Introduction to Applied Sociology*;[20] Lazarsfeld did not think that any more grandiose title was justified.

Whether or not the methodology of the utilization of research has a future in the profession is hard to say. Perhaps some portions will be subsumed under the sociology of sociology. Others might be encompassed within the burgeoning field of applied sociology; the two Readers on Lazarsfeld's seminar reading list in 1966 have multiplied to nearly twenty. Perhaps the area of most intense activity will be the question of how to train young sociologists for the role of practitioner. Lazarsfeld and Merton long ago advocated a professional school for research in human affairs.[21] They proposed the creation of an institution similar to a medical school in that it would teach the substantive fundamentals of the social sciences together with the research techniques applicable to problems in public administration, marketing, law, or politics. That proposal never found support. Perhaps another one will.

Shortly before his death, Lazarsfeld was engaged in plans for a new and improved second edition of the *Applied Sociology* book. This time, he was thinking of using assistants from the Vienna Institute for Advanced Studies. Had he lived on to carry out those plans, the circuit of the Transatlantic transfer would have been complete.

Notes

1. "A Memoir in Honor of Professor Wold," in T. Dalenius, G. Karlsson and S. Malmquist, eds., *Scientists at Work—Festschrift in Honor of Herman Wold*. Uppsala, Sweden: Almquist and Wiksells, 1970, 79.

2. Robert K. Merton, "The Role of Applied Social Science in the Formation of Policy: A Research Memorandum," *Philosophy of Science* XVI (1949), 161–181.

3. Robert K. Merton, Leonard Broom and Leonard S. Cottrell, Jr., eds., *Sociology Today*. New York: Basic Books, 1959.

4. "Instructions to Session Chairmen for the 1962 Conference of the American Sociological Association," n.d.

5. "American Sociological Association Program," August 29–September 2, 1962.

6. Letter dated November 6, 1962.

7. "Introduction," in Paul F. Lazarsfeld, William H. Sewell, Harold Wilensky, eds., *The Uses of Sociology*. New York: Basic Books, 1967.

8. Lee J. Cronbach and Patrick Suppes, *Research for Tomorrow's Schools*. New York: Macmillan, 1969.

9. Raymond Boudon, "An Introduction to Lazarsfeld's Philosophical Papers," in Paul F. Lazarsfeld, *Philosophie des Sciences Sociales*. Paris: Gallimard, 1970.

10. "The Policy Science Movement (An Outsider's View)," *Policy Sciences* 6 (1975), 211–222.

11. "First International Congress of Social Sciences of the Luigi Sturzo Institute," Rome, September 5–10, 1967.

12. Paul Lazarsfeld and Jeffrey Reitz, *Toward a Theory of Applied Sociology*. New York: Columbia University Bureau of Applied Social Research, November 1970.

13. *The Consequences of the Study of Federal Student Loan Programs*. New York: Columbia University Bureau of Applied Social Research, 1970.

14. Joel I. Brooke, *The Utilization of Basic Social Research: A Case Study*. New York: Columbia University Bureau of Applied Social Research, 1972; Douglas McDonald, *Some Problems in the Organization and Use of Social Research in the U.S. Navy*. New York: Columbia University Bureau of Applied Social Research, 1971; Ann Pasanella and Janice Weinman, *The Road to Recommendation*, ONR Technical Report No. 3. New York: Columbia University Bureau of Applied Social Research, 1973. See also Jeffrey G. Reitz, *The Gap Between Knowledge and Decision in the Utilization of Social Science*, ONR Technical Report No. 1. New York: Columbia University Bureau of Applied Social Research, 1972; Douglas McDonald and Paul Lazarsfeld with the assistance of A. Halberstam, *Some Problems of Research Organization*, ONR Technical Report No. 6. New York: Columbia University Bureau of Applied Social Research, 1973; Jeffrey Reitz, *Social Interaction Between Policymaking and Social Scientists*, ONR Technical Report No. 4. New York: Columbia University Bureau of Applied Social Research, 1973.

15. James S. Coleman, "The Social Structure Surrounding Policy Research," in Ann K. Pasanella, ed., *Sociological Knowledge for Action.* Forthcoming.

16. Martin Jaeckel and Paul F. Lazarsfeld, "The Uses of Sociology by Presidential Commissions," in Mirra Komarovsky, ed., *Sociology and Public Policy.* New York: Elsevier, 1975.

17. Ruth Love, "Using a Dissemination Service." New York: Columbia University Bureau of Applied Social Research, 1974.

18. Joel Brooke, *A Survey of Social Researchers' Attitude Toward Utilization,* ONR Technical Report No. 2. New York: Columbia University Bureau of Applied Social Research, 1973.

19. Norman P. Hummon and Patrick Doreian, *Formal Approaches to Applied Social Research,* ONR Technical Report No. 7. New York: Columbia University Bureau of Applied Social Research, 1975.

20. Paul F. Lazarsfeld and Jeffrey G. Reitz with the collaboration of Ann K. Pasanella, *An Introduction to Applied Sociology.* New York: Elsevier Scientific Publishing, 1975.

21. "A Professional School for Training in Social Research," 1950. Reprinted in Paul F. Lazarsfeld, *Qualitative Analysis.* Boston: Allyn and Bacon, 1972. (Editors' note: see the chapter in this volume by Charles Y. Glock, "Organizational Innovation for Social Research and Training.")

PART 2

QUANTITATIVE METHODS AND REASONING

7. GENERATING MODELS AS A RESEARCH STRATEGY

Raymond Boudon

It is hardly an exaggeration to say that one of the main paradigms of modern empirical research in sociology is defined by the seminal papers of Paul Lazarsfeld on the logic of survey analysis and particularly on spurious correlations.[1] Lazarsfeld's ideas on the analysis of statistical relations in empirical research stimulated Herbert Simon's interest. Simon's paper on spurious correlations, in turn, stimulated the interest of several others. Finally, Lazarsfeld's ideas crystallized into what was to be known as "causal analysis," and causal analysis has become widely used in empirical research.[2]

But the interpretation of a statistical table or of a set of statistical tables seldom ends with causal analysis. Consider for instance the well-known example reported by Stouffer and his coworkers in the first volume of *The American Soldier*. Kendall's and Lazarsfeld's presentation of the finding is the following:[3] "Chart IX in I, 252, shows (on a personal level) that soldiers who were promoted were, as one would expect, considerably more optimistic about general promotion chances in the Army than those who were not promoted. But, in addition, a unit comparison between Military Police and the Air Corps is also presented. We learn that the promotion chances in the Military Police were much poorer than in the Air Corps. And yet the satisfaction with promotion in the Military Police was considerably higher among all subgroups." This analysis of the Chart IX of *The American Soldier* is a "causal analysis" (of an intuitive type) of the complicated structure relating individual satisfaction to two independent variables (individual promotion or not, belonging to a unit where promotion is frequent or not). The analysis displays a complicated interaction effect between the individual and what, since Lazarsfeld, would be called the contextual variable.

However, this causal analysis does not explain the chart. It simply summarizes it. This is made clear by Lazarsfeld's comment which proposes the following

51

theory to *explain* the chart (in the strong sense of the word *explain,* that is, making understandable:[4] "The promoted man in an advantageous unit enjoys his own promotion less and the non-promoted man resents his setback more. This would explain the positive association between promotion and approval of the promotion system based on personal data and the negative correlation between promotion chances and approval based or unit rates."[5]

What Lazarsfeld proposes in this last passage is a generating theory from which the statistical structure can be derived. This example is paradigmatic: *understanding* a statistical structure means in many cases building a generating theory or model (in the case where the theory need be formalized and has actually been) that includes the observed empirical structure as one of its consequences.[6]

Although sociological methodology has essentially devoted its attention in the last decade to such areas as causal analysis and, thanks in great part, to Lazarsfeld's original impulse, has made a considerable progress in this respect, it seems to me that a major task for the future will be to learn how to build generating theories to *explain* statistical structures.

In the following, I will offer a number of examples of generating theories, in most cases very simple, which I happened to develop for substantive rather than methodological reasons. I mean that my purpose in building them was to understand the *meaning* of some statistical structures which I had met in the course of various empirical researches.

Example 1: The *American Soldier* Game

It can be interesting to begin with an alternative explanation using a generating model of the above-mentioned finding from *The American Soldier.* As is well known, this finding has given rise to much theoretical research. It is related for instance to the development of frequently used concepts such as *relative deprivation* or *reference group.*[7] This is easy to understand, but the finding is puzzling. Moreover, it recalls some other famous but equally puzzling sociological statements such as Tocqueville's[8]—that in the years preceding the 1789 Revolution, dissatisfaction was higher in the parts of France where people in the average were better off and had more favorable expectations; or Durkheim's[9]— that satisfaction is greater in a system where the desires of the individuals are bounded. Such statements or findings are probably fascinating because, although counterintuitive, they correspond to common-sense experience.

An interesting and plausible explanation, to me at least, is the following. Let us consider a set of N persons, each knowing nothing about the others, except that they are N altogether. Imagine further that each of these N persons is faced with the decision—either enter in a competitive game or not. The competition game itself is of the simplest type: a fixed maximum number of winners (n) is assumed, and it is supposed that each will win an amount B; these winners will be drawn randomly from the persons who will have chosen to pay an amount C (with $C < B$), for the right to be admitted into the lottery. Let us further assume some theory of risk bearing—for instance, that each of the N persons would prefer playing rather than not, provided that the expected net gain is greater than some positive quantity h.

This model describes, though obviously in a very simplified fashion, a type of competition structure which frequently occurs in the real social life. A high school graduate, facing the eventuality of entering some prestigious institution of higher education, can be generally assumed to have a more or less precise evaluation of the number of students who will be accepted and of the number of students who are as good as he is himself. However, he will not generally know whether the others will or not actually "invest" and try to enter the institution. A soldier will in the same way often have a rough estimation of the number of soldiers who can plausibly be promoted over a period of time and of the number of eventual candidates who would be as qualified as he is himself.

Consider now two arithmetical applications of the model: in the first, we suppose, say, that $N = 20$, $B = 4$, $C = 1$, $n = 10$, $h = 1$; that is, that the size N of the group is 20, the maximum number n of winners is 10, the cost C of entry is 1, the value B of the benefit is 4, and h, the minimal value of the expected gain for the potential players to participate, is 1.

What will happen in this case? The model generates a competitive game which should be represented by a 20-dimensional payoff matrix. Fortunately, this matrix can be summarized, however. This can be done by considering a player whom we will call *Ego* and by considering the payoffs associated to each of the strategies opened to him as a function of the number of others choosing a given strategy. This summarization is made possible by the fact that the model considers the potential players as undistinguishable, so that the payoffs *Ego* can expect depend exclusively on the *number* of others choosing a given strategy and not on the identity of the players. Now, according to the model, every potential player has two strategies—playing or nonplaying. The value of *nonplaying* is zero. The value of *playing* depends on the number of others who choose the same strategy. Thus, let us call *Ego* one of the potential players. If either nobody beside him or 1, or 2, or . . . 9 persons beside him play the game, he will earn an amount worth 4 to a cost of 1, that is, a net gain of 3, as the total number of players will in none of these situations exceed the number of possible winners. If ten persons beside him play the game, he will earn a net gain of $4 - 1$ with probability 10/11, as in this case eleven persons altogether play the game whereas the maximum number of winners cannot exceed ten. This says that *Ego* will be exposed to lose 1, the price of his participation to the lottery, that is, to get a net gain of -1 with probability 1/11. In this case his expected net gain is $(4 - 1) \cdot (10/11) - 1 \cdot (1/11) = 2.6$. If eleven persons beside him play the game, he will get a net gain of $4 - 1$ with probability 10/12 and lose 1 with probability

2/12. His expected net gain in this case is $(4 - 1) \cdot (10/12) - 1 \cdot (2/12) = 2.3$. These very simple computations can be extended to the other possible cases. Their result is given in Table 1.

The interesting feature is that in all cases the strategy *playing* gives to *Ego* an outcome which he prefers to the outcome guaranteed by the alternative strategy. In the worst possible assumption he can make (all, that is, the 19 other potential players, beside him, choose to play), the lottery gives him an expected net gain of 1, which, according to the assumption of the model, he prefers to the certainty of a zero gain, which is guaranteed to him by the alternative strategy. Let us recall indeed that by assumption a player prefers a lottery giving him an expected gain to a fixed sum provided that the expected gain exceeds the fixed sum by at least *h*, which has been supposed equal to 1. Consequently, playing is a dominant strategy for *Ego*: independently of the number of others who could choose to play, *Ego* should prefer to play rather than not. But this is, of course, true of all the potential players, as *Ego* is just any of them. Consequently, all will play. But, if all do so, ten will earn an amount worth 4 to a cost of 1, that is, will get a net gain of +3, whereas ten will earn an amount worth zero to the same cost, that is, will get a net loss of −1. The model generates a situation in which, if all behave rationally, ten people will be satisfied and ten will be frustrated. The structure of the situation of competition is such that playing is an appealing strategy for all. But the number of losers is high.

Let us now imagine a situation similar to the previous one except for one parameter: assume as previously that $N = 20, B = 4, C = 1, h = 1$, and change the value of *n* from 10 to 5. That is, there can be now at most five winners. In other words, the overall expectations open to the group as a group are now less favorable than in the previous case: the objective chances of upward mobility are now lower. An analysis similar to the previous one shows easily that, for *Ego,* the strategy *playing* is preferable for him to the strategy *nonplaying* provided that the number of other players does not exceed nine. In the case where this number is exactly nine, the expected net gain associated with the lottery *Ego* is faced with if he chooses to play is 1. Because this expected gain exceeds by 1 unit the net gain of zero he would get from not playing the game, he will play (Table 2). But, when the number of other players exceeds nine, *Ego* should, according to the assumption prefer nonplaying to playing, as playing gives an expected net gain smaller than 1.

It is interesting to note that the change in the value of the parameter *n* changes the whole structure: Whereas in the former case all participants had a dominant strategy, in the latter none of the participants has a dominant strategy. In other words, he cannot say absolutely which of his strategies is better as this depends on the number of others who will choose such and such strategy. But, according to the assumptions, he does not know (nor do the others) how many people will select which strategy. The best thing he can do in this situation appears at first sight as strange: if *Ego* is a rational player, he would flip a coin to determine whether or not he should play. Flipping a regular coin with probabili-

TABLE 1. Values of *Ego*'s Strategies as a Function of the Number of Others Choosing the Strategy "Playing"

				Number of Others Choosing the Strategy "Playing"									
	0	1	2	...	9	10	11	12	...	17	18	19
Strategies of *Ego*												
Playing	3	3	3	...	3	(2.6)	(2.3)	(2.1)	...	(1.2)	(1.1)	(1)
Not playing	0	0	0	...	0	0	0	0	...	0	0	0

Figures in parentheses represent *expected* net gains.

TABLE 2. Values of *Ego*'s Strategies as a Function of the Number of Others Choosing the Strategy "Playing"

				Number of Others Choosing the Strategy "Playing"									
	0	1	...	4	5	6	7	8	9	10	11	...	18	19
Strategies of *Ego*														
Playing	3	3	...	3	(2.3)	(1.9)	(1.5)	(1.2)	(1.0)	(0.8)	(0.7)	...	(0.1)	(0.0)
Not Playing	0	0	...	0	0	0	0	0	0	0	0	...	0	0

Figures in parentheses represent *expected* net gains.

ties .5 associated with the two possible outcomes is an equilibrium strategy in the sense that no potential player has an interest in choosing another one. Indeed, if he would do so (for instance if he would flip a coin with probabilities .6 or .4 rather than .5 associated to one of the outcomes), he would contribute to diminish the value of his own expected net gain. Thus (assuming for the sake of simplicity that heads and tails will appear *exactly* as frequently), the outcome of the game will be that ten players will "choose" not to play, that ten will play and that, among the latter, five will win and five lose (it is interesting to note that the outcome of the game would be the same if the N members of the population were randomly and sequentially selected, each being informed of the strategy chosen by the members drawn before him).

Let us now compare the two situations just analyzed. In the first one, a greater proportion of people is promoted; however, the proportion of people dissatisfied with the system is greater, since ten have invested and gained nothing from their investment, while in the second case only five people have lost their investment. Certainly the feeling of frustration must be greater among those who have invested in the game and derived nothing from it than among those who have "rationally" decided not to invest. The former cannot fail to be painfully affected by seeing that other people who have invested the same amount as themselves are rewarded whereas they get nothing.

The model generates in summary a *structure* similar to *The American Soldier* finding, to Tocqueville's "law," or to Durkheim's statement that a society that offers more mobility *can* simultaneously generate more dissatisfaction. It is an example of a generating theory. It is interesting in the sense that it can be indefinitely complicated: Thus, B can be made a decreasing function of n (the more people are honored, the smaller the honor). The potential players can be divided into classes. Thus, it can be supposed that a class of potential players will be characterized by a value h_1, greater than the value h_2 characterizing the other class. This is a way of simulating the idea that people with lower resources are less prone to risk bearing. Various assumptions can be made on the information of the participants and so on. I do not want to go here into the detail of these possible complications. The main point which I want to make is that the model provides an example of a generating theory whence consequences corresponding to a number of counter intuitive or at least puzzling empirical findings can be easily derived, as well as many other consequences.[10]

Example 2: An Example of Overinvestment Effects

The second example is a variant of the first. I was puzzled in the course of a study on short-term institutions of higher education in France by a number of observations which I found hard to reconcile with one another: Short-term (two years) institutions of higher education appeared in view of the statistics of enrollments to have little attraction to students, who preferred in large majority the traditional long-term (four or five years for the *licenced* degree) institutions of higher education. However, scholarships were more readily available in the two-year institutions. On the other hand, *average* income appeared empirically about the same for the students from the two-year institutions as for the "licencies" (four or five years) from the traditional system. The *variance* of income was for its part greater for the long-term students, however: the licencies were more likely to get a level of income much lower or much higher than the average income. Let us add that the minority of students who had chosen the two-year system of higher education appeared satisfied. However, given the available data, it is impossible to know whether they were more satisfied than the long-term students. Also, the two-year students appeared to rank the two-year institutions higher in many respects (quality of teaching, probability of finding a job after completion of studies, etc.) than the traditional long-term institutions. On the whole, most of the empirical findings gave the impression that the two-year institutions were attractive both objectively and subjectively as far as clear conclusions can be derived in this latter respect from the feeling of satisfaction expressed by the two-year students.[11] This appeared in contradiction to the fact that the number of enrollments remained very modest in comparison to the enrollments in the traditional long-term system.

Of course, many interpretations can be given of the apparent contradictions; for example, the long-term institutions are not more rewarding socially and economically, but they are more fun. But it may be interesting to examine whether the counterintuitive finding (apparently attractive institutions attract few potential candidates) does not simply derive from the structure of the competition process generated by the institutional framework.

So, let us assume that the choice the students are confronted with is the following: either choose a *short-term institution,* less costly, on the average socially as rewarding as the long-term one, or a *long-term institution,* more costly, on the average socially not more rewarding than the short-term institution, but associated with a higher probability than the short-term institution of rewards both higher and lower than the average. This is, reduced to its simplest logical form, the type of choice that appears empirically as implicitly proposed to the students.

The prediction likely to be made intuitively from this description of the logic of the choice offered to the participants is probably that the short-term institutions should be attractive. This is probably the kind of consideration that the political authorities had in mind when they developed these institutions. However, it is possible to show that the structure of the competition process does not *necessarily* make the short-term institutions very attractive.

Assume that N, the number of participants, is 20; that B_s and C_s, the benefit and the cost associated to the short term, are, respectively, 2 and 1; and that the cost C_L of the long term is equal to 2. As for the benefit associated to the long term, we will assume that long-term students will receive a reward worth 4 but that a reward of this level can be given at most to six people. If more than six students choose the long term, if for instance eight choose the long term altogether, two of them will receive a reward worth 3. More precisely, we will assume that rewards worth 4 can be attributed at most to six people and that rewards worth 3 at most to eight people. Finally, if more than $6 + 8 = 14$ students choose the long term, rewards worth 2 will have to be attributed. This simple model describes more or less the type of choice that is offered to actual students: either choose a short-term institution and be sure to derive from a moderate investment a moderate return or choose the long term which requires a higher investment and whose return is less predictable (more widely scattered) and depending on the number of candidates choosing the same strategy. As in the previous example, let us assume that h is positive. That is, we assume that people prefer a lottery with an expected gain g to a certain gain k, if g is greater than k by some positive quantity.

Let us now see what a rational player would do in the case of this example. The short-term strategy gives a net gain of 1 (benefit 2, cost 1) with certainty. The long-term strategy gives a net gain of 2 (benefit 4, cost 2) with certainty if not more than six people altogether, that is, not more than five people beside *Ego* choose the same strategy. In the case where, say, eight people altogether, that is, seven people beside *Ego* would choose the long-term strategy, each would get 4 from his investment of 2, for a net gain of 2, with probability 6/8, whereas he would get 3 from his investment of 2, for a net gain of 1 with probability 2/8. In that case the expected net gain of each of the players would be $2 (6/8) + 1 (2/8) = 1.7$. The structure of the game can be summarized, as in the previous case, by a table giving the returns *Ego* can expect from the two alternative strategies (here, long-term strategy versus short-term strategy) as a function of the number of others choosing the strategy "long term" (table 3).

Assume, for instance, that $h = 0.4$. Following the kind of analysis used in the previous example, the best strategy for each of the participants would be to choose the strategy "long term" with a probability 14/20. So that (assuming *exactly* fourteen persons would actually choose the long-term strategy if each would choose the equilibrium strategy) the outcome of the game would be that, among the fourteen players, six would get a net gain of 2 (benefit 4, cost 2) whereas eight people would get a net gain of 1 (benefit 3, cost 2), that is, a return from their investment which makes them in a situation exactly similar to the one they would have known had they chosen the alternative strategy. Though attractive, the short-term strategy would have attracted a moderate number of students: six. Making the value of h lower makes the outcome still more dramatic. Thus, with $h = 1$, all students except one choose the long term according to the prediction of the model. In that case five students get a net gain of zero from their investment in the long-term educational system, a return lower than the one they would have derived from the short-term system. Thus, at equilibrium, the situation is similar to the one observed in reality: with $h = 1$, most students choose the long-term institution; the average net benefit is about

TABLE 3. "Values" of *Ego*'s Strategies as a Function of the Number of Students Choosing the Strategy "Long Term"

Strategies of *Ego*	0	1	2	...	5	6	7	...	9	...	13	...	18	19
								Number of Others Choosing the Strategy "Long Term"						
Long term	2	2	2	...	2	(1.8)	(1.7)	...	(1.6)	...	(1.4)	...	(1.1)	(1)
Short term	1	1	1	...	1	1	1	...	1	...	1	...	1	1

Figures in parentheses correspond to *expected* gains.

the same for the long- and the short-term students; a noticeable proportion of the long-term students get a net benefit higher than the net benefit accruing to the short-term students; symmetrically, as in reality, a noticeable proportion of the former get a net benefit lower than the latter.

I can, of course, not discuss in detail the underlying assumptions of the model, or argue in detail why it is a more or less realistic description of the empirical situation I originally considered, or present a more general formalization going beyond the arithmetic example considered here, or even suggest possible variations, which, of course, are numerous and some of them obvious. My point is that the model provides a generating theory from which the apparent "contradictions" of the observed data can be "solved." In other words, the model generates for some sets of values of the parameters outcomes whose structure is comparable to what can be observed in the real world—rational men placed in competition structures with given characteristics can behave so as to give the superficial impression of behaving irrationally.

Example 3: The Generation of Educational and Social Inequalities

The first two examples of generating models presented in the previous sections have the common feature of using game theory. They have the advantage of suggesting that game theory can be used in areas of sociological research where it is not traditionally used. Other classical examples of the use of game theory or at least of the game theoretical conceptual framework in generating models used to explain statistical structures can easily be given. One interesting example in this respect is Olson's theory which explains why the number of members of a political party or of a union is generally much lower than the number of people getting benefits from the union or supporting the party.[12] Olson's theory is a good example of a generating theory from which a number of characteristics of empirical data on the level of participation in voluntary associations can be explained.

But the notion of generating theory or model does not necessarily imply the use of game theory. At a very general level, a generating theory can be typically described as a theory containing two logical core elements: (1) a description of the logic postulated to regulate the actions of the individuals observed in a survey or some other kind of observation from which quantitative data are derived and (2) a description of the social constraints within which the logic of individual action develops.

The third example is drawn from my work on educational opportunity.[13] It will not be presented in detail. One problem I met in this work was to explain why social mobility did not seem empirically to be affected by the increase in the equality of educational opportunity which had taken place since World War II in all Western societies contrary to the intuitive assumption that says that more equality in education between the social classes should diminish social heritage. Empirical observations revealed (1) that educational disparities between classes diminish in a steady and moderate fashion during the two decades following World War II in Western societies and (2) that the structure of intergenerational social mobility remained more or less constant in the same countries. Also, mobility appears empirically as very similar in countries very different from one another in many respects including the degree of class disparities with regard to education. That this empirical finding was counterintuitive is confirmed by the interest raised and the amount of further research generated by Lipset and Bendix's monograph where it was first presented.[14]

It is not possible to present in detail here the generating model which I have used to interpret these "contradictions" or at least puzzling findings. Its main logical components are the following.

1. A theory of individual decision with regard to education. This theory is a rational theory, similar to the one presented in the previous secton, but complemented by some ideas drawn from the reference group theory.

2. A definition of the constraints generated by the structure of the educational system. One essential constraint in this respect is that any educational system necessarily offers to the cohorts who come through it a sequence of choices corresponding to alternatives unequally rewarding for the individual. This ideal typical structure of the educational system has the consequence that the effects of the logic of individual decisions are of an exponential nature.

3. A theory of the overtime change from one cohort to the next of the structure (in the sense of the parameters) of the individual decision process.

4. A generation from the previous components of the model of typical overtime (from one cohort to the next) change in a number of distributions; overtime change in the proportion of students with a given level of school achievement and from a given social origin who reach each of a number of possible levels of school attainment; overtime change in the social composition of the student body at each educational level, and so on.

5. A theory of the allocation of individuals at the various levels of the social structure as a function of educational level.

6. A generation from the previous components of the model of fictitious intergenerational mobility matrices, showing that, under broad circumstances, a decrease in the level of class disparities with regard to education can be accompanied by no increase in the level of intergenerational social mobility, even though, as is assumed by the model, those with a relatively higher level of educational attainment are relatively privileged in the status allocation process.

On the whole, the model generates a number of statistical outcomes. More precisely, it gives specific predictions not on the numerical values, but on the structural properties of the relations between various subsets of variables including time, age, school achievement, social origin, social status, educational level, and the like. Thus, it shows, as we have just seen, that (under broad and specific circumstances) equalization of educational disparities does not generate a decrease of intergenerational social heritage. It shows also that countries very different with respect to educational disparities between classes are not necessarily very different with regard to intergenerational social mobility. It "predicts" the structural change in the composition of the student body at various educational levels one should expect to observe under given assumptions and so on.[15]

I recalled briefly this example because it illustrates a case in which the number of statistical structures predicted by the model is much greater than in the previous examples. The model is a kind of theoretical machinery able to generate a number of predictions on the structure of the relations concerning various subsets of the above-mentioned list of variables. In other words it relates a number of empirical statistical tables such as overtime change in the number of students at each educational level, overtime change in the composition of the student body, overtime change in the structure of social expectations associated with a given educational level, overtime change in the structure of intergenerational mobility, for instance.

But, whereas the model is much more complicated than those of the previous sections, it is of the same nature in the sense that it is characterized by the fact that its axiomatics include a specific theory of individual action as well as a description of the structural constraints in the framework in which individuals act, whereas its consequences include a number of specific predictions at the level of aggregate statistical relations between the variables included in the model.

The notion of generating model is, I believe, a fundamental one for the sociology of tomorrow. It is a way of reconciling sociological theory and statistical analysis, quantitative analysis and *understanding* in the Weberian sense. It avoids, by essence so to say, the pitfalls of atomism as well as of sociologism. By contrast with sociologism, which tends to make the individuals the mere products of social structures, the notion of generating models imply the definition of a logic of individual action, decision, or behavior. By contrast with atomism, generating models go beyond mere averaging of individual behaviors. In a generating model, individual actions are *aggregated*: the outcome of this aggregation depends on the individual logic of action or behavior as it is hypothesized by the generating model and on the assumptions made relatively to the social context within which individuals act.

Obviously, this notion is not new. It can be found implicitly in the work of many classical sociologists such as Tocqueville or Durkheim, not to mention more modern works. Lazarsfeld's interpretation of the famous finding from *The American Soldier* is an example of a generating theory of a verbal type. Tocqueville and Durkheim have also presented generating theories of their important finding according to which satisfaction is not necessarily a monotonically increasing function of mobility. Nonverbal generating theories, that is, generating models, are not very frequent in sociology. They are much more often used by economists, for instance. In sociology, descriptive statistical models such as the regression models used in causal analysis are much more frequently used than generating models.

However, generating models have the advantage that they can contribute to increase our *understanding* of the statistical structures that we observe in empirical research. Certainly, the notion of generating models suggests a synthesis between some of Lazarsfeld's main areas of investigation: the analysis of statistical relations, the relationship between the statistical analysis and the interpretation of statistical tables, the logic of individual action, the relationship between the logic of individual action and the social context within which individuals behave.

Notes

1. Patricia L. Kendall and Paul F. Lazarsfeld, "Problems of Survey Analysis," in Merton and Lazarsfeld, eds., *Continuities in Social Research,* Glencoe, Ill., The Free Press, 1950, pp. 133–96; "Interpretation of statistical relations as a research operation", in Paul F. Lazarsfeld and Morris Rosenberg, ed., *The Language of Social Research,* Glencoe, Ill., The Free Press 1955, pp. 115–25.

2. Herbert Simon, "Spurious Correlation: A Causal Interpretation," *Journal of the American Statistical Association,* 49 (September 1954), pp. 467–479. It would be impossible to give here a list of references on causal analysis.

3. Patricia L. Kendall and Paul F. Lazarsfeld, "The Relation between Individual and Group Characteristics in *The American Soldier,*" in Paul F. Lazarsfeld and Morris Rosenberg, pp. 290–297.

4. Obviously, analyzing the statistical data of Chart IX with the help of the regression techniques used in modern "causal analysis" would not explain (in the strong sense of making understandable, *verständlich*) the structure either. The main difference between the intuitive causal analysis of the type often used by Lazarsfeld and the regression techniques used in modern causal analysis is that the latter provide a quantification of the effects.

5. Patricia L. Kendall and Paul F. Lazarsfeld, "The Relation between Individual and Group Characteristics in *The American Soldier,*" in Paul F. Lazarsfeld and Morris Rosenberg, p. 295.

6. I borrow the expression "generating model" from T. J. Fararo, "The Nature of Mathematical Sociology," *Social Research,* 36, 1 (Spring 1969), 75–92.

7. For a general discussion of these concepts, see W. G. Runciman, *Relative Deprivation and Social Justice.* Berkeley: University of California Press, 1966.

8. A. de Tocqueville, *Oeuvres complètes, l'Ancien Régime et la Révolution.* (Paris: Gallimard, 1951), pp. 222–223.

9. E. Durkheim, *Le Suicide,* p. 277.

10. Raymond Boudon, *La Logique de la frustration relative* (unpublished).

11. The model described in this section as well as the empirical data that inspired it are presented in R. Boudon, Ph. Cibois, and J. Lagneau, "Enseignement supérieur court et pièges de l'action collective," *Revue française de Sociologie,* XVI, 159–88, and "Short Higher Education and the Pitfalls of Collective Action," *Minerva,* 14, 1 (Spring 1976), 33–60.

12. Mancur Olson, *The Logic of Collective Action.* Cambridge: Harvard University Press, 1965.

13. Raymond Boudon, *Education, Opportunity and Social Inequality.* New York, Wiley, 1974.

14. Seymour Martin Lipset and Reinhard Bendix, *Social Mobility in Industrial Societies.* Berkeley: University of California Press, 1963.

15. T. Fararo, "A Mathematical Analysis of Boudon's IEQ Model," *Social Sciences Information,* 15, 2–3 (1976), 431–475.

8.   THE MEANING OF CAUSAL ORDERING

Herbert A. Simon

The topic of causal analysis (alias "path analysis"), and the closely allied topics of structural equation estimation and identification, have accumulated a large literature in the past couple of decades, both in the field of economics, where most of the underlying theory was developed, and in sociology and political science, where a great many applications and extensions of the theory have taken place. Since the history of these topics is being treated in another essay in this volume, I will not concern myself with it here. Nor will I undertake an expository account of the statistical techniques to which causal analysis has given rise. A number of excellent expositions of these techniques are readily available: among them are Blalock's *Causal Inferences in Nonexperimental Research* (1964), Fisher's *The Identification Problem in Econometrics* (1966), and the three recent survey volumes, *Sociological Methodology, 1970,* edited by Borgatta and Bohrnstedt, *Causal Models in the Social Sciences* (1971), edited by H. M. Blalock, and *Structural Equation Models in the Social Sciences* (1973), edited by Goldberger and Duncan.

I will assume that my readers are familiar with this technical material, or at least with its existence, and that they have been appropriately instructed, edified, and perhaps even confused by the lush jungle of technique contained in it. My purpose here is to cut away some of this exuberant growth so that we may examine the conceptual seeds and roots from which it has sprouted. I will be concerned, not with the methods of causal analysis, but with its purposes. What questions does causal analysis seek to answer, and how does it answer them?[1]

The discussion in this paper, as in much of the literature of causal analysis, will be limited to linear systems. I should call attention, however, to Paul Lazarsfeld's important contributions to the case of discrete, and especially dichotomous, variables. Lazarsfeld's insistence on the importance of prior knowledge for the making of causal attributions is especially relevant to the discussion here.

65

The Identification Problem

The topic of causal analysis is inextricably interwoven with the identification problem. In this section, I should like to introduce that problem in the simplest cases of two to four variables. All of the important issues will be illustrated by these examples, so that we will not need to concern ourselves with complex situations involving larger numbers of variables.

Let us suppose that, for a sample of adults, we have measures of their total number of years of schooling (x) and of their verbal abilities (y). Now we might be interested in how people's verbal abilities affect the amount of education they obtain. In this case, it would be natural to write

(1) $$x = Ay + B.$$

By the usual method of least squares, or by any other curve-fitting procedure, we could then estimate the coefficients, A and B, of eq. (1) and could interpret A as expressing the expected number of years of additional education for each unit increase in ability as measured by the test. However, this inference would make any thoughtful person nervous. Isn't the relation exactly the reverse of the one we have assumed? Isn't it amount of education that determines the score on the verbal ability test? In that case, we should have written

(2) $$y = Cx + D.$$

Again, we could estimate the coefficients, C and D. If the fit of the data to a straight line were very close, we would have, approximately, $C = 1/A$. But now we would interpret C as expressing the average increase in verbal ability produced by each additional year of education. Although there is a simple arithmetic relation between A and C, the two interpretations of them are entirely different.

The difference in interpretation arises, not from the algebra—the two equations are algebraically indistinguishable, each being derivable from the other—but from our implicit attributions of two completely different *causal mechanisms* to them. We would write the first equation if we thought there was a causal mechanism that determined, at each stage in the educational process, which students would continue and which would terminate their educations, and if these decisions depended upon the students' verbal abilities. We would write the second equation if we thought that the process of education operated as a causal mechanism gradually increasing students' measured verbal abilities. The two equations are not, therefore, simply different notations for the same proposition. They represent two substantively distinct theories about the phenomena.

Clearly it is of great practical and theoretical importance to decide which interpretation is correct. The difference between them will reveal itself whenever we intervene to alter the mechanism in order to affect the consequences.[2] If the first tells the whole story, then continuing the education of a person beyond the point predicted by his verbal ability score will not be expected to raise that score, nor will curtailing the education lower it. If the second is fully correct, then the reverse is true: changing the number of years of education will indeed change the verbal scores. Nothing in the data themselves favors either one of these interpretations.

Suppose we believe that, in actual fact, both mechanisms are operative—that verbal ability does indeed increase with increasing amounts of education but that verbal ability also determines how long a person will pursue his formal education. Then both an equation of the form 1 and an equation of the form 2 will hold between the variables x and y. But, if this is so, then, from an estimating standpoint, we are in an even more difficult situation than before, for the simultaneous operation of the mechanisms described by eq. 1 and 2 determines unique equilibrium values for both x and y. If both mechanisms are operating, our observations will not lie on a particular straight line at all, but will fall at a single point. The observations will not determine the coefficients, A and C in eq. 1 and 2, for there is an infinity of pairs of straight lines that pass through the equilibrium point. A pair can be found having any desired value whatsoever of the coefficients.[3]

Of course, actual observations will contain errors of "noise" and hence will not all fall on a single point but will be clustered about it. However, the analysis we wish to carry out here does not depend at all on the presence or absence of random error in the measurements, so we will treat them as though they were precise and would, in fact, all fall on one point, provided both equations held.

To account for the linear relation actually observed between the variables, we will have to postulate that one, or both, of the equations is modified by the influence of some additional variable. Let us suppose, for example, that verbal ability is determined not only by years of schooling, but also by native aptitude which we will assume can be measured by something called "IQ." (The example is meant to be entirely hypothetical and not to imply that I believe that any existing measure of intelligence can be regarded as a valid yardstick of "native aptitude.") Under this assumption, eq. 2 will have to be replaced by

$$(2') \qquad\qquad y = Cx + Dz + E,$$

where z is IQ. Now any set of observations satisfying both eq. 1 and 2' will, in fact, have a slope in the (x, y) plane equal to A, and hence that slope can be interpreted as the amount of increase in education, at equilibrium, that will be produced by a unit increase in verbal ability (regarding the latter an an independent variable). Specifically, we will have

$$(3) \qquad\qquad A = \left(\frac{\sigma_x}{\sigma_y}\right) r_{xy} = \frac{\sigma_x}{\sigma_y},$$

the last equality deriving from our assumption that eq. 1 holds exactly, so that $r_{xy} = 1$. On the other hand, we still cannot make estimates of C and D that would separate out the effect upon y of x from the effect of z. We can only estimate

$$(4) \qquad \frac{D}{(1 - CA)} = \frac{\sigma_y}{\sigma_z} ,$$

the complex coefficient on the left side of eq. 4 being the *net* effect of a unit change in IQ upon verbal ability, taking into account both the direct effect (eq. 2′) and the indirect effect through the change in amount of schooling (the feedback to eq. 2′ through the mechanism of eq. 1). Notice that eq. 3 and 4, and the conclusions we have drawn from them, depend critically upon the assumption that z does not appear in equation 1, that is, that IQ exerts no direct effect upon amount of schooling completed, but influences schooling only indirectly through its effect upon verbal ability.

Instead of introducing IQ as a new independent variable, we might have introduced some variable (w, say) to measure social facilitation or discouragement of the continuation of schooling. This new variable would be introduced into equation 1, as one of the direct determinants of amount of schooling, rather than eq. 2, as a direct influence upon verbal ability. We would then have the new equation

$$(1') \qquad x = Ay + Bw + F.$$

In this case, the original eq. 2 could be used, with the observed data, to estimate C:

$$(5) \qquad C = \left(\frac{\sigma_y}{\sigma_x}\right) r_{xy} = \frac{\sigma_y}{\sigma_x} .$$

Notice that we arrived at an estimate of A in eq. 3 and, alternatively, at an estimate of C in eq. 5, simply by making different assumptions about what third variable was affecting the behavior of the system. We used exactly the same data (the standard deviations of the variables x and y) to estimate both C and A. And, indeed, in the absence of statistical distributions, C is simply the reciprocal of A, as we had been led to expect earlier. What is still more peculiar about the situation is that, in estimating these parameters, we did not even have to observe the values of the third variable we introduced, for these values do not enter into the parameter estimation in any way, and we obtain the same parameter estimate no matter what these values might be. The critical new information, which allows us to estimate A from eq. 1 and 2′, whereas we could not from eq. 1 and 2, was simply the *a priori* information that a third variable existed that had a direct effect upon one of the two postulated mechanisms but not on the other. Hence, the third variable, which is assumed to have this effect, need not be observable at all, nor does our observing it or not observing it change the assumptions we have to make in order to guarantee the estimatability (ie., identifiability) of coefficients in the original equations.

If we postulate that both of the auxiliary variables, z and w, are present, with w appearing only in eq. $1'$ and z only in eq. $2'$, then the state of identifiability of the coefficients changes again. In this case, we can estimate each of the coefficients, A, B, C, D, provided that z and w are observable variables. In the special case, for example, where $r_{zw} = 0$, it is easy to show that

$$(6) \qquad A = \left(\frac{r_{xz}}{r_{yz}}\right)\left(\frac{\sigma_x}{\sigma_y}\right), \text{ whereas}$$

$$(7) \qquad C = \left(\frac{r_{yw}}{r_{xw}}\right)\left(\frac{\sigma_y}{\sigma_x}\right).$$

There is nothing special about the particular examples I have chosen for purposes of illustration. In any case whatsoever, detection of a linear relation between two variables does not tell us which of the variables is causing the other to change. Indeed, it may be the case that each is influencing the other to some extent. Alternatively, neither variable may be driving the other directly, but both may be determined by some third, observed or unobserved, variable. For example, suppose that z and w were the same variable and that both A and C were zero (no direct relation between x and y). Then it is easily shown that the slope of the regression of y on x is simply $\left(\frac{\sigma_y r_{yz}}{\sigma_x r_{xz}}\right)$. Under the assumptions we have been making, the correlation between x and y would still be unity. This is the classical case of spurious correlation.

I have carried through these examples in nonstochastic form to show that, at its root, the problem of identifying the coefficients of regression equations is not a statistical problem that would disappear if we were able to make all measurements with perfect accuracy and to observe all the variables involved in the postulated relations. Even under these circumstances, we must make *a priori* assumptions about the mechanisms that underlie the behavior of the variables if we are to estimate the coefficients. And, in general, the assumptions we make will allow us to estimate some, but not all, of the coefficients.

What does it mean to say that we must make *a priori* assumptions in order to construct identified models of the phenomena we are seeking to explain? The whole procedure has a suspiciously circular appearance. The special characteristic of scientific theories—as distinguished from theological or metaphysical ones—is that they should be based on fact and testable by empirical evidence. What becomes of the empirical foundation of science if we demand *a priori* assumptions at the very core of our theory construction? To see what is involved, we must explore more deeply the nature of the "mechanisms" that the specific equations in a system of relations among variables are supposed to represent.

What Are Mechanisms?

I have introduced the notion of "mechanism" informally, assuming that the reader already has an intuitive notion of what is meant by the term. We need now to make that notion somewhat more explicit, although I do not know how to formalize it completely. If we see a heavy object suspended above the ground, we look for the wire that is holding it up. In the absence of a wire, or other visible support, we try to conceive of other ways in which a force could be exerted on the object to oppose the force of gravity: a magnet somewhere in the vicinity, perhaps? or a vertical air jet from below? or perhaps someone has discovered an effective gravity shield and has installed it here?

In many, but not all cases, a mechanism means something visible which experience tells us is capable of producing the observed effect. If the mechanism is not itself visible, then there must be some detectable circumstances that tell us it is present. (Gravitational force is exerted upon a body when it is near the surface of the earth or some other massive body; magnetism, when an object made of magnetic material is present.) Our belief in a gravity shield would depend on there being specified independent tests of whether the shield was present or absent.

Our suspicion of ESP rests in considerable measure upon the absence of independent indications of mechanism or of specifications of what the character of such a mechanism might be. In any case where one person's behavior influenced another's, we would expect to see some form of visual, tactile, or auditory communication between them. If it could be shown, as ESP experiments attempt to show, that the second person could not have been aware of the behavior of the first, we would be at a loss to explain the influence exerted on the second person's behavior—and most of us would be dissatisfied with our understanding of the outcome until we had identified a possible transmission mechanism.[4]

Notice that, when we postulate a mechanism to explain a particular phenomenon, we are importing into the explanation our knowledge, or supposed knowledge, of the world gained from previous experience with related phenomena. When we postulate that a wire is supporting the suspended body, our postulate incorporates our previous experience with wires and strings; when we postulate that it is being held up by a magnet, we reflect our prior experience with magnets. If we are skeptical of the gravity shield explanation, it is because we are not aware of any previous successes in blocking the force of gravity and cannot specify the kinds of materials that would produce that effect or where they would have to be located.

Mechanism is closely related to the ideas of lawfulness and of reducibility. When consistent relations have been observed between phenomena, we postulate a law or "mechanism" connecting them, and our confidence in the mechanism increases if we are able to decompose it, in turn, into familiar lawful relations of a simpler kind. There is a certain boot-strapping character to this kind of reasoning. In Bayesian fashion, we explain a specific empirical relation on the basis of a mechanism that we already believe in because of previous experience with similar empirical relations. But we should not be distressed at the infinite regress of explanation that this implies. Mechanisms and laws are theoretical constructs that are derived *inductively* from empirical evidence but are not derivable *deductively* from that evidence. We can never show that a particular mechanism did, in fact, cause certain phenomena; we can only show that this mechanism *could* have produced the phenomena—that, if the mechanism had been at work, the phenomena would have appeared.

Thus, the *a priori* assumptions we use in identifying equations are not prior to all experience; they are only prior to the particular data we are seeking to analyze. They represent laws of qualitative structure (Newell and Simon, 1976) derived inductively from such common experiences as observing that forces are usually exerted by stretched (but not loose) strings on the objects connected to them or that unsupported bodies are usually accelerated toward the earth. *A priori* assumptions are closely analogous to the prior probabilities that enter into Bayesian statistical theory: they provide a means for linking a particular experiment or observation with the whole body of knowledge already available, in order to arrive at a proper interpretation of the new information.[5]

The Specification of Mechanism

In our hypothetical example of a theory connecting schooling, verbal ability, IQ and socioeconomic status, we saw that different *a priori* assumptions led to very different interpretations of the observed regression coefficient connecting the first two variables. We saw, further, that observation of the exogenous variables—IQ and socioeconomic status—would not by itself remove the ambiguity of specification of the mechanisms. Additional identifying assumptions had to be made. We have suggested that these assumptions have their sources in prior experience. More specifically, there appear to be at least three broad classes of such sources: experimental manipulation, temporal ordering, and observation of "tangible" links between phenomena.

Experimentation

What could it mean operationally to distinguish between amount of schooling being causally determined by verbal ability, on the one hand, and verbal ability being determined by amount of schooling, on the other? Consider the following thought experiment. We divide a group of children randomly into ten subgroups, and specify for each a different amount of schooling, from one to ten years. At the end of ten years, we measure the average verbal ability of each subgroup. This experiment amounts to disabling the first of the two causal mechanisms proposed above (eq. 1). If that were the only mechanism involved in the relation between schooling and verbal ability, we would expect to find no significant differences among the experimental groups. If the second mechanism (eq. 2) were at work, we would expect the groups with larger amounts of schooling to exhibit greater verbal ability. If both mechanisms were at work, we would expect to find such a relation, but a smaller one than in a control population where each student had been allowed to terminate his schooling voluntarily. Hence, a basic technique for determining *a priori* assumptions is to exercise experimental control over the phenomena, randomizing treatments where appropriate, to eliminate the operation of mechanisms other than the ones in which we are interested.

Of course the world will not permit us to perform the experiment outlined above. Sometimes, however, such experiments, or approximations to them, are performed accidentally—that is, different groups of people are subjected to different treatment under conditions in which we cannot see that any systematic rule determined which persons experienced which treatment. Notice the key characteristic of such experiments, whether they are carried out deliberately or by accident. We test for the presence of a causal mechanism by comparing the relation between dependent and independent variables in several experimental groups that have been equated (by randomization or otherwise) with respect to everything relevant except the value of the independent variable. We can accomplish this only to the extent that the independent variable is controllable independently of other variables that might affect the dependent variable. When we try to test a mechanism with naturally occurring data, it is this latter independence that must concern us; we must be wary of possible connections between independent and dependent variables through other, spurious, links.

Temporal Ordering

Another source of identification of mechanisms derives from the postulate that causation cannot work backward through time. If we have variables measured at different points in time, then the earlier variable may exert a causal influence on the later, but not the later on the earlier. Thus, if we had measures of IQ taken at the time schooling began and measures of verbal ability taken later, then IQ could affect verbal ability, but not verbal ability IQ. The fact that two variables, measured at different points in time, covary does not mean, however, that there is necessarily a causal mechanism connecting them. The correlation may be spurious, in that both are affected by a third, common, variable.

In the social and behavioral sciences, the use of temporal relations to infer the direction of causation is beset with an additional difficulty. Human beings can form expectations of future events, and, if their expectations are reasonably accurate, the future event may be the best predictor of the expectation. This is not, of course, a case of the future influencing the past, because the expectations are not actually determined by the future event but by current knowledge that is predictive of that event. Nor, of course, do the expectations normally cause the future event (although in the case of so-called self-confirming predictions they may); their relation is mediated by the laws that govern the system whose behavior is being predicted and by the actor's knowledge of these laws.

For the reasons mentioned in the previous two paragraphs, temporal precedence does not always imply causal precedence. Nevertheless, ordering in time does provide one of the most powerful means available to us for specifying the mechanisms operating in a system. The principal care we must take when we make use of this means is to be alert for the presence of additional variables, beyond those specifically represented in our model, that may operate simultaneously on several of the variables that are represented, so as to produce spurious correlation between them.

"Tangible" Links

Finally, as the earlier comments on ESP indicate, in theories in the social and behavioral sciences, we frequently employ the postulate, "If no communication, then no influence," to exclude variables from particular mechanisms and to seal off, conceptually, the system we wish to study from larger systems in which it may be embedded.

The important method of comparative statics, employed in a great deal of economic analysis, depends upon the assumption that variables can be ignored if they are only weakly linked to the phenomena under study. Thus, the demand for a product might be described as depending on the price of that product, and perhaps the prices of one or two close substitutes, but not directly depending on the price of other commodities. A good theoretical justification can be given for the practice of ignoring weak linkages, especially in studies concerned with short-run effects (Simon and Ando, 1961).

A corollary to the "no communication, no influence" postulate is the postulate that only those stimuli, or aspects of stimuli, to which a person attends can affect his behavior. A variety of techniques are available—at the most microscopic level, recording a subject's eye movements—for controlling or ascertaining the range and direction of attention and, hence, for choosing a small subset of the total situation as relevant to the postulated mechanisms of behavior.

Spatial propinquity can also be a basis for marking off the boundaries of mechanisms. A city or a metropolitan area tends to be a useful unit for analysis because the network of communications *within* its boundaries is dense as compared with the communications *across* its boundaries. In the modern world, this principle must, of course, be applied with caution. Modern telecommunications make it possible to create highly interdependent systems whose components are widely dispersed. Thus, one would be careful in using geographical propinquity to draw the boundary of a subpart of a formal organization; a matrix showing relative frequencies of communication among its elements would provide a more informative and reliable basis for identifying particular mechanisms.

Formal Representation of Identifying Assumptions

A few words need to be said about the ways in which the *a priori* assumptions enter into the equations of a theory. Each such assumption must operate to reduce the number of independent parameters (i.e., coefficients in the equations) that are to be estimated from the data. The assumptions take three principal forms: (1) the omission of particular variables from particular equations, (2) the assumption that two or more coefficients are identical or always equal in value, and (3) the assumption that particular pairs of variables are uncorrelated.

All theory building proceeds on the "empty world assumption"—that most things are not related directly to most other things. In general, we require affirmative reasons for including a variable in an equation. Although this is an indispensable principle for theory building, it exposes us continually to the danger of spurious correlation via omitted common variables. We are safest in those circumstances where we already have a sufficiently strong theory to recognize the possible channels of influence, and where we can therefore apply the principle mentioned earlier—if no communication, then no influence—to exclude variables from equations. A particular case of this principle is the application of time's arrow to exclude variables measured at later times from equations that determine the values of earlier variables. In general, exclusion of variables from equations (zeroes in the matrix of coefficients) is probably the most common form taken by identifying assumptions.

The assumption that two or more coefficients are equal usually stems from some kind of postulate of homogeneity or symmetry in the system under study. Such postulates are very often tenable as applied to physical systems; much less often, unfortunately, in application to social or behavioral systems. The assumption, for example, in classical physics, that the gravitational constant is everywhere the same is a powerful source of identifiability of models in celestial mechanics.

Let me give a hypothetical example of how assumptions of equality of coefficients might be used in the theory of interpersonal influence. Suppose that we have two equations, formally identical with eq. 1 and 2', but where x is now the position of one person on a particular attitude scale and y the position of another person, under conditions where the two persons are engaged in trying to persuade each other to change attitudes, and where z represents other influences upon y. We saw earlier that the coefficients C and D of eq. 2' were not identifiable in this model. If, however, we make the assumption that $C = A$ (the two persons are equally influential and influenceable), then we can solve for A as before, obtaining 3, and moreover, from 4, we will have

(8) $$D = \frac{\sigma_y^2 - \sigma_x^2}{\sigma_y \sigma_x},$$

so that D is now identified. It must be emphasized again, however, that setting two or more coefficients equal is an empirical assumption, which is to be made only when it is empirically justified, and not just for convenience in estimating coefficients.

If two variables are both observed, then their actual correlation can be determined, and there is no need to make assumptions about their statistical distribution. In the case of unobserved variables, however (e.g., "disturbances" in equations), the assumption that they are uncorrelated provides additional identification for the system under study. The case of three variables and three mechanisms, each subject to disturbance, is treated in Simon, 1954, Section 4 (reprinted in Blalock, 1971, Chapter 1). In that discussion, identification is achieved by a combination of the assumption that particular variables are absent from particular equations and that the disturbances are mutually independent.

On "Automatic" Science

Causal analysis is a technology—a set of procedures that can be applied to data with the aim of discovering underlying causal relations among variables. As with all technologies, one of its functions is to eliminate the need for thought or, at least, for difficult, problem-solving thought. A person who seeks to solve a simple algebraic problem without a thorough grounding in the techniques of algebraic manipulation has to think very hard and even then may not succeed in reaching a solution. A person who has acquired algebraic skills may solve the problem by applying a nearly automatic algorithm, that is, almost without thinking.

The danger, of course, with a technology of analysis lies in the very automaticity of its use. Someone may learn the technique and how to apply it without ever understanding its conceptual basis and the limits of its validity and applicability. It is hard to find a tool of scientific analysis that has not been abused by mindless application. The most blatant examples of such abuse come from the realm of statistics, particularly hypothesis-testing techniques and factor analysis.

A statistics recipe book performs for its user essentially the same function as a book of etiquette: it tells him what to do on each occasion without requiring him to ponder on why he is doing it. "Divide the variance into its components, compute the value of z for each, and assign it to the appropriate significance level"; or "extract successive factors from the correlation matrix, applying a significance test to each one until the increment of variance extracted is no longer significant." In this way, variance analysis and factor analysis become tools for doing "automatic" science, the laying on of magic formulas whose meanings are purely conventional, and hence don't call for hard thought in either their application or their interpretation.

Unfortunately, the mindless use of statistical techniques produces meaningless results. For example, findings are interpreted without any regard for the difference between the technical meaning of "statistically significant" and the meaning of "significant" in everyday language. Thus a one percent difference between two numbers is described as "highly significant" because, under the null hypothesis, it has a very low probability of occurrence. The question is seldom asked whether the one percent difference is of any *importance*.

Similarly, standard statistical tests like the *t*-test or the chi-square test, whose rationale relates exclusively to testing null hypotheses, are actually applied to test the "significance" of the deviation of data from an explicit theoretical model. But these abuses of statistics from mindless application are not the topic of this paper, and I have inveighed against them elsewhere (Gregg and Simon, 1967; Simon, 1968). Let me return to the subject of causal analysis.

Causal analysis is not immune from this danger of thoughtless application. I would like to comment here upon two misuses of the technique that are all too common. The first is the practice of making identifying assumptions on the basis of their convenience for the computation of parameter estimates rather than on the basis of their empirical plausibility. The second is the practice of using normalized "path coefficients" instead of regression coefficients to describe the relations among variables.

Improper Identification

In the typical identification problem, we have a set of theoretical equations connecting some variables and a set of observations of those variables. We wish to estimate the coefficients of the equations, and, if possible, we wish to ascertain also whether the theoretical equations fit the observed data well or badly. To do this, we form certain estimating equations—that is, new equations that express the coefficients of the original, theoretical equations as functions of the observations—and solve them for the coefficients. Having estimated the coefficients, we then substitute the estimated values in the theoretical equations and use the resulting numerical equations to judge how well the data fit the theory. In what follows, I will assume, just to make matters a bit more specific, that all of the theoretical relations with which we shall be concerned are linear.

There are a large number of ways in which we can form equations for estimating the coefficients of the theory. In the case of a relation between two variables, we can, for example, simply select two observations of the pair of variables, determine the straight line passing through them, and use the slope and intercept of that line as estimates of the corresponding coefficients of the linear equation postulated by the theory. Of course, if we had selected a different pair of observations, we would have obtained different estimates. To treat all of the data points as equally informative, we generally form some symmetric function of them to make the estimate; the method of least squares is one way of doing this. It gives us estimates for the coefficients that, in a certainly precise sense, provide the best fit, on average, of data points to theory.

To obtain unique estimates of a set of variables, we must provide exactly as many linear estimating equations as we have variables to be estimated. Some of these estimating equations are provided by the theoretical equations themselves; the remainder must be derived from the identifying assumptions. As we have seen, the number of variables to be estimated can be reduced by assuming specific coefficients to be zero or pairs of coefficients to be equal, or new equations can be introduced by assuming that various pairs of observed or unobserved variables are uncorrelated. Each of these assumptions is an empirical postulate about the phenomena under study. It is illegitimate to assume, for example, that residuals are uncorrelated simply because additional identifying assumptions are needed. If such assumptions are made, they can greatly alter the estimates of the coefficients—that is, of the magnitudes of the causal connections among the variables.

If a system is underidentified through lack of an empirical basis for making a sufficient number of identifying assumptions, then the safest procedure is to consider alternative models, obtained by introducing alternative assumptions, and to test the sensitivity of the coefficients of the theory to changes in the underlying model. If the sensitivity is low, then errors in the identifying assumptions are not causing much damage; if it is high, then it becomes clear that the coefficient values are not being determined by the observed data alone but are being much influenced by the questionable identifying assumptions.

Coefficients are most easily estimated when the system is just identified— that is, when the number of estimating equations, including those provided by the identifying assumptions, is just equal to the number of distinct coefficients to be estimated. However, prior knowledge about the phenomena may suggest a greater number of identifying assumptions, thus producing an overidentified system. The temptation should be resisted to throw away the "superfluous" postulates. First, there now exist a number of techniques, having satisfactory statistical properties, for estimating the coefficients of overidentified systems. Second, when a system is just identified, it will always yield consistent estimates of the coefficients and, hence, will provide no test of the correctness of the model. When a system is overidentified, it may prove impossible to arrive at consistent estimates of the coefficients that satisfy all of the assumptions of the model. Hence, in this case, the theory can be tested at the same time that its coefficients are estimated.

This discussion can be summarized in one general piece of advice: Assumptions made to identify a system of equations are empirical assumptions about the phenomena the equations describe. Hence, faithfulness to what is known about the phenomena rather than statistical convenience or elegance must govern the choice of these assumptions.

Correlation Coefficients or Regression Coefficients

The earliest development of causal analysis, due to Sewall Wright (1921), occurred in the context of research in genetics. In this context, the main question to be answered by estimating coefficients is the relative contribution made by each of the independent variables to the determination of the dependent variable. Under these conditions, no information is lost if all of the variables are normalized by dividing each by its standard deviation. Hence, much of the work in this area that follows Wright's tradition of "path analysis" is expressed in terms of these normalized variables, that is, in terms of correlation coefficients instead of regression coefficients.

In a 1960 paper, printed as Chapter 6 in Blalock (1971), Wright defends the use of the normalized coefficients. His arguments are primarily based on statistical convenience together with the notion that the purpose of these coefficients is to measure "the relative direct contributions of variability of the immediate causal factors to variability of the effect in each case." He then illustrates his argument with a genetic example, where the path coefficients have a clear interpretation in terms of genetic theory.

For most social and behavioral science applications of causal analysis, however, the situation is quite different. In such applications, the standardized coefficients do not generally have any invariant meaning when transfered from one situation to another. This is readily illustrated by a well-known problem of prediction.

Suppose that we wish to examine the relation between college aptitude scores (x) and performance in college (y). We obtain values of x and y from a population of students, and compute the regression of y on x, using least squares, say. We obtain an estimate, A, of the slope of the regression, and r_{xy}, of the correlation between the two variables. Which of these coefficients, A or r, gives us the best information about the relation between aptitude and academic performance?

In general, we will have used the aptitude scores as one basis for selecting students. Hence, the population on which the relation between aptitude and performance was measured contains mainly the upper part of the distribution on the aptitude measure. What would have been the values of A and r if all of the applicants had been admitted? Under fairly weak assumptions about the population distributions, the value of A estimated for the original sample provides an unbiased estimate of A for the entire population; but the sample value of r will be substantially smaller than the population value. More specifically, $r_{xy} = r_{x'y'}(\sigma_x/\sigma_{x'})$, where x' and y' are the values of the variables measured over the entire population instead of the sample selected for admission. Thus, if the upper half of the population were admitted, we might expect the standard deviation of aptitude in the selected group to be only about half of the standard deviation in the original group, with a corresponding reduction in the coefficient of correlation. But the expected value of the unstandardized regression coefficient would not be changed, it would remain invariant.

As our theories of phenomena become stronger and take on a quantitative rather than a merely qualitative character, we wish to take seriously the actual numerical values of the coefficients that measure the strength of connection between variables. But "strength" here indicates some underlying theoretical parameter that is not a mere artifact of our sampling procedures or the range of variation in the independent variable. As a general rule, the regression coefficients in properly specified models provide such invariant parameters, whereas the standardized coefficients—the correlation coefficients—do not. For this reason, the quite frequent use of partial correlation coefficients rather than partial regression coefficients in causal diagrams is regrettable.

Once again we see the dangers of "automatic" science. It is appealing to use, once and for all, a "normalized" statistic like the correlation coefficient. It provides us with a measure, which must always lie between zero and one, of "strength of association" between two variables. But just what is the operational meaning of "strength of association"? This strength, as measured by the correlation coefficient, will always vary with the range of variation of the independent variable. And, with rare exceptions like the genetic example used by Wright, this range of variation is an artifact of the particular experimental or observational situation from which the data were drawn, not an intrinsic characteristic of the phenomena. The real "strength of association" we usually wish to measure is the magnitude of change in the dependent variable that will be produced by a unit change in the independent variable—that is, the partial regression coefficient.

Conclusion

Scientific inquiry is concerned not only with discovering quantitative relations between variables, but also with interpreting these relations in terms of the underlying causal mechanisms that produced them. Without a knowledge of these mechanisms, we cannot predict how variables will co-vary when the structure of the system under study is altered, either experimentally or by changes in the world around us.

Determining the causal mechanisms that control phenomena is an inductive task. No finite body of data can point unequivocally to one particular causal model and exclude all others. We need not be overly concerned with this, for we have long since reconciled ourselves to the fact, pointed out by Popper, that theories can be disproved by evidence but can never be established irrevocably.

In discovering the mechanisms that govern some system of phenomena and measuring their strength, the data from each experiment or set of observations must be interpreted in terms of our prior knowledge of the world. In particular, to specify the mechanisms of a model, we must be prepared to make *a priori* assumptions that cannot be derived from the data we are examining. These assumptions play the same role as Bayesian prior distributions play in the Bayesian approach to statistical inference.

There is always a temptation to shrink from the difficult task of grounding identifying assumptions in empirical and theoretical knowledge and to select them instead on grounds of statistical convenience or simplicity. This is a temptation that is worth resisting if we wish to arrive at a real understanding of the phenomena we are studying. In this as in other decisions associated with our statistical methods, it is a snare and a delusion to seek out "automatic" techniques that can be applied without careful consideration or that are neutral with respect to the substance of our theories. It is not enough to learn the etiquette book. The reason (or lack of reason) for its rules must be understood as well.

Notes

1. The papers collected in Blalock (1971) raise and discuss many of the issues considered here. I would call attention particularly to Chapters 1, 2, 5, 7, 9 and 10 in that volume.

2. Such interventions are referred to in the literature of identification as "changes in structure."

3. This difficulty, sometimes called the "confluence problem," was first pointed out by Ragnar Frisch.

4. The peculiarity of claims for phenomena like ESP is not that they postulate new causal mechanisms—newly postulated forces have been no novelty in contemporary physics—but that the advocates of ESP generally exhibit more interest in denying mechanism than in identifying and characterizing the mechanism that might produce the claimed effects. The very fact that the phenomenon is described as "extrasensory" rather than "sixth-sensory" reveals the bias against postulating mechanism to account for the effects.

5. As a matter of fact, Kadane (1974) has shown that it is possible to give an explicitly Bayesian account of the identification problem. The basic idea is simply to introduce a prior probability distribution over the ensemble of admissible models. This formulation makes clear the relation of the identification problem with the general problem of theory induction.

References

BLALOCK, II. M., JR. *Causal Inferences in Nonexperimental Research.* Chapel Hill: University of North Carolina Press, 1964.

BLALOCK, H. M., JR., ed., *Causal Models in the Social Sciences.* New York: Aldine/Atherton, 1973.

BORGATTA, F. F., and G. W. BOHRNSTEDT, eds., *Sociological Methodology, 1970.* San Francisco: Jossey-Bass, 1970.

FISHER, FRANKLIN M. *The Identification Problem in Econometrics.* New York: McGraw-Hill, 1966.

GOLDBERGER, A. S., and O. D. DUNCAN, eds., *Structural Equation Models in the Social Sciences.* New York: Seminar Press, 1973.

GREGG, LEE W., and H. A. SIMON. "Process Models and Stochastic Theories of Simple Concept Formation," *Journal of Mathematical Psychology* 4 (1967), 246–276.

KADANE, JOSEPH B. "The Role of Identification in Bayesian Theory," in S. E. Fienberg and A. Zellner, eds., *Studies in Bayesian Econometrics and Statistics.* Amsterdam: North-Holland Publishing Company, 1974.

NEWELL, ALLEN, and H. A. SIMON. "Computer Science as Empirical Inquiry: Symbols and Search," *Communications of the ACM,* 19 (1976), 113–126.

SIMON, H. A., and A. ANDO. "Aggregation of variables in dynamic systems." *Econometrica,* 29 (1961), 111–138.

SIMON, H. A. "On Judging The Plausibility of Theories," in B. van Rootselaar and J. F. Staal, eds., *Logic, Methodology, and Philosophy of Sciences III.* Amsterdam: North-Holland Publishing Company, 1968.

WRIGHT, SEWALL. "Correlation and Causation," *Journal of Agricultural Research,* 20 (1921), 557–585.

9.   PANELS AND TIME SERIES ANALYSIS: MARKOV CHAINS AND AUTOREGRESSIVE PROCESSES

T. W. Anderson

1. Introduction

One of the innovations in social research made by Paul F. Lazarsfeld was the development and application of panel surveys. In this design a sample of individuals is interviewed at several points in time; the resulting data are sequences of responses. The techniques and objectives were described by Lazarsfeld, Berelson, and Gaudet in *The People's Choice* (1944). That study was based on repeated interviews of many voters in Erie County, Ohio, in 1940. Each respondent was asked in May, June, July, August, September, and October for which party (or candidate) the respondent intended to vote. For some purposes the responses to this question were coded as Republican, Democrat, and "Don't Know"; that is, each person at each time was put into one of three categories. The records of the 445 persons who responded to all six interviews can be considered as 445 observations (or "realizations") from a probability distribution of such records (that is, a segment of a stochastic process).

A discrete-state, discrete-time Markov chain can serve as a model for panel data. The development of this model and appropriate statistical techniques, illustrated by the survey of vote intention, was reported as Part VI (March 22, 1951) of the Rand study, "The Use of Mathematical Models in the Measurement of Attitudes," directed by Lazarsfeld. An exposition of the model and its applications (which was taken from the research memorandum) appeared as

This research was supported by the Office of Naval Research Contract N00014-75-C-0442, Stanford University. Reproduction in whole or in part is permitted for any purpose of the United States Government. The author is indebted to Persi Diaconis, Neil Henry, and Paul Shaman for reading an earlier version of this essay and making helpful suggestions.

the first chapter of *Mathematical Thinking in the Social Sciences*, edited by Lazarsfeld. The statistical methodology, developed further in collaboration with Leo Goodman, appeared later.

In some panel surveys the responses may be quantitative, such as answers to the question, How many hours did you spend last month reading the newspapers? In economic surveys the questions are more likely to produce numerical answers: How many hours did you work last week? How much money did you spend on groceries last month? A possible model for time series consisting of measurements on one or more continuous variables is a univariate or multivariate autoregressive process. The statistical methods for autoregressive processes have been developed mainly for one observed time series, that is, the record of one unit of observation. However, a characteristic feature of panel data is that there are available the records of several units of observation. Of course, such repeated measurements occur in other situations. A psychologist may obtain a test score on several individuals at several points in time; a physician may read blood pressures of several patients daily.

The purpose of the present paper is to review some statistical methods for Markov chains and present similar methods for corresponding problems in autoregressive processes in the case of repeated measurements. The statistical problems treated are those presented by Anderson and Goodman (1957) and suggest that other procedures for Markov chains have their analogs for autoregressive processes. The development of the methods for autoregressive processes and proofs of the mathematical statements are by Anderson* (1978).

Each section of this paper is divided into three subsections, the first dealing with the Markov chain model, the second treating the autoregressive model, and the third displaying correspondences between the two models. Section 2 defines the models and reviews some of their properties. Section 3 discusses summary data and estimates of parameters. Section 4 develops tests of hypotheses.

2. Probability Models for Time Series

2.1. A Markov Chain Model for Discrete Data

A Markov chain can serve as a model for the probabilities of a sequence of statistical variables that take on a finite set of values. Let the values or states or categories be labeled $1, \ldots, m$, and let x_t be the statistical variable at time t, $t = 1, \ldots, T$. For instance, $x_1 = 2$ might denote an individual holding opinion 2 (Democrat) at the first interview (May). Then a Markov chain model specifies the probability of state j at time t given state i at time $t - 1$

---

*Statistical methods for a single observed series from a Markov chain have been discussed extensively by Billingsley (1961). The autoregressive process with one observation on the series is treated in depth in Anderson (1971). Bartlett (1951) developed some methods in the context of a single observation. See Goodman (1973) for more references.

(2.1)
$$Pr\left\{x_t = j | x_{t-1} = i\right\} = p_{ij}(t), \qquad i,j = 1, \ldots, m.$$

These transition probabilities satisfy the conditions $p_{ij}(t) \geqslant 0$ and

(2.2)
$$\sum_{j=1}^{m} p_{ij}(t) = 1, \qquad i = 1, \ldots, m.$$

While the period of observation is usually finite ($t = 1, \ldots, T$), the stochastic process may be defined for all integers, $t = \ldots, -1, 0, 1, \ldots$. In any case, there is a marginal distribution of the statistical variable at each time point; the probability of state i at time t is denoted $p_i(t) [p_i(t) \geqslant 0, \Sigma_{i=1}^{m} p_i(t) = 1]$. The joint probability that $x_{t-1} = i$ and $x_t = j$ is $p_i(t-1)p_{ij}(t)$; thus, the marginal probability that $x_t = j$ follows from the marginal distribution at $t - 1$ by

(2.3)
$$\sum_{i=1}^{m} p_i(t-1) p_{ij}(t) = p_j(t), \qquad j = 1, \ldots, m.$$

To describe the probabilities of the observed random variables ($t = 1, \ldots, T$), it is only necessary to prescribe the vector $p(1) = [p_1(1), \ldots, p_m(1)]'$ and the matrices $P(t) = [p_{ij}(t)]$, $t = 2, \ldots, T$. The distinguishing feature of a Markov chain is that the conditional probability of x_t given the entire past $x_{t-1}, x_{t-2}, \ldots$ depends only on the immediately preceding variable x_{t-1}.

In many situations the transition probabilities are homogeneous; that is, $p_{ij}(t) = p_{ij}$ or $P(t) = P, t = \ldots, -1, 0, 1, \ldots$. Then the marginal distributions are homogeneous, that is, $p(t) = p$, and the process is stationary. In this case, (2.3) is

(2.4)
$$\sum_{i=1}^{m} p_i p_{ij} = p_j, \qquad j = 1, \ldots, m.$$

The matrix form of (2.4)

(2.5)
$$p'P = p'$$

shows that p is a left-sided characteristic vector of P corresponding to a characteristic root of 1, that is, a root of $|P - \lambda I| = 0$ of 1. The equations (2.2) can be written $P\epsilon = \epsilon$, where $\epsilon = (1, \ldots, 1)'$; thus ϵ is a right-sided characteristic vector of P corresponding to a characteristic root of 1. There are m characteristic roots $\lambda_1 = 1, \lambda_2, \ldots, \lambda_m$; each root satisfies $|\lambda_i| \leqslant 1$. The Markov chain is called irreducible if the root of 1 is of multiplicity 1; then there is a positive probability of going from one state to another in some interval of time. In that case p is determined uniquely by (2.5) and the normalization $p'\epsilon = 1$.

In a more general model the probability of a state at time t may depend on the states at several time points earlier. For example, a second-order stationary chain is defined by the transition probabilities

(2.6)
$$Pr\left\{x_t = k | x_{t-2} = i, x_{t-1} = j\right\} = p_{ijk}, \qquad i,j,k = 1, \ldots, m,$$

where $p_{ijk} \geqslant 0$ and $\Sigma_{k=1}^{m} p_{ijk} = 1, i,j = 1, \ldots, m$. Higher-order chains and nonstationary chains are defined similarly. For some purposes it is convenient to

redefine states so as to construct a Markov (first-order) chain that is mathe-
matically equivalent to this second-order chain. For example, if $m = 2$, let $\tilde{x}_t = 1$
if $x_{t-1} = 1, x_t = 1, \tilde{x}_t = 2$ if $x_{t-1} = 1, x_t = 2, \tilde{x}_t = 3$ if $x_{t-1} = 2, x_t = 1$, and
$\tilde{x}_t = 4$ if $x_{t-1} = 2, x_t = 2$. Then the matrix of transition probabilities for $\tilde{x}_t$ is

$$(2.7) \quad \tilde{\mathbf{P}} = \begin{bmatrix} p_{111} & p_{112} & 0 & 0 \\ 0 & 0 & p_{121} & p_{122} \\ p_{211} & p_{212} & 0 & 0 \\ 0 & 0 & p_{221} & p_{222} \end{bmatrix}$$

The Markov chain model also includes multivariate cases. In case of two
dichotomous variables $y_t = 1$ or 2 and $z_t = 1$ or 2, define x_t by $x_t = 1$ if $y_t = 1$,
$z_t = 1, x_t = 2$ if $y_t = 1, z_t = 2, x_t = 3$ if $y_t = 2, z_t = 1$, and $x_t = 4$ if $y_t = 2, z_t = 2$.

The model may be further developed to include effects of other variables by
stratification. If there is a discrete conditioning variable, the transition probabilities can depend on it; that is, the (homogeneous) transition probabilities in the
hth stratum may be set $[p_{ij}^{(h)}]$.

From a statistician's viewpoint the Markov chain model is constructed from a
family of elementary multinomial distributions; in the case of a dichotomous
item (that is, two states) these are Bernoulli distributions. Each conditional
distribution is such a discrete distribution The appropriate statistical procedures
for a Markov chain are similarly developments of methods for multinomial
distributions.

2.2 An Autoregressive Process

An autoregressive process can serve as a model for a sequence of continuous
random variables or a sequence of vectors whose components are continuous
random variables. In the first-order (Markov) autoregressive process the p-
component vector y_t has a conditional expected value of $B(t)y_{t-1}$ given y_{t-1},
$y_{t-2}, \ldots$, where $B(t)$ is a $p \times p$ matrix and the disturbance (or innovation)
$u_t = y_t - B(t)y_{t-1}$ is statistically independent of $y_{t-1}, y_{t-2}, \ldots$. The model
may be written

$$(2.8) \qquad\qquad y_t = B(t)y_{t-1} + u_t.$$

Then u_t is a sequence of independent (unobservable) random vectors with
expected values $\mathcal{E}u_t = 0$, covariance matrices $\mathcal{E}u_t u_t' = \Sigma_t$, and u_t independent
of $y_{t-1}, y_{t-2}, \ldots$. Let the covariance matrix of y_t be $\mathcal{E}y_t y_t' = F_t$. Then from
(2.8) and the independence of y_{t-1} and u_t we deduce

(2.9) $$F_t = B(t)F_{t-1}B(t)' + \Sigma_t.$$

If the observations are made for $t = 1, \ldots, T$, the model may be specified by the marginal distribution of y_1 and the distributions of $u_2, \ldots, u_T$. In particular, if y_1 and the u_t's are normal, the model for the observation period is specified by $F_1, B(2), \ldots, B(T), \Sigma_2, \ldots, \Sigma_T$.

When the autoregression matrices are homogeneous, that is, $B(t) = B$ and the u_t's are identically distributed with mean 0 and covariance matrice Σ, the process is stationary if the characteristic roots of B are less than 1 in absolute value and the process is defined to $t = \ldots, -1, 0, 1, \ldots$ or y_1 is assigned the stationary marginal distribution. In this case the covariance matrix of y_t is

(2.10) $$F = \sum_{s=0}^{\infty} B^s \Sigma B'^s,$$

and the covariance of y_t and y_s is

(2.11) $$\mathcal{E}y_t y_s' = B^{t-s}F, \qquad s \leqslant t.$$

[Note that $F = F_t = F_{t-1}$ satisfies (2.9) for $B(t) = B$ and $\Sigma_t = \Sigma$.]

A second-order stationary autoregressive vector process may be defined by

(2.12) $$y_t = B_1 y_{t-1} + B_2 y_{t-2} + u_t.$$

This model can be written as a first-order process by writing

(2.13) $$\tilde{y}_t = \tilde{B}\tilde{y}_{t-1} + \tilde{u}_t,$$

where $\tilde{y}_t = (y_t', y_{t-1}')'$, $\tilde{u}_t = (u_t', 0)'$, and

(2.14) $$\tilde{B} = \begin{pmatrix} B_1 & B_2 \\ I & 0 \end{pmatrix}.$$

The characteristic roots of $\tilde{B}$ are the roots of $|-\lambda^2 I + \lambda B_1 + B_2| = 0$. For a stationary process these roots are to less than 1 in absolute value. (See Anděl [1971], for example.)

The autoregressive processes appropriate to several subpopulations (strata) may be different. In the homogeneous first-order case the matrix of coefficients and the covariance matrix in the hth stratum may be $B^{(h)}$ and $\Sigma^{(h)}$.

The autoregressive process is constructed from multivariate regressions. In (2.8), for example, the vector y_{t-1} constitutes the "independent variables" and the vector y_t constitutes the "dependent variables" in ordinary regression. To a large extent the statistical methods for autoregressive models are regression or least squares procedures.

2.3. Correspondence between Markov Chains and Autoregressive Processes

The discrete variable x_t that takes the values $1, \ldots, m$ can be replaced by the m-component vector z_t in which the ith component is 1 if $x_t = i$ and is 0 if $x_t \neq i$. If we define ϵ_i to be the m-component vector with 1 as the ith component and 0 as the other components, we can define z_t as ϵ_i when $x_t = i$. Then

$$(2.15) \qquad Pr\{z_t = \epsilon_j | z_{t-1} = \epsilon_i\} = p_{ij}(t), \qquad\qquad i, j = 1, \ldots, m.$$

Thus the conditional expectation of z_t given the past is

$$(2.16) \qquad \mathcal{E}(z_t | z_{t-1}, z_{t-2}, \ldots) = \mathcal{E}(z_t | z_{t-1}) = P(t)' z_{t-1}.$$

If we let $v_t = z_t - P(t)' z_{t-1}$, then (2.16) implies $\mathcal{E} v_t = 0$ and

$$(2.17) \qquad \mathcal{E} v_t z_{t-s}' = \mathcal{E}\mathcal{E}(v_t | z_{t-1}, z_{t-2}, \ldots) z_{t-s}' = 0, \qquad s = 1, 2, \ldots$$

The latter yields

$$(2.18) \qquad \mathcal{E} z_t z_{t-1}' = P(t)' \mathcal{E} z_{t-1} z_{t-1}'.$$

Note that here v_t has a singular distribution since $\epsilon' v_t = 0$. Conditional on $z_{t-1} = \epsilon_i$, the variance of the jth component of v_t is $p_{ij}(t)[1 - p_{ij}(t)]$ and the covariance between the jth and kth components is $-p_{ij}(t) p_{ik}(t)$, $j \neq k$. The unconditional variance is $\sum_{i=1}^{m} p_i(t-1) p_{ij}(t)[1 - p_{ij}(t)]$, and the unconditional covariance is $-\sum_{i=1}^{m} p_i(t-1) p_{ij}(t) p_{ik}(t), j \neq k$.

The properties of a Markov chain are similar to those of an autoregressive model, defined by (2.8), in that the conditional expectation of the observed vector z_t given the past is a linear function of the immediately preceding observed vector z_{t-1}. The autocovariances of z_t can be obtained from (2.18) in a manner analogous to that of the autoregressive model. In particular, in the stationary case (2.11) holds with $y_t y_s'$ replaced by $z_t z_s'$, B by P' and F by $\mathcal{E} z_{t-1} z_{t-1}' - \mathcal{E} z_{t-1} \mathcal{E} z_{t-1}' = \mathcal{E} z_{t-1} z_{t-1}' - pp'$; then $f_j = p_j - \sum_{i=1}^{m} p_i p_j^2$ and $f_{jk} = -\sum_{i=1}^{m} p_i p_j p_k, j \neq k$. The representation of the Markov chain differs from the autoregressive process in that the covariance matrix of the residual v_t is singular and depends on z_{t-1} in the conditional distribution; while v_t is uncorrelated with z_{t-1}, it is not statistically independent of z_{t-1}. We also note that the characteristic roots of B are less than 1 in absolute value, but one root of P (when P is irreducible) is exactly 1, corresponding to characteristic vectors of p on the left and ϵ on the right; ϵ is the characteristic vector of F corresponding to a root of 0. In the following pages the parallels between the two processes are used to suggest methods and derivations for one model from the other.

3. Estimation of Parameters

3.1. Estimation of Transition Probabilities

An observation on an individual consists of the sequence of states for T successive time points. For example, the $T = 6$ successive monthly party preferences of a voter might constitute such a sequence. Let $x_{t\alpha}$ be the state of the αth individual at the tth time, $\alpha = 1, \ldots, N, t = 1, \ldots, T$. The observed sequence $x_{1\alpha}, \ldots, x_{T\alpha}$ is considered an observation from the Markov chain specified by the set of probabilities $[p_i(1)], [p_{ij}(2)], \ldots, [p_{ij}(T)]$. The probability of a given sequence of states $x(1), \ldots, x(T)$ is

$$(3.1) \qquad p_{x(1)}(1) p_{x(1)x(2)}(2) \ldots p_{x(T-1)x(T)}(T).$$

The parameters to be estimated from a sample are the marginal probabilities $[p_i(1)]$ and the transition probabilities $[p_{ij}(2)], \ldots, [p_{ij}(T)]$. The observed sequences are considered as independent observations from the model defined by (3.1).

Let $n_{ij}(t)$ be the number of observed individuals in state i at time $t - 1$ and j at time t, and let

$$(3.2) \quad n_i(t-1) = \Sigma_{j=1}^m n_{ij}(t) = \Sigma_{k=1}^m n_{ki}(t-1), \quad i = 1, \ldots, m, t = 2, \ldots, T.$$

The set $n_{ij}(t), i, j = 1, \ldots, m$, for each t constitutes the frequencies of individuals in state i at time $t - 1$ and state j at time t and would usually be recorded in a two-way table; the row totals are $n_i(t - 1), i = 1, \ldots, m$, and the column totals are $n_j(t), j = 1, \ldots, m$.

A sufficient set of statistics for the model (3.1) is $n_{ij}(t), i, j = 1, \ldots, m$, $t = 2, \ldots, T$; statistical inference need only use this information. The maximum likelihood estimates of the parameters are

$$(3.3) \qquad\qquad \hat{p}_i(1) = \frac{n_i(1)}{N}, \qquad\qquad i = 1, \ldots, m,$$

$$(3.4) \qquad \hat{p}_{ij}(t) = \frac{n_{ij}(t)}{n_i(t-1)}, \qquad i,j = 1, \ldots, m, t = 2, \ldots, T.$$

The estimates are in effect estimates of multinomial probabilities. The estimates satisfy $\hat{p}_i(1) \geqslant 0, \Sigma_{i=1}^m \hat{p}_i(1) = 1, \hat{p}_{ij}(t) \geqslant 0$, and $\Sigma_{j=1}^m \hat{p}_{ij}(t) = 1$.

Now consider the case of homogeneous transition probabilities, but with the initial probabilities $p_i(1)$ arbitrary. Then a sufficient set of statistics is $n_i(1)$, $i = 1, \ldots, m$, and

$$(3.5) \qquad\qquad n_{ij} = \sum_{t=2}^T n_{ij}(t), \qquad\qquad i,j = 1, \ldots, m.$$

The two-way table of frequencies (3.5) is the sum of the $T - 1$ two-way tables with entries $n_{ij}(t)$. [However, $n_i(1)$ is not a marginal total of this table.] The maximum likelihood estimates are (3.3) and

(3.6)
$$\hat{p}_{ij} = \frac{n_{ij}}{n_i^*}, \qquad i, j = 1, \ldots, m,$$

where $n_i^* = \Sigma_{j=1}^m n_{ij}$.

In an alternative model the states at the initial time $t = 1$ are considered as given; that is, $x_{1\alpha}$, $\alpha = 1, \ldots, N$, are treated as nonstochastic. Then $n_i(1)$, $i = 1, \ldots, m$, are considered as given, that is are parameters, not statistics. The sufficient set of statistics is the set $n_{ij}(t)$, $t = 2, \ldots, T$, or n_{ij}, $i, j = 1, \ldots, m$ as the case may be.

In the case of homogeneous transition probabilities, it may be desired to treat the process as stationary; the marginal probability distribution $[p_i]$ is determined by $[p_{ij}]$ as the solution to (2.4); in particular, the initial distribution $[p_i(1)]$ must be $[p_i]$. A sufficient set of statistics is $n_i(1)$, $i = 1, \ldots, m$, and n_{ij}, $i, j = 1, \ldots, m$. While the parameter set can be reduced to $[p_{ij}]$, the maximum likelihood estimates are not (3.6) in this case because the likelihood function depends on $n_i(1)$ and $p_i(1) = p_i$, $i = 1, \ldots, m$, the latter being functions of $[p_{ij}]$. The estimates are too complicated to give explicitly.

To assess sampling variability and to evaluate confidence in inferences, it is desirable to know the distributions of the estimates. Since the exact distributions for given sample sizes are too complicated to be useful, we consider "large-sample theory." Anderson and Goodman (1957) developed asymptotic theory for the number of observations N getting large; this large-sample theory is appropriate for panel studies where the number of time points is small (sometimes $T = 2$) and the number of respondents is large. When the transition probabilities are homogeneous, the parameters do not depend on the time t except the initial probabilities $[p_i(1)]$; then it is meaningful to consider asymptotic distributions as $T \to \infty$. This theory is appropriate when the data consist of one (or several) long series; the measurements are not necessarily repeated. Bartlett (1951) gave some of this theory. In general, when a limiting distribution holds for $T \to \infty$, it will hold for arbitrary N; in fact, with proper normalization the same limiting distribution holds for $N \to \infty$ and fixed T. In such a case we will say the limit holds as N and/or $T \to \infty$. [In mathematical terms the error is arbitrarily small if N is sufficiently large or T is sufficiently large, or both.]

The asymptotic theory for $N \to \infty$ is the usual multinomial theory, for the N observations on the chain are independent. Then by the usual multinomial theory $\sqrt{N}[\hat{p}_i(1) - p_i(1)]$, $i = 1, \ldots, m$, have a limiting normal distribution with means 0 and covariance matrix $[p_i(1)\delta_{ij} - p_i(1)p_j(1)]$, where $\delta_{ii} = 1$ and $\delta_{ij} = 0$, $i \neq j$. If $p_i(t - 1) > 0$, the set $\sqrt{n_i(t - 1)}[\hat{p}_{ij}(t) - p_{ij}(t)]$, $j = 1, \ldots, m$, have a limiting normal distribution with means 0 and covariance matrix $[p_{ij}(t)\delta_{jk} - p_{ij}(t)p_{ik}(t)]$; the sets for different values of i and/or different values of t are independent in the limiting distribution. The limiting distribution of the estimates of the rows of the transition probability matrices is the same as that of estimates of independent multinomial distributions.

If the transition probabilities are homogeneous and the chain is irreducible, then for each i the set $\sqrt{n_i^*}\,(\hat{p}_{ij} - p_{ij})$, $j = 1, \ldots, m$, has a limiting normal distribution with means 0, variances $p_{ij}(1 - p_{ij})$ and covariances $-p_{ij}p_{ik}$, $j \neq k$, and the sets for different values of i are independent in the limiting distribution. The limits in the homogeneous case are valid as $N \to \infty$ and/or $T \to \infty$.

3.2. Estimation of Autoregressive Coefficients

Let $\mathbf{y}_{t\alpha}$ be the p-component vector of measurements of the αth individual at the tth time point, $\alpha = 1, \ldots, N$, $t = 1, \ldots, T$. The model is a first-order autoregressive model (2.8) with $\mathbf{u}_t$ having the normal distribution $N(\mathbf{0}, \Sigma_t)$ and $\mathbf{y}_1$ having the normal distribution $N(\mathbf{0}, \mathbf{F}_1)$. The probability density of the sequence $\mathbf{y}_{1\alpha}, \ldots, \mathbf{y}_{T\alpha}$ for a given α is

$$
\begin{aligned}
\text{(3.7)} \quad & (2\pi)^{-Tp/2}\,|\mathbf{F}_1|^{-\frac{1}{2}}\,\prod_{t=2}^{T}|\Sigma_t|^{-\frac{1}{2}} \\
& \times \exp\left\{-\tfrac{1}{2}\left[\mathbf{y}_{1\alpha}'\mathbf{F}_1^{-1}\mathbf{y}_{1\alpha} + \sum_{t=2}^{T}(\mathbf{y}_{t\alpha} - \mathbf{B}(t)\mathbf{y}_{t-1,\alpha})'\Sigma_t^{-1}(\mathbf{y}_t - \mathbf{B}(t)\mathbf{y}_{t-1,\alpha})\right]\right\}.
\end{aligned}
$$

Then a sufficient set of statistics for $\mathbf{F}_1$, $\mathbf{B}(2)$, $\ldots$, $\mathbf{B}(T)$, Σ_2, $\ldots$, Σ_T is $\sum_{\alpha=1}^{N}\mathbf{y}_{t\alpha}\mathbf{y}_{t\alpha}'$, $t = 1, \ldots, T$, and $\sum_{\alpha=1}^{N}\mathbf{y}_{t-1,\alpha}\mathbf{y}_{t\alpha}'$, $t = 2, \ldots, T$. The maximum likelihood estimates of the parameter matrices are

$$
\text{(3.8)} \qquad \hat{\mathbf{F}}_1 = N^{-1}\sum_{\alpha=1}^{N}\mathbf{y}_{1\alpha}\mathbf{y}_{1\alpha}',
$$

$$
\text{(3.9)} \quad \hat{\mathbf{B}}(t) = \sum_{\alpha=1}^{N}\mathbf{y}_{t\alpha}\mathbf{y}_{t-1,\alpha}'\left(\sum_{\alpha=1}^{N}\mathbf{y}_{t-1,\alpha}\mathbf{y}_{t-1,\alpha}'\right)^{-1}, \qquad t = 2, \ldots, T,
$$

$$
\text{(3.10)} \quad \hat{\Sigma}_t = N^{-1}\sum_{\alpha=1}^{N}\left(\mathbf{y}_{t\alpha} - \hat{\mathbf{B}}(t)\mathbf{y}_{t-1,\alpha}\right)\left(\mathbf{y}_{t\alpha} - \hat{\mathbf{B}}(t)\mathbf{y}_{t-1,\alpha}\right)',
$$
$$
t = 2, \ldots, T.
$$

The components of $\hat{\mathbf{B}}(t)$ are least squares estimates. [See Anderson (1958), Chapter 8, and Anderson (1971), Chapter 5, for example.]

The assumption that the autoregression matrices are homogeneous and the disturbances identically distributed leads to considerable simplification.

The sufficient set of statistics for F_1, B, and Σ is $\sum_{\alpha=1}^{N} y_{1\alpha} y_{1\alpha}'$, $\sum_{t=2}^{T} \sum_{\alpha=1}^{N} y_{t\alpha} y_{t\alpha}'$, $\sum_{\alpha=1}^{N} y_{T\alpha} y_{T\alpha}'$, and $\sum_{t=2}^{T} \sum_{\alpha=1}^{N} y_{t\alpha} y_{t-1,\alpha}'$. The maximum likelihood estimate of F_1 is (3.8) and the maximum likelihood estimates of the other matrices are

$$(3.11) \qquad \hat{B} = \sum_{t=2}^{T} \sum_{\alpha=1}^{N} y_{t\alpha} y_{t-1,\alpha}' \left(\sum_{t=2}^{T} \sum_{\alpha=1}^{N} y_{t-1,\alpha} y_{t-1,\alpha}' \right)^{-1},$$

$$(3.12) \quad \hat{\Sigma} = [N(T-1)]^{-1} \sum_{t=2}^{T} \sum_{\alpha=1}^{N} (y_{t\alpha} - \hat{B} y_{t-1,\alpha})(y_{t\alpha} - \hat{B} y_{t-1,\alpha})'.$$

An alternative model is to consider $y_{1\alpha}$, $\alpha = 1, \ldots, N$, as nonstochastic or fixed and treat $y_{t\alpha}$, $t = 2, \ldots, T$, $\alpha = 1, \ldots, N$, conditionally. Then the maximum likelihood estimates of B and Σ are (3.11) and (3.12).

When $y_{1\alpha}$ is considered to have the marginal normal distribution determined by the stationary process, the covariance matrix F_1 is a function of B and Σ as given by (2.10). Then the maximum likelihood estimates are much more complicated. [As $T \to \infty$, (3.11) and (3.12) are asymptotically equivalent to the maximum likelihood estimates, but not as $N \to \infty$.]

We now consider the asymptotic properties of the estimates as $N \to \infty$ and/or $T \to \infty$. As $N \to \infty$, $\hat{F}_1$, $\hat{B}(t)$, and $\hat{\Sigma}_t$ are consistent estimates of F_1, $B(t)$, and Σ_t, $t = 2, \ldots, T$, respectively. The elements of $\sqrt{N}[\hat{B}(t) - B(t)]$ have a limiting normal distribution with means 0 and covariances constituting the Kronecker product $\Sigma_t \otimes F_{t-1}^{-1}$, $t = 2, \ldots, T$. The matrix F_{t-1} is estimated consistently by $(1/N)\sum_{\alpha=1}^{N} y_{t-1,\alpha} y_{t-1,\alpha}'$.

In the case of homogeneous autoregressive coefficients, regardless of the distribution of $y_{1\alpha}$, $\alpha = 1, \ldots, N$, and of the value of N, as $T \to \infty$ $\hat{B}$ and $\hat{\Sigma}$ are consistent estimates of B and Σ, respectively, and $\sqrt{T}[\hat{B} - B]$ has a limiting normal distribution with means 0 and covariance constituting $(1/N)\Sigma \otimes F^{-1}$. The matrix F is consistently estimated by $[1/(T-1)N] \sum_{t=2}^{T} \sum_{\alpha=1}^{N} y_{t-1,\alpha} y_{t-1,\alpha}'$.

If T is fixed and $N \to \infty$, $\sqrt{N}(\hat{B} - B)$ has a limiting normal distribution with means 0 and covariances constituting $\Sigma \otimes (\sum_{t=2}^{T} F_t)^{-1}$.

3.3 Correspondence of Sufficient Statistics and Estimates in Markov Chains and Autoregressive Processes

In Section 2.3 a Markov chain was represented as a vector process with $z_t = \epsilon_j$ with conditional probability $p_{ij}(t)$ given $z_{t-1} = \epsilon_i$. From this definition we can write the second-order moment matrices for the Markov chain as

$$(3.13) \qquad \sum_{\alpha=1}^{N} z_{t\alpha} z_{t\alpha}' = \sum_{i=1}^{m} n_i(t) \epsilon_i \epsilon_i',$$

which is a diagonal matrix with $n_i(t)$ as the ith diagonal element, and

$$(3.14) \qquad \sum_{\alpha=1}^{N} z_{t-1,\alpha} z_{t\alpha}' = \sum_{i,j=1}^{m} n_{ij}(t)\epsilon_i\epsilon_j' ,$$

which is an $m \times m$ matrix with $n_{ij}(t)$ as the i,jth element. Note that the elements of (3.13) can be derived from the elements of (3.14). Here (3.14) for $t = 2, \ldots, T$ constitute a sufficient set of statistics for the inhomogeneous Markov chain. The estimates (3.4) constitute elements of the matrix estimates (3.9) under this correspondence. If the transition probabilities are homogeneous with arbitrary initial probabilities, a sufficient set of statistics is (3.13) for $t = 1$ and

$$(3.15) \qquad \sum_{t=2}^{T} \sum_{\alpha=1}^{N} z_{t-1,\alpha} z_{t\alpha}' = \sum_{i,j=1}^{m} n_{ij}\epsilon_i\epsilon_j' .$$

The estimates (3.6) are elements of (3.11).

4..Tests of Hypotheses

4.1. Tests for Markov Chains

The tests for Markov chains presented in this section were developed by Anderson and Goodman (1957); they can be applied for any value of $T(\geqslant 2)$ and for large N. Bartlett (1951) developed some of the tests as valid for one observed sequence of states from a homogeneous chain when $T \to \infty$. For convenience, we shall assume $p_{ij}(t) > 0$ and $p_{ij} > 0$ as the case may be. Some of the procedures were illustrated in Anderson (1954). In Section 4.2 test criteria for the corresponding hypotheses for autoregressive models are given (in the same sequence), and in Section 4.3 the correspondences are discussed.

Specified Probabilities. In the homogeneous chain to test the null hypothesis that $p_{ij} = p_{ij}^0, j = 1, \ldots, m$, where the set p_{ij}^0 are specified, for a given i one can use the criterion

$$(4.1) \qquad n_i^* \sum_{j=1}^{m} \frac{(\hat{p}_{ij} - p_{ij}^0)^2}{p_{ij}^0} ,$$

which under the null hypothesis has a limiting χ^2-distribution with $m - 1$ degrees of freedom as $N \to \infty$ and/or as $T \to \infty$. The criteria for different i are asymptotically independent. To test the null hypothesis, $p_{ij} = p_{ij}^0$, $i, j = 1, \ldots, m$, the sum of (4.1) over i can be used; it has a limiting χ^2-distribution with $m(m - 1)$ degrees of freedom when the null hypothesis is true. These criteria are analogs of the χ^2 goodness-of-fit criterion for multinomial distributions. The test procedures can be inverted in the usual fashion to obtain confidence regions for the transition probabilities.

Homogeneity. In treating panel data the investigator may question whether conditions change enough over the time of observation to require the use of an inhomogeneous chain. To test the null hypothesis that $p_{ij}(t) = p_{ij}, t = 2, \ldots, T$, for some $p_{ij}, i, j = 1, \ldots, m$, one may use the criterion

$$(4.2) \qquad \sum_{t=2}^{T} \sum_{i,j=1}^{m} n_i(t-1)\frac{[\hat{p}_{ij}(t) - \hat{p}_{ij}]^2}{\hat{p}_{ij}} .$$

Under the null hypothesis this criterion has a limiting χ^2-distribution with $m(m-1)(T-2)$ degrees of freedom as $N \to \infty$. If one thinks of the set of probabilities $p_{ij}(t)$ and the set of frequencies $n_{ij}(t)$ in (three-way) $m \times m \times (T-1)$ arrays, the criterion (4.2) is the usual χ^2-criterion for testing the independence of the categorization (i, j) and the classification t.

Independence. If $p_{ij} = p_j, i = 1, \ldots, m$, for some $p_j, j = 1, \ldots, m$, the random variable x_t is independent of x_{t-1} in a homogeneous Markov chain. To test the null hypothesis of independence one may use the criterion

$$(4.3) \qquad \sum_{i,j=1}^{m} n_i^* \frac{(\hat{p}_{ij} - \hat{p}_j)^2}{\hat{p}_j} ,$$

where $\hat{p}_j = \Sigma_{i=1}^{m} n_{ij}/[N(T-1)], j = 1, \ldots, m$. Under the null hypothesis the criterion has a limiting χ^2-distribution with $(m-1)^2$ degrees of freedom as $N \to \infty$ and/or $T \to \infty$. The criterion is the χ^2-criterion for independence in the two-way table $\{n_{ij}\}$.

Given Order. An investigator may consider a more elaborate model in which the probability of a state observed at time t depends on the state observed in the last r time points. He may question whether it would be appropriate to use a model of lower order. Independence is order $r = 0$; in the previous section this hypothesis was tested against the alternative that $r = 1$. As another example, we consider testing the null hypothesis that a homogeneous second-order chain is first-order, that is, that $p_{ijk} = p_{jk}$ for some suitable p_{jk} ($p_{jk} \geq 0, \Sigma_{k=1}^{m} p_{jk} = 1$).

In a second-order homogeneous chain with $n_i(1)$ and $n_{ij}(2)$ as given [or $p_i(1)$ and $p_{ij}(2)$ as arbitrary], the maximum likelihood estimates of p_{ijk} are $\hat{p}_{ijk} = n_{ijk}/n_{ij}^*, i, j, k = 1, \ldots, m$, where $n_{ijk} = \Sigma_{t=3}^{T} n_{ijk}(t), n_{ij}^* = \Sigma_{k=1}^{m} n_{ijk}$, and $n_{ijk}(t)$ is the number of observations of state i at $t - 2, j$ at $t - 1$, and k at t. Then a criterion for testing that an assumed second-order chain is actually a first-order chain is

$$(4.4) \qquad \sum_{i,j,k=1}^{m} n_{ij}^* \frac{(\hat{p}_{ijk} - \hat{p}_{jk}^*)^2}{\hat{p}_{jk}} ,$$

where $\hat{p}_{jk}^* = \Sigma_{i=1}^{m} n_{ijk}/\Sigma_{i=1}^{m} n_{ij}^*$. When the null hypothesis is true, (4.4) has a limiting χ^2-distribution with $m(m-1)^2$ degrees of freedom as $N \to \infty$ and/or $T \to \infty$.

Several Chains Identical. A population may be stratified into several subpopulations and the transition probabilities may be different. Suppose we have N_h observations from a Markov chain with transition probabilities $p_{ij}^{(h)}$, $h = 1, \ldots, s$, and we wish to test the null hypothesis that the chains are identical, that is, that $p_{ij}^{(h)} = p_{ij}$, $h = 1, \ldots, s$ for some p_{ij}. Let $\hat{p}_{ij}^{(h)}$ be the maximum likelihood estimate of the transition probability from the hth sample, and let $\hat{p}_{ij}^{(\cdot)}$ be the estimate based on all s samples under the assumption of the null hypothesis. The criterion is

$$(4.5) \qquad \sum_{h=1}^{s} \sum_{i,j=1}^{m} n_i^{*(h)} \frac{[\hat{p}_{ij}^{(h)} - \hat{p}_{ij}^{(\cdot)}]^2}{\hat{p}_{ij}^{(\cdot)}},$$

which has the χ^2-distribution with $(s-1)m(m-1)$ degrees of freedom under the null hypothesis as $N_h \to \infty$ and/or $T \to \infty$.

4.2. Tests for Autoregressive Processes

The hypotheses about the matrices of autoregressive coefficients considered in this section correspond to those concerning Markov chains presented in Section 4.1. The development and application of test procedures are based on asymptotic theory as $N \to \infty$ and/or $T \to \infty$. The procedures are analogs of procedures in multivariate regression. [See Anderson (1958), Chapter 8, for example.] For many hypotheses there are choices of test criteria that have the same limiting distributions under the respective null hypotheses. We have usually chosen a trace criterion (the Lawley-Hotelling criterion in the case of a linear hypothesis) as the criterion most similar to the criterion for the corresponding hypothesis about Markov chains.

Specified Autoregressive Matrices. If the autoregression matrices are the same, that is, $\mathbf{B}(2) = \ldots = \mathbf{B}(T) = \mathbf{B}$, one can test the null hypothesis that $\mathbf{B}$ is a specified $p \times p$ matrix $\mathbf{B}^o$ by use of the criterion

$$(4.6) \qquad tr(\hat{\mathbf{B}} - \mathbf{B}^o) \sum_{t=2}^{T} \sum_{\alpha=1}^{N} \mathbf{y}_{t-1,\alpha} \mathbf{y}'_{t-1,\alpha} (\hat{\mathbf{B}} - \mathbf{B}^o)' \mathbf{\Sigma}^{-1}.$$

As $N \to \infty$ and/or $T \to \infty$, this criterion has a limiting χ^2-distribution with p^2 degrees of freedom. Other criteria, such as the likelihood ratio criterion, could be used. A confidence region for $\mathbf{B}$ consists of all matrices $\mathbf{B}^o$ such that (4.6) is less than a suitable number from the χ^2-tables.

Equality of Autoregression Matrices Given Equality of Covariance Matrices. Suppose $\mathbf{\Sigma}_t = \mathbf{\Sigma}$, $t = 2, \ldots, T$, for some covariance matrix $\mathbf{\Sigma}$; consider testing the null hypothesis $\mathbf{B}(t) = \mathbf{B}$ for some matrix $\mathbf{B}$. The criterion

$$(4.7) \qquad tr \sum_{t=2}^{T} [\hat{\mathbf{B}}(t) - \hat{\mathbf{B}}] \sum_{\alpha=1}^{N} \mathbf{y}_{t-1,\alpha} \mathbf{y}'_{t-1,\alpha} [\hat{\mathbf{B}}(t) - \hat{\mathbf{B}}]' \hat{\mathbf{\Sigma}}^{-1}$$

has a limiting χ^2-distribution with $(T-2)p^2$ degrees of freedom as $N \to \infty$ when the null hypothesis is true.

Independence. In the first-order autoregressive model independence at different time points is identical to $\mathbf{B}(2) = \ldots = \mathbf{B}(T) = \mathbf{0}$ or in the homogeneous case $\mathbf{B} = \mathbf{0}$. In the latter case the null hypothesis of independence is that the auto-regression matrix is the zero matrix and the criterion given $\Sigma_2 = \ldots = \Sigma_t$ is (4.6) with $\mathbf{B}^o = \mathbf{0}$.

Given Order. The second-order homogeneous process is defined by (2.12). It is a first-order process if $\mathbf{B}_2 = \mathbf{0}$. To test this null hypothesis we need estimates of $\mathbf{B}_1$ and $\mathbf{B}_2$

(4.8)
$$[\hat{\mathbf{B}}_1 \hat{\mathbf{B}}_2] = \left[\sum_{t=3}^{T} \sum_{\alpha=1}^{N} \mathbf{y}_{t\alpha} \mathbf{y}'_{t-1,\alpha} \quad \sum_{t=3}^{T} \sum_{\alpha=1}^{N} \mathbf{y}_{t\alpha} \mathbf{y}'_{t-2,\alpha} \right]$$
$$\left[\begin{array}{cc} \sum_{t=3}^{T} \sum_{\alpha=1}^{N} \mathbf{y}_{t-1,\alpha} \mathbf{y}'_{t-1,\alpha} & \sum_{t=3}^{T} \sum_{\alpha=1}^{N} \mathbf{y}_{t-1,\alpha} \mathbf{y}'_{t-2,\alpha} \\ \sum_{t=3}^{T} \sum_{\alpha=1}^{N} \mathbf{y}_{t-2,\alpha} \mathbf{y}'_{t-1,\alpha} & \sum_{t=3}^{T} \sum_{\alpha=1}^{N} \mathbf{y}_{t-2,\alpha} \mathbf{y}'_{t-2,\alpha} \end{array} \right]^{-1}.$$

These are maximum likelihood estimates if $\mathbf{y}_{1\alpha}, \mathbf{y}_{2\alpha}, \alpha = 1, \ldots, N$, are considered as fixed. The covariance matrix Σ is estimated by

(4.9)
$$\hat{\Sigma} = [N(T - 2)]^{-1} \sum_{t=3}^{T} \sum_{\alpha=1}^{N} [\mathbf{y}_{t\alpha} - \hat{\mathbf{B}}_1 \mathbf{y}_{t-1,\alpha} - \hat{\mathbf{B}}_2 \mathbf{y}_{t-2,\alpha}]$$
$$[\mathbf{y}_{t\alpha} - \hat{\mathbf{B}}_1 \mathbf{y}_{t-1,\alpha} - \hat{\mathbf{B}}_2 \mathbf{y}_{t-2,\alpha}]'.$$

A criterion for testing the null hypothesis is

(4.10)
$$tr\hat{\mathbf{B}}_2 \left[\sum_{t=3}^{T} \sum_{\alpha=1}^{N} \mathbf{y}_{t-2,\alpha} \mathbf{y}'_{t-2,\alpha} - \sum_{t=3}^{T} \sum_{\alpha=1}^{N} \mathbf{y}_{t-2,\alpha} \mathbf{y}'_{t-1,\alpha} \right.$$
$$\left. \left(\sum_{t=3}^{T} \sum_{\alpha=1}^{N} \mathbf{y}_{t-1,\alpha} \mathbf{y}'_{t-1,\alpha} \right)^{-1} \sum_{t=3}^{T} \sum_{\alpha=1}^{N} \mathbf{y}_{t-1,\alpha} \mathbf{y}'_{t-2,\alpha} \right] \hat{\mathbf{B}}'_2 \hat{\Sigma}^{-1}.$$

Under the null hypothesis the criterion has a limiting χ^2-distribution with p^2 degrees of freedom as $N \to \infty$ and/or $T \to \infty$.

Several Processes Identical. Consider testing the null hypothesis that the matrices of autoregressive coefficients of s first-order homogeneous autoregressive processes with identical covariance matrices Σ are equal on the basis of N_h observed time series of length T from the hth process, $h = 1, \ldots, s$. If $\hat{\mathbf{B}}^{(h)}$ is the estimate of the matrix for the hth process, $\hat{\mathbf{B}}$ is the pooled estimate of the hypothetically equal matrices, and $\hat{\Sigma}$ is the pooled estimate of Σ, a criterion for testing the null hypothesis is

(4.11)
$$tr \sum_{h=1}^{s} (\hat{\mathbf{B}}^{(h)} - \hat{\mathbf{B}}) \sum_{t=2}^{T} \sum_{\alpha=1}^{N_h} \mathbf{y}^{(h)}_{t-1,\alpha} \mathbf{y}^{(h)'}_{t-1,\alpha} (\hat{\mathbf{B}}^{(h)} - \hat{\mathbf{B}})' \hat{\Sigma}^{-1}.$$

Under the null hypothesis this has a χ^2-distribution with $(s-1)p^2$ degrees of freedom.

4.3. Correspondence of Tests

The matrix $\mathbf{P}$ has $m(m-1)$ elements to specify because the sum of elements in each row is 1, while the matrix $\mathbf{B}$ has p^2. In most cases, if a χ^2-test for a hypothesis about $\mathbf{P}$ or $\mathbf{P}(t)$ has as the number of degrees of freedom a multiple of $m(m-1)$, the corresponding test for $\mathbf{B}$ or $\mathbf{B}(t)$ has the same multiple of p^2 as the number of degrees of freedom. According to the correspondence set up in Section 3.3., n_i^* is the ith diagonal element of the diagonal matrix $\Sigma_{t=2}^{T} \Sigma_{\alpha=1}^{N} z_{t-1,\alpha} z_{t-1,\alpha}'$ and the diagonal matrix with diagonal elements $1/p_{ij}$ is a generalized inverse of the limiting covariance matrix of $\sqrt{n_i^*}(\hat{p}_{i1} - p_{i1}), \ldots, \sqrt{n_i^*}(\hat{p}_{im} - p_{im})$. Then the sum of (4.1) over i and (4.6) correspond as criteria for specified matrices.

Since $n_i(t-1)$ is the ith diagonal element of $\Sigma_{\alpha=1}^{N} z_{t-1,\alpha} z_{t-1,\alpha}'$ of the representation for the Markov chain, (4.2) and (4.7) correspond as tests of homogeneity.

For independence (4.3) corresponds to (4.6) with $\mathbf{B}^o = \mathbf{0}$; in the discrete case the covariance matrix of $\hat{p}_{ij}$ does not depend on i. The correspondence between degrees of freedom, however, is $(m-1)^2$ and p^2 because independence in the discrete case is not defined by setting $\mathbf{P} = \mathbf{0}$. (Independence is $\mathbf{P} = \epsilon p'$.)

For testing whether a second-order model is actually first-order criteria (4.4) and (4.10) correspond. In the latter $\hat{\Sigma}$ could be replaced by (3.12), which is a consistent estimate of Σ when the null hypothesis is true, or $\hat{\Sigma}$ could be replaced by the matrix in brackets divided by $N(T-2)$. Note the degrees of freedom are $m(m-1)^2$ and p^2, respectively.

To test equality of matrices criteria (4.5) and (4.11) correspond.

Personal Note. In a sense, this paper is a continuation of discussions of mathematical models and statistical methods that Paul and I had for the last 30 years. One contrast in our interests is that Paul was more interested in discrete data (particularly dichotomies) while I have been more interested in continuous data (particularly normally distributed). Another contrast is that in mathematical developments Paul preferred model building and analysis of ideal data, and I have emphasized statistical inference. My contribution here demonstrates some of our mutual, as well as dissimilar, interests in the area of time series analysis for repeated measurements. My great sorrow at Paul's death is made a little more poignant at the time of reviewing this paper by the realization that although it was written for him it will not be read by him.

References

ANDĚL, JIRI. "On the Multiple Autoregressive Series," *Annals of Mathematical Statistics*, 42 (1971), 755–759.

ANDERSON, T. W. "Probability Models for Analyzing Time Changes in Attitudes," Part VI, *The Use of Mathematical Models in the Measurement of Attitudes*, Research Memorandum, Project Rand. Santa Monica, Calif.: The Rand Corporation, 1951.

ANDERSON, T. W. "Probability Models for Analyzing Time Changes in Attitudes," in Paul F. Lazarsfeld, ed., *Mathematical Thinking in the Social Sciences*. Glencoe, Ill.: The Free Press, 1954, 17–66.

ANDERSON, T. W. *An Introduction to Multivariate Statistical Analysis*. New York: Wiley, 1958.

ANDERSON, T. W. *The Statistical Analysis of Time Series*. New York: Wiley, 1971.

ANDERSON, T. W. "Repeated Measurements on Autoregressive Processes," *Journal of the American Statistical Association*, 73 (1978), 371–378.

ANDERSON, T. W. and LEO A. GOODMAN. "Statistical Inference about Markov Chains," *Annals of Mathematical Statistics*, 28 (1957), pp. 89–110.

BARTLETT, M. S. "The Frequency Goodness of Fit Test for Probability Chains," *Proceedings of the Cambridge Philosophical Society*, (1951), 86–95.

BILLINGSLEY, PATRICK. "Statistical Methods in Markov Chains," *Annals of Statistics*, 32 (1961), 12–40.

GOODMAN, LEO A. "Causal Analysis of Data from Panel Studies and Other Kinds of Surveys," *The American Journal of Sociology*, 78 (1973), 1135–1191.

LAZARSFELD, PAUL F., BERNARD BERELSON, and HAZEL GAUDET. *The People's Choice*, 2nd edition. New York: Columbia University Press, 1948.

10. PURPOSIVE ACTORS AND MUTUAL EFFECTS

James S. Coleman

Prologue

Among the central characteristics of Paul Lazarsfeld's style in social research has been his ability to set other persons to work on problems which he himself has formulated and partially solved. An example is latent structure analysis, which in Lazarsfeld's hands was only in part an analytical tool. In part it was a set of problems generated by a central idea, through which Lazarsfeld stimulated numbers of his colleagues, students, and others to work.

A classic example of this intellectual style is the 16-fold table problem, or the problem of mutual dependence among two attitudes measured at two points in time in panel data. Lazarsfeld's principal contribution was not that he definitively solved the problem, but that he *saw* a problem and posed it for himself and others. Though he himself gave a partial solution to the problem, with an index of mutual effects,[1] he was not satisfied with this and continued not only to work on it himself (see Lazarsfeld, 1973), but also to push others to attempt solutions. Again, many of his colleagues, students, and others, have fashioned significant portions of their careers through work on the problem that Lazarsfeld posed.[2]

The major stimulus to my work in mathematical sociology, including the central conception in *Introduction to Mathematical Sociology* (Chapters 3, 4, 5, 6) and subsequent work (1964b, 1968) was this 16-fold table problem. More recently, my work in mathematical sociology has involved models of purposive action, with different intellectual origins and addressed to different intellectual problems. Yet I found myself recently drawn back to the 16-fold table problem; perhaps it is impossible to leave entirely the problems which initiated one's intellectual activity. This paper is the consequence of that continued pull, an amalgam of the problem set by Lazarsfeld and the models of purposive action with which I have recently worked. It is a measure of Lazars-feld's influence that, despite the shift of orientation from causal to purposive models of action, I return to the problem that he posed.[3]

Part I: Outline of the Model

A Special Case of the 16-Fold Table Problem

Consider a situation in which two persons have a relationship and also have attitudes or behavior in a given area. We can ask two questions. First, assuming that the relation continues, we can ask whether the attitudes or behavior of each of the two persons are influenced by the attitudes or behavior of the other. Second, if we no longer assume that the relation will continue, we can ask whether divergence in attitude or behavior affects its continuation, and if so, to what degree. More generaly, the problems are those examined by Lazarsfeld and Merton in a paper on homophily (1954): the tendency of those who are alike in some respect to come together as friends and the complementary process by which those who are friends come to share the same values.

These complementary processes may be studied through panel analysis, examining at two or more points in time both the attitudes or behavior of the members of the sample and the presence or absence of friendship ties. And it is possible to construct statistical measures to show the degree to which the complementary processes operate. A number of such measures applicable to such data have been devised since Lazarsfeld formulated the problem.

What I want to do here is somewhat different: to lay out a model of rational behavior, and, then by viewing the observed data as outcomes generated by purposive action on the part of the members of the sample, to use the observed data to estimate something about the purposes or interests of those who are observed in the panel. This attempt will not be wholly successful in addressing these problems in this manner but will be a beginning toward their solution.

I will first lay out the framework of the model of purposive action in the context of the problem at hand and then will show how the data may be used in conjunction with the model.[4] To fix ideas, I will refer to data on marijuana use from Kandel's research, analyzed elsewhere by her (1976).

The use of marijuana was measured for students in five high schools in the fall and spring of the 1971–1972 school year. We can ask how their friendships affected their use of marijuana and how their similarity of behavior toward marijuana affected their friendship. Or, in a purposive framework, we can ask the relative strength of their interests in marijuana use and in their friends, as well as the strength of their interests in their friends' marijuana behavior.

We will begin for simplicity with consideration of a restricted social system, which fits the 16-fold table problem, and will ask at the outset only a portion of the questions. That is, we will consider friendships already in existence, remaining unbroken over the period of the panel, and will ask only about changes in marijuana use, not about changes in friendship.

Consider a social system composed of the following actors:

1. Friend A (He may be distinguished according to some criterion, such as the younger of the two, or the one with higher grades in school, etc. Or we may not distinguish him from his friend. In this exposition, we will assume that he is distinguished on some dimension from his friend.)

2. Friend B
3. Other actors with interests in A's marijuana use
4. Other actors with interests in A's not using marijuana
5. Other actors with interests in B's marijuana use
6. Other actors with interests in B's not using marijuana

The social system contains two events to which the actors are linked in two ways: they each have some *control* over one or both events, and they each have an *interest* in the outcome of one or both events. The events are marijuana use by A and B, each with two outcomes: use or nonuse.

The "other actors" in the system are not present in the data and are introduced only to account for the changes that are not in accord with either A's or B's interests. In effect, they absorb the otherwise unexplained changes. Actor 3 is introduced to account for the unexplained changes of A toward marijuana use, actor 4 is introduced to account for the unexplained changes of A away from marijuana use, and so on.

For similar technical purposes, four more events are added to the system, each corresponding to one of these external actors. Proceeding in this way, each actor begins with full control over his "own" event, though the contents of events 3 to 6 are left unspecified. Then the exchanges of control that are assumed to take place between times 1 and 2 consist of each actor's giving up some control over his own event to gain control over other events in which he is interested. In this process, the actors and events 3 through 6 stand for all the other relations in which A and B are involved that lead them to modify their behavior in ways not accounted for by this relationship itself.

The system, then, although it consists of only two identified actors—A and B—and two identified events—A's and B's marijuana use—includes also four additional unidentified actors and four additional unidentified events. As indicated above, each actor begins with full control over his "own" event. The structure of interests will be identified in a later section.

The interest matrix is denoted by $\mathbf{X}$, with elements x_{ji}, where x_{ji} is the fraction of actor j's interest in event i. There is also a matrix $\mathbf{S}$ denoting the direction of interests, with elements s_{ji}. If j is interested in a positive outcome of event i (that is, his marijuana use), $s_{ji} = +1$, and, if j is interested in a negative outcome (no use), $s_{ji} = -1$. For each actor, the sum of x_{ji} over the set of six events is 1.0. (By definition of actors 3, 4, 5, and 6, they have interests in only one event, but A and B may have interests not only in their own behavior, but also that of their friend.)

Control of events is denoted by a matrix **C**, with elements c_{ij}, the fraction of control over event i by actor j. The sum of control by all actors over event i is 1.0. We think of this control as the "initial control," and the system of action consists of each actor exchanging control to gain control of events in which he has a great deal of interest. This leads to a different configuration of "final control" or "effective control."

The system of exchange generates several things: first, it allows us to express the relative power of each actor in the system, and conjointly, the relative value of each event in the system. These are

a. The power (r_j) of each actor is the control he has over events, weighted by the value of each event:

$$(1) \qquad r_j = \sum_{i=1}^{m} v_i c_{ij}.$$

b. The value (v_i) of each event is the interest each actor has in the event, weighted by the power of the actor:

$$(2) \qquad v_i = \sum_{j=1}^{n} r_j x_{ji}.$$

If we know the interests and control, then it is possible to solve for values or power, obtaining first one, and from it the other. For example, substituting in eq. 2 the value for r_j given in eq. 1:

$$(3) \qquad v_i = \sum_{j=1}^{n} \sum_{k=1}^{m} v_k c_{kj} x_{ji}.$$

Equations of the form of eq. 3 form a set of simultaneous equations, one for each event i, which may be solved for the set of v_i, and then in turn by use of eq. 1, for the set of r_j.

Once the values of events and power of actors are known, then it is possible to see what the final control or effective control of each event by each actor will be. I will not derive it here, but, if each actor behaves according to a reasonable definition of rationality, the effective control after exchanges, denoted by b_{ij} will be

$$(4) \qquad b_{ij} = x_{ji} \frac{r_j}{v_i}.$$

That is, the effective control by actor j over event i is his interest in the event, adjusted by the ratio of his power to the value of the event.[5]

Although other quantities may be derived from the model, the only one of interest to us here is the outcome of the event. The probability of a positive outcome of the event is equal to the effective control held by those actors who are interested in a positive outcome. If all control is held by them, the outcome will be positive with certainty; if half is held by them, the outcome will be positive with probability 0.5; if none, the outcome will be negative with certainty. Using the quantities defined above, the probability of a positive outcome of event i (denoted by p_i) is

(5) $\qquad p_i = \sum_j b_{ij}, \qquad$ summed only over actors for whom $s_{ji} = +1$.

The usual application of this model has been to begin with known values of interest (X) and control (C) and then to use these to calculate the power of actors, the value of events, the effective control of events, and the probabilities of positive outcomes in all events. However, the strategy we will use here will be different: to begin with observed otucomes of events, then to use these to estimate effective control of each actor, and, from that, by making some assumptions about initial control, to infer interests of actors. That is the general outline of the strategy to be employed below.

Part II: Interdependence of Friends in Marijuana Use

Application of the Model and Estimation of Effective Control

A 16-fold table representing marijuana use of pairs of friends is given in Table 1. Rows of the table show persons classified according to their marijuana use in the fall of the school year; columns show their use in the spring.

We will consider each friendship pair as a social system of the sort discussed in the preceding section. The events under consideration are in the spring. Each event can have two outcomes, so there are four possible combinations of outcomes, one represented by each column in the table. Row 1 consists of 43 replications of a given type of social system, one in which we assume that the interests of A and B toward both their own use and that of their friend are positive. Let us consider the outcome of event 1 (A's use in the spring) first and examine the configuration of effective control. At this point, all we know is that the direction in which effective control will be exerted is the direction of interest and, by eq. 4, that where there is no interest, there will be no effective control.

Thus for social systems of this type, the probability of a positive outcome is given by summing the effective controls for those actors with positive interests:

(6) $\qquad\qquad\qquad p_1 = b_{11} + b_{12} + b_{13}.$

For each of the four types of social systems represented by the four rows, we can write an equation for the probability of a positive outcome (indicating the row by the second subscript on p_1)

TABLE 1 Marijuana Use of Friends in Fall and Spring

	Fall		Spring				
Row	A	B	A Yes B Yes	A Yes B No	A No B Yes	A No B No	Total
1	Yes	Yes	27	5	6	5	43
2	Yes	No	7	16	1	9	33
3	No	Yes	6	1	20	18	45
4	No	No	19	14	15	436	484
	Total		59	36	42	468	605

Actors	Direction of Interest	Effective Control
1 (boy A)	positive	b_{11}
2 (boy B)	positive	b_{12}
3	positive	b_{13}
4	negative	b_{14}
5	none	0
6	none	0

$$(7) \quad \begin{aligned} p_{11} &= b_{11} + b_{12} + b_{13} \\ p_{12} &= b_{11} \qquad\quad + b_{13} \\ p_{13} &= \qquad\quad b_{12} + b_{13} \\ p_{14} &= \qquad\qquad\qquad b_{13} \end{aligned}$$

The b's are unknown values of effective control. But the p's, as probabilities of a positive outcome, can be estimated by the actual proportions of students in each of the types of social systems that were using marijuana in the spring. For example, the estimate of p_{11} is 32/43. If we denote the estimates of p's and b's by p_{ik}^* and b_{ij}^*, the b_{ij}'s may be estimated by the three equations below:[6]

$$(8) \quad \begin{aligned} b_{11}^* &= \frac{1}{2}(p_{11}^* + p_{12}^* - p_{13}^* - p_{14}^*) \\ b_{12}^* &= \frac{1}{2}(p_{11}^* + p_{13}^* - p_{12}^* - p_{14}^*). \\ b_{13}^* &= \frac{1}{4}(3p_{14}^* + p_{12}^* + p_{13}^* - p_{11}^*) \end{aligned}$$

Since $b_{11} + b_{12} + b_{13} + b_{14} = 1$, then b_{14} is estimated as $1 - b_{11}^* - b_{12}^* - b_{13}^*$. In an exactly analogous way, the effective control for the second event may be estimated by the actual outcomes in the spring:

$$(9) \quad \begin{aligned} b_{21}^* &= \frac{1}{2}(p_{21}^* + p_{22}^* - p_{23}^* - p_{24}^*) \\ b_{22}^* &= \frac{1}{2}(p_{21}^* + p_{23}^* - p_{22}^* - p_{24}^*). \\ b_{25}^* &= \frac{1}{4}(3p_{24}^* + p_{22}^* + p_{23}^* - p_{21}^*) \end{aligned}$$

As for event 1, since $b_{21} + b_{22} + b_{25} + b_{26} = 1$, then b_{26} is estimated as $1 - b_{21}^* - b_{22}^* - b_{25}^*$.

Using the data from Table 1, together with eq. 8 and 9,

$b_{11}^* = .609$		A's effective control over his own behavior
$b_{12}^* = .067$		B's effective control over A's behavior
$b_{13}^* = .078$		Others' effective control over A's behavior in a positive direction
$b_{14}^* = .245$		Others' effective control over A's behavior in a negative direction
$b_{21}^* = .181$		A's effective control over B's behavior
$b_{22}^* = .516$		B's effective control over his own behavior
$b_{25}^* = .066$		Others' effective control over B's behavior in a positive direction
$b_{26}^* = .237$		Others' effective control over B's behavior in a negative direction

These data show that for both members of the pair the major control over marijuana use is exercised by the person himself, through his own prior behavior. The friend exercises some control, though not much, as do those with an interest in the person's use of marijuana. The major external control is exercised by those against his use. There is some difference here for the two friends. Though the friends are not distinguished according to a dimension such as age (older and younger) or another dimension, there is an asymmetry, for A is the person who named B as his best friend in school. We would expect, for that reason, that, if there were a difference, it would be in the direction of greater control by B over A's behavior, but the data show somewhat greater control by A.

Estimation of Interest of Each Friend in His Own and Other's Behavior

As indicated in an earlier section, each actor's interest determines the allocation of his resources which gain him effective control over events he is interested in. If A is greatly interested in B's behavior, he will end up with a good deal of effective control over it, limited only by his resources and his other interests. Going back to eq. 4, the relation is

$$(10) \qquad b_{ij} = x_{ji} \frac{r_j}{v_i}.$$

Now, since we have estimates of the b's for events 1 and 2, if certain assumptions can be made about the structure of the interest and control matrices which will allow expression of the relative sizes of value and power, then we can estimate the interests themselves.

As indicated earlier, the control matrix is taken to be one in which each actor, including the four external actors, has control over the event representing his behavior. The external actors are assumed to have interests only in the events 1 (for actors 3 and 4) and 2 (for actors 5 and 6). Actor 1 (friend A) is assumed to have interests in his own behavior, in that of B, and in that of actors 3 and 4. (The last is what induces him to give up control of a portion of his behavior to actors 3 and 4). Actor 2 (friend B) has a similar interest structure. The interest matrix is as follows:

	E_1	E_2	E_3	E_4	E_5	E_6
A_1	x_{11}	x_{12}	x_{13}	x_{14}	0	0
A_2	x_{21}	x_{22}	0	0	x_{25}	x_{26}
A_3	1	0	0	0	0	0
A_4	1	0	0	0	0	0
A_5	0	1	0	0	0	0
A_6	0	1	0	0	0	0

It is possible to obtain estimates for interests in events directly from the estimates of effective control, as follows: First, we note that each pair of actors who have a potential exchange relation (i.e., each with an interest in what the other controls) do not have any indirect links through mutual exchanges with other actors. This means that the value of A_j's actions that A_i comes to gain control of equals the value of A_i's actions that A_j comes to gain control of, or for all actors i, j:

$$(11) \qquad v_j b_{ji} = v_i b_{ij}$$

But since each actor j has initial full control over event j, $r_j = v_j$ for all actors j, so that eq. 11 becomes

$$(12) \qquad r_j b_{ji} = r_i b_{ij}.$$

However, eq. 10 together with the fact that $r_j = v_j$ implies that $r_i b_{ij} = r_j x_{ji}$. This together with eq. 12 implies that $x_{ij} = b_{ji}$ for all i and j. Thus, the interest of actor i in event j equals the effective control of actor j over event i, when each actor j initially controls event j.[7] If 1 is uninterested in 2's behavior, then 2 has no leverage over him with which to change his behavior. And vice versa. In terms of the example, since actor 2's effective control over 1's marijuana use is .067 and 1's effective control over 2's use is .181, this means that actor 2 shows over twice as much interest in 1's behavior as 1 does in 2's.

More generally, in this application, the interest of each actor in another's behavior (which the other initially controls) is exhibited by the control that the other is able to exercise over his behavior. The estimates of the interests of actors 1 and 2 in each event are

Estimates of Interests

	E_1	E_2	E_3	E_4	E_5	E_6
A_1	.609	.067	.078	.245	0	0
A_2	.181	.516	0	0	.066	.237

Power of Each Friend and of Outside Actors
and Value of the Behavior of Each

Now that estimates of interest are found, it becomes possible to estimate the power of each actor in the system and the value of A's behavior and B's behavior. It is simplest to estimate the latter first. This could be done by solving the set of simultaneous equations (3), but this is almost done already, since the v_i's can readily be expressed in terms of v_1. First, using eq. 4,

$$b_{12} = x_{21} \frac{v_2}{v_1},$$

but $x_{21} = b_{21}$, so that substituting and expressing in terms of v_2 gives

$$v_2 = \frac{b_{12}}{b_{21}} v_1.$$

This means that the value of actor 2's behavior in the system relative to that of actor 1 is his control over 1's behavior, relative to 1's control over his.

All the other v_i's can similarly be expressed either in terms of v_1 or v_2, so using this together with the fact that $\Sigma v_i = 1$ gives, after some algebra,

$$(13) \qquad v_1 = \frac{b_{21}}{b_{21}(1 + b_{13} + b_{14}) + b_{12}(1 + b_{25} + b_{26})},$$

and using the estimates of b_{ij}'s from the example, the v_i are estimated as

$$v_3 = .043$$
$$v_1 = .554 \qquad v_4 = .136$$
$$v_2 = .205 \qquad v_5 = .014$$
$$v_6 = .049$$

The power of each actor is, as we have seen, equal to the value of his behavior in the system, so that these estimates are also estimates of the power of each actor. The power of actor 1 (friend A) relative to actor 2 reflects the fact that he is able to exercise stronger effective control over 2's marijuana use than 2 is over his. And the power of both 1 and 2 relative to the external actors reflects the fact that most of their marijuana use or nonuse at time 2 is predicted by (controlled by) their own use at time 1 or the other's use at time 1; not a great deal of their behavior at time 2 is unaccounted for.

Part III

Expansion to Consider Relative Interests in the Relationship as well as the Behavior

Now we are in a position to expand the system to consider an additional event: the continuation of the relation or its breakup and the formation of a new relation. Now, rather than four initial types of systems, there are eight: four sets of friendship pairs as described in the preceding sections, differing in their initial behavior states, and four sets of pairs, arbitrarily formed from the larger group, who are not friends at the first time point. Data for the example of marijuana use examined in the preceding sections are presented in Table 2.[8]

The upper left quadrant can be recognized as the data shown in Table 1, consisting of all the friendships that remained friends at time 2. (Alternatively, for the calculations of the preceding sections, the sum of the upper left and upper right quadrants could have been used.)

There are two related questions to be added here to those examined earlier: (1) How does the friendship respond in its continuing or failing to continue, to similarity or difference in the behavior (marijuana use) of its members? and (2) How do pairs who are not friends respond, in becoming friends or failing to, to the similarity or difference in behavior of the members of the pair?[9] These questions could be partitioned further by asking, for example, how the friendship in which at least one member uses marijuana responds to the use by both or by only one, as a question different from that of how the friendship in which at least one member does not use marijuana responds to the use by one member or by neither. Or the two questions could be combined into one, by asking how a pair (whether friends or not) responds (by possibly breaking up if a friendship exists or forming if one does not exist) to similarity or difference in use. Here we will examine the two questions separately, remaining at the intermediate level of specificity. Thus we will analyze the upper and lower sections of the table separately. (However, to obtain an estimate for the control of the friendship over its own continuation, we must analyze the lower half of the table first and use an estimate of the external control from that half to separate out the control exercised by the friendship and that exercised by external actors toward its continuation. The reasons for this will be evident in analysis of the upper half.)

In each of the two analyses, there is an additional event beyond that of the previous analysis, defined slightly differently in the two cases: in the upper half the event is continuation of the friendship (+) or breakup (−) and in the lower half of its formation of a friendship (+) or not (−).

Table 2

Marijuana Use	Friends	Friends at Time 2 (+)				Not Friends at Time 2 (−)				
	A B	A B ++	+−	−+	−−	++	+−	−+	−−	
+	+ +	27	5	6	5	4	3	4	1	55
+	+ −	7	16	1	9	2	7	2	6	50
+	− +	6	1	20	18	6	1	9	7	68
+	− −	19	14	15	436	4	9	14	124	635
−	+ +	11	1	2	2	347	178	170	84	795
−	+ −	3	5	1	8	292	2,865	139	1,369	4,682
−	− +	4	2	9	10	316	155	4,530	1,705	5,621
−	− −	4	11	11	147	244	2,380	2,628	25,621	31,046

The pair is regarded as a new actor, with initial control over this new event and with an interest in that event (and in the events controlled by "its" external actors). In addition, when the pair is a friendship pair, it has an interest in the marijuana use of its members, an interest in that use being alike.

This latter interest is the interest which in the previous analysis was attributed to each of the members, as interest in marijuana use of the other.

Estimation of Effective Control

Among the friendship pairs each member of the pair has an interest in his own or nonuse of marijuana and an interest in maintaining or breaking the relation (depending on the similarity or difference of his friend's marijuana behavior). Among the nonfriendship pairs, the latter interest is an interest in forming a friendship if their marijuana use (or nonuse) is alike.

As in the previous analysis, with the new event and new actor, two additional external actors and two additional events are included, to account for the changes in friendship which are otherwise unaccounted for.

For the friendship pairs, the upper half of the table, the structure of interest is as given below. (The new event is inserted as event 3, with the previous external events moved from 3 through 6 to 4 through 7, and the two new external events are 8 and 9.)

Interest Matrix for Friendship Pairs

		E_1	E_2	E_3	E_4	E_5	E_6	E_7	E_8	E_9
Friend A	A_1	x_{11}	0	x_{13}	x_{14}	x_{15}	0	0	0	0
Friend B	A_2	0	x_{22}	x_{23}	0	0	x_{26}	x_{27}	0	0
Friendship pair	A_3	x_{31}	x_{32}	x_{33}	0	0	0	0	x_{38}	x_{39}
	A_4	1	0	0	0	0	0	0	0	0
	A_5	1	0	0	0	0	0	0	0	0
	A_6	0	1	0	0	0	0	0	0	0
	A_7	0	1	0	0	0	0	0	0	0
	A_8	0	0	1	0	0	0	0	0	0
	A_9	0	0	1	0	0	0	0	0	0

For the nonfriendship pairs, the interest structure is the same, except for the absence of x_{31} and x_{32}. That is, if the pair is only an artificially constructed pair, it cannot exercise control over the two persons' behavior.

For the lower half of the table, the structure of interests leading to a positive outcome (marijuana use or creation of a friendship) gives the probabilities of a positive outcome shown as follows for events 1, 2, and 3 in the four rows of the table (labeled 5 through 8):

$$p_{15} = b_{11} + b_{14} \qquad p_{25} = b_{22} + b_{26} \qquad p_{35} = b_{31} + b_{32} + b_{38}$$

$$p_{16} = \qquad b_{14} \qquad p_{26} = \qquad b_{26} \qquad p_{36} = \qquad b_{38}$$

$$p_{17} = b_{11} + b_{14} \qquad p_{27} = b_{22} + b_{26} \qquad p_{37} = \qquad b_{38}$$

$$p_{18} = \qquad b_{14} \qquad p_{28} = \qquad b_{26} \qquad p_{38} = b_{31} + b_{32} + b_{38}$$

These equations show that the interests in a positive outcome on marijuana use, events 1 and 2, are only those of the users, plus external actors 4 and 6. For the formation of a friendship, the two members of the pair have a positive interest when marijuana use or nonuse is alike, and external actor 8 has a positive interest. (Actor 3, the pair, has a negative interest, as does external actor 9.)

The effective controls, b_{ij}'s, can be estimated, using these equations, together with the proportions positive at time 2, which are estimates of the p_{ik}'s:

(14)

$$b_{11}^* = \frac{1}{2}(p_{15}^* + p_{16}^* - p_{17}^* - p_{18}^*)$$

$$b_{14}^* = \frac{1}{2}(p_{17}^* + p_{18}^*)$$

$$b_{22}^* = \frac{1}{2}(p_{25}^* + p_{27}^* - p_{26}^* - p_{28}^*)$$

$$b_{26}^* = \frac{1}{2}(p_{26}^* + p_{28}^*)$$

$$b_{31}^* + b_{32}^* = \frac{1}{2}(p_{35}^* + p_{38}^* - p_{36}^* - p_{37}^*)$$

$$b_{38}^* = \frac{1}{2}(p_{36}^* + p_{37}^*)$$

Note that b_{31} and b_{32} cannot be estimated separately. When the members' marijuana use (or nonuse) is alike, both have interests in a friendship; when it is different, both have interests opposed. For this reason, we will simply assume that $b_{31} = b_{32}$, recognizing that the further analysis contains that assumption.

From Table 2, the proportions of positive outcomes for each of these events for each of the four rows are

Using eq. 14, this gives the following estimates for the b_{ij}'s:

$b_{11}^* = .591$ A's effective control over his own behavior

$b_{14}^* = .085$ Others' with positive interests effective control over A's behavior

$b_{22}^* = .574$ B's effective control over his own behavior

$b_{26}^* = .093$ Others' with positive interests effective control over B's behavior

	p^* (proportion positive)		
Row	E_1	E_2	E_3
$E_1\ E_2\ E_3$			
5 + + −	.675	.667	.020
6 + − −	.676	.093	.004
7 − + −	.085	.667	.004
8 − − −	.085	.093	.006

Row	E_1	E_2	E_3
$E_1\ E_2\ E_3$			
1 + + +	.709	.745	.782
2 + − +	.640	.240	.660
3 − + +	.206	.603	.662
4 − − +	.072	.082	.762

$b_{31}^* + b_{32}^* = .009$	A's and B's effective control over friendship formation
$b_{31}^* = b_{32}^* = .0045$	A's (or B's) effective control over friendship formation
$b_{38}^* = .004$	Others' with positive interests effective control over friendship formation

By subtraction from 1.0, $b_{15} = .324$, $b_{27} = .333$, and $b_{33} + b_{39} = .987$. The latter two b_{ij}'s cannot be separated because interests of those two actors are directed against friendship formation in all four rows. Only by considering the upper half of the table will it be possible to obtain separate estimates for these, with a caveat introduced by the recognition that the event as defined is slightly different.

Because in a system in which all pairs with direct links have no indirect links, $x_{ji} = b_{ji}$ for all i and j (see p. 105), we can immediately write the x_{ji}'s for the first three rows of the interest matrix except for x_{33}, since b_{33} cannot be extricated from $b_{33} + b_{39}$. Because of this, we will analyze the upper half first, to allow separating b_{33}, b_{38}, and b_{39}.

For the upper half of the table, the probabilities of a positive outcome are (I will use the same subscripts, even though the estimates of the b's and x's will be different in the two halves of the table except for b_{33} and b_{39})

$$p_{11} = b_{11} + b_{13} + b_{14} \qquad p_{21} = b_{22} + b_{23} + b_{26} \qquad p_{31} = b_{31} + b_{32} + b_{33} + b_{38}$$

$$p_{12} = b_{11} + b_{14} \qquad p_{22} = b_{23} + b_{26} \qquad p_{32} = b_{33} + b_{38}$$

$$p_{13} = b_{13} + b_{14} \qquad p_{23} = b_{22} + b_{26} \qquad p_{33} = b_{33} + b_{38}$$

$$p_{14} = b_{14} \qquad p_{24} = b_{26} \qquad p_{34} = b_{31} + b_{32} + b_{33} + b_{38}$$

Estimates of the b_{ij}'s, using these equations, are

$$b_{11}^* = \frac{1}{2}(p_{11}^* + p_{12}^* - p_{13}^* - p_{14}^*)$$

$$b_{13}^* = \frac{1}{2}(p_{11}^* + p_{13}^* - p_{12}^* - p_{14}^*)$$

$$b_{14}^* = \frac{1}{4}(3p_{14}^* + p_{12}^* + p_{13}^* - p_{11}^*)$$

$$b_{22}^* = \frac{1}{2}(p_{21}^* + p_{23}^* - p_{22}^* - p_{24}^*)$$

$$b_{23}^* = \frac{1}{2}(p_{21}^* + p_{22}^* - p_{23}^* - p_{24}^*)$$

$$b_{26}^* = \frac{1}{4}(3p_{24}^* + p_{22}^* + p_{23}^* - p_{11}^*)$$

$$b_{31}^* + b_{32}^* = \frac{1}{2}(p_{31}^* + p_{34}^* - p_{32}^* - p_{33}^*)$$

$$b_{33}^* + b_{38}^* = \frac{1}{2}(p_{32} + p_{33})$$

Again, b_{31}^* and b_{32}^* are not separable, nor are b_{33}^* and b_{38}^*. As before, b_{15}^* and b_{27}^*, and this time b_{39}^*, are estimated as 1.0 minus the other b_{ij}^*'s on the event.

The proportions of positive outcomes for these four rows are, from Table 2, From these p_{ik}^*'s, the b_{ij}^*'s can be estimated, using eq. 15:

b_{11} = .536	A's effective control over his own behavior
b_{13} = .102	Friendship's (A_3's) effective control over A's behavior
b_{14} = .088	Others' with positive interests effective control over A's behavior
b_{22} = .513	B's effective control over his own behavior
b_{23} = .150	Friendship's (A_3's) effective control over B's behavior
b_{26} = .086	Others' with positive interests effective control over B's behavior
$b_{31} + b_{32}$ = .111	A's and B's effective control over friendship's continuation
$b_{31} = b_{32}$ = .0555	A's (or B's) effective control over friendship's continuation
$b_{33} + b_{38}$ = .661	
b_{15} = .274	Others' with negative interests effective control over A's behavior

$$b_{27} = .251 \qquad \text{Others' with negative interests effective control over B's behavior}$$

$$b_{39} = .228 \qquad \text{Others' with negative interests effective control over the friendship}$$

To estimate the values of b_{33} and b_{38} in the upper half, we will use b_{38}^* from the lower half, which gives for the upper half

$$b_{33}^* = .657$$

$$b_{38}^* = .004$$

Similarly, for the lower half, we will use b_{39}^* from the upper half to obtain separate estimates for b_{33} and b_{39}:

$$b_{33}^* = .759$$

$$b_{39}^* = .228$$

With these estimates, the interest structure for the upper half of the table is

Interests for Friendship Pairs

	E_1	E_2	E_3	E_4	E_5	E_6	E_7	E_8	E_9
A_1	.536	0	.102	.088	.274	0	0	0	0
A_1	0	.513	.150	0	0	.086	.251	0	0
A_3	.0555	.0555	.657	0	0	0	0	.004	.228

This shows that A has lesser interest in the friendship than does B, resulting from the fact that his marijuana use is less often changed by it than B's. This is an example of Willard Waller's principle of least interest: the principle that the member of a relation with less interest in the relation has greater power in it. Here, we observe the power through the changes in behavior and infer the interest. The friendship, as a corporate actor, has less interest in the members' behavior than they in the friendship, because the friendship's continuation is less affected by the members' divergence in marijuana use than either members' marijuana use is affected by the friendship.

It is useful to compare the interest structure among the nonfriends:

Interests for Nonfriendship Pairs

	E_1	F_2	E_3	E_4	E_5	E_6	E_7	E_8	E_9
A_1	.591	0	0	.085	.324	0	0	0	0
A_2	0	.574	0	0	0	.093	.333	0	0
A_3	.0045	.0045	.759	0	0	0	0	.004	.228

In this case, the interest of the pair in the members' marijuana use (deriving from the marijuana use's control over friendship formation) is less than a tenth as large as in the case of the friendship pairs. Each of the actors has somewhat greater control over his own behavior among the nonfriends (deriving from the lesser change among the nonfriends).

Estimation of Value of Events and Power of Actors

From these interests, it is possible to use eq. 3 to estimate the value of each event (and since $r_i = v_i$, the power of each actor). The equation for v_1 in the system of friendship pairs comes out to be:

$$v_1 = \frac{x_{31}x_{23}}{x_{31}x_{23}(1 + x_{14} + x_{15}) + x_{13}x_{32}(1 + x_{26} + x_{27}) + x_{13}x_{23}(1 + x_{28} + x_{29})}$$

After substituting in estimated values and solving for all v_i's,

$v_1 = r_1 = .220$	Friend A
$v_2 = r_2 = .150$	Friend B
$v_3 = r_3 = .405$	Friendship pair
$v_4 = r_4 = .019$	External actor
$v_5 = r_5 = .060$	External actor
$v_6 = r_6 = .013$	External actor
$v_7 = r_7 = .038$	External actor
$v_8 = r_8 = .002$	External actor
$v_9 = r_9 = .092$	External actor

The measures of power show that the friendship relation is about twice as powerful (in its ability to change members' behavior) as the marijuana use (or nonuse) interests of either of them is—though A shows, as before, somewhat more power than B. The power of the external actors derives both from the power of the actor whose behavior they are interested in and their effective control over that actor. These measures of power again reflect Willard Waller's principle of least interest: the more powerful are those that show less interest in the others' behavior.

For the lower half of the table, there is an anomaly. Close inspection of the structure of interests will show that there is not a single interdependent system. There is one system of actors (and events) 1, 4, and 5; another of actors (and events) 2, 6, and 7; and a third of actors (and events) 3, 8, and 9. It is possible to calculate the power of each actor within each of these three systems, but not across systems. Furthermore, actor 3 has an interest in events 1 and 2 in the first two systems, with no reciprocating interest from any actor in system 1 or 2. This means that the third system is not independent but, rather, dependent on the first and second systems. The third actor, the pair, has no power at all, for it drains into actors 1 and 2 through the interest of the pair in the two actors' behavior.

Perhaps this is only as it should be: a wholly artificial pair, which is not an actual relationship, could hardly have power in a social system. However, it would be more satisfying if the problem could have been formulated in a different way to obviate this difficulty. For example, sacrificing the notion that each actor has initial control over a single event, we could have dispensed with the artificial pair altogether, and given actors 1 and 2 each 0.5 initial control over the third event, the formation of a relationship. In that case, keeping all other actors and events, there would have been an interdependent system. However, just as it was not possible to distinguish, in the above analysis, b_{31} and b_{32}, it would again not be possible to do so, and, although the system would have been more aesthetically satisfying, it would not have led to a determinate calculation of the relative power of actors 1 and 2.

Conclusion

The present paper constitutes a marriage between problems of data analysis, which have ordinarily been looked at solely in a "causal" rather than a "purposive" framework, and a theoretical model of purposive action. The problem is a special case of 16-fold table problem introduced by Paul Lazarsfeld in the late 1940s, a case in which any mutual effects are between members of a friendship pair, rather than between attitudes. In this context of social interdependence rather than intraindividual interdependence, the purposive framework of ideas fits naturally and leads to perfectly sensible interpretations. This raises the question of whether the same formal framework might not have a reasonable interpretation for the case of intraindividual interdependence, where the variables are attitudes of a single person, rather than two. If so, this would allow calculation of the power of attitudes in a system of attitudes, exactly as was calculated in part 1 of this paper. Although I am not prepared to say that such an interpretation can be found, the general approach appears of sufficient promise to warrant work in that direction.

Notes

1. The first presentation of this index seems to have been in an undated mimeographed paper of Lazarsfeld at the Bureau of Applied Social Research, about 1947.

2. People who have worked on this problem include Donald Campbell (1961, 1971), Leo Goodman (1973a, 1973b), and Raymond Boudon (1968).

3. I am extremely indebted to Dr. Denise Kandel for sending to me at a time when I was thinking of models of purposive action a case of the 16-fold table problem, involving pairs of friends in high school and marijuana smoking, part of her analysis of drug use in high school. Although I had worked extensively on a comparable problem earlier, it had not occurred to me to look at it again through the different lenses provided by a new conceptual framework until Dr. Kandel presented me with the problem and the data.

4. The model has been described in detail in J. Coleman (1973a, 1973b).

5. In Coleman (1973b), the final or effective control is derived as maximization of utility, where utility gained from control over an event follows the Weber Fechner law, which gives a particular functional form to the general principle of declining marginal utility.

6. The structure of the estimates for b_{11} and b_{12} is evident from eq. 7. For b_{13}, the estimate is obtained by substituting for b_{11} and b_{12} in each of the equations (7), then summing the four equations and dividing by 4.

7. More generally, if the number of events and actors is the same, even if C is not an identity matrix, the value may be calculated, since, by two applications of eq. 1, $VC = VB$. After solving for value, power may be calculated from eq. 1, and then interests from eq. 4.

In substantive terms, this means that we infer an actor's interest in his friend's behavior by the degree of control that his friend is able to exercise over his behavior.

8. The lower right quadrant of Table 2, pairs who were neither friends in fall or spring, was constructed by estimating the numbers of pairs of each category, based on the responses of persons in the sample. First, the number of positive and negative A's and B's in the fall were determined:

A	Yes	105
A	No	703
B	Yes	123
B	No	685

The total of 808 persons with matched friends represented .38 of the total population, giving 2,126.32 as the total population. Pairs were formed only within schools (five schools), within the same sex, and within the same grade (four grades), since all friendship choices were within school and most were of the same sex and grade. It was assumed then that the effective target population for each of these 808 persons was within his own school-sex-grade group. This implies that the total population must be divided by $5 \cdot 2 \cdot 4 = 40$. It was also assumed that the target population had the same proportion of users at times 1 and 2 as the B's at times 1 and 2. Thus the target population of users for each person was estimated as $123/(.38 \cdot 5 \cdot 2 \cdot 4) = 8.092$, and the target population of nonusers was $685/(.38 \cdot 5 \cdot 2 \cdot 4) = 45.066$. Since among the sample of persons naming friends (the A's) there were 105 users and 703 nonusers, the estimate of the number of pairs of each type was given by 105 or 703 times the appropriate target population:

Yes	Yes	850
Yes	No	4,732
No	Yes	5,689
No	No	31,681

From these numbers were subtracted the friendship pairs of each type, giving

Yes	Yes	795
Yes	No	4,682
No	Yes	5,621
No	No	31,046

The A's and the B's in these pairs were assumed to change independently, in the same proportions as the A's and the B's in the sample of pairs. Thus, for example, of the A's who were positive at time 1, $(27 + 5 + 7 + 16 + 4 + 3 + 2 + 7)/105$, or .676 were positive at time 2, and, of the B's who were positive at time 1, $(27 + 6 + 6 + 20 + 4 + 4 + 6 + 9)/123$, or .667 were positive at time 2. Thus the proportion of AB pairs who were both positive at time 1 and both positive at time 2 would be $.676 \cdot .667 = .451$. These proportions were calculated for all 16 cells and multiplied by the appropriate marginal above. Thus $795 \cdot .451 = 358$. Then the actual friendships that formed by time 2 of each type were subtracted from these numbers: $358 - 11 = 347$. This gave the number for the cell in the table, as the estimate of the number of pairs of each behavior type in each school-grade-sex group who were not friends at either fall or spring.

9. If the friendship were defined asymmetrically, then the examination would proceed differently, with a table four times as large as Table 2, consisting of four sets of four rows each. The first set would consist of pairs in which both A and B named each other as best friends at time 1, the second would consist of pairs in which A named B, but B did not name A, the third pairs in which B named A but A did not name B, and the fourth pairs in which neither named the other as a friend. However, in this analysis, we treat the friendship as a symmetric relation, either existing or not existing.

References

BOUDON, R. "A New Look at Correlation Analysis," in H. M. Blalock and A. D. Blalock, eds., *Methodology in Social Research*. New York: McGraw Hill, 1968, pp. 199–235.

CAMPBELL, D. T. "Temporal Changes in Treatment-Effect Correlation: A Quasi-Experimental Mode for Institution Records and Longitudinal Studies," in G. B. Glass, ed., *The Promise and Peril of Educational Information*. Princeton, N.J.: Educational Testing Service, 1971, pp. 93–110.

CAMPBELL, D. T. and K. N. CLAYTON. "Avoiding Regression Effects in Panel Studies of Communication Impact." *Studies in Public Communication*, 3 (1961), 99–117.

COLEMAN, J. S. *Introduction to Mathematical Sociology*. New York: The Free Press of Glencoe, 1964(a).

COLEMAN, J. S. *Models of Change and Response Uncertainty*. Englewood Cliffs, N.J.: Prentice-Hall. 1964(b).

COLEMAN, J. S. "The Mathematical Study of Change," in H. M. Blalock and A. D. Blalock, pp. 428–478.

COLEMAN, J. S. "Systems of Social Exchange." *Journal of Mathematical Sociology*, 2 (1972), 145–163.

COLEMAN, J. S. *Mathematics of Collective Action*. Chicago: Aldine, 1973.

GOODMAN, L. "Causal Analysis of Data from Panel Studies and Other Kinds of Surveys." *American Journal of Sociology*, 78 1973(a), 1135–1191.

GOODMAN, L. "The Analysis of Multidimensional Contingency Tables When Some Variables Are Posterior to Others: A Modified Path Analysis Approach." *Biometrika*, 60 1973(b), 179–192.

KANDEL, D. B. "Similarity in Real Life Adolescent Friendship Pairs." (mimeographed). Columbia University, June 1976.

LAZARSFELD, P. F. "Mutual Relations over Time of Two Attributes: A Review and Integration of Various Approaches," in M. Hammer, K. Salzinger, and S. Sutton, eds., *Psychopathology*, New York: Wiley, 1973.

LAZARSFELD, P. F. and R. K. MERTON. "Friendship as Social Process: A Substantive and Methodological Analysis," in M. Berger, T. Abel, and C. Page, eds., *Freedom and Control in Modern Society*. New York: Van Nostrand, 1954.

11. THE ANALYSIS OF QUALITATIVE VARIABLES USING MORE PARSIMONIOUS QUASI-INDEPENDENCE MODELS, SCALING MODELS, AND LATENT STRUCTURES

Leo A. Goodman

1. Introduction

To illustrate the use of the models and methods to be discussed in the present article, we shall reanalyze the data in Table 1, a $2 \times 2 \times 2 \times 2$ contingency table presented earlier by Stouffer and Toby (1951, 1962, 1963) and considered also by Lazarsfeld and Henry (1968) and Goodman (1974a, 1975). This table describes the observed response patterns of respondents to questionnaire items on role conflict. It cross-classifies 216 respondents with respect to whether they tend towards universalistic values (+) or particularistic values (−) when responding to each of four questionnaire items, where each questionnaire item pertains to a different situation in which there is role conflict. The letters A, B, C, and D in Table 1 denote the dichotomous variables associated with the four questionnaire items (or the four situations of role conflict).

Table 1 describes a four-way contingency table (in particular, a $2 \times 2 \times 2 \times 2$ table) obtained by cross-classifying individuals with respect to four dichotomous variables (A, B, C, and D). The models and methods to be discussed in the present article can be applied more generally to m-way contingency tables (for $m = 2, 3, 4, \ldots$) obtained by cross-classifying individuals with respect to m polytomous (not necessarily dichotomous) variables.

We shall begin our analysis of Table 1 by considering first the simple model H_0 which states that the four variables (A, B, C, and D) in the four-way contingency table are mutually independent. This model has the advantage of being simple and parsimonious, but it usually has the disadvantage of not being congruent with the observed data in the contingency table. When the independence

This research was supported in part by Research Contract No. SOC 76-80389 from the Division of the Social Sciences of the National Science Foundation.

119

TABLE 1. Observed Cross-Classification of 216 Respondents with Respect to Whether They Tend Toward Universalistic (+) or Particularistic (−) Values in Four Situations of Role Conflict (A, B, C, D)

Response Pattern Item A B C D				Observed Frequency
+	+	+	+	42
+	+	+	−	23
+	+	−	+	6
+	+	−	−	25
+	−	+	+	6
+	−	+	−	24
+	−	−	+	7
+	−	−	−	38
−	+	+	+	1
−	+	+	−	4
−	+	−	+	1
−	+	−	−	6
−	−	+	+	2
−	−	+	−	9
−	−	−	+	2
−	−	−	−	20

model H_0 is not congruent with the observed data, various modifications of this model can be considered. We shall show here how the independence model H_0 can be replaced by various quasi-independence models, by the corresponding scaling models associated with these quasi-independence models, and by latent structures that fit the data. In addition, we shall show how to obtain more parsimonious quasi-independence models, scaling models, and latent structures that also fit the data. Although the usual quasi-independence models, scaling models, and latent structures are less parsimonious than the corresponding independence model H_0, we shall present later herein particular quasi-independence models, scaling models, and latent structures that (1) are "as parsimonious" as the independence model H_0, and (2) fit the data in Table 1 better than model H_0.

The scaling models introduced in Goodman (1975) were developed there primarily using the quasi-independence concept. There is a wide class of models, including these scaling models and other related models (e.g., the mover-stayer model), which can be developed using the quasi-independence concept. All of these models can also be formulated using the latent structure concept. They are special kinds of latent structures. In the present article, we shall develop further these special kinds of latent structures and other latent structures as well.

The independence model H_0 will be discussed in Section 2, the quasi-independence models in Sections 3 and 4, the corresponding scaling models in Section 5, and the latent structures in Section 6.

2. The Independence Model

In order to examine the independence model H_0 in some detail, we need to introduce some mathematical notation. For the situation in which there are four dichotomous variables $(A, B, C,$ and $D)$, we let (i, j, k, l) denote the response pattern in which the variables $A, B, C,$ and D are at response levels $i, j, k,$ and l, respectively (for $i = 1, 2; j = 1, 2; k = 1, 2; l = 1, 2$). With respect to Table 1, level 1 on a given dichotomous variable denotes a positive (+) response, and level 2 denotes a negative (−) response. [Thus, for example, the response pattern $(1, 2, 1, 2)$ corresponds to the pattern $(+, -, +, -)$ in Table 1, and the observed frequency of this pattern in the table is 24.] We let π_{ijkl}^{ABCD} denote the probability of obtaining response pattern (i, j, k, l); we let π_i^A denote the probability of obtaining response level i on variable A; and we let π_j^B, π_k^C, and π_l^D be defined similarly.

Consider now the simple model H_0 which states that variables $A, B, C,$ and D are mutually independent. Using the notation defined in the preceding paragraph, model H_0 can be expressed as follows:

$$(1) \qquad \pi_{ijkl}^{ABCD} = \pi_i^A \, \pi_j^B \, \pi_k^C \, \pi_l^D .$$

Equation (1) states that the probability of obtaining response pattern (i, j, k, l) on the joint variable (A, B, C, D) is simply the product of the relevant probabilities π_i^A, π_j^B, π_k^C, and π_l^D pertaining to variables $A, B, C,$ and D, respectively.

Since there are two levels pertaining to the dichotomous variable A (viz., $i = 1, 2$), there will be two probabilities, π_1^A and π_2^A, associated with this variable. However, since the two levels are mutually exclusive and exhaustive, these probabilities will satisfy the condition that

$$(2a) \qquad \sum_{i=1}^{2} \pi_i^A = 1.$$

Similarly, the probabilities π_j^B, π_k^C, and π_l^D will satisfy the following conditions:

$$(2b) \qquad \sum_{j=1}^{2} \pi_j^B = 1,$$

$$(2c) \qquad \sum_{k=1}^{2} \pi_k^C = 1,$$

$$(2d) \qquad \sum_{l=1}^{2} \pi_l^D = 1.$$

When the probabilities π_1^A, π_1^B, π_1^C, and π_1^D are known, the remaining probabilities π_2^A, π_2^B, π_2^C, and π_2^D can be determined using eq. (2a), (2b), (2c), and (2d), respectively. Thus, we can think of the four probabilities π_1^A, π_1^B, π_1^C, and π_1^D as a basic set of parameters associated with model H_0.

Since there are 2^4 possible response patterns (i, j, k, l) pertaining to the joint variable (A, B, C, D), there will be 2^4 probabilities, π_{ijkl}^{ABCD} (for $i = 1, 2; j = 1, 2;$ $k = 1, 2; l = 1, 2$), associated with this joint variable. However, since the 2^4 response patterns are mutually exclusive and exhaustive, these probabilities will satisfy the condition that

$$(3) \qquad \sum_{i,j,k,l} \pi_{ijkl}^{ABCD} = 1.$$

When the first $2^4 - 1$ probabilities [say, π_{ijkl}^{ABCD} for all (i, j, k, l) except (i, j, k, l) $= (2, 2, 2, 2)$] are known, the remaining probability (viz., π_{2222}^{ABCD}) can be determined using eq. (3). Thus, we can think of the $2^4 - 1$ probabilities as a basic set of parameters associated with the $2 \times 2 \times 2 \times 2$ contingency table.

When the $2 \times 2 \times 2 \times 2$ contingency table can be described by the simple model H_0, the basic set of $2^4 - 1$ parameters can be replaced by the basic set of four parameters associated with model H_0. Thus, fifteen parameters (i.e., $2^4 - 1 = 15$) are replaced by only four parameters under model H_0. To test model H_0, there will be $15 - 4 = 11$ degrees of freedom.

As we noted earlier, model H_0 has the advantage of being simple and parsimonious, but it usually has the disadvantage of not being congruent with the observed data in the contingency table. For example, when this model is used with the data in Table 1, the expected frequencies estimated under the model do not fit the data well (see Table 2), and the corresponding values obtained for the goodness-of-fit chi-square and the likelihood-ratio chi-square turn out to be 104.11 and 81.08, respectively (see Table 3).[1] Since there were eleven degrees of freedom for testing model H_0, the discrepancy between the observed frequencies and the corresponding expected frequencies estimated under model H_0 is statistically significant.

Since the simple model H_0 is not congruent with the observed data, we shall now consider various modifications of this model. In the next section, some quasi-independence models that are congruent with the data will be presented.

3. Quasi-Independence Models

The independence model H_0 states that the responses on variables $A, B, C,$ and D are mutually independent when all 2^4 response patterns (i, j, k, l) are considered; that is, the model states that the product formula (1) holds true for all 2^4 response patterns. A quasi-independence model would state that the responses on variables $A, B, C,$ and D are "mutually independent" when a specified subset of the 2^4 response patterns is considered (with the concept of mutual independence appropriately redefined); that is, the model would state that the product formula (1) holds true for the specified subset of the 2^4 response patterns (with the parameters in the model appropriately redefined).[2] Un-

TABLE 2. Observed and Estimated Expected Frequencies for the Stouffer-Toby Data under Models H_0, H_1, and H_2

Response Pattern Item				Observed Frequency	Expected Frequency Estimated Under		
A	B	C	D		Model H_0	Model H_1	Model H_2
+	+	+	+	42	13.63	–	–
+	+	+	–	23	30.31	–	20.19
+	+	–	+	6	7.11	4.72	5.50
+	+	–	–	25	28.67	–	25.96
+	–	+	+	6	17.71	5.99	5.92
+	–	+	–	24	20.83	24.74	27.93
+	–	–	+	7	12.89	7.56	7.61
+	–	–	–	38	28.67	–	35.91
–	+	+	+	1	2.83	1.14	1.10
–	+	+	–	4	7.98	4.73	5.18
–	+	–	+	1	0.89	1.44	1.41
–	+	–	–	6	4.94	5.97	6.66
–	–	+	+	2	7.79	1.83	1.52
–	–	+	–	9	7.98	7.57	7.17
–	–	–	+	2	2.44	2.31	1.95
–	–	–	–	20	7.54	–	–

der the independence model H_0, all 2^4 observed frequencies are considered, whereas, under a quasi-independence model, only the observed frequencies corresponding to the specified subset of response patterns are considered, and the remaining observed frequencies are blanked out. Both the expected frequencies estimated under the independence model H_0 and the corresponding expected frequencies estimated under quasi-independence models can be obtained, for example, from the computer program ECTA.[3] These expected frequencies are presented in Table 2 for the independence model H_0 and for two quasi-independence models, H_1 and H_2, which we shall consider next. (For additional discussion of quasi-independence models, see, e.g., Goodman, 1968, 1975.)

Let U denote the specified set of response patterns that is to be considered under the quasi-independence model, and let S denote the remaining response patterns (viz., the response patterns that are not included in set U). The observed frequencies pertaining to the response patterns in set U are to be considered under the quasi-independence model, and the observed frequencies pertaining to the response patterns in set S are to be blanked out. In different substantive contexts, different response patterns will be included in set U (with the remaining response patterns in set S). (For some illustrative material, see, e.g., Goodman, 1969, 1972, 1975.)

For Table 1, consider for the moment the special case where the observed frequencies are zero for all response patterns other than those listed as follows:

(4) $(1,1,1,1), \quad (1,1,1,2), \quad (1,1,2,2), \quad (1,2,2,2), \quad (2,2,2,2).$

[In other words, the observed response patterns do not include any patterns other than (+, +, +, +), (+, +, +, −), (+, +, −, −), (+, −, −, −), and (−, −, −, −).] If this special case were true, we would have a Guttman scale where all respondents are scalable (see, e.g., Guttman, 1950). In actual fact, as we see from Table 1, the response patterns other than those listed in (4) also do occur, and the (nonzero) observed frequencies corresponding to these response patterns are relevant in determining the extent to which the respondents are not scalable.

We shall now let set U consist of the response patterns other than those listed in (4), and thus set S will consist of the response patterns in (4). Since there were five response patterns in set S, there will be $2^4 - 5 = 11$ response patterns in set U. The quasi-independence model H_1 states that the responses on variables $A, B, C,$ and D are quasi-independent when eleven response patterns in set U are considered. In other words, this model states that, when the "scale-type" patterns in (4) are excluded from consideration, the responses on variables $A, B, C,$ and D are quasi-independent. Since we consider here only response patterns that are *not* scale-type patterns, it might seem reasonable to expect the quasi-independence model H_1 to be true.

Under the quasi-independence model H_1, we consider eleven response patterns, whereas, under the independence model H_0, we considered $2^4 = 16$ response patterns. Five less response patterns are considered under model H_1 than were considered under model H_0. In testing model H_1, there will be five less degrees of freedom than there were in testing model H_0. There were eleven degrees of freedom in testing model H_0 (as noted in Section 2), and thus there will be $11 - 5 = 6$ degrees of freedom in testing model H_1.

The expected frequencies estimated under model H_1 fit the data in Table 1 very well (see Table 2), and the corresponding values obtained for the goodness-of-fit chi-square and the likelihood-ratio chi-square are 1.01 and 0.99, respectively (see Table 3).[4] Since there were six degrees of freedom for testing model H_1, the discrepancy between the observed frequencies and the corresponding estimated expected frequencies under H_1 is not statistically significant.

A great improvement in the fit is obtained when the independence model H_0 is replaced by the quasi-independence model H_1. (The difference between the corresponding chi-square values obtained under models H_0 and H_1 can be assessed, using $11 - 6 = 5$ degrees of freedom.) On the other hand, model H_1 is less parsimonious than model H_0.[5] We shall next consider a quasi-independence model, H_2, which is more parsimonious than model H_1.

Instead of deleting all five scale-type response patterns listed in (4), as was done under model H_1 (see Table 2), we now consider the quasi-independence model H_2 obtained when only the two extreme response patterns,

(5) $(1, 1, 1, 1)$ and $(2, 2, 2, 2)$,

are deleted. Model H_2 states that, when the two extreme response patterns in (5)

TABLE 3. Chi-Square Values for Some Models Applied to
the Stouffer-Toby Data

Model	Degrees of Freedom	Goodness-of-Fit Chi-Square	Likelihood-Ratio Chi-Square
H_0	11	104.11	81.08
H_1	6	1.01	0.99
H_2	9	2.28	2.28
H_2'	10	2.42	2.39
H_2''	11	2.85	2.72
M_1	6	2.72	2.72
M_1'	8	2.84	2.89
M_1''	10	4.34	4.39
M_1'''	10	4.52	4.55
M_1''''	11	6.01	6.26

are excluded from consideration, the responses on variables A, B, C, and D are quasi-independent.

By applying to the quasi-independence model H_2 the same kinds of methods used earlier with H_1, we find that the estimated expected frequencies under H_2 continue to fit the data (see Table 2), and the corresponding chi-square values continue to be small (see Table 3). Model H_2 is more parsimonious than model H_1. (Compare the nine degrees of freedom for model H_2 with the six degrees of freedom for H_1.)

From the above comparison of models H_1 and H_2, we can see that one way to obtain more parsimonious quasi-independence models is to delete fewer response patterns under the model. In the next section, we shall present a different way to obtain more parsimonious models.

Before closing the present section, we take note of the fact that, although our attention has been focused here on the four-way contingency table having four dichotomous variables, the models and methods presented in this section (and in other sections of the article) can be applied more generally to m-way contingency tables (for m = 2, 3, 4, ...) having m polytomous (not necessarily dichotomous) variables. With respect to the quasi-independence models, see, for example, Goodman (1968, 1969a). It is also possible to extend the general formulation of the scaling models in Goodman (1975) to the case where the variables are polytomous, and the general methods of latent structure analysis in Goodman (1974a, 1974b) can be applied directly to the polytomous case. (With respect to the number m of variables under consideration, in scaling and latent structure analysis attention is usually focused on the case where m = 3, 4, ... ; but the general methods in Goodman [1974a] can also be applied directly to the case where m = 2, and the general formulation in Goodman [1975] can be extended to this case.)

4. More Parsimonious Quasi-Independence Models

For expository purposes, we return for the moment to the independence model H_0 applied to the $2 \times 2 \times 2 \times 2$ contingency table. We noted earlier in Section 2 that there were four basic parameters (π_1^A, π_1^B, π_1^C, π_1^D) associated with the four dichotomous variables A, B, C, and D in model H_0. Consider for the moment the special case where these four parameters satisfy the condition that

(6) $$\pi_1^A = \pi_1^B = \pi_1^C = \pi_1^D.$$

Equation (6) states that the probability of obtaining response level 1 on variable A is equal to the corresponding probability for variable B, which in turn is equal to the corresponding probability for variable C, which in turn is equal to the corresponding probability for variable D. When this condition is satisfied, the four parameters (π_1^A, π_1^B, π_1^C, π_1^D) can be replaced by a single parameter (say, π_1), the probability of obtaining response level 1 (which would be the same in this case for variables A, B, C, and D). Since the four parameters can be replaced by a single parameter, the restricted model thus obtained when eq. (6) is satisfied is more parsimonious than the original independence model H_0. Since the four parameters can be replaced by a single parameter, there will be three more degrees of freedom in testing the restricted model than in testing model H_0. There were eleven degrees of freedom in testing model H_0 (as noted in Section 2), and thus there will be $11 + 3 = 14$ degrees of freedom in testing the restricted model.

Instead of considering the special case where all four parameters in (6) are equal to each other, we could consider the case where two or three of the parameters are equal. For example, suppose that the equality held true for two of the parameters, says, π_1^B and π_1^C. In that case, eq. (6) would be replaced by

(7) $$\pi_1^B = \pi_1^C,$$

the two parameters (π_1^B and π_1^C) could be replaced by a single parameter, and there would be one more degree of freedom in testing the restricted model in which eq. (7) is satisfied than in testing model H_0.

Instead of considering the special case where the parameters in (6) or in (7) all refer to response level 1, we could consider the case where some of these parameters refer to response level 2. For example, suppose that the probability of obtaining response level 1 on variable A was equal to the probability of obtaining response level 2 on, say, variable D. In that case, eq. (6) and (7) would be replaced by

(8) $$\pi_1^A = \pi_2^D,$$

the two parameters (π_1^A and π_2^D) could be replaced by a single parameter, and there would be one more degree of freedom in testing the restricted model in which eq. (8) is satisfied than in testing model H_0.

Conditions of the kind described by (7) and (8) can be combined in various ways. For example, suppose that *both* equalities in (7) and (8) held true. In that case, conditions (7) and (8) would be replaced by the condition that

(9) $$\pi_1^B = \pi_1^C \text{ and } \pi_1^A = \pi_2^D,$$

the two parameters π_1^B and π_1^C could be replaced by a single parameter, *and* the two parameters π_1^A and π_2^D could also be replaced by a single parameter (the four parameters π_1^B, π_1^C, π_1^A, π_2^D could be replaced by two parameters), and there would be two more degrees of freedom in testing the restricted model in which condition (9) is satisfied than in testing model H_0.

The preceding comments in this section were concerned with modifications of the independence model H_0 obtained by imposing restrictions upon the parameters in the model. The *restricted* independence models thus obtained are more parsimonious than the (unrestricted) model H_0. Similar kinds of restrictions can be imposed upon the parameters in the quasi-independence models.[6] To estimate the expected frequencies under the *restricted* independence models, the method used earlier for the (unrestricted) model H_0 can be applied (see note 1), with the estimates of the parameters (π_1^A, π_1^B, π_1^C, π_1^D) appropriately modified; and, similarly, to estimate the expected frequencies under the *restricted* quasi-independence models, the method used for the corresponding unrestricted quasi-independence model can be applied, with the iterative procedure that estimates the parameters in the model appropriately modified.[7]

In the preceding section, we found that the quasi-independence model H_2 fit the data well, it was more parsimonious than the quasi-independence model H_1, which also fit the data well, and it was less parsimonious than the independence model H_0, which did not fit the data. We shall now show how to make model H_2 more parsimonious, using the general approach presented earlier in the present section.

Let us now consider the *restricted* quasi-independence model H_2' obtained from model H_2 by imposing upon the parameters in this model a restriction analogous to (7). There will be one more degree of freedom in testing model H_2' than in testing model H_2. Since there were nine degrees of freedom in testing model H_2 (as noted in the preceding section), there will be ten degrees of freedom in testing model H_2'. As we see from the corresponding chi-square values in Table 3, model H_2' fits the data well, and it is more parsimonious than model H_2.[8]

Consider next the *restricted* quasi-independence model H_2'' obtained from model H_2 by imposing upon the parameters in this model a restriction analogous to (9). There will be two more degrees of freedom in testing model H_2'' than in testing model H_2. Since there were nine degrees of freedom in testing model H_2, there will be eleven degrees of freedom in testing model H_2''. As we see from the chi-square values in Table 3, model H_2'' also fits the data well, and it is more parsimonious than models H_2 and H_2'.

Note that a test of model H_2'' has as many degrees of freedom associated with it as does a test of the independence model H_0.[9] Model H_2'' can serve here as an example of how the independence model H_0 (and the related quasi-independence models H_1 and H_2) can be modified in order to obtain models that are parsimonious and that fit the data. The methods used here to obtain the modified model can be applied more generally to other quasi-independence models.

5. Scaling Models and More Parsimonious Scaling Models

Associated with each quasi-independence model considered earlier herein, there is a corresponding "scaling model" of the kind introduced in Goodman (1975). The unrestricted quasi-independence models H_1 and H_2 can be rewritten as unrestricted scaling models, and the restricted quasi-independence models H_2' and H_2'' can be rewritten as restricted scaling models. With each of these scaling models, we can estimate the proportion of "intrinsically scalable" individuals and the proportion of "intrinsically unscalable" individuals in the population under consideration,[10] and we can also estimate various other parameters of interest in the model (e.g., the distribution of the intrinsically scalable individuals among the different "scale-type" response patterns). The estimated parameters under each of these scaling models will be included in Table 4. How well each of these scaling models fits the data can be assessed in the same way that was described earlier herein for assessing the fit of the corresponding quasi-independence model. For further discussion of these scaling models, and the methods of estimation and testing associated with these models, see Goodman (1975). To save space here, we shall not go into these matters in this article.

With the quasi-independence model H_1 considered earlier herein, we viewed the response patterns listed in (4) as the "scale-type" patterns, whereas, with the quasi-independence model H_2 (and with H_2' and H_2''), we replaced this set of patterns by the smaller set of extreme response patterns listed in (5). With different sets of response patterns viewed as the "scale-type" patterns, different scaling models can be obtained. This approach to scaling led to the introduction of the demi-scales, demi-demi-scales, biform scales, and various multiform scales described in Goodman (1975). To save space here, we again refer the interested reader to that article for a discussion of these scales.

As we noted earlier, the various scaling models introduced in Goodman (1975) can be viewed as special kinds of latent structures. We shall comment further on the relationship between scaling models and latent structures near the end of the next section.

6. Latent Structures and More Parsimonious Latent Structures

Stouffer and Toby (1951, 1962, 1963) and Lazarsfeld and Henry (1968) analyzed Table 1 using a particular five-class restricted latent structure (viz., the latent distance model), and they concluded that the underlying latent variable pertaining to universalistic versus particularistic values could be described by the five latent classes in that model. In contrast to that conclusion, we shall show here that a simpler latent structure is congruent with these data.

Consider now a four-way contingency table which cross-classifies a sample of n individuals with respect to four manifest *polytomous* variables A, B, C, and D. If there is, say, some latent *dichotomous* variable X, so that each of the n individuals is in one of the two latent classes with respect to this variable, and within each latent class the manifest variables (A, B, C, D) are mutually independent, then this two-class structure would serve as a simple explanation of the observed relationships among the variables in the four-way contingency table for the n individuals. More generally, if the latent variable X is *polytomous* with T latent classes, so that each of the n individuals is in one of the T latent classes with respect to this variable, and within each latent class the manifest variables (A, B, C, D) are mutually independent, then this T-class latent structure would serve as an explanation of the observed relationships among the variables in the four-way contingency table (see, e.g., Lazarsfeld, 1950, and Lazarsfeld and Henry, 1968).

As earlier herein, we let π_{ijkl}^{ABCD} denote the probability that an individual will be at level (i, j, k, l) on the joint variable (A, B, C, D), and similarly we let π_{ijklt}^{ABCDX} denote the probability that an individual will be at level (i, j, k, l, t) on the joint variable (A, B, C, D, X).[11] The latent structure model can be expressed as follows:

$$(10) \qquad \pi_{ijkl}^{ABCD} = \sum_{t=1}^{T} \pi_{ijklt}^{ABCDX} ,$$

where

$$(11) \qquad \pi_{ijklt}^{ABCDX} = \pi_t^X \, \pi_{it}^{\bar{A}X} \, \pi_{jt}^{\bar{B}X} \, \pi_{kt}^{\bar{C}X} \, \pi_{lt}^{\bar{D}X} .$$

Here π_t^X denotes the probability that an individual will be at level t on variable X; also $\pi_{it}^{\bar{A}X}$ denotes the conditional probability that an individual will be at level i on variable A, given that he is at level t on variable X; and π_{jt}^{BX}, π_{kt}^{CX}, π_{lt}^{DX} denote similar conditional probabilities. Equation (10) states that the individuals can be classified into T mutually exclusive and exhaustive latent classes, and eq. (11) states that, within the tth latent class, the manifest variables (A, B, C, D) are mutually independent $(t = 1, \ldots, T)$.

For simplicity, let us consider first the special "latent structure" M_0 in which there is only *one* latent class (i.e., where $T = 1$). For this simple model, we see that $\pi_1^X = 1$, and the formulae (10)–(11) turn out to be equivalent to the product formula (1). Thus, the special "latent structure" M_0 is equivalent to the independence model H_0. As we noted in Section 2 (see, e.g., Table 3), model M_0 (= H_0) does not fit the data in Table 1. The estimated parameters for this model are included in Table 4.[12]

We consider next the latent structure M_1 in which there are *two* latent classes (i.e., where $T = 2$). Applying to this model the general methods developed in Goodman (1974a, 1974b), we obtain the chi-square values for M_1 included in Table 3 and the corresponding estimated parameters for M_1 in Table 4. From the chi-square values for M_1 in Table 3, we see that this model fits the data well. Model M_0 (= H_0), which had eleven degrees of freedom, did not fit the data, but model M_1, which has six degrees of freedom, does fit the data well.

Model M_1 for Table 1 states that (1) there is a single latent *dichotomous* variable X pertaining to "universalistic versus particularistic latent values," and (2) this latent variable alone can explain the observed relationships among all four manifest variables (A, B, C, D) in the contingency table. From the estimated parameters for M_1 in Table 4, we see that, with respect to the joint manifest variable (A, B, C, D), the "modal response levels" are (1, 2, 2, 2) and (1, 1, 1, 1), for latent classes 1 and 2, respectively; and the former latent class is modal, since $\hat{\pi}_1^X = .72$. Thus, individuals in the modal latent class tend to be at manifest response level 2 (i.e., "intrinsically" particularistic), except for the response level on variable A, and individuals in the nonmodal latent class tend to be at manifest response level 1 (i.e., "intrinsically" universalistic). The $\hat{\pi}_t^X$ for model M_1 in Table 4 estimate the distribution of the latent *dichotomous* variable X, and the other estimated parameters for this model can be used to estimate the effect of variable X upon each manifest variable (A, B, C, D).[13]

Latent structures can be modified to obtain more parsimonious models using methods similar to those used earlier herein to modify the quasi-independence model H_2 to obtain the more parsimonious models H_2' and H_2''. We shall now illustrate this by showing how the latent structure M_1 can be modified.

Equation (7) for model H_0 (= M_0) stated that the probability of obtaining response level 1 on variable B was equal to the coresponding probability for variable C. A related kind of condition for latent structure M_1 can be expressed as follows:

$$(12) \qquad \pi_{1t}^{\bar{B}X} = \pi_{1t}^{\bar{C}X}, \qquad\qquad \text{for } t = 1, 2.$$

Equation (12) states that the conditional probability that an individual will be at response level 1 on variable B (given that he is at level t on latent variable X) is equal to the corresponding conditional probability for variable C. We next consider the *restricted* latent structure M_1' obtained from model M_1 by imposing condition (12) upon the parameters in the model. In this case, the two parameters $\pi_{11}^{\bar{B}X}$ and $\pi_{11}^{\bar{C}X}$ can be replaced by a single parameter *and* the two parameters $\pi_{12}^{\bar{B}X}$ and $\pi_{12}^{\bar{C}X}$ can be replaced by a single parameter (the four parameters $\pi_{11}^{\bar{B}X}$, $\pi_{11}^{\bar{C}X}$, $\pi_{12}^{\bar{B}X}$, $\pi_{12}^{\bar{C}X}$ can be replaced by two parameters), so there would be two more degrees of freedom in testing the *restricted* latent structure M_1' in which

TABLE 4. Estimated Parameters in Some Models Applied to the Stouffer-Toby Data

Model	Latent Class t	$\hat{\pi}_t^X$	$\hat{\pi}_{1t}^{\bar{A}X}$	$\hat{\pi}_{1t}^{\bar{B}X}$	$\hat{\pi}_{1t}^{\bar{C}X}$	$\hat{\pi}_{1t}^{\bar{D}X}$
$M_0 \ (=H_0)$	1	1.00	.79	.50	.51	.31
M_1	1	.72	.71	.33	.35	.13
	2	.28	.99	.94	.93	.77
M_1'	1	.72	.71	.34	.34	.13
	2	.28	.99	.93	.93	.77
M_1''	1	.77	.73	.36	.36	.16
	2	.23	.99	.99	.99	.84
M_1'''	1	.74	.73	.34	.34	.15
	2	.26	.98	.98	.98	.73
M_1''''	1	.70	.69	.31	.31	.14
	2	.30	.96	.96	.96	.69
H_1	0	.68	.77	.38	.44	.19
	1	.18	1.00	1.00	1.00	1.00
	2	.03	1.00	1.00	1.00	.00
	3	.03	1.00	1.00	.00	.00
	4	.03	1.00	.00	.00	.00
	5	.05	.00	.00	.00	.00
H_2	0	.78	.80	.42	.44	.17
	1	.18	1.00	1.00	1.00	1.00
	2	.05	.00	.00	.00	.00
H_2'	0	.78	.80	.43	.43	.17
	1	.17	1.00	1.00	1.00	1.00
	2	.05	.00	.00	.00	.00
H_2''	0	.77	.81	.43	.43	.19
	1	.17	1.00	1.00	1.00	1.00
	2	.05	.00	.00	.00	.00

eq. (12) is satisfied than in testing model M_1. Since there were six degrees of freedom in testing model M_1 (see Table 3), there will be eight degrees of freedom in testing model M_1'. As we see from the chi-square values in Table 3, model M_1' fits the data well, and it is more parsimonious than model M_1.

From the estimated parameters for models M_1 and M_1' in Table 4, we see that the estimates for M_1 do not satisfy a condition analogous to (12) but that the estimates for M_1' do. Using the estimated parameters for M_1' in Table 4, we can provide the same kind of description of this model as we did earlier herein for M_1.

The restricted latent structures M_1'', M_1''', and M_1'''' in Tables 3 and 4 were obtained from M_1' by methods similar to those used to obtain M_1' from M_1.[14] For model M_1'', the additional conditions imposed upon M_1' were

$$(13) \qquad \pi_{12}^{\bar{A}X} = \pi_{12}^{\bar{B}X}, \quad \pi_{11}^{\bar{D}X} = \pi_{22}^{\bar{D}X} ;$$

for model M_1''', the additional conditions imposed upon M_1' were

(14)
$$\pi_{12}^{\bar{A}X} = \pi_{12}^{\bar{B}X}, \quad \pi_{11}^{\bar{A}X} = \pi_{12}^{\bar{D}X};$$

for model M_1'''', the additional conditions imposed upon M_1' were

(15)
$$\pi_{12}^{\bar{A}X} = \pi_{12}^{\bar{B}X}, \quad \pi_{11}^{\bar{A}X} = \pi_{21}^{\bar{B}X}, \quad \pi_{11}^{\bar{A}X} = \pi_{12}^{\bar{D}X}.$$

The utility of these kinds of conditions, and their interpretation in terms of "error rates," is discussed further in Goodman (1974b). From the corresponding chi-square values for models M_1'', M_1''', and M_1'''' in Table 3, we see that these models also fit the data and that they are more parsimonious than M_1 and M_1'.

Note that a test of model M_1'''' has as many degrees associated with it as does a test of the independence model M_0 $(=H_0)$.[15] Model M_1'''' can serve here as an example of how the independence model M_0 (and the related latent structure M_1) can be modified to obtain models that are parsimonious and that fit the data. The methods used here to obtain the modified model can be applied more generally to other latent structures.

We return now briefly to the quasi-independence models and the corresponding scaling models discussed earlier. As we noted, the quasi-independence models can be rewritten as scaling models that can in turn be expressed as latent structures. Applying the general methods developed earlier for estimating the parameters in the quasi-independence model, we can estimate the proportion π_0 of "intrinsically unscalable" individuals (see Goodman, 1975), and then we can extend these methods to obtain estimates of the proportion of individuals in each "intrinsically scalable" category. For example, for model H_1 considered earlier herein, there will be an "intrinsically unscalable" class of individuals, and then five "intrinsically scalable" categories pertaining to the five scale-type response patterns in (4). The "intrinsically unscalable" class and the five "intrinsically scalable" categories can be viewed as latent classes, and, for expository purposes, we number these latent classes from zero to five, with the "intrinsically unscalable" class numbered zero.[16] Applying to the data in Table 1 the methods developed for the analysis of the quasi-independence model H_1, we find that the proportion π_0 in the "intrinsically unscalable" class is estimated by $\hat{\pi}_0 = .68$ (see Goodman, 1975), and then the corresponding estimates for the proportion π_t in the tth "intrinsically scalable" classes ($t = 1, 2, \ldots, 5$) turn out to be

(16) $\hat{\pi}_1 = .18, \quad \hat{\pi}_2 = .03, \quad \hat{\pi}_3 = .03, \quad \hat{\pi}_4 = .03, \quad \hat{\pi}_5 = .05,$

where these five latent classes are numbered in the same order as the corresponding five scale-type response patterns in (4).

Having presented results obtained for the quasi-independence model H_1, we could also present the corresponding results for the other quasi-independence models, H_2, H_2', and H_2''.[17] These results are included in Table 4.[18]

Except for the independence model H_0, each of the other models considered in Tables 3 and 4 is congruent with the observed data in Table 1. Considering the various models that fit a given set of data, the choice among them would depend, in part, on which models are more meaningful in the particular substantive context. An additional criterion to assist in making this choice when comparing several models of the same general kind (e.g., models H_1, H_2, H_2', and H_2'', or models M_1, M_1', M_1'', M_1''', and M_1'''') is the criterion of parsimony. When comparing several models of the same general kind, the more parsimonious model for a given set of data is preferable.[19] Of course, the choice of the more parsimonious model for a given set of data does not imply that the less parsimonious models are dismissed entirely as possible models for the data.[20]

Applying the criterion of parsimony to the models in Table 3 that fit the data would lead to the selection of models H_2'' and M_1'''' for these data.[21] Since models H_2'' and M_1'''' are quite different kinds of models, our inability to choose between them on the basis of the results in Table 3 may be due to the fact that the data described in Table 1 are not from a particularly large sample. If additional data were obtained, the relative merits of models H_2'' and M_1'''' would probably become more apparent. Indeed, with additional data, our assessment of the relative merits of each of the models considered in the present article might turn out to be quite different from the present assessment.

We have presented in this article various simple quasi-independence models, scaling models, and latent structures that fit the data in Table 1. In addition, other latent class and latent distance models could be applied to these data;[22] but to save space we shall not go into this here. The interested reader can compare the results presented in the present article with results obtained using various other latent class and latent distance models.[23] As we have already noted, considering the various models that may fit a given set of data, the choice among them would depend, in part, on which models are more meaningful in the particular substantive context, and on the other considerations discussed above.

Notes

1. The expected frequencies estimated under the independence model H_0 can be calculated using formula (1), with the probabilities on the right side of the formula replaced by the corresponding observed proportions. (Thus, the probabilities π_1^A, π_1^B, π_1^C, and π_1^D in formula (1) can be replaced by the corresponding observed proportions; viz., .79, .50, .51, and .31, respectively.) The estimated expected frequencies and the corresponding chi-square values, in Tables 2 and 3, for model H_0 and for the quasi-independence models H_1 and H_2 discussed in the next section, can be obtained, for example, from the computer program ECTA (Everyman's Contingency Table Analyzer), prepared by R. Fay and the author and available from the author.

2. To avoid possible misunderstanding, we shall henceforth use the term "quasi-independence" rather than the term "independence" (or "mutual independence") when a specified subset of the 2^4 response patterns is considered.

With the usual definition of the parameters in the *quasi*-independence model, these parameters are *not* probabilities, although they are related to such probabilities (see, e.g., Goodman, 1968, 1975).

3. Of course, the expected frequencies estimated under the independence model H_0 can be calculated directly using the explicit formula (1), as indicated in note 1; but the expected frequencies estimated under the quasi-independence models to be considered can*not* be calculated in such a simple way—an iterative procedure is needed for that calculation. This procedure is incorporated in the computer program ECTA (see note 1). In the same way that the independence model H_0 can be replaced by quasi–independence models, the more general loglinear model (see, for example, Goodman, 1970, 1978) can be replaced by corresponding "quasi–loglinear models," and ECTA can be used for this purpose as well.

4. For the estimated parameters under model H_1 and the other models considered in this article, see Table 4.

5. For the analysis of a given set of data (for example, a four–way contingency table), we can compare two models with respect to their parsimony by comparing the number of degrees of freedom associated with each model, or equivalently by comparing the number of parameters in the basic set of parameters associated with each model. The less parsimonious model will have less degrees of freedom associated with it, and it will have more parameters in its basic set of parameters. There are five less degrees of freedom associated with H_1 than with H_0, and there are (in a certain sense) five more parameters in the basic set of parameters associated with H_1 than with H_0.

6. As we noted earlier, with the usual definition of the parameters in the *quasi*-independence model, these parameters are *not* probabilities, although they are related to such probabilities.

7. The appropriate modification for restricted quasi-independence models was described in Goodman (1975, pp. 766-767). Since the quasi-independence models in that article could be rewritten as latent structures (see, e.g., Goodman, 1975), and the restricted quasi-independence models could be rewritten as restricted latent structures, the computer program used to analyze both restricted and unrestricted latent structures (see Goodman, 1974a, 1974b) could also be used with the restricted and unrestricted quasi-independence models.

8. For additional discussion of model H_2' (and the other models considered in this section and in the following section), see Goodman (1975). For the estimated parameters under model H_2' (and the other models considered in the present article), see Table 4.

9. A comparison of the fit obtained with models H_0 and H_2'' should, strictly speaking, take account of the fact that model H_0 might normally be applied without earlier examination of the data, whereas the particular model H_2'' would normally be applied after some earlier examination of the data. The general problem associated with the effects of scanning or ransacking a body of data (and with sequential and/or simultaneous inference) is important in the comparison of H_0 and H_2'' and in other comparisons as well, and it should not be overlooked; but discussion of this topic here would take us too far afield. (For discussion of somewhat related matters, see, for example, Goodman, 1969a.)

10. For the "intrinsically unscalable" individuals in the population, their responses on variables, A, B, C, and D are mutally independent. For the "intrinsically scalable" individuals in the population, their response patterns correspond to their "scale type". (For further details, see Goodman, 1975, and the discussion near the end of Section 6 herein.)

11. Variables, A, B, C, and D are *manifest* polytomous variables here, whereas variable X is a *latent* polytomous variable. There are T latent classes with respect to variable X, with the latent classes numbered from 1 to T (i.e., $t = 1, \ldots, T$).

12. For comments on the estimation of the parameters in model M_0 ($= H_0$), see note 1.

13. For comments pertaining to the path diagram associated with this model and the calculation of the corresponding path coefficients, see Goodman (1974b).

14. The restricted latent structures M_1' and M_1'' were considered in Goodman (1974a); see models H_7 and H_8 in that article.

15. The comments in note 9 pertaining to H_0 and H_2'' can be applied here to M_0 and M_1''''. These comments apply also to various other comparisons in the present article.

16. Model H_1 can be formulated as a special kind of latent structure in which the latent variable X has in total six latent classes. (With respect to model H_1, we number these latent classes from zero to five rather than from one to six as would be obtained with the general formulation of latent structures presented earlier in this section; see note 11 and formulas (10)–(11).) The "intrinsically unscalable" class (i.e., latent class zero) is essentially different from the five "intrinsically scalable" classes (i.e., latent classes one to five), since special kinds of restrictions are imposed upon the conditional probabilities ($\pi_{it}^{\bar{A}X}$, $\pi_{jt}^{\bar{B}X}$, $\pi_{kt}^{\bar{C}X}$, $\pi_{lt}^{\bar{D}X}$) pertaining to the latter classes (where $t = 1, 2, 3, 4, 5$) which are not imposed upon the conditional probabilities pertaining to the former class (where $t = 0$). For further details, see note 10 and Table 4 herein, and Section 6 of Goodman (1975).

17. Some of these results (but not all of them) were included in Goodman (1975).

18. For the sake of convenience, the results for models H_1, H_2, H_2', and H_2'' in Table 4 are presented there using the same notation as was used earlier for the latent structures in that table. (This could be done since the quasi–independence models and the corresponding scaling models could be rewritten as latent structures.) However, it may be worthwhile to point out that these results could also be presented in a somewhat different format that might be more readily understandable to some readers. For an example of this alternative presentation, see the discussion of model H_1 in Goodman (1975).

19. We are concerned here with the case where each of the models to be considered is congruent with the observed data, and comparisons between the corresponding chi–square values (obtained by calculating the difference between corresponding chi–squares) lead to the choice of the more parsimonious model. Of course, when this is not the case, we reject models that are not congruent with the observed data, and we reject the more parsimonious model if the chi–square comparisons indicate that it should be rejected.

20. As we have already noted, we are concerned here with the case where each of the models to be considered is congruent with the observed data. If additional data were obtained, we might find that the more parsimonious model no longer fit the data whereas the less parsimonious models may continue to fit the data.

21. We shall not consider here whether the kind of model represented by H_2'' (and the related models H_1, H_2, and H_2') is more meaningful in the particular substantive context than is the kind of model represented by M_1'''' (and the related models M_1, M_1', M_1'', and M_1'''). (This is an interesting and important topic, but it is beyond the scope of the present article.) Although the chi-square values for H_2'' in Table 3 are somewhat smaller than the corresponding values for M_1'''', the difference in itself would not warrant the choice of H_2'' over M_1''''.

22. Of course, still other kinds of models could also be considered.

23. See, for example, Stouffer and Toby (1951, 1962, 1963), Lazarsfeld and Henry (1968), and Goodman (1974a, 1974b, 1975). The methods for analyzing the quasi–independence models and the corresponding scaling models presented herein and in Goodman (1975) are somewhat easier to apply than the corresponding methods for latent class and latent distance models.

References

GOODMAN, LEO A. "The Analysis of Cross-Classified Data: Independence, Quasi-Independence, and Interactions in Contingency Tables with or without Missing Entries," *Journal of the American Statistical Association, 63* (1968), 1091–1131.

GOODMAN, LEO A. "How to Ransack Social Mobility Tables and Other Kinds of Cross Classification Tables, " *American Journal of Sociology, 75* (1969a), 1–40.

GOODMAN, LEO A. "On the Measurement of Social Mobility: An Index of Status Persistence," *American Sociological Review, 34* (1969b), 831–850.

GOODMAN, LEO A. "The Multivariate Analysis of Qualitative Data: Interactions Among Multiple Classifications." *Journal of the American Statistical Association, 65* (1970), 226–256.

GOODMAN, LEO A. "Some Multiplicative Models for the Analysis of Cross-Classified Data," *Proceedings of the Sixth Berkeley Symposium on Mathematical Statistics and Probability,* (1972), 649–696.

GOODMAN, LEO A. "Exploratory Latent Structure Analysis Using Both Identifiable and Unidentifiable Models," *Biometrika, 61* (1974a), 215–230.

GOODMAN, LEO A. "The Analysis of Systems of Qualitative Variables When Some of the Variables Are Unobservable. Part I: A Modified Latent Structure Approach," *American Journal of Sociology, 79* (1974b), 1179–1259.

GOODMAN, LEO A. "A New Model for Scaling Response Patterns: An Application of the Quasi-Independence Concept," *Journal of the American Statistical Association, 70* (1975), 755–768.

GOODMAN, LEO A. *Analyzing Qualitative/Categorical Data: Log-Linear Models and Latent-Structure Analysis.* Cambridge: Abt Books, 1978.

GUTTMAN, LOUIS. "The Basis for Scalogram Analysis," in Samuel A. Stouffer et al., eds., *Measurement and Prediction, Studies in Social Psychology in World War II*, Vol. IV. Princeton, N.J.: Princeton University Press, 1950, pp. 60–90.

LAZARSFELD, PAUL F. "The Interpretation and Computation of Some Latent Structures," in Samuel A. Stouffer et al., eds., *Measurement and Prediction, Studies in Social Psychology in World War II*, Vol IV. Princeton, N.J.: Princeton University Press, 1950, pp. 413–472.

LAZARSFELD, PAUL F., and NEIL W. HENRY. *Latent Structure Analysis.* Boston: Houghton-Mifflin, 1968.

STOUFFER, SAMUEL A., and JACKSON TOBY. "Role Conflict and Personality," *American Journal of Sociology*, 56 (1951), 395–406. Reprinted in Samuel A. Stouffer, *Social Research to Test Ideas.* New York: Free Press, 1962. Reprinted in part in Matilda White Riley, *Sociological Research: A Case Approach.* New York: Harcourt, Brace and World, 1963.

12. THE CHOICE AXIOM AFTER TWENTY YEARS

R. Duncan Luce

This survey is divided into three major sections. The first concerns mathematical results about the choice axiom and the choice models that devolve from it. For example, its relationship to Thurstonian theory is satisfyingly understood, and there are certain interesting statistical facts. The second section describes attempts that have been made to test and apply these models. The testing has been done mostly, though not exclusively, by psychologists; the applications have been mostly in economics and sociology. Although it is clear from many experiments that the conditions under which the choice axiom holds are surely delicate, the need for simple, rational underpinnings in complex theories, as in economics and sociology, leads one to accept assumptions that are at best approximate. And the third section concerns alternative, more general theories which, in spirit, are much like the choice axiom.

Perhaps I had best admit at the outset that, as a commentator on this scene, I am qualified no better than many others and rather less well than some who have been working in this area recently, which I have not been. My pursuits have led me along other, somewhat related routes. On the one hand, I have contributed to some of the recent, purely algebraic aspects of fundamental measurement (for a survey of some of this material, see Krantz, Luce, Suppes,

This essay is a slightly abridged version of the article, with the same title, which appeared in the *Journal of Mathematical Psychology*, 15(1977), 215–233. Copyright 1977 by Academic Press. Reprinted with permission. The material on rankings has been deleted and that on Tversky's elimination-by-aspects model abbreviated. The references to rankings are Atkinson, Bower, and Crothers (1965, pp. 150–155), Block and Marschak (1960), Chakrabarti (1969), Georgescu-Roegen (1958, 1969), Luce (1959, pp. 68–74), Marschak (1960), and Skvoretz, Windell, and Fararo (1974).

Drs. D. M. Green, T. Indow, A. A. J. Marley, P. Suppes, A. Tversky, and J. I. Yellott, Jr. commented on an earlier draft of this essay. In several cases, errors of fact or interpretation were pointed out as well as various omissions and obscurities; my thanks to each for his thoughtful remarks.

and Tversky, 1971). And on the other hand, I have worked in the highly probabilistic area of psychophysical theory; but the empirical materials had led me away from axiomatic structures, such as the choice axiom, to more structural, neural models which are not readily axiomatized at the present time. After some attempts to apply choice models to psychophysical phenomena (discussed later in its proper place), I was led to conclude that it is not a very promising approach to these data, and so I have not been actively studying any aspect of the choice axiom in over 12 years. With that understood, let us begin.

Mathematical and Statistical Results

The Choice Axiom

Anyone reading this article is probably already familiar with the choice axiom (axiom 1: Luce, 1959), so I confine myself to a brief reminder. One part says that, if a choice set S contains two elements, a and b, such that a is never chosen over b when the choice is restricted to just a and b, then a can be deleted from S without affecting any of the choice probabilities. The other, more substantive part, concerns choice situations where all the deletions of the first part have been carried out. Suppose R is a subset of S, then the choice probabilities for the choice set R are assumed to be identical to the choice probabilities for the choice set S conditional on R having been chosen, that is, for a in R,

$$P_R(a) = P_S(a|R).$$

Several easy consequences of this are that the ratio $P_R(a)/P_R(b)$ is independent of R (the constant-ratio rule), that the pairwise probabilities satisfy

$$P(a, b)\,P(b, c)\,P(c, a) = P(a, c)\,P(c, b)\,P(b, a)$$

(the product rule), and that there exists a numerical ratio scale v over T such that for all a in R,

$$P_R(a) = \frac{v(a)}{\sum\limits_{b \text{ in } R} v(b)}.$$

We say $v(a)$ is a response strength associated with response a, and the axiom implies response probability is proportional to response strength. This representation is closely related to the logit analysis used in statistics. For two-element choice sets, it was proposed earlier by Bradley and Terry (1952), and so some authors (e.g., Suppes and Zinnes, 1963) refer to these as BTL models. Others, especially economists, refer to it as the strict utility model. As Fantino and Navarick (1974) note, it recurs repeatedly in people's thinking about choice probabilities.

The Relation to Thurstone's Theory

It was apparent from the outset that in many situations the numbers predicted by the choice axiom differ but little from those predicted by the special case of Thurstone's discriminable dispersion model (called the random utility model by economists and probit analysis by statisticians) in which the random variables are independent, are normally distributed, and have the same variance. Indeed, the paired comparison situation leads to the logistic distribution for the choice model and the normal ogive for Thurstone's, and these are well known to be very similar except in the tails. One study (Burke and Zinnes, 1965) aimed at empirical tests concerned ways to try to maximize the difference between the two models. Large differences in the prediction of $P(a, c)$ in terms of $P(a, b)$ and $P(b, c)$ arise only when one of these probabilities is very near 0 and the other is very near 1, but it is not practical to estimate such extreme values with sufficient accuracy to make the test workable.

The first major step in understanding the exact relationship between these two models, due to Block and Marschak (1960), is the theorem that, for any system of probabilities satisfying the choice axiom, there is an independent Thurstone model defined on the whole real line that yields these probabilities. Their proof was very indirect and later E. Holman and A. A. J. Marley (reported in Luce and Suppes, 1965) gave a direct proof. In particular, an independent Thurstone model with random variables of the form

$$P(X \leqslant t) = f(t)^{v(x)}, \quad f(-\infty) = 0, \quad f(\infty) = 1, \quad -\infty < t < \infty$$

yields the choice model. If one restricts this to random variables that differ only in their means—a shift family—then one obtains the double exponential[1] of the form

$$P(X \leqslant t) = e^{-e^{-\alpha t + \beta}}.$$

A question not then answered, and only recently resolved by McFadden (1974) and independently and under appreciably less restrictive conditions[2] by Yellott (1977), is whether this distribution is unique or not. That is, while we can reproduce any set of probabilities satisfying the choice axiom by using appropriate double exponential distributions, can we do the same thing with some different distribution? The answer is No, provided that the Thurstone model is restricted to a shift family and that the choice set has at least three elements. This is by no means obvious, nor is it easy to prove. The case of just binary choices is more complex; Bradley (1965) discussed it.

In the course of investigating this problem, Yellott has brought to our attention two related facts. The first, which was also pointed out earlier in the context of paired comparison models by Thompson and Singh (1967) (see also Beaver and Rao, 1972), is that the double exponential distribution arose very many years ago in statistics (Fisher and Tippett, 1928; Gumbel, 1958) as an answer to the question: given n independent, identically distributed, random variables, what is the asymptotic ($n \to \infty$) distribution of the maximum? This is similar to the question answered in the central limit theorem, but with "maximum" substituted for "average" (or "sum"). There are various possibilities, one of which is the double exponential that arises when the underlying distribution has an exponential tail.

The second fact is a new and very pretty result, which, had Thurstone known it, might have led him to postulate the double exponential rather than the normal distribution. Yellott asked and answered the following question. Suppose choices are determined by a Thurstone model involving random variables that are independent and a shift family and that the choice probabilities exhibit the following plausible invariance property: let each element of a choice set be replicated k times—think of choices among books or phonograph records with several identical copies of each—the probability of choosing any particular element is independent of the value of k. Yellott has shown that under this invariance assumption the distributions in the Thurstone model must be double exponentials, and hence the choice axiom must hold. In many contexts, Yellott's condition is so compelling that his theorem means that Thurstone's model with a shift family of independent random variables and the choice axiom stand or fall together.

It should be noted that Yellott's invariance condition is closely related to Debreu's (1960) counter-example to the choice axiom: Suppose that a person is indifferent between a and b and a' and b, $P(a, b) = P(a', b) = \frac{1}{2}$ and that a and a' are very similar so $P(a, a') = \frac{1}{2}$. Because of the similarity of a and a', Debreu contends $P_A(a) = P(a, b) = \frac{1}{2}$, where $A = \{a, a', b\}$. However, according to the choice axiom

$$P(a', b) = P(a, b) \text{ iff } P_A(a) = P_A(a')$$

$$P(a', a) = P(a', b) \text{ iff } P_A(b) = P_A(a),$$

whence $P_A = \frac{1}{3} < P(a, b)$. The key difference between Yellott and Debreu is that the former uses equal numbers of replications whereas the latter does not.

Limit Properties

Let L_n denote a probability distribution on the first n integers, $n \geqslant 2$. Steele (1974) called a sequence of such distributions, $n = 2, 3, \ldots$, a *Luce process* provided they exhibit the constant-ratio rule; that is, for each $m < n$ and for $i, j \leqslant m$,

$$\frac{P_n(i)}{P_n(j)} = \frac{P_m(i)}{P_m(j)}.$$

Next, let us define for each L_n a measure P_n on the unit interval by placing atoms at the points k/n, $1 \leqslant k \leqslant n$, with mass $P_n(k)$. Using the results of Karamata (1933) on regularly varying functions, Steele showed that if the sequence L_n is a Luce process and if the associate measures P_n converge in distribution to P, then for some α, $0 \leqslant \alpha \leqslant \infty$, $P[0,x] = x^\alpha$. So far as I know, this result has yet to be put to use.

Discard and Acceptance Mechanisms

Luce (1960) suggested that choices may be effected by systematically discarding elements from a choice set. If so and if we denote the probability of discarding b from A by $Q_A^*(b)$, then a natural inductive hypothesis is

$$P_A(a) = \sum_{b \text{ in } A - \{a\}} Q_A^*(b)P_{A - \{b\}}(a).$$

There it was shown that if the choice axiom also holds, then

$$Q_A^*(b) = \frac{1 - P_A(b)}{|A| - 1},$$

where $|A|$ is the number of elements in A. So in this very special case the choice probabilities can arise from a discard mechanism.

Marley (1965) studied the problem more generally. We say the choice probabilities satisfy *regularity* if, for a in $A \subseteq B$, $P_A(a) \geqslant P_B(a)$. This is a very weak property which almost everyone believes to be true of choice probabilities. However, as Corbin and Marley (1974) have pointed out, even it may not always be true. For example, a guest in deference to his host selects the second most expensive item on a menu; this choice of course will be altered by adding an entree more expensive than any on the current menu. Marley showed that regularity is sufficient, but not necessary, for the discard equation to hold, that the discard probabilities are unique when the inequality in regularity is strict, and he gave an expression for them.

Following Marley (1968), let P^* denote aversion probabilities, that is, $P_A^*(a)$ is the probability that a is selected from A as the least desired element. One can define an acceptance condition that parallels the discard one by

$$P_A^*(a) = \sum_{b \text{ in } A - \{a\}} Q_A(b)P_{A - \{b\}}^*(a).$$

These two conditions, discard and acceptance, are called strong if $Q^* = P^*$ and $Q = P$.

Another plausible relation between the two kinds of probabilities is Marley's *concordant condition*

$$P_A(a)P_{A - \{a\}}^*(b) = P_A^*(b)P_{A - \{b\}}(a).$$

He showed that the concordant condition implies that both the strong discard and the strong acceptance conditions hold but that neither set of choice probabilities can satisfy the choice axiom.

Applications

As we see in the next section, psychologists have been at pains to test the adequacy of the choice axiom as a descriptive model, but there has been relatively little application of it as the foundation of some other theory. I made some attempts in Luce (1959, 1963) and Luce and Galanter (1963) to build a psychophysical theory on it, and Nakatani (1972) and Shipley (1965) extended those ideas, but realistically I do not think that it has been a particularly successful program.

In sociology, there are two large texts on mathematical sociology. There is a brief mention of the choice axiom in the introduction to Coleman (1964), but he does not appear to employ it later, whereas Fararo (1973) devotes much of one of 25 chapters to expositing the idea. However, so far as I can see, nothing is really built on it.

In economics, there appear to be two sorts of applications. One is typified by the work of McFadden and his colleagues (for a survey, see McFadden, 1976) in which different possible models of choice are used to fit empirical data that arise in economic contexts of some complexity. This work is more in the spirit of data handling and reduction of statistics than of economic theory. The other, which is more deeply theoretical, attempts to reconstruct the foundations of rational economic theory, basing it on probabilistic rather than algebraic assumptions. Work of this sort was initiated by Georgescu-Roegen (1936, 1958). The latter paper raised the key questions: "I. What axioms are logically necessary and experimentally justified, to relate the multiple choice probability to that of the binary choice? II. Granted these axioms, what is the reflection of the 'average' demand into the binary choice map?" Halldin (1974) undertook the investigation of the second question on the assumption that the choice axiom is a reasonable answer to the first question. As he pointed out, the choice axiom is a possible probabilistic formulation of ". . . a leading . . . and powerful . . . principle in the traditional economic theory of consumer behavior: by the definition of rationality, the choice made from any given budget set B depends exclusively on the ordering of the alternatives in B." He proceeds to develop on this foundation a generalization of the classical theory of demand. He summarizes his results as follows. "On the basis of Luce's theory then, we conclude that whereas the mode or most probable demand of the uncertain consumer will always coincide with his classical and optimal demand, his mean or expected demand will not, that is, his expected demand will not reveal preferences as demand reveals preferences in the classical case, nor can it be identified with the demand he would have if, as in classical theory, his preferences were perfectly certain."

Experimental Tests

By now, quite a variety of experiments have either been performed to test or been interpreted in terms of the choice axiom, and so it is helpful to group them into related categories. Even so, only the briefest mention of individual studies is possible. I have elected to group most of the animal studies together at the end.

Binary Data

Because the choice axiom implies the binary constraint

$$\frac{P(a, b)\, P(b, c)\, P(c, a)}{P(b, a)\, P(c, b)\, P(a, c)} = 1,$$

known as the product rule, binary (paired comparison) data provide an indirect test of the axiom. This property is equivalent to the binary choice model of Bradley and Terry (1952),

$$P(a, b) = \frac{v(a)}{v(a) + v(b)}.$$

In an early paper on taste preferences, Hopkins (1954) used Bradley's (1953) estimation scheme and a χ^2 evaluation and found the Bradley-Terry model satisfactory. Burke and Zinnes (1965) fitted both the binary Thurstone and the Bradley-Terry model to three published sets of data—Gulliksen and Tukey (1958), in which 200 subjects evaluated pairs of handwriting specimens; Guilford (1954), in which a single subject judged each pair of weights 200 times; and Thurstone (1959), in which 266 subjects judged the seriousness of crimes. They estimated two of the three probabilities, predicted the third, and used χ^2 as a measure of goodness of fit. Thurstone's data were indecisive and the other two favored the Thurstone model. As they pointed out, assigning all of the variability to just one of the three probabilities is not really very satisfactory. Hohle (1966) carried out another analysis of existing data: lifted weights (Guilford, 1931), preferences among vegetables (Guilford, 1954), samples of handwriting (Hevner, 1930), and numerousness (Hohle). His more sophisticated analysis involved maximum likelihood estimates for the scale values of both the Bradley-Terry and Thurstone models and evaluated the fit in terms of $-2 \ln \lambda$, where λ is the likelihood ratio, which is asymptotically distributed as χ^2. By this test, the Bradley-Terry model was favored, although in over half of the comparisons the discrepancies were significant. In the worst case, the average absolute deviation was .032. Skvoretz, Windell, and Fararo (1974) used as stimuli two sets of five occupations each, with one occupation in common. A group of 79 subjects were presented with all 36 pairs and asked to "choose that occupation which, *in general*, you accord a higher social standing." Using Bradley's procedures, these were fitted to the binary model and the appropriate χ^2 test yielded $p > .25$. So, for the average subject, the binary model fit very well. Later, under rankings, I discuss other data from this study.

Several authors, probably motivated by Debreu's (1960) counter-example to the choice axiom (actually, to simple scalability; see below), have emphasized the need to take into account similarity relations among the stimuli. Restle (1961) proposed a binary choice theory that has recently been generalized by Tversky (1972a, b) to arbitrary sets of alternatives. Rumelhart and Greeno (1971) designed a study in which certain subgroups of stimuli were similar, but different groups were not. Their data clearly disconfirmed the Bradley-Terry model and were consistent with the Restle model. Their procedure of estimation was criticized by Edgell, Geisler, and Zinnes (1973), but their conclusion was not altered by correcting the estimates.

Nonbinary Data: The Constant Ratio Rule

The constant ratio rule (CRR) (Clarke, 1957) version of the choice model has attracted considerable attention, especially as a way of dealing with confusion matrices. Early studies include Anderson (1959), Clarke (1957, 1959), Clarke and Anderson (1957), and Egan (1957a, b). These authors all concluded that the CRR is reasonably satisfactory. Later studies along much the same lines, including Atkinson, Bower, and Crothers (1965, pp. 146–150, analyzing the data of W. K. Estes), Hodge (1967), Hodge and Pollack (1962), Pollack and Decker (1960), and Waganaar (1968), continued to interpret the data as reasonably favorable, although not always. Hodge (1967, p. 435) put it this way: "Taken as a whole, the predictions are good enough to make the CRR a useful tool in designing practical stimulus displays and response systems (cf., Engstrand & Moeller, 1962). As a model of choice behavior, however, the rule as presently formulated is somewhat unsatisfactory. The results of the present experiment and those of Hodge and Pollack demonstrate that the CRR has difficulty predicting the response proportions of single dimensional ensembles, especially when the 2 by 2 matrices involve variations in the spacing-range conditions and practice on the task."

But even the apparently favorable cases are cast into doubt by Morgan (1974) who worked out a likelihood ratio test for the CRR and reexamined some of the published data, which he found departs significantly from predicted values. His discussion of the difficulties in running a suitable experiment to test the CRR is illuminating.

Yellott and Curnow (1967) ran a study in which one of three possible target letters was flashed briefly at random in a 4 × 4 matrix along with 15 other non-target letters. On some trials the subject had all three responses available, and on the remainder one of the two incorrect responses was eliminated by the experimenter after the presentation and before the response. Assuming that choices were a mixture of guesses and observations, it was found that the choice axiom accounted well for the data of the four subjects. When an error was made, on trials for which all three responses were available, they required a second choice. These were not well predicted, but they argued that this is not a satisfactory test of the choice axiom because of sequential effects introduced by the selection of trials.

Tversky (1972b) conducted a psychophysical and two preference studies of the CRR. The psychophysical data exhibited no significant departure, but in the preference data the observed binary proportions were larger than those predicted from trinary data. This is plausible in the light of his model, which generalizes both Restle and the CRR (see below), in which stimulus similarity plays a role.

Nonbinary Data: Response Biases

In Luce (1959) and more fully in Luce (1963), a class of models was developed in which the scale values associated with responses are decomposed multiplicatively into two factors, a response bias b_j associated solely with the response and a stimulus factor, η_{ij} being the impact of stimulus i on response j. The choice axiom then yields the form

$$P(r_j \mid s_i) = \frac{\eta_{ij} b_j}{\sum_k \eta_{ik} b_k}.$$

In the latter paper I attempted, with some degree of success, to use this to account for various psychophysical data, but certain phenomena proved recalcitrant to this approach. Perhaps the most striking of these occurs in absolute identification, where the information transmitted for stimuli spread over a large range grows almost linearly with log n until about $n = 7$ at which point it becomes constant (Miller, 1956) or for 10 or more stimuli it grows linearly with range up to a point (15-20 decibels in auditory intensity) after which its rate is greatly reduced (Braida and Durlach, 1972). Indeed, until very recently no model has successfully accounted for these phenomena (Luce, Green, and Weber, 1976).

Shipley and Luce (1964) collected considerable data (weights) and attempted to fit them with this model with, at best, modest success. Shipley (1965) collected additional auditory data and found that the simple model would not do, and she developed a number of elaborate modifications of it which, however, have not been pursued. Townsend (1971) fit the model to an alphabet confusion matrix with rather better results. Broadbent (1967) argued that it is a suitable model to explain the word-frequency effect in the perception of words, but his interpretation was sharply questioned by Catlin (1969) and Nakatani (1970) and defended by Treisman (1971).

Nakatani (1968, 1972) proposed a generalization of the response bias model which he calls confusion-choice recognition theory. He has had success in fitting it to word recognition data. For a summary, see Luce and Green (1974, p. 307).

β-Learning Model

The form of biased choices just described suggested (Luce, 1959) a possible mechanism for learning, not unrelated to the linear operator models then in vogue. The idea was that on trial n there is a set of response strengths $v_n(a)$, a in A, and, if alternative a is selected on trial n, then depending on the outcome it is changed to $\beta v_n(a) = v_{n+1}(a)$ on trial $n + 1$. A positive reinforcement corresponds to $\beta > 1$ and a negative one to $0 < \beta < 1$. In terms of the probabilities, these operators are nonlinear, but they exhibit instead of linearity the very powerful property of commutativity. This captures a learning process in which there is no forgetting or attenuation of the past.

Mathematical properties of these operators were investigated by Bush (1960), Kanal (1960, 1962a, 1962b), Lamperti and Suppes (1960), and Luce (1959). In Luce (1964) whole families of commutative operators were investigated and, in general, were shown to behave much like the β model. Bush, Galanter, and Luce (1959) conducted some experimental tests of the model, using animals, but their conclusions were sharply questioned by Sternberg (1963, pp. 96–97) who pointed out that optimal estimates of the parameters were considerably different from their nonoptimal ones.

Simple Scalability

Although the evidence so far reviewed makes one suspicious that the choice axiom is not terribly accurate empirically, to me the most compelling data against it are the several studies that were explicitly designed to undermine the whole broad class of models satisfying simple scalability. Luce and Suppes (1965) defined the *constant utility models* to be those for which there is a real-valued function u over alternatives and real functions F_n on n real arguments such that

$$P_A(a_1) = F_n[u(a_1); \ u(a_2), \dots, u(a_n)],$$

where $A = \{a_1, a_2, \dots, a_n\}$. If, in addition, we assume that F_n is strictly increasing in the first argument and strictly decreasing in the remaining $n - 1$, then we say *simple scalability* holds. Tversky (1972a) showed this to be equivalent to the following simple observable property called *order independence*: for a, b in $A - B$ and c in B,

$$P_A(a) \geqslant P_A(b) \text{ iff } P_{B \cup \{b\}}(c) \geqslant P_{B \cup \{a\}}(c),$$

provided none of the probabilities is 0. This generalizes earlier results on binary simple scalability (Krantz, 1967; Tversky and Russo, 1969) which had been shown to be equivalent to each of the following well-known properties:

Strict stochastic transitivity: $P(a, b) \geqslant \frac{1}{2}$ and $P(b, c) \geqslant \frac{1}{2}$ imply $P(a, c) \geqslant$ max $[P(a, b), P(b, c)]$, and $>$ in either hypothesis implies $>$ in the conclusion.

Substitutability: $P(a, c) \geqslant P(b, c)$ iff $P(a, b) \geqslant \frac{1}{2}$.

Independence: $P(a, c) \geqslant P(b, c)$ iff $P(a, d) \geqslant P(b, d)$.

To begin with, against simple scalability is Debreu's (1960) example. It was raised against the choice axiom, but the argument actually only uses order independence. Almost everyone, including me, agrees that Debreu is empirically correct, and so simple scalability must be wrong.

Empirically, we also have several unambiguous studies. Coombs (1958) showed that preferences among shades of gray include triples of alternatives, which he could identify on the basis of his unfolding ideas, that violate strict stochastic transitivity and hence simple scalability (the full impact of his result was not fully realized by most of us at the time). Chipman (1960) found in a study of subjective probability that he could reject strict stochastic transitivity for six of ten subjects. Krantz (1967) showed that substitutability, and hence simple scalability, failed for judgments about monochromatic colors. Whether or not one alternative can be substituted for another was found to be context dependent. And Tversky and Russo (1969) exhibited failures of independence, and hence simple scalability, in judgments of the relative size of simple geometric figures that varied in two dimensions. "It was found that the similarity between stimuli facilitate the discrimination between them. But since the similarity between two stimuli can be varied without changing their scale values, simple scalability, and hence independence, must be violated." (p. 11)

These results are deeply disturbing because their variety of domains make it difficult to see in what domain simple scalability, let alone the choice axiom, may hold. And at the same time, all the data reported are in large part consistent with simple scalability, and so it is difficult to abandon the idea completely. As we shall see, Tversky was led from these problems to his choice-by-elimination model, but even that may not be without problems.

Expected Random Utility (Thurstone) Model

Becker, DeGroot, and Marschak (1963b), drawing upon a theoretical analysis in Becker, DeGroot, and Marschak (1963a), designed a study of choices among gambles which had the following property. No expected random utility model predicts that one of the alternatives (which was an average of the other two) in each choice set would ever be chosen. There were 25 such sets and 60 of the 62 subjects selected the forbidden alternative at least once in 25 times. This study casts doubt upon just about any way of generalizing the expected utility property in a probabilistic context.

Animal Data

In his text, Greeno (1968) analyzed several sets of data. Food preferences of rats (Young, 1947) gave good agreement with the product rule. However, the proportions of time spent in alternative activities (Allison, 1964) did not satisfy the product rule very well. And finally, monkey data on times devoted to activities allowed good predictions.

By far the most systematic program of animal research that bears on these matters is that of R. J. Herrnstein and his collaborators. He has concerned himself with choice situations defined in an operant framework in terms of different keys associated with different reinforcement schedules. The behavior observed is key presses and reinforcements received. The major generalization from those data is that strength of responding is proportional to its relative rate of reinforcement. Put more formally, if there are n alternative responses, r_i denotes the number of reinforcements delivered per ith response, r_0 is a constant, and R_i is the number of occurrences of response i, then

$$R_i = \frac{kr_i}{\sum_{j=0}^{n} r_j}.$$

If P_i denotes the proportion of i responses, then

$$P_i = \frac{R_i}{\sum_{j=1}^{n} R_j}$$

$$= \frac{kr_i / \sum_{j=0}^{n} r_j}{\sum_{j=1}^{n} kr_j / \sum_{h=0}^{n} r_h}$$

$$= \frac{r_i}{\sum_{j=1}^{n} r_j},$$

which of course is the choice axiom representation, but with the scale value having an explicit empirical interpretation.

For a general discussion of these ideas, summaries of the data, and more detailed references, see Fantino and Navarick (1974), Herrnstein (1970, 1974), and de Villiers and Herrnstein (1976). Herrnstein and Loveland (1976) have studied the product rule during extinction trials and found that the choice axiom prediction is not nearly as extreme as the data.

Generalizations

As we have seen, there is much evidence that choices are not generally governed by axioms as simple as the choice axiom. Indeed, the difficulty pervades the whole broad class of models exhibiting simple scalability. That being so, various other approaches have been taken.

There is of course the general class of Thurstone models, which economists call random utility models. These are the ones with a random variable U_a associated with each response alternative and the assumption that

$$P_A(a) = Pr(U_a \geqslant U_b \text{ for all } b \text{ in } A).$$

Mostly, only independent random utility models have been used; these are ones in which the random variables are assumed to be independent of each other. As Tversky (1972b) pointed out, a familiar example (Luce and Raiffa, 1957, p. 375) makes clear that this model will not suffice. Consider nearly equivalent trips to Paris and to Rome, and let the added symbol + denote some minor added benefit, such as a slight reduction in price. It is evident that for a = either Paris or Rome, $P(a+, a) = 1$, but that it is quite possible for both P(Paris+, Rome) < 1 and P(Rome+, Paris) < 1. Assuming an independent Thurstone model, the first two equalities imply no overlap between the distributions of a and $a+$ for a = Paris and a = Rome, whereas the last two inequalities imply an overlap between Paris+ and Rome and between Rome+ and Paris. These statements are mutually inconsistent for independent random variables.

So the only remaining real possibility that retains the intuitive idea of a utility indicator is some form of nonindependent Thurstone model. Although Restle (1961) and Eisler (1964) have suggested binary generalizations, it was not until Tversky (1972a, 1972b) (see also Corbin and Marley, 1974) that a full generalization was proposed. Tversky suggested that each alternative is characterized by a set of aspects, that each person has a weighting function over aspects, and that choices are effected as follows. An aspect is selected with a probability proportional to its weight and all alternatives not having that aspect are covertly eliminated; this process is repeated until a unique choice is made. He showed this implies there is a function U over the subsets of the universal set such that the choice probabilities are related by

$$P_A(a) = \frac{\sum\limits_{B, B \cap A \neq A} U(B) P_{A \cap B}(a)}{\sum\limits_{B, B \cap A \neq \phi} U(B)}.$$

This model reduces to the choice model in the special circumstance where the pairs of alternatives are aspect disjoint. Furthermore, for binary alternatives, it is equivalent to Restle's (1961) model. But perhaps its nicest feature is the number of desirable consequences that can be derived from it. Tversky (1972a) showed that it implies regularity (see the section on Discard and Acceptance Mechanisms), moderate stochastic transitivity: if $P(a, b) \geqslant \frac{1}{2}$ and $P(b, c) \geqslant \frac{1}{2}$, then $P(a, c) \geqslant \min [P(a, b), P(b, c)]$; and $P_{\{a,b,c\}}(a) \geqslant P(a, b) P(a, c)$. The latter multiplicative inequality was generalized in Sattath and Tversky (1976) to $P_{A \cup B}(a) \geqslant P_A(a) P_B(a)$. Thus, it and regularity provide lower and upper bounds on $P_{A \cup B}(a)$ in terms of $P_A(a)$ and $P_B(a)$. It will be recalled that regularity is a condition that nearly everyone believes to be true of most choices. And whereas strong stochastic transitivity (max for min above), which is equivalent to binary simple scalability, has been rejected in data, moderate stochastic transitivity has not been.

Conclusion

After somewhat less than 20 years, where does the choice axiom stand? As a descriptive tool, it is surely imperfect; sometimes it works well, other times not very well. As Debreu and Restle made clear and as has been repeatedly demonstrated experimentally, it fails to describe choice behavior when the stimulus set is structured in such a way that several alternatives are treated as substantially the same. It probably also fails whenever the experimental subjects have the belief—which I fear may often be the case—that they should employ the response alternatives about equally often. This tends to introduce some form of response bias which can well differ from one experimental run to another. Keep in mind that, once we enter the path of strict rejection of models on the basis of statistically significant differences, little remains. To the best of my knowledge, the only property of general choice probabilities that has never been empirically disconfirmed is regularity—a decrease in the choice set does not decrease the probability of choosing any of the remaining alternatives—but even that looks suspect in a Gedanken experiment. Despite these empirical difficulties, there remains a tendency to invoke the choice axiom in many behavioral models—often implicitly. This is partly because it is so simple and the resulting computations are so easy.

Perhaps the greatest strength of the choice axiom, and one reason that it continues to be used, is as a canon of probabilistic rationality. It is a natural probabilistic formulation of K. J. Arrow's famed principle of the independence of irrelevant alternatives, and as such it is a possible underpinning for rational, probabilistic theories of social behavior. Thus, in the development of economic theory based on the assumption of probabilistic individual choice behavior, it can play a role analogous to the algebraic rationality postulates of the traditional theory.

However long the choice axiom may prove useful, at least during the 1960s and 1970s it contributed to the interplay of ideas about choices that arose in economics, psychology, and statistics.

Notes

1. There is a good deal of terminological confusion. Sometimes the Laplace distribution is called the double exponential, whereas $e^{-e^{-x}}$ is often called the log Weibull distribution because the distribution e^{-x^k}, $x \geq 0$, is known as the Weibull distribution. Both Holman and Marley and McFadden stated the result in Weibull form, but, to have the variables run from $-\infty$ to ∞, Yellott uses the double exponential form.
2. McFadden's proof is more restrictive in two respects. He assumed that the distribution of the random variable is translation complete and that there are infinitely many objects of choice; neither is required in Yellott's proof.

References

ALLISON, J. "Strength of Preference for Food, Magnitude of Food Reward, and Performance in Instrumental Conditioning," *Journal of Comparative and Physiological Psychology,* 57(1964), 217–223.

ANDERSON, C. D. "The Constant-Ratio Rule as a Predictor of Confusions Among Various Stimuli of Brief Exposure Duration," *Technical Note, AFCRC-TN-58-60.* Hearing and Communication Laboratory. Bloomington: Indiana University, 1959.

ATKINSON, R. C., G. H. BOWER, and E. J. CROTHERS. *An Introduction to Mathematical Learning Theory.* New York: Wiley, 1965.

BEAVER, R. J., and P. V. RAO. "The Use of Limit Theorems in Paired and Triple Comparison Model Building," *Journal of Mathematical Psychology,* 9(1972), 92–103.

BECKER, G. M., M. H. DEGROOT, and J. MARSCHAK. "Stochastic Models of Choice Behavior," *Behavioral Science,* 8(1963a), 41–55.

BECKER, G. M., M. H. DEGROOT, and J. MARSCHAK. "An Experimental Study of Some Stochastic Models for Wagers," *Behavioral Science,* 8(1963b), 199–202.

BLOCK, H. D., and J. MARSCHAK. "Random Orderings and Stochastic Theories of Responses," in I. Olkin, S. Ghurye, W. Hoeffding, W. Madow, and H. Mann, eds., *Contributions to Probability and Statistics.* Stanford, Calif.: Stanford University Press, 1960, pp. 97–132.

BRADLEY, R. A. "Some Statistical Methods in Taste Testing and Evaluation," *Biometrics,* 9(1953), 22–38.

BRADLEY, R. A. "Another Interpretation of a Model for Paired Comparisons," *Psychometrika,* 30(1965), 315–318.

BRADLEY, R. A., and M. E. TERRY. "Rank Analysis of Incomplete Block Designs. I. The Method of Paired Comparisons," *Biometrika,* 39(1952), 324–345.

BRAIDA, L. D., and N. I. DURLACH. "Intensity Perception II. Resolution in One-Interval Paradigms," *Journal of the Acoustical Society of America,* 51(1972), 483–502.

BROADBENT, D. E. "Word-Frequency Effect and Response Bias," *Psychological Review,* 74(1967), 1–15.

BURKE, C. J., and J. L. ZINNES. "A Paired Comparison of Pair Comparisons," *Journal of Mathematical Psychology,* 2(1965), 53–76.

BUSH, R. R. "Some Properties of Luce's Beta Model for Learning," in K. J. Arrow, S. Karlin, and P. Suppes, eds., *Mathematical Methods in the Social Sciences, 1959.* Stanford, Calif.: Stanford University Press, 1960, pp. 254–264.

BUSH, R. R., E. GALANTER and R. D. LUCE. "Tests of the 'Beta Model,' " in R. R. Bush and W. K. Estes, eds., *Studies in Mathematical Learning Theory.* Stanford, Calif.: Stanford University Press, 1959, pp. 382–399.

CATLIN, J. "On the Word-Frequency Effect," *Psychological Review,* 76(1969), 504–506.

CHAKRABARTI, S. K. "A Note on the Relation Between Binary and Multiple Choice Probabilities," *Econometrica,* 37(1969), 726–727.

CHIPMAN, J. S. "Stochastic Choice and Subjective Probability," in D. Willner, ed., *Decisions, Values and Groups,* Vol. 1. New York: Pergamon, 1960, pp. 70–95.

CLARKE, F. R. "Constant-Ratio Rule for Confusion Matrices in Speech Communication," *Journal of the Acoustical Society of America,* 29(1957), 715–720.

CLARKE, F. R. "Proportion of Correct Responses as a Function of the Number of Stimulus-Response Alternatives," *Journal of the Acoustical Society of America,* 31 (1959), 835.

CLARKE, F. R., and C. D. ANDERSON. "Further Test of the Constant-Ratio Rule in Speech Communication," *Journal of the Acoustical Society of America,* 29(1957), 1318–1320.

COLEMAN, J. S. *Introduction to Mathematical Sociology.* Glencoe, Ill.: Free Press, 1964.

COOMBS, C. H. "On the Use of Inconsistency of Preferences in Psychological Measurement," *Journal of Experimental Psychology,* 55(1958), 1–7.

CORBIN, R., and A. A. J. MARLEY. "Random Utility Models with Equality: An Apparent, but not Actual, Generalization of Random Utility Models," *Journal of Mathematical Psychology,* 11(1974), 274–293.

DEBREU, G. "Review of R. D. Luce, Individual Choice Behavior: A Theoretical Analysis," *American Economic Review,* 50(1960), 186–188.

DE VILLIERS, P. A., and R. J. HERRNSTEIN. "Toward a Law of Response Strength," *Psychological Bulletin,* 83(1976), 1131–1153.

EDGELL, S. E., W. S. GEISLER III, and J. L. ZINNES. "A Note on a Paper by Rumelhart and Greeno." *Journal of Mathematical Psychology,* 10(1973), 86–90.

EGAN, J. P. "Message Repetition, Operating Characteristics, and Confusion Matrices in Speech Communication," *Technical Report* 57-60. Hearing and Communication Laboratory. Bloomington: Indiana University, 1957a.

EGAN, J. P. "Monitoring Task in Speech Communication," *Journal of the Acoustical Society of America,* 29(1957b), 482–489.

EISLER, H. "A Choice Model for Paired Comparison Data Based on Imperfectly Nested Sets," *Psychometrika,* 29(1964), 363–370.

ENGSTRAND, R. D., and G. MOELLER. "The Relative Legibility of Ten Simple Geometric Figures," *American Psychologist,* 17(1962), 386.

FANTINO, E., and D. NAVARICK. "Recent Developments in Choice," in G. H. Bower, ed., *The Psychology of Learning and Motivation,* Vol. 8. New York: Academic Press, 1974, pp. 147–185.

FARARO, T. J. *Mathematical Sociology.* New York: Wiley, 1973.

FISHER, R. A., and L. H. C. TIPPETT. "Limiting Forms of the Frequency Distribution of the Largest or the Smallest of a Sample," *Proceedings of the Cambridge Philosophical Society,* 24(1928), 180–190.

GEORGESCU-ROEGEN, N. "The Pure Theory of Consumer's Behavior," *Quarterly Journal of Economics,* 50(1936), 545–593.

GEORGESCU-ROEGEN, N. "Threshold in Choice and the Theory of Demand," *Econometrica,* 26(1958), 157–168.

GEORGESCU-ROEGEN, N. "The Relation Between Binary and Multiple Choices: Some Comments and Further Results," *Econometrica,* 37(1969), 728–730.

GREENO, J. G. *Elementary Theoretical Psychology.* Reading, Mass.: Addison-Wesley, 1968.

GUILFORD, J. P. "Some Empirical Tests of the Method of Paired Comparisons," *Journal of Genetic Psychology,* 5(1931), 64–77.

GUILFORD, J. P. *Psychometric Methods,* 2nd ed. New York: McGraw-Hill, 1954.

GULLIKSEN, H., and J. W. TUKEY. "Reliability for the Law of Comparative Judgment," *Psychometrika,* 23(1958), 95–110.

GUMBEL, E. J. *Statistics of Extremes.* New York: Columbia Press, 1958.

HALLDIN, C. "The Choice Axiom, Revealed Preferences, and the Theory of Demand," *Theory and Decision,* 5(1974), 139–160.

HERRNSTEIN, R. J. "On the Law of Effect," *Journal of the Experimental Analysis of Behavior,* 13(1970), 243–266.

HERRNSTEIN, R. J. "Formal Properties of the Matching Law," *Journal of the Experimental Analysis of Behavior,* 21(1974), 159–164.

HERRNSTEIN, R. J., and D. H. LOVELAND. "Matching in a Network." *Journal of the Experimental Analysis of Behavior,* 26(1976), 143–153.

HEVNER, K. "An Empirical Study of Three Psychophysical Methods," *Journal of Genetic Psychology,* 4(1930), 191–212.

HODGE, M. H. "Some Further Tests of the Constant-Ratio Rule," *Perception & Psychophysics,* 2(1967), 429–437.

HODGE, M. H., and I. POLLACK. "Confusion Matrix Analysis of Single and Multidimensional Auditory Displays," *Journal of Experimental Psychology,* 63(1962), 129–142.

HOHLE, R. H. "An Empirical Evaluation and Comparison of Two Models for Discriminability Scales," *Journal of Mathematical Psychology,* 3(1966), 174–183.

HOPKINS, J. W. "Incomplete Block Rank Analysis: Some Taste Test Results," *Biometrics,* 10(1954), 397–399.

INDOW, T. "On Choice Probability," *Behaviometrika,* 2(1975), 13–31.

KANAL, L. *Analysis of Some Stochastic Processes Arising From a Learning Model.* Ph.D. dissertation. Philadelphia: University of Pennsylvania, 1960.

KANAL, L. "A Functional Equation Analysis of Two Learning Models," *Psychometrika,* 27(1962a), 89–104.

KANAL, L. "The Asymptotic Distribution for the Two-Absorbing Barrier Beta Model," *Psychometrika,* 27(1962b), 105–109.

KARAMATA, J. "Sur un mode de croissance régulière: Théorèmes fondamentaux," *Bulletin de la Société Mathématique de France,* 61(1933), 55–62.

KRANTZ, D. H. "Rational Distance Functions for Multidimensional Scaling," *Journal of Mathematical Psychology,* 4(1967), 226–245.

KRANTZ, D. H., R. D. LUCE, P. SUPPES, and A. TVERSKY. *Foundations of Measurement,* Vol. 1. New York: Academic Press, 1971.

LAMPERTI, J., and P. SUPPES. "Some Asymptotic Properties of Luce's Beta Learning Model," *Psychometrika,* 25(1960), 233–241.

LUCE, R. D. *Individual Choice Behavior.* New York: Wiley, 1959.

LUCE, R. D. "Response Latencies and Probabilities," in K. J. Arrow, S. Karlin, and P. Suppes, eds., *Mathematical Methods in the Social Sciences, 1959.* Stanford, Calif.: Stanford University Press, 1960, pp. 298–311.

LUCE, R. D. "Detection and Recognition," in R. D. Luce, R. R. Bush, and E. Galanter, eds., *Handbook of Mathematical Psychology,* Vol. 1. New York: Wiley, 1963, pp. 103–189.

LUCE, R. D. "Some One-Parameter Families of Commutative Learning Operators," in R. C. Atkinson, ed., *Studies in Mathematical Psychology.* Stanford, Calif.: Stanford University Press, 1964, pp. 380–398.

LUCE, R. D., and E. GALANTER. "Discrimination," in R. D. Luce, R. R. Bush, and E. Galanter, eds., *Handbook of Mathematical Psychology*, Vol. 1, New York: Wiley, 1963, pp. 193–243.

LUCE, R. D., and D. M. GREEN. "Detection, Discrimination, and Recognition," in E. C. Carterette and M. P. Friedman, eds., *Handbook of Perception*, Vol. II. New York: Academic Press, 1974, pp. 299–342.

LUCE, R. D., D. M. GREEN, and D. L. WEBER. "Attention Bands in Absolute Identification," *Perception & Psychophysics*, 20(1976), 49–54.

LUCE, R. D., and H. RAIFFA. *Games and Decisions.* New York: Wiley, 1957.

LUCE, R. D., and P. SUPPES. "Preference, Utility, and Subjective Probability," in R. D. Luce, R. R. Bush, and E. Galanter, eds., *Handbook of Mathematical Psychology*, Vol. 3. New York: Wiley, 1965, pp. 249–410.

MARLEY, A. A. J. "The Relation Between the Discard and Regularity Conditions for Choice Probabilities," *Journal of Mathematical Psychology*, 2 (1965), 242–253.

MARLEY, A. A. J. "Some Probabilistic Models of Simple Choice and Ranking," *Journal of Mathematical Psychology*, 5(1968), 333–357.

MARSCHAK, J. "Binary-Choice Constraints and Random Utility Indicators," in K. J. Arrow, S. Karlin, and P. Suppes, eds., *Mathematical Methods in the Social Sciences, 1959.* Stanford: Stanford University Press, 1960, pp. 312–329.

MCFADDEN, D. "Conditional Logit Analysis of Quantitative Choice Behavior," in P. Zarembka, ed., *Frontiers in Econometrics.* New York: Academic Press, 1974, pp. 105–142.

MCFADDEN, D. "Quantal Choice Analysis: A Survey," *Annals of Economic and Social Measurement*, 5(1976), 363–390.

MILLER, G. A. "The Magical Number Seven, Plus or Minus Two: Some Limits on Our Capacity for Processing Information," *Psychological Review*, 63 (1956), 81–97.

MORGAN, B. J. T. "On Luce's Choice Axiom." *Journal of Mathematical Psychology*, 11(1974), 107–123.

NAKATANI, L. H. *A Confusion-Choice Stimulus Recognition Model Applied to Word Recognition.* Ph.D. dissertation. Los Angeles: University of California, 1968.

NAKATANI, L. H. "Comments on Broadbent's Response Bias Model for Stimulus Recognition," *Psychological Review*, 77(1970), 574–576.

NAKATANI, L. H. "Confusion-Choice Model for Multidimensional Psychophysics," *Journal of Mathematical Psychology*, 9(1972), 104–127.

POLLACK, I., and L. DECKER. "Consonant Confusions and the Constant-Ratio Rule." *Language and Speech*, 3(1960), 1–6.

RESTLE, F. *Psychology of Judgment and Choice.* New York: Wiley, 1961.

RUMELHART, D. L., and J. G. GREENO. "Similarity Between Stimuli: An Experimental Test of the Luce and Restle Choice Models." *Journal of Mathematical Psychology*, 8(1971), 370–381.

SATTATH, S., and A. TVERSKY. "Unite and Conquer: A Multiplicative Inequality for Choice Probabilities," *Econometrica*, 44(1976), 79–89.

SHIPLEY, E. F. "Detection and Recognition: Experiments and Choice Models," *Journal of Mathematical Psychology*, 2(1965), 277–311.

SHIPLEY, E. F., and R. D. LUCE. "Discrimination among Two- and Three-Element Sets of Weights," in R. C. Atkinson, ed., *Studies in Mathematical Psychology*. Stanford, Calif.: Stanford University Press, 1964, pp. 218–232.

SKVORETZ, J., P. WINDELL, and T. J. FARARO. "Luce's Axiom and Occupational Prestige: Test of a Measurement Model," *Journal of Mathematical Sociology*, 3(1974), 147–162.

STEELE, J. M. "Limit Properties of Luce's Choice Theory," *Journal of Mathematical Psychology*, 11(1974), 124–131.

STERNBERG, S. "Stochastic Learning Theory," in R. D. Luce, R. R. Bush, and E. Galanter, eds., *Handbook of Mathematical Psychology*, Vol. 2. New York: Wiley, 1963, pp. 1–120.

SUPPES, P., and J. L. ZINNES. "Basic Measurement Theory," in R. D. Luce, R. R. Bush, and E. Galanter, eds., *Handbook of Mathematical Psychology*. New York: Wiley, 1963, Vol. 1, pp. 1–76.

THOMPSON, W. A., JR., and T. SINGH. "The Use of Limit Theorems in Paired Comparison Model Building," *Psychometrika*, 32(1967), 255–264.

THURSTONE, L. L. *The Measurement of Values*. Chicago: University of Chicago Press, 1959.

TOWNSEND, J. J. "Theoretical Analysis of an Alphabetic Confusion Matrix," *Perception & Psychophysics*, 9(1971), 40–50.

TREISMAN, M. "On the Word Frequency Effect: Comments on Papers by J. Catlin and L. H. Nakatani," *Psychological Review*, 78(1971), 420–425.

TVERSKY, A. "Choice by Elimination," *Journal of Mathematical Psychology*, 9(1972a), 341–367.

TVERSKY, A. "Elimination by Aspects: A Theory of Choice," *Psychological Review*, 79(1972b), 281–299.

TVERSKY, A., and J. E. RUSSO. "Substitutability and Similarity in Binary Choices," *Journal of Mathematical Psychology*, 6(1969), 1–12.

WAGENAAR, W. A. "Application of Luce's Choice Axiom to Form-Discrimination," *Nederlands Tijdschrift voor de Psychologie*, 23(1968), 96–108.

YELLOTT, J. I., JR. "The Relationship Between Luce's Choice Axiom, Thurstone's Theory of Comparative Judgment, and the Double Exponential Distribution," *Journal of Mathematical Psychology*, 15(1977), 109–144.

YELLOTT, J. I., JR., and P. F. CURNOW. "Second Choices in a Visual Span of Apprehension Task," *Perception & Psychophysics*, 2(1967), 307–311.

YOUNG, P. T. "Studies of Food Preference, Appetite, and Dietary Habit: VII. Palatability in Relation to Learning and Performance," *Journal of Comparative and Physiological Psychology*, 40(1947), 37–72.

13. SOCIAL EXCHANGE AND CHOICE

Anthony Oberschall

The empirical analysis of action (EAA hereafter) developed by Paul Lazarsfeld and his associates (Lazarsfeld and Rosenberg, 1955, section V) was an important advance in sociology. EAA consists of a theoretical scheme and a set of research techniques for understanding choices made repeatedly and under similar circumstances: consumer choices, choice of residential location, choice of occupation, voting (choice of a candidate for political office). The scheme consists of a representation of the process of choice itself from its initial to final stage, an actor with predispositions and resources (the individual's initial preferences and information about alternatives), and a social milieu (group, neighborhood, social network) in which social influences are exercised on the actor during the process of choice. A systematic ordering of the important variables in the choice process is called an accounting scheme. Thus, in voting, the citizen has initial political preferences and perceptions and information about parties, candidates, and issues which are reinforced, modified, and augmented by social influences and the political campaign before he makes a final choice.

EAA is not based on a rigorous model of choice from which deductions are made. The relative importance of various influences on choice, and the interaction of predispositions and influences, are established inductively by multivariate statistical analysis. Another step is sometimes taken by aggregating the scattered individual choices to produce a global outcome. In the case of voting, the sum of individual choices determines a winner. EAA has established the importance of group influences and social milieu in a wide range of choice situations. It allows a compact description of empirical regularities.

I wish to thank Dr. J. Lachman for advice and assistance and the Guggenheim foundation for awarding me a fellowship that made this work possible.

158

Two limitations should be pointed out. Perhaps because EAA does not lend itself easily to it, choice situations in which outcomes are interdependent with other's choices (choice of spouse, of a collaborator at work) have not been studied within its framework. Social interaction of this reciprocal, given-and-take variety has been typically studied in small groups with techniques quite different from EAA. Second, the absence of a concept of rational choice has prevented the use of deduction as a theoretical tool in EAA. Despite many empirical findings, knowledge has not been systematically codified. No system of propositions exists for application across all choice situations. This is surprising since the subject matter of EAA overlaps with that of an important branch of economics, microeconomic theory. Microeconomic theory deals in a quite general way with choice among alternative courses of action when resources constrain choice and makes use of a model of choice from which systematic deductions are made under a variety of circumstances.

In this paper, I will explore the application of a microeconomic model to social interaction where actors make interdependent choices under resource limitations. I will first present an elementary (and necessarily simplified) outline of some aspects of the microeconomic approach and point out similarities and differences with EAA. I will illustrate its application to an instance of social interaction described at great length by Blau (1963). Space limitations do not permit a comprehensive discussion of the advantages and limitations of the microeconomic approach in sociological applications.

Outline of the Microeconomic Approach*

Microeconomic theory employs four key concepts: utility, diminishing marginal utility from additional units of a good, a resource stock or budget which constrains choice, and maximization of utility subject to the budget constraint. People pursue objectives subject to certain constraints. The structure of preferences—and hence of objectives to be pursued—is represented by a "utility function." If an actor prefers A to B, he derives more satisfaction, or utility, from A than from B. An actor is assumed to be able to rank alternatives in order of preference. The preferences of a rational actor are transitive: if he prefers A to B, and B to C, he will prefer A to C. It is not necessary to assume a cardinal measure of utility, nor interpersonal utility comparisons.

The specific mathematical form of the utility function embodies certain other behavioral assumptions as well. For example, one frequently assumes that, although "more" of a good is preferable to less, the added satisfaction of "more" declines as the amount at hand increases. This is referred to as "diminishing marginal utility."

An actor can derive a particular level of utility from many different combinations of A and B. The locus of all such combinations in the case of two com-

*This outline is based on Henderson and Quandt (1971), Chapter 2.

modities or activities is called an indifference curve and will have a convex shape. The slope of the indifference curve measures the rate at which the actor is willing to substitute A for B to maintain the same level of utility. The slope will vary as a function of the amount of A and of B the actor already possesses or has performed. The overall steepness of the indifference curve (its overall convex shape) is a function of the actor's relative preferences for A and for B. A collection of indifference curves corresponding to different levels of utility is called an indifference map. Holding one activity or commodity constant and increasing the other lands the actor on a higher indifference curve, as does increasing both at the same time.

The concept of a resource stock or budget expresses the idea that choice is a function of resource limitations and of costs in addition to one's preferences. In many microeconomic applications, the budget constraint is expressed as the income of the consumer which he allocates to various combinations of commodities, each having a price (per unit cost). In other situations, the budget is expressed as a time constraint, or a combination of income and time constraints.

The solution of the choice situation is provided by the final element of the microeconomic approach, maximization of utility subject to the budget constraint. In common-sense terms this merely means that, given an actor's preferences and his resource limitations, he will choose that combination of commodities or activities which will provide him with the maximum of satisfaction. In the case of two commodities or activities the solution will be at the point of tangency of his budget line and an indifference curve.

Three kinds of deductions are made from the model. Given a particular resource constraint, how do the actor's choices change if his preferences change? Given the same preferences, but a change in his budget, how do his choices change? And given the same preferences and same budget, but a change in the "prices" of the activities or commodities, what choices will he then make?

Some possible objections to the microeconomic approach have to be dealt with. It is alleged that an "economic" model is inapplicable in social interaction because "sociological" variables cannot be expressed in monetary units. Nothing in the approach, however, requires that the variables in the model and the budget constraint be expressed in dollars and cents or that they be converted into dollar equivalents.

Another objection deals with the maximization of utilities. Without going into a long debate on this controversial point, one might answer that most people in many choice situations come close enough to maximizing satisfaction so that the approach is a useful simplification of reality over a wide range of social processes.

A further objection deals with the existence of a whole series of costs associated with making choices (transaction costs, information costs, etc.). But these associated costs can be entered into the resource constraint or budget explicitly and do not prevent the use of the microeconomic approach.

A final objection to the approach in sociological applications might be that choices are often interdependent. Since I shall develop at some length an application of the microeconomic approach in a situation where choices are interdependent, this objection as well must be qualified.

The microeconomic approach bears some similarities and differences to the EAA. The concept of predispositions—the actor's preferences—correspond to the concept of a utility function. But, in EAA, preferences may change in the course of the choice process, whereas in the microeconomic model the utility function remains constant. There is another way of drawing the contrast. In EAA, the actor is not fully aware of his preferences initially. He discovers them as a result of acquiring more information about alternative choices and about the preferences others have in his social milieu. The second element in EAA, the influence process, bears some similarities with the concept of a budget constraint, but it is not as precisely spelled out. As a budget constraint limits the combination of commodities or activities that the consumer can purchase or engage in, so the influences deriving from a fixed social milieu set limits to the kinds of information and social pressures the actor is subject to. Lastly, in EAA, though the actor does seek to achieve a balance between his preferences and conforming to significant others in his social milieu, he does not seek to maximize an explicit utility function. It is the combination of a specific utility function, a budget constraint, and maximization of the utility function subject to the budget constraint that allows deductions to be made in the microeconomic approach. The EAA model incorporates greater diversity of behavior and a more complex environment at the cost of a more limited ability to draw deductive conclusions.

Social Exchange in a Federal Enforcement Agency

The model to be discussed was inspired by a well-known study of a federal enforcement agency by Peter Blau (1963). He studied the interactions of enforcement agents in an office. The work was demanding and highly professional. Their decisions had to be based on complex regulations and had to stand up in court. The agents' decisions were reviewed by a supervisor whose evaluation of their performance influenced their careers. Errors in the application of the regulations weighed heavily against an agent. Some agents were more competent than others in the performance of their tasks. Under the circumstances, agents turned to one another for information and for advice to save time and to reduce the chances of error.

The model deals with the pattern of consultation that Blau observed in the group, in particular the interaction between more competent and less competent agents and its consequences for an informal status hierarchy in the group.

Consultation takes time. Getting advice increases the performance of the less competent advice seeker; at the same time, giving advice diminishes the output of the more expert consultant. In return for his advice, the consultant obtains respect and approval, that is, a public recognition of his greater competence, from the advice seeker, which then increases the consultant's standing in the group. I shall refer to "standing" in the group hereafter simply as "status."

The situation has all the necessary elements for an application of the microeconomic approach. There are two choices for the consultant and the advice seeker: they allocate their time between doing their own work and consultation. Each agent makes choices subject to a budget constraint, in this case the total amount of time he works in the office. Both work output and status have the property of declining marginal utility for the agents. We finally assume that both agents seek to maximize their utility, which is a function of work output and status. Under these circumstances, one wants to find out the extent of consultation that will take place in a consultant-advice seeker pair, the rate (price) at which advice is exchanged for status, the status differentiation that develops as a result of consultation, and the manner in which consultation changes the work output of both.

Work output and status are not measured in monetary units. Nor is there an externally set "price" at which advice is traded for status. The choices of the two agents are linked in two ways. Time spent in consultation is the same for both, and the transfer rate of advice for status results from the interaction of the agents as each seeks to maximize his utility.

However, the exchange taking place differs from pure economic exchange in one important respect. In an apples-for-oranges exchange, the total number of apples and oranges in the possession of an exchange pair remains constant. In my model, the output gain of the advice seekers does not necessarily equal the output loss of the consultant, and there is no loss of expertise by the consultant equal to a permanent gain to the advice seeker. On the contrary, what is transferred from consultant to advice seeker—the analog of apples—is the time spent in advising, and it is given in exchange for status, the analog of oranges. Thus the budget constraint must be stated in terms of a time budget, not in terms of a stock of advice (e.g., good ideas) or in terms of units of work output.

Although the situation described by Blau is more complex, since there are many agents with varying levels of expertise and since even competent agents occasionally seek advice, my model will deal with a single consultant-advice seeker pair and assumes that advice flows only from the more competent to the less competent agent, whereas status flows only in the opposite direction.

The Model

The letter and subscript i represent the consultant, and j stands for the less competent advice seeker. Status s_i^o and s_j^o represent their initial status endowments. We shall assume that the total amount of status $s_i + s_j$ in the pair is a fixed quantity and that the status gained by i during the exchange is exactly equal to the status given up by j: $\Delta s_i = -\Delta s_j$. We further assume that the exchange of status for advice can be represented by $\Delta s_i = bt_a$, where b is the transfer rate of status for advice and t_a is the time spent in consultation.

The consultant i works at the output rate a, and j works at the rate c, with $a > c$. As a result of the consultation, j raises his output rate from c to a for a limited period of time: $t_a = kt_{a_j}$, where t_{a_j} is the length of time that j works at the output rate a as a result of getting advice. For instance, if k is a sixth, ten minutes consulting increases j's output rate for one hour.

The factor k measures the usefulness of advice and will be called the index of usefulness. The smaller k, the longer j is able to utilize i's advice for increasing his output rate, that is, the more useful the advice. Suppose advice is sought on a particular point of information specific to a particular case. Then the advice received would be useful only for a limited amount of time, and one would expect k to be close to one. But if advice is given on a general principle or procedural question that can be repeatedly applied, k would be closer to zero.

Both i and j have a time budget that constrains their choice. For i, $t_a + t_{w_i} = T_i$: time spent consulting plus time spent working on his own case load equals total time at his disposal. For j, the time budget is a somewhat different expression: $t_a + t_{a_j} + t_{w_j} = T_j$. His total time is the sum of time he spends consulting, working at the rate a after getting advice, and working at the rate c using his wits alone.

The Cobb-Douglas utility function commonly used in economics is appropriate for the behaviors assumed in the model. Thus we assume that $u_i(w, s) = w_i^\alpha s_i^\beta$, and $u_j(w, s) = w_j^\gamma s_j^\delta$, and that $\alpha + \beta = 1, \gamma + \delta = 1$. If α is large relative to β, the expert consultant can be said to be relatively "work oriented"; if α is small relative to β, he is "status oriented." The same interpretations hold for j when γ is large or small relative to δ.

We have now defined all the symbols, made the assumptions and specified the relationships between variables necessary for proceeding to a solution of the exchange model.

For person i,

(1) $w_i = at_{w_i}$, since he does not produce an output during time t_a spent consulting,

(2) $\Delta s_i = s_i - s_i^0 = bt_a$, status gain is directly proportional to time spent giving advice,

(3) his budget constraint is $t_a + t_{w_i} = T_i$,

(4) his utility function is $u_i = w_i^\alpha s_i^\beta$; $0 \leqslant \alpha, \beta \leqslant 1$; $\alpha + \beta = 1$.

Similarly for person j,

(5) $w_j = ct_{w_j} + at_{a_j}$, since he works at the output rate c for t_{w_j} and the rate a for t_{a_j} and produces no output during t_a,

(6) $\Delta s_j = s_j - s_j^o = -bt_a$, since $\Delta s_i = -\Delta s_j$,

(7) his budget constraint is $t_a + t_{wj} + t_{aj} = T_j$, and

(8) $t_a = kt_{aj}$,

(9) his utility function is $u_j = w_j^\gamma s_j^\delta$; $0 \leqslant \gamma, \delta \leqslant 1; \gamma + \delta = 1$.

The solution proceeds as follows. Since the utility function is expressed in terms of w and s and the budget constraint in terms of time, one must first express the budget constraint in terms of w and s, which can be done from eq. 1 to 3 and 4 to 7. (One could also do the opposite and express the utility function in terms of t_w and t_a.) Then we maximize i's utility function subject to his budget constraint. From the resulting equations, a demand function for Δs_i is obtained which expresses the amount of status sought by i as a function of b, the transfer rate. A similar procedure is followed for j, but in this case, a supply function for Δs_j in terms of b is obtained. The conditions for a maximum are then studied to determine what restrictions, if any, should be imposed on the parameters. After that step, the supply of s is equated to the demand for s, and we solve for b, the transfer rate. Following that, one can solve for Δs_i, Δs_j, t_a, t_{wj}, t_{wi}, w_i, and w_j in terms of the parameters s_i^o, s_j^o, T_i, T_j, a, c, k, α, β, γ, and δ. Further possible restrictions on the parameters are examined to make sure that the solutions are realistic (e.g., the time variables have to be positive values). Finally, the solutions are studied as functions of the parameters, and interpretations for the findings are given.

The Expert Consultant's Maximization of Utility Function Subject to His Budget Constraint.

From eq. 1, $t_{wi} = w_i/a$, and from eq. 2, $t_a = (s_i - s_i^o)/b$. Substituting into eq. 3, the budget constraint can be expressed as a function of w_i and s_i:

(10) $$\frac{w_i}{a} + \frac{s_i - s_i^o}{b} = T_i.$$

For an interior solution to exist for the constrained maximization problem, it is necessary that the constraint have a negative slope. Since $w_i = -(a/b)s_i + aT_i + (a/b)s_i^o$, and a and b are always positive numbers, this condition is met. (It is worth noting that $1/a$ and $1/b$ are analogous to "prices" in the usual budget constraint in the theory of consumer behavior, where the consumer purchases two commodities q_1 and q_2 having prices p_1 and p_2 with a total income of Y, that is, $q_1p_1 + q_2p_2 = Y$.) To maximize u subject to the budget constraint, one forms the Lagrange function $v_i = u_i + \lambda[(w_i/a + (s_i - s_i^o)/b - T_i)]$. The first order conditions for utility maximization are that $\partial v_i/\partial w_i = 0$, $\partial v_i/\partial s_i = 0$,

$\partial v_i/\partial \lambda = 0.$* Differentiating and eliminating λ from the first two equations, one obtains $w_i = \alpha a s_j/\beta b$. Substituting w_i into the third equation, one obtains the demand function for s_i

(11)
$$s_i = \frac{\beta T_i}{\alpha + \beta} b + \frac{\beta}{\alpha + \beta} s_i^o .$$

Since we are interested in the demand for Δs_i, and $\Delta s_i = s_i - s_i^o$,

(12)
$$\Delta s_i = \frac{\beta T_i}{\alpha + \beta} b - \frac{\alpha}{\alpha + \beta} s_i^o.$$

For a demand function, one expects that demand for a good increases as price decreases. Since $1/b$ is analogous to price, one expects $\partial \Delta s_i/\partial(1/b) < 0$. Equation 12 meets this condition, since, if $1/b$ decreases, b increases, and if b increases, by eq. 12, Δs_i increases.

The Advice Seeker's Maximization of His Utility Function Subject To his Budget Constraint.

Eliminate t_{a_j} from eq. 5 and 7 by means of eq. 8, and rewrite the budget constraint in terms of w_j and s_j. The budget constraint now becomes

(13)
$$\frac{w_j}{c} + (s_j^o - s_j) \frac{c(1 + k) - a}{bko} - T_j.$$

For an interior solution to exist, the budget constraint must have a negative slope, that is, we require that

(14)
$$c(1 + k)a < 0,$$

or alternatively,

(15)
$$c(1 + k) < a.$$

Inequality (eq. 14) is a condition of exchange. If it is not met, no consultation will take place between i and j. Inequalities 14 and 15 imply that the parameters a, c, and k must take on only those values for which j increases his output if he consults over what his output would be if he didn't, that is, consultation takes place only if it increases j's output. If the competence gap is large ($a - c$ is large), the inequality will hold over a greater range of values for k. Thus the greater the competence gap, the more likely that conditions for consulting exist.

*A further (second-order) condition for the existence of a constrained maximum is that $\partial^2 u_i/\partial w_i^2 (\partial u_i/\partial s_i)^2 - 2(\partial^2 u_i/\partial w_i \partial s_i)(\partial u_i/\partial w_i)(\partial u_i/\partial s_i) + (\partial^2 u_i/\partial s_i^2)(\partial u/\partial w)^2 < 0$. This expression becomes the requirement that $-(\alpha + \beta) < 0$, which is always true since $\alpha + \beta = 1$.

One now proceeds in the same manner as earlier in the case of i. Maximizing u_j subject to the constraint eq. 13 yields the supply function

$$(16) \qquad -\Delta s_j = s_j^o - s_j = \frac{\gamma}{\gamma + \delta} s_j^o - \frac{T_j kc}{[a - c(1 + k)]} b \frac{\delta}{\gamma + \delta} .$$

For a normal supply function, one expects supply to increase as price increases. Here, again, it is $1/b$, not b, which is analogous to price. Thus one expects $\partial(-\Delta s_j)/\partial \frac{1}{b} > 0$. If $1/b$ increases, b diminishes, and, by eq. 16, if b diminishes, $-\Delta s_j$ increases. Equation 16 thus exhibits the desired property of a supply function. The second-order condition for the existence of a constrained maximum in j's case is that $-(\gamma + \delta) < 0$, which is always true since $\gamma + \delta = 1$.

The Transfer Rate b

To solve for b, the transfer rate of status for advice time, we equate quantity of supply and demand for status, that is, $\Delta s_i = -\Delta s_j$. From eq. 12 and 16,

$$\frac{\beta}{\alpha + \beta} T_i b - \frac{\alpha}{\alpha + \beta} s_i^o = -\frac{\delta}{\gamma + \delta} \frac{kcT_j}{[a - c(1 + k)]} b + \frac{\gamma}{\gamma + \delta} s_j^o ,$$

and solving for b, one gets, assuming $\alpha + \beta = 1, \gamma + \delta = 1$,

$$(17) \qquad b = \frac{\alpha s_i^o + \gamma s_j^o}{\beta T_i + \delta kcT_j/[a - c(k + 1)]} \qquad \text{where } a - c(k + 1) > 0.$$

In this expression, b is always positive, as the transfer rate should be, and possesses the following properties:

$$(18) \qquad \frac{\partial b}{\partial a} > 0, \frac{\partial b}{\partial c} < 0.$$

The transfer rate increases as the expertise of the consultant increases, and it decreases as the competence level of the advice seeker increases. These deductions agree with common sense. Greater competence is more highly rewarded. The transfer rate will be greater as the competence gap $(a - c)$ is greater.

$$(19) \qquad \frac{\partial b}{\partial k} < 0.$$

The transfer rate decreases as k increases. The higher k, the less "useful" is the advice to j. Inequality eq. 19 can be interpreted to mean that the less useful the advice to j, the lower will be the transfer rate, that is, the lower will be his status payment per unit advice to i.

$$(20) \qquad \partial \frac{\partial b}{T_i} , \partial \frac{\partial b}{T_j} < 0.$$

The greater the total time available for i and for j, the lower the transfer rate. If i and j have less time available, b increases: it becomes more costly for j to seek i's advice.

$$(21) \qquad \frac{\partial b}{\partial s_i^o} > 0, \quad \frac{\partial b}{\partial s_j^o} > 0.$$

The transfer rate b varies positively with the size of the initial status endowments. Since the total amount of status in the pair is constant, these deductions are of limited interest, since the effects offset each other.

$$(22) \qquad \frac{\partial b}{\partial \alpha} > 0, \quad \frac{\partial b}{\partial \beta} < 0.$$

If i were more work oriented, b would increase; that is, i would extract more status per advice from j, all else remaining constant.

$$(23) \qquad \frac{\partial b}{\partial \delta} > 0, \quad \frac{\partial b}{\partial \delta} < 0.$$

If j were more work oriented, the transfer rate would be greater. He would be willing to pay more status for the same amount of advice.

Putting eq. 22 and 23 together, one would predict b to be especially high when a work-oriented consultant interacts with a work-oriented advice seeker and to be especially low when two status-oriented agents engage in consultation. The consequence of these relationships will be that, *for the same amount of consultation*, less status differentiation will occur in a status oriented pair than in a work-oriented pair.

Consultation Time t_a

If b is solved in eq. 17 in terms of the model parameters, t_a can be obtained either from eq. 6 and 16 or from eq. 2 and 12. If that is done,

$$(24) \quad t_a = \frac{\beta\gamma T_i s_j^o - \alpha\delta T_j s_i^o kc[a - c(k+1)]}{\alpha s_i^o + \gamma s_j^o}, \text{ where } a - c(k+1) > 0.$$

Two conditions, however, must be met. First, advice time t_a cannot exceed the maximum amount of advice that i can make use of. Since t_a plus t_{a_j} cannot exceed t_j, it implies that $t_a(1 + 1/k) \leqslant T_j$.

The second condition is that advice time t_a must be positive, which is met only if the numerator of eq. 24 is positive. That is true so long as

$$(25) \qquad \frac{a - c(k+1)}{kc} > \left(\frac{s_i^o}{s_j^o}\right)\left(\frac{\alpha/\beta}{\gamma/\delta}\right)\left(\frac{T_j}{T_i}\right).$$

Inequality eq. 25 puts some restrictions on the value of the parameters for consultation to take place. The left-hand side of eq. 25 is the ratio of output gain realized by j to normal output (without advice). Since in many applications T_i and T_j will be equal, it follows from inequality eq. 25 that, for a given amount of output gain to be realized by j, the chances of consultation are higher when the initial status endowments are about the same ($s_i^o/s_j^o > 1$). Moreover, the chances of consultation are higher when a status-oriented consultant ($\alpha/\beta < 1$) is sought out by a work-oriented advice seeker ($\gamma/\delta > 1$) than vice-versa.

Assuming that eq. 25 holds, one can show that $\partial t_a/\partial s_i^o < 0$, and $\partial t_a/\partial s_j^o > 0$, which imply that consulting time varies positively with lower initial status differences. One can further show that $\partial t_a/\partial \beta > 0$ and that $\partial t_a/\partial \gamma > 0$, which implies that advice time varies positively with the status consciousness of the consultant and the work orientation of the advice seeker. (Conversely, t_a varies negatively with the work orientation of the consultant and the status consciousness of the advice seeker.) Further, $\partial t_a/\partial a > 0$, and $\partial t_a/\partial c < 0$, which implies that advice time varies positively with the expertise of the consultant and negatively with the ability of the advice seeker and, therefore, positively with the competence gap ($a - c$). Finally, $\partial t_a/\partial k < 0$, which implies that advice time varies positively with the usefulness of advice for j (when k increases, usefulness diminishes). These predictions are subject to empirical testing.

Status Gain and Loss

Once b has been obtained, Δs_i can be determined from eq. 12 and s_i from eq. 11. Since $\Delta s_i = -\Delta s_j$, the value of Δs_j is also readily obtained and one needs only examine the relationships between changes in Δs_i and parameter changes to establish how Δs_j varies with those parameters.

From eq. 12,

$$\Delta s_i = \beta T_i b - \alpha s_i^o = \frac{\beta T_i (\alpha s_i^o + \gamma s_j^o)}{\beta T_i + [\delta k c T_j/a - c(k + 1)]} - \alpha s_i^o.$$

From this equation it follows that, all else held constant,

$$(26) \qquad \frac{\partial(\Delta s_i)}{\partial a} > 0,$$

as i's expertise increases, i's status gain increases (and j's status loss increases).

$$(27) \qquad \frac{\partial(\Delta s_i)}{\partial c} < 0,$$

as j's competence level increases, i's status gain decreases (and j's status loss decreases).

$$(28) \qquad \frac{\partial(\Delta s_i)}{\partial k} < 0,$$

as k increases (the advice is less useful to j), i's status gain decreases (and j's status loss decreases).

So far the deductions for b and Δs_i are similar. But alternative preference structures may have a different effect on b than on Δs_i, since they will also affect t_a and, through t_a, react back on Δs_i. Thus

$$(29) \qquad \frac{\partial(\Delta s_i)}{\partial\alpha} < 0,$$

an increase in work orientation of the consultant will result in a lesser status gain for him (and less of a status loss for j), despite the fact that $\partial b/\partial\alpha > 0$.

Although b increases as α increases, consulting time decreases even more. The net impact of an increase in α is thus to diminish status differentiation.

$$(30) \qquad \frac{\partial(\Delta s_i)}{\partial\gamma} < 0, \qquad \text{if } \frac{a - c(k+1)}{kc} > \frac{\alpha s_i^o T_j}{\beta s_j^o T_i}.$$

$$> 0, \qquad \text{if } \frac{a - c(k+1)}{kc} < \frac{\alpha s_i^o T_j}{\beta s_j^o T_i}.$$

The net effect on status differentiation of a change in j's preferences will depend upon which of these inequalities applies. Since eq. 25 is a condition for the exchange occurring at all, the status gain of the consultant will tend to vary negatively with the work orientation of the advice seeker.

Work Output

Once consulting time t_a has been obtained, budget constraints eq. 3 and 7 allow the solution for t_{w_i}, t_{w_j}, and t_{a_j}, and eq. 1 and 5 provide the solution for w_i and w_j. Since t_a varies inversely with w_i, the effect of parameter changes upon i's output is just the opposite to its effect on t_a. But, since w_j varies directly with t_a, alternative parameter values have the same effect on w_j as on t_a.

It is also possible to show that the difference between the pair's total output with consulting and total output without consulting, ΔW, is determined by the following inequalities:

$$(31) \qquad \Delta W > 0, \qquad \text{if } \frac{a - c}{a + c} > k.$$

$$\Delta W = 0, \qquad \text{if } \frac{a - c}{a + c} = k.$$

$$\Delta W < 0, \qquad \text{if } \frac{a - c}{a + c} < k.$$

Since k is inversely related to the usefulness of advice for j, it will be seen that, as usefulness decreases (k increases), the combination of values of a and c for which ΔW is positive becomes limited. In particular, if two agents are close in competence ($a - c$ is small), usefulness has to be very great for ΔW to be greater than zero. If the competence gap is large ($a - c$ is large), ΔW can be positive for a wider range of k.

Some Conclusions

The values of the actors (expressed in the parameters α and β, and γ and δ) have to be explicitly introduced into the model to enable deductions to be made. Under some circumstances, no consulting will take place at all, or else its likelihood will be low (e.g., if the competence difference is slight or if a work-oriented consultant deals with a status-oriented advice seeker). The "price" of advice in status terms (b) varies positively with the competence difference, with the usefulness of the advice and with the degree of work orientation of the two actors. It varies negatively with total work time. Interestingly, then, when a pair of actors both value work output highly, the price of advice will be especially high, and, when they are both status oriented, the price will be low.

The amount of consulting will vary positively with the degree of status consciousness of the expert and the degree of work orientation of the advice seeker and will vary positively with lower initial status differences. If low status difference can be thought of as a "democratic" setting and high status difference as a "hierarchic" setting, one would hypothesize from the model that more consulting takes place in a democratic setting if, paradoxically, the expert is hierarchy minded (i.e., status oriented) and the advice seeker unconcerned with hierarchy (i.e., places low value on status relative to work output).

In a hierarchic setting, because of inequality eq. 25, the likelihood that consultation will take place at all is lower to begin with than in a democratic milieu, though consultation is possible if the competence gap is wide.

Finally, greater status differentiation results in consulting pairs if the competence gap is large and if both actors are status conscious than if the competence gap is small and if both are work oriented.

Deductions and Findings

The model that was abstracted here from Blau's description of the federal enforcement agency is at once simpler and more complex than the account he provided. It is simpler because we have considered only interaction between a pair of agents whereas Blau analyzed interaction among a larger number of group members. Our account is also simpler because it does not take into account the observed mutual consultations between agents who have the same competence level. Lastly, Blau observed a pattern of friendly social intercourse in addition to consulting relationships, both in the office and during the lunch breaks, through which agents established bonds of liking for one another that in the aggregate produced cohesion in the group. All this is ignored in the model presented here.

The model is, on the other hand, more complex, since in addition to the agents' competence level, it takes into account their preferences, that is, the degree of work and status orientation. These preference, as we have seen, play an important role in the model. Furthermore, k, the index of usefulness of advice for j, was introduced and proves to be important in the model. Despite these differences between Blau's account and the model, three observations he makes can be compared with deductions from the model.

1. Blau states that the more expert a consultant, the greater will be the price of the advice in status terms. Our eq. 19, $\partial b/\partial a > 0$, predicts such a relationship.

2. Blau notes that competence was correlated with popularity as a consultant. If "popularity" implies that the amount of time spent in consulting was greater, it agrees with our deduction that the greater the expertise of the consultant, the more time he spends consulting (i.e., that $\partial t_a/\partial a > 0$).

3. Blau also notes that in a regular consulting pair one agent usually had quite a lot more competence than the other. This observation agrees with the deduction that, for consultation to occur at all, the greater a and the smaller c, the greater the range of values of k for which consultation will occur, since we require that $c(1 + k) < a$. Inequality 31 also indicates that the greater competence differences ($a - c$) are associated with high likelihood that output in the pair will increase if consultation takes place. One would expect that to be the case for a regular consulting pair.

Blau himself has presented a formal model of interaction in the federal enforcement agency (1964, pp. 168–179). He too makes use of the assumptions and techniques of economic analysis: utility functions, convex indifference curves, the concept of a budget constraint, and maximization of utilities. Nevertheless, his model differs in some crucial respect from the one presented here. Though Blau does not state the model in terms of equations and uses instead a graphic presentation (the Edgeworth box) to describe the consultant-advice seeker interaction, the difference is more fundamental than techniques of analysis.

The two variables K and H in Blau's exchange model (using his notation) are similar to w and s in my model. Blau represents the interaction between consultant and advice seeker as $\Delta H_i = -\Delta H_j$ and $-\Delta K_i = \Delta K_j$. The exchange in this formulation is analogous to a pure barter exchange of apples for oranges where the total stock of apples and oranges possessed by both parties remains constant.

It is not, however, realistic to assume that $-\Delta K_i = \Delta K_j$, since the loss of output of the consultant can be greater than, equal to, or less than the work output gain of the advice seeker, depending upon inequality eq. 31. The Edgeworth box representation of the exchange cannot have K or W as one of its two dimensions, since pure exchange assumes fixed stocks. Instead the relevant dimension has to be time spent working, which does exist as a fixed stock $(T_i + T_j)$. Advice can then be represented as a transfer of t_a time from i to j. This leads to major changes from the pure exchange representation, since the output rates a and c and the factor k have to be introduced explicitly. These parameters are central for the model and for the deductions. My model thus combines exchange of status and advice and production of work output. These correspond to the two goals of the actors, advancement in one's peer group and advancement in the formal bureaucracy.

Many social interactions are probably not pure exchange but consist of a mixture of consumption, exchange, and production. What is sought is not a direct transfer of a good or a service. Instead, a factor of production is obtained from an interaction partner. The consultant's advice becomes a factor of production for the advice seeker. Other interactions are undertaken for producing a joint product (a game of tennis) and cannot be realistically represented as a net transfer of anything from one actor to another. In many interactions what is produced or exchanged is not a fixed quantity of a commodity or of an attribute: sentiments of friendship, love, approval might grow in both members of an interaction pair, as might sentiments of dislike and disapproval, unconstrained by a fixed stock of sentiments. Simple two-party exchange models must be expanded to encompass such situations, if indeed they can apply at all.

Blau also assumes that the transfer rate b is based on a social norm of fairness (pp. 174-175). To be sure Blau is ambivalent on this score, since he thinks that, in a group in which several consultants and advice seekers compete for advice and status, supply and demand will influence the transfer rate. In my model, b is explicitly determined by supply and demand and by the assumption that $\Delta s_i = b t_a$, that is, that status change is directly proportional to time spent giving advice, with the transfer rate b the factor of proportionality. This last assumption must be defended on empirical grounds as describing the behavior of the interacting parties. Without it, the model could not be solved for a determinate value of b. The transfer rate would then depend on the bargaining power of the two parties.

Sensitivity of Deductions and Assumptions

To what extent do the deductions depend on specific assumptions made in the formulation of the model? To answer this question, we examine that effects of alternative assumptions.

1. It was assumed that with t_a time units of advice person j works at the expert's output rate a for t_a/k length of time. Suppose that one assumes that j achieves an output rate that will be more than c but less than a as a result of

getting advice, that is, that *j*'s output rate will be $c + h(a - c)$, $0 \leqslant h \leqslant 1$ (when $h = 1$, we are back to the original assumption). If this were the case, condition 14 for an exchange to occur at all becomes

(14') $$\frac{c(k + h)}{h} < a.$$

As before the interpretation of this inequality is that *j*'s output if he consults must exceed his output if he didn't consult.

If one solves the model using the same steps as earlier, one obtains

(17') $$b' = \frac{\alpha s_i^o + \gamma s_j^o}{\beta T_i + [\delta k c T_j / ha - c(k + h)]}.$$

It can be observed that the sign and position of a, c, and k in eq. 17' and in eq. 17 are the same. Thus $\partial b'/\partial a > 0$, $\partial b_i/\partial c < 0$, $\partial b'/\partial k < 0$, with the same interpretations as earlier. Since $\partial b'/\partial h > 0$, on condition that $(a - c) > 0$, (which is always true), the transfer rate increases with h. The factor h can be thought of as a measure of the extent to which the expertise of the consultant is imparted to the advice seeker during the consultation. The deductions from the model, with a somewhat more general assumption about productivity gains from advice, remain the same.

2. We have assumed that no permanent learning takes place as a result of advice, that is, c is a constant. If one assumed that c is instead a function of t_a, the amount of time spent in consultation, a more complicated mathematical model would result. But, within the framework of our assumptions, it is possible to make deductions about the effects of an increase of c upon consultation (from whatever sources, including learning): $\partial b/\partial c < 0$, $\partial t_a/\partial c < 0$ (if $a > c(k + 1)$, a necessary condition for any exchange at all), and $\partial(\Delta s_i/\partial c < 0$. Consequently, as c increases, one predicts that the transfer rate decreases, consultation time decreases, and status differentiation in the pair decreases, until at some point inequality $a > c(k + 1)$ no longer holds, and no more consultation will occur.

3. It was assumed that k, the index of usefulness of advice, is a constant over all consulting interactions. If the advice *j* obtains varies in usefulness across consultations, k would be variable. In the model, k can be thought of as the expected value of the distribution of k. Over a large number of problems giving rise to consultation, k has an average value. If the usefulness of advice *j* obtains permanently changes such that the average value of k increases or decreases, it is possible to make predictions from the model by noting that $\partial b/\partial k < 0$, $\partial t_a/\partial k < 0$, and $\partial(\Delta s_i)/\partial k < 0$, as has already been made.

4. We have assumed that $s_i + s_j = s_i^o + s_j^o$ and thus also that $\Delta s_i = -\Delta s_j$. There is a fixed stock of status in the interaction pair. Status is relative, not absolute: *i*'s status is defined relative to *j*, and *j*'s relative to *i*. These are necessary assumptions for solving the model, for otherwise supply could not be equated to demand, and b would not be determinate. One might object that no concrete

good or service actually changes hands in a transfer of status (as money would if apples are purchased, or in a barter exchange, apples would for oranges). Since status is a relatively intangible attribute, $\Delta s_i = -\Delta s_j$ might be thought an unrealistic assumption. How can i ensure that j accords him just that much superior status? Can he not be misled into thinking that j holds him in higher regard than is actually true?

There are nonetheless visible and public signs of superior status in social interaction. Numerous small services (opening a door, fetching a cup of coffee, waiting rather than be waited upon, ...) and public acts of deference (not interrupting a higher-status speaker but putting up with his interruptions, making favorable comments to third parties, ...) are instances of these. A greater status gap is marked by more frequent and more important unilateral services and displays of deference. These advantages of status are routinely policed in daily interaction. Should j not confer on i the marks of superior status, i would soon notice and terminate his consulting relationship with j.

The model also makes use of the idea of an initial status endowment s_i^0 and s_j^0. How these initial status endowments are arrived at is left unspecified. They might be based on ranking in the bureaucratic hierarchy (e.g., civil service grade), a more diffuse societal status (e.g., amount and kind of education), or some combination of both. Initial status endowments are not important in setting the transfer rate b, since they enter expression 17 in symmetrical fashion. They are important for advice time t_a in eq. 24 and in eq. 25. If the initial status endowment difference is large, t_a is likely to be of short duration, or else no consulting is likely to take place at all.

Conclusion

Unlike a pure exchange model of social interaction, the inclusion of additional interaction partners and of additional variables into a model of the type developed here (a mixture of exchange and of production) cannot be done in routine fashion. With more than two group members, the utility function for status in the group obtained by means of bilateral exchanges may turn out to be more complex than a simple extrapolation from the two-actor model might suggest and so would, consequently, the demand and supply functions for status. If an additional variable has no fixed stock, or if it is produced rather than exchanged in the interaction, as sentiments of mutual attraction might well be, the model may have to be reformulated altogether. Extensions of the two-actor, two-variable model await future work. They will have to be undertaken if a rigorous theory of status differentiation and group cohesion is to be developed. The microeconomic approach that I have applied provides a promising start. It will require, however, creative ideas and novel departures, for the tools of microeconomic theory cannot be routinely applied to social processes by simply plugging sociological variables into existing formulae and equations.

I have applied a microeconomic model to a social interaction situation that results in differentiation in a group. Building on the work of Paul Lazarsfeld, I have also tried to extend it in two directions, one substantive and the other methodological. The situation analyzed consists of interdependent choices, and the technique used allows for deductive rather than inductive theorizing.

References

BLAU, PETER 1963 *The Dynamics of Bureaucracy*. Chicago: University of Chicago Press, 2nd ed.

BLAU, PETER 1964 *Exchange and Power in Social Life*. New York: Wiley.

HENDERSON, JAMES and RICHARD QUANDT 1971 *Microeconomic Theory*. New York: McGraw-Hill.

LAZARSFELD, PAUL and MORRIS ROSENBERG 1955 *The Language of Social Research*. Glencoe, Ill.: The Free Press.

14. VIGNETTE ANALYSIS: UNCOVERING THE NORMATIVE STRUCTURE OF COMPLEX JUDGMENTS

Peter H. Rossi

Introduction

Human existence may be viewed in part as threading one's way through a succession of choice points, most quite trivial, but some quite critical for the life experiences that depend on the alternatives chosen. Each such choice point involves making an implicit or explicit judgment about the relative desirability of the alternatives involved. The more trivial choice points, such as choosing which street to take on a journey to work, may be settled more or less "automatically" by evoking long-standing decisions. The more important choice points, such as whether to apply for another job, may involve considerable explicit weighing of the positive and negative factors of each alternative, attempting to arrive at a net balance that would clearly point in one direction or the other.

The judgments made at choice points are rarely made *de novo*. Such choices usually are aided by the existence of more or less fixed preference schedules among objects and actions belonging to more or less homogeneous classes. Thus, one may have a more or less fixed preference schedule for foods, for television programs, for work tasks, and so on, each preference schedule containing an ordering of objects or actions in terms of greater or lesser desirability, The origins of such preference schedules are through learning from others and from direct experience with alternatives. Nor are such schedules fixed forever; the ordering of items on a particular schedule may change over time and may shift as a set of choices actually made produces changes in the saliency of alternatives.

To some degree each individual within a society may be conceived of as having an idiosyncratic set of preference schedules; indeed this is the basis of the common observation that there are differences in taste. Yet, the features common to all preference schedules must be considerable, accounting in large part for the observed uniformities in market behavior, media listening and viewing ratings, and similar phenomena. Indeed, it is quite likely that interindividual differences are minor in comparison to interindividual consensuses in preference schedules. Hence, it is possible to discern an American schedule of food preferences or of standards of beauty, with individual Americans holding idiosyncratic preferences that may be regarded as variations on main themes.

According to this conception of human judgments, there exists a very large collective component to such judgments that consists of the evaluative principles that are shared collectively among the members of a society. Of course, this is another way of saying that important components of social systems are normative structures.

In any particular empirical choice situation, however, it is difficult to discern the normative or evaluative principles at work, as a particular choice situation may involve very complex alternatives, each containing several characteristics, each evoking different preference schedules. Thus, although a widespread consensus may favor meat over leafy vegetables as food, a particular set of dishes on a menu may involve choosing among varying mixtures of meats, vegetables, and other ingredients. Preference hierarchies at a particular moment may be affected by previous meals eaten recently, and so on. Similarly, two jobs offered may involve different salaries, working conditions, varying expectations about length of tenure, and hours. The complexities of actual choice situations makes it difficult to discern the general principles that underly the choice behaviors that ensue, since any particular choice outcome may in one case be sensitive to one preference schedule and in another sensitive to another preference schedule.

Vignette analysis, the technique to be described in this chapter, has been devised to help in the unraveling of choice behavior. The objective is to uncover the underlying collective preference schedules concerning some domain of objects or actions. The technique is applicable to certain types of judgments about complex alternatives about whose constituent characteristics some *a priori* knowledge is available. And it has proved useful in developing measures of the prestige standing of complex households, judgments about the punishment to be meted out to convicted offenders, decisions about the just wages to be given to incumbents of particular jobs, and similar problems.

Lazarsfeld's Contribution to Vignette Analysis

There is a very special reason for presenting this technique in a volume of papers offered in honor of Paul Lazarsfeld. The fact of the matter is that Paul Lazarsfeld provided me with the ideas that form the basic principles of the developed technique. When I told Paul two years ago that he had made this contribution, he did not remember the occasion. Of course, students take their professors' remarks more seriously than the professors often do and remember them better.

Lazarsfeld provided me with the basic idea of vignette analysis in the course of criticizing a draft of my dissertation, a writing that provided me with credentials and then fortunately slipped into the oblivion that it well deserved. My dissertation was a critique of measures of social status using the conceptual framework of latent structure analysis to assess the various procedures used in the then extant social stratification literature.

In the dissertation I discussed, among other approaches, August B. Hollingshead's solution to the problem of obtaining social status measures for high school students in Morris, Illinois.[1] His approach was to use a number of knowledgeable residents of Morris as judges who rated the social standing of each of the high school students' families. The average of such ratings given was then used to measure the social standings of each of the families rated. I wrote in the draft that I thought Hollingshead's approach to be ingenious but only applicable to communities small enough that enough knowledgeable residents could be found who were acquainted with most of the families in the town. Lazarsfeld's almost indecipherable marginal comments on this section suggested that the way to generalize Hollingshead's approach was to create "vignettes" describing fictitious families whose essential status characteristics (occupation, ethnicity, educational attainment, place of residence, etc.) would be described in thumbnail sketches. Such vignettes given to a representative sample of a large community would yield the principles underlying status judgments that could then be applied to real families that had similar characteristics. The vignettes, Lazarsfeld further suggested, should be constructed by systematically varying the combinations of characteristics so that an analysis could discern how such characteristics were combined to form an overall status judgment.

I incorporated Lazarsfeld's suggestion into my thesis and filed the idea away for future exploitation. It has taken a goodly number of years for that germ of an idea to develop into the technique that is to be described in this chapter. The lengthy gestation was partly a matter of having been distracted by other concerns but also partly because the technology did not exist in earlier years that makes the technique workable. Interestingly enough, another Lazarsfeld, Paul's son Robert, made a strong contribution to its development, having worked for me for a year as a computer programmer developing the program that makes the generation of vignettes a simple and manageable task.

An Outline of the Vignette Technique

The vignette technique as it eventually evolved is applicable to the study of any problem in which evaluations are to be made by persons concerning complicated objects. Since the technique was developed initially to study social status,

I will use that substantive area in this exposition of the technique. Later in this chapter I will indicate some of the other substantive areas to which the technique has been applied.

The presenting problem is how to measure the social status of households, the basic units of social stratification. As conventionally presented in the literature of social stratification,[2] the social status of a household is its evaluation in the eyes of other members of society. But households vary widely—in composition, in the occupations held by household members, in ethnic origins, and so on. A critical issue in social stratification research is the manner in which such diverse characteristics are taken into account by members of a society in making status judgments. For example, most conventional measures of household social status use some combination of the head of the household's occupational and educational attainment, but that procedure ignores the occupational and educational attainments of other persons in the household as well as other household characteristics that have been viewed in the social stratification literature as relevant.

The vignette solution to this problem is to obtain social status ratings on households that vary in composition and characteristics by analytically deriving the principles underlying the ways in which the raters arrive at overall status through combining the influences of the set of characteristics to be found in a household. The households being rated are described in short vignettes that are printed by computer on cards, a format that facilitates the rating task.

The critical feature of the vignette technique is that the vignettes are created by a computer program that randomly assigns values to each of the vignette characteristics; the end result is that the correlations among vignette characteristics are much lower than are those in the "real world," and they are often zero. In practice it is necessary to place some restrictions on the random association of vignette characteristics to eliminate absurd combinations, for example, physicians with less than college education or couples with children who are older than their parents.

Because the number of possible combinations of characteristics can rapidly mount to astronomical proportions, it is not possible to present a rater with all possible vignettes. Rather, the strategy is to present each respondent with a fair sample of that "universe" of all possible combinations, such samples having the same statistical properties of the "universe."

There are some very desirable features of the technique as described so far. First, because each characteristic is randomly associated (within limits of reasonableness) with every other characteristic, the multicollinearity of the "real" world is avoided. In the real world, occupational and educational attainment typically correlate around .6; in the vignette world, the correlation can be lowered to zero. Because the respondent is confronted with statistically infrequent combinations, one is forced to make judgments that are more indicative of the preference ordering held. Thus, in the vignette world, working wives hold down higher-status jobs than their husbands as frequently as husbands stand in the same position vis-à-vis their wives.

A second desirable characteristic is that it is possible to construct vignettes using relatively large lists of characteristics. Thus in the study we will describe households that consist of husbands and wives who are described in terms of six dimensions, a vignette taking on one value from each dimension, the total of *unique* vignettes capable of being generated from these lists being of the order of 100×10^6.

Finally, the results are capable of being analyzed by sophisticated multivariate techniques, in this case by multiple regression. The analysis yields a regression coefficient for each characteristic (and interaction terms among characteristics) that represents the "collective" principles used in combining vignette characteristics in arriving at social status judgments for households.

Vignette Analysis Applied to Household Social Status Ratings

The study to be described was based on a national sample of approximately 500 adults, each of whom were asked to rate on a nine-point scale the "social standing" of households described on a pack of 60 cards. Some of the vignettes described one-person households, some households consisted of husbands and wives only, other more complicated households consisted of married couples and their adult children, and there were a few cases of men and women living together who were not married. For the purposes of this illustration we will only consider those vignettes that described a husband and wife household.

Concerning each household, the vignettes contained the following information:

1. Husband's occupation: selected from among occupational titles for which NORC prestige scores were available. Including "unemployed" for 10 percent of the vignettes.

2. Wife's occupation: Selected from the same pool, and including "housewife" as an occupation for 25 percent of the vignettes.

3. Husband's educational attainment: In single years from seventh grade to college graduate.

4. Wife's educational attainment: Same as husband's.

5. Ethnicity: Selected from among ethnicities for which NORC prestige scores were available.

6. Housing occupied: Six descriptions ranging from renting an apartment to owning a detached home.

In addition to rating each vignette on a nine-point scale, respondents were asked a few background questions enabling a characterization of respondent socioeconomic status.

The 496 respondents each rated 40 vignettes for a total of 19,840 vignettes. Usable ratings were obtained on 19,702 vignettes out of the total that they were asked to respond to. Each rating was converted to VPRES, a linear transformation producing a number ranging from 0 to 100 a metric that is comparable to the standard NORC prestige scores. In addition, since we anticipated that respondents might vary one from the other in the range of ratings and the means they use, we standardized each respondent's score distribution by normalizing to a mean of zero and a standard deviation of one. The resulting score is shown as ZPRES in the tables that follow.

The analysis of the VPRES and ZPRES scores is fairly straightforward. Each of the scores for each of the vignettes is regressed on the characteristics of the vignettes, as shown in Table 1. The top panel of Table 1 contains the zero-order relationships among the vignette characteristics and the two transformed ratings VPRES and ZPRES. Note that the correlations among vignette characteristics are small,[3] indicating that the computer followed directions. The correlations involving the two transformed ratings, VPRES and ZPRES, however, are not artifacts of the design of vignettes but empirical findings.

The bottom panel of Table 1 displays the regression statistics for the analysis of the ratings. The left-hand columns show the regression coefficients for VPRES, and the right-hand columns show the corresponding coefficients for ZPRES. Since VPRES has a more substantive meaning, being calibrated in the same scale in which occupational prestige has been measured, the discussion will mainly center on the coefficients associated with VPRES. However, it should be noted that, when the differences among individuals in mean ratings and ratings variability (ZPRES formulation) are held constant, the total amount of variation explained by the vignette characteristics is enhanced. This indicates that there are tendencies among individuals to rate all vignettes higher or lower and to use a greater or smaller number of rating intervals.

A modest amount of variance in the ratings is explained by the vignette characteristics, .192 in the case of VPRES and .278 in the case of ZPRES. Part of the unexplained variance may be accounted for by "errors" in ratings made by the respondents, and part may be accounted for by the fact that in some vignettes a particular respondent may have fastened on one of the vignette characteristics as the main cue while in another vignette a different characteristic may have provided a guide. We are unable to distinguish between the two sources of unexplained variance except to note that the unexplained variance increases with the complexity of the vignettes. That is, when the number of characteristics in a vignette description is increased, the amount of variance explained tends to decline, suggesting that the more descriptive material is included in vignettes the more "error" is generated.

The regression coefficients indicate that respondents take into account all the descriptive statements presented to them in the vignettes in arriving at their assessments. However, the information is not weighted equally. Occupational attainment counts more heavily than any other characteristic, with educational attainment a close second. Furthermore, descriptive statements about husbands count more than corresponding information about wives. In general, these find-

TABLE 1. Regression of Vignette Social Standing Ratings on Vignette Characteristics

A. Zero-Order Correlations Among Vignette Characteristics and Ratings

	Husb. Ed.	Wife Ed.	Ethn.	Husb. Occ.	Wife Occ.	VPRES	ZPRES
Husb. educ.		-01	00	32	-01	24	30
Wife educ.			01	-03	31	17	20
Ethnicity				-01	00	05	06
Husb. occ.					-03	32	38
Wife occ.						20	24
VPRES							86

B. Regression Statistics

	VPRES			ZPRES		
	b	Beta	T	b	Beta	T
Husband's occ. (NORC score)	.451	.283	16.5	.021	.356	22.0
Wife's occ. (NORC score)	.359	.228	12.6	.017	.286	16.7
Wife by Husband's Occ. Interaction	-.001	-.043	1.9	-.000	-.076	-3.5
Husb. ed. (years)	1.248	.163	23.8	.059	.201	31.2
Wife ed. (years)	.912	.118	17.4	.041	.142	22.0
Ethn (NORC score)	.092	.048	7.4	.004	.057	9.4
Housewife dummy	3.090	.052	7.0	.112	0.50	7.1
Unempl. dummy	-11.300	-.067	-9.1	-.493	-.072	11.1
Housing type	.148	.072	11.2	-.006	0.83	13.7
Intercept	-3.195			-2.460		
R =	.438			.520		
R^2 =	.192			.278		
N =	19,510(a)			19,423(a)		

(a) Missing values lower the N.

ings scarcely constitute a surprise, although the details can hardly have been anticipated in advance.

Centering our attention on the coefficients associated with VPRES for each point of a husband's occupational prestige score, the household is given .45 points in household prestige, whereas the corresponding coefficient for wives' occupational prestige is .36, a weighting that accords to wives' achievement .8 that of husbands' achievements. A similar proportionality applies to educational attainment: each additional year of education attained by a husband provides 1.2 points in household prestige whereas the same contribution of a wife yields .9 points.

An interaction term for husband and wife occupation almost reaches statistical significance, indicating a slight tendency to discount the occupational attainment of a household when both husband and wife have high occupational attainment. Surprisingly (at least to us), there is a relatively slight contribution of household ethnicity to household prestige, less than that of housing type.

Two dummy variables have been entered into the analysis marking respectively the designation of wife as a "housewife" and husbands as "unemployed." All other things being equal, a family that has its female member described as a housewife is given a slight increment (3 points) in comparison to other households.[4] Husbands whose occupational description was that of "unemployed" contributed a large decrement to the household's prestige of 11.3 points.

The beta coefficients shown in Table 1 can be used to gauge the relative importance of the types of descriptive statements entered into the vignettes. However, the reader should bear in mind that, since the variances in descriptions are completely artifacts of the design, the betas are standardized to a constructed world in which the variables are distributed rectangularly rather than as they are in the empirical world.

The relatively low amounts of variance explained in the analyses of Table 1 suggests that there is considerable variation around the tendencies described by the coefficients displayed in Table 1. These collective tendencies cannot be considered as very strongly defined since there is so much in the way of variation in ratings that cannot be explained by the vignette descriptions. This leads rather naturally to the question of whether or not some of the variation can be captured by considering characteristics of the respondents. Perhaps respondents vary in their ratings in some systematic ways that can be interpreted as indicating substantial subgroup differences in underlying evaluative principles employed. For example, persons high in social status may rate households differently from low-status persons, perhaps accenting occupational achievements as against education.

To answer some of these questions, Table 2 contains the regressions of the ratings on selected respondent characteristics. Note that in the VPRES regression only a very small amount (.013) of variance is accounted for by respondent characteristics, whereas in the ZPRES regression the amount of variance explained is so small that it is essentially zero. The differences between the

**TABLE 2. Regression of Vignette Social Standing Ratings
on Respondent Characteristics**

Respondent Characteristics	VPRES			ZPRES		
	b	*Beta*	*T*	*b*	*Beta*	*T*
Sex (M = 1, F = 2)	−.739	−.014	−1.84	−.006	−.003	−.41
Race (NW = 1, W = 0)	3.933	.051	3.67	−.020	−.007	−.49
Age (years)	−.048	−.030	−3.68	.000	.008	.98
Education (years)	−.324	−.037	−3.61	−.001	−.004	−.40
Income (000)	.117	.029	3.30	−.000	−.000	−.01
Household prestige score (a)	−.084	−.049	4.60	.000	.001	.07
Intercept	58.500			.034		
R =	.113			.015		
R² =	.013 F = 30.4			.000 F = .546		
N =	16,541			16,541		

(a) Household prestige score computed using weights derived from this study and applied to relevant characteristics of household members.

VPRES and ZPRES regressions indicate that respondents differ mainly in the scaling factors that they apply to their ratings. Some respondents tend to rate all vignettes higher (or lower) than other respondents, and some put more variation into their ratings than others. Specifically, blacks are more likely to rate the vignettes higher than whites, and older persons tend to rate lower, along with the better educated and those of higher socioeconomic status. In short, the systematic variation that can be captured by these respondent characteristics is so small that we can consider the regression statistics of Table 1 to mirror fairly well the underlying rating principles employed by Americans as they assess the social status of households about which they are presented a limited amount of information.

Other Applications of the Vignette Technique

The vignette technique can be usefully applied to other substantive areas going considerably beyond the study of social status alone. The general class of problems to which the technique is applicable is comprised of issues involving understanding the principles underlying judgments of complex circumstances. It is especially appropriate where the judgments involved are those made with comparative frequency. The applications listed as follows exemplify those characteristics.

A very natural extension of the study of household social status was to the issue of distributive justice income.[5] To household vignettes we randomly attached a set of earnings, and respondents were asked whether the persons portrayed in the vignettes were fairly paid, overpaid, or underpaid. The subsequent analysis provides an understanding of certain basic issues in the theory of distributive justice. For example, is a person's earnings justified more by his needs than by his accomplishments? Are two earners in a family viewed as being entitled to have a combined income that is the sum of what they would be entitled to as single earners? Is equal pay for equal work a principle of judgment or equity, or should the pay accorded to blacks or women be scaled down?

A second application has been to the field of criminal justice. To gauge the receptivity of public officials to reform of state corrections system involving the use of community facilities—halfway houses, part-time incarceration, and the like—we constructed vignettes describing hypothetical convicted offenders whose criminal offense, age, and previous record were systematically varied.[6] Public officials ranging from governors to members of the bar were asked to judge what would be the appropriate sentence for each of the convicted offenders depicted in the vignettes. Analyses centered on whether certain groups of elites used different judgment principles than others, for example, was the sentencing behavior of criminal court judges different from that of prison officials or leading members of the bar?

A closely related application has been to the definition of child abuse, an area in which legislation and practice is not very clearly defined. Vignettes were constructed depicting an act that was possibly abusive to a child, a description of the victim in terms of age and sex, a description of alleged abuser in terms of relationship to the victim, and a short description of the outcome of the abusive act. The vignettes were given to a sample of adults in the Los Angeles metropolitan area,[7] who were asked to rate the "seriousness" of the events depicted in the vignettes. The analyses yielded seriousness scores for potentially abusive acts and the extent to which the seriousness of acts was modified by characteristics of the victim and characteristics of the perpetrator.

A final example may suffice: Lenore Weitzman has been employing the technique in her study of the no-fault divorce law in California. Family court judges and family law counselors were given sets of vignettes that depicted hypothetical couples coming before the family court. Each vignette described the couple in demographic and socioeconomic terms, and the respondents were asked to judge how child custody awards and property settlements would be made in such cases. The analyses will center on whether judges and lawyers still use a criterion of fault in allocating child custody and in the division of common property.

Unresolved Issues

It has been a long time since Lazarsfeld scribbled his comments on the margins of the draft of my dissertation. And it will be some time before the vignette technique becomes entrenched as a common tool in social research. Although the technique has been demonstrated to be workable in that vignettes can be produced and respondents can react apparently sensibly to them, it is not at all clear whether the results have any validity. All that has been demonstrated so far is that the ratings of respondents are lawful: We cannot yet tell whether their ratings resemble closely the judgments that would be made when presented with concrete instances in which they would have to make similar judgments. Other unresolved issues include certain arcane statistical problems related to the use of vignettes as the unit of analysis with some degree of autocorrelation among the vignettes rated by particular individuals.

If these issues can be solved satisfactorily, the vignette technique will become, it is hoped, a part of standard repertory for social researchers. It would also represent another Lazarsfeld contribution to the repertory.

Notes

1. August B. Hollingshead, *Elmtown's Youth*. New York: Wiley, 1949.

2. See, for example, Bernard Barber, *Social Stratification*. New York: Harcourt Brace, 1957.

3. Restricting professional occupations (e.g., physician, lawyer, etc.) to college graduates produced the relatively high correlations (.3) between occupation and education.

4. Actually we coded housewife as having an occupational prestige score of 26.9, a number arrived at through research on prestige scores for largely female occupations (see Christine A. Bose, *Jobs and Gender: Sex and Occupational Prestige*. Center for Metropolitan Planning and Research, Baltimore: Johns Hopkins, 1973).

5. Wayne Alves and Peter H. Rossi, "Who Should Get What? Fairness Judgments of the Distribution of Earnings," *American Journal of Sociology*, 84, 3 (November 1978), 541–565.

6. Richard Berk and Peter Rossi, *Prison Reform and State Elites*. Cambridge, Mass.: Ballinger, 1977.

7. Karen Garrett and Peter H. Rossi, "Judging the Seriousness of Child Abuse," *Medical Anthropology*, 2, 1 (Winter 1978), 1–48.

PART 3

QUALITATIVE METHODS AND REASONING

15. MARX'S GENERAL AND MIDDLE-RANGE THEORIES OF SOCIAL CONFLICT

Lee Benson

Why study human behavior?[1] According to Karl Marx, to change the world. More precisely, to change the world into a better world. Still more precisely, to develop theories useful to human beings struggling to create a better world—a world in which human beings realize their innate need and capacity to live in cooperative harmony with each other and with Nature and to function as free, creative, self-actualizing, communal, social individuals.[2]

That goal inspired Marx's lifelong work. As he conceived it, the fruitful study of human behavior required development of a unified, historical, social science. There could be "only one [social] science, the science of history . . . the real, positive science . . . of the practical activity, of the practical processes of development of men."[3] His "real, positive science," however, was a *critical* historical social science that effectively integrated normative and empirical theory.[4] To what extent did Marx develop such a science? That question, I believe, is *the* question around which we should systematically organize the enterprise of social science—if we aim to practice Francis Bacon's profession, the advancement of learning for "the relief of man's estate."

When we make the validity of Marx's theories the central problem of social science, do we stack the deck in their favor? Not at all. If his theories are false, a large-scale systematic program to assess and revise them would demonstrate that to be the case more convincingly than, for example, Daniel Bell succeeds in doing in his writings on "the end of ideology," and "the coming of postindustrial society."

Indisputably, Marx ranks as the most influential social theorist of all time. The validity of his theories has functioned, therefore, as *something like* the central problem of twentieth-century social science. But on all sides, the "great debate" on Marx has strongly tended to be more ideologic than scientific. (Unless noted otherwise, *Marx* stands for the collaborative team of Marx and

189

Engels.) That is a large claim. For the sake of this essay's argument, let us assume it to be warranted. What, then, is to be done to reduce the role of ideology in the scholarly assessment of Marx's theories? That is a hard problem for which this essay provides no master solution. But it does suggest a procedure to reorient the debate so that it focuses more on Marx and less on Marxologists.

Marx understandably did not present his ideas as a body of clear, internally consistent theories. Generations of specialized scholars continue to produce conflicting interpretations of "what Marx really said." The conclusion seems reasonable, therefore, that we cannot expect to show one interpretation of a text (or set of texts) to be the only possible *true* interpretation. If that conclusion is granted, it then seems advisable to concentrate scholarly energies on assessing Marx's theories rather than (endlessly) redescribing or criticizing them. Specify a class of behavior. Then specify the theories about it that might reasonably be attributed to Marx. Finally, we can proceed to assess the probable validity of each of those theories and abandon, or revise, or replace the ones we regard as invalid.

This procedure is more easily outlined than carried out.[5] But our ability to carry it out would be increased, I believe, if we follow Robert Merton's lead and systematically distinguish between Marx's general and middle-range theories.[6] Guided by Merton's distinction between levels of theory, a collaborative group of scholars might be able to codify the multiplicity of brilliant, but contradictory, ideas scattered throughout Marx's writings into a unified, multi-leveled, general theory of social conflict and human behavior.

Having outlined a procedure to assess Marx's theories, I try to carry it out—to a limited extent. Thus, rather than present a range of possible interpretations, I restrict attention to what is taken to be Marx's *valid* general theory of social conflict and *invalid* middle-range theory of social conflict in the capitalist epoch. Put another way, this essay aims to strengthen the credibility of Marx's general theory by showing that it logically requires a middle-range *reference-group* theory of conflict in the capitalist epoch rather than a *social-class* theory of conflict.

Marx's General Theory of Social Conflict

Marx's general theory of social conflict represents one of what Merton characterizes as "all-inclusive systematic efforts to develop a unified theory that will explain all the observed uniformities of social behavior, social organization and social change."[7] We can describe Marx's general theory of social conflict as a general theory of human behavior, past, present and future.

Critics caricature Marxism, I believe, when they describe it as a general theory of capitalism and its transcendence by socialism. That is a special theory of Marxism, that is the subject of Marxism on the middle-range level of theory. On the level of general theory, in the sense that Darwinism is a general theory of biological evolution, Marxism is an all-inclusive theory of societal evolution, or the worldwide historical functioning, development, and transformation of human societies. (We speak of "societies" for brevity's sake; it is human beings, not societies, that evolve.)

Just as Darwinism invokes natural "forces" of *chance variation* and *natural selection* to explain biological evolution, Marxism invokes human "forces" of *induced variation* and *conscious selection* to explain societal evolution. It is a general theory of the origin, evolution, and eventual abolition of social conflict as the motor, the driving force of human social development in successive historical epochs from primitive communism to advanced communism. At its highest level of generality, Marxism is a theory of the historical processes that function to narrow the gap between the human potential generated by biological evolution and the human reality generated by societal evolution.

Marx's theories of the cosmos and of human nature led him to develop a general theory of human behavior that differs radically from all theories that postulate the inevitability of social conflict. Such theories, Marx argued, are best understood as ideologies developed to *justify* stratified societies of various types. Social conflict is not inflicted on men by some (illusory) supernatural entity, not mandated by Nature, and not immutably rooted in human nature by some biological trait. To replace such ideological explanations and justifications of conflict, Marx asserted a basic theoretical proposition: Irrespective of the level of material production and technological and institutional development, in any society *unequal access to the basic resources needed to sustain life invariably creates a culture that engenders significant social conflict of some type.* (Unequal access is, of course, a complex concept. It refers to economic phenomena that derive from different types of inegalitarian control of resources, for example, ownership, authority, force. As types of inegalitarian control differ, so types of conflict differ. And inegalitarian societies with similar modes of production may differ significantly in their magnitude and type(s) of social conflict depending upon, among other things, their political systems.)

According to Marx, men *invented* and developed social conflict while actively pursuing their ends. On a societal level, they had found that unequal access to the basic resources needed to sustain life aided them in their daily conflict with Nature. On balance, social inequality, in its myriad forms and consequences, functioned to increase men's society-wide capacity to produce their means of subsistence. When each society (or interacting cluster of societies) is viewed as a separate entity, the interactive processes that historically link inequality, increased productive capacity, and social conflict are neither universal nor unilinear. Societal evolution (like biological evolution) shows dead-ends and regressions. Suppose, however, that we view all societies as components of an increasingly interactive, extraordinarily complex, worldwide system, particularly after the breakthrough to capitalism had been achieved. Then, Marx theorized and predicted, the interactive processes among inequality, increased productive capacity, and social conflict would continue to accelerate until men achieved a highly advanced mode of production. Having achieved that mode of production, after millennia of struggle against Nature and each other, men then will be able, and impelled, to abolish social conflict—both intrasocietal and inter-societal.

Marx's general theory is truly general. It comprehends both the existence and nonexistence of social conflict, and it elegantly explains its origin, development, and eventual abolition. Apart from his theory's influence on the course of history, is there reason to think it valid? Yes. In a desperately compressed essay, however, I cannot try to show what I believe to be the case—that the historical record strongly supports Marx's general theory of social conflict. Instead, I try to do two things: (1) to show that Marx greatly weakened the credibility of his general theory by illegitimately deriving from it an invalid social-class theory of conflict in the capitalist epoch and (2) to suggest how we might replace the middle-range theory by a more credible Marxian-Tocquevillian reference-group theory that both logically derives from, and supports, Marx's general theory of social conflict and human behavior.

Disentangling the General Theory and Middle-Range Theories

As I read Marx, his basic concept is mode of production, not social class. He asserted a mode-of-production general theory of social conflict and human behavior rather than a social-class general theory. In support of this reading of Marx, consider Engels's famous eulogy:[8]

> It was precisely Marx who had first discovered the great law of motion of history, the law according to which all historical struggles, whether they proceed in the political, religious, philosophical or some other ideological domain, are in fact only the more or less clear expression of struggles of social classes, and that the existence and thereby the collisions, too, between these classes *are in turn conditioned by the degree of development of their economic position, by the mode of their production and of their exchange determined by it* [emphasis added]. This law . . . has the same significance for history as the law of the tranformation of energy has for natural science. . . .

Marx's historical orientation required him to confront an immensely difficult problem: What criterion could be used to order the entire history of humanity (subdivided into "real" societies) that was parsimonious, logically consistent, empirically operational, and theoretically fruitful? His solution was to divide human history into successive epochs, differentiated by one universal variable, the dominant mode of production in the societies that constituted the world of humanity.

Marx's mode-of-production general theory logically led him to insist that apparently similar phenomena actually differ significantly when they occur in different historical epochs (and in societies with different historical configurations of modes of production).[9] His general theory thus required him to derive significantly different middle-range theories of social conflict for different epochs. Not to do so is to be unhistorical and, therefore, in the most basic sense, *un-Marxian*. Yet that is precisely what he failed to do.

Marx assumed, for example, that proletarian-capitalist struggles in the capitalist epoch would not significantly differ from capitalist-feudal lord struggles in the feudal epoch. That assumption can easily be shown to contradict historical reality. Does that finding invalidate Marx's general theory? Not at all. That is just what we should expect to find when we legitimately use Marx's general theory to reconstruct and explain social conflict in epochs dominated by such different modes of production as manorial feudalism and industrial capitalism. Paradoxically, therefore, when we show the errors in Marx's social class theory of conflict in the capitalist epoch, we strengthen the credibility of his mode-of-production general theory of social conflict. Less paradoxically, I shall argue, Marx did not logically derive his theory of social conflict in the capitalist epoch from his general theory.

Nonsocial Groups and Social Groups

This critique of Marx's middle-range theory requires us to develop an *abstract* typology of social groups that can be used to classify *concrete* groups, that is, groups of people who share some distinctive attribute or set of attributes (e.g., demographic, ecological, political). To begin with, I restrict the term *group* to relatively large aggregates of individuals (several hundred or more). I also define the terms *group* and *social group* to mean different things. The more inclusive term *group* can be dichotomized into *nonsocial group* and *social group*.

Etymologically, *social* refers to the *quality of relationships* among individuals grouped together. The members of any *social* group, identified by a specified attribute or set of attributes, have *some significant* degree of association, or alliance, or sociability, or communality—relational qualities lacking among the individuals said to constitute a nonsocial group.

Unless we assume what we must demonstrate, no specified attribute intrinsically identifies the individuals who possess it as members of a social group, except for attributes such as membership in an *organized* group, for example, a religious denomination. Mere existence is not consciousness. To claim that a specified social group exists, therefore, we must do more than show that a number of individuals possess some common attribute (or set of attributes). We must also show that the common attribute is possessed by individuals who, in one way or another, consider themselves to be positively related.

We can carry the argument further. A good theory of social conflict requires us to do more than distinguish between nonsocial groups and social groups; we must be able to distinguish among social groups that vary significantly in their degree of communality. A typology, in ascending order of communality, distinguishes three *abstract* types of social group: (1) interest or associational group, (2) quasi-communal or limited-communal group, and (3) communal group.

Contemporary examples help make the distinctions clear. Members of the National Association of Manufacturers and of the American Historical Association are members of interest groups; Hutterites, Amish, Hasidic Jews, and Mormons are members of communal groups. In stark outline, I sketch an abstract typology of groups ordered from least to greatest potentiality for becoming communal:[10]

Typology of (Large) Groups

1. Nonsocial group
    1.1. Statistical aggregate
    1.2. Demographic or ecological group
    1.3. Categorical group
2. Social group
    2.1. Interest or associational group
    2.2. Quasi-communal or limited-communal group
    2.3. Communal group

Economic-Interest Group, Social Class, Cultural Group

Marx conceived *social class* to comprehend both subjective and objective components. By definition, social classes in capitalist societies had to be based on a combination of objective economic attributes (e.g., kind and amount of property, occupation, income). But, if shared objective economic attributes were not accompanied by subjective consciousness, according to Marx, individuals did not function as members of a social class. In my terms, they then functioned as members of a nonsocial demographic or categorical group that could become a social class. Put another way, Marx tried to develop a theory of capitalist society that predicted and explained the evolution of demographic and categorical groups into social groups, at first, of the interest-group type, then ascending the scale of communality to full-fledged communal groups, that is, social classes.

Marx emphasized the radical differences between economic-interest groups and social classes. For example, he theorized that capitalism must increasingly produce proletarians, that is, industrial factory workers, who, despite their own inclinations, would first be forced to form an economic interest-group and then would go on to develop, more voluntarily as it were, increasingly higher levels of class consciousness. ("Marxists" who inflate the term *proletarian* to encompass all poor, propertyless individuals or all wage earners thereby dissolve Marxism either into atheoretical, sentimental populism or useless formalism.) To support the argument that it was un-Marxian of Marx to predict the formation of a communal proletarian social class, I shall argue that capitalism inevitably produces multicultural societies, greatly magnifies the scope and intensity of cultural group conflicts, and thus fragments rather than unifies "the proletariat."

As defined by Marx, social classes are based on economic attributes. As defined here, *cultural groups* are based on one or more of four related kinds of attributes: (1) ethnic ("race" is treated as an inclusive form of ethnicity—so inclusive as to have limited utility), (2) linguistic, (3) religious, and (4) territorial. As the term cultural group suggests, members of a concrete social group based on one or more of those four kinds of attributes share a distinctive cultural system, that is, a belief system that significantly differs from the belief systems of all other social groups. At the least, members of a cultural group share some significant degree of consciousness of kind based upon the *previous* existence of a distinctive cultural system (e.g., contemporary white Southerners in the United States).

Multicultural Society, Archetypal Society

For my purposes, the concept *multicultural society* is restricted to complex societies whose population includes two or more large-scale cultural groups. Large-scale refers to numerical size and simply connotes a significant percentage of the total population.

Multicultural societies differ in obvious respects. It is therefore necessary to develop a typology of multicultural societies (including, of course, the negative type, i.e., culturally homogeneous society),[11] but I here note only that multicultural societies existed before the capitalist epoch. Before capitalist expansion created a world market and unprecedented patterns of migration, multicultural societies primarily took the form of an imperial center governing conquered societies that maintained their distinctive cultures. In the capitalist epoch, multiculturalism became increasingly characteristic of almost all societies, among other reasons, because of more or less individual migration (voluntary or forced) or some combination of conquest and migration, religious cleavages and uneven regional economic development. Marx therefore erred badly when he chose France as the archetypal society to develop his theory of social conflict in the capitalist epoch, more precisely, when the Hegelian strain in his thinking led him to combine France and England to create an ideal-type society for analysis.

Tocqueville treated America, not France or England, as the archetypal society to test and develop a theory of social conflict in the capitalist epoch. In doing so, he was more Marxian than Marx. Two quotations from Engels's letters illustrate the basic point. Written in 1886 and 1890, they constitute variations on a theme he increasingly emphasized. To specify that theme succinctly, I have spliced the quotations together:[12]

. . . America after all is the ideal of all bourgeois: a country rich, vast, expanding, with purely bourgeois institutions unleavened by feudal remnants of
[or?] monarchical traditions, and without a permanent and hereditary proletariat . . . America is so purely bourgeois, has no feudal past at all and is
therefore proud of its purely bourgeois organization. . . .

America is the archetypal capitalist society in two senses. First, as Engels saw,
despite capitalist plantation slavery in the South, its history is the history of the
capitalist society least encumbered by "passive survival of antiquated modes of
production" (Marx's methodological criterion). Second, given the nature of the
capitalist mode of production, as societies became increasingly capitalist after
1500, they became increasingly multicultural. American history exemplifies that
process in its clearest form; it is the development of a multicultural society *à la
mode capitaliste*, that is, by essentially individualistic migration (voluntary and
forced) of members of different cultural groups from economically troubled
areas to rapidly developing capitalist areas. (That capitalist process, of course,
can now be increasingly observed in Western Europe, with results increasingly
analogous to those exemplified by American history.)

What happens when we see the significance of what Marx's economic determinist blinders kept him from seeing: that the normal operations of capitalism
strongly tend to produce multiculturalism? *We then see that American history
serves as the strategic natural experiment to develop and test conflicting middle-
range theories of social conflict in capitalist societies in the capitalist epoch.*
(Russia and India might serve as archetypal semicapitalist and colonial societies
in the capitalist epoch. Space considerations prevent discussion here of the
methodological advantages and disadvantages of archetypal case studies as
against comparative case studies. Given vast resources and a truly integrated
team of area specialists, comparative historical studies undoubtedly are preferable to archetypal historical studies. But to my knowledge, those two conditions
have never been satisfied. Until they can be satisfied, at least on pragmatic
grounds, the archetypal case study seems the preferable research strategy.)

Reference Groups

Marx's and Engels's middle-range theory of social conflict in the capitalist
epoch forced them to develop an underdeveloped form of the reference-group
concept. They did not use that term, of course; Herbert Hyman coined it in
1942. Much more significantly, until Engels finally broke free of the fetters of
economic determinism in 1893, they conceived of membership reference groups
in single-attribute rather than multiple-attribute terms. And unlike modern
theorists, they devoted little attention to nonmembership reference groups.

The core idea around which the reference-group concept has developed
informs Marx's most sweeping proposition: "It is not the consciousness of men

that determines their existence, but, on the contrary, their social existence determines their consciousness."[13] By *consciousness*, Marx referred to two radically different things, best suggested by posing two questions: Which social groups do men identify with (positively and negatively)? What are the belief systems and behavior patterns of the social groups that men identify with positively and negatively and, as a result of that identification, develop the belief systems and behavior patterns characteristic of members of specified groups?

As I have suggested in a previous essay, what might be called Marx's "Hegelian materialism" induced him to conceive social existence in narrowly economic determinist fashion and to reduce the complex relationships between social existence and consciousness to a one-sided process of reflection. (During the 1890s, I will show in another essay, Engels struggled to exorcize the Hegelian component from the Marxist theory of consciousness.) Marx unwarrantedly assumed that only economic attributes could function as the *real* basis of social groups that served their members as reference groups, that is, that "determine their consciousness." And he made another unwarranted assumption. As I have noted, he assumed that "men can [truly] orient themselves only negatively to members of other social classes [than the one to which they were eligible to belong]."[14]

Modern reference-group theory, I believe, primarily derives from and is heavily indebted to Marx's efforts to show that "social existence determines consciousness." But it has advanced much beyond him. For present purposes, I need only note that one version of reference-group theory has clarified and extended the concept so that it is no longer fettered by Marx's economic determinist assumptions.[15]

In that conception of reference groups, economic *and* noneconomic attributes can function as significant, real bases of social groups from which human beings derive both their positive and negative orientations. Consciousness may also be significantly influenced by *positive* identification with social groups to which individuals do *not* belong. Thus extended, the reference-group concept helps us see that, in complex multicultural capitalist societies, individuals are highly likely to have multiple identities that may significantly influence their consciousness. Once we see that, we can work to transcend Marx's social class theory of confict and develop a Marxian-Tocquevillian reference group theory of conflict in the capitalist epoch.

Conflicting Middle-Range Theories of Social Conflict

During the summer of 1843, while struggling to find a solution to the problem of human emancipation, Marx converted himself from radical democracy to communism. His conversion owed much to intensive reading in political theory and history (particularly the history of the French Revolution).[16]

Marx's central problem (like Tocqueville's) had preoccupied Rousseau and Hegel. In modern society, a radical dualism developed between men's functioning economically as atomistic egoists and politically as public-spirited members of the commonwealth. How could the resultant severe strains be overcome?

Hegel answered, dialectically. The strains produced by the dualism between man as *homme* and as *citoyen* could be overcome by the modern state. However, for the state to do that required, among other things, a "professional bureaucracy whose exclusive assigned mission is to look after the 'universal interests of the community,' hence a 'universal class'."[17]

In an essay entitled "Contribution to the Critique of Hegel's Philosophy of Right," Marx accepted Hegel's general dualistic mode of thought but rejected his particular solution. To overcome the severe strains in modern society did require a "universal class." Contrary to Hegel, however, the state could not impartially stand over exploiter and exploited. The truly universal class was the proletariat—the universal class whose sufferings would force it to redeem suffering humanity, unite men in a true commonwealth, and thereby achieve real rather than partial human emancipation.[18]

Marx completed that first proletarian "manifesto" in January, 1844. Its nuances need not concern us. What requires comment is this: When Marx first predicted the coming of the proletarian revolution, he argued from Hegelian dualistic, "dialectical" premises, not from a complex mode-of-production theory of social conflict in the capitalist epoch. That theory was not developed by Marx and Engels until 1845–1846 (in *The German Ideology*), *after* Marx had tried to turn Hegel "upside-down" in order to substitute the Proletariat for the Prussian Bureaucracy as the Universal Class.

To create a mythic theory about how the proletariat functions in capitalist society, Marx forced himself to disregard (among other things) the radical differences between feudalism and capitalism. For example, he knew that Tocqueville had emphasized the key role legal distinctions play in the formation and cohesion of social groups (e.g., legal equality dissolves social groups based on economic inequalities). But, in an essay written in late 1843 ("On the Jewish Question") that cites Tocqueville's *Democracy in America*, Marx argued, in effect, that Tocqueville failed to understand that differences in "private property, education, occupation" produced social-class divisions in societies characterized by equality of legal condition. Contrary to Tocqueville, he argued that equality of legal condition does not inhibit development of class distinctions based on inequalities of material condition.[19]

When Marx presented that argument, he had not yet developed his general theory of social conflict based on the mode of production concept and appears to have read little, if anything, "on capitalism or political economy...."[20] But that general theory and concept helps us see that Marx's argument was fallacious precisely because it ignored the *radical differences* between capitalist and precapitalist inegalitarian modes of production.

To maintain the Hegelian-inspired notion that the proletariat would function as the *universal class*, Marx ignored the fact that the concept, class, when applied to human beings in society, rested on property distinctions established by law. It was an "un-Marxian" error of staggering proportions to imagine that once legal distinctions which simultaneously grouped and stratified men were abolished, classes would function in capitalist societies as they had in legally stratified precapitalist societies. Tocqueville knew better. But, intoxicated by the French Revolution and conditioned by Hegelian idealism, in the two essays of 1843-1844 cited previously, Marx casually dismissed legal status as a significant determinant of class cohesion and conflict. That dismissal permitted him to greatly exaggerate economic exploitation as the *source* of consciousness and the cement of *class* cohesion. Thus he created a mythic proletariat that would become a revolutionary cohesive social class with the development of industrial capitalism, as he thought that the French bourgeoisie had become with the development of commercial capitalism. Having created that mythic proletariat as the agent of human emancipation, he never could free himself from his own creation. I say that not to condemn Marx but to understand him.

Bourgeoisie Under Feudalism, Workers Under Capitalism

In 1845, Marx and Engels published *The Holy Family*, a lengthy work in which their paid their severe disrespects to young Hegelian former comrades-in-arms. Anti-Hegelian in its proclamation of the coming proletarian triumph, it was thoroughly Hegelian in its *a priori* anti-empirical spirit, astonishing claims to omniscience, and distorted perceptions of empirical reality.[21]

Among other misperceptions, Marx and Engels deluded themselves about the degree of class consciousness attained by the English and French workers in 1845—a recurrent delusion that afflicted them throughout their lives. To understand rather than merely deplore that delusion, we must note that Marx and Engels badly underestimated the extent to which class consciousness would be inhibited by the dependence of the modern capitalist mode of production upon legally free and physically mobile workers. Legal freedom, physical mobility, the occupational differentiation and mobility inevitable in rapidly expanding capitalist economies, these and numerous other conditions worked powerfully against the development of proletarian class consciousness. And the absence of proletarian class consciousness, of course, also worked powerfully against *capitalist* class consciousness, that is, class consciousness based not on hereditary differences in legal status, but on differences in property, sources of income, or occupation.

Marx and Engels also badly underestimated the consequences of other phenomena inherent in capitalism: (1) The legal equality required for the full development of capitalism made it a radically different mode of production from any other inegalitarian mode of production; *when not crystallized in hereditary legal status, economic exploitation* was insufficient to produce class consciousness; (2) capitalist societies become multicultural societies; (3) in multicultural capitalist societies, the antagonistic overall culture produced by antagonistic relationships among human beings engaged in the production of their means of subsistence induces them to try to find material security, a sense of personal worthiness, and communality in antagonistic cultural groups rather than in antagonistic social classes.

Because the Hegelian strain in their thought hindered them from seeing the consequences of those (and other relevant) phenomena, Marx and Engels dogmatically clung to the mechanistic formula that the workers under capitalism would become class conscious in more or less the same way that the burghers had become class conscious under feudalism.[22] That formula increasingly diverged from reality. But they continued to cling to it. Their Hegelianism convinced them that they could penetrate beneath outward appearances to see "what the proletariat is" and to predict "what it consequently is historically compelled to do." Self-deluded by that Hegelian conviction, on the eve of the outburst of nationalism that manifested itself during the Revolutions of 1848, they misperceived reality and saw a world in which:[23]

> National difference and antagonisms between peoples are vanishing daily more and more owing to the development of the bourgeoisie, to freedom of commerce, to the world market, to uniformity in the mode of production and in the conditions of life corresponding thereto.

Had Marx and Engels not been so fixated on the Hegelian dialectic that forced them to construct, in their imagination, a revolutionary universal class out of the heterogeneous mass of workers produced by capitalist development, they might have seen that the capitalist mode of production inevitably produced multiculturalism. Stripped of German Hegelianism, French bourgeois class-struggle ideology, and English Smithian-Ricardian economic determinism, Marx's mode-of-production general theory of social conflict could have led him in 1848 to make a valid claim of this sort:

> National differences and antagonisms between peoples are *simultaneously increasing* and *decreasing daily* more and more owing to the development of the bourgeoisie, to freedom of commerce, to the world market, to uniformity in the mode of production and in the conditions of life corresponding thereto.

The Irish Question and "False Consciousness"

For some time after the Revolutions of 1848 collapsed, Marx clung to the delusion that his social-class theory of social conflict was correct. As each economic downturn approached, his hopes soared—only to plummet again as the crisis came and went without the occurrence of anything that resembled the predicted revolution. With the benefit of hindsight, we can now easily see what Marx failed to see, namely, that economic attributes, in rapidly expanding capitalist societies, are at best more likely to function as the bases of a large number of competing economic interest groups than as the bases of two (or three) increasingly communal classes. As later Marxists came to recognize, most notably Lenin, trade unions strongly tend to produce "economism," not revolutionary proletarian consciousness. Contrary to Marx's simplistic theory and wishful thinking, trade unions actually work against the development of a communal proletarian social class.[24]

History has "taught" that lesson to Marxists. But it has taken a heap of history for them to learn it. As late as the mid-1860s, Marx had not yet learned it. He recognized, however, that some changes had to be made in his social-class theory of conflict in the capitalist epoch. His first significant modification was Hegelian in form and content. Although simplistic and shallow, it represented considerable progress from his contemptuous dismissal in 1848 of such "vanishing" cultural attributes as ethnicity, nationality, and religion.

During the mid-1860s, England was by far the most industrially developed country in the world. To quote Marx, it was "the most important country for the workers' revolution, and moreover the *only* country in which the material conditions for this revolution have developed up to a certain degree of maturity."[25] England satisfied his conditions for the existence of a revolutionary proletarian social class. But the class did not exist. Simple things like that cause problems for theorists. Rather than revise his class struggle theory, Marx tried to save it by invoking the Hegelian theory of "false consciousness." (He did not actually use that term, of course; it subsequently came to be used, however, for the theory that he did invoke.)

As emphasized above, the intellectual debris that Marx carried over from Hegelianism included the Messianic notion of the master theorist who knew better than real-life actors why they did what they did and what they would have to do, whatever their conscious ideas and intentions. Why didn't English workers do what History required them to do? Because they permitted themselves to be deceived about their *real* identity, Marx answered.

English workers consciously thought of themselves as Englishmen rather than as workers. More precisely, they thought of themselves as English Protestants whose main enemies were Irish Catholics, particularly the Irish Catholic workers who constituted a growing proportion of the "English" labor force. Having hit upon that explanation in 1869–1870 for the failure of his theory to manifest itself in reality, Marx, understandably enough, became convinced that the "Irish Question" was the most important question facing the communist movement. It had to be solved, Irish liberation had to be won, before the English workers could play their historical role, that is, create a communal proletarian class and begin the international revolution.[26]

The argument can be reformulated in more general terms. History had falsified the predictions that Marx made during the 1840s. Trying to save his class-struggle theory, he acknowledged that individuals in multicultural capitalist societies had multiple attributes that could "determine" their consciousness—multiple attributes around which social groups might form and function as reference groups for their members' consciousness and behavior. But only one *real* type of attribute existed, Marx assumed, economic attributes. A more arbitrary, dogmatic, and illogical assumption is hard to imagine. By the mid-1860s, however, to save his class-struggle theory, Marx had to imagine it.

Once the false-consciousness assumption was granted, the rest was easy. The English ruling classes, precisely because they were the *ruling* classes, controlled "the means of mental production." Controlling the means of mental production, and fully conscious of their class interests, they skillfully manipulated the consciousness of English Protestant and Irish Catholic workers. As a result, those workers failed to recognize *their* class interest. Instead of fighting their real capitalist enemies and oppressors, they permitted the antagonisms engendered by the capitalist mode of production to be artificially diverted into cultural group channels and fiercely fought each other. Artful aristocrats and capitalists manipulated, divided and conquered them.[27]

Criticism of Marx's false "solution" to his theoretical problem is best postponed until I analyze the strongly "revisionist" letter that Engels wrote in 1893 to explain cultural group conflict in the United States. Here I have simply called attention to Marx's claims that the English ruling classes consciously created cultural group conflict and kept it "artificially" alive, that international conflicts primarily were ploys designed to prevent proletarian internationalism, and that the ruling classes primarily maintained their rule because they used a Machiavellian strategy to divide and conquer the workers whose common exploitation would otherwise have united them.

America: Exception or Archetype?

For obvious reasons, the "national question" was particularly important in the United States. After Marx died in 1883, Engels took over the job of combatting the sectarianism plaguing the American "workers' movement." Moreover, the country's rapid industrialization made Engels want to keep close contact with American correspondents. As a result, his letters help us see how continuous confrontation with the actual course of American development forced Engels to repudiate idealist Hegelian dualism and eventually to comprehend the heterogenous reality of complex, multicultural, capitalist societies.

In 1886, Engels frequently corresponded with the American translator of his celebrated book, *The Condition of the Working Class in England*. By June, Engels had become exhilarated by the way "the American working class is moving. . . ." He viewed America as, in effect, the archetypal capitalist society, *the country where capitalism could best be observed.* Six months later, Engels was even more euphoric. He had convinced himself that the class consciousness of American workers now equaled that of European workers.[28] Euphoria, however, was short-lived. By August 1887, Engels bemoaned "the gigantic nature of the mistakes they [i.e., the Americans] make" and admitted that "the movement" would "travel in tremendous zigzags and seem to be moving backwards at times. . . ."[29] And by February 1890, he had reversed his argument of January 1887 that the American working class moved so fast because on that "favoured soil . . . no medieval ruins bar the way. . . ." Now he explained that Americans[30]

> . . . are most conservative—just *because* America is so purely bourgeois, has no feudal past at all, and is therefore proud of its purely bourgeois organization. . . .

Engels recognized that cultural group conflicts significantly contributed to the lagging development of the American movement. But, as indicated in a letter of March 1892, he still clung to Marx's Hegelian notion of false consciousness manipulated by Machiavellian capitalists.[31]

> . . . a permanent native-born working class . . . [has] organized itself on trade-union lines to a great extent. But it still occupies an aristocratic position and wherever possible leaves the ordinary badly paid occupations to the immigrants, only a small portion of whom enter the aristocratic trade unions. But these immigrants are divided into different nationalities, which understand neither one another nor, for the most part, the language of the country. *And your bourgeoisie knows much better even than the Austrian government how to play off one nationality against the other* [emphasis added]: Jews, Italians, Bohemians, etc., against Germans, and Irish, and each one against the other, so that differences in workers' standards of living exist, I believe, in New York to an extent unheard of elsewhere. . . . Once the Americans get started [however], it will be with an energy and impetuousness compared with which we in Europe shall be mere children.

In December 1893, the reality principle finally broke through the Hegelian-inspired delusion Engels and Marx had shared about the proletariat as the *universal class* destined to redeem the suffering of mankind. Engels's analysis specifically referred to American conditions. We can now extend his analysis and observe that the conditions he referred to were not uniquely American. On the contrary. They increasingly prevailed in advanced capitalist countries, *as capitalism rid them of precapitalist survivals and made them more like America.* To study and explain social conflict in capitalist societies, Engels's analysis helps us see, we should study and explain the *archetypal* capitalist society, America—something that Tocqueville had seen much more clearly than Marx (perhaps because he had never been deluded by Hegelianism and its propensity to substitute subjective ideal-type models for objective empirical reality).

In the following letter, Engels argued that the weaknesses of American socialism were due to much more basic conditions than egotistical squabbles among German emigrés. Those squabbles certainly cause[32]

much harm, but, on the other hand, it is not to be denied that American conditions involve very great and peculiar difficulties for a steady development of a workers' party.

First, the Constitution, based as in England upon party government, which causes every vote for any candidate not put up by one of the two governing parties to appear to be *lost*. And the American, like the Englishman, wants to influence his state; he does not throw his vote away.

Then, and more especially, immigration, which divides the workers into two groups: the native-born and the foreigners, and the latter in turn into 1) the Irish, 2) the Germans, 3) the many small groups, each of which understands only itself: Czechs, Poles, Italians, Scandinavians, etc. And then the Negroes. *To form a single party out of these requires quite unusually powerful incentives. Often there is a sudden violent élan, but the bourgeois need only wait passively, and the dissimilar elements of the working class fall apart again* [emphasis added].

Third, through the protective tariff system and the steadily growing domestic market the workers must have been exposed to a prosperity no trace of which has been seen here in Europe for years now (except in Russia, where, however, the bourgeois profit by it and not the workers).

A country like America, when it is really ripe for a socialist workers' party, certainly cannot be hindered from having one by the couple of German socialist doctrinaires.

Compare Engels's explanation of "the failure" of the American proletariat to constitute a communal social class with Marx's explanation of "the failure" of the English proletariat to constitute a communal social class. Engels transcends Marx.

Marx's 1870 explanation is contrary to fact, simplistic. It exhibits an embarrassing awe of the Machiavellian ruling classes and elitist intellectual contempt for the puppetlike workers. It is shallow in its understanding of primary socialization processes, the web of kinship, the nature of social bonds, the density and spontaneity of primordial relationships in complex multicultural capitalist societies, the powerful and pervasive influence of language on culture and consciousness. At bottom, it expresses an ambivalent elitist-populistic pathetic lament against rich folks' smartness and power, poor folks' dumbness and impotence.

To do justice to the subtleties of Engels' explanation would require lengthy analysis. Here I can only note that he transformed a Hegelian false-consciousness pseudo-explanation into a Marxian explanation of social group conflict in a capitalist culture whose ethos proudly proclaims the war of all against all in the production of the means of subsistence. *That capitalist ethos, Marxism postulates, penetrates the deepest levels of personality to train and condition human beings to feel antagonistic, express antagonisms, and act antagonistically.* Engels invoked that postulate to explain the fragmented working class produced by American capitalism.

In place of Marx's argument that artful capitalists *artificially* divided workers, Engels theorized that the complex set of tendencies inherent in the natural processes of capitalism strongly tended to produce disunity and antagonism among workers whose *relationships of reproduction* naturally conditioned them to identify with social groups whose cultural systems differed and conflicted. "To form a single party out of these [members of radically different cultural groups]," Engels observed, "requires quite unusually powerful incentives. Often there is a sudden violent *élan*, but the bourgeois need only wait passively, and the dissimilar elements of the working class fall apart again." What made them dissimilar? Millennia of different modes of production, millennia of different conditions of social existence, millennia of life in societies and communities with different cultures and historics. All this amounts to Engels's invoking, in opposition to Marx, one of Marx's most powerful propositions concerning the complex relationships between social existence and consciousness: "The tradition of all the dead generations weighs like a nightmare on the brain of the living."[33]

History, not artful capitalists, naturally conditioned the dissimilar consciousness of workers in the quintessentially capitalist society, America. What capitalism did was to bring into close physical and symbolic proximity workers who imbibed radically different cultures with their mothers' milk in a society whose mode of production and overall culture engendered and exalted conflict. Capitalism naturally brought workers into conflict, capitalists did not have to do that. Contrary to Marx's conspiracy notion, capitalists, *for good capitalist reasons*, normally tended to discourage cultural-group antagonisms among their workers (except occasionally, as a strike-breaking tactic). They knew that such antagonisms adversely affected productivity and profits. Thus an intensive study of Milwaukee workers from 1883 to 1914 found that "The various nationality groups . . . were not permitted [by employers] to carry their antagonisms into the shop, for workers who argued among themselves posed a threat to industrial discipline. . . . In fact, in most shops in the city it was already [1900] the rule that workers had to bury their ethnic hostilities while on the job."[34] That finding, of course, is consistent with Engels's analysis—and should surprise no one familiar with workers' proclivities and capitalists' calculations.

By 1893, Engels recognized that the state of "social existence" and "consciousness" in America represented, in archetypal form, the natural outcome of Marx's brilliant predictions in the *Communist Manifesto*:[35]

> In place of the old local and national seclusion and self-sufficiency, we have intercourse in every direction, universal interdependence of nations. . . . The bourgeoisie . . . compels all nations, on pain of extinction, to adopt the bourgeois mode of production; it compels them to introduce what it calls civilization into their midst, i.e., to become bourgeois themselves. In a word, it creates a world after its own image.

But a bourgeois world is a world of legal equality of status, a world of rapid economic expansion and change, a world of wholly unprecedented occupational diversity and mobility, a world of migrating peoples who strongly tend to cling to the cultures from which they were uprooted or uprooted themselves, a world of intensely nationalist multicultural societies wracked by intrasocietal and intersocietal cultural conflict. In such an increasingly complex, hostile and alienated world, Engels finally understood in 1893 after the course of events in the real world helped him to free himself of fifty years of Hegelian delusions of a universal class, a multiplicity of cultural groups are much more likely than two antagonistic economic classes to serve men as reference groups—to provide them with identity, communality, protection from hostile others, solidarity and strength in pursuit of material interest, a sense of worthiness, value-systems to help orient their lives, life-styles to practice, a living space in which they can try to escape from alienation and feel at home.

Engels's analysis supports this proposition: Cultural attributes have much greater potential than economic attributes to function as the basis of social groups that have a "sacred" rather than a "profane" character. As a result, cultural groups rather than economic groups tend strongly to function as the *primary* reference groups that men "naturally" turn to when they engage in the myriad types of conflict endemic in the capitalist epoch (e.g., conflicts over beliefs, status, material resources). To say that in no way substitutes cultural determinism for economic determinism. Among other reasons for rejecting cultural determinism, as I have hinted, is recognition of three contradictory processes obviously at work in the contemporary world: *ethnocentrism, cosmopolitanism,* and *atomism* (labels, I trust, descriptive enough to convey my meaning without further specification). I cite those phenomena to support the general proportion that, in the capitalist epoch, no simple formula can credibly identify and explain the complex relationships between social existence and the consciousness of groups and individuals.

My argument does not deny the significance of conflicts over material resources within and between multicultural societies during the capitalist epoch. What it does deny is that these conflicts primarily take the dualistic form predicted by Marx. Specifically, it denies the validity of Marx's Hegelian-inspired dualistic middle-range theory that in "the epoch of the bourgeoisie" society would split "up more and more into two great hostile camps, into two great classes directly facing each other: Bourgeoisie and Proletariat."[36] That has not happened. And, according to Marx's mode-of-production general theory of social conflict, it should not have happened. He mistakenly predicted that it would happen because, in the world in which he thought and worked, the proletariat was the only agent of human emancipation that he could foresee.

My explanation of Marx's error may be wrong. Little matter. What matters is this: From Marx's valid general theory, I suggest, we can logically derive a middle-range reference group theory that simultaneously avoids the eclectic vacuity of "pluralism" and explains the extraordinary variety of social groups evident in the modern world, including cohesive *preference groups* whose members have similar cognitive and normative beliefs (i.e., values, attitudes, opinions) but vary widely in their demographic, ecological or categorical attributes. To develop that theory, however, requires intensive, systematic, and cumulative historical studies. I have argued that we can help satisfy that requirement, and thereby contribute towards realization of Marx's goal, development of a critical historical social science. We can do so by treating American history as a strategic natural experiment to test and develop a Marxian-Tocquevillian reference-group theory of social-group conflict and cohesion in the capitalist epoch.

Notes

1. The beginning of this essay is the appropriate place to note my heavy intellectual debt to Paul Lazarsfeld. It was only after I began to work with him at Columbia in 1952 that I began to see how one might go about the *scientific* study of human behavior. His extraordinary contributions to the logic of concept clarification, as well as to the methodology of quantitative and qualitative research, have strongly influenced my orientation to historical studies. Space constraints, alas, prevent me from trying to show explicitly how those contributions might powerfully help us carry out a scientific program to assess Marx's theories.

2. Space constraints force resort to documentation of the most elementary type, that is, identification of sources directly referred to in the text rather than detailed justification of my reconstruction of Marx's theories.

3. Here I have spliced together, in context, two quotations. Loyd D. Easton and Kurt H. Guddat, eds., *Writings of the Young Marx on Philosophy and Society* Garden City, N.Y.: Anchor Books, 1967, pp. 408, 415.

4. Here I have extended to *critical historical social science*, the important concept, *critical social science*, impressively developed by Mihailo Markovic. See his *From Affluence to Praxis* Ann Arbor: University of Michigan Press, 1974, pp. 45–69.

5. Another major obstacle to the *scientific* assessment of Marx's theories is their historical character. Historians have not been trained or equipped to test theories systematically. Nonhistorians have not been trained or equipped to do historical research systematically. As a result, assessment of Marx's theories has fallen into the interstices of the fragmented social scientific enterprise. How to overcome that fragmentation is a large question. I call attention to it to avoid any implication that the procedure outlined in the text is presented as a sure-fire panacea to cure the ideological ills plaguing the assessment of Marx. For discussion of the argument that scientific historiography is indispensable to the development of powerful social scientific theories, see Lee Benson, *Toward the Scientific Study of History* Philadelphia: Lippincott, 1972, pp. 1, 225–340, and *passim*.

6. Robert Merton, *On Theoretical Sociology* New York: Free Press, 1967, pp. 39–72.

7. *Ibid.*, p. 39.

8. Karl Marx, *The Eighteenth Brumaire of Louis Bonaparte* New York: International Publishers, 1963, p. 14.

9. For clear statements of Marx's proposition, see a letter he wrote in 1877 conveniently reprinted in Lewis S. Feuer, ed., *Marx and Engels: Basic Writings on Politics and Philosophy* Garden City, N.Y.: Anchor Books, 1959, pp. 438–441; his "Afterword To The Second German Edition" of *Capital* New York: International Publishers, 1967, Vol. 1, pp. 12–20; the "Author's Preface to the Second Edition," *Eighteenth Brumaire*, pp. 8–9.

10. Here I have developed ideas sketched in Lee Benson, "Group Cohesion and Social and Ideological Conflict: A Critique of Some Marxian and Tocquevillian Theories," *American Behavioral Scientist*, 16 (May–June 1973), 753–754.

11. I have sketched such a typology in an unpublished paper, Lee Benson, "Marx's General and Middle-Range Theories of Social Conflict," discussion paper presented to the Faculty Seminar on Multicultural Societies, University of Pennsylvania, April 15, 1976, (mimeo), pp. 36–38.

12. For the letters I have spliced together, in context, see Karl Marx and Frederick Engels, *Letters to Americans, 1848-1895* New York: International Publishers, 1953, pp. 157–158, 224–226. For Marx's methodological observations on case studies as a means to develop general theories, see *Capital*, Vol. 1, pp. 7–8.

13. See the discussion in Benson, in *American Behavioral Scientist*, 745–747.

14. *Ibid.*, 749–750.

15. See the two chapters on reference-group theory, the first of them in collaboration with Alice S. Rossi, in Robert Merton, *Social Theory and Social Structure* New York: Free Press, 1957, pp. 225–386.

16. Richard N. Hunt, *The Political Ideas of Marx and Engels: Marxism and Totalitarian Democracy, 1818-1850* University of Pittsburgh Press, 1974, pp. 54–55.

17. *Ibid.*, pp. 54–55.

18. Marx's text is conveniently found in T. B. Bottomore, ed., *Karl Marx: Early Writings* New York: McGraw-Hill, 1963, pp. 57–59.

19. *Ibid.*, pp. 11–12.

20. Hunt, *Political Ideas of Marx and Engels*, pp. 52–53.

21. The text is found in Easton and Guddat, eds., *Writings of the Young Marx*, p. 368.

22. C. J. Arthur, ed., *Karl Marx and Frederick Engels: The German Ideology* New York: International Publishers, 1970, pp. 82–83; Dirk J. Struik, ed., *Birth of the Communist Manifesto* New York: International Publishers, 1971, pp. 90–91, 96–102.

23. *Ibid.*, p. 100.

24. For a recent statement, see Richard Hyman, "Workers Control and Revolutionary Theory," in Ralph Miliband and John Saville, eds., *The Socialist Register: 1974* London: Merlin Press, 1974, p. 271.

25. An entire volume has been published on *Ireland and the Irish Question: A Collection of Writings by Karl Marx and Frederick Engels* New York: International Publishers, 1972. In particular, see pp. 126–70, 272–301.

26. *Ibid.*, pp. 272–301.

27. *Ibid.*, pp. 292–295.

28. Marx and Engels, *Letters to Americans*, pp. 157–158; W. O. Henderson and W. H. Chalmers, eds. and trans., *Friedrich Engels: The Condition of the Working Class in England* Stanford: Stanford University Press, 1968, pp. 352–354.

29. Marx and Engels, *Letters to Americans*, pp. 189–190.

30. *Ibid.*, pp. 224–225.

31 *Ibid.*, pp. 242–243.

32. *Ibid.*, pp. 257–258.

33. Marx, *Eighteenth Brumaire*, p. 15.

34. Gerd Korman, *Industrialization, Immigrants, and the Americanizers: The View From Milwaukee, 1866–1921* Madison: State Historical Society of Wisconsin, 1967, pp. 65–66.

35. Struik, ed., *Communist Manifesto*, 93. Throughout this essay, I have tried to distinguish among Marx's different theories. In effect, my argument is that Marx's mode-of-production theory is the *real* [sic] theory; economic determinism is what Marx failed to free himself from but, alas, bequeathed to whole generations of Marxists and researchers influenced by Marx.

36. Struik, ed., *Communist Manifesto*, p. 90.

16. ETHICAL AND PRACTICAL DILEMMAS OF FIELDWORK IN ACADEMIC SETTINGS: A PERSONAL MEMOIR

David Riesman

I begin by saying something about the influence that Paul Lazarsfeld had on my development as a sociologist and that he and his colleagues at the Bureau of Applied Social Research have had (along with others), on my curiosity concerning the processes of interviewing and of survey research. Then, I turn to the Teacher Apprehension Study, published under the title *The Academic Mind* (Lazarsfeld and Thielens, 1958) and to Lazarsfeld's invitation to me to assess the quality and accuracy of the interviewing in that survey. Finally, I turn to some of the ethical and practical problems—and for me, ethical problems are never abstractly separate from pragmatic dilemmas—which fieldwork in academic settings entails: problems raised for me in the most intense form in the Teacher Apprehension Study itself.

The Lazarsfeldian Influence

Lazarsfeld's interest in my work and our early contacts were influential in persuading me to leave teaching law for sociology. During the time that I was a law student, my teacher and friend, Carl Friedrich, had helped introduce me to contemporary European social science and to the then nascent and important work in public opinion polling during the 1930s. (The hope I then held may

I am indebted to two of the editors, Robert K. Merton and James S. Coleman, for extraordinarily penetrating criticisms of earlier drafts; also to helpful criticisms by Charles Y. Glock, Herbert Hyman, who are also fellow contributors; and under pledge of confidentiality, Everett C. Hughes and Donald Light. I also want to acknowledge the help of the Hazen Foundation and the Lilly Endowment, support which made work on this essay possible.

seem quixotic today: namely, that surveys concerning political attitudes would make the American polity more responsive to actual opinion rather than to what politicians, publicists, and lobbyists could mobilize in the name of the public.)

When in 1937 I became a law professor at Buffalo, Friedrich invited me to contribute a monograph on civil liberties to a volume that he and Edward Mason were editing. My general approach was social-psychological, looking at the political context of freedom of speech, noting the linkage of interests and idealisms that one had to weigh in the face of competing interests and values. Concurrently, I began a comparative study of defamation in the United States and in other countries to see what words meant in different cultural settings, and why, for example, the British took libel seriously whereas the Americans assumed that one ought to be able to "take it";[1] I was also curious as to why in a Viennese tenement house people brought suits for slander when they were insulted, as against the punch in the mouth or "playing the dozens" more characteristic of subcultures within the United States (Riesman, 1942a, 1942b, 1942c).

My law professor friends, most of them concerned with large questions of public law, thought all this was interesting but could not respond to it in a collegial way; but Lazarsfeld, Harold Lasswell, Robert and Helen Lynd, Erich Fromm, and Marie Jahoda did respond to this work; their own very diverse kinds of work stimulated me.

It would be out of place here to record all the generosities and accidents that made it possible for me to shift my calling in line with my new sense of colleagueship, including Edward Shils's omnivorous reading which had led him to discover my essay on civil liberties and Everett Hughes's teaching and encouragement after I came to Chicago. But I do want to take account briefly of the impact on me in 1948 when, taking a leave of absence at Yale and in company with Nathan Glazer, I began to study in detail the procedures of interviewing and the design and interpretation of surveys. I read interviews and discussed the meaning of opinion—and also of those who on polls registered "no opinion"—with Herbert Hyman and Paul Sheatsley in what was then the eastern office of NORC in New York City (Riesman and Glazer, 1949). Previously, Nathan Glazer had worked with a group of Columbia graduate students meeting on Saturday mornings at the office of the Bureau of Applied Social Research to analyze interviews done by C. Wright Mills's students the previous year and on which the latter's book, *White Collar*, was based. With Mills's permission, Glazer and I reanalyzed the interviews which along with others provided a kind of test as we explored typologies used in *The Lonely Crowd*; the triad of anomie, adjustment, and autonomy drew particularly on the concepts of Robert K. Merton's seminal paper, "Social Structure and Anomie" (Merton, 1938). The concerns of Lazarsfeld and his circle at the Bureau were formative in much of the work that led to *The Lonely Crowd* and *Faces in the Crowd*, including the study of mass media, the panel studies of voting behavior, and the explorations of patterns of personal influence. (See, e.g., Wolfe and Fiske in Lazarsfeld and Stanton, 1949; Lazarsfeld and Merton, 1948; Lowenthal, 1944.)

It is hard to give a sociology student today a sense of the excitement that surrounded the Bureau of Applied Social Research in the decade 1948–1958— an atmosphere from which I learned and drew colleagueship and friendship. It was a shop where all kinds of studies were underway and in which substantive explorations of then relatively new areas (such as changes in individual voting behavior over a series of elections, studies of medical schools, explorations of audiences and of communicators and various elites) were proceeding simultaneously with methodological inquiries, such as the possibilities of contextual analysis of interviews by examining, as was to be done in the Teacher Apprehension Study, the effect of peer climates of opinion on individual respondents—on these intertwined substantive and methodological topics, ideas were freely shared, hunches tried out, languages of social research elaborated. Paul Lazarsfeld, impresario and orchestrator of the often quite individualistic work of the shop, insisted on self-consciousness about the nature of such enterprises (see, e.g., Lazarsfeld, 1961).

Research Program on the Interview

Greatly influenced by these exposures to a shoplike atmosphere, I sought to recreate in a small way two similar ventures at the University of Chicago: first, the Center for the Study of Leisure, for which I recruited Rolf Meyersohn, who had worked at the Bureau and, second, what I termed the Interview Project, aimed at studying, mainly through secondary analysis, the interview process where my principal collaborator was Mark Benney, a researcher and writer associated with Mark Abrams in London, and my other collaborator, the late June Sachar Ehrlich, who had also worked at the Bureau of Applied Social Research. Examining the history of the survey interview, we were interested in its use as a mode of exchange among people of different social classes, ethnic groups, political persuasions and cultural styles; and we were interested in what survey analysts speak of as "interviewer effects," that is, how (if at all) perceptions of the interviewer affected responses of interviewees on matters of supposed fact as well as opinion.

When the late Samuel A. Stouffer published his book, *Communism, Conformity, and Civil Liberties* (Stouffer, 1955), he undertook to interview simultaneously a sample of the general population and a subsample of local "community leaders" such as mayors, bar association presidents, PTA heads, and many others. In addition, he used two interviewing staffs, the National Opinion Research Center at the University of Chicago, with many of whose officials we had already been working, and the American Institute of Public Opinion (the Gallup Poll), to see whether what we came to call the "house-styles" of different interviewing agencies produced different results in interviews on controversial political questions. Domestic communism, real and alleged, was such an issue in the era to which Senator Joseph McCarthy gave his name, though many local vigilantes and inquisitors were also active. We found that, despite considerable differences in education, sophistication, and tolerance between the "typical" Gallup and "typical" NORC interviewer, their exceptional conscientiousness, ability, and professionalism compensated for house-style differences and brought about a striking similarity of results, both with the (more or less elite) sub-samples and the national cross-section (Riesman, 1956a; cf. Riesman, 1956b).

Lazarsfeld's interest in the sociology of higher education extended far beyond the question as to how applied work done in centers or institutes meshed with the usually less problem-oriented and more guild-oriented work of academic departments. He had written an essay, "Innovation in Higher Education," which is undated but which, I believe, was a contribution to a collection he had persuaded his Columbia University colleague Bernhard J. Stern to edit (Stern, 1953). When I came to the University of Chicago, my own interest in higher education became more focused under the guidance of Everett C. Hughes, who helped me realize the usefulness of Robert Park's ecological concepts, applied to the way in which whole systems related symbiotically or competitively to each other and, vis-à-vis higher education, to the fashions in which colleges and universities (and, of course, also units within them) competed in what was not then wholly a national catchbasin for students and faculty, for friends and renown. I took every opportunity for a speaking engagement or professional meeting to learn more about the enormous diversity of American higher education, private and public, Catholic, Protestant, and more or less secular; I was keeping notes on the visits but had no organized plan of research, let alone a conceptual scheme to help me master the bewildering variety of competing enterprises now still further enlarged by the designation "post-secondary education." Hughes's students constituted no shop; in the study of institutions, they generally preferred the mode of participant observation, supplemented by interviews.[2]

Surveying the Surveyors: *The Academic Mind*

Into this constellation of interests, capacities, and lacunae, Lazarsfeld had come, in the spring of 1955, to ask me to do a rapid followup study of the Academic Freedom Survey he had just completed for Robert Hutchins's Fund for the Republic. Hutchins had declared in 1954 that the spirit of the academic profession in America was being crushed by the then current investigations of subversion on the nation's campuses.

Lazarsfeld took the initiative to propose a study that would seek to discover to what degree faculty members were apprehensive as the result of McCarthyism; what if any protections they had against attack from colleagues, administrators, trustees, and regents; and, on the other hand, to what extent they felt isolated, reported or spied upon by students, undefended by colleagues, threatened by administrators or by hostile outside agencies.[3] In exploring the depth, significance, and extent of apprehension—for example, if teachers were censoring books they used, what they said in class, how they communicated with their colleagues and outside publics—Lazarsfeld saw an opportunity to put to use the Bureau's research program he had initiated on "contextual analysis." He decided to follow Samuel Stouffer's lead in employing two interviewing staffs (NORC again and Elmo Roper). He also chose a mode of sampling that took small academic departments as total units as well as individuals within larger ones.

As described in the acknowledgements of *The Academic Mind: Social Scientists in a Time of Crisis*, which eventuated from the study, Lazarsfeld used as colleagues to help him develop a questionnaire fellow members of his season at the Center for Advanced Study in the Behavioral Sciences at Palo Alto during the academic year, 1954-1955. In a carefully stratified sample of accredited colleges and universities based on the development of quality indices and somewhat weighted on the side of the more prestigeful institutions, 182 institutions were chosen at random, and the president of each was asked for permission to have interviewers work on the college premises. Twenty schools refused to participate—and while in one or two such instances, snobbery toward or hostility about sociology, questionnaires, and other such forms of low-life (as viewed from the height of the dominant humanities) may have been involved, most refusals seemed based on fear, and hence provided inferential evidence on issues of academic freedom; the study ended up with 165 schools and 2,451 respondents, all of them social scientists. In accordance with standard practice, some of the best interviewers of both NORC and Roper conducted a pretest, both agencies combined on an elaborate set of specifications to instruct interviewers in what was for many, familiar with shorter interviews with often less formidable respondents, a comprehensive guide as to what the study involved and how they should proceed.

The survey finally went into the field in the spring of 1955. Friction developed almost immediately at a number of colleges and with a number of respondents, some of whom communicated directly with Paul Lazarsfeld, others with Robert Hutchins, still others complaining to the interviewer, breaking off interviews or otherwise indicating that they thought the interview "loaded" (this tended to be a right-wing or conservative reaction), the interviewer inept, or the questionnaire faulty, or both (a common reaction among high-status respondents in leading institutions);[4] that the whole idea of a study was an irrelevant distraction when what was needed was action against McCarthy (what, in my later field report, I termed the "activist" response which was rather uncommon), and in many places the fear that the questionnaires would somehow fall into the hands of the department chairman, the president, the FBI, or the investigating committee. (Such fears were in general more likely at more traditional or despotically run institutions.)

Lazarsfeld recognized that these reactions to the survey were data of course highly relevant to the survey's principal concerns. He also thought it important to see whether an independent investigator would find that the complaints against the survey and some of the interviewing were valid; thus it occurred to him that it would be desirable to have someone like myself be the one to do another survey. This would involve reinterviewing some of the respondents, talking to some of the interviewers, and occasionally triangulating what transpired between particular respondents and particular interviewers. I might also be able to contribute to what the questionnaires themselves and the interviewers' reports already revealed about whether the "house-style" differences between Roper and NORC had in any way affected the accuracy and quality of the interviewing.

Lazarsfeld's invitation was responsive to my own interest in civil liberties, my curiosity about college communities, and my wish to learn more from the Bureau of Applied Social Research about interviewing and survey methods. I was fortunate, because of the quarter system, to be able to obtain a leave from the University of Chicago, and, with my colleague, Mark Benney, I went off almost at once on the trail of the survey. We began work at the Bureau in order to steep ourselves in the actual interviews before starting out to do our own survey of the survey.

When I had been a respondent to the survey interview myself, I recognized the inevitable conflict between individual idiosyncracy and comparability; I was not troubled that some of the personal experiences I had had during what the study came to call "the difficult [McCarthy] years" could not be captured by a survey aiming at comparability; and I felt that my interviewer had probed adequately for side comments in case I wanted to elaborate on these. While this was, of course, a one-shot interview, rather than a panel study (cf. Lazarsfeld 1940; Berelson, Lazarsfeld, and McPhee, 1954), the questionnaire gave ample room for the respondent's own historical comparisons, and I assumed that Lazarsfeld would be able to use cross-tabulations to tease out latent variables where others saw only obvious marginals.

It was not, however, until I had had an opportunity to read all the interviews that I fully appreciated the extent to which the survey was adapted to the academic avant-garde in which I myself lived, and was often perceived as irrelevant or tangential in those institutions which my follow-up report referred to as "traditional" colleges.

Even though the questionnaire had not been designed with their specific and, among themselves, quite divergent issues of potential apprehension other than McCarthyism, it nevertheless managed to capture more of the preoccupations in such colleges than many faculty members themselves, who objected to the survey, were able to recognize. Faculty trained in leading institutions, some of whom were, of course, to be found in the more traditional colleges, often had familiarity with the procedures of survey research agencies and what turned out to be a justified confidence in their scrupulousness about confidentiality; many other respondents, however, who had never before seen a survey, let alone a survey interviewer, were afraid of it.[5]

In reading the interviews from professors in high-status, relatively well-protected colleges and universities, I found the interviewer recording many negative comments concerning the survey, which she sometimes summarized in her report (most of the interviewers were women) turned in along with the interviews to the home office. There were many reactions that might be termed Luddite, not only from political theorists, historians, geographers and others, but also from some sociologists who objected to surveys and to quantification in principle. There were other reactions which struck me as symptoms of the narcissism endemic especially in the higher reaches of academia—narcissism sometimes so strong that questions were misinterpreted to damn the survey for omitting a topic that was in fact included. Even Lazarsfeld's personal friends in academia had fault to find, neglecting to notice his gifts in making use of not always perfect data. Then, of course, hostilities aroused by the topic itself, again in the avant-garde which might feel that it had not been as brave as it ought to have been vis-a-vis McCarthyism, were often vented on the interviewer herself, who tended, like the proverbial ambassador from an enemy kingdom, to be shot as the bearer of bad tidings.[6]

A friend has written somewhere that a paranoid is a person who lacks the insensitivity of the normal person to the hostility all around him. I have already remarked that some respondents had feared that their remarks might fall into the hands of investigating committees or, possibly, the FBI. Yet the fact is that very few respondents had anything to report that would put them on a national "enemies list." Rather, among the more traditional colleges, the fears were principally of potential local enemies: a Protestant or Jew or even lay Catholic teaching in a college dominated by a conservative diocese or religious order; a Missouri Synod Lutheran with inclinations to theological unorthodoxy; a professor anxious about what his students might report concerning his classes to his colleagues, dean, or president.

In contrast, in the most secure and selective institutions where faculty were more liberal and where the issue of McCarthyism was often regarded as passé, there was almost a feeling of insult at being questioned by what I came to term the "young girl in a red hat" who could not possibly understand the sophisticated intricacies of the academics' responses.[7]

After Mark Benney and I had steeped ourselves in the interviews, we chose 40 colleges and universities to represent various levels of academic quality, all located between Minnesota in the Northwest and North Carolina in the Southeast—making this regional selection in order to save money, time, and wear and tear of travel. Where two colleges in the sample were geographically close (sometimes the same interviewers had worked at them), we would often visit both institutions, sometimes discovering that an interviewer who had been regarded with disdain at an avant-garde college was seen as highly professional at a neighboring major state university more exposed to McCarthyite apprehensions and pressures. It turned out that much of the faculty was away in the summer, and we had frustrating experiences of not finding people we had arranged to interview; as I describe in my report in *The Academic Mind*, this unavailability was, on occasion, the result of administrative pressure.[8]

Both with our academic and survey research informants, I sought to practice a code of mutuality: my more or less dialectical interviewing style took for granted the respondents' sharing similar interests and concerns. (In fact many of the survey interviewers turned out to be members of the ACLU, more concerned with civil liberties than the majority of their academic respondents.)

On returning to the University of Chicago, Mark Benney and I developed a followup questionnaire which we sent both to some faculty we had missed at colleges we had visited and to a few new colleges to cover areas where we felt our own nonrandom sampling had been deficient. In this questionnaire, sent to respondents at 45 colleges who returned 432 mailed questionnaires (a 45 percent return), we asked two interrelated questions:

"Do you think that—in spite of any specific reservations you might have had about the Study a generally true and fair image of your attitudes to academic freedom was elicited by the questionnaire?

Do you think that the interviewer got down a generally fair and true record of your attitudes?"

In sharp contrast to the impression left by a number of often vehement criticisms voiced concerning the survey, 85 percent said "yes" to the first of these questions (5 percent said "no"; 10 percent, "don't know"), and 78 percent checked "yes" to the second question (3 percent said "no"; 19 percent, "don't know"—the latter sometimes observing that they "didn't see what she wrote"). As Lazarsfeld and Thielens noted in their own discussion, the Teacher Apprehension Survey was not a census in which every respondent counts one and no more than one; conceivably, the dissatisfied minority included many who would have had more of relevance to say if they had felt the questionnaire and/or the interviewer to have been appropriate. Nevertheless, in light of the fact that at least 30 percent of our mail questionnaire respondents were sharply critical of the original questionnaire, their overwhelming admission that it accomplished at least a substantial part of its aims gave me the basis for saying, along with other evidence, based on our institutional visits and our discussions with interviewers, that the survey rested on substantially accurate reports of respondents' attitudes and that, where errors of commission or omission occurred, these did not affect the overall conclusions of the study.[9]

The group I brought together at the University of Chicago, led by Mrs. Elizabeth Drake, to help analyze the mail questionnaires was, of course, familiar with the limitations of such questionnaires based on unevenness of response. One pattern emerged which said something about the complex cultural climate of that epoch, namely, that right-wing faculty members, when they did send questionnaires back, often did so anonymously as they were permitted to do and attacked the survey as many had the first time around as biased in a pro-communist direction, or at least in the direction of liberals to prove that faculties had been unjustly or unduly frightened by McCarthyism. Both the original survey and my own questionnaire served to remind such individuals of the irritating liberalism of the leading academic centers that Hutchins, Lazarsfeld, and I were all seen as representing, not to speak of the Ford Foundation. Though the original survey in fact gave them the opportunity, which some made use of, to mention pressure against them from liberal colleagues, many had so stereotyped the questionnaire as not to "hear" this opening. Conversely, in what my report describes as the upper-middle reaches of academia, with faculty of avant-garde quality but not with avant-garde protections, both the original survey and my followup served as reminders that somebody cared, and it was here that one found often the most diligent and concerned respondents who made an effort to be responsible in their answers and generally felt that they had succeeded. (For details of the mail questionnaires, see Lazarsfeld and Thielens, 1958, pp. 269 ff.)

Quantitative and Qualitative Surveys Compared

Lazarsfeld and I had planned a second volume in which we would discuss many issues that had to be cut out of both my own truncated field report and the analysis of the Survey that he and Thielens had drastically condensed. I had recruited some graduate students, including Michael Maccoby and Lawrence Kohlberg, to work on a typology of colleges and vignettes of colleges, for example, based on the interviews, my visits, and the mail returns. We had written memoranda on the problems that arose because the Survey was confined to social scientists, on the assumption that they were on the whole the most threatened group during "the difficult years." But, on a number of campuses, the "controversial" faculty were in the art department or in English literature, or in philosophy, or in mathematics and theoretical physics, or (very rarely) in education. Such people felt left out of the Survey, and sometimes their social science colleagues concluded that the result was to limit the Survey's full scope. Yet the line had to be drawn somewhere, if one was doing the kind of sample survey that Lazarsfeld had initiated rather than the kind of "snowball" interviewing I would sometimes do in which one faculty member would lead me to another in a department outside the area of the Survey or to a beleaguered administrator who had himself become a cause célèbre. There were ingenious interviewers who did the interviews in their cars to avoid the possibility of being observed or even overheard, but there were no interviewers who felt authorized to do what I did at a Negro college, which was to go around one evening and talk to a black minister involved in labor organizing to see whether the picture of 100 percent Americanism presented to me at the college was in his judgment the straight story or not—he said it was. Neither of us managed to foresee that this would be one of the colleges where, only seven years later, one of the first college sit-ins occurred. At the same time, such somewhat journalistic forays on my part presented ethical questions.

For example, I had constantly, at the more traditional colleges, to think about what if any harm might come to a faculty member who was seen talking to a professor from the University of Chicago, regarded as a subversive university operating on behalf of the subversive Fund for the Republic. Getting the story was important, but not so important as to justify harm or, in most cases, feared or perceived danger of harm to individuals.

Before visiting a college, Mark Benney and I would study catalogs and, on arriving there, would first look at bulletin boards, the student bookstore, read the student press, and sometimes find the student editors extremely useful informants. We tried to sense the micro-climates of different enclaves on a campus, some of which could be developed from the original Survey through contextual analysis, but some of which escaped that net.

The second volume never came to fruition. Hence, the memoranda June Sachar Ehrlich wrote on the different "house-styles" of Roper and NORC are reflected only marginally in *The Academic Mind*. We concluded, as already indicated, that they did not affect the results, but this did not mean that there were not interesting differences worth further exploration.

I remember a conversation with Lazarsfeld in which we concluded that our two quite different procedures on the whole came to quite similar results; that mine would of course have been impossible without his original survey as a starting point; but that I learned some things that his survey failed to turn up. However, the things I learned from my own survey and questionnaire I knew with much less certainty because of the lack of any systematic sampling or the intricate procedural safeguards built into the original survey design.

Of one thing I could be quite sure. There had been no case of interviewers' betraying their trust either to college authorities or to governmental ones. This was so whatever their personal beliefs: even though their personal tolerance might not extend to those they considered reactionaries or radicals, their professional tolerance did. All this made me think that interviewing is a kind of "women's liberation" for some. It was interesting to discover, moreover, that even very conservative interviewers were far more tolerant than their husbands vis-à-vis the "Reds" at the local college—just as liberal or even radical interviewers patiently heard out reactionary professors.

The results of our re-study seemed to show that the stratified random sample and the structured interview, constructed so that many issues are approached from variant perspectives and at different points in sequence and carried in the hands of a well-educated and carefully instructed interviewer, sufficed for an overall judgment on most issues of the impact of McCarthyism upon academic social scientists. The Survey also located the types of institutional contexts where those pressures had been felt most heavily—namely, those institutions, often major state universities, where eminent liberal-to-radical faculty felt exposed even though they might not consciously bow to pressures. But, for case studies of individual variability in the face of such pressure, one would have needed to use interviewers who were considered the peers of their respondents and who knew enough about the particular issues on that particular campus to probe intensively in an almost psychoanalytic way to uncover shades of feeling that had perhaps been repressed—although in fact a number of the structured interviews evoked torrents of feeling and some took as long as six hours for the hapless interviewers whose fingers got blisters and cramps from endless writing.

Many respondents on the original survey, to use Paul Lazarsfeld's own analogy, were like patients who could not believe that their doctor could possibly diagnose their ailment since he spent so little time with them and did not get their full life histories. But the quantitative survey instrument, like the diagnostic tools of the physician, can often reveal what is latent to the academic "patients" themselves.[10]

Ethical Dilemmas of Field Research in Academe

As my own work after the Teacher Apprehension Study turned almost exclusively to the sociology of higher education, I continued in the wake of that study to assume that there was a single academic procession that could be ranked by the sort of quality indices developed by Lazarsfeld and later used by Carnegie Commission surveys, themselves designed and used by individuals (Martin Trow and S. M. Lipset) who had had their first exposure to survey research method at the Bureau of Applied Social Research. I made use of the Merton distinction of locals and cosmopolitans (Merton, 1949) as well as following trails of personal influence that ran from major graduate schools to the many former teachers colleges that were seeking to become regional universities (cf. Katz and Lazarsfeld, 1955). I also took for granted that imitation of the national academic leaders was distorted by misperceptions of the direction being taken by the latter, but I did not seriously doubt that there was a model of research-oriented universities toward which institutions aspired, sometimes under the impetus of ambitious administrators working with apathetic faculty, sometimes vice versa. In fact, in the quarter century since the Teacher Apprehension Survey was conducted, we have in academic as in other respects become a far more national society; we have many more cosmopolitans (some of whom also have institutional loyalty) and many fewer locals (many of whom are local by default, often union members with little if any institutional loyalty).

However, once I began to study individual institutions in quasi-ethnographic detail, I tended to become more the historian and less the generalizing sociologist—more convinced of the idiosyncrasy of particular institutions and of a lack of any consensus within or among institutions, as to where the whole academic procession should be headed. There were breaks in the procession and institutions with radically different goals, or what Gerald Grant and I have come to term telic reformist or revolutionary aims (Grant and Riesman, 1975). James

S. Coleman has argued cogently that even the subunits of the major research-oriented universities do not all share the same goals and values (Coleman, 1973).

Yet it remains true that only a relatively small number of institutions has a sufficient distinctiveness of aim to avoid the not-so-hidden injuries of invidiousness in a society where egalitarianism means that there are no good alibis for not getting to the top, wherever the top may be located. Even in the experimenting colleges, which have sought a special mandate, exclusively and uniquely theirs, there can nevertheless often be detected an effort to legitimate the enterprise by norms that have some universal applicability. In fact, to the college ethnographer, as to the historian, there are many more institutions which claim to be unique than in fact are so: the novelty, something after the fashion of a cargo cult, may lie in the persuasive relabeling of a tradition. Thus, the researcher who values diversity faces another dilemma. If the institution is described in its actuality, its own sense of mystique may be imperiled; it becomes a "case," an instance of a larger human drama.

There are ethical and practical traps in responding to such misgivings and antagonisms. It is easy to fall into the mucker pose sometimes assumed by the already established and to emphasize one's own critiques of the limitations of Ivy League institutions (cf. Cottle, 1973). Or one can let attacks pass without response, possibly leading the protagonist to believe that one is in agreement, whereas in fact one is only attentive and silent. As already indicated, I think that, except for the very shyest and most withdrawn among academic faculty and administrators, nondirective interviewing is less fruitful than a more dialectical approach; hence silence in one area and responsiveness in others may lead to a misreading of one's own views. Furthermore, I could not slip inconspicuously into a classroom in the way that a younger person could who might "pass" as a student and, of course, in any case would always try to make clear my purpose before visiting a college and ask permission of particular faculty before visiting classes. But such a request may put the faculty member on the spot. He or she may not want to seem apprehensive about a visit from a presumably critical colleague, and the liberty of refusal is thus somewhat constrained. In the effort to turn respondents into informants and then into quasi-co-researchers, I sometimes inadvertently introduced tensions and difficulties.

Thus, field research which values diversity creates its own kind of dilemma. As institutions are described in detail—including such basic matters as budget, governance, attrition and other details shared with other institutions with which they can then be compared—the members of what is in effect a "mystery cult" may feel that their mystique is imperiled by "mere" facts. What had been for them fully idiosyncratic then becomes a "mere case." What is to the researcher an instance of a larger human drama may be to those on the scene far less valuable in not being portrayed as entirely unique.

Possible injuries to a college's mystique are only one of a number of the ethical dilemmas of ethnographic research on academic institutions—dilemmas to which I want now to turn.

That I came from the University of Chicago and, later, from Harvard, generally provided me with adequate entrée if I wanted to study an academic institution. But my personal and institutional status also created obstacles among people who, at many academic levels, would attribute particular kinds of snobbery to a professor at a major university, or who might in some cases be envious or otherwise antagonistic.

If I asked to visit a class—and of course I would never visit without asking—I generally felt that some comment on the visit was required, almost as in the case of "de-briefing" of "subjects" in a social-psychological investigation. Hence, I would often arrange to take the professor in question out to lunch or dinner afterwards when there would be a chance to talk about the class and assimilate any misgivings the faculty member may have had about how things went or how, if there was discussion, the students performed. Of course, unobtrusive measures where they could be employed avoided such moral engagements, and my collaborators and I made use of these whenever we could, as I had done in the original Teacher Apprehension Study: again the student bookstore, student papers, bulletin boards, patterns of student traffic, athletic activities (including the tonal and choreographic qualities of marching bands), and the kinds of recorded data on colleges compiled by Alexander Astin and his collaborators over many years (e.g., Astin, 1965) could be scrutinized without personal involvement.

Anthropologists who study nonliterature peoples have an easier time: those they write about are not likely to read what is said about them nor, despite all the current breast-beating about "imperial" anthropology, are those who are studied likely to be harmed—if anything, the opposite, for anthropology has helped to create a climate critical of colonialism and even of "modernization."

But, if one writes about colleges, one is writing about institutions that are perishable and about individuals whose careers can be made or broken by what is said about them or their institutions or both. Researchers doing community studies in the United States had developed a tradition of using pseudonyms: "Middletown," "Yankee City," "Elmtown," "Plainville, U.S.A.," or "Good Fortune." When Joseph Gusfield, Zelda Gamson, and I began a study of two new colleges in the public system of Michigan, we referred to Detroit as "Midwest City" and gave the colleges similarly uninteresting names (see, e.g., Gusfield and Riesman, 1968). We also assured administrators and faculty at the two colleges, when we were making our contracts of entrée, that we would disguise the names of individuals except for the top leadership and that we would submit for criticism any drafts of what we wrote about the institutions, both to make sure that, as the British say, we "got it right" and to uncover possible sources of harm either to individuals who might be identified or to the institutions.

In these judgments, we followed the practice of *The Academic Mind* itself, in which the colleges included are named in an appendix, but all quotations from respondents are anonymous, and some identifying details are changed or omitted. We were guided also by the tradition of community studies and, in addition, by my experience with the Vassar studies directed by Nevitt Sanford which led me to believe that a college generous enough to open itself to scrutiny should not suffer harm as a result—just as Bennington College should not suffer from Theodore Newcomb's well-known early work there (Newcomb, 1943). True enough, Howard Becker, Blanche Geer, Everett Hughes, and Anselm Strauss were intending to name the University of Kansas Medical School in *Boys in White* and did so, and *Making the Grade*, by Becker, Geer, and Hughes, names the University of Kansas as the locale. But in our own work we felt that we were dealing with vulnerable fledgling institutions, more easily harmed than a major medical school or one of the great state universities that dominates higher education in its state.

Burton Clark has pointed out that innovative institutions tend to have a saga: the product of a particular history and perhaps particular progenitors (Clark, 1970). In what is perhaps the most brilliant work of institutional history, Martin Duberman's *Black Mountain*, the defunct college is of course named, but so are individuals who are still alive or whose descendants are still alive (Duberman, 1972). Plainly, if one is to do any kind of "natural history" of an academic enterprise, one needs to know something of the founding fathers (or in the case of women's colleges, sometimes the founding mothers); there are frequently schisms, because it is rare that visionary founders can carry out their visions. Lazarsfeld helped alert me to the search for and analysis of deviant cases. And I have been especially interested in those founders who have remained in office and seen an institution beyond its initial vision—playing the roles both of Joseph Smith and of Brigham Young. (In fact, a very large number of founders turn out to have had at some time a religious call, some exposure to a divinity school or novitiate, before turning to an academic vocation.)

After we had published several articles about the two Michigan colleges, using pseudonyms for the institutions, we concluded that we had been mistaken. It made no sense to call Detroit "Midwest City." Nor did it make sense to disguise the fact that Oakland was founded originally as a branch of Michigan State University and that Monteith was a subcollege of Wayne State University. Indeed, in understanding the institutions we were examining, it was important to know that their fate in part depended on the vicissitudes of the auto industry and that the United Auto Workers and labor in general were strong in the state. It was important to know that the colleges existed in a state where public higher education has had virtual hegemony. We also reemphasized our wish to submit drafts of what we might publish to faculty, administrators, and in some cases students at the institutions in question, not only for their help in correcting us in errors of fact or interpretation, but also to make as certain as possible that what we wrote would not be likely to damage the institutions or individuals.

Yet, what is one to do when one has interviewed a top official who has agreed to be named, and then sends him a draft of a chapter in which he resolutely denies saying what one knows he has said? (I have taken notes, and I have dictated those notes immediately afterward, and they are congruent with everything else I know about the individual in question, not only from talking with him a number of times, but also from hearing him talked about by others.) What was said seemed in no conceivable way damaging either to the individual or to the institution. I felt bound to eliminate the quotation, yet I felt a certain dishonesty in doing so, moderated by the realization that the omission changed nothing essential in the story.

But, if individuals and institutions' leaders can be overprotective, we have also found that they can be insufficiently guarded. For example, faculty members at a regional state college might be principally concerned with their immediate physical locale, not appreciating, at least until recently, the degree to which they were part of an increasingly centralized statewide system whose officials might use what was written about the college as ammunition in allocating scarce resources, permitting new postbaccalaureate programs to be developed and so forth. Correspondingly, my collaborators and I have felt at times that the judgment as to potential harm could not be left to even a very large number of readers at a particular college or university. For example, a draft that Gerald Grant and I wrote about a particular campus was severely criticized by some readers on the campus because we wrote nothing about the severe drug problems in the dormitories. Nor had we noted the fact that some faculty, and not only the younger ones, openly used marijuana and occasionally stronger drugs with students. But we felt that this was exactly the kind of information that regents or a legislature could use to punish a campus even though it would be possible to say that there is hardly any campus outside the fundamentalist belt, and perhaps even there, where people cannot be found smoking marijuana.

One cannot work at a college over a period of years without forming attachments to the people in it. Anthropologists face the hazard of going native; we of becoming therapist-counselors or indeed, unless we are exceedingly watchful, of becoming part of the public relations network of the institution as it seeks to maintain and enhance its viability.

Gerald Grant and I studied a sample of more or less experimental colleges, and concluded that it is best to use actual names of institutions, faculty and staff.[11] Otherwise, the researcher is not held to standards of reliability, being always able to contend that shadings of the truth were necessary for purposes of disguise. But, if individuals are named, they must accept the fairness of what is said about them; in one case in which an individual has preferred not to be named, we have left that person out of the story altogether—fortunately for us, the person was not central to the account.

Just as someone may be startled to hear his or her own voice on a tape recorder, so a person we have interviewed may feel at a minimum annoyed and at a maximum betrayed on reading a draft of what we propose to write. Our work proceeds, in fact, by the successive approximations of a series of drafts. We share our rough and preliminary draft with a few insiders, asking them to keep it confidential so that no one will be hurt by errors that may exist or by secrets that must be kept from enemies of the institution. On the basis of often extremely lengthy and cogent criticisms—often so full and careful that it is not an exaggeration to speak of these respondents as co-researchers—we write another draft, to which we give somewhat wider circulation. Commonly this sequence is followed by a re-visit, in which the revised draft is discussed with participants and questions are raised by us if not by them as to the possibilities of harm resulting from eventual publication.[12]

As anyone knows who has done this type of research, one is regarded as either too kind or too harsh. We are aware that, if sometimes we are too kind to visible faculty and administrators we have named, it is because we know "too much." But we also must ask ourselves whether, if we conclude that an institution is damaging to faculty or students, we should consider our responsibility to be comparable to that of the Federal Trade Commission or Consumers' Union, namely, to expose the evil so that students and faculty will be warned away and public or private funds not wasted in a time of shrinking resources. Fortunately, none of the institutions we have studied has been in our judgment one jump ahead of the sheriff—perhaps if it were, we would steer clear of it, for exposé is not the function of our research.

If the dilemma between candor and damage should become too great, we might decide not to publish. In marginal cases the hope would be that time would heal certain wounds, that leading actors would move on to other and presumably safer posts, and that the dangers of contemporary history would be obviated by becoming past history. But, while to some we may seem too kind, to others who are devotees of the more experimental or offbeat institutions, we are likely to seem not kind enough, for in their view no outsider can possibly do justice to the full significance of their enterprise. I have in mind here institutions that have something of a sacred quality for their members, especially faculty who, by their dedication, have generally chosen to render themselves invisible in the cosmopolitan world of their disciplines; it is understandable that in the light of their sacrifices, they want to believe in the utter uniqueness of their institution.

The two St. John's Colleges (Annapolis and Santa Fe) offer an illustration. Gerald Grant and I both admire them for their sturdy opposition to all the current fads of innovation: relevance, student co-determination, experiential learning, and so on. In a sense, they are among the most innovative of American colleges, because they have (along with Shimer College) stayed the same while almost everyone else has changed. Their faculty are acolytes to the only slowly changing roster of the Great Books and are required eventually to teach every subject in the curriculum and thus are discouraged from becoming visible specialists in any. The two colleges keep to a high order of seriousness and, perhaps for this reason, have had a hard time recruiting enough capable students to enlarge the applicant pools. However, it is an experiment that may come into its own again, with the signs of renewed interest already apparent in the study of the classics, particularly Greek, today.

The true devotees of St. John's believe that no outsider can understand them—certainly no sociologist, a vulgar guild which does not exist at St. John's. Every misunderstanding in our first drafts was pounced on to prove that we were unredeemable outsiders; every interpretation was challenged on the ground that one could only know the College from within (Merton, 1972). Faculty who believe that one does not understand the St. John's curriculum until one has spent nearly a lifetime in teaching it naturally think that the short visits we have paid to the colleges are proof of our frivolity. Such reactions can of course be turned into data for the researcher. They make clear the extent of the total dedication demanded of the non-celibate scholastics who make up the "archons" (as the leading faculty are termed at St. John's, since there are no faculty ranks).

However, I find the argument of the insider against the outsider unpersuasive, whether it is black against white, women against men, or the indigenous people objecting to the visiting anthropologist. One needs both perspectives; one needs to know more than one place. Indeed one has to get outside of one's own place in order to judge it.

The Lazarsfeldian Perspective

Lazarsfeld was trained in philosophy, mathematics, and psychology. He was at home in more than a single country; today his influence radiates throughout the academic and intellectual worlds of social science, both through his remembered presence and his voluminous writings and the work of generations of "Young Turks" who emerged from the Bureau of Applied Social Research with both shared and personal agendas.[13]

In carrying out the disaggregation of aggregate data to discover typologies, Lazarsfeld never lost sight of the fact that the distinction between a "case" and a "case history" is inevitably blurred and that, where such data are examined in sufficient detail, many typological instances turn out to be "deviant cases." Lazarsfeld brought a historian (Sigmund Diamond) into the Columbia Sociology Department, and in his panel studies he was interested in trajectories as against the flat contemporaneity of the single-shot survey (even when one asks for retrospctive data). He was endlessly interested in continuities in social research. Furthermore, in survey research and in institutional studies, Lazarsfeld had invariably been curious about the particular subject of his research, as well as inventive about method, nor did he disdain concern for public policy—always asking not only who is paying the bills but who is in fact the client, or group of clients, of any particular investigation.

Lazarsfeld used to remark that he undertook the Teacher Apprehension Study because it gave him a chance to put to work his passion for newly discovered contextual analysis. But, as the Marxists say, it was no accident that the subject was academic freedom: he cared about that. In these post-McCarthy days, it seems safe to say that he had a lifelong nostalgia for socialism, Vienna style, disguised in what seemed the ultra-American regalia of an empirically minded institution-building, intellectually adventurous, and wide-ranging social scientist.

Notes

1. The historian John Demos has alerted us to the extent of litigiousness over slander in the Puritan era in New England.

2. This style of work is illustrated in Becker, Geer, Hughes, and Strauss, 1961 and Becker, Geer, and Hughes, 1968—both based on work at the University of Kansas. I was a reader and commentator on the field notes that fed into this work. Everett Hughes and Robert Park had visited Lazarsfeld in his early Newark shop in the 1930s and had come away with great admiration for his versatility; to this day, Hughes has shared my belief in the greatness of Lazarsfeld's creative vitality and intellectual range.

3. One outside source of possible support and frequent pressure whose power impressed me in the course of my own later investigation was both the student and local press, whose influence depended on local context—for example, attacks from the *Chicago Tribune* did not trouble University of Chicago faculty members when Robert Hutchins was president of the University and treated the *Tribune* with insouciant contempt (Riesman, 1958).

4. The Smith College social science faculty delivered a joint protest directly to Hutchins, attacking the whole procedure for its supposed crudities and inability to capture, through a questionnaire handled by a nonsocial scientist interviewer seen as a typical market research type, all the nuances and shadings of respondents' attitudes.

5. Since *The Academic Mind*, published by the Free Press, is out of print, readers who would like access to a cogent review essay on the book, which summarizes both its methods and conclusions, would profit from Kelman, 1959.

6. It would be an interesting study in itself to see how, even in more agreeable times than the McCarthy era, professors who have generally regarded ourselves as an aggrieved and misunderstood minority treat those who come to us as suppliants of lower status: college travelers for textbook companies; survey interviewers; and in the better colleges, administrators.

7. Scorn for survey interviewers could be found inside as well as outside the social sciences, sometimes reflecting the class bias of the educated upper-middle class toward "mere" jobholders who did apparently routine work in comparison to their own presumably more meaningful careers. It may be that the women's movements would today heighten such reactions. I had come to the study with a great respect for survey interviewers; I came away from the Teacher Apprehension Study with even greater respect for both the Roper and NORC sets of interviewers—for their shrewdness as well as their indefatigability, their almost unfailing conscientiousness (in an era of hedonism, sometimes a devalued trait), their ingenuity, and even cheerfulness in the face of obstacles. (Incidentally, it was a blessing that the interviews were not tape-recorded, which would have brought us "too much" data at too high a cost, the greater part of it surplus.)

8. The late Mark Benney has given a colorful, if not always wholly accurate, account of our joint expedition in his witty and poignant autobiography (Benney, 1966).

9. For example, it was interesting to find that on the whole the younger and more liberal NORC interviewers obtained or at any rate wrote down more free-answer comments than the Roper interviewers, but much of this difference depended on the ecological distribution of interviewers and interviewees in view of the different sampling points of the two agencies, the far greater experience of the Roper interviewers, and the fact that many respondents in the more traditional colleges were familiar with the name Roper—a name that may have been a negative asset for some in the avant-garde. We secured the ages of all the interviewers and matched them to respondents' ages (we wish we could have had photographs also!) but did not find age to be a variable affecting response (cf. Benney, Riesman, and Star, 1956). Sex as such did not seem to make any difference either; there were 250 women respondents, and only a handful of male interviewers. We also had opportunities to discuss the quality of the interviewing with the home-office staff of both agencies as well as with Louis Harris and Clara Shapiro.

10. For a collection of essays discussing, on the one hand, the advantages of deviant case analysis and, on the other, special problems of classification and construction of questionnaires, see Lazarsfeld and Rosenberg, 1955; also, see Lazarsfeld and Henry, 1968; Merton, 1947.

11. When it comes to using the actual names of students, we find the problem more complex. Students often have almost a cult of candor, and it puts them on the spot to ask if we may quote something they said; we use the names of students only in exceptional circumstances, as for example in an article on New College in Sarasota where, with his permission, I used a student's long letter about the college for excerpts printed separately that gave a better impression of the intellectual style of the college than anything I might have written. (Riesman, 1975a). A few critics have contended that in using students' names we violate guidelines if not imperatives concerning research on "human subjects." We recognize that there is a psychological age of consent that may not be identical with adulthood as defined politically or legally.

12. The "participants" include those who have left. Many within an institution, however, naturally resent our interviewing dissidents who have left, feeling that they bear a grudge or are disloyal—yet for our purposes, like student drop-outs, they are part of the relevant universe.

13. This *Festschrift* itself should provide some indication of what seems to me a unique phenomenon; one might find an earlier illustration, for example, in Charles Y. Glock's contribution concerning consumer research to *The Uses of Sociology* (Glock, 1967; see also Glock, Chapter 5 of this volume). I should perhaps add that the Michigan Survey Research Center and companion Institute for Social Research have also been shops with a tradition of continuing investigation, such as in the case of the often inventive and invariably educative Detroit Area Studies undertaken with each new cohort of students.

References

ASTIN, ALEXANDER 1965 *Who Goes Where to College?* Chicago: Science Research Associates.

BECKER, HOWARD S., BLANCHE GEER, and EVERETT C. HUGHES 1968 *Making the Grade: The Academic Side of College Life.* New York: Wiley.

____, BLANCHE GEER, EVERETT C. HUGHES, and ANSELM STRAUSS 1961 *Boys in White: Student Culture in Medical School.* Chicago: University of Chicago Press.

BENNEY, MARK 1966 *Almost a Gentleman.* London: Peter Davies.

____, DAVID RIESMAN, and SHIRLEY A. STAR 1956 "Age and Sex in the Interview," *American Journal of Sociology* 62 (September), 143–152.

BERELSON, BERNARD, PAUL F. LAZARSFELD, and WILLIAM N. McPHEE 1954 *Voting.* Chicago: University of Chicago Press.

CAPLOW, THEODORE 1964 *Principles of Organization.* New York: Harcourt Brace, pp. 213–216.

CLARK, BURTON R. 1970 *The Distinctive College: Antioch, Reed, and Swarthmore.* Chicago: Aldine.

COLEMAN, JAMES S. 1961 *The Adolescent Society.* New York: Free Press.

____, 1973 "The University and Society's New Demands upon It," in Carl Kaysen, ed., *Content and Context: Essays on College Education.* New York: McGraw-Hill Carnegie Commission Series, pp. 359–399.

COTTLE, THOMAS J. 1973 "The Pains of Permanence," in Bardwell Smith, ed., *Tenure: Pro and Con.* San Francisco: Jossey-Bass, pp. 9–33.

DEMOS, JOHN 1975 *Symposium on Sociology and the American Past,* Eastern Sociological Society Annual Meetings, March 28.

DUBERMAN, MARTIN 1972 *Black Mountain: An Exploration in Community.* New York: Dutton.

GLOCK, CHARLES Y., and FRANCESCO M. NICOSIA 1967 "The Consumer," in Paul F. Lazarsfeld, William H. Sewell, and Harold L. Wilensky, *The Uses of Sociology.* New York: Basic Books, Chapter 12, pp. 363 ff.

GRANT, GERALD, and DAVID RIESMAN 1975 "An Ecology of Academic Reform," *Daedalus* 104 (Winter), 166–191.

GUSFIELD, JOSEPH, and DAVID RIESMAN 1968 "Innovations in Higher Education: Notes on Student and Faculty Encounters in Three New Colleges," in Becker, Geer, Riesman, and Weiss, eds., *Institutions and the Person: Essays Presented to Everett C. Hughes.* Chicago: Aldine, 165–199.

JENCKS, CHRISTOPHER, and DAVID RIESMAN 1969 *The Academic Revolution.* New York: Doubleday Anchor (now a University of Chicago paperback).

KATZ, ELIHU, and PAUL F. LAZARSFELD 1955 *Personal Influence.* Glencoe, Ill.: The Free Press.

KELMAN, HERBERT C. 1959 "Apprehension and Academic Freedom," *Public Opinion Quarterly*, 23 (Summer), 181–188.

LAZARSFELD, PAUL F. 1937 "Some Remarks on the Typological Procedure in Social Research," *Zeitschrift für Sozialforschung*, 119–139.

LAZARSFELD, PAUL F. 1940 "Panel Studies," *Public Opinion Quarterly*, 4: 122–128.

LAZARSFELD, PAUL F. 1961 "Observations on the Organization of Empirical Social Research in the United States," *Information*. International Social Science Council, Paris, France, 29, 1–35.

_____ , BERNARD BERELSON and HAZEL GAUDET 1968 *The People's Choice*. New York: Columbia University Press (3rd ed.)

_____ , and NEIL W. HENRY 1968 *Latent Structure Analysis*. Boston: Houghton Mifflin.

_____ , and ROBERT K. MERTON 1948 "Mass Communication, Popular Taste, and Organized Social Action," in Lyman Bryson, ed., *The Communication of Ideas*. New York: Harpers, pp. 180–219.

_____ , and MORRIS ROSENBERG, eds. 1955 *The Language of Social Research: A Reader in the Methodology of Social Research*. Glencoe, Ill.: The Free Press, Sections Ie and IIc.

_____ , and WAGNER THIELENS, JR. 1958 *The Academic Mind: Social Scientists in a Time of Crisis*. New York: The Free Press.

LOWENTHAL, LEO 1944 "Biographies in Popular Magazines," in Paul Lazarsfeld and Frank Stanton, eds., *Radio Research, 1942–43*. New York: Duell, Sloan and Pearce, pp. 504 ff.

MERTON, ROBERT K. 1938 "Social Structure and Anomie," *American Sociological Review*, 3 (October), 672–682.

MERTON, ROBERT K. 1947 "Selected Problems of Fieldwork in the Planned Community," *American Sociological Review*, 12 (June), 304–312.

MERTON, ROBERT K. 1949 "Patterns of Influence: A Study of Interpersonal Influence and Communications Behavior in a Local Community," in Lazarsfeld and Stanton, eds., *Communications Research 1948–49*. New York: Harpers, pp. 180–219.

MERTON, ROBERT K. 1972 "Insiders and Outsiders: An Essay in the Sociology of Knowledge," *American Journal of Sociology*, 72 (July), 9–47.

NEWCOMB, THEODORE M. 1943 *Personality and Social Change: Attitude Formation in a Student Community*. New York: Holt.

RIESMAN, DAVID 1942a "Civil Liberties in a Period of Transition," Carl J. Friedrich and Edward S. Mason, eds., *Public Policy*, Volume 3. Cambridge, Mass.: Harvard Graduate School of Public Administration, pp. 33–96.

RIESMAN, DAVID 1942b "Democracy and Defamation," *Columbia Law Review*, 42 (May), 727–780; 1085–1123; 1282–1318.

RIESMAN, DAVID 1942c "The Politics of Persecution," *Public Opinion Quarterly*, 6 (Spring) 41–56.

RIESMAN, DAVID 1952 *Faces in the Crowd*. New Haven, Conn.: Yale University Press.

RIESMAN, DAVID 1956a "Orbits of Tolerance, Interviewers, and Elites," *Public Opinion Quarterly*, 20:49–73.

RIESMAN, DAVID 1956b "The Sociology of the Interview," *Midwest Sociologist*, 18 (Winter), 3–15.

RIESMAN, DAVID 1958a *Constraint and Variety in American Education.* Lincoln, Nebr.: University of Nebraska Press.

RIESMAN, DAVID 1958b "Interviewers, Elites, and Academic Freedom," *Social Problems*, 6 115–126.

RIESMAN, DAVID 1958c "Academic Freedom and the Press" *Forum, The University of Houston Quarterly* (May), pp. 1ff.

RIESMAN, DAVID 1975a "New College," *Change* 7 (May), 34–43.

RIESMAN, DAVID 1975b "The Future of Diversity in a Time of Retrenchment," *Higher Education*, 4, 461–482.

____, and NATHAN GLAZER 1949 "The Meaning of Opinion," *Public Opinion Quarterly*, 12, 633–648; reprinted in Riesman, *Individualism Reconsidered.* Glencoe, Ill.: The Free Press, 1954, pp. 492–507.

____, JOSEPH GUSFIELD, and ZELDA GAMSON 1975 *Academic Values and Mass Education.* New York: McGraw-Hill paperback.

SANFORD, NEVITT, ed. 1962 *The American College: A Psychological and Social Interpretation of the Higher Learning.* New York: Wiley.

STERN, BERNHARD J. 1953 "Historical Materials on Innovation in Higher Education." Mimeograph report submitted to the Rockefeller and Ford foundations, May.

STOUFFER, SAMUEL A, 1955 *Communism, Conformity, and Civil Liberties.* New York: Doubleday.

TROW, MARTIN, et al. 1975 *Teachers and Students.* Carnegie Commission on Higher Education. New York: McGraw-Hill.

WHYTE, WILLIAM F., JR. 1943 *Street Corner Society.* Chicago: University of Chicago Press.

WOLFF, KATHERINE M. and MARJORIE FISKE 1949 "The Children Talk About Comics," in Paul F. Lazarsfeld and Frank Stanton, eds., *Communications Research: 1948–49.* New York: Harper, pp. 20–26.

17. ON FOLLOWING IN SOMEONE'S FOOTSTEPS: TWO EXAMPLES OF LAZARSFELDIAN METHODOLOGY

Hanan C. Selvin

Although the metaphor in the title of this paper appears to have a single and straightforward meaning, I suggest that in the history of science it has at least three distinct meanings. The first and most literal is essentially to put one's foot exactly in the footprints of the leader, to march where he marched and at the same gait. In the history of science—or, more generally, in the history of ideas—this may well be the most common pattern, appearing in such forms as the master and his disciples; the jointly authored paper by a senior and a junior scholar; and the "office," "laboratory," or "school" often associated with the leader's name.

The second meaning of following in someone's footsteps is not to imitate or copy, but to use the leader's footprint as a guide—to develop new methods to work on the same kinds of problems that had interested him or to use his methods to work on new kinds of problems. In some cases, this may lead to the rejection of the leader-follower relationship by either member, as when Marx announced that he was not a Marxist or when Freud's disciples, Jung and Adler among others, rejected some key premises of the leader, while still calling themselves psychoanalysts.

A third kind of footstep following, not explored in this paper, is to go where the leader *would have gone* had he faced the same situations as the follower.

As originally planned, this was to have been a joint paper with Christopher Bernert on the recent history of causal analysis, and there is hardly a paragraph that has not benefited from our work on that subject. I am grateful to Michael Miciak for research assistance and for a critical reading of an early draft. Special thanks must go to David Caplovitz for his penetrating criticisms of an earlier draft; I wish I could have heeded more of them. Most of all, however, I want to thank Herman O. Wold, who in his so-called "retirement" is not only writing and publishing more than most people half his age, but is also one of the world's most diligent and helpful correspondents. In the fall of 1976 he even found the time to visit Stony Brook for a few days and to spend several long sessions explaining recent developments in econometrics, his own and others'.

This kind can be described as *taking the role* of the leader; in effect, putting oneself inside the leader's head and asking what he would have done in the situation the follower faces. This may even take the form of an imaginary historical experiment, as in asking what Durkheim would have done in his study of suicide if he had used the statistical tools of correlation and regression, which were undergoing separate development during the same decade (Selvin, 1976).

For simplicity, I suggest short labels for the two types of leader-follower relationships to be examined here: *imitating* and *following*. To *imitate* is to do what the leader has already done, as nearly as possible—to apply his insights, his theories, and his methods to the same kinds of problems on which he worked. To *follow* is to pattern oneself after the leader but to change one or more key elements—to choose different methods for reaching his goals or to use his methods for reaching different goals.

Since one purpose of this volume is to honor Paul Lazarsfeld, I want to honor him by presenting examples of my following in his footsteps in both major senses of the phrase. Moreover, in view of his oft-expressed interest in the ways in which research, whether empirical or methodological, is actually carried out, I shall include some biographical details, both his and mine.

Imitating

Although I do not remember the date of this story, I do remember that it took place during a cocktail party in the Lazarsfelds' West 85th Street apartment and that Wag Thielens and I were chatting with Paul; this probably places it during the early stages of the work that led to *The Academic Mind* (Lazarsfeld and Thielens, 1958).

"How did it happen, Paul," I asked, "that you didn't go on in mathematics [the field in which he had taken his Ph.D. in Vienna]?"

"Ach," he replied, with a deprecatory shrug of his shoulders, "I decided that I would rather be a second-rate psychologist or sociologist than a third-rate mathematician!"

There are two points to this little story. The more obvious is that Paul characteristically understated his qualities in adopting those two ordinal numbers. The second point is that, although I did not know it at the time, I have imitated Paul in this decision, abandoning mathematics (and, at different times, economics, physics, and my family's retail furniture business) for the pursuit of sociological methodology and empirical social research.

On a more intellectual plane, the first serious work of methodology to which I turned after leaving graduate school at Columbia was the algebraic derivation of his famous "elaboration formula."[1] I wanted to show that Paul had been wrong in omitting the numerical coefficients of the formula, that these coefficients contained important substantive and methodological implications.

Trying to beat the Master at his own game is, I soon came to realize, a poor strategy. It gradually became clear to me that the omitted coefficients only complicated the algebra without adding anything to the methodology.

Another example of imitating, but with a higher methodological payoff, came two years later in a joint attempt by Martin A. Trow and myself to make sense of the well-known classification of empirical studies as either "descriptive" or "explanatory," a distinction for this purpose that we had learned from Herbert H. Hyman's classic *Survey Design and Analysis* (1955). During the preceding year the Berkeley Department of Sociology had engaged in that favorite pastime of would-be leading graduate departments—the reorganization of the graduate curriculum. Perhaps because there were so many new members in the department who had not yet had time to build up a vested interest in one or another method of research, and also because there were so many of us who had been either graduate students or faculty members at Columbia (Kingsley Davis, Nathan Glazer, William Kornhauser, Seymour Martin Lipset, Leo Lowenthal, Philip Selznick, and Trow and myself), the new curriculum included a required two-semester course in methods of research for first-year graduate students; the planned course closely resembled the famous Sociology 195–196, long required of first-year graduate students at Columbia.[2]

It fell to Trow and me to give this course for the first time in 1958–1959, and I was to give it for each of the next four years, always with another former Columbia student (Charles Y. Glock and William L. Nicholls II).[3] Trow and I decided to have the students read several important works of empirical social research, which we would then explicate[4] in what we fondly hoped would be a Lazarsfeldian manner.

One more element in this story deserves mention: the presence in this class of an unusually bright and skeptical group of graduate students who bedeviled us with searching questions at every turn. Those whose names most readily come to mind after eighteen years include Nicholas Jay Demerath III, David Nasatir, Emmanuel Schegloff, and Maurice Zeitlin.

It was my turn to give the first lecture on the half-dozen important empirical studies that we had selected, and I proceeded to apply the descriptive–explanatory typology to them. The lecture was a disaster! I didn't like the typology, and neither did Trow or the students. The next day, it was Trow's turn to lecture, and, as often happens in such jointly taught courses, he picked up the ball where I had left it. In attacking this Lazarsfeldian problem of classifying study designs, or, better, study *aims*, he went about it in a thoroughly Lazarsfeldian way—by *substructing* the descriptive-explanatory typology (Lazarsfeld, 1937 [1972]).[5] The process of substruction consists essentially in discovering or constructing a small number of dimensions, or variables, that underlie a set of qualitative types.

The two dimensions in Trow's substruction amount essentially to answers to the following two questions:

1. Does the investigator seek to describe some antecedently defined population?
2. Is he interested in identifying patterns of causal relations?

By *antecedently defined population* we mean a population that was of interest to someone *before* the investigator began his work. Consider, for example, the "target population" in the long-term series of studies on American voting behavior conducted by the Survey Research Center of the University of Michigan (Campbell et al., 1966), which is the set of legally qualified voters in the United States. This population obviously existed long before the Ann Arbor investigators began their studies, and it is of interest to many people, not least being the chairmen of the two major political parties. An example of a more nearly distinctive Lazarsfeldian target population is the audience watching some program on network television; again, this audience existed apart from any theoretically oriented research that might be done on it. A third example is a set of students at some college or university that might serve as subjects for an investigation in psychology or sociology; once again, these students constitute a population of interest to many people—administrators, faculty, community, and parents—before, and apart from, any research. In short, the population at issue here is not one that is created by the investigator.

For the purposes of this typology, it does not matter whether the investigator studies the entire population or selects a properly designed sample. Obviously, only in the third example given—the study of a particular college or university— would studying the entire target population be feasible, but feasibility is not at issue here.

In sharp contrast to the intention of the investigator in each of these three examples—to describe some aspects of a *real* population—are those studies in which the investigator works with *available cases*, which represent no real population. Instead, they constitute what Philip Hauser (in Deming, 1950, p. 14) has aptly called a *chunk*. And, as I have argued elsewhere (Hirschi and Selvin, 1967 [1973], ch. 13), it makes little sense to try to consider a chunk as a sample from some hypothetical universe of possibilities.

The answer to the second question is less obvious. The point is whether or not the investigator cares about the *effects* of some independent variable(s), the causes of some dependent variable(s), or both. The methodological explicator will be able to answer this question by looking for such indicators of an interest in causality as cause-and-effect language, the use of three-variable tables to test for spuriousness or for the presence of an intervening variable, and the use of path diagrams. Since these two dimensions are conceptually and empirically independent, and each involves a single dichotomy, they combine to yield the four types shown in Figure 1.

Figure 1. A Typology of Study Aims

Does the investigator seek to describe an antecedently defined population?

		YES	NO
Is the investigator interested in causality?	YES	Descriptive-Explanatory	Purely Explanatory Studies
	NO	Purely Descriptive	Nonstudy

Purely Descriptive Studies

Studies in this category range from the simplest market-research investigation—say, a hotel owner who leaves a postcard questionnaire in each room to determine the quality of his service—to the U.S. Bureau of the Census, whose decennial censuses and monthly sample surveys may well be the world's largest and most proficiently conducted descriptive surveys. Note that this characterization of the Census Bureau's aims refers to the aims in the minds of the senior officials of the Census Bureau, not the aims in the minds of researchers who may use Census Bureau data for substantive or theoretical purposes. From the standpoint of the Census Bureau, then, the sample survey that led to the Blau and Duncan study, *The American Occupational Structure* (1962), was a descriptive study; what Blau and Duncan aimed to do with the data is another story (discussed in the following paragraphs).

Purely Explanatory Studies

Most laboratory experiments in social psychology are of this type. Students in such courses are required to spend a fixed number of hours as experimental subjects, and they usually choose the experiments in which they are most interested. Subjects in such experiment(s) constitute a self-selected chunk. At the other extreme in size, but nevertheless of the same type, are the Kinsey studies of sexual behavior (Kinsey et al., 1948, 1953). Large as these "samples" are, they are nevertheless chunks (Cochran et al., 1968 [1950]).

Descriptive-Explanatory Studies

These studies aim *both* to describe certain aspects of a real population and to investigate causal relations within that population. The Blau and Duncan study sought to measure certain characteristics of the United States population and of important components of that population. It also sought to account for the variation in certain key variables, such as the level of attained occupational prestige achieved by respondents. Another example of this important type is Samuel A. Stouffer's *Communism, Conformity, and Civil Liberties* (1955), in which he measured the extent to which the American adult population was frightened by "the threat of Communism." He sought to account for variations in this fear. Note, however, that the ancillary study of community leaders in a dozen middle-sized cities, which Stouffer conducted to refine some of his causal hypotheses, is clearly an explanatory study; this particular chunk of middle-sized cities cannot represent the United States as a whole or even the population living in middle-sized cities.

Nonstudy

As Lazarsfeld pointed out (Lazarsfeld, 1937 [1972]), one virtue of the systematic construction of typologies is that it often uncovers logically possible types that the impressionistically constructed typology did not include. Such a logical possibility is the nonstudy, which seeks *neither* to describe some real population nor to investigate causal relations. Examples of this type are now fortunately rare, but they were common in journals of psychology and sociology before World War II, with titles such as "Attitudes of College Sophomores Toward War" or "How Youth Feels about the Depression."

The application of a Lazarsfeldian method to a Lazarsfeldian problem has produced useful results. The new typology is clearer and easier to apply than the old, and it appears to be valuable in explicating the reports of empirical social research.

Following

The problem that provides me with an example of *following* arose when Travis Hirschi and I were seeking to explicate one of the few methodological problems in which Paul Lazarsfeld appears to have had no interest, if indeed such problems exist. Although he reported having been interested in the work of the Chicago urban ecologists while he was still in Vienna, he had not, to my knowledge, worked systematically with city blocks or census tracts.[6] By applying Lazarsfeldian concepts of causal analysis to an important ecological study, I hoped to illuminate the question of whether or not valid causal analysis is even possible in such studies.

The problem first began to take shape when Hirschi and I were trying to explicate the analysis in Bernard Lander's *Towards an Understanding of Juvenile Delinquency* (1954; Hirschi and Selvin [1973, 1967], ch. 9). Lander had data on seven characteristics of the 155 census tracts of Baltimore from the 1950 Census, as well as the delinquency rate for each tract. In brief summary, one part of Lander's argument runs like this:

> The areal variables of median years of education, percent non-white, and percent of houses that are dilapidated are all associated statistically with the delinquency rate; these variables, however, are not causes of delinquency, since they are merely indicators of the more fundamental and unmeasurable variable of *anomie*, and it is the anomie that causes the delinquency.

Among the methodological issues here are the ecological fallacy, the illegitimate substitution of a relation between properties of such aggregates as census tracts for the desired relation between properties of the component individuals (Hirschi and Selvin, 1973 [1967], ch. 15), and the invocation of a "false criterion of non-causality" (Hirschi and Selvin, 1973 [1967] ch. 8, "measurable variables are not causes").

Rather than pursue these problems, which appear to be reasonably well understood by many sociologists, I want to turn instead to a problem that, as far as I know, has received no attention at all: the conditions under which one may legitimately draw causal inferences from areal, or other aggregate data.

Common sense is an unusually poor guide here. Consider, for example, Lander's apparent assumption that his independent variables, such as "percent non-white," were causally prior to his dependent variable, the rate of delinquency. On the individual level, of course, it would be hard to argue otherwise. One's race is determined at the moment of conception, and one's status as a delinquent comes much later. On the ecological level, however, it is easy to argue that a high rate of delinquency will drive, or has driven, many whites out of slum areas, so that the delinquency rate actually operates prior to "percent non-white."

Although Hirschi and I suggested several ways in which Lander might have determined the causal order of his variables, and, although earlier work by Lazarsfeld (1972 [1946]) and later work by Pelz and Andrews (1964) have set forth powerful statistical procedures for determining the relative causal priority of pairs of reciprocally interacting variables, I nevertheless had a nagging sense that it might not even be possible to establish a meaningful causal order between ecological variables. It is only in the last few months that I have learned of an answer to this question—or, rather, that there is a more fundamental question, entirely unknown to Hirschi and me.

In connection with a study of the recent history of causal analysis which I had been conducting with Christopher Bernert, I had occasion to write Herman

Wold to ask him to describe the history of his own interests in causal analysis. I learned two things from Wold's long and detailed answer: the general point that sociologists wishing to do serious work on the methodology of causal analysis must be familiar with recent work in econometrics,[7] and the specific point that

> ... Ragnar Bentzel and Bent Hansen in an important paper showed that if the data of a [recursive] system are aggregated over time, say from monthly to yearly periods, the resulting system will be interdependent. Clearly, the Bentzel-Hansen paper went a long way towards a reconciliation of the arguments for and against interdependent systems.
>
> It is a question whether Bentzel-Hansen's paper suffices to establish the interdependent system as an operative tool. Reference is made to Werner Meissner's important analysis of interdependent systems from the point of view of cybernetics (control theory). Meissner argues that a control system must have a causal structure that can be simulated on the computer, but interdependent systems cannot be simulated (Wold, 1976).

For the reader unfamiliar with econometric terminology, I shall decompose this paragraph and its implications into a few relatively simple propositions:

1. It is always possible to give meaningful causal interpretations to *recursive systems*, those in which each variable depends only on variables causally prior to it in the system; in other words, there are neither "feedback loops" nor pairs of variables that simultaneously affect each other.

2. It is impossible to make meaningful *causal* statements about *interdependent systems*. These are systems with feedback loops or with pairs of variables that simultaneously and reciprocally affect each other.

3. The paper by Bentzel and Hansen cited by Wold shows that if a recursive system is aggregated over any of three "domains of aggregation"—over variables, over time, or over individuals—the system becomes interdependent.

To understand the bearing of these three assertions on Lander's analysis, and on causal analysis such as Lander conducted, it will be useful to state two propositions about Lander's analysis, one inferential and the other obvious:

1. I infer that the theories of delinquency and, more generally, of deviance on which Lander drew were all theories in which the unit of analysis is the individual. Thus Merton's "Social Structure and Anomie" (1938) deals with the ways in which individuals located in various parts of the social structure responded to socially induced pressures to strive for certain culturally approved goals with the socially structured means available to them.

2. Lander's data are aggregated in all three of the ways discussed by Bentzel and Hansen: various violations of the law are combined into one overall rate of delinquency for each census tract; the independent variables are variously aggregated over time (median monthly rent) and over blocks and tracts (over crowding).

Proposition 3 and these two statements about Lander's analysis seem to me to destroy any possibility of making meaningful causal inferences in Lander's data. These arguments, however, are perfectly general, and I believe that they apply to any attempt at causal analysis with aggregate data, *where the theories are derived from propositions about individual behavior.* If this analysis is correct, what should urban ecologists do in the future when they want to make causal statements?

As I see it, there are several possible lines of action open to causally-oriented urban ecologists:

1. They can try to find logical or methodological errors in my analysis or in that of Bentzel and Hansen, on which it is partially based.

2. They can accuse me of heresy, ignorance, or other shortcomings and derelictions, as did some of the early critics of my 1957 paper on tests of significance.

3. They can abandon the attempt to construct recursive systems in ecological analyses and, therefore, causal inferences from such data. Most large-scale econometric models—say, those of whole economies—are interdependent systems, but this has not kept them from being both practically and theoretically meaningful.[8]

4. Investigators of ecological data might abandon altogether the use of what Lazarsfeld has called "analytic" variables or what Hagstrom and I have called "aggregative" variables—properties of higher-level units derived by taking some parameter of the distribution of a lower-level characteristic over the units constituting the higher level (Kendall and Lazarsfeld, 1955 [1950]; Lazarsfeld and Menzel, 1972 [1961]; Selvin and Hagstrom 1959). They would then work *only* with "global" (Lazarsfeld) or "integral" (Selvin and Hagstrom) variables; examples include the spatial distribution of recreational facilities in each census tract; the number, training, and behavior of the police in each area and the treatment of crime news in the mass media. But even this draconian measure may be insufficient in the light of the Bentzel and Hansen argument, for it still seems impossible to avoid aggregation over time, and this alone will turn the otherwise recursive system into an interdependent one and thus preclude the analyst from making causal inferences.

5. Finally, ecologists wanting to make causal statements might rely on propositions about the behavior of individuals, using the properties of their ecological units as *contextual variables.*[9] One might then be led to propositions of the following form: the effect of an individual's education on the probability of his becoming a delinquent depends on the social integration of the area in which he lives.[10]

In truth, I do not feel altogether confident about the validity of the above arguments, but bitter experience has taught me that there are risks attendant on being a methodologist. Nevertheless, my Master was never one to shun controversy, and, following him, I cannot do so either.

Notes

1. This formula shows how the numerical association between an independent variable and a dependent variable can be decomposed into the weighted sum of two first-order partial associations (between the independent variable and the dependent variable, with the effect of the "test factor" removed) and the unweighted sum of the product of the two "marginal" associations (between each of the two original valuables and the test factor). (See Lazarsfeld, 1955 [1946], pp. 116–125). In the algebraically correct formula there is a numerical coefficient or "weight" that multiplies each partial association, but Lazarsfeld leaves these coefficients out of his published discussions.

2. For an analysis of the way in which this course was taught around 1950 and of the effects of taking the course on the subsequent graduate careers of the students, see Wright (1954).

3. Glock and Nicholls were omitted from the list of former Columbians mentioned above because they had not yet joined the department at that time, nor had William Petersen, another former Columbian. Lest anyone misunderstand the significance of this longer list of former Columbians, be it noted that Glazer left Berkely after only a year or two and, by 1965, Petersen, Lipset, and I had also left. In all fairness, I should point out, neither among the former students nor the former faculty was there unanimous support for Lazarsfeldian methodology; rather than attempt the impossible task of even roughly quantifying each person's support for Paul's ideas, I have left the list unedited.

4. For Lazarsfeld's own account of what he means by *explication*, see the Introduction to Lazarsfeld and Rosenberg (1955). Conversations with him during the past few years indicated that he still emphasized the central role of explication in the work of methodologists.

5. Three comments are relevant here: (1) Although all of Lazarsfeld's methodological discussions of typology construction involve the qualitative determination of the "underlying dimensions," such procedures as factor analysis and his own latent-structure analysis accomplish this task quantitatively; see, for example, Selvin in Tanur (1972, ch. 45). In the use of expressions such as "discover underlying factors," there is an unfortunate bit of misleading epistemology long in use by psychologists; it seems to me clearer, more honest and less pretentious to speak of "constructing new variables" from the given variables. (3) The reader familiar with linear algebra may think of the substructed dimension as constituting a quantitative "basis" for the qualitative types, in the sense that each type can be constructed from the regions defined by several dimensions.

6. The content of these two sentences, believed to be the case by many sociologists, including the editors of this volume, who had known and worked with Paul at length, turn out to be entirely wrong! The missing link was supplied by William S. Robinson, who told me that, as I had conjectured, Paul had indeed led him to study the problem of ecological correlations (Robinson, 1950; see also Hirschi and Selvin, 1972 [1967], ch. 15, for later work on this and related problems). Robinson reports that he and Paul first investigated the problem

empirically, discovering rapidly that the individual correlations and ecological correlations are essentially independent of each other. However, it was only when Robinson realized several years later that analyses of co-variance provided an appropriate formalization for this problem that he was able to write his justly famous paper of 1950. Although this choice of mathematical formulization did not involve Lazarsfeld, the history of this paper is altogether Lazarsfeldian in spirit (my own judgment, not necessarily Robinson's).

7. Although sociologists have more to learn from econometricians in this respect than vice versa, Wold credits certain sociologists—among them, Otis Dudley Duncan and Robert M. Hauser—for working out ways to include hypothetical and unmeasurable variables in a path analysis (Wold, 1976).

8. One does not need recursive systems or causal interpretations to gain scientific understanding. Thus Boyle's Law and Charles's Law relate the pressure, volume, and temperature of an "ideal" enclosed gas to form an interdependent system.

9. Robert M. Hauser (1970) argues persuasively that many analyses purporting to show "contextual effects" actually represent the effects of uncontrolled or poorly controlled individual-level variables. See, also, the subsequent exchange between Hauser and Allen H. Barton.

10. Hagstrom and I (1963) argued that Durkheim, Blau, and Davis had all trivialized the study of contextual effects by limiting the descriptions of their contexts to single variables; this is why I have chosen a composite variable, "social integration," in the preceding example. For serious discussion of this and related points, see the exchange between Davis (1963), Selvin-Hagstrom (1963), and Selvin (1968).

References

BAKAN, DAVID 1967 *On Method: Toward a Reconstruction of Psychological Investigation*. San Francisco: Jossey-Bass.

BLAU, PETER M., and OTIS DUDLEY DUNCAN 1967 *The American Occupational Structure*. New York: Wiley.

CAMPBELL, ANGUS, et al. 1966 *Elections and the Political Order*. Ann Arbor, Mich: Survey Research Center, Institute for Social Research.

COCHRAN, WILLIAM G., et al. 1968 [1950] *Statistical Problems of the Kinsey Report on Sexual Behavior in the Human Male*. Westport, Conn.: Greenwood.

COLEMAN, JAMES S. 1956 "Appendix I" in S. M. Lipset, J. S. Coleman, and M. Trow, *Union Democracy*. New York: Free Press.

DAVIS, JAMES A. 1963 "Group Variables," *American Sociological Review*, 28 (October), 814.

DEMING, WILLIAM E. 1950 *Some Theory Sampling*. New York: Wiley.

HAUSER, ROBERT M. 1970 "Context and Consex: A Cautionary Tale," *American Journal of Sociology*, 75 (January), 645–664.

HIRSCHI, TRAVIS M., and HANAN C. SELVIN 1973 [1967] *Principles of Survey Analysis*. New York: Free Press.

HOGBEN, LANCELOT 1958 *Statistical Theory*. New York: Norton.

HYMAN, HERBERT H. 1955 *Survey Design and Analysis*. New York: Free Press.

KENDALL, PATRICIA L. 1957 "Note on Significance Tests," In R. K. Merton, G. G. Reader, and P. L. Kendall, eds., *The Student Physician*. Cambridge, Mass.: Harvard University Press, Appendix D, pp. 301–305.

——, and PAUL F. LAZARSFELD 1955 [1950] "The Relation between Individual and Group Characteristics in *The American Soldier*," in Paul F. Lazarsfeld and Morris Rosenberg, eds., *The Language of Social Research*. New York: Free Press, pp. 290–296.

KINSEY, ALFRED, et al. 1948 *Sexual Behavior in the Human Male*. Philadelphia: Saunders.

KINSEY, ALFRED, et al. 1953 *Sexual Behavior in the Human Female*. Philadelphia: Saunders.

LANDER, BERNARD 1954 *Towards an Understanding of Juvenile Delinquency*. New York: Columbia University Press.

LAZARSFELD, PAUL F. 1955 [1946] "Interpretation of Statistical Relations as a Research Operation," in P. F. Lazarsfeld and Morris Rosenberg, eds., *The Language of Social Research*. New York: Free Press, pp. 116–125.

LAZARSFELD, PAUL F. 1972 [1937] "Some Remarks on Typological Procedures in Social Research," in P. F. Lazarsfeld, Ann K. Pasanella, and Morris Rosenberg, eds., *Continuities in the Language of Social Research* New York: Free Press, 99–106.

LAZARSFELD, PAUL F. 1972 [1946] "Mutual Effects of Statistical Variables," in P. F. Lazarsfeld, Ann K. Pasanella, and Morris Rosenberg, eds., 1972, pp. 388–398.

——, and HERBERT MENZEL 1972 [1961] "On the Relation Between Individual and Collective Properties," in P. F. Lazarsfeld, Ann K. Pasanella, and Morris Rosenberg, eds., 1972, pp. 225–236.

——, ANN K. PASANELLA, and MORRIS ROSENBERG, eds. 1972 *Continuities in the Language of Social Research*. New York: Free Press.

——, and MORRIS ROSENBERG, eds. 1955 *The Language of Social Research*. New York: Free Press.

——, and WAGNER THIELENS, JR. 1958 *The Academic Mind*. New York: Free Press.

MERTON, ROBERT K. 1938 "Social Structure and Anomic," *American Sociological Review*, 3 (October), 672–682.

——, GEORGE G. READER, and PATRICIA L. KENDALL, eds. 1957 *The Student Physician*. Cambridge, Mass.: Harvard University Press.

MORRISON, DENTON E., and RAMON HENKEL, eds. 1970 *The Significance Test Controversy: A Reader*. Chicago: Aldine.

NAMBOODIRI, N. KISCHMAN, LEWIS F. CARTER, and HUBERT M. BLA-

LOCK, JR. 1975 *Applied Multivariate Analysis and Experimental Designs*. New York: McGraw-Hill.

PELZ, DONALD C., and FRANK M. ANDREWS 1964 "Detecting Causal Priorities in Panel Study Data," *American Sociological Review*, 29 (December), 836–848.

ROBINSON, WILLIAM S. 1950 "Ecological Correlation and the Behavior of Individuals," *American Sociological Review*, 15 (June), 351–356.

SELVIN, HANAN C. 1955 "The Uses and Misuses of Significance," in *The Effects of Leadership: Climate and Individual Characteristics of the Non-duty Behavior of Army Trainees: An Exploratory Report*. New York: Bureau of Applied Social Research, Columbia University, Appendix D.

SELVIN, HANAN C. 1968 "Computer Analysis of Observational Data," in *Calculus et Formalizations dans les Sciences de l'Homme*. Paris: Edition du Centre de la Recherche Scientifique.

SELVIN, HANAN C. "Varieties of Military Leadership," in Judith M. Tanur, ed., *Statistics: A Guide to the Unknown*. San Francisco: Holden-Day, pp. 253–265.

SELVIN, HANAN C. 1976 "Durkheim, Booth and Yule: The Non-diffusion of an Intellectual Innovation," *European Journal of Sociology*, 17 (May), 39–52.

———, and WARREN HAGSTROM 1963 "The Empirical Classification of Formal Groups," *American Sociological Review*, 28 (June), 399–411.

STOUFFER, SAMUEL A. 1955 *Communism, Conformity and Civil Liberty*. Garden City, N.Y.: Doubleday-Anchor.

TANUR, JUDITH M., ed. 1972 *Statistics: A Guide to the Unknown*. San Francisco: Holden-Day.

WOLD, HERMAN 1956 "Causal Inference from Observational Data," *Journal of the Royal Statistical Society* (A), 119 Part I, 28–50.

WOLD, HERMAN 1976 "Open Path Models with Latent Variables: The NIPALS (Non-Linear Iterative Partial Least Squares) Approach," Uppsala, (unpublished).

WRIGHT, CHARLES R. 1954 "The Effect of Training in Social Research," Ph.D. dissertation. New York: Columbia University.

18. DISPOSITION CONCEPTS IN BEHAVIORAL SCIENCE

Morris Rosenberg

Although most behavioral scientists spend much of their time studying dispositions, few pause to consider the distinctive nature of this concept. A disposition refers *not* to a state or condition of the individual, but in the words of Pap (1958:426) to "a tendency to react in a certain way to a certain kind of stimulus (in a generalized sense of stimulus)." Although Pap speaks of stimulus whereas Hempel (1952) refers to "circumstances," they are not in essential disagreement.

Consider the concept "elastic." When we say that a piece of material is elastic, we do not mean that it is in process of being stretched; we mean that it is *capable* of being stretched. It may, in fact, spend its entire existence without actually being stretched, but it is still legitimate to characterize it as elastic, since it would stretch if the proper pressure were applied to it. Similarly, we say that a piece of copper is a good electrical conductor, even if electricity is not induced in it; that glass is brittle, even if not broken; and so on. In physical science such concepts as soluble, fissionable, catalyzer, electrical resistance, fragile, meltable all possess dispositional characteristics.

If disposition concepts play an important role in physical science, they are of far greater importance in behavioral science. McDougall (1938) referred to "tendencies as indispensable postulates of all psychology." Most of the major dependent variables of survey research are essentially dispositional concepts.

Most of us, then, are engaged in studying not only what is but what could be or tends to be. Take the concept of "liberalism." This is an attitude toward a certain set of social and political objects. A "liberal" is one who, at election time, may be expected to vote for the liberal candidate; when asked to give an opinion about social welfare measures, the liberal would be expected to ex-

---

Portions of this essay were presented as part of the W. I. Thomas Lecture at the University of Tennessee in 1966. I am indebted to the late Professor Gordon A. Allport who made a number of valuable suggestions at that time.

press support of them. When we characterize him as liberal, we are essentially describing how that person *would* behave (or respond, think, or feel) *if* he or she were in a situation in which liberalism was relevant.

Precisely the same is true of *traits* (physical courage, generosity, morality); of *abilities* (intelligence, musical skill, artistic talent); of *reflexes* (the Babinski reflex, heat or cold sensitivity); of *habits* (brushing one's teeth, eating at a certain time, watching a recurrent television program); of *values* (beliefs in democracy, equality, success); of *drives* (sex, safety, belongingness, self-actualization); of *personality characteristics* (authoritarianism, compulsiveness, extraversion); or of *powers* or "tendencies" generally. These are all dispositions—tendencies to respond; they represent the major dependent variables of most sociological research and are important both as independent and dependent variables in psychological research.

It is important to differentiate such dispositions from specific responses, acts, or events. The brittleness of glass refers to a response tendency, whereas the actual shattering of the windowpane is an event. Political liberalism is the disposition, whereas the vote for the liberal candidate on election day is the act, response, or event.

From his earliest studies of the empirical analysis of action through his trail-blazing work on voting behavior, market behavior, and so on, Paul F. Lazarsfeld was deeply interested in the study of behavior or events. At the same time, Lazarsfeld (1958; 1959a) made extremely important contributions to the study and classification of dispositions. Since human dispositions are so numerous and diverse, a good classification is no easy matter. Donald Campbell (1963) claims there are at least 80 different classifications of dispositions in the literature. In addition, dispositions have been differentiated in terms of means and ends, in terms of physiological and cultural determinants, in terms of moral desirability, in terms of whether they are cardinal, central, or secondary, motivational and stylistic (Allport, 1961).

One of the most ingenious classificatory schemes is Lazarsfeld's heuristic typology of dispositions involving the location of all dispositions within a three-dimensional property space. As Lazarsfeld notes (1959a:8),

> A scrutiny of various texts shows that three dimensions dominate the discussion. One is generality and specificity (e.g., a personality trait that can be exhibited in many substantive spheres versus an interest usually directed toward a limited object). Another may be described as degree of directiveness (e.g., an attitude versus a desire for something, the former being more of the passive, the second more of the driving kind). The third dimension relates to the time perspective (e.g., a plan or an expectation spans the future; an urge or a perceptual bias focuses on the present).

Dichotomizing these three dimensions yields eight types which subsume most of the multitudinous dispositions that personality and social psychologists consider: preferences and opinions; general traits and attitudes; wants or needs; directional traits; expectations; tendencies or inclinations; intentions or plans;

and, generally, "motivation." Since natural language tends to be imprecise, the ideas here are better communicated by the location along the three dimensions specified by Lazarsfeld than by reference to the available terms.

It is worth calling special attention to one of these dimensions, namely, the passive-driving dimension, since it plays a large role both in physical and human dispositions. At the extreme of passivity are certain dormant potentialities docilely awaiting the conditions for their activation. Thus, the dispositions to shiver or sweat are not dynamic ones, urgently seeking expression, but passive ones, awaiting heat or cold to activate them. Somewhat more driving or dynamic would be such dispositions as attitudes or traits. An attitude, to be sure, is dormant until it is activated by some circumstance, but some dispositions are easily activated whereas others are not. Thus, an ardent radical will start talking politics at the drop of a hat; a very wide range of stimuli will activate such an easily triggered disposition. Finally, some dispositions are extremely dynamic; such would be true of many drives and desires. The sex drive at a certain period of life would be the most conspicuous example. Similarly, an artist, composer, or writer may have a pressing drive to create, a drive which urgently seeks expression, requiring only certain conditions to unchain, unleash, or release it.

Criticisms of Dispositions

By now a small industry has emerged devoted to the study of human dispositions. Psychologists in the area of tests and measurements have devoted decades to the development and refinement of aptitude, attitude, and personality tests, and the rash of measurement instrument inventories appearing in recent years (Robinson and Shaver, 1973; Shaw and Wright, 1967; Bonjean, Hill, and McLemore, 1967; Miller, 1964; etc.), chiefly devoted to the measurement of dispositions, attests to the widespread interest in this area among sociologists. Yet it may be worth pausing to ask, what do we really mean when we call someone liberal, or alienated, or misanthropic, or prejudiced, or other-directed? Do we mean anything at all? Is it worth knowing? What are its drawbacks and limitations?

Historically speaking, the rise of disposition research has been accompanied by a corresponding rise in disposition criticism, and the two have proceeded apace. Blumer has criticized dispositions because they are unobservable,[1] La-Piere (1934) because they are poor predictors of behavior (a view loudly echoed in recent years by Deutscher [1966; 1973] and others), and Skinner (1953) because they are tautological or superfluous. Furthermore, in thinking of dispositions as potentials or tendencies, Nelson Goodman (1954) has questioned whether potentials or possibilities have any meaning (especially insofar as they are counterfactual conditionals), and Hartshorne and May (1928) long ago called into question the presumed reality of response tendencies by providing empirical evidence[2] that the postulated response tendencies did not in fact exist.

Since space limitations prevent me from dealing with all these as well as certain other equally serious criticisms of dispositions, I would like to focus on two arguments: (1) the contention that, causally speaking, dispositions are tautologies and (2) the contention that they are weak predictors of behavior or events. Both of these criticisms are, I believe, true. I would superimpose on this admission the paradoxical assertion that dispositions still remain the fundamental subject matter of social psychological research.

Dispositions as Tautologies

In ordinary discourse, we are prone to say that rubber stretches because it is elastic, gasoline burns because it is inflammable, glass shatters because it is brittle, people attack school busses because they are prejudiced, children get high marks because they are smart, and so on. Such statements plainly imply that dispositions are capable of participating in causal statements—that they have causal efficacy.

It is neither frivolous nor carping to ask whether such statements have any meaning whatever. What do we actually mean when we say that rubber stretches because it is elastic? We are saying nothing more or less than that rubber stretches because it is stretchable. Each of us may say with a straight face that paper burns because it is combustible without realizing that we are only saying that paper burns because it can burn. When we attribute Jones's handsome charity donation to his generosity, we are saying nothing more enlightening than that he behaved generously because of his tendency to behave generously—scarcely a dazzling insight and certainly causally suspect.

The role of such circular reasoning in the history of science has not always been trivial. This point is well illustrated in the notorious history of "phlogiston." One problem that bedeviled early scientific theory was why things burned. To explain this phenomenon, the concept of phlogiston—the material substance that makes things burn—was introduced and enjoyed wide currency; things burned because they contained phlogiston. The error here lay in attributing a material reality to what was in fact a disposition.

Similarly, Pap (1962) reminds us of the Molière physician who, taxed to explain why opium caused such drowsiness, attributed it to opium's "dormitive powers." If the reader assumes that the progress of medicine has rendered such reasoning archaic, I can only mention the case of a friend who, recovering from a severe bout of flu, asked his doctor why he felt so tired and was told that this reaction was due to "post-influenza fatigue."

The circularity of dispositions to some extent is due to the methodology used to study them. We can never study someone's sunny disposition directly but can only infer it from his ready laughter or other indicators. Search as we may, we will never see intelligence; we can only infer it from answers to tests, problems solved, modes of speech, and so on. Thus, the alleged cause, which presumably accounts for the overt response, can only be inferred from the response. In other words, although the disposition is said to be the cause of the response, all we ever can observe is the response, not the disposition. In Weissman's (1965: 162) words, "The actuality that is prior to potentiality in knowledge is the actuality that succeeds potentiality in time."

If dispositions are tautologies, is there any point in studying them? One reason to do so is that some tautologies are fruitful; despite their circular nature, they contribute to understanding. Generally, tautologies are experienced as fruitful when it is not self-evident *which* disposition underlies the concrete behavior. Assume that someone gives a large donation to the Givers Fund. Which disposition does it reflect—generosity? conformity? guilt? spite of the IRS? It might be any of these and more. Lazarsfeld has shown that just as an indicator is a concrete manifestation of an abstract concept, so an act, event, or response is assumed to be a specific expression of a general disposition. (Lazarsfeld, 1958; 1959a)

Examples are easily at hand. In developing her theory of neurosis, Horney (1945) differentiated three interpersonal orientations of people: those who move toward people, those who move against people, and those who move away from people. A study of occupational choice (Rosenberg, 1957) showed a correspondence between these general orientations and the tendency to select occupations in which such orientations tend to be expressed. Such results simply express a tautology: those who enjoy working with people and helping others tend to select occupations (such as teaching or social work) which enable them to work with people and help others. The reason such a tautological finding is not necessarily trivial is that when we focus on the specific act—selecting teaching, science, medicine, business—it is not obvious which of many general possible dispositions may be reflected in the act.

Similarly, when people tell us that the general public is not qualified to vote on today's complex issues, that government officials are unresponsive to the needs of the average man, that people who talk politics without knowing what they are talking about should be kept quiet, and so on, it may not be immediately apparent that these responses to "political" questions are in part overt manifestations of an underlying disposition of misanthropy. In this event the tautology would be experienced by many as an increment to knowledge.

Dispositions and Behavior

A case can be made for the assertion that dispositions are not only tautological, but unobservable, nonmaterial, and vague as well. The pragmatically oriented social scientist may live comfortably with these criticisms by the simple expedient of ignoring them, but the effort to shove down his throat the further charge that dispositions are useless for predicting actual behavior can only activate his disposition to gag. Yet far and away the most prominent and pressing criticism of dispositions today revolves about the issue of behavior. In recent years, Irwin Deutscher (1966; 1973) has resumed the vigorous challenge to attitude research launched over 40 years ago by LaPiere (1934). We are interested, he says, in social behavior, but attitudes often do not effectively predict behavior. And Deutscher is unquestionably right; one cannot tell very much what a person will do by finding out what he thinks, feels, and wants. As Merton (1948) long ago pointed out, prejudice does not always lead to discrimination nor does discrimination always reflect prejudice.

Social scientists have characteristically responded to this problem by sharpening and refining their research instruments. Although none but the cantankerous can quarrel with a solution so redolent of virtue, the point is that even the most impeccable methodology cannot overcome the fact that knowledge of general dispositions alone cannot possibly predict actual behavior very well.

The reason, I believe, cuts deeply and is rooted in the very nature of human dispositions. As noted earlier, Hempel (1952) speaks of dispositions as potentials or tendencies of objects to respond in certain ways "under specifiable circumstances." "Under specifiable circumstances!" These three innocent little words generate the most monumental difficulties.

Although efforts have been made to classify dispositions, the classification of circumstances has generally been ignored. Yet, without some ordering or classification of the endless variety of circumstances, the task of predicting real-life behavior becomes well-nigh hopeless. Without making any claim for completeness, I would like to point out how varied are the meanings which fall under the rubric of the term "circumstances."

The most familiar sense in which the concept of circumstance applies is in the narrow sense of "stimulus." The sight of a beggar arouses one's generous or sympathetic impulses. A picture of a communist leader arouses one's feelings about communism. Such stimuli, it may be noted, may derive either from *external* or *internal* sources. If a stranger starts a political conversation, this would be an external stimulus. An example of an internal stimulus would be a train of association which carries one's thoughts to a topic that causes one to express one's views to a person present (Mead, 1934). A slight twinge in the arm stimulates a hypochondriacal disposition and sends one rushing for an aspirin. Such stimuli may be purposive or accidental.

A second sense in which the term circumstance is used is that of "providing an opportunity" for a disposition to express itself in behavior. A skilled piano player can only express this disposition in behavior if a piano is present. We do not think of the piano simply as a stimulus but as indispensable equipment allowing the piano skill to be expressed in behavior. Similarly, a person disposed to vote Republican has no opportunity to do so until election day.

A third meaning of circumstance refers to a certain condition of the "field" or environment. Thus a person may only be able to read if there is silence in the house. An artist may be unable to paint in an ordinary room but able to do so in a studio.

Circumstances may also mean the availability of "power" or "resources." A youth's disposition to leave home may not be converted into behavior until he is old enough to support himself. The field of advertising constantly creates dispositions favorable to products; the activation of these dispositions in the individual case must, however, depend on the availability of money. Many dispositions never achieve behavioral expression because people lack the power or resources to realize them.

Another circumstance which may "release" a disposition is a change in the anticipation of the consequences issuing from the behavior. Needless to say, many dispositions do not achieve behavioral expression because of anticipation of the possible consequences. A man disposed to lie, cheat, swindle, or rape will usually refrain from doing so out of fear of the probable consequences. It thus follows that a change in the anticipated consequences may be the circumstances that result in the expression of the disposition. A faculty member disposed to criticize his department chairman may do so *after* he gets tenure. A man with homicidal tendencies may release this disposition when thrown into contact with a military enemy. The disposition is thus activated when circumstances permit it to be expressed with impunity.

The circumstance perhaps most familiar to the sociologist is the role context. As Allport (1966:1) observes, "Every parent knows that an offspring may be a hellion at home and an angel when he goes visiting. A businessman may be hardheaded in the office and a mere marshmallow in the hands of his pretty daughter." Similarly, William James (1950:294) noted that "many a youth who is demure enough before his parents and teachers swears and swaggers like a pirate among his 'tough' young friends."

The "circumstances" that permit, allow, or stimulate the conversion of dispositions into action are, then, extremely varied. They may be thought of as cues, stimuli, triggers, releasers, necessary or sufficient conditions, and so on. Lacking knowledge of the stimuli, opportunities, environmental conditions, resources, anticipated consequences, or role contexts, the ability to predict specific behavior from general dispositions is usually weak.

The issue of circumstances is thus absolutely critical to the entire question of predicting behavior or events from knowledge of dispositions. In this regard, however, two issues must be separated: (1) the determinacy of circumstances and (2) the specification of circumstances.

Determinacy of Circumstances

As social scientists, many of us are busily at work seeking to ascertain whether people are authoritarian, other-directed, anomic, radical, Machiavellian, misanthropic, politically tolerant. Assuming that we have gained such knowledge, can we say much about behavior? One reason we cannot derives from a particular characteristic of many dispositions, namely, their "openness." As Weissman (1965:55) says, "This openness is pre-supposed when we say that a mind or object is qualified to initiate or undergo a change without stipulating when or where the change will occur, or the specific identity of the causal conditions whose satisfaction will be sufficient to make it occur; thus some dogs are likely to bark anytime, anywhere, and at nearly any provocation."

Though the social scientist may know someone's response tendencies and even the types of circumstances which can activate them, what he is unable to predict is *whether* the circumstances will actually occur. Assume that we describe a man as courageous. On this basis we predict that, if he passes a burning building with a child inside, he is likely to attempt to rescue that child. What we cannot predict is whether, where, when, and so on he will ever *pass* a burning building with a child inside. Similarly, although we may predict that an honest man will return a found wallet, we cannot predict whether, when, or where he will find a wallet.

To those who bemoan the dire straits of the behavioral sciences, some consolation may be afforded by the fact that the physical sciences are in the same fix. When a physicist claims that a block of uranium is "fissionable," he makes no prediction about the fission of that particular uranium. When we attribute to metal the disposition of thermal conductivity, we are describing how it would behave if it were heated. What we do not specify is where, when, or by what means a particular bar of metal will actually conduct heat.

Max Weber (1949:118) was explicit in recognizing the limitation of science with respect to determinate predictions about objects. He quotes E. Meyer as follows: "Natural science can assert . . . that when dynamite is set on fire an explosion will take place. But to predict whether and when in a specific instance this explosion will take place . . . that is impossible."

If it is meaningful to say that a piece of metal has the disposition of thermal conductivity even if it is never heated, then we are obviously dealing with a counterfactual conditional. It is equivalent to the statement that a person has musical talent even if he has never struck a note. But plainly if we assign to objects dispositions that may never be expressed in behavior, then the ability to predict behavior from dispositions is modest. Over and above these logical considerations, however, is the more general fact of indeterminacy. The social scientist is no more able to predict the totality of social behavior than the physical scientist to predict the totality of physical behavior. Fortunately, neither the social nor the physical scientist is interested in explaining or predicting the totality of behavior. One only specifies that, *if* the circumstances (or, more generally, the supplementary causal conditions) obtain, then, given the disposition, certain behavior will result.

Specification of Circumstances

But, whereas physical and social science are alike in their inability to specify whether the necessary conditions for the activation of dispositions will obtain, they differ in a critical regard—the *specification* of circumstances. The contrast is apparent. Ice will melt if sufficient kinetic energy is applied; glass will shatter if subjected to a blow; copper will conduct if a current is induced in it; and so on. With most human dispositions, on the other hand, the *definition* fails to specify the circumstances that will activate them. An authoritarian person will behave in a certain way if—what? A courageous person will act bravely if—what? In behavioral science, not only are we unable to predict whether the required supplementary causal conditions will obtain, but we are also unable to specify what these supplementary causal conditions are. Though we know the disposition, we do not know the circumstances required for it to be expressed in action.

No less important is the fact that the same behavior may express different dispositions. Assume that there are two men in combat, each of whom destroys an enemy machine gun nest. For the first man this is an expression of courage; fearless of his own life, he stealthily approaches the enemy and flings a grenade at the enemy gun. For the second man it is an expression of an excruciating fear attaining the level of panic. In a terror so intense that he is deprived of reason, this soldier wildy flings his grenades at the enemy. The behavior of both men is the same, but the disposition expressed by the behavior is completely different.

Not only may the same behavior reflect different dispositions, but different behavior may reflect the same disposition. Assume that a man has the trait of "kindness." This disposition may be expressed in his behavior to his wife, his children, his employees, destitute or needy people, animals, sick people, and so on; it may be expressed in a manner, a tone of voice, consideration of other people's feelings, giving gifts, sending cards, making monetary contributions, consoling crying children. This man's kindness will probably not be expressed in *all* these ways; it may be expressed in some but not in others.

Or take a group of people who are "generous." One person expresses this generosity in large contributions to charity; a second in frequent gifts to one's family; a third in picking up the check for a party at a restaurant; a fourth in giving to beggars. As Lazarsfeld (1959b) expressed it, the relationship of the overt indicator to the underlying disposition is probabilistic. If all we know about someone is that he is generous, our ability to predict *how* this generosity will be expressed is not great.

But probably the most fundamental reason why dispositions cannot perfectly predict behavior is the existence of contradictory dispositions. If one of these dispositions finds behavioral expression in a particular circumstance, then the other is necessarily excluded from expression (or some compromise is effected). A familiar example is role conflict. As a father one should spend time with his family, but as a businessman he should devote his efforts to work. Confronted with the decision of whether to take his family on a camping trip for two weeks, obviously one of his dispositions cannot be fully realized in behavior.

But role conflict is only a specific example of a much more general process. Given the enormous variety of dispositions that each of us has and the great range of situations in which we find ourselves, we constantly confront contradictory dispositions. In the abstract, no contradiction may be apparent, but in the concrete situation it is. For example, there is obviously no contradiction between being a Republican and desiring to get along well with people. But assume that a Republican is among a group of Democrats who are talking politics. If the individual expresses his or her political attitudes, then the person's behavior contradicts his or her disposition toward interpersonal harmony. If that person nods agreement in order to avert conflict, the individual's behavior violates his or her political attitude. Similarly, there is no logical contradiction if a businessman is prejudiced and also desires to make a profit. It only becomes a contradiction the moment a black customer walks into his shop. As soon as this happens, one of his dispositions *cannot* correspond to his behavior.

Usefulness of Dispositions

In light of the fact that dispositions are tautological and poor predictors of behavior, as well as being unobservable, nonmaterial, and vague, why are social scientists so busily engaged in studying attitudes, such as those toward the president, the Soviet Union, or the press; personality characteristics, such as authoritarianism, other-directedness, self-esteem; values, such as success, individualism, equality of opportunity; aptitudes and abilities, such as mechanical aptitudes or intelligence; and so on? The answer is simple: the reason that we study dispositions is because we must. If it is impossible to live with dispositions, it is even less possible to live without them.

One reason for our interest in dispositions is their extraordinary *generality*. Herein lies their great power for social science. In calling a person conservative, or generous, or authoritarian, or polite, we are implicitly predicting his responses in many thousands of situations, however widely separated in time and space. Think of what is meant by describing a person as "tactful." In the course of a single day, he will have a number of opportunities to display this quality, and this will go on day after day, week after week, year after year. In calling someone tactful, then, we are literally predicting his behavior in thousands of situations and suggesting that his behavior will differ from that of a "tactless" person in these many situations. The same is true if we call someone honest, or sociable, or kind. Each casual characterization of an individual in terms of even a minor attitude, trait, value is in fact a broad behavioral prediction. It is based on an implicit assumption regarding the stability and consistency of human responses.

Though the existence of such consistency has been challenged by Hartshorne and May (1928), it is an assumption that remains indispensable to the search for lawful relations.

Without such disposition concepts, the scientist is lost in the welter of the concrete. Every individual act or interaction is unique, idiosyncratic, and unduplicable, never before existing, never to be repeated. In the absence of the assumption of dispositions, it is conceptually unmanageable. Only by responding in terms of the elements common to widely diverse situations can we even begin to know how to respond in the thousands of situations that constitute the substance of our actual lives.

Since the social scientist is interested in man, he must be concerned with that which is important to men. This, then, is the second reason for the concern with dispositions, namely, that they are so important to the behavioral scientist because they are so important to his subjects. Gordon Allport (1935: 806) discussed this point with reference to attitudes. He said,

> Without guiding attitudes the individual is confused and baffled. Some kind of preparation is essential before he can make a satisfactory observation, pass suitable judgment, or make any but the most primitive reflex type of response. Attitudes determine for each individual what he will see and hear, what he will think and what he will do. To borrow a phrase from William James, they "engender meaning upon the world"; they are our methods for finding our way about in an ambiguous universe.

If attitudes and habits, even broadly conceived, have such psychological significance for the individual, then the full range of dispositions (including "powers," skills, traits, or, more generally, personality qualities) must have overwhelming importance. Nothing so important to men can legitimately escape the close and careful attention of the student of man.

A third reason for our interest in dispositions lies in their importance for rational action. To make our decisions in terms of what objects could be, might be, or tend to be rather than in terms of what they are may appear to be the height of irrationality. This practice, it should be noted, has not gone unchallenged. Indeed, propositions referring to potentials which are not in fact actualized are known as counterfactual (or contrafactual) conditionals which, according to Nelson Goodman (1954), have no more reality than occult capacities.

Yet all of us in fact consider it rational to respond in terms of a nonexistent potentiality. For example, we say that gasoline will ignite if a flame is brought close to it. How many of us laugh derisively at the idea, contending that we are simply referring to a nonexistent response potential, and how many carefully keep the lighted match far away? Those of us who value our safety act in terms of this nonexistent potential, even though this potential is never realized; indeed, we are at considerable pains to ensure that it is never realized. We say that porcelain will shatter if it strikes a hard surface, and, if we value the porcelain, we make special efforts to preclude the activation of this potential. In other words, we respond to objects not only in terms of what they are, but also in terms of their response potentials.

It is quite impossible to make any rational decision in the absence of assumptions about human dispositions, including our own. We respond in one way to a kind person, in another way to a cruel one; in one way to a bold person, in another to a timid one; in one way to a friendly person, in another to a hostile one; and so on. The same applies to our own dispositions, as George Herbert Mead (1934) observed. Rational action is thus predicated on assumptions about the dispositions of others and ourselves.

Fourth, it is necessary to use dispositions because of their explanatory and theoretical significance. They are to a substantial extent the basis for the change of the S-R (stimulus-response) formula to the S-O-R (stimulus-organism-response) formula. For, in much of social science research, the aspect of the "organism" which enters into the S-O-R sequence is the individual's dispositions. It is essentially for this reason that Lazarsfeld (1959b:481) and Allport (1962) suggest that dispositions may be viewed as "intervening variables"—intervening between stimulus and response or between environment and behavior.

Without reference to dispositions, one simply has a mechanical relationship between stimulus and response; one operates on the assumption of an "empty organism." Dispositions help to explain, to make sense of, such S-R relationships. They thus have theoretical value in enabling one to understand action which would otherwise remain unexplained or incomprehensible.

Finally, we must study dispositions to understand behavior. In light of our earlier recital of the many compelling reasons why knowledge of human dispositions cannot effectively predict concrete behavior, this statement may appear strange in the extreme. Yet the seeming contradiction is easily resolved by recognizing the following: to assert that dispositions rarely *predict* behavior is not to suggest that they do not *cause* behavior. The earlier discussion notwithstanding, we can flatly assert that dispositions *always* determine behavior. This assertion appears to fly squarely in the face of the evidence of Deutscher (1966; 1973), LaPiere (1934), Wicker (1969), and others, demonstrating that people's attitudes, traits, and the like often do not correspond to their acts and, in fact, to our own contention that it is impossible for dispositions and behavior to correspond perfectly. How can this uncompromising assertion be defended?

Let us consider LaPiere's (1934) classical study of the discrepancy between expressed attitudes and overt behavior. When LaPiere asked a number of innkeepers and hotel owners whether they would accommodate Orientals, most replied in the negative, but, when confronted by a well-dressed Oriental couple in the company of a well-spoken Caucasian applying for accommodations, they complied without demur. Seemingly, their dispositions had little to do with their behavior.

But the paradox is easily resolved if one asks, *which* dispositions? The researcher may think that one attitude should cause behavior, whereas it is another attitude that is actually responsible. LaPiere feels that prejudice toward Orientals should be associated with discrimination toward Orientals, but the innkeeper has other dispositions as well: a disposition to avoid insulting a person to his face; a disposition to avoid unpleasantness, hostility, recrimination; a desire to please; a wish to rent his room for profit; a fear of possible legal consequences of discrimination; and so on. All these are also dispositions, and it is one of these, rather than prejudice, that determines the innkeeper's behavior. The fact that a *particular* disposition does not cause behavior does not mean that the behavior is not caused by dispositions; it simply means that the *researcher* has picked the wrong disposition as a basis for predicting the particular behavior.

A critical problem in predicting from a general disposition to a specific act or event, then, is that every individual is equipped with a multiplicity of dispositions and every act may reflect a multiplicity of dispositions. If one wishes to predict whether someone will discriminate, it is not enough to know whether he is prejudiced. To improve behavioral predictions, one would also have to study other dispositions, such as his attitudes toward the American Dream, toward the desire for profit, toward maintaining the high regard of his neighbors, toward wanting to be well-liked by everyone, and so on. The analyst who decides that the *only* relevant disposition is prejudice will surely find a discrepancy between the attitude and behavior.

Instead of focusing exclusively on particular dispositions, then, greater attention must be given to the study of dispositional structures, including the strength, priority, or hierarchy of individual dispositions. This point has been brought home to us with great vividness by one of Lazarsfeld's (1959a) three dimensions of disposition, namely, the passive-driving dimension. Nothing is more apparent than the differential strength or drive of dispositions. As noted earlier, some dispositions are dynamic, urgently seeking expression, whereas others are passive, supinely awaiting some stimulus or other activating circumstance to bring them to the fore. Allport (1961:372-373) observes that "dispositions range from absorbing passions, through mild predilections, to mere manners. . . . Some are compelling, self-active, the very steam boilers of life. Others are stylistic and instrumental . . .". A man may abandon his home and roots to advance his occupational goals, but he will not do so because he dislikes the state flag or national anthem. To predict behavior, we must know more than what the disposition is; we must also know whether it is, in the words of Allport, "cardinal, central, or secondary."

With reference to any specific act, it is probable that more than one disposition is implicated. Actual behavior, then, will usually reflect either the victory of a superordinate disposition over others or a compromise among dispositions of varying strength. This is as true of physical as of human dispositions. For the physical scientist, the very problem of explaining the specific behavior of objects lies precisely in taking account of the competing tendencies of objects. On the basis of a knowledge of dispositions, he will calculate that the physical object will respond as a vector of different fields of force or that one force will totally overcome another. But that force X completely overcomes force Y—that, in a given case, centripetal force overcomes centrifugal force, that the application of heat overcomes the bonding forces of molecules—does not deter the physical scientist from attributing centrifugal or bonding forces to objects. I see no reason to think that the relationship of human dispositions to behavior differs in any essential way. To predict behavior, then, we must study not dispositions but disposition structures—their degree of dynamism and their hierarchical ordering within the individual's phenomenal field—and apply this knowledge to specific acts or events.

It should be apparent that the aim of this paper has not been to bury dispositions nor to praise them, but to attempt to elucidate their nature, to point to some of their strengths and weaknesses, and to hint at some directions for further work. A number of sociologists have criticized dispositions and a far larger number have studied them, but Paul F. Lazarsfeld is among the very few to have explicitly called attention to them and, in the process, to have advanced our understanding through his ingenious classification of dispositions and his explanation of their causal significance. In this area, as in so many others, we would be well advised to follow his lead.

Notes

1. In a critique of *The American Soldier* studies at the Annual Meetings of the American Sociological Society in about 1950, Blumer pointed out that, although thousands of attitude studies had been done, no one had ever seen an attitude. Yet Hempel (1952) stresses that scientific progress has depended fundamentally on unobservables.

2. Not proof, as the reanalysis of Hartshorne and May's own data by Roger Burton (1963) showed.

References

ALLPORT, GORDON W. 1935 "Attitudes," in G. Murchison, ed., *Handbook of Social Psychology*. Worcester, Mass.: Clark University Press, pp. 798-884.

ALLPORT, GORDON W. 1961 *Pattern and Growth in Personality*. New York: Holt, Rinehart and Winston.

ALLPORT, GORDON W. 1962 "Prejudice: Is It Societal or Personal?," *Journal of Social Issues* 18(2) 120-134.

ALLPORT, GORDON W. 1966 "Traits Revisited," *American Psychologist*, 21 (January), 1-10.

BONJEAN, C., R. J. HILL, and S. O. McLEMORE 1967 *Sociological Measurement: An Inventory of Scales and Indices.* San Francisco: Chandler Publishing Company.

BURTON, ROGER V. 1963 "Generality of Honesty Reconsidered," *Psychological Review*, 70 (November), 481–499.

CAMPBELL, DONALD T. 1963 "Social Attitudes and Other Acquired Behavioral Dispositions," in S. Koch, ed., *Psychology: A Study of a Science*, New York: McGraw-Hill, Vol. 6., pp. 94–172.

DEUTSCHER, IRWIN 1966 "Words and Deeds: Social Science and Social Psychology," *Social Problems*, 13 (Winter), 235–254.

DEUTSCHER, IRWIN 1973 *What We Say—What We Do: Sentiments and Acts.* Glenview, Ill.: Scott, Foresman.

GOODMAN, NELSON 1954 *Fact, Fiction and Forecast.* London: Athalone Press.

HARTSHORNE, H. and M. A. MAY 1928 *Studies in Deceit.* New York: Macmillan.

HEMPEL, CARL G., 1952 "Fundamentals of Concept Formation in Empirical Science," in *International Encyclopedia of Unified Science*, Vol II, No. 7. Chicago: University of Chicago Press.

HORNEY, KAREN 1945 *Our Inner Conflicts.* New York: Norton.

JAMES, WILLIAM 1950 *The Principles of Psychology.* New York: Dover. (Copyright, 1890, by Henry Holt).

LaPIERE, RICHARD 1934 "Attitudes vs. Actions," *Social Forces*, 13 (March), 230–237.

LAZARSFELD, PAUL F. 1958 "Evidence and Inference in Social Research," *Daedalus*, 87. (Fall), 99–130.

LAZARSFELD, PAUL F. 1959a "Reflections on Business," *American Journal of Sociology*, 65 (July), 1–31.

LAZARSFELD, PAUL F. 1959b "Latent Structure Analysis," in S. Koch, ed., *Psychology: A Study of a Science*, Vol. 3. New York: McGraw-Hill, pp. 476–543.

LAZARSFELD, PAUL F. 1959c "Problems in Methodology," in R. K. Merton, L. Broom and L. S. Cottrell, Jr., eds., *Sociology Today.* New York: Basic Books, pp. 39–78.

LAZARSFELD, PAUL F. 1966 "Concept Formation and Measurement in the Behavioral Sciences," in G. DiRenzo, ed., *Concepts, Theory and Explanation in the Behavioral Sciences.* New York: Random House, pp. 144–204.

McDOUGALL, WILLIAM 1938 "Tendencies as Indispensable Postulates of All Psychology," *Proceedings of the XI International Congress of Psychology, 1937.* Paris: Alcan, pp. 157–170.

MEAD, GEORGE HERBERT 1934 *Mind, Self and Society.* Chicago: University of Chicago Press.

MERTON, ROBERT K. 1948 "Discrimination and the American Creed," in R. M. MacIver, ed., *Discrimination and National Welfare.* New York: Harpers, pp. 196–126.

MILLER, D. C. 1964 *Handbook of Research Design and Social Measurement*. New York: McKay.

PAP, ARTHUR 1958 *Semantics and Necessary Truth*. New Haven, Conn: Yale University Press.

PAP, ARTHUR 1962 *An Introduction to the Philosophy of Science*. New York: Free Press of Glencoe.

ROBINSON, JOHN, and PHILIP SHAVER 1973 *Measures of Social Psychological Attitudes*, rev. ed. Institute for Social Research. Ann Arbor: University of Michigan.

ROSENBERG, MORRIS 1957 *Occupations and Values*. Glencoe, Ill.: The Free Press.

SHAW, M. E., and J. M. WRIGHT 1967 *Scales for the Measurement of Attitudes*. New York: McGraw-Hill.

SKINNER, B. F. 1953 *Science and Human Behavior*. New York: Macmillan.

WEBER, MAX 1949 *The Methodology of the Social Sciences*. Glencoe, Ill.: The Free Press.

WEISSMAN, DAVID 1965 *Dispositional Properties*. Carbondale: Southern Illinois University Press.

WICKER, ALLEN 1969 "Attitudes Versus Actions: The Relationship of Verbal and Overt Behavioral Responses to Attitude Objects," *Journal of Social Issues*, 25 (Autumn), 41–78.

PART 4

SUBSTANTIVE
SOCIAL RESEARCH

19. IMMIGRATION, CITIZENSHIP, AND SOCIAL CHANGE: INTENTION AND OUTCOME IN AMERICAN HISTORY

Sigmund Diamond

I have elsewhere paid tribute to Paul Lazarsfeld's influence in teaching us how to ask the question "Why?" correctly.[1] But I have special reason for being grateful to his persistence in asking "Why?" in matters in which to ask that question, so I believed, was to reveal the naivete of the questioner. When I first came to Columbia University almost a quarter century ago, as a historian in a department of sociology, I met regularly with Lazarsfeld and a few other colleagues to consider what a program in historical sociology might be. "Why do we feel we must know the history of something before we think we understand it?" Paul kept asking. I never gave him an answer then, because, I am afraid, I thought the question did not really deserve one. Years later I learned what I did not know then—that Paul had been concerned with the question for a long time. In his "Principles of Sociography," written in 1933, the third commandment reads: "Contemporary information should be supplemented by information on earlier phases of whatever is being studied."[2] Like other commandments, even better known, that one has not always been observed, not even by Paul, but we live in the faith that it is useful to respect standards to which we fail to conform; and I, for one, have appropriated Paul's question—and dictum—as if they were my own. The essay that follows has no citation to Lazarsfeld, Paul Felix, but I know how much it owes to that deceptively simple "Why?"

The Problem Stated

In a general history of American immigration, two periods of special importance in the history of the peopling of the United States—the early seventeenth century, when the bases of North American social structure were established,

263

and the late nineteenth and early twentieth centuries, when the United States was transformed into an industrial society—are characterized in such a way as to stress the essential conservatism of the earlier migration and the greater radicalism of the later.

Concerning the earlier migration, Professor Jones writes:

> But whatever their motive for migration, the vast majority appear to have had no quarrel with the greater part of their heritage. They thought of America in the same way that John Donne in 1622 thought of England, namely, as "the suburbs of the Old World."

In contrast with the conservatism of the seventeenth-century immigrant, only too happy to create on the shores of the New World a suburb of the Old World, stands the desire for change—even to the point of radicalism—of many of the immigrants of the late nineteenth century. "During the forty-year debate on immigration that culminated in the enactment of the restrictive laws of the 1920's," writes Professor Jones:

> nativists repeatedly linked immigrants as a class with extreme political radicalism. The charge was not lacking in plausibility, for each of the revolutionary and extreme radical movements which arose in the United States during this period possessed a large foreign-born population.[3]

The warrant for Professor Jones's characterization of the first of these periods of immigration history as conservative, the second as radical, rests on the assumption that the outcome of an event is the same as the intention of those who precipitated it. If immigrants come with conservative intentions, the consequences of their acts will be conservative; if they come with radical intentions, the consequences of their acts will be radical. Social analysis is, however, so much concerned with accounting for the discrepancy between the intention of the actor and the outcome of his acts that it seems unpardonable for an historian to assume that the character of the first determines the character of the second. But my concern is less with uncovering Professor Jones's error than with reversing the emphasis of his conclusion, a conclusion that is concurred in, I believe, by many historians of immigration to the United States. To insist on the radical consequences of early seventeenth-century immigration and on the conservative consequences of late nineteenth-century immigration might sound as though my intention were to test the limits of perversity. But though my theme may be perverse, and also my conclusions, I shall open on a note of impeccable orthodoxy, with a text from Adam Smith. In a section entitled "Causes of the Prosperity of New Countries," Adam Smith writes: "The colony of a civilized nation which takes possession, either of a waste country, or one so thinly inhabited, that the natives easily give place to the new settlers, advances more rapidly to wealth and greatness than any other human society," because the settlers bring with them superior economic institutions, "a knowledge of agriculture and other useful arts," and the habits of disciplined, orderly work and government.[4]

Writing early in the nineteenth century, Herman Merivale in his *Lectures on Colonization and Colonies* took up Adam Smith's theme and offered an explanation to account for the materialism of colonial societies made up through migration from the mother country:

> In such community the mere wants of life are abundantly supplied, but not supplied without labour. There is none of that depressing poverty which elsewhere weighs down the energies of large masses of mankind. . . . On the other hand, everything which adorns human life . . . is either difficult of acquisition or unattainable. The colonist has little temptation to long for the enjoyment of such superfluities, for the stimulus of envy is wanting; he does not see them heightening the pleasures of others, and therefore thinks little of them. . . . He is in danger, therefore, of sinking into a state of listless and inglorious indolence. . . .
>
> To counteract this tendency, he has only what may almost be termed the abstract desire of accumulation; I mean the desire of amassing wealth, unconnected with the passion for its enjoyment. . . . the love of accumulation must, in all communities, be among the most important sources of national activity—in new communities, it is the only one. Money-making becomes the popular passion. The acquisition of wealth confers the only substantial title to public regard.[5]

"The acquisition of wealth confers the only substantial title to public regard"—in one form, the thought is a tiresome, even if true, cliché of the critics of American society; in another, it is an aspect of American society, derived from the immigrant character of its colonial origins, that is offered in explanation of its rapid economic growth.

In the early summer of 1853 the yacht North Star, bearing on board the most renowned American businessman of the day, Commodore Cornelius Vanderbilt, steamed into the port of London in the course of a world cruise. The occasion provided the London *Daily News* with an opportunity to explain why men of his type had greater prestige in the United States than in England:

> America . . . is the great arena in which the individual energies of man, uncramped by oppressive social institutions, or absurd social traditions, have full play, and arrive at gigantic development. . . . The great feature to be noted in America is that all its citizens have full permission to run the race in which Mr. Vanderbilt has gained such immense prizes. In other countries, on the contrary, they are trammelled by a thousand restrictions. . . . Your men of rank here—your makers of millions for themselves and tens of millions for the country—too often spend their time, their intellect, their labor, in order that they may be able to take rank among a class of men who occupy their present position in virtue of what was done for them by some broad-shouldered adventurer, who, fortunately for them, lived eight hundred years ago in Normandy. . . .
>
> It is time that the millionaire should cease to be ashamed of having made his own fortune. It is time that parvenu should be looked on as a word of

honor. It is time that the middle classes should take the place which is their own, in the world which they have made.... The Montmorencis, the Howards, the Percys, made the past world—and they had their reward. Let them give place to better men.[6]

If the London *Daily News* is to be believed, the businessman was remaking the world, he was remaking it faster in the United States than elsewhere, he was more rewarded for his efforts in the United States than in England, and he was able to do so because of a veritable revolution that had occurred in American social institutions and social traditions. How do these facts of social behavior and social belief relate to the colonial condition singled out by Adam Smith and Herman Merivale as decisive in explaining both American economic growth and the character of American society?

Structure and Values Transformed

The fact is that a broad spectrum of feudal and other restraints and restrictions, the absence of which, according to both Merivale and the London *Daily News*, was responsible for the special character of American society, was present at the start of American history.

Consider the words of the Fundamental Constitutions of the Carolinas, written by John Locke:

> Each signiory, barony, and colony, shall consist of 12,000 acres; the eight signiories being the share of the eight proprietors, and the eight baronies of the nobility; both which shares . . . are to be perpetually annexed, the one to the proprietors, the other to the hereditary nobility. . . .[7]

Or consider the instructions given to Sir Thomas Gates by the Virginia Company on the eve of his departure for Jamestown in May 1609:

> You must devide yor people into tennes twenties & so upwards, to every necessary worke a competent nomber, over every one of wch you must appointe some man of Care . . . to oversee them and to take dayly accounte of their laboures, and you must ordayne yt every overseer of such a nomber of workemen Deliver once a weeke an accounte of the wholle committed to his Charge. . . . You . . . shall call them together by Ringinge of a Bell and by the same warne them againe to worke.[8]

What needs to be explained is why the forms of social organization implied by such statements—forms of social organization which imposed harsh discipline to fix people permanently into the positions allotted them by superior authority—changed so drastically and in ways calculated to release enormous amounts of human energy. It would not be too much to say that the first North American revolution was not that of 1776 and was not essentially political in character at all; it took place in the early seventeenth century and was marked by the contrast between the rigor and severity of the first social order established in the colonies and the far greater equalitarianism and mobility of the society that supplanted it.

The keynote of all North American colonial societies in their initial stages was labor discipline, and the essential purpose of their institutions was to guarantee order and stability through the attachment of each person to the position allowed him by the provision of incentives to assure docility and sanctions to punish disobedience. To Englishmen and Frenchmen of the seventeenth century, no attribute of society was more important than order, and no state of affairs was more greatly to be shunned than social disorder. What the founders of the earliest North American colonial settlements attempted to do was to establish orderly, disciplined societies of officials and workmen in which each man would know his position and behave in the way defined as appropriate. In Virginia and orderly, disciplined societies of officials and workmen in which each man would know his position and behave in the way defined as appropriate. In Virginia and the Carolinas and other proprietary colonies and in New France, the authorities worked toward the creation of some form of manorial system established on the basis of the labor of imported peasants. In Massachusetts it was assumed that a carefully sifted population would discipline itself by voluntary acceptance of a code of religious values.

Though the plans that were devised to give effect to this desire to achieve social order were, in general, eminently rational and in accord with then widely accepted notions for the attainment of social stability, they suffered from a fatal flaw; reality was far different from what the North American colonizers expected. For the leaders of the Virginia enterprise, the first permanent English colony in North America, the model was the East India Company, and the dream was to reproduce the Spanish looting of a continent. But conditions in Virginia were not those of India or Mexico and Peru. "It was the Spaniards good hap," wrote Captain John Smith later,

> to happen in those parts where were infinite numbers of people, whoe had manured the ground with that providence that it afforded victuall at all times; and time had brought them to that perfection they had use of gold and silver, and the most of such commodities as their countries afforded; so that what the Spaniard got was only the spoile and pillage of those countries people, and not the labours of their owne hands. . . .
>
> But we chanced on land, even as God made it. . . . Which ere wee could bring to recompence our paines, defray our charges, and satisfie our adventurers; wee were to discover the country, subdue the people, bring them to be tractable civil and industrious, and teach them trades that the fruits of their labours might make us recompence, or plant such colonies of our owne that must first make provision of how to live of themselves ere they can bring to perfection the commodities of the countrie.[9]

Unlike the Spaniards, then, who established their New World societies in areas where there was already a large and, to a degree, tractable labor force, the English and French colonizers had to recruit their labor force. The concessions they offered to recruit and motivate a labor force that was adequate both quantitatively and qualitatively made it impossible to reproduce the rigidity of social structure characteristic of contemporary Europe or to maintain for any considerable time the harshness and rigor characteristic of their initial efforts at society building. To discipline a labor force was one thing; to recruit and motivate it, quite another. The solution that was adopted to solve the second problem made it impossible to solve the first problem in the anticipated way, and the result was a veritable social revolution in the early seventeenth-century colonies.

From the very outset, it was necessary to offer substantial inducements to recruit a voluntary labor force. These concessions varied consideraly from time to time and from place to place: the importation of women to be distributed as wives (which converted a labor camp into a community); increasing opportunity to trade; the granting of certain legal and political rights ("No man will go from hence to have less liberty there than here");[10] and, above all, the promise of easy access to the ownership of land. In short, the major concession offered to recruit and motivate the population was the promise of social mobility. But the concessions offered to entice a labor force to migrate across the Atlantic and to accept the discipline of society had, in fact, the effect of reducing the likelihood that that discipline would be accepted. Instead of docility there was disobedience; instead of stability, disorder. And where disobedience and disorder were both consequences of the means by which the country was peopled and also requirements for survival within it, it was inevitable that older definitions of freedom would need to be broadened and new social institutions created.

The first permanent English colony in North America, Jamestown, was a private estate, which, in the absence of an amenable local labor force, was worked on the basis of imported, that is, immigrant, labor. Basic policies were laid down in London by the shareholders of the Virginia Company; the management was entrusted to agents of the shareholders; and the supervision of those whose labor in Virginia was necessary for the attainment of the Company's objectives was placed in the hands of officials appointed in London. So far as the immigrant labor force was concerned, the role that was envisaged for them by the Company can easily be inferred from the sermon preached by the Reverend William Crashaw on the departure of Governor de la Warr to Virginia: ". . . the basest and worst men trained up in a severe discipline, sharp lawes, a hard life, and much labour, do prove good members of a Commonwealth. . . . The very excrements of a full and swelling state . . . wanting pleasures, and subject to some pinching miseries," will become "good and worthie instruments."[11]

Clearly, few immigrants would have been willing to face the dangers of the Atlantic passage and the terrible uncertainty of life in the New World if all that had been offered them were "severe discipline, sharp lawes, a hard life, and much labour." In fact, of course, that was not all that was offered them. Wives, opportunities for trade, political rights, and, above all, the right to acquire land were offered as concessions to induce immigrants to enter the labor force. Social order, the Company had hoped, would be achieved by fixing each man to a position in its table of organization, but as a result of the concessions offered to get immigrants to accept those positions, each person in Virginia had become the occupant of several statuses; for now there were rich and poor in Virginia, masters and servants, landowners and renters, old residents and newcomers, married and single, men and women, and the simultaneous possession of these statuses involved the holder in a network of relationships, some congruent and some incompatible with his organizational relationship.

Fluidity replaced stability, disobedience replaced deference. Writing about the upstart behavior of Virginians once landless, now landowners, Secretary of State John Pory wrote to Sir Dudley Carleton:

> Our cowekeeper here of James Citty on Sundays goes accowtered all in freshe flaminge silke; and the wife of one that in England had professed the black arte, not of a scholar, but of a collier of Croydon, wears her rough bever hatt with a faire perl hat band.[12]

The signal that the rigorous discipline the Virginia Company sought to impose could not survive the granting of the concessions offered to recruit an immigrant labor force came when those sworn to uphold that discipline—the very leaders of the Company—subverted it. "The servants you allow them," Captain John Smith wrote the Company concerning its officials in Virginia, "they plant on their private lands, not upon that belongeth to their office, which crop alwaies exceeds yours...."[3] "Such an Antipathy is there between theyr vast Comands and our grumbling Obedience," Sir Francis Wyatt wrote from Jamestown to his father in England: "Mingling matters of honor and profitt often overthrow both. ... I often wish little Mr. Farrar here that to his zeale he would add knowledge of this Contrey."[14]

In 1607, when Jamestown was founded, there had been no "Contrey," only the Virginia Company. It was the Company's fate to have created a country and to have destroyed itself in the process.

In New England men were not, as in Virginia, the occupants of a status in the table of organization of a business enterprise. It was assumed that the discipline that lay at the basis of Puritan state and society would be the product of the voluntary acceptance by a carefully sifted population of a code of religious values and the institutions designed to make them effective. But even though the basis of social order in New England was less external than in Virginia, more a matter of the acceptance of certain moral and religious precepts, the fact is that it, too, could not withstand the corrosive effects of the concessions offered to raise the level of motivation of an immigrant society. The same ethic that attempted to check the free play of egoism on behalf of "the good of the community" fostered the development of egoism. Not only did the religious precepts of Puritanism systematize the virtues making for economic success, but the leaders of the community deliberately stimulated men's hopes of rising in the world as the major incentive to increase labor productivity when the colonies

faced starvation and ruin. Given the opportunities for the economic exploitation of the New World that existed, it proved impossible for the Puritan leaders
to keep egoism and discipline in tandem. Once self-interest had been given free
rein, it could not again be exorcised no matter how sharply the leaders called the
populace to account for their sins and no matter how poignantly they evoked
the memory of olden days when duty called one to action on behalf of community rather than self. What the founders did to motivate an immigrant population to behave in the ways expected of them made it impossible to maintain
order in the ways that had been anticipated, and the rigor and severity of the
first social order in New England broke down.

In 1653, Captain Robert Keayne, one of the richest Boston merchants of
his period, wrote a 158-page will in which he attempted to justify the behavior
that, some years before, had resulted in his being censured for having been drunk
and for having sold his goods at too high a price. It is significant that Keayne
ultimately justified himself by appeal to the very ethic that the founders of the
community had relied on to help create the good society, ceaseless energy and
constant striving in economic matters: "My account books will testify to the
world on my behalf that I have not lived an idle, lazy, or dronish life nor spent
my time wantonly, fruitlessly or in company-keeping as some have been too
ready to asperse me or that I have had in my own time . . . many spare hours to
spend unprofitably away or to refresh myself with recreations . . . but have
rather studied and endeavored to redeem my time as a thing most dear and
precious to me and have often denied myself in such refreshings that otherwise I might lawfully have made use of."[15]

In 1653, the same year in which Keayne wrote his will, William Bradford,
the governor of Plymouth Colony, was reading over the history he had written
of the colony he had led for many years. He had written in 1617 that the Pil-
grims had pledged themselves to continue as they were, "knite together as a
body in a most stricte and sacred bond and covenante of the Lord . . . straitly
tied to all care of each other's good, and of the whole by every one and so
mutually." When he reached that passage he turned the page and wrote on the
back: "But (alass) that subtill serpent hath slylie wound in himselfe under faire
pretences of necessitie and the like, to untwiste these sacred bonds and ties, and
as it were insensibly by degrees to dissolve, or in a great measure to weaken, the
same."

What Bradford did not realize was that the "subtill serpent" which he felt
was responsible for the destruction of Pilgrim society and Pilgrim character
had been invited into the community to help that society get established. At the
outset, when fields had been tilled in common and the produce equally shared,
Bradford tells us, the harvests were poor; the young refused to work for the old,
some wives objected that their husbands were, in effect, working for other
women. "The experience that was had in this common course and condition,
tried sundrie years, and that amongst godly and sober men," Bradford writes,
"may well evince the vanitie of that conceite of Plato's and other ancients,

applauded by some of later times;—that the taking away of propertie and bringing in community into a commonwealth would make them happy and flourishing. . . . For this communitie . . . was found to breed much confusion and discontent, and retard much imployment that would have been to their benefite and comfort." To raise the level of productivity, concessions had to be offered—the land was divided and given out in individual plots. But now Bradford learned to his dismay that the dissolving effects of economic opportunity could not be restricted solely to the economy, that the moral discipline of Puritanism could not withstand corrosion:

Also the people of the plantation began to grow in their owtward estats . . . by which means corne and catle rose to a great prise, by which many were much inriched and commodities grue plentifull; and yet in other regards this benefite turned to their hurte, and this accession of strength to their weakness. For now as their stocks increased, and the increase vendible, ther was no longer any holding them togeather, but now they must of necessitie go to their great lots . . . . By which means they were scatered all over the Bay, quickly, and the towne, in which they lived compactly till now was left very thine, and in a short time almost desolate . . . . And others still break away . . . thinking their owne conceived necessitie, and the example of others, a warrente sufficient for them. And this, I fear, will be the ruine of New-England . . . & will provock the Lords displeasure against them.[16]

In brief, the seventeenth-century immigrants to North America may indeed have been conservative in intention and outlook, but the society they created in the New World was not simply a "suburb of the Old World." In language that Herman Merivale would have understood, the essential difference between New World and Old World society lay in the greater possibility of social mobility in the former—acquiring the wealth and status that gave claim to public regard. And this social mobility was a structural consequence of the explosion that had occurred in the first colonial social order as a result of the need to offer concessions to recruit an immigrant labor force. Despite their conservative intentions, the founders of North America found they could establish societies only by being revolutionary.[17]

Structure and Values Ratified

The ideology that developed in connection with these changes in social structure—an ideology in which both social esteem and self-respect were largely dependent upon occupational success—is an old story that needs no retelling here, except perhaps to point out that its appearance in the most incongruous places is testimony to its strength and persistence. Consider, for example, the biography of one Antonio Lombardo, an immigrant who made good in the Promised Land:

He was one of hundreds who cheered joyously when, from the deck of the steamer, they saw the Statue of Liberty and the skyline of New York, their first sight of the fabled land, America . . . . In his heart was a great hope and a great ambition.

After he had landed he paid his railroad fare to Chicago and came here with just $12 as his initial capital. Mr. Lombardo, however, accepted the hardships as part of the game, and with confidence in his own ability and assurance of unlimited opportunities began his career. He became an importer and exporter . . . . Like most successful men he has received much but given more to the community in which he lives. It is to such men that America owes her greatness.[18]

The tenacity of this ideology on the popular imagination becomes clear when we realize that Mr. Lombardo was no ordinary businessman, but a leader of the Chicago Mafia.

Mr. Lombardo was no ordinary businessman, but he was an ordinary immigrant, one of the millions who came during the late nineteenth and early twentieth centuries; and the connection between that ideology and immigration is a complex one. Seventeenth-century immigrants, despite their conservative intentions, destroyed a social order and created a new ideology. Late nineteenth-century immigrants, despite their more reformist intentions, ratified existing social structure and social values instead of nullifying them.

The effect of immigration on establishing certain trades and industries in the United States, what immigration meant by way of providing necessary skills and capital, its relation to the business cycle and to the introduction of machinery—much of this is now known. Europe was the great pool which met American requirements for industrial labor; immigration was the plebiscite by which the trained and the untrained, the skilled and the unskilled voted their approval of the structures which allowed them to alter the circumstances of their own lives and ratified the character of American industrial society.[19] I should like now to suggest how immigration and labor discipline were connected and why the later immigration confirmed existing institutions and values instead of nullifying them.

One part of the story—the way in which advantage could be taken of competing nationalities to squeeze more production out of them—is epitomized in the statement of the superintendent of Andrew Carnegie's Braddock steel mill in 1875: "We must be careful of what class of men we collect . . . . We must steer clear as far as we can of Englishmen, who are great sticklers for high wages, small production and strikes. My experience has shown that Germans and Irish, Swedes and what I denominate 'Buckwheats'—young American country boys, judiciously mixed, make the most effective and tractable force you can find. Scotsmen do very well, are honest and faithful, Welsh can be used in limited numbers."[20] I have been told by men who worked in the automobile industry in the 1920s and 1930s that there was then practiced what they called the Balkanization of the assembly line—placing a foreman of one nationality over workmen of another so that ethnic loyalty would not interfere with the task of production; indeed, so that ethnic enmity might be a spur to production. That ethnic enmity had consequences for labor discipline was a commonplace. John Powell wrote from Luzerne City, Pennsylvania, to his brother in Wales on June 21, 1871, about the end of a six-month coal strike: "It is true that they got a number of old, spineless Irish to be blacklegs (turncoats) at one of the pits and succeeded in getting hundreds of soldiers to guard them . . . . Had it not been for those old Irish we could have won a complete victory two months sooner had they been as united as the Welsh." A Welsh iron-puddler reported in 1888: "Competition is strong now and the companies are taking advantage of this to employ Poles, Hungarians, Negroes, and foreigners unused to that kind of work and in this way making the old workmen idle. It is a good thing that Welshmen understand every kind of work better than they do, so that the Welsh get the jobs of foremen because they must have some experienced men who they can trust . . . ." No industry and no ethnic group could claim immunity. He "was only a Hunky," said a Pittsburgh steelworker about a shopmate, "and no decent American would have anything to do with him—for, be it said, we workers have our classes the same as other people." Speaking of the Italian millhands in Lawrence, Massachusetts, in the early 1900s, one worker said: "The little jests that break the monotony of millwork are impossible when a 'dago' is working next to you; if you joke him, he will stick a knife into you." As a result, foremen usually put the "impulsive, industrious, erratic" Italians by themselves in the spinning rooms. Small wonder, then, that employers made the collection of information about the ethnic composition of their potential labor force a matter of first importance; ethnicity became a determinant of labor relations policy. The employment manager of a company "must not only be aware of the location of all the groups of foreign settlement in the community, but he must become personally acquainted with the individual boarding bosses, steamship agents, clergymen, and other influential agents . . . . These are his supply depots, and only by perpetual, personal reconnoitering can he remain familiar with the quantity and quality of available applicants."[21]

Nor was it only ethnic enmity that led to labor discipline; the sheer fact of ethnicity itself was conducive to labor docility or, when conflict did erupt, to limited industrial conflict rather than to unlimited social warfare. Referring to the twelve-hour day, an immigrant steelworker commented: "A good job, save money, work all time, go home, sleep, no spend"—and thereby revealed himself to be the very model of docility. Millions of the so-called New Immigrants at the end of the nineteenth century had only the most marginal connection with American society. To begin with, vast numbers came with the sole thought of saving enough money to purchase land on their return, and millions did return. They were in the United States but not of it, leaving their families behind and living, isolated, in boarding houses in ethnic enclaves. Describing his life, a Polish steelworker said: ". . . just like horse and wagon. Put horse in wagon, work all day. Take horse out of wagon—put in stable. Take horse out of stable, put in wagon. Same way like mills. Work all day. Come home—go sleep. Get up—go work in mills—come home."[22] Even when they did not have the incentive of saving to purchase a farm in Poland or Italy to keep them at their jobs, vast numbers of immigrants related their new experience in America to their old experience in Europe in such a way as, again, to lead to acceptance of industrial discipline. Having had no previous experience with the group he was now entering, having been socialized into a previous society to which—in a variety of fundamental ways—he remained committed, the immigrant did not criticize the new society from the standpoint of a native who may have suffered grievous economic or social or psychic losses in the transition to an industrial society, nor could he criticize it because it failed to measure up to expectations derived from a previous condition he had never experienced. Early in the nineteenth century, the New England textile mill owners were constrained to adopt certain social policies to accommodate community standards concerning the meaning of individualism and expectations regarding the nature of factory labor. With the coming of the immigrant, such constraints were no longer felt: "Only when the advent of the immigrant made it no longer necessary for the manufacturer to gain the support of the community in order to secure his labor force, was he freed from the need of guaranteeing the social welfare of his workers."[23]

How natives and immigrants understood their own history affected their response to industrialization and, therefore, the policy adopted by employers to attract a labor force. In the seventeenth century, the need to attract a voluntary immigrant labor force entailed the payment of an extraordinarily high price—a fundamental change in the character of the social order. In the early nineteenth century, native labor was dear, and the price paid to command it included the provision of a variety of social welfare programs. But the later immigrants had no historical reasons to be prejudiced against mill work, they had no standing in the community which required the mill owner to make provision for anything but wages, and they had all sorts of reasons to be unusually diligent workers, ready to accept the introduction of new machinery and the authority of their superiors, willing to work at a fast pace and at wages the natives scorned.[24]

But there is another equally important aspect of the relationship between immigration and labor discipline—the way in which, under conditions of constant immigration, the method of proving one's American nationality came to be acceptance of the structure and values of American society. How to prove one's Americanness has never been an easy problem, but it has been especially difficult for the labor movement. Has the labor movement of any other country had to prove, in quite the same way, that it was English, French, or Italian?

To define Americanism as acceptance of a particular kind of social system and ideology has been used as a weapon in industrial disputes especially since the late nineteenth century. On September 12, 1912, after a textile strike in Lawrence, Massachusetts, the anarchist Carlo Tresca organized a great demonstration in honor of Anne Lo Pezzi, a worker who had been killed during the strike; 3,000 workers marched behind the slogan, "No God, No Country." On October 12, Columbus Day, 32,000 workers—led by immigrants—marched behind the slogan, "For God and Country."[25] The great steel strike of 1919, coming in the wake of the Americanization movement of World War I and the frightened reaction to the Bolshevik revolution, provides abundant evidence of the use of the identification of Americanism and a particular social philosophy to throw the labor movement on the defensive. Speaking to a group of Cleveland steelworkers during the war, Captain J. C. Curran of the Emergency Fleet Corporation used words that must have fallen like sledge hammers on the ears of his immigrant audience:

> In looking over this sea of faces I notice that quite a number of you come from lands beyond the sea. You are welcome in America, no matter what country you came from. But . . . remember this much, as you have all the privcleges of the native-born American, you have likewise the same obligations. . . . You are expected to fight by their side, and if you are not willing to do that, then, damn you, go back to the country from whence you came.[26]

In October 1918, a subsidiary of U.S. Steel asked each employee to sign a "Pledge of Patriotism" for "loyalty to our country and to the company for which I work." By the time the strike erupted, the company and its supporters had had considerable experience with using the symbols of national loyalty. "Have you heard it," a New Kensington, Pennsylvania, steelworker asked, "that great piece of rotten trickery that the employer is using? No man can be a loyal American worker unless he is a scab." When it was all over, the newspaper of the striking union sadly concluded, "In the end, many strikers only returned to work because they called themselves good loyal Americans."[27]

With the passage of time, the criterion of American loyalty began to shift from what it seemed to be at the start of American national history: from loyalty implicit in the act of immigration itself, which indicated a willingness to cut the ties that bound the immigrant to an older set of institutions and beliefs, to a more active test of loyalty, a demonstration of willingness to accept the system within which American enterprise had developed. The process by which one part of American society—the economic system—became identified with the nation itself has a history too complex to be inquired into here, but the consequences of that identification may easily be inferred from the statement of an American journalist in 1919: "You cannot be against the capitalistic system and still for America; you cannot apologize for that system or feel ashamed of it and still be a good American. You cannot indeed be a good American in the sense of being loyal to American traditions, unless you are proud of the capitalistic system."[28] If to believe that was the prerequisite for being an American, it would be difficult to conceive of any more subtle—or powerful—means of converting an immigrant population into a disciplined labor force.

But for an immigrant to make an offer of proof of his Americanness was not entirely a consequence of coercion; it was also a consequence of his own desire—

and to satisfy his desire there was a mechanism at hand, the acquisition of the legal and political rights of citizenship. "Citizenship," as T. H. Marshall has taught us, "is a status bestowed on those who are full members of a community. All who possess the status are equal with respect to the rights and duties with which the status is endowed." Citizenship has an integrating effect; it connotes that all are equal who are fully members of a community, and it rests that membership on "loyalty to a civilization which is a common possession." In this, it stands in contrast to the notion of class, which, however defined, is an expression of social and economic inequality. It was Marshall's purpose not only to reveal the historical development of the concepts of citizenship and class, but to probe the subtle dialectic that binds them, each so different from the other, so firmly together. The extension of citizenship has modified class structure by providing political means through which social reforms are achieved and by abating the harshness of class conflict through fostering loyalties and values which, by being common to all the members of the society, counteract the circumscribed and therefore divisive loyalties of class.[29]

The documents of the history of immigration to the United States read like a gloss on Marshall's text, for they reveal that the immigrants, in their pursuit of the legal rights of citizenship, learned the political skills that made it possible to mitigate the harshest effects of social inequality and accepted the values that enabled them to live from day to day, often in the most degrading circumstances, in the belief that the United States was, literally, their country. Writing in 1838 from Ohio to his father in England, weaver and farmer Edward Phillips said: "The laws are excellent, within the reach of every man, and every man of 21 years of age has a vote in choosing the law givers. There is none to [sic] high that the law canot [sic] reach him, nor none so low that it will not protect. The path to science, to wealth, and to heaven is open to all. . . . Your sons have the privilege of becoming the greatest men in the nation. In fact this is a free country." Writing to his brother and sister in Shropshire from Illinois in 1865, John Griffiths explained why he had not replied to the last letter he had received in 1860: "In the first place, we, the American people, were contending for our Constitutional liberty against a Slaveholding Arristocracy [sic] which as [sic] turned out to be one of the bloodiest wars that history as [sic] recorded, and I did not want any of my relations to come here until I saw which would gain the victory, Slavery or Freedom." The acquisition of the political rights of citizenship conveyed an intoxicating sense of power to many immigrants who saw in those rights a weapon with which to belabor those who had greater economic and social power, but it did not make them, in the short run, more understanding of the struggle of others to achieve those same rights, not even when they too were immigrants. Struck Pittsburgh steel mills are being worked by nonunion unskilled labor, H. J. Thomas told his family in Wales, "the sweepings of foreign countries, Swedes and Bohemians . . . brought here to make good the shortage by the aristocratic elements. . . . Let the masters remember that the balance of power is in the hands of the sons of toil by the ballot box." It had been different in England, as William Winterbottom told his brother in 1895: "We was planted and reared on what we know to be a verry [sic] small Island furnished with Lords Barons Kings and we thare [sic] dependents and Subjects we had no say in the Matter only work and Obay just animals."[30]

Immigrants from England may have been the first to acquire the rights of citizens and to be transformed by them, but the vision of the potentiality of citizenship was hardly their monopoly: "I am polish man," an anonymous immigrant wrote to the Massachusetts Commission on Immigration in 1914:

> I want be american citizen—and took here first paper in 12 June N 625. But my friends are polish people—I must live with them—I work in shoes shop with polish people—I stay all the time with them—at home—in the shop—everywhere. I want live with American people, but I do not know anybody of American. I go 4 times to teacher and must pay $2 weekly. . . . The teacher teach me—but when I come home—I must speak polish and in the shop also. In this way I can live in your country many years—like my friends—and never speak-write good english—and never be good American citizen. I know here many persons, they live here 10 or moore [sic] years, and they are not citizens, they don't . . . know geography and history of this country, they don't know constitution of American. —nothing. I don't like be like them. . . . I want go from them away. But where? Not in the country, because I want go in the city, free evening schools and learn. I'm looking for help. . . . Perhaps you have somebody, here he could help me.[31]

Mary Antin wrote the story of her immigrant experience in Boston as if she had read *Citizenship and Social Class* fifty years before it was written. In the middle of her second year in school, she learned about George Washington. She compared herself, a Jewish girl from Poland, to the first president of the United States, and suffered from the comparison, but from her new-born humility came a sense of dignity she had never known before:

> . . . this George Washington, who died long before I was born, was like a king in greatness, and he and I were Fellow Citizens. . . . It thrilled me to realize what sudden greatness had fallen on me; and at the same time it sobered me, as with a sense of responsibility. I strove to conduct myself as befitted a Fellow Citizen. . . .
>
> What more could America give a child? Ah, much more! As I read how the patriots planned the Revolution, and the women gave their sons to die in battle, and the rejoicing people set up the Republic, it dawned on me gradually what was meant by my country. The people all doing noble things, and striving for them together, defying their oppressors, giving their lives for each other—all that it was that made my country. . . . The Country was for all the Citizens, and I was a Citizen.[32]

Impelled by coercion and desire to become Americans, the immigrants of the late nineteenth century entered a school of citizenship which did not remake them into a single mold, but which introduced them to a set of beliefs and practices that made it possible for them to withstand the severities of their lives, to alter the society in which they lived, to identify with what they had once wanted only to have a symbiotic relation to. From the kingdom of necessity, where they had been subjects, they had migrated to the republic of freedom, where they had become citizens.

We are now in a position to suggest an answer to the question with which we began. It is not too paradoxical to say that the immigrants of the seventeenth century, desiring nothing so much as to remain loyal Englishmen, nevertheless created a new society and a new nationality, while the immigrants of the late nineteenth century, considerably more reformist, ended by accepting the institutions and values their immigrant forebears had established. When the cost of labor is dear enough, the price we pay for it is massive social change; when the cost of labor is more moderate, we need make only adjustments.

Lazarsfeld's Question Revisited

I still do not know *the* answer to Paul Lazarsfeld's question, but I keep working at it, and I am in a position now to indicate—as this essay suggests—a set of provisional answers, some of which are tied to the circumstances of the time and place we have studied, others of which—of a more general character—can be stated in more abstract fashion.

We, as social analysts, must have historical knowledge in order to know what historical knowledge was held by those we are studying, for, as our essay demonstrates, how the actors in any situation behave depends in part on how they have assimilated and understood their own history. Historical knowledge is a prerequisite, moreover, for the very generation of new problems for social inquiry, problems which cannot even rise to the level of consciousness if phenomena are viewed only in their contemporary aspect. "There is no nature in an instant," Whitehead wrote; to investigate a situation within too limited a time-span is to blind oneself to aspects of it which take longer to manifest themselves.

But the territory we enter, once we embark on the journey suggested by Lazarsfeld's question, takes us as close as we are likely to come to some of the problems that lie at the center of our discipline and, indeed, of our lives.

Scholarship in the social sciences is littered with the relics—some ruined, some still standing—of theories and explanations that assumed an identity between intention and outcome; the second was born from the womb of the first, the first was implicit in the child it created. That there is a relation between the two is true enough, but the relation is far more likely to be devious than direct, and the effort to explore that relation discloses a problem that stands at the center of all serious social analysis: What are the constraints imposed by social structure on the human will? Man is born free but everywhere he is in chains, Rousseau said. Perhaps; but there can be no doubt that everywhere man proposes and everywhere his proposals are deflected from the paths they were intended to traverse. Hell is other people, said Sartre; sometimes the deflections are caused by the conflict of wills and intentions. Hell is one man alone in a room, said Pascal; sometimes the deflections are caused by the consequences of the very activities we engage in that seemed to be required to make a reality of intention. That the exploration of the reasons for the gap between intention and outcome takes us close to the core of social existence is clear, and it is equally clear that the exploration cannot be carried out except with substantive historical knowledge and the knowledge of how to conduct historical research. If the field of sociology is marked with the toppled remains of monumental theoretical structures that collapsed because of the flaw of assuming the equation of intention and outcome, so, too, the field of historiography is similarly littered—littered with once-accepted explanations which assumed an historical past of the phenomena they were intended to explain, a past which found the origin of present social institutions and social practices to lie in the intentions of those whose activities set them on their way. A genuflection before the altar of historical explanation may be more ritual piety than scholarship; if so, it is not good enough, nor are assumptions about what the past must have been. That historical past must be reconstructed in the same detail and with the same care as any other aspect of social analysis, if we are to be able to ask ourselves the question, How does social organization deflect and constrain will?, and if we are to be able to see the variety of ways in which those constraints operate. The circumstances of the time and place we have studied here have disclosed an enormous gap between the intentions of immigrants to America and the outcome of their efforts to realize those intentions and, in addition, a mechanism to explain the gap between intention and outcome. The ebb and flow in the supply and demand for labor intervened between intentions and consequences in ways unforeseen by both the providers and the purchasers of labor, making some behave more "radically" than they had intended, others, more "conservatively."

But this is a mechanism that explains the circumstances of the case we have studied, and surely there is no reason to believe that it is a general explanation of how social organization constrains human purpose. "God breaketh not all men's hearts alike," Richard Baxter wrote, and we are led to hope from the study of the causes of our fathers' heartbreaks—which is the study of history—that perhaps we may spare our children some.

Notes

1. Sigmund Diamond, "Some Early Uses of the Questionnaire: Views on Education and Immigration," *Public Opinion Quarterly*, XXVII (Winter 1963), 528–542.

2. David S. Landes and Charles Tilly, eds., *History as Social Science: Report of the History Panel, the Behavioral and Social Science Survey* (Englewood Cliffs, N.J.: Prentice-Hall, 1971), p. 72.

3. Maldwyn Allen Jones, *American Immigration* (Chicago: The University of Chicago Press, 1960), pp. 9, 229.

4. Adam Smith, *An Inquiry into the Nature and Cause of the Wealth of Nations*, James E. Thorold, ed., 2nd ed. (Oxford: Clarendon Press, 1880) pp. 144–145.

5. Herman Merivale, *Lectures on Colonization and Colonies* (London: Oxford University Press, Humphrey Milford, 1928), pp. 612–613.

6. London *Daily News*, June 4, 1853, quoted in John Overton Choules, *The Cruise of the Steam Yacht North Star* (Boston: Gould and Lincoln, 1854), pp. 58–61.

7. *Old South Leaflets* No. 172, p. 2.

8. Susan Myra Kingsbury, ed., *Records of the Virginia Company* (Washington, D.C.: U.S. Government Printing Office, 1906–35), III, p. 21.

9. John Smith, *Description of Virginia and Proceedings of the Colonie* (Oxford: 1612) in Lyon Gardiner Tyler, ed., *Narratives of Early Virginia* (New York: C. Scribner's Sons, 1907), p. 178.

10. Quoted in Perry Miller, "Religion and Society in the Early Literature: The Religious Impulse in the Founding of Virginia," *William and Mary Quarterly*, 3d ser., VI (1949), p. 31.

11. *A Sermon Preached in London before the Right Honourable Lord la Warre, Lord Governor and Captaine Generall of Virginia* (London: 1610), quoted in Miller, p. 37.

12. Pory to Carleton, September 30, 1619, in Tyler, ed. *op. cit.*, p. 285.

13. John Smith, *Generall Historie*, in Tyler, ed., *op. cit.*, p. 356.

14. Kingsbury, ed., *Records*, III, p. 237.

15. Quoted in Bernard Bailyn, ed., *The Apologia of Robert Keayne* (New York: Harper & Row, 1965), pp. 73–74.

16. *Bradford's History "Of Plimoth Plantation"* (Boston: Wright & Potter Printing Co., 1928), pp. 42, 163, 361–363.

17. The argument advanced here has been developed in greater detail in Sigmund Diamond, "From Organization to Society: Virginia in the Seventeenth Century," *The American Journal of Sociology*, LXIII (March 1958), 457–475; *id.*, "An Experiment in Feudalism: French Canada in the Seventeenth Century," *The William and Mary Quarterly*, 3d ser., XVIII (January 1961), 3–34; *id.*, "Le Canada francais au XVII siecle: un société préfabriqué," *Annales: Economies-Sociétés-Civilisations*, XVI (Winter 1961), 317–353; *id.*, *The Creation of Societies in the New World* (Chicago: Rand McNally, 1963).

18. Quoted in Fred D. Pasley, *Al Capone: The Biography of a Self-Made Man* (Garden City, N.Y.: I. Washburn, 1930), pp. 226–227.

19. Rowland Berthoff, *An Unsettled People: Social Order and Disorder in American History* (New York: Harper and Row, 1971), pp. 325–326; Brinley Thomas, *Migration and Economic Growth*, 2nd ed. (Cambridge: University Press, 1973), passim.

20. Quoted in James H. Bridge, *The Inside Story of the Carnegie Steel Company* (New York: Aldine, 1903), p. 81.

21. The quotations may be found in Alan Conway, ed., *The Welsh in America: Letters from the Immigrants* (Minneapolis: University of Minnesota Press, 1961), pp. 191, 194; David Brody, *Steelworkers in America: The Nonunion Era* (New York: Russell and Russell, 1970), p. 42; Donald F. Cole, *Immigrant City: Lawrence, Massachusetts, 1845–1921* (Chapel Hill: University of North Carolina Press, 1963), p. 116; Brody, *op. cit.*, p. 109.

22. Quoted in Brody, *op. cit.*, p. 100; John Fitch, "The Closed Shop," *The Survey*, November 8, 1919, p. 91.

23. Caroline F. Ware, *The Early New England Cotton Manufacture: A Study in Industrial Beginnings* (Boston: Houghton Mifflin, 1931), p. 8.

24. Gerald Rosenbloom, *Immigrant Workers* (New York: Basic Books, 1973), pp. 28–38, 130–133.

25. Cole, *op. cit.*, pp. 195–196.

26. Quoted in David Brody, *Labor in Crisis: The Steel Strike of 1919* (Philadelphia and New York: Lippencott, 1965), p. 72.

27. Brody, *ibid.*, p. 74; Brody, *Steelworkers*, p. 259; *The Amalgamated Journal*, November 13, 1919, p. 10.

28. Quoted in *The New Republic*, XXI (December 24, 1919), p. 120.

29. T. H. Marshall, *Class, Citizenship, and Social Development* (New York: Doubleday, 1965), pp. 92, 101 ff.

30. The quotations are from Charlotte Erickson, *Invisible Immigrants* (London: Weidenfeld & Nicolson, 1972), pp. 271, 200; Conway, *op. cit.*, pp. 229–230; Erickson, *op. cit.*, p. 234.

31. Quoted in Oscar Handlin, ed., *Immigration as a Factor in American History* (Englewood Cliffs, N.J.: Prentice-Hall, 1959), pp. 163–164.

32. Mary Antin, *The Promised Land* (Boston: Houghton Mifflin, 1912), pp. 222–224.

20.　THE EFFECTS OF UNEMPLOYMENT: A NEGLECTED PROBLEM IN MODERN SOCIAL RESEARCH

Herbert H. Hyman

"UNEMPLOYMENT. *See* Employment and Unemployment" the *International Encyclopedia of the Social Sciences*, published in 1968, instructs the modern reader seeking knowledge on the topic. So guided, the reader then locates a long and learned article treating problems of the definition of unemployment and accurate measurement of its extent, reporting rates for various countries and times, noting that during the great depression of the 1930s the rate soared to an eighth to a fifth of the labor force in Western European countries but up to "as much as a quarter of the American" workers, and that in contrast with the low rates in Western Europe in the 1950s and 1960s "unemployment in the United States ... failed to fall below 5% in any year after 1957 (through 1964)." If the Encyclopedia article were being written now—in late 1975— the author would have added that the American rates have gone as high as 9 percent.

Given these dismal facts, the author properly discusses in detail the causes of unemployment. What about its consequences? After presenting the extreme rates in certain subgroups of American workers (between 8 percent and 15 percent in the 1950s and 1960s), he tells us, "It is hardly necessary to elaborate upon the social and political ... consequences of these high unemployment rates." True to his word, the author says no more. That one bland sentence is not merely empty of content and uninformative to the reader concerned about the sociological, psychological, and political implications of unemployment. It encourages false, unfortunately plausible, beliefs that the consequences are obvious, uniform, and well established. Indeed they are far from obvious and are highly variable depending on the dispositions of the individuals who become unemployed and on the duration of their unemployment, and on the social and cultural context in which the unemployed are embedded. That much we surely know about the forms of unemployment *in the great depression* from the many studies in the 1930s when some writers, notably Lazarsfeld, warned us that their knowledge of those historical patterns—however extensive—was still deficient.

The reader who turns to the original *Encyclopedia of the Social Sciences*, published in 1935, for knowledge of the effects of unemployment receives a very different course of instruction. A Whorfian might even make something out of the fact that the old course was given under a different, less attractive title. The article then was called "*Unemployment*." Like its counterpart thirty years later, it is focused mainly on the nature and magnitude of unemployment and its causes, but the opening sentence on the effects of unemployment quickly sounds a different note. "The *disastrous* consequences of *prolonged* unemployment, both for the individual and for society, can be indicated only briefly here" (italics supplied). Not true to his word, that author describes in about 350 words many of the varied and subtle effects then documented and their dependence on duration of the experience, the individual's characteristics, and social institutions. The more obvious effects, "suffering and misery for the unemployed worker and his family, even when some measure of public support guarantees against outright starvation," are mentioned first, before listing the break-up of homes, the sharp rise in the number of children who became inmates of state institutions, the malnutrition of those who remained in school, the emergence of armies of wandering and demoralized, homeless children, the humiliation in accepting charity, the loss of an orderly existence in the absence of the routine of regular work, the progression with time from rebellion through desperation to resignation, the strengthening of the repressive powers of the state against the spectre of revolutionary acts by the unemployed All these and other effects are noted, located in particular settings, and their dynamics and shadings suggested despite the compression imposed.

The contrast between the two articles typifies the scientific treatment and concern accorded the problem in the old and new era. The encyclopedias are simply symbols of their times, as anyone can sense who examines the literature for treatments of the problem.[1] Indeed a strict empiricist would have to admit that he knows very little about the social-psychological consequences of being unemployed in the 1950s or later because of the neglect of such research in the last twenty-five years, and any cautious scholar, learning how variable, complex, and contingent the effects were in the past, would surely hesitate to generalize about the consequences of modern unemployment on the basis of findings anchored only in a distant and different world

How strange it is that we stopped studying so important and persistent a problem, that we consigned ourselves to ignorance and helplessness by neglecting our professional duties as applied social researchers, that we have missed great opportunities as basic researchers to explore these deep experiences and observe powerful forces penetrating to the hearts of individuals and institutions and the counterforces that provide defenses against these invaders. Surely it is important to ask ourselves why we stopped such valuable studies, and it is not just an academic question. The problem is all around us. Alas, the human subjects for our studies still number into the millions. The paths of study were laid out for us by such pioneers as Lazarsfeld, and there are some other short cuts to knowledge that I may be able to suggest.

More than forty years have passed since Lazarsfeld and his collaborators began their studies of the effects of unemployment, leading to a series of publications in the years 1932-1938.[2] In celebrating his long and distinguished career, I stress those early achievements in the hope that it will remind us of that neglected, almost lost, tradition of research and lead us to revive it. Indeed it was only the very special task of preparing this contribution, leading me naturally to contemplate and review Lazarsfeld's long life, that shocked me into recognition of the neglect.

Mine is only one case, but a compelling one to cite. I personally knew all the major collaborators, Philip Eisenberg, Hazel Gaudet, Marie Jahoda, Mirra Komarovsky, Samuel Stouffer, Bohdan Zawadski, Hans Zeisel. I knew the work and had recently referred to it in writing about the early *history* of survey methods. Yet its relevance to our times had been lost upon me, and I did not notice the neglect until given the special stimulation of this occasion. How strange. But no more peculiar than the recent case of the encyclopedia author, who, despite his assignment, cited not a single one of the 112 references conveniently listed in the Lazarsfeld 1938 review of the literature on "The Psychological Effects of Unemployment."[3]

Current research on the problem does not come naturally to us. If anything, it seems—quite unnaturally—lost to sight even though the journalists, preempting our role, write frequent vivid reports of their own "research." One recently went so far as to conduct a telephone survey among the 50,000 employees of the bankrupt W. T. Grant Company who were "being discharged without termination pay, without salary for untaken vacation time and without normal bonuses." The survey "disclosed widespread shock, bitterness and disillusion" (*The New York Times*, November 15, 1975, p. 35).

The modern reader of the Jahoda-Lazarsfeld-Zeisel monograph on Marienthal cannot help but experience the pathos of a community so deeply and pervasively afflicted in 1931-1932 by unemployment and the consequent poverty. In 77 percent of the 478 families, no member had employment and all were dependent on meager biweekly unemployment insurance benefits—until those had been exhausted—and they received emergency assistance—until that was exhausted—and they survived solely by their own resourcefulness. "When a cat or dog disappears, the owner no longer bothers to report the loss; he knows that someone must have eaten the animal, and he does not want to find out who. . . . Once in a long while . . . someone turns out to be improbably resourceful. One man, for instance, who knows every plant and animal in the area, who can imitate the call of every bird, established himself—admittedly without a license—as a temporary dealer in 'minor livestock'" (pp. 22-23). On the day before the scheduled biweekly relief payment, the enumeration of the lunches the children brought to school established that 50 percent had "nothing or dry bread." The "diet sheets" for enumerating the number and character of meals eaten over a week established that 69 percent of the families ate no meat at all throughout the week or only on one of the days.

Reading such horrendous reports, the thought that crosses the modern reader's mind, as Lazarsfeld remarks in his retrospective foreword to the 1971 edition, "is that the findings may be out of date and out of place." Our unemployment certainly is not as pervasive, the *average* level of *objective* deprivation not as severe, and the reader might therefore conclude that the social and psychological effects currently are modest in magnitude, perhaps negligible, and not worthy of study. Lazarsfeld reminds us that "the substantive problem is still very much with us" in 1971, and one could go further. Who can prejudge the psychophysics of such processes—asserting that so and so many units of starvation equals a quantum of psychological devastation, that the shape of such functions is linear or has some other obvious contour, that the first little bit of unemployment has very little effect and that the threshold to deep psychological changes is not crossed until the most extreme and prolonged deprivation occurs, that a certain amount of sustenance and support—no matter how and when provided—reverses the process and restores the soul. These are empirical questions for which we do not yet have the answers, and research under conditions of unemployment that differ from those in Marienthal or elsewhere in the great depression is just what we need to obtain the answers.

Admittedly, the 77 percent rate in Marienthal was three times the rate that America experienced in the Great Depression and about nine times our worst recent rates. But this only raises other empirical questions about what might be called the social-psychophysics of these processes. How big is big? It would be unwarranted to assume that the prevalence of unemployment must reach the extreme level of Marienthal before the community is shattered. Although our rates are much lower, some millions of workers are unemployed and millions more in the families of unemployed breadwinners are in turn affected. Since the dark days of the Depression, the absolute numbers who have experienced the effects of unemployment ironically have grown simply because of the increase in population. For example, the 6.8 percent of our labor force who were unemployed in 1958 numbered some 4,600,000, whereas the 8.7 percent who were unemployed in 1930 numbered about 4,300,000.[4] The 8,000,000, about 8 percent of the labor force, who were unemployed in October, 1975 equaled in numbers those who were unemployed in 1931 when the rate hit almost 16 percent.[5] The consequences of varying numbers, proportions, and geographical clusterings of unemployed certainly are complex and befuddle the mind, but surely should make us start, not stop, research.

Jahoda, Lazarsfeld, and Zeisel go so far as to suggest that a *lower* rate may have an even *more* destructive effect in what surely is a remarkable anticipation of reference group theory and the concept of relative deprivation. "In places where not all people are pushed out of work at the same time, neglect and despair may set in at an earlier stage when the level of income is still higher. Comparison with the surrounding world seems to play its part in matters of mood and attitude" (p. 82). At another point they remark on "the peculiarly uniform and hence unifying situation in Marienthal. Everyone ... bears the same lot" (p. 41), and in the opening pages of their original monograph they stress the special context, "We were dealing with a community that was totally unemployed. In the absence of comparable studies of partially unemployed communities, it cannot be said with certainty to what extent the unemployed individual in the midst of an otherwise working community—say, in a big town—differs from the unemployed individual who lives in a place where everybody is out of work." Then they tentatively advance the suggestion that "for various reasons a closed rural community finds it *easier* to keep functioning over an extended period of time" (p. 3, italics supplied).

Effects involving feelings of relative deprivation and, in turn, injustice, as these historic observations suggest, may be greater when unemployment is less prevalent, and then become focused on the social order. But it is also possible that one is more likely to interpret his own unemployment as a *personal* failure when he is part of a small minority rather than when everyone else is unemployed.[6] *The New York Times* recently reported the case of Mr. Prato, "for 10 years ... a proud laborer" who after five months of unemployment looks at his sleeping sons and thinks, "I brought them into the world, and I can't even provide for them. *You* feel like a failure. Less than a man" (italics supplied, November 2, 1975).[7]

In a situation like Marienthal, although hope springs eternal in an occasional human breast—witness F. W. "Who during the first year of unemployment sent off 130 applications for jobs without receiving a single answer" (p. 93), when all come to see that no one can find work, hopelessness prevails. Even F. W. "was now reduced to complete despair." "None of these would at first understand that they were all in the same predicament together. 'When it began, I thought my husband was the only one who couldn't find work, and I kept sending him off to look for some" (p. 79). In the contrasted situation where a majority remain employed, some of the unemployed may still hope and try, since they perceive that jobs, though scarce, do exist and that the competitors are not legion.[8] The consequences of various levels of unemployment, mediated through such perceptual and cognitive processes, are most complex. Unraveling and establishing them surely requires empirical work in settings where the rates are low and moderate as well as high.

To read these classic studies is to experience not only pathos, but also serendipity and irony,[9] and to become captivated by the simple, but elegant, instruments and methods devised. The young school children (circa age ten) of Marienthal and in a control group from neighboring, less afflicted, villages were asked to write an essay on "What I Want for Christmas". "The presents the children of Marienthal wanted cost only about one-third as much as the presents the other children hoped to get. And the children barely dared openly to state even these modest wishes. ... They usually started with an introductory sentence like 'If my parents weren't out of work' " (p. 58). For those who theorize in terms of fantasy and wish fulfillment, it is an unexpected finding, and for anyone it will suggest how far the harsh realities of unemployment can invade even the world of childhood.

This promising method was extended. An essay competition for older children was organized on the subject "How I See My Future." The prize was a pair of new trousers—clearly a strong incentive in light of the inventories presented on the clothing the families owned. It "came to nothing because of lack of response" (p. 9). Only fifteen essays were received, five of these from apprentices who were currently employed, most other youths being unable to contemplate or plan their futures and thus having nothing to write. The few such who did participate "expressed only general hopes about a better future, . . . about the world revolution that would liberate the oppressed, but nothing about their own particular future" (p. 62). From a statistician's point of view, the method is a loser. To a thoughtful methodologist, it is a sure winner, whichever way it works. The replies are informative; the nonreplies are equally revealing of the loss of hopes and plans.

The same kind of method was also used for adults. About sixty life histories were collected in Marienthal, most of them revealing that "the adult no longer has any specific designs for the future" (p. 59). This method was used on a grand scale in 1931 in Poland,[10] the money prizes offered for the best autobiographies of the unemployed netting almost 800, of which a series of 57 were analyzed by Zawadski and Lazarsfeld. For the many who equate unemployment *only* with privation, and for those who think most unemployed are shirkers who desire only to be fed, a few brief passages in that analysis may shatter such ideas. "A peculiar change takes place in the world of values of the unemployed in regard to work. One has the impression that the writers cannot find words sufficiently enthusiastic to describe the value and dignity of work. A 28-year-old metal worker complains that 'Fate has not granted it to me to enjoy the pleasure and happiness that work gives'" (p. 233).[11] The suffering that comes from privation is compounded by "many other sufferings which result from changed social status. Through many subsequent degradations these people lose their sense of human dignity. . . . Most of them are ashamed" (p. 238). Zawadski and Lazarsfeld remark, "In spite of the theme of degradation which appears so often, it is not the injury to social pride, nor the feeling of sinking in the social hierarchy, but a more general and deep-rooted motif that is mentioned most often and most bitterly: it is the feeling of being superfluous, and, bound up with it, the feeling of aimlessness, of mere vegetation" (p. 240).

These old, but indelible, passages teach us that unemployment is not simply privation, and they should suggest to modern researchers that unemployment can have profound effects, even in the absence of privation. The distinction between unemployment and poverty deserves special attention. The facile and false identification of the two entities may, so it seems to me, have contributed to the recent and strange neglect of research on the effects of unemployment.

Some individuals with meager resources, of course, become poverty-stricken and suffer privation almost immediately after becoming unemployed, and most individuals, if they remain unemployed long enough, finally sink into poverty. But long before that moment, they may experience the sense of being superfluous, of losing dignity, of vegetating, that Zawadski and Lazarsfeld described as stemming from the loss of that valued entity, work, and not from privation. Because the unemployed are often dressed in rags, we do not look below that surface for other causes of the effects. Surely, there are some fortunate individuals who, no matter how long they are unemployed, will never experience poverty or end up in rags. They may have inherited wealth or married into it or struck it rich once. To some observers the plight of the rich unemployed (not the idle rich) may appear comical or no plight at all. Certainly no one would suggest that their suffering is harsh, but, if they are seeking work and cannot find it, their unemployment also may have painful and profound effects.

The executives the Braginskys studied in 1974 were nowhere near the poverty line when they became unemployed. One mentions his "few thousand in the bank," a lot more than many employed have, and two-thirds of them, as noted, were quickly rescued by a new job. Nevertheless, they suffered severe and lasting effects. The Braginskys speak like Durkheim: "The higher one's status and the more sudden one's fall, the greater the impact." Obviously they are not speaking about poverty which comes, at least for these classes, by slow degrees.

Just as one may show that unemployment is not necessarily, often not, accompanied by poverty, so, too, one can show that poverty is often not accompanied by unemployment. As Secretary Wilbur Cohen and Eugenia Sullivan of HEW reported in the mid-1960s, a striking feature of individuals or families in poverty in America is that they are over age sixty-five. The resourceful lady who solved her poverty, as the journalists reported, by eating cat food (not the cat as in Marienthal) was old. Although the distinction may seem academic to the common man, she and other old people, no longer being members of the labor force, are not "unemployed." Families headed by domestic workers or farm laborers also have a very high incidence of poverty, not because of unemployment but because of the low wages.[12] Indeed, as Bremner shows in his historical work on "the discovery of poverty in the United States," poverty in the past frequently arose not because of unemployment, but because those who were working were exploited, not paid a living wage.[13]

Perhaps the fact that we do not make the necessary distinction between poverty and unemployment and a typological classification of all the various combinations of the two entities, but remain fixated on the most dramatic pattern—unemployment with poverty, may account for our neglect of comprehensive research on the effects of unemployment. When we have studied the effects of poverty—not that we have studied it enough—we assume that we have automatically completed our studies of unemployment, when, in truth, we have hardly begun to cover the range of such studies. When we find instances of unemployment without the accompaniment of poverty—common now but rare in the depression—perhaps we regard these forms as too trivial to study, inconsequential in their effects. In the rare instances where we do study unemployment accompanied by poverty, we may miss a good deal of the process, focusing only on the dynamics that flow from the poverty.

The reader of *Marienthal* (and other works of the period) learns a large repertory of methods: the systematic collection of personal documents such as essays and life histories, of households records of diet and clothing, the enumeration of school children's lunches not only on the day before the payment of benefits but on the day *after* when, in contrast with a "rational" model of saving and spreading out of meager resources, the previously empty lunch boxes would often be filled, for example, with a "salami sandwich, two doughnuts, and a piece of chocolate" (p. 55), the systematic keeping of time budgets revealing how empty the free time was, the observation of walking behavior and counts of how many times the men stopped because they were on their way to nowhere and in no hurry to get there (in contrast with the women who still had their domestic duties to claim all their time and hurry them on their way), the analysis of existing records such as library circulation, where "the number of loans dropped from 1929 to 1931 by 49 percent" (p. 38), although the former borrowing charge had been dropped and the collection had been enlarged, and association membership where the only two out of all the political, cultural, recreational, or other such groups to show an increase in membership were an organization that ran a nursery school and a cremation society.

Such sad, often ironic and unexpected, findings on the effects of pervasive or prolonged unemployment should stimulate new research into the problem, and the simple yet informative methods pioneered so long ago should encourage us to start and guide our steps. Those who are interested, but who cannot see undertaking expensive and laborious new field studies, or who regret the neglected opportunities of the last twenty-five years and cannot see any way to redress that neglect, may appreciate some short cuts through the avenue of secondary analysis.

At least thirty-six times since 1951, the Gallup Poll measured the perception of threat of local unemployment with the indicator, "Do you think there will be more people out of work or fewer people out of work in this community in the next six months?" In its national, general social surveys in 1973 and 1974, NORC enumerated the *current* labor force status of both the respondent and spouse, determining whether the individuals were employed or unemployed and seeking work. In addition, the *history* of unemployment was determined by the question, "At any time during the last ten years, have you been unemployed and looking for work for as long as a month?" In a quick search of my own files (not of the comprehensive records of the various archives), I found four other NORC national surveys where the individual's membership in the labor force and current unemployment had been measured with more or less refined instruments, one in 1965, one in 1966, one in 1968, and the one in 1973 using quite an elaborate battery for careful measurement and enumerating the unemployment of the spouse as well as the respondent. The Survey Research Center national panel study, with waves in 1958 (when unemployment hit 6.8 percent of the labor force) and 1960, enumerated the unemployment of the individual at each of those points and permits one to trace effects as a person moves in and out of that status. All these surveys are accessible to analysts, contain collateral items, such as age, sex, position in the family, number of dependent children, income, and so on to refine the measurement, and taken together provide a wide range of dependent variables—political, social and others—to trace the effects of unemployment in the contrasted contexts of various times and places.

The availability of all these data may make it seem all the more strange that we have neglected the problem, but that is easily understood. If one does not have a prior interest in a problem, one is unlikely to search for relevant data and learn how researchable it is—unless he stumbles onto the materials and appreciates them, or they are described in ways that are seductive.[14] I present a few preliminary analyses of some of these data to illustrate the opportunities.

In Table 1, based on the NORC national social surveys for 1973 and 1974, individuals who had been unemployed for at least one month in the previous ten years are compared in outlook on life with individuals who had no such history of unemployment. The comparison is restricted to white males all of whom are currently employed. Thus race, sex, and current labor force status cannot confound the comparisons. All the men are aged thirty to sixty-five, to increase the homogeneity of the two groups, and to ensure that all would have been in the labor force for the entire period and had ample and equal opportunity to experience unemployment. There was no need to control other major social variables that some might regard as causes of past unemployment and also as possible explanations of the findings. The distributions by size of community and region of residence, total family income in the previous year, and educational attainment are similar and not significantly different for the contrasted groups. (A propos of poverty, the median family income in 1972 of the unemployed group was $11,250.) The overall similarity may seem startling, but when one realizes that—given enough time—even the well-trained and advantaged worker in the favored environment is vulnerable to an episode of unemployment, it is no longer so surprising.

That a period of unemployment—even of short duration and long ago—has *any* lasting effect on a group later so advantaged would be an unexpected finding. That it makes so big and consistent a difference in outlook—if not on every test of the hypothesis—is truly surprising. That unemployment is not forgotten with the passage of time and can lead to a misanthropic view of society and a pessimistic view of life seems the proper, albeit provisional, conclusion to draw.

Table 2 traces three groups of workers via the SRC panel study to see whether their outlooks changed as their fortunes fluctuated. The data for group C show that those who fortunately were employed both in 1958 and 1960, at the times when they were interviewed, remained unchanged in their view of life.

TABLE 1. Outlook on Life as Affected by History of Previous Unemployment

		Among Currently Employed White Males Aged 30 to 65 Who Had		
		Been Unemployed in Past 10 Years	Never Unemployed in Past 10 Years	Chi-Square P-Value
Rate self "very happy"	1973(a)	19%	42%	.001
	1974(b)	20	39	.05
Agree that "the lot of the average man is getting worse, not better"	1974	74	49	.001
Agree that "hardly fair to bring child into world with way things look for future"	1974	35	27	N.S.
People mostly "look out for themselves" rather than "trying to be helpful"	1973	61	43	.01
Most people "try to take advantage of you" rather than "trying to be fair"	1973	61	31	.001
"Can't be too careful in dealing with people" rather than "most can be trusted"	1973	66	38	.001
Agree that "most people don't really care what happens to the next fellow"	1974	60	56	N.S.

NS –
(a) The sizes of the unemployed and employed groups in 1973 were 70 and 240, respectively.
(b) In 1974, the sizes of the unemployed and employed groups were 50 and 231, respectively.

TABLE 2.   Changes in Outlook as Affected by Fluctuations in Employment (a)

	Sometimes Not Sure Life Works Out as I Want	Have My Share of Bad Luck	Usually Have to Change Personal Plans
A. Unemployed in 1958 and Employed in 1960 (N-14)			
Response in 1958	86%	39%	57%
1960	64	23	50
Net decline in pessimism	−22%	−16%	−7%
B. Employed in 1958 and Unemployed in 1960 (N-19)			
Response in 1958	68%	40%	47%
1960	68	50	59
Net increase in pessimism	0%	+10%	+12%
C. Employed in 1958 and Employed in 1960 (N-1,008)			
Response in 1958	51%	27%	41%
1960	53	27	37
Net change	+2%	0%	−4%

Apart from work, each group, of course, may have experienced many things in the two years—growing old, the death of a family member, winning a lottery—which could have altered outlook on life. But there is no reason to believe that such vicissitudes of fortune would affect one group more than another. That past or present unemployment can sour a person's view of life is surely the conclusion to hold provisionally while social researchers, challenged by the persistent problem, undertake definitive studies.

The data for group A show that those who were unemployed in 1958 but who were employed when interviewed again in 1960 experienced a marked decline in pessimism. The data for group B show that those whose fortunes had reversed, taking them out of the ranks of the employed in 1958 and into unemployment in 1960, experienced a marked increase in pessimism. The three groups were not matched on any other variables since they are not directly compared with each other. Each group is compared with itself at two contrasted points in its career and thus acts as its own equivalent control group.

The findings must be treated cautiously, since groups A and B are tiny in size but do suggest that the worker's outlook can be depressed by unemployment, perhaps even temporary in character, and restored by employment. The latter process may seem to contradict the earlier findings on the traumatic effects of *past* unemployment. Group A, however, can hardly be described as having been converted into incurable optimists on the basis of the 1960 pattern. And, granted that it is dangerous to compare the different groups, it is noteworthy that group A—like group C in being employed in 1960, but with a history of *past* unemployment in 1958—is the more pessimistic group in 1960.

In 1913, R. H. Tawney stated that in some areas needing reform "practical action is delayed by the absence of sufficient knowledge," but he also warned us that many times "the continuance of social evils is not due to the fact that we do not know what is right, but to the fact that we prefer to continue doing what is wrong."[15] In celebrating Lazarsfeld's career, I have traced the paths he took long ago to knowledge of an important social problem. Once again we must follow in his footsteps. But he would be the first to urge us to apply the knowledge we shall obtain and to take the right course of action.

Notes

1. Although my assertion is not based on a rigorous and large-scale content analysis, it is also not based on casual impressions. The cumulative index to the first fifty volumes of *Social Forces* for the years 1922–1972 lists thirteen articles under the heading "Unemployment," eleven appearing prior to the year 1950. The two recent ones, both by the same author, deal with the unemployment of nonwhites but not with the effects. The cumulative index to the first thirty-one volumes of the *Public Opinion Quarterly* 1937–1967 has no heading "Unemployment," but, under other headings, Eva Mueller's study in 1966 is the only relevant article. It elegantly analyzes the effects of the individual's own unemployment and of the level that prevails, but it is limited to such effects on consumer confidence. The cumulative index to the first seventy volumes of the *American Journal of Sociology* 1895–1965 lists forty-two articles on "Unemployment," only two of which are after 1950, and one of these, by Street and Leggett, is restricted to ideological effects among unemployed Negroes. In the cumulative index to the *American Sociological Review* for the first twenty-five

volumes up to 1960, "Unemployment" is not a heading, the reader being referred to "Employment," where I find one article between 1950–1960 that perhaps treats the consequences of unemployment. A check of later *ASR* volumes through 1970 shows only one article that definitely treated effects of unemployment, again written by John Leggett. (A second article perhaps should be counted.) Thus *one* lone scholar is responsible for half of the negligible total, four articles, found in thirty-five volumes of the two journals since 1950.

I shall have more to say about the literature on poverty, which in my judgment is not critical to the argument, but the findings under that rubric in the indexes do not change my conclusion. In the *AJS*, only one of twenty-four articles on "poverty" appeared after 1950. That one, by W. F. Ogburn, did not deal with its consequences. Thirteen articles on "Poverty" appeared in *Social Forces*, three appearing after 1950. Two treat the notion of a "culture of poverty," the third deals with students at Negro colleges from poverty backgrounds and thus seem dubious evidence against my assertion. In the chapter on "Urban Poverty and Social Planning" in *The Uses of Sociology*, published in 1968, Gans remarks, "Except for Harold Sheppard's work on unemployed auto workers in South Bend, not yet in book form, no sociologist seems to have published empirical studies of the effects of unemployment and poverty since Marie Jahoda, Paul Lazarsfeld, and Hans Zeisel wrote *The Unemployed of Marienthal* in 1932, and this book has not yet been translated into English." (See Paul F. Lazarsfeld, William H. Sewell, Harold L. Wilensky, eds., *The Uses of Sociology*. New York: Basic Books, pp. 475–476.) Understandably, Gans says almost nothing about *effects*. The chapter treats causes of *poverty* and programs to reduce it, bringing in the particular effects, reduced aspirations, when they in turn become "causes" that perpetuate poverty and reduce the success of ameliorative programs that have not taken such causes (effects) into the planning. This encyclopedic volume also has a chapter on "Unemployment, Manpower and Area Development" by Harold Sheppard, which again treats mainly the causes of unemployment. The only effect discussed in detail is the *migration* of the unemployed in their search for work.

This is in no way to suggest that studies of general causes, or of those special effects which prevent the individual from solving his problem of unemployment thus becoming causes of prolonged unemployment, are unimportant. But the broad study of effects is equally important. As Gans shows, if not for the study of effects, one *cause* of prolonged unemployment would not have been established. That "cause" was first documented in Marienthal, when as Lazarsfeld tells us in a foreword written "Forty Years Later" to the first English edition (1971), "One of the main theses . . . was that prolonged unemployment leads to a state of apathy in which the victims do not utilize any longer even the few opportunities left to them. The vicious circle between reduced opportunities and reduced level of aspiration has remained the focus of all subsequent discussions" (p. vii).

The occasional journal article stands out in such splendid isolation that it underscores the recent neglect. One such study conducted during the 1961 recession found that among high-status individuals, "the longer their unemployment, the more defensive and self-critical" they became. No such negative effects were found for low-status individuals, documenting that the effects are varied and contingent and suggesting to the authors that unemployment is perceived as personal failure in the higher classes but as society's fault in the lower classes. See J. D. Goodchilds and E. E. Smith, "The Effects of Unemployment as Mediated by Social Status," *Sociometry*, 26 (September 1963), 287–293.

2. Paul Lazarsfeld, "An Unemployed Village," *Character and Personality*, (December 1932), 147–151. B. Zawadski and P. F. Lazarsfeld, "The Psychological Consequences of Unemployment," *Journal of Social Psychology*, 6 (May 1935), 224–251. Samuel A. Stouffer and P. F. Lazarsfeld, *Research Memorandum on the Family in the Depression*. Social Science Research *Council Bulletin No. 29*, 1937. Philip Eisenberg and P. F. Lazarsfeld, "The Psychological Effects of Unemployment," *Psychological Bulletin*, 35 (June) (1938), 358–389. Hazel Gaudet and P. F. Lazarsfeld, "Who Gets a Job," paper read at meetings of the Eastern Psychological Association, 1938. Marie Jahoda, Paul F. Lazarsfeld, and Hans Zeisel, *Marienthal: The Sociography of an Unemployed Community*, Chicago: Aldine-Atherton, 1971. (The original was first published in German in 1933 under the title, *Die Arbeitslosen von Marienthal*.)

A study of changes in the father's authority following prolonged unemployment, in families where he had been the sole earner, was conducted in Newark in the winter of 1935 by Mirra Komarovsky in collaboration with Lazarsfeld. It first appeared in 1940 but is available only in a 1971 reprint edition. (See Mirra Komarovsky, *The Unemployed Man and His Family*. New York: Octagon Books, 1971.)

3. Given the thoroughness of the review, some minor items were included, but surely many of the major works were worthy of citation thirty years later. R. C. Angell's monograph, the Stouffer-Lazarsfeld "SSRC Bulletin on the Family in the Depression" (one of thirteen bulletins sponsored by the Council Committee on Studies of the Depression), and the Jahoda-Lazarsfeld-Zeisel monograph on *Marienthal* are examples.

4. There is no need for an elaborate technical discussion of errors in these estimates, or the comparability of the statistics over time (the early estimates being derived by methods other than labor force surveys), or the obscurities created by using crude rates of unemployment for the national labor force rather than refined rates, for example, unemployment in urban areas, among heads of households, or the rate of unemployment of a prolonged character, or the number of "hidden unemployed" advisedly not included in such statistics but whom the common man might rightly regard as "unemployed." However one looks at the data, one cannot escape the fact that the problem is still with us, implicates millions of individuals, and may in some sectors and groups have risen to extreme levels. Although difficulties in the definition of unemployment and in the corresponding measurements are not essential to our discussion, it is relevant to note what appears to be a change in the standards or scales of judgment currently used by some to weigh the severity of unemployment. Those who regard 3–4 percent unemployment as "minimal" or "normal" have effectively redefined that as the zero point of their scale. Thus, 5–6 percent unemployment becomes very close to bottom. By such reanchoring of scales, unemployment rates that once were matters of grave concern are no longer judged to be "problems."

5. If we make the well-founded assumption that humans do not forget the past and can be permanently scarred by it, all these figures which represent only the rate during a given short interval of time understate the effects of cumulative unemployment. Many of those unemployed today are not the same people as those unemployed half a year ago.

Using regular reports of the Census Bureau, Lebergott found that in 1956, a year of prosperity when the average number of unemployed at any one point was 2.5 million, a total of 10.0 million workers had been unemployed at some time during that year. Cumulating over a *single* year increased the total fourfold. Thus the rates of 5 percent or more we have had for many years imply that unemployment is a basic fact of life for about one-fifth of American workers in every year. (See Stanley Lebergott, ed., *Men Without Work: The Economics of Unemployment.* Englewood Cliffs, N.J.: Prentice-Hall, 1964, pp. 47, 53, n. 69.) The Braginskys provide empirical evidence on the persistent effects of *past* unemployment. They conducted initial interviews with a group of about fifty unemployed men who had previously held secure and high status professional or managerial posts and a reinterview about three months later. At that point about two-thirds had found jobs, but the cynicism toward society observed initially "was not only still prominent but had actually increased. . . . The trauma leaves a permanent scar . . . long after the victim moves out of surplus status and back into the social mainstream." (See D. D. and B. M. Braginsky, "Surplus People: Their Lost Faith in Self and System," *Psychology Today* 9 (August 1975), 68–72. That the *past level* of unemployment in an area, as well as the individual's own past unemployment, can have an enduring effect was documented in the Michigan 1956 election survey. (See Angus Campbell et al., *The American Voter.* New York: Wiley, 1960, p. 383.)

6. This particular consequence of the level is suggested by Eisenberg and Lazarsfeld in their review of the general literature. "We must distinguish between mass layoffs and partial firings, much or little unemployment in a given trade, early and late depression periods. When few people are being fired, the unemployed may be justified in feeling inferior; at other times he may have the dubious consolation that he is not the only one" (*op. cit.*, p. 361). One of the few studies in the modern period was based on analysis of 500 psychiatric case records that had been collected during 1946–1951, a time of high employment and prosperity. Mr. D, "who had withdrawn from association with his friends into a life of almost total isolation because of his shame and guilt at not having a job during a period of full employment" is a classic illustration of the pattern Lazarsfeld suggested. [See Stanley A. Leavy and Lawrence Z. Freedman, "Psychopathology and Occupation. Part I, Economic Insecurity," *Occupational Psychology*, 35 (January and April 1961), 23-35.

7. This recent case recalls an ingenious hypothesis about the effect of the prevailing level advanced by Stouffer and Lazarsfeld in their monograph on *The Family in the Depression.* "The probability of an unemployed husband losing prestige in the eyes of his wife (or authority in the eyes of his children) varies inversely with the proportion unemployed of fellow workers in the same occupation at the same income level" (*op. cit.*, p. 89). On the basis of psychological studies during the depression, Plant suggested that the father's loss of authority, in turn, impaired the formation of the children's ideals. The father,

normally the ego-ideal, was undermined especially when his deficiencies were so easily observable, because he was home so much in very crowded quarters as a result of the idleness and poverty. (See James S. Plant, *Personality and the Cultural Pattern*, New York: Commonwealth Fund, 1937.)

8. A lovely solution to a puzzling finding in a classic American study also suggests the operation of such factors. Rundquist and Sletto studied a group of unemployed young adults, almost all under the age of twenty-five, and a control group of young employed individuals in Minneapolis around the time of the bottom of the depression. Mean scores of the two groups were close together and the differences nonsignificant on economic radicalism, general adjustment, and "morale" (very similar in content to what is now called anomia), *objective* unemployment thus seemingly having no effect. However, when the aggregate groups were subdivided by their expectations, those *employed* who were very *uncertain* that their jobs would last had scores on the various scales as "bad" as, often "worse" than, the unemployed who were very uncertain of finding work. The *unemployed* who were very *certain* of finding work had scores as "good" as, often "better" than, the employed who felt very certain of keeping their jobs. Clearly, individuals can begin to count themselves in the ranks of the unemployed before they ever make the descent, and others can see themselves as employed before they begin the ascent. These perceptual and cognitive processes may be governed to some degree by autistic factors but certainly must be reflections of the objective level that prevails and the way the trend is running. (See Edward A. Rundquist and Raymond F. Sletto, *Personality in the Depression*. Minneapolis: University of Minnesota Press, 1936, esp. pp. 170, 223, 338.)

9. Perhaps the most ironic finding occurred in the case described by Stouffer and Lazarsfeld where the apathy of one husband, a common and normally destructive effect of prolonged unemployment, led the wife to report, "My husband doesn't have any push, but I like him that way" (*op. cit.*, p. 95).

10. The method was also used in the United States. (See Marion Elderton, ed., *Case Studies of Unemployment*. Philadelphia: University of Pennsylvania Press, 1931, esp. p. 385.)

11. As previously described in Marienthal and stated here, the hope of the unemployed "becomes constantly weaker, when they see the futility of effort" (*op. cit.*, p. 235), and the search for work, however much it may be valued, ceases.

12. Wilbur J. Cohen and Eugenia Sullivan, "Poverty in the United States," *HEW Indicators*, (February 1964), pp. vi–xxii.

13. Robert H. Bremner, *From the Depths: The Discovery of Poverty in the United States*. New York: New York University Press, 1956. In his classic survey of poverty in York, England in 1899, Rowntree found that in 52 percent of the families in "primary poverty" the chief wage earner was "in regular work, but at low wages." This was the major cause, the death of the chief wage earner being next most important and responsible for the poverty of 16 percent of the families. The chief wage earner being out of work was the least important factor, accounting for only 2 percent of the cases. His underscored conclusion was, "the wages paid for unskilled labor in York are insufficient to provide food, shelter, and clothing adequate to maintain a family of moderate size in a state of bare

physical efficiency." (See B. Seebohm Rowntree, *Poverty: A Study of Town Life*, London: Macmillan, 1902, pp. 119–133.)

14. As Lazarsfeld tells us in an autobiographical essay, the very first diffusion of the Marienthal findings was done in seductive fashion. An American visitor to Vienna had seen some of the work in progress and on his return wrote an article in the *Nation*, 136 (January 4, 1933), called "When Man Eats Dog." That's *news*, as everyone knows, but the *Nation* and the news of forty years ago is long since forgotten. (See P. F. Lazarsfeld, "An Episode in the History of Social Research: A Memoir" in *Perspectives in American History*, Vol. 2. (Cambridge, Mass.: Charles Warren Center for Studies in American History, Harvard University, 1968, and Robert N. McMurey, "When Man Eats Dog," *Nation*, 136 (January 4, 1933), 15–18.)

15. R. H. Tawney, "Poverty as an Industrial Problem, 1913," quoted in Bremner, op. cit., p. 9.

21. WITH WHAT EFFECT? THE LESSONS FROM INTERNATIONAL COMMUNICATIONS RESEARCH

Elihu Katz

I

In 1953, at the height of the Cold War, the *Public Opinion Quarterly* produced a special issue on international communications research, marking the grand opening of the world to the communications research fraternity. Devoted to various aspects of studying communications and propaganda outside the United States, the issue also marked the completion by the Bureau of Applied Social Research of the heroic study of public opinion and communication in six countries of the Middle East (Glock, 1952-1953; Sills and Ringer, 1952-1953).[1] This series of surveys for the Voice of America still serves as a model for national audits of communication behavior.

Inspired by this achievement, Paul Lazarsfeld (1952-1953) wrote a "prognosis" for the new field which constitutes the introductory essay for the special issue. International research on mass communication, Lazarsfeld believed, would attract major attention, talent, and support. Examination of the mass media in comparative context, he thought, would liberate communications research from its specifically American setting. It would enlarge our view of the workings of mass media as social institutions and of the cultural, social and psychological processes through which influence flows.

The paper gives particular emphasis to the developing nations. Lazarsfeld thought that the effect of mass communications—and the interpersonal networks to which they are linked—would be more visible in less complex societies. He assumed, as did others, that the media would figure prominently in the drive toward modernization and that communications research would take the lead in assessing the progress of innovation. The result, presumably, would be reflected in enhanced recognition of the role of the mass media among the agents of change and of the place of communications research among the social sciences.

Twenty five years later, George Wedell and I, together with Dov Shinar and Michael Pilsworth, have just completed a qualitative study of the situation of broadcasting in eleven countries which are roughly representative of the ninety-one independent countries which qualified as developing in 1974 on the basics of UNCTAD data.[2] The study was concerned (1) with the process whereby broadcasting was introduced and institutionalized in these countries, that is, with the mutual accommodation of broadcasting and the other social institutions; and (2) with the role of the media in nation building, that is, with the extent to which the media are fulfilling the promise invested in them. We had good reason to suppose that there would be considerable disparity between promise and performance (Katz, 1973a; Katz and Wedell, 1974).

This paper will summarize what we—and others—have learned about the promise and performance of broadcasting and of broadcasting research, in the third world. The starting point in both cases is Paul Lazarsfeld's prognosis. Specifically, three broad themes in Lazarsfeld's paper will be addressed: (1) the role of mass media in the contact among cultures, (2) the relationship between the organization of the media and the content of the programs, and (3) the effects of mass communication on modernization.

II

Lazarsfeld was right in presuming that international communications research would flourish. But there are at least two additional assumptions implicit in his expectations. One of these is that the media would be "there", that is, that the nations would adopt and install the broadcast media and place them in the service of development goals. A second assumption is that researchers would systematically pursue the effects of the media not only at the institutional level, but among the people, and not just in the towns, but in the villages.

As it turns out, both assumptions raise problems. Attention to these is prerequisite to responding to the three questions.

Broadcasting in the Service of Development?

When we began our study, we thought we would find broadcasting explicitly linked to development planning, at least rhetorically. But not so. Despite the best efforts of communications theorists and the active prodding of international organizations, the media have hardly begun to be harnessed to serious developmental goals.[3]

Indeed, broadcasting—even radio broadcasting—is not yet universally available. The developing countries are concentrated in the tropical zones, and over-the-air systems of distribution are subject to tropospheric interference. Even when the signal is receivable, the sets are still to arrive in many places. Latest statistics continue to show great disparities among the regions of the world in the ownership of radio sets, with Africa and South Asia lagging farthest behind. While the *rate* of growth has accelerated rapidly (Frey, 1973), Africa has only lately exceeded the UNESCO "minimum" of 50 sets per thousand people (See Table 1).

The launching of television in the Third World coincides with early planning for modernization and with the need to stabilize new regimes and establish their legitimacy. The rhetoric of certain nations makes this clear. Television is being introduced, they sometimes say, for three reasons—to contribute to national integration, to promote economic development, and to stimulate cultural self-expression. But we found little of this is in actual evidence—in the location of transmitters, in the distribution of receiving sets, or in the content of what is broadcast.

Even though each one of the eleven countries we studied has introduced television broadcasting, the availability of the signal is everywhere limited.[4] Indeed, it can be said that television has not moved very far out of the major cities in all of the developing countries. There could hardly be more convincing evidence that the leaders and planners do not assign very high priority to television in their development plans. Even where there is electricity and where the signal does reach beyond the cities, the price of sets often exceeds a native farmer's annual income, sometimes by two or three times.

Concerted Study of Media Effects?

The other assumption, also widespread, is that researchers in international communications would devote themselves primarily to systematic study of the processes of political, social, and technical development. Lazarsfeld hoped that new methods would be developed for observing the interaction of cultural values, media use, and sociometric networks.

Early research began that way. Lerner's (1958) reworking of the Bureau materials on the Middle East (Glock, 1952-1953) is considered the classic text for study of the role of the media in political mobilization. Lerner attempted to

TABLE 1. Mean Total Sets per Thousand Population for All Countries in Our Sample in Each Area, 1973-1974

	Radio	TV
Africa	68	6
Asia	49	6
Central America	231	60
South America	275	89

demonstrate empirically that exposure to mass communications would equip peasants with opinions about their world and with "empathy", that is, the ability to perceive and identify with the social, political and technical needs of new nationhood beyond the confines of their experience in extended family and village. Thus would radio listening and newspaper reading become the socio-psychological bricks of nation building, the modern-day equivalent of the painful process of actual movement from countryside to city which charac-terized modernization in the West. The mass media would drive a wedge between the generations, leaving the village elders to brood over tradition while their sons, reinforced by the media, took the great leap forward.

If Lerner is the prophet of international communications, Schramm (1964) is its priest. More reserved than Lerner, Schramm tried to instruct the new nations in the functions and effects of mass communications. Translating Lerner from the political to more technical and educational realms, Schramm is careful to emphasize—extrapolating from domestic American studies—that deep-rooted attitudes cannot be changed by exposure to the media alone. Instrumental practices of various kinds which do not conflict with tradition of belief may, however, be quite responsive to change.

Thus, the Center for International Studies at MIT (Lerner's home base) became the major focus for studies of communication and political development while the Institute for Communications Research at Stanford (Schramm's base), and its satellites became the spearhead for studies of communications and socio-economic modernization. Frey (1973) reviews the work of both groups. The prolific work of Rogers and his associates (1969, 1971, 1973) deserves mention, bridging, as it does, the tradition of research on the diffusion of innovation in American rural sociology and the more macroscopic inclinations of the MIT-Stanford axis. Probably the largest concentrations of evaluation studies are to be found in the area of family planning (Berelson, 1965) and in the use of broadcasting for instruction in schools.

Before the answers were in, however, some communications theorists and researchers began to veer away from traditional studies of modernization. Schiller (1969), for example, views broadcasting as an extension of western imperialism. In alliance with the local elite, which broadcasting helps to estab-lish, and with the multinational corporations, broadcasting introduces con-sumerism, individualist striving, repression of class conflict, belief in progress and the other trappings of westernization (Elliott and Golding, 1974). By motivating individuals to aspire to mobility and higher standards of living, these scholars say that the media are creating the kind of consumer demand which maintains the dependence of the developing countries on the economies of the West. If the true goal of national liberation is to break the cycle of exchanging primary prod-ucts for finished ones, the media and other agents of modernization are subvert-ing that goal.

The effect of this criticism was not, of course, to discredit the influence of mass communication, but it did deflect attention from simple studies of *effect* to studies of the *content* of mass communications (Mattelart, 1973) and to the imbalance of communications flow from the metropolitan capitals of the West to the developing world (Nordenstreng and Varis, 1973; Tunstall, 1976). A further result was that certain social scientists were led to exact a new promise from the media—that they should contribute to authentic cultural expression. Some theorists would reject this possibility out of hand. Clifford Geertz (1973, p. 270), for example, classes the mass media with the agents of "epochalism" which are vying with the agents of "essentialism" for the definition of the identity of the new nation. This struggle between keeping pace with the present and finding roots in the past, says Geertz, sets in on the morning after, when the firecrackers simmer down and the nation awakens to the loneliness of independence. But others are more optimistic, insisting that the media can serve as agents of cultural continuity helping to find contemporary relevance in certain of the traditional values in the folk or classical arts.

Bennett (1974, and in UNESCO, 1974) can be numbered among the optimists. In his proposal for media development for rural Thailand, he argues not only against dissonant foreign influences—such as consumption, violence, cupidity, and jealousy—but even against the message of home-made instructional broadcasts which reflect, he says, a deeply rooted *Asian* attitude that leaving home and farm and getting still another certificate is the aim of life. Bennett argues for media and messages that will gratify the needs of the farmer who is staying home.

Thus, there have been important shifts in the character of international communications research over the two and a half decades. First, and most recent, is the shift away from economic and political development to a concern with culture—domestic and imported. Second, there is a shift from study of the manifest message of the media to the more latent images in which media messages come packaged. This is, of course, a classic issue in media research. Third, there has been a movement away from the study of individual effects to a study of the effects of mass media on the more macroscopic level.

A fourth shift in communications research is reflected in the insistence that the nation-state should not be treated as a distinct unit of analysis. National systems of broadcasting, it is argued, are linked inexorably with international networks of content and control and they must be analyzed in that context (e.g., Cardona, 1975).

In summing up, we should point out the irony that the new nations—despite their fear of the imposition of alien culture—are probably moving in the direction of increased mobilization of the media for development, whereas the researchers—without abandoning the assumption that the effects of the media are great—are much more interested in the so-called "consciousness industry", that is, in media content and control. With the consequent decline in evaluation research, there appear to be more true believers but less proof as time goes by.

III

Now that we have some idea of how the new nations have responded to the broadcast media and how research has responded to the opportunity of studying them comparatively, we turn to the substance of Lazarsfeld's proposals for comparative research. Three areas of interest central to his "prognosis" have been singled out, and we here address ourselves to each.

Culture Contact

A first theme which looms large is study of the role of mass media as brokers in the flow of influence across cultural boundaries. It is this focus which Lazarsfeld sees contributing importantly to the other social sciences. Arguing that communication is one of the mechanisms through which change occurs in culture contact, he predicts that communications research will be recognized as "a part of anthropology which has so far been neglected, the study of the processes by which the various cultures influence each other."

The first thing that needs to be said in response is that the implication of *mutual* influence is incorrect. The flow of influence, so far, is almost all in one direction—from the metropolitan centers of Western broadcasting to the developing countries. Thus, 30–75 percent of the television programs in the eleven countries we studied are imported from the West, as is much of the music on radio. The United States is the major exporter regardless of the cultural background of the country. England and France are important sources for their former colonies, and there is some exchange with other countries sharing the same language. Japan is now a program supplier to South East Asia, but exchanges between neighbors are rare.

Even the home-made programs are often imitations of Western models and some of the companies which market television films also sell program formats so that a children's program or a quiz program can be replicated by local producers. Thus the American-inspired soap opera is the most widely diffused "local" production in the world; it is the main staple of South American television. In Brazil, for example, three locally produced soap operas consume the whole of prime time every night.

The flow of news is even more unidirectional. Radio and television organizations subscribe to the international wires and the international news film services, based in London, Paris and New York, and the presentation of the news—like the presentation of programs—is in direct imitation of the metropolitan centers. The series of terse, disconnected news items presented in staccato fashion by a team of breathless announcers dressed in the latest London fashions is the usual format of the major news program (Katz, 1973b).

Indeed, there is little to see of indigenous culture on the television screen. Even cultures with rich visual traditions such as Thailand and Iran have little to show of their heritage on television. There are, of course, programs set aside for regional and national folklore, but the *style* of what one sees is apparently uninfluenced by tradition. There is no evident effort—as there is, say, in the modern architecture of these countries—to incorporate elements of the tradition or symbolic expressions of continuity. Experimentation with the adaptation of indigenous forms was more characteristic of the earliest days of television—in Thailand, for example—than currently. Inevitably, it seems, the standards and styles of the West become the models for programming just as they are for equipment layout and maintenance and for organization. As a result, producers are caught up in the glamor of metropolitan cultures and, in the process, forget their own.

The rise of radio and television is associated with the decline in the traditional arts, both classical and popular (McCormack, 1969; Kato, 1975). The relationship is not necessarily causal, though broadcasting probably plays a part in keeping people home—and thus away from the tea-house, the theater, and the temple fair. Altogether, the routine of nonstop broadcasting is probably undermining "the sense of occasion" which was the mark of participation in culture.

Why has it happened this way? The first and most obvious reason is the dependence of the developing countries on the technology of the West. Only now have certain of the countries in our sample begun assembly of radio and television receiving sets; production and transmission equipment are still wholly imported from the West. In addition, these countries were dependent on Western financing—either in the form of colonial or postcolonial subventions, in the form of international development investments from such as the World Bank, or in the form of commercial investment on the part of overseas broadcasters or multinational advertisers who saw a potential market for their products or sets in the developing countries. Programs, and programming ideas, arrived through these same channels.

Less obvious, perhaps, is the influence of the complexity and cost of television production. The innocent decision to broadcast five or six hours per night (2,000 hours per year!) is an automatic invitation to "Kojak" and "Kung-Fu." It is cheaper to buy abroad than to produce even the most modest of local productions. And what is more, there isn't enough talent, or budget or infrastructure in the arts allied to broadcasting (writers, film-makers, actors, graphic artists) to cope with the number of broadcast hours. This demand for imported material is complemented by the energetic sales departments of the American and European television and film companies and by the Information Services of the various foreign embassies. The eagerness to supply is sometimes seen as part of a campaign to westernize the developing world (Schiller, 1969; Mattelart, 1973), but, even if that is so, one cannot reckon without the voracious demand for material to fill time.

Another factor is the difficulty of transplanting the traditional arts to a studio from the village green or fairgrounds. Not all are performing arts, and the idea of an audience—even an unseen one—may disturb. Moreover, the technical problems of outside broadcasting are far greater. There is also the problem of limited repertoire. Many of the classical and folk arts have strictly circumscribed repertoires which are rapidly exhausted by the mass media. An exception may be found in the troubadour-like arts, which have traditionally refreshed themselves by improvised reference to current events. These arts apparently succeed very well on radio and television; we have examples from Thailand (Tambiah, 1968) and from Senegal.

Thus, we have some answers—at the macro level at least—of how broadcasting serves as a mechanism for the introduction of cultural change, how it disconnects people from their own cultures and channels the flow of intercultural influence. Indeed, broadcasting itself—as technology, organization, content—is an example of the diffusion of innovation across cultural boundaries. Like all innovations, it has had to accommodate to local conditions, particularly to direct political control. Nevertheless, the resultant flow of ideas seems so pervasive that many countries of the Third World are calling for a halt to the "free flow of information" and for more "authenticity" in programming.[5]

Although much more might be said on the institutional level, the problem is that we have so little to say on the level of viewers and listeners in village or town. Analysis of the expressive—rather than instrumental—uses of mass communications hardly exists. Impressionistically, one senses that the mass media are less revolutionary than institutional or content analysis implies. There is some ethnographic data. Mosel (1963), for example, argues that broadcasting has been assimilated to the traditional passivity and playfulness of rural Thailand. In his analysis of Somali Nomads, Lewis (1968) suggests that radio fits, but also transforms, nonliterate cultures. But we have very little of this kind of anthropology (Goody, 1968) and even less of the elementary sort of communications research which is needed in order to identify the cultures in which "Kojak" or "Lucy" outdraw home-produced programs and to explain why.[6]

Broadcasting Structures and Program Output

Lazarsfeld was also interested in the nexus of control-organization-output-taste. What is the influence of different economic and political systems on the control of broadcasting organizations? What is the relationship between different types of organization and program output? How does output affect taste? Here Lazarsfeld expressed interest in European broadcasting systems no less than those of the developing world.

The one aspect of Western broadcasting which has not been transplanted to the developing world is the cardinal tenet of "freedom of expression." Whereas American and British technology, organization, and a wide variety of program material successfully crossed the oceans, the notion that broadcasting and government should be separated from one another did not survive the journey. Of the three major Western systems, only the French—which, until recently, was directly associated with the Ministry of Information—serves as a usable model in the developing world. Whether there is nominal public control and direct government operation, as in most of Africa, or private ownership, as in most of South America, or mixed systems, such as in parts of Asia, there is very strong and unmasked political control by government.

One would expect there to be differences in output between commercial systems and systems that are government owned and operated, even bearing in mind that the latter also usually sell advertising time. One would expect the former to be more entertaining and the latter more didactic. Similarly, one would expect differences among nations that have only one national television network, nations that have two networks under the same management, and nations that have two or more competing networks under different managements. These, of course, are Lazarsfeld's questions concerning the relationship between broadcasting structure and output.

Few differences are evident, however, at least at the superficial level of categories of content. Regardless of the type of system, radio broadcasting everywhere consists of about 20-30 percent informational content and 50-60 percent music. Television consists of about 30 percent information and 70 percent entertainment. Imported foreign material, as already noted, makes up between 30-75 percent of output but the mode is about 50 percent (see Table 2).

Country-by-country analysis does show certain interesting variations. Thus, radio in Tanzania and Senegal broadcasts more information, current affairs, and education. Even Tanzania's commercial service devotes 38 percent of its programs to information. In the case of television, the African countries Algeria, Nigeria, Senegal—broadcast relatively more information and less entertainment than the private (or at least not exclusively government) stations of Brazil, Peru, and Thailand. But this difference is probably a result of the low levels of finance available to more African broadcasters. "Information" programs usually take the form of live studio broadcasts, the cheapest use of resources. Moreover, there is no systematic difference between African countries and the others in the proportion of television programs imported and home-produced.

More refined analysis can be performed, of course, on the actual schedules themselves. It is not enough to show that ratios of information to entertainment do not differ markedly in different kinds of broadcasting structures and under different sorts of regimes or that the ratio of imported to domestic programming is the same. There remains the question of what *kinds* of entertainment and information (see Table 3).

In fact, however, the imported programs—50 percent of television hours—tend to be standard American: the action-adventure series and the family-situation serial. Everywhere—regardless of type of regime or broadcasting system—American programs outnumber all others. Even in countries which are culturally related—such as Cyprus to Greece or Algeria to France—U.S. programs predominate. But ideology makes way for "L'Homme de Fer" [sic] in Algeria or for "Kojak" or "Gunsmoke" or "Family Affair." Each of these and many

TABLE 2. Proportion of Television Programs Imported versus Home-Made. 1973–1974

	Indonesia[d]	NBC	Nigeria WNTV	BCNN	Senegal	Algeria	Thailand[d]	Iran[b]	Cyprus[c]	Brazil[a]	Peru[d]
Imported	35	30	55	55	75	50	50	40	65	57	60
Home-made	65	70	45	45	25	50	50	60	35	43	40

Source: Information provided by respective organizations.
(a) All channels. (b) National network. (c) Channels 1 and 2. (d) Channels 4 and 5.

TABLE 3. Evening TV Program Schedules in Seven Countries, Saturdays 1974

July 19, 1974 Nicosia, CBC	July 19, 1974 Singapore, Ch. 5	July 26, 1974 Lagos, NBC	July 19, 1974 Tehran, NIRT	July 19, 1974 Brasília, Globo	April 15, 1974 Algiers, RTA	July 19, 1975 Bangkok, Ch. 7, 5c
6:30 News	5:55 Children	6:00 News (Int'l)	6:00 Puppets	6:00 "The Wonderful World of Disney" (U.S. series)	5:45 "Western Affair" (U.S. series)	6:00 Popular Music (Thai)
6:35 Puppets	6:20 Consumers' Guide	6:05 Sports	6:15 Physical Education for Teenagers	7:15 "Bravo" (serial)	6:55 "Ivanhoe" (U.K. serial)	6:30 Documentary (Thai)
6:50 "Gun-smoke" (U.S. series)	6:30 News	7:00 News (Nat'l)	6:40 Educational Program	8:00 News	7:20 Puppet Festival	7:00 "Devil Man" (Japanese series)
7:40 "Human Stories" (Greek series)	6:35 "Wheeler" (U.S. cartoon)	7:05 "Bar Beach Show"	7:00 Sports News	8:30 "Escalada" (serial)	7:30 Magazine of the East (regional news)	7:30 Play (Thai)
8:30 News	7:00 Family Time	8:00 Play of the Week	7:15 Children's Story	9:00 "Kojak" (U.S. series)	8:00 News	7:50 Folklore (Thai)
9:00 News (Turkish)	7:30 News	9:00 News	7:30 "Family Affair" (U.S. serial)	10:00 *Crooks and Coronets* (U.S. feature film)	8:25 "Family Affair" (U.S. serial)	8:00 News
9:10 Music with Theodorakis	7:45 "Harry Secombe Show" (U.K.)	9:15 "Matters of the Moment"	8:00 Air Force (Foreign?) serial	12:00 *Cry Rape* (U.S. feature film)	8:50 Press Review	8:30 Classical Music (Thai)
9:55 "Anthology: Murder" (U.S. series)	8:35 "Streets of San Francisco (U.S. series)	10:00 Feature Film (U.S.)	8:30 News		9:05 *Fernande* (French feature film)	9:00 "Thrill-seeker" (U.S.? series)
11:10 News	9:30 News	11:00 News	9:00 Friendly Countries		10:00 News	9:45 Feature Film (Thai)
	9:55 "Gomer Pyle" (U.S. comedy serial)		10:00 "Days of Our Lives" (U.S. serial)		10:50 Variety Show	
	10:25 "Callan" (U.K. series)		10:25 "Mister Know It All" (comedy)			
	11:20 Feature Film (U.S.)		10:30 "On the Way" (political discussion)			
			11:00 Football (Iran vs. USSR)			

other favorites commanded prime-time positions in several countries during the period of our study.

But it would be unfair not to point out some of the differences in emphasis. Prime time in Brazil, for example, is the domain of the *telenovela,* the home-made soap operas which take up almost the whole of the weekday evenings. Algeria programs instructional broadcasts in the early evening and imports from Lebanon, Bulgaria, France, and England; one has the impression that Algerian television—like its French model—is working to appeal to a more highbrow standard. Cyprus imports from Greece, Thailand is taking an impressive number of programs from Japan. Thailand and Nigeria offer home-made drama.

But, altogether, the rhythm of the evening hours is very much the same everywhere: shows for children and sometimes instruction in the early evening; a family comedy; the news; a series or serial, sometimes a show; and a feature film. Documentaries are almost unrepresented in this sample, and the same paucity is evident in the field of discussion. Curiously, the quiz seems unpopular. The high degree of uniformity in television programming, both in flow and content, appears to be a response to several kinds of constraints. Television is the medium of the whole family; it must take account of family members' availability by age and sex; it must feed the voracious transmitters with a constant supply of programs and thus must depend on the very few places in the world where programs are stockpiled; it must, it seems, live up to the expectation that it will entertain, and in rather specific ways (see Williams, 1974). Thus, many small European countries, even rich ones like Sweden, import a third or more of their television programs.[7] And even Russia, we are told (Powell, 1975), has abandoned television to entertainment.

Nor does competition make much difference. Competing channels usually present the same fare. Thus, on Monday, July 15, 1975, at 8:30 P.M., for example, the viewers of Bankok could choose among three American series: "Manhunt" (Channel 3), "FBI" (7c), and "Get Christy Love" (7, 5c). On a June Saturday night in Teheran, the viewer had a choice of "Family Affair" and "Days of Our Lives" on one channel and "The Bold Ones" and "Kojak" on the other. The examples are handpicked, of course, for the choices sometimes include—as in Thailand on July Sundays—wrestling, "Disney," or "Hawaii Five-O." Singapore has a more indigenous channel 8 and a more cosmopolitan channel 5. But, on the whole, competition leads to sameness—as it did in Britain—except when the competitors are both operated under one direction and an explicit effort is made to create choice.

It follows that the structure of control, the ideological commitment, or the competitive broadcasting does very little to alter the patterns of program output. Public ownership, more guided development, Anglo-French versus American-influenced systems may have some effect. Cultural orientations, too, such as those of Algeria (to France), or Cyprus (to Greece) or Nigeria (to England) also show through. But, by and large, the answer to Lazarsfeld's question about the relationship between structure and output is remarkably unsociological. Change the regime, change the broadcast organization, introduce competition, and the program schedule remains essentially unaltered. "Kojak" is in the box.

With What Effects?

Third, Lazarsfeld predicted that comparative research would find the study of media effects "less discouraging." Whereas the isolation of a single stimulus is all but impossible in modern societies which are deluged by competing and confounding stimuli, he felt that traditional societies responding to the introduction of a new medium, a new message, or a technical innovation would stand still long enough to be studied. "We can expect," he writes, "that in a fairly stable situation, such as we might find among one or two countries of the East, the Point Four program, for example, might have noticeable and rather speedy effects."

Perhaps there *are* one or two countries of the East which fit that description. From the point of view of the research fraternity, Taiwan is probably a good example. Studies of modernization in areas such as family planning, for example, show that the message and techniques of social change have had noticeable and speedy effects (Freedman et al., 1964-1965).

But Taiwan also proves the rule that innovations in traditional societies are almost as difficult to study as innovations in modern societies. The fact is that social and technical changes come not one at a time but in packages. Modernizing influences are interrelated. At both the individual and aggregate levels, exposure to mass media is correlated with years of schooling, literacy, size of farm, trips to the city, empathy, innovativeness, achievement motivation, and so on. Just as the study of media effects was confounded by other "modern" stimuli in the West, so the study of media effects is confounded by other "modernizing" stimuli in the developing countries. The media have a part in all of this, but the extent of their direct contribution, and whether they are cause or effect of other aspects of modernization, is all but impossible to assess.

At the individual level, the data relating media use to modernizing attitudes and practices of peasants seem consistent and persuasive. There are not very many such studies—fewer than Lazarsfeld's prognosis implied—but they demonstrate quite strong correlations between media exposure and modernity, even when other variables are taken into account. Literacy is even more strongly related. Rogers (1969) and Frey (1973) both review the correlational studies. More recent evidence comes from Inkeles and Smith (1974) who insist that their data, though cross-sectional, should probably be read causally: the mass media induce (urban) working men to hold modern attitudes—to feel efficacious, for example. In his own study, Frey (1973) also advances a causal argument.

To a certain extent, then, it is fair to argue—as Lazarsfeld predicted—that the mass media have an identifiable share in the modernization of individual attitudes and practices. Indicators of economic and political modernity such as empathy, the ability to take the role of the other, innovativeness in agriculture and in the home, or participation in political affairs can be shown to be related to mass-media exposure. And the magnitude of the correlations—even when other variables are held constant—is impressive compared with comparable studies in modern societies. But, nevertheless, it is clear that the intervening variables—social status, for example—do reduce these relationships substantially (Rogers, 1969) and that it is better to speak, as does Frey, in terms of two sets of variables, one defining "exposure to change" and the other "cognitive flexibility." The first group includes urbanization, literacy, mass-media exposure, and schooling, and the second group encompasses empathy, innovativeness, tolerance of deviant behavior, open-mindedness, and other elements of individual modernity.

Moreover, studies that have taken a closer look at the influence of mass communication are at pains to point out what the media do not or cannot do. Thus, Hornik (1974) and others before him point out that there is no evidence to support the assertion that media glamor is responsible for a "revolution of rising frustrations" (Lerner, 1963) or, indeed, for any kind of revolution at all—either at the individual or the national levels. Societies which have more developed mass media have not experienced greater instability. Individuals who have access to the media tend to be more satisfied with their lives—not necessarily because of the media—than those who have not. In questioning this part of Lerner's thesis, Hornick's data offer support for Lerner's suggestion that the "psychic mobility" made possible by the media may serve as a substitute for physical mobility. The data show that adolescents whose parents recently acquired a television set became *less* interested in moving to the city. This is a nice echo of what the manager of a local TV station in Iran told us: A highly respected local physician had been intending to leave for Tehran because he longed for the life of the big city. But television came to Jazd, and he found that he now felt himself part of the cosmopolitan world and changed his mind about leaving.[8]

Still more microscopically, it turns out that the mass media are most effective at the "awareness" stage in the adoption of innovation and hardly at all at the point of decision to adopt. Decisions to innovate in developing societies are even more dependent on friends and neighbors than they are in developed ones. Indeed, the "two-step flow of communication" is on display in many village communities where the village chief or local influential own a radio or read a newspaper and then pass on what they have seen or heard. The evidence that the mass media skip a generation and support the modernizing young against their parents is very sparse; Rogers (1969) suggests that this may be the case in modern, but not in traditional Colombian villages.

Indeed, the same intervening variables which act to speed, or retard, the flow of mass communications in modern societies have been rediscovered in traditional ones (Lazarsfeld and Merton, 1948). If it is true that China has been as successful in its use of the media as is sometimes claimed, it is almost certainly because of monopolization (Pool, 1973). Unlike Russia, which is reached by foreign broadcasts, radio in mainland China is limited, almost without exception, to the national broadcasting service which is distributed, in large measure, to wired, one-channel sets. And where the media are associated with diffusion of change, it is certainly because of canalization, whereby the new is linked symbolically with an already established attitude (Katz, 1974). Most important of all is the role of supplementation. The media are at their most effective when they link up with a social infrastructure which is dedicated to doing a certain job, such as when the media reinforce the work of the agricultural agent, the farm forum, the literacy corps, the health worker, the local influential. By the same token, the media have not proven good substitutes for teachers even when they are carefully programmed for instruction. They provide supplementation and support for teachers. They are at their best when they are accompanied by, or constrain, curricular reform. But these adhesions make it difficult to evaluate the direct contribution of the media.

At the aggregate level, the influence of the media is even more difficult to assess. Frey (1973) reviews several studies which have tried to fit national data to Lerner's causal model which leads from rates of urbanism to rates of literacy to mass media growth to political participation (such as voting rates). The variables are surely related—all the studies agree—but the sequence of their causal links is not clear; the one that stands up best in Frey's survey of these studies is the one linking media exposure to political participation.

IV

It is for the reader to decide how far we have advanced toward answering Lazarsfeld's questions. My own feeling is that we do not have enough to show.

Partly, as elaborated in Section II, this is because the developing nations themselves have been rather slow to respond to the media of mass communication. The diffusion of radio is still incomplete, and television—in many areas—is only beginning. The peasants, who are the focus of development efforts, are typically last on line. Partly, it is because the focus of research itself has changed. The current interest in the international flow of news and entertainment and in their symbolic content, has been accompanied by a corresponding shift away from the study of more formal efforts to achieve change and from the survey method of evaluation.

To Lazarsfeld's question concerning the process of intercultural influence, we could explain how the media filter in alien content and filter out indigenous culture—even when no such intention exists.

To the question of the relationship between structure and program output, we could answer that some aspects of culture and structure do peek through into content: political control, colonial background, determination to effect change, private versus public ownership. But more than variation, we see sameness. The constraints which guide the transplantation of the media from Western centers to the developing countries go some distance in explaining the process whereby the world is becoming "culturally homogenized."

To the narrow question of whether and how media induce modern attitudes and behavior, we could answer that the media have a share in this, but, just as in modern society, one cannot understand the influence process without reference to the norms and networks in which people are enmeshed. Exposure to the mass media is part of a package of "exposure to change" which is associated with open-mindedness. But it is not always clear which comes first.

Although the causal links are no more clear on the aggregate level, several comparative studies do suggest that the rate of media exposure increases the extent of political participation. We do know that the state, everywhere, deploys the media to promote loyalty to the center. Where transmission and reception facilities are available, the national language is heard and spread. Images of the leaders appear nightly on television, enplaning and deplaning. The King of Thailand may be seen in his traditional role as distributor of bounty to the needy or the disaster-stricken. The ruling generals of Brazil and Peru are omnipresent. At the aggregate level, a good case can be made that the media are, indeed, agents of national integration just as the printed word was in the West. Intuitively, Deutsch (1953) and Innis (1951) seem well supported; but we do not know for sure.

We simply have not gotten close enough to the larger questions. We continue to speculate about the effects of print on Western civilization, but we have not been able to devise systematic methods for studying the deeper effects of the introduction of radio or television. Where we had the chance, as in Israel or South Africa, we settled for rather too narrow definitions of effect (Katz and Gurevitch, 1976; Harrison and Ekman, 1976). Given the slow progress of television into the hinterlands, however, it may not be too late to examine whether and how the media contribute to national integration, or whether it is true that the latent message of the media is that of competitive striving and the celebration of progress, or the ways in which American family comedies or action/ adventure programs are understood, or, indeed, whether McLuhan (1964) is right or wrong in alleging that the technology of the media influence our most fundamental processes of perception and cognition.

Notes

1. Almost 2,000 completed interviews were obtained from urban and rural areas in Greece, Turkey, Iran, Egypt, Lebanon, Jordan, and Syria. There was a report on the data from each country as well as a comparative report on the four Arabic countries. Daniel Lerner (1958) incorporates these reports which repre-

sent the teamwork, in various coalitions, of Lerner, G. K. Schueller and M. Stycos (Turkey), J. M. Stycos (Jordan), W. N. McPhee and R. Meyersohn (Lebanon, Syria), B. Ringer and D. Sills (Iran), P. L. Kendall and B. B. Ringer (Egypt), and P. L. Kendall and E. Katz (four Arabic countries).

2. The eleven countries are Algeria, Brazil, Cyprus, Indonesia, Iran, Nigeria, Peru, Senegal, Singapore, Tanzania, and Thailand. Reports on broadcasting and national development in each of these countries as well as an overall report by Katz and Wedell (1975) have been submitted to the sponsors, the Ford Foundation and the International Broadcast Institute. I wish to thank Michael Pilsworth for his helpful advice on the present paper.

3. Head (1974) comes to the same conclusion.

4. Of course, the variability among countries is very great; India, for example, has 25 sets per 1,000 people; Lebanon has 419.

5. For understandable reasons, certain liberal and opposition groups in the developing countries are very fearful of the call for cultural authenticity in programming. They prefer "Kojak" to a coalition of traditionalists and authoritarians. This is a major focus of argument in the developing world. (Katz, 1977).

6. In certain countries, we found American imports among the most popular programs; in others, particularly in Africa, this was not the case. It is our impression, however, that home-produced soap opera outdraws American series and serials almost everywhere, despite (or perhaps because of) the great disparity in sheer technique and showmanship.

7. Britain, by contrast, permits only 14 percent importation.

8. Every self-respecting international communications researcher has to have a Middle Eastern anecdote.

References

BENNETT, NICHOLAS, 1974. "Planning for the Development of Educational Media in Thailand," *Educational Broadcasting International*, 176–179.

BERELSON, BERNARD, ed., 1965. *Family Planning and Population Programs*. Chicago: University of Chicago Press.

CARDONA, ELIZABETH de, 1975. "Multinational Television," *Journal of Communication*, 25, 122–127.

DEUTSCH, KARL W., 1953. *Nationalism and Social Communication*. New York: Wiley.

ELLIOTT, PHILLIP, and PETER GOLDING, 1974. "Mass Communication and Social Change," in E. de Kadt and G. Williams, eds., *Sociology and Development*. London: Tavistock, 229–254.

FREEDMAN, RONALD, JOHN Y. TAKESHITA, and T. H. SUN, 1970. "Fertility and Family Planning in Taiwan: A Case Study of the Demographic Transition," *American Journal of Sociology*, 70, 16–27.

FREY, FREDERICK, W., 1973. "Communication and Development," in Ithiel de Sola Pool, Wilbur Schramm, et al., eds., *Handbook of Communication*. Chicago: Rand McNally, 337–432.

GEERTZ, CLIFFORD, 1973. *The Interpretation of Cultures*. New York: Basic Books.

GLOCK, CHARLES Y., 1952–53. "The Comparative Study of Communications and Opinion Formation," *Public Opinion Quarterly*, 16, 512–523.

GOODY, JACK, ed., 1968. *Literacy in Traditional Societies*, London: Cambridge University Press.

HARRISON, RANDALL, and PAUL EKMAN, 1976. "TV's Last Frontier: South Africa," *Journal of Communication*, 26, 102–109.

HEAD, SYDNEY W., ed. 1974. *Broadcasting in Africa*. Philadelphia: Temple University.

HORNIK, ROBERT C., 1974. "Mass Media Use and the 'Revolution of Rising Frustrations': A Reconsideration of the Theory," *Papers of East West Communications Institute*, 11.

INKELES, ALEX, and DAVID H. SMITH, 1974. *Becoming Modern: Individual Change in Six Developing Countries*. London: Heinemann.

INNIS, HAROLD A., 1951. *The Bias of Communication*. Toronto: University of Toronto Press.

KATO, HIDETOSHI, 1975. "Essays in Comparative Popular Culture," *Papers of the East-West Communication Institute*, 13.

KATZ, ELIHU, 1971. "Television Comes to the Middle East," *Transaction*, 8, 42–50.

——— , 1973a. "News from the Global Village: The Structure of Television in Developing Countries," *The Listener*, 89,

——— , 1973b. "Television as Horseless Carriage," in Gerbner, Melody and Gross, eds., *Communications Technology and Social Policy*. New York: Wiley.

——— , 1974. *On the Use of the Concept of Compatibility in Research on the Diffusion of Innovation*. Jerusalem: Israel Academy of Science, Proceedings.

KATZ, ELIHU, and E. G. WEDELL, 1977, with Dov Shinar and Michael Pilsworth. *Broadcasting in the Third World: Promise and Performance*. Cambridge, Mass.: Harvard University Press.

KATZ, ELIHU, and MICHAEL GUREVITCH, 1976. *The Secularization of Leisure: Culture and Communication in Israel*. London: Faber and Faber.

KATZ, ELIHU, 1977. "Cultural Continuity and Change: The Role of Mass Media," in Tehranian and Hakimzadeh, eds., *Communication Policies in Rapidly Developing Societies*. London: Routledge & Kegan Paul.

LAZARSFELD, PAUL F., 1952–1953. "The Prognosis for International Communications Research." *Public Opinion Quarterly*, 481–490.

LAZARSFELD, P. F., and R. K. MERTON, 1948. "Mass Communication, Popular Taste and Organized Social Action," in Lyman Bryson, ed., *Communication of Ideas*. New York: Harper, pp. 95–118.

LERNER, DANIEL, 1958. *The Passing of Traditional Society: Modernizing the Middle East.* New York: Free Press.

_____ , 1963. "Toward a Communication Theory of Modernization," in L. W. Pye, ed., *Communications and Political Development.* Princeton, N.J.: Princeton University Press.

LEWIS, I. M., 1968, "Literacy in a Nomadic Society: The Somali Case," in Jack Goody, ed., *Literacy in Traditional Societies.* London: Cambridge University Press.

MATTELART, ARMAND, 1973. "Mass Media and the Socialist Revolution: The Experience of Chile," in G. Gerbner, L. Gross, and W. H. Melody, eds., *Communications Technology and Social Policy.* New York: Wiley.

McCORMACK, THELMA, 1969. "Folk Culture and the Mass Media," *European Journal of Sociology*, 10, 220–237.

McLUHAN, MARSHALL, 1964. *Understanding Media*, New York: McGraw-Hill.

MOSEL, JAMES N., 1963. "Communication Patterns and Political Socialization in Transitional Thailand," in L. W. Pye, ed., *Communications and Political Development.* Princeton, N.J.: Princeton University Press.

NEURATH, PAUL M., "Radio Farm Forums as a Tool of Change in Indian Villages," *Economic Development and Cultural Change*, 10, 275–283.

NORDENSTRENG, KAARLE, and TAPIO VARIS, 1976. "Television Traffic: A One-Way Street?," *UNESCO Reports and Papers on Mass Communication*, #70.

OLSON, DAVID E., ed., 1974. *Media and Symbols.* Chicago: University of Chicago Press.

POOL, ITHIEL de SOLA, 1973. "Communication in Totalitarian Societies," in Ithiel de Sola Pool, Wilbur Schramm, et al., eds., *Handbook of Communication.* Chicago: Rand McNally.

POWELL, DAVID E. 1975. "Television in the USSR," *Public Opinion Quarterly*, 39, 287–300.

ROGERS, EVERETT M., with LYNNE SVENNING, 1969. *Modernization Among Peasants: The Impact of Communication.* New York: Holt, Rinehart and Winston.

ROGERS, EVERETT M., with F. FLOYD SHOEMAKER, 1971. *Communication of Innovations: A Cross-Cultural Approach.* New York: Free Press.

ROGERS, EVERETT, 1973. *Communication Strategies for Family Planning.* New York: Free Press.

SCHILLER, HERBERT I., 1969. *Mass Communication and American Empire.* Boston: Beacon Press.

SCHRAMM, WILBUR, 1964. *Mass Media and National Development: The Role of Information in the Developing Countries.* Stanford, Calif.: Stanford University Press.

SILLS, DAVID L., and BENJAMIN E. RINGER, 1952–1953. "Political Extremism in Iran: A Secondary Analysis of Communications Data," *Public Opinion Quarterly*, 16, 689–701.

TAMBIAH, S. J., 1968. "Literacy in a Buddhist Village in North-East Thailand," in Jack Goody, ed., *Literacy in Traditional Societies*. London: Cambridge University Press.

TUNSTALL, JEREMY, 1976. *The Media are American*. London: Constable.

UNESCO, 1974. *Interim Report of Pre-Feasability Study Team*, Bangkok.

WILLIAMS, RAYMOND, 1974. *Television: Technology and Cultural Form*. London: Fontana.

22. THE CHANGING SOCIAL ORIGINS OF AMERICAN ACADEMICS

Seymour Martin Lipset and Everett C. Ladd, Jr.

Most watchdogs of higher education will agree that the extraordinary growth in the numbers of students in college and graduate school since World War II has profoundly altered the quality of American life. A college education is generally correlated with liberal values in such areas as civil rights and civil liberties. And college graduates strongly support change in cultural orientations and life-style expectations.[1] In 1900, only 238,000 students—a little over 2 percent of the 18- to 24-year-old population—went to college. At the end of World War II the figure had climbed to 2,078,000, and by 1975, 9.7 million—over one-third of the 18- to 24-year olds—enrolled in accredited institutions of higher education.[2] These expanding numbers have meant expanding educational opportunities for the underprivileged and more chances for upward mobility. If any doubt exists that education is more equitably distributed in America than elsewhere, one has only to look at the figures for higher education—the proportion of students enrolled here is far higher than in European countries. What is more, studies of professionals in many economically developed nations confirm that, once out of college, a significantly higher percentage of Americans from disadvantaged backgrounds are employed in professional fields.[3]

Clearly, then, expanded numbers of students have meant a democratization of our society. But what of faculty, whose numbers have also swelled? Has an expanding professoriate in a society increasingly self-conscious about inequality become a source of upward mobility? Has a significant increase occurred in the proportion of the faculty coming from lower-status backgrounds, from economically disadvantaged groups, or from underrepresented minorities? In 1900

We are particularly indebted to Clark Kerr and Martin Trow of the Carnegie Commission (Council) on Higher Education for the use of their 1969 faculty survey, which was collected under the direction of Trow. Our 1975 Survey was collected with support from a grant from the Spencer Foundation. We have previously reported on these surveys in Everett Ladd and S. M. Lipset, *The Divided Academy: Professors and Politics* (New York: The Norton Library, 1976), and in a series of articles published in *The Chronicle of Higher Education* from September 1975 to June 1976.

there were just 24,000 faculty—a mere 0.08 of 1 percent of the labor force. By the close of World War II, their numbers had jumped to 126,000, and by 1975 670,000 faculty members accounted for 0.71 percent of the labor force— an eightfold increase over 1900. Some students of higher education, David Riesman among them, have maintained that in the post-World War II years the university has become more meritocratic—placing greater weight on ability rather than on social background in faculty selection as well as student admission.[4] Certainly, in recent years the university has placed increasing emphasis on redressing past inequities through affirmative action hiring programs. Given the attempts to make the university more meritocratic and to expand opportunities to underrepresented or disadvantaged groups, we set out to examine just how much democratization has actually taken place within the faculty ranks.

Little survey data on the social origins of faculty were collected prior to 1969. In that year 60,000 randomly selected faculty filled out questionnaires in a project under the auspices of the Carnegie Commission on Higher Education. In a second study, directed by us in 1975, questionnaires were completed by approximately 3,500 respondents, comprising a cross-section of all college and university faculty. This second survey inquired into background factors not covered in the Carnegie study—particularly the respondent's ethnic origin, family denominational affiliation, and assessment of family economic status during his or her high school years.[5]

As a partial substitute for past surveys, we also compared the responses of the various age cohorts—professors in their twenties, with colleagues in their thirties, forties, and so forth. Presumably if academe has increasingly democratized its employment patterns, the younger a faculty member, the less privileged his or her background.

Socioeconomic Background

Not surprisingly perhaps, faculty members apparently still come largely from middle-class family backgrounds. Both the 1969 and 1975 surveys point to the professions and small business as the largest occupational categories for the fathers of professors. Two-fifths come from professional, semiprofessional, and managerial families, and another fifth are from business backgrounds. Only one-quarter are of working-class origin. Yet in 1950, when the fathers of most of today's faculty were occupationally active, 70 percent of all American males were in manual or white-collar and sales positions (see Table 1).

Even the breakdown by age cohorts—though it reveals major differences in paternal occupational backgrounds—does not suggest an opening to the less privileged. Essentially, younger faculty are less likely to be children of farmers or small businessmen and more apt to have fathers in professional (particularly managerial and semiprofessional) employment. This trend is not peculiar to the

TABLE 1. Occupations of Fathers of American Academics, 1969 and 1975, and of the Male Labor Force in 1950 (as percentages of *n*)

	1969 Survey Distribution (n = 60,028)	1975 Survey Distribution (n = 3,536)	Males in Labor Force, 1950 (n = 42,722,000)
College, university teacher/administrator	4%	4%	0.5%
Elem., sec. school teacher/administrator	3	3	0.6
Other professional	15	16	2.6
Managerial and semi-professional	16	17	10.2
Owner, large business	2	1	0.4
Owner, small business	18	18	3.3
White collar	8	7	12.6
Farmer	10	8	9.8
Skilled worker	16	17	23.6
Semi-skilled and unskilled Workers	8	9	33.6
Armed services	1	1	0.9

Source: Data on the proportion of the total male labor force in 1950 employed in the various occupational groups are from *Historical Statistics of the United States, Colonial Times to 1970*. Washington, D.C.: U.S. Government Printing Office, 1976, pp. 139–145.

academy but corresponds to changes in the composition of the labor force. The telling fact is that faculty under 35 are no more likely to have fathers in semi- or unskilled trades, or in white-collar jobs, than are their older colleagues.

What also emerges from these studies is that academics are the offspring of a disproportionately well-educated group of parents, at least on the paternal side. This becomes clear if we compare data from both studies with the census report for all males in 1950. In that year only 12 percent of American adult men were college graduates, but the figures for fathers of college faculty taken in 1969 and 1975 were 22 percent and 23 percent. On the graduate level the divergence was even more striking. Only 2 percent of the general male population did graduate work in 1950 compared with 17–18 percent for the faculty fathers in 1969 and 1975.

Respondents to our 1975 sample were also asked to describe their family status while they were in high school, as "wealthy," "above average," "average," "somewhat below average," or as "poor." The largest segment (42 percent) reported "average," possibly a synonym for middle class. More faculty said that they were below average (36 percent) than above (23 percent). The 10 percent of self-reported "poor" origins far outnumbered the 2 percent "wealthy."

Breaking these figures down by age, though, reveals that changes have occurred, but not in the direction one would expect. The proportion of faculty reporting "poor" origins has declined from 14 percent among those aged 50 and older to 6 percent among those under 30 years. Combining "below average" and "poor" yields a shift from 41 percent among older faculty to 23 percent among the young. Conversely, the proportion reporting "wealthy" or "above-average" family economic background is greatest among the more recent recruits to academe (29 percent) and smallest among the oldest cohort (19 percent). Contrary to the assumption that the growth of academe results in a faculty drawn increasingly from less privileged origins, the subjective reports by academics indicate that the expanding profession has been recruiting from more privileged sectors.

These surprising changes in the socioeconomic background of professors may reflect recent changes in the status and political influence of the universities themselves. In two comprehensive surveys of the way in which Americans evaluate the relative prestige of occupations, the National Opinion Research Center in 1947 and 1963 found that "college professor" ranked close to the top among 90 occupations in both years. Only major political jobs (Supreme Court justice, governor, and federal cabinet member), physicians, and some scientists outranked the professor. The job title, "professor," was evaluated in both years more positively than "lawyer," "members of the board of directors of a large corporation," "mayor of a large city," "banker," and "owner of a factory that employs about 100 people." For most occupational rankings little change occurred over the sixteen-year interval. But the evaluation of "college professor" improved slightly. And the categories that moved up most were the scientific occupations closely related to the academy—"scientist, government scientist, chemist, nuclear physicist, psychologist, sociologist, biologist, economist."[6] The increased career attractiveness of the professoriate during the post-World War II period is also reflected in undergraduate career choices at prestigious schools during the 1950s and 1960s. According to one authoritative study of liberal arts colleges, by Donald Akenson and Lawrence Stevens, the proportion of students of high academic attainment from high-status background stating that they planned a scholarly career rose from the freshman to the senior year. Those drawn to business careers increasingly came from the academically least successful half of the graduating seniors.[7]

That academia is drawing increasing proportions of faculty from more privileged backgrounds appears to be an anomaly. A number of national studies of social mobility suggest that opportunities "to enter high-status occupations appear to have improved in successive cohorts of U.S. men for at least the last 40 years." That is, in many professions the more privileged positions are increasingly being filled by men from less well-to-do backgrounds.[8]

According to a *Scientific American* survey of the backgrounds of top executives of the 600 largest U.S. nonfinancial corporations, as of 1964 the business elite had recruited from less privileged elements in a way that had never been true before in American history. As the study notes,[9]

Only 10.5 percent of the current generation of business executives . . . are sons of wealthy families; as recently as 1950 the corresponding figure was

36.1 percent, and at the turn of the century, 45.6 percent. . . . Two-thirds of the 1900 generation had fathers who were heads of the same corporation or who were independent businessmen; less than half of the current generation had fathers so placed in American society. On the other hand, less than 10 percent of the 1900 generation had fathers who were employees; by 1964 this percentage had increased to nearly 30 percent.

Surprisingly, both to scholars in the field and to those radicals convinced that a mature capitalism would become increasingly rigid, a number of underlying structural trends that *were expected to limit mobility* appear, in fact, to be responsible for *its extension*: the replacement of the family-owned enterprise by the public corporation, the bureaucratization of American corporate life, the recruitment of management personnel from the ranks of college graduates, and the awarding of higher posts on the basis of a competitive promotion process similar to that which operates in government bureaucracy. Because of the spread of higher education to the children of the working classes, the ladder of bureaucratic success is increasingly open to those from poorer circumstances. Privileged family and class backgrounds continue to be enormous advantages, but training and talent make up for them in an increasing number of cases.

Thus we have a seemingly contradictory set of findings. On the one hand, the expansion of higher education into wider and less privileged sectors of American life and the growth of occupations and professions requiring higher education have significantly increased the proportions of the disadvantaged in high-status occupations generally and in the summits of big business in particular. On the other, a greatly expanded professoriate is drawing from wealthier, rather than from less privileged, family origins. Only when we recognize the increasing desirability of scholarly work do we begin to understand its attraction for the more privileged, whose backgrounds give them an advantage in the competition for admission to the best graduate departments and ultimately thereby to the professoriate.

Class background bears not only on who becomes a professor, but even more closely on where he or she teaches. Just as students from well-to-do, better educated families are more likely to qualify for selective colleges, secure higher grades, and do graduate work in distinguished institutions, so high family status affects the attainments of faculty. Analyses of both the 1969 and 1975 surveys yield comparable findings. The more prestigious, research-oriented institutions have drawn their professors disproportionately from the higher social strata. Faculty offspring do best of all. They are most likely to be found in the top schools, suggesting that family culture plays a major role in transmitting the ability to do well academically. Trailing them are the children of the middle class, with the progeny of big business and professional families doing better than others. Conversely, academics from working-class and farm backgrounds turn up most heavily in the lower-status colleges (see Table 2).

A similar relationship exists between parental education and academic achievement. The more years of schooling that faculty parents have, the higher

TABLE 2. Academic Position of Faculty by Their Social Backgrounds, 1975 Occupation

	Standing of Faculty Member's School*			
Father's occupation	Tier 1	Tier 2	Tier 3	Tier 4
College university teacher/ administration (n = 176)	39%	31%	22%	8%
Elementary sec. school teacher/administration (n = 106)	26	23	34	16
Other professional (n = 106)	25	23	21	31
Managerial and semi-professional (n = 607)	23	21	25	31
Owner, large business (n = 44)	32	22	17	28
Owner, small business (n = 600)	23	19	25	33
Farm owner/manager (n = 319)	23	23	25	29
Other white collar/ clerical/sales (n = 266)	27	23	23	27
Skilled wage worker (n = 550)	17	15	27	41
Semi-skilled and unskilled laborer (n = 264)	17	16	25	43
Armed Forces (n = 30)	14	22	32	32

*Institutions were ranked on the basis of a three-item index of academic standing, including SAT scores required for admission (selectivity), research expenditures adjusted for the number of students (research), and total institutional expenditures, also adjusted to a per student basis (affluence). All colleges and universities were arrayed on this index, with raw scores ranging from 3 (highest standing) to 27 (lowest). Tier 1 schools are those with index scores of 3 to 9; tier 2, 10 to 15; tier 3, 16 to 21; and tier 4, 22 to 27.

The above distributions are from the 1975 survey, but the much larger 1969 survey yielded essentially the same findings.

the status of the institution where their offspring teach. Nearly two-thirds of those whose mothers did not complete high school were teaching in the least prestigious colleges as compared to one-third of the offspring of mothers with postgraduate education.

Nor do these indicators of family socioeconomic background—father's occupation and education, mother's education and subjective reports on family economic status when in high school—correlate only with the prestige of the university. They also influence publication record, receipt of research support, and teaching load. The higher the family status of the respondents, the lower their teaching load, the more likely they are to have received research grants, and the more they have published. These relationships hold for those at different age levels and in the various disciplines.

In large measure family background also determines faculty's conceptions of their roles. Those from more privileged origins are more likely to prefer research to teaching. Among those of wealthy backgrounds 47 percent favor research, as do a third of those from above-average-income families; this compares to less than a quarter of faculty from average or below-average income homes. And, as Martin Trow and Oliver Fulton have shown, there is a strong relationship between research orientation and actual activity.[10]

Religion and Ethnicity

If the expanded professoriate has not broadened its class origins, it has expanded its religious, ethnic, racial, and sexual base. The faculty is now less decisively white Anglo-Saxon Protestant than before World War II and more female than before the 1960s.

The 1975 survey permits for the first time a detailed portrait of religious and ethnic background. Previously, we had precise information only on the basic religious breakdown—the percentage of Catholics, Protestants, and Jews, and the racial groups. But to place all Protestants in one category is to conceal enormous variations among denominations. The basic data from the two surveys refer to family of origin rather than to the respondent's own religious affiliation (see Table 3).

Our figures show a strikingly large representation (33 percent) of Jews, Calvinists (Presbyterians and Congregationalists), and Episcopalians, compared to their proportion in the public at large (11 percent), but an underrepresenta-

TABLE 3, 1969 and 1975. Distribution of Religious Background of Faculty and of the General Public

Religious Background	All Faculty 1969	1975	General Public	College-Educated Population
Jewish	9%	10%	3%	5%
Catholic	19	18	27	28
Other	4	5	1	1
None	3	5	3	3
Protestant				
Baptist	NA	9	23	17
Methodist	NA	14	14	16
Lutheran	NA	7	8	7
Presb./Cong.	NA	17	6	11
Episcopalian	NA	6	2	4
Mormon	NA	2	(a)	(a)
Quaker Unitarian	NA	1	(a)	(a)
Other	NA	6	10	8

NA – Data not available.
(a) Less than 1 percent.
Source: For general public and college-educated population, National Opinion Research Center Social Surveys, 1972–1976.

tion of Baptists and Catholics. Baptists are clearly the least represented group in academe, constituting a quarter (23 percent) of the public and but 9 percent of professors. Catholics comprise 27 percent of the national population, but only 18 percent of the faculty.

In major research-oriented universities, the variations are even more striking. Jews are 3 percent of the public but 20 percent of all academics in the more prestigious institutions. The 2 percent of the general public who are Episcopalians contribute 9 percent of the high-tier professoriate, whereas the 5 percent who are of Calvinist religious background form almost a fifth of faculty teaching at major universities. Conversely, 23 percent of the population who are Baptists supply but 6 percent of those at leading institutions, whereas the slightly larger Catholic population is represented by 17 percent of the faculty at such schools.

These variations correspond generally to the educational and occupations attainments of the denominations thirty years ago, when most of today's academics were in school or college. In 1945–1946, a detailed study based on 12,000 interviews drawn from Gallup surveys reported that the best educated denominations were the Episcopalians, Congregationalists, and Presbyterians. Over a fifth were college graduates. They also had the highest proportions by far in professional employment (17–20 percent). Jews followed, as the next best educated group (16 percent college trained), with the second highest proportion of professionals (14 percent). Baptists, Catholics, and Lutherans had the lowest proportions of those finishing college (6–8 percent) and a comparably low number of professionals.[11]

Stephen Steinberg's analysis of 1969 data on the religious background of graduate students—those who will provide the next generation of faculty—found similar relationships. Jews were the most overrepresented group among graduate students planning a career in college teaching at 16 percent; 20 percent were Catholics, and 52 percent were Protestant. Over a quarter of the Jewish graduate students (27 percent) were at a top-ranking university as compared with 15 percent of the non-Jews. The Protestant denominations varied among graduate students in much the same way as among faculty. There was a much larger proportion of Presbyterians, Congregationalists, and Episcopalians in the ranking universities than they formed in the public or among graduate students. Baptists, on the other hand, were considerably underrepresented.[12]

From the 1969 Carnegie data, whose massive sample of 60,000 faculty permitted a detailed breakdown of religious representation by age, we can see that the proportion of Jews has increased dramatically over time, while the ratio of Catholics has also gone up significantly. Among those 65 and older in 1969, 4 percent were Jewish and 14 percent Catholic. The corresponding figures for those under 25 were 12 percent Jewish and 21 percent Catholic.[13] As Andrew Greeley points out, the rapid economic and educational progress Catholics have made in the larger community is paralleled by the increasing proportion of younger Catholic faculty in higher education.[14] Catholics, however, still remain underrepresented within the upper echelons of the profession.

A goodly majority of them (56 percent) were found in 1975 in lower-tier institutions. Only the much poorer Baptists had a larger percentage in such schools. The lesser accomplishments of the Catholics appear to reflect the relatively low economic and educational status of the Catholic community three decades ago.

Our 1975 data also suggest some shifts over time among Protestant denominations. Comparing older and younger faculty, one sees a marked decline in proportions of Methodists and Lutherans. The former constituted 19 percent of those 60 and over and 12 percent among the under 30, whereas the latter formed 8 percent of the over-60 group and 4 percent of the under 30 cohort.

Though it is difficult to pinpoint the precise sources of variation among the different denominations, at least two factors stand out—scholarly propensities of different groups related to religious-cultural factors and class background. The first set of variables has been held to explain not only the exceptional record of Jews in academe, but what Thorstein Veblen referred to as their "intellectual preeminence."[15]

There is considerable evidence, from studies of science in the Middle Ages to contemporary analyses of the backgrounds of Nobel Prize winners and of scholars in various countries, including the Soviet Union, attesting to Jewish intellectual achievements. In seeking to explain these findings, we have written elsewhere,[16]

> The greater commitment of Jewish academics to the intellectual role and activities clearly has its roots in Jewish culture. . . . Presumably, the status given to the religious scholar and the activities of the mind remains within secularized Jewish culture, transferred in large part to the intellectual and his work. Some evidence that the intellectual orientation of the current crop of Jewish faculty members is not due to the greater educational and intellectual achievements of their parents may be seen in the fact that they come from less educated families, which were less represented in the teaching professions and in other occupations requiring high levels of education, than the families of the Gentile professors. . . . Thus though the Jewish professors must have absorbed their drive for intellectual accomplishment in their home environment, more of them than of their non-Jewish colleagues were the "first-generation" of their families to attend college.

The 1969 survey confirms that a Jewish background facilitates intellectual achievement. In general, the higher the education faculty parents had, the more likely their offspring were to be located in the research segments of academe. But Jewish professors stood out, even among those with fathers who had attended graduate school. Over half of such Jews (56 percent) indicated a preference for research rather than teaching, in contrast to 31 percent of the Catholics and 30 percent of the Protestants. Only 18 percent of the Jews from such highly educated family backgrounds reported no scholarly publications in the last two years. The comparable figures for Catholics and Protestants were 47 percent and 44 percent, respectively. Fully 50 percent of the Jews were in major research universities, as compared with 16 percent of the Catholics and 25 percent of the Protestants.

Our 1975 survey provides further evidence that Jews continued to form a disproportionately high segment of academe generally and of the better institutions in particular, despite lower socioeconomic origins than their successful Protestant colleagues. The fathers of faculty of Episcopalian, Congregational-Presbyterian, and Quaker or Unitarian background were more likely than those of the Jews to have attended college and/or occupied professional positions.

The 1975 data also point up the relation of ethnic origin to academic attainment. The most significant inequities involve blacks and persons of Latin American origin. Constituting about 11 percent of the general public, blacks remain only 3 percent of the professoriate, with the proportion essentially unchanged over the six-year period. They are no more heavily represented in the young faculty cohorts than in the older, and close to two-thirds are clustered at schools of the lowest range. Hispanics, who comprise 4 percent of the population, are only 1 percent of academe, but they may have increased their representation in the younger faculty ranks. The fact that this category includes not only the more deprived publics of Mexican and Puerto Rican background, but a significant minority of well-educated, middle-class immigrants from Cuba and parts of South America, may explain why one-quarter of Hispanic faculty teach in upper-tier institutions. On the whole, though, blacks and Hispanics are among the most underprivileged and least educated groups in the population; perhaps that is why they have made such little headway in entering faculty ranks during a decade of affirmative action policies. An analysis of U.S. Census data by Richard Freeman also indicates that the ratio of black faculty and administrators to total faculty remained the same for men (.025) and moved up slightly for women (from .045 to .054) between 1960 and 1970. "Relative to their proportion of the population . . . Japanese Americans and [American] Indians made especially large gains."[17]

It should be noted that, although the proportion of black faculty does not appear to have grown, there is clear evidence that the demand has increased. Analyzing the data from the 1969 Carnegie Survey and one conducted in 1973 by the American Council on Education, Freeman finds that "Black faculty received more job offers than whites. . . . Within similar institutions, black male faculty appear to have obtained a 7-8 percent ($1,200) income advantage over whites with what appear to be the same academic skills. A sizeable premium was accorded to black scholars with many publications in 1973 as a result of a substantial increase in the marginal value of an article for black faculty between 1969-73, which suggests that the pressures of that period raised the reward to quality."[18]

At the other end of the achievement spectrum are the faculty of Asian (mainly Chinese and Japanese) descent who formed 1.5 percent of all faculty in 1975, two-and-one-half times their proportion in general population. In both 1969 and 1975, about one-third of all Asian professors taught in major research universities, a larger percentage than any other ethnic or religious group except for the Jews. By contrast, in 1969 only 5 percent of black faculty were at the most prestigious scholarly institutions, a figure which increased to 17 percent in 1975. (These differences in part reflect contrasting family backgrounds. Only one-quarter of the fathers of black faculty attended college, as compared to 50 percent of the fathers of Asians.) The findings from our sample survey conform to the census data. These show[19]

> that some minorities, notably Japanese and Chinese Americans, were well-represented among faculty in both 1960 and 1970, having proportions employed above those of the majority white population. Indeed a remarkable 3.5 percent (male) and 1.6 percent (female) of [all] Chinese Americans were college and university professors or administrators in 1970. American Indians, Filipinos, and persons of Spanish origin, on the other hand, were, like blacks, relatively underrepresented.

From all indications, the proportion of minority faculty is not likely to grow in the near future. Lucy Sells of the American Sociological Association has shown that in 1975–1976 non-Asian minorities secured only 5.3 percent of all doctorates obtained by U.S. citizens. Almost half of these, however, were in the field of Education. Blacks earned slightly less than 3 percent of all Ph.D.s awarded in the social sciences and only 1 percent in the physical sciences. Chicanos and Puerto Ricans secured about 1 percent in both (see Table 4).

Persons tracing their ancestry back to the British Isles and northern Europe still comprise a full three quarters of the professoriate, substantially higher than their 60 percent of the population at large. In fact, however, the English, Scots and Welsh, who are slightly over one-third of the faculty and a fifth of the public, account for all of this margin. Irish, Germans, and Scandinavians are found within academe in about the same proportions as outside. Italians and non-Jewish East Europeans are somewhat underrepresented (see Table 5).

Faculty Women

Women have been in a better position than black, Hispanic, or American Indian minorities to take advantage of the increased commitment to affirmative action policies since, as a group, they do not come from economically or educationally deprived families. A full 61 percent of all black professors reported a "poor" or "below-average" family status when they were in high school, as contrasted to 28 percent of white females. Still, the progress of women in the professoriate appears excruciatingly slow. According to U.S. government statistics, their proportion has crept upward from 19.6 percent in 1963–1964, to 20.6 percent in 1972–1973, and 21.3 percent in 1975–1976. Recent gains have been rather striking within the slim crop of faculty fresh out of graduate school.

TABLE 4. Fields of Doctorates Awarded to U.S. Citizens, by Ethnicity of Recipient, 1975-1976 (a)

Field	All Recipients (n = 26,993)	Black (n = 989)	American Indian (n = 143)	Chicano (n = 240)	Puerto Rican (n = 63)	Asian American (n = 286)	Total Minorities (n = 1,721)
Education	25.0%	61.2%	33.6%	31.2%	27.0%	13.6%	45.6%
Social Sciences	19.9	16.1	16.1	17.5	25.6	12.6	16.0
Arts and Humanities	16.6	8.9	25.2	24.6	7.9	10.5	12.7
Professions	4.3	3.5	1.4	2.5	6.3	5.6	3.7
Life Sciences	14.5	5.6	10.5	12.5	14.3	20.3	9.7
Physical Sciences	13.6	3.6	9.8	7.9	12.7	17.1	7.3
Engineering	6.2	1.1	3.5	3.8	6.3	20.3	5.1
Total	100.1%	100.0%	100.1%	100.0%	99.9%	100.0%	100.1%

Source: Commission on Human Resources, National Research Council, 7-16-76 Printout. Compiled by Lucy W. Sells, Executive Specialist for Minorities and Women. American Sociological Association.
(a) Data may not add to 100 percent due to rounding.

TABLE 5. Ethnic Origins of Faculty and of the General Public, 1975 (column percentages)

	Faculty	General Public (a)
British Protestant	33%	16%
British Catholic	2	1
Irish Protestant	6	7
Irish Catholic	5	4
German/Austrian Protestant	17	14
German/Austrian Catholic	4	4
Scandinavian	5	7
Italian	4	6
East European, non-Jewish	5	5
East European, Jewish	8	2
Other European, non-Jewish	5	3
Other European, Jewish	1	(b)
Hispanic	1	4
Black	3	11
Asians	1.5	(c)

Source: The general public data are from a merged data set including 1972, 1973, 1974, 1975, and 1976 NORC General Social Survey data.
(a) The percentages for the general public do not add to 100; some respondents refused to classify themselves as to ethnic background, whereas others were of sufficiently diverse backgrounds that they cannot be located in the table's fifteen categories.
(b) Less than 1 percent.
(c) No reliable estimate is possible from these data, but the census estimate for Asians is 0.6 percent.

Women in 1975 were over a third of all full-time faculty under age 30, by far their largest share since World War II of this professorial "entering class." A 1976 study by the National Science Foundation of scientists (including social) and engineers employed full-time by universities and colleges indicates that this "was the second consecutive year that their [women's] numbers have increased by 5 percent," whereas for men, the "rate of increase was only 2 percent in each of the last two years."[20] These findings coincide with the results of a detailed statistical study of first-job placements among new holders of Ph.D. degrees that "earlier discrimination in teaching appointments disappeared by 1973."[21] But more curiously, however, the gains in employment do not apply to "senior faculty positions where the percentage of women full professors and associate professors fell between 1974 and 1975 and salary disparities between male and female professors grew."[22]

The recent growth in the proportions of women in academe does not come as the culmination of a pattern of slow steady progress. In fact, the proportion of women in academe was *declining* from the 1930s through to the last decade. U.S. Office of Education data indicate that the high point for women faculty as a percentage of the total was reached in 1930—at *32.5 percent*. By 1960 it had fallen to 19.4 percent. The biggest increase occurred during the suffragette struggle for the vote, when women jumped from 18.9 percent in 1910 to 30.1 percent in 1920.[23] The period from the Great Depression of the 1930s to the early 1960s has been described by Jessie Bernard as "the great withdrawal."

During the 1920s, 15 percent of all Ph.D.s were obtained by women. Their proportion declined to 12 percent during the 1930s and reached a low of 9 percent in the 1940s and 1950s.[24] Bernard pointed out that the drop-off appeared to be "the result of a declining supply of women offering their services" much more than of a "declining demand.... The picture seems to be one not of women seeking positions and being denied but rather one of women finding alternative investments of time and emotion more rewarding...".[25] Some analysts of this phenomenon have related it to a change in values which pressed women in the years following World War II into "a headlong flight into maternity. Whether they wanted babies or not, they felt they should want them."[26]

Women faculty appear to come from somewhat higher social backgrounds than do their male counterparts. For example, just 21 percent of the women in the 1975 sample are the offspring of blue-collar workers as against 27 percent of the men. At the other end of the occupational ladder, a larger proportion of women than of men were the children of owners of large businesses. In that same sample, a significantly higher percentage of male faculty (38 percent) than of women (28 percent) perceived themselves coming from deprived "poor" or "below-average" circumstances at the time they were in high school. Women faculty were also likely to have better educated parents. And the younger women come from the most privileged backgrounds in the whole profession.

These patterns are not new. Earlier studies of students planning to go on to graduate school as well as of graduate students indicate that the class background of the women among them was, "in general, higher than that of men who do as measured by father's education, occupation, or income."[27]

The question inevitably arises, then, even though women started from a higher social position than men, why have they wound up teaching in less prestigious schools? In 1975, women comprised only one-sixth of all academics in the major research universities, but they made up a full third of the faculty in schools of the lowest scholarly standing. Patricia Graham points out "they make up a much smaller percent of the faculties of the most prestigious institutions, particularly in the tenured ranks, where the proportion in arts and science faculties at Harvard is 3%, at Yale 1.6%, at Princeton 1%, at Stanford 5%, at Berkeley 5.6%, at Chicago 5%, and at Columbia 5%."[28] As we have seen, there is a strong correlation between family background and the niche found in the profession for the entire professoriate. But women, presumably through some mix of discrimination and cultural imperatives, go against the grain—starting out from a high socioeconomic position and ending up at institutions oriented to more teaching and less research.

Thus, after close to a decade of considerable ferment surrounding their position in higher education and a sharp increase in their numbers among graduate students and new faculty entrants, women as a group occupy very much the same status within academe as they did in 1969. Thirty-four percent of male faculty in the 1975 study were full professors, but only 18 percent of the women (see Table 6). Nearly half of the men, compared to only a quarter of the

TABLE 6. Professional Status of Men and Women in the Faculty, 1975 (column percentages)

	Men (n = 2861)	Women (n = 644)
Full professors	34%	18%
Teach eleven hours or more per week	45	38
Publications last two years		
None	46	61
Five or more	12	4
Received research grants in last year	46	27
At lower-tier (tiers 3 and 4) colleges and universities	53	64

women, reported receiving some form of research grant in the previous year. As a group, the women teach a lot more and write a lot less. And curiously, as Laura Morlock notes, "these differences between time spent in research and teaching are greater in universities than in two-year or four-year colleges. In other words, *women are most likely to spend less time in research than their male colleagues in precisely those institutions with the best research facilities.*"[29]

Among the young academics the inequities are even more striking. Just 15 percent of these younger men are instructors, the status of 41 percent of the women. Whereas 21 percent of the men had become associate or full professors before age 35, only 8 percent of the women had reached those ranks. Five times as many men reported a high rate (five or more works in the past two years) of publication.

The 1975 survey continued to reveal a pattern of "segregation" by discipline also. Women are still only 5 percent of all natural science faculty at major research universities. However, they comprise a full half of all academics teaching at lower-tier schools in a cluster of applied disciplines which historically have been "women's fields"—education, library science, nursing, child development, and home economics. Again, our data suggest that changes in the distribution of academic women, by field and type of school, are occurring very slowly (see Table 7).

The sex distribution of graduate school degrees, enrollment, and applications imply that this pattern of sex segregation by discipline and by concentrations within the disciplines is bound to continue. In 1974, though women secured 19 percent of all doctorates, they received less than 10 percent of those in agriculture, business and management, computer and information sciences, economics, engineering, mathematics, chemistry, physics, and geology. Women's strongest fields were nursing (100 percent), home economics (64 percent), foreign languages (44 percent), library science (40 percent), letters and English (32 percent).[30]

TABLE 7. Location of Women Faculty, by Discipline Group and Type of School (row percentages)

	1969	1975
Natural Sciences		
Major universities	5%	5%
Middle tier	7	11
Lower tier	13	10
Social Sciences		
Major universities	13	18
Middle tier	20	19
Lower tier	26	28
Applied "women's fields"		
Major universities	37	43
Middle tier	44	39
Lower tier	51	50

The proportion of females enrolled in graduate school has steadily increased during the 1970s, but, as of the academic year 1974–1975, relatively few were studying for advanced degrees in the more quantitative fields. Thus women constituted a majority of the graduate students in education, the health professions, English, foreign languages, home economics, and library science. Slightly over a quarter of those in the biological and social sciences were female. They were, however, a seventh or less of those enrolled in business, engineering, economics, computer sciences, and the physical sciences.[31]

These continued sex-related variations do not appear to result from admissions barriers. A study of graduate school admissions at the University of California at Berkeley revealed that women tended to apply to departments with a high ratio of applicants to places, largely those that did not require mathematical preparation. As the authors of the study pointed out, "Women are shunted by their socialization and education towards fields of graduate study that are generally more crowded, less productive of completed degrees, and less well funded, and that frequently offer poorer professional employment prospects."[32]

Alan Bayer and Helen Astin and Michael Faia have reported that the average salary of academic women in the early 1970s was $3,500 less than that of men and that much of this gap resulted from differences in rank, years of employment, field of specialization, involvement in research, and university setting.[33] It should be noted though that the main precipitants of the sex-related income variations appear to be not explicit discrimination within given institutions and departments, but the location of women disproportionately in lower-paying sectors and disciplines and/or their lesser involvement in activities associated with more rapid promotion and high salaries.

That women do less well subsequently than men is, of course, in part the result of discrimination and societal values and structure, but it may also be a matter of choosing less rewarded roles. Though research is much more heavily rewarded than teaching, leading to job offers from prestigious institutions, early tenure, rapid promotions, higher salaries, and lighter teaching loads, women profess to have *much less interest in research*. In 1975, only 17 percent (contrasted to 28 percent of men) stated that their interests lay primarily in that direction. Among women under 35, preference for research rose to 23 percent, but this was still far below the 38 percent figure for younger males.

The more positive attitude of women toward teaching shows up in responses to a number of other questions. Thus, a much higher proportion "strongly agree" that "teaching effectiveness, not publications, should be the primary criterion for promotion." A third of the male faculty but only a quarter of the females agree: "No one can be a good teacher unless he or she is involved in research." It is clear that these variations in attitudes are linked to actual behavior.

Although various socially imposed constraints—such as family responsibilities—might intrude to prevent women from doing research, they cannot stop women from *wanting* to do research. Part of the reason why academic women get less research support and publish less is because they are less interested in the research enterprise. It is easy to say that the sources of this lower commitment to research are largely "cultural," and almost certainly the observation is true. But recognition of the cultural antecedents is not very helpful to a personnel committee seeking to evaluate the achievements of candidates for positions. The problem posed has been well stated by Helen Astin and Alan Bayer.[34]

Sex discrimination in academe does not begin when a women accepts an appointment at a college or university. Rather it is rooted in the cumulative effects of early childhood socialization for "appropriate" sex role behavior and attitudes, differential treatment and expectations of girls and boys by their parents, teachers, and peers throughout adolescence and early adulthood, and differential opportunities for admission to undergraduate and graduate school. . . . As a result, when women enter teaching careers in colleges and universities they have interests, aspirations, expectations, educational backgrounds, and experiences that differ from those of their male counterparts.

As faculty members, women experience a second barrier to equality with men: the academic reward system is biased toward behaviors and activities exhibited more often by men than women. Indeed, the academic reward system was established by men, so rewards go primarily to those women who accept and exhibit men's criteria for academic rewards.

Some of the trends discussed here may be altered as academe enters a period of economic austerity, declining student-age cohorts, and minimal expansion of the number of faculty positions. The opportunities for those groups seeking to enlarge their involvement in the universities, particularly women and racial minorities, will be more and more limited in an increasingly competitive labor market. Allan Cartter reported in 1972 that "current trends imply the virtual disappearance of the under 35 age group from the teaching ranks."[35]

These changes in the economic situation within academe are producing increased resistance on the part of white males to affirmative action programs which give special preference or quotas to women and minorities. And, as Alice Rossi, perhaps the most prominent feminist leader in academe, has noted, such "responses will not necessarily be instances of sexism, but simply responses to pressure on academe to begin some rational contraction . . . alarms sounded against a tightening market for sons and male students."[36] In a much more competitive buyer's market, traits associated with success in academe—class and educational background, for example—will possibly count for even more in the future. The outsiders who come knocking on the door of the Faculty Club in the early 1980s may find it even more difficult to gain entrance than in past decades.

Notes

1. See, for example, Daniel Yankelovich, *The New Morality* (New York: McGraw-Hill, 1974). See, also, by S. M. Lipset, *Rebellion in the University* (Chicago: University of Chicago Press, 1976), esp. pp. xxviii–1.

2. These data are from *Historical Statistics of the United States, Colonial Times to 1970* (Washington, D.C.: U.S. Government Printing Office, 1975), pp. 382–383; *Statistical Abstract of the United States, 1976* (Washington, D.C.: U.S. Government Printing Office, 1976), p. 141; and U.S. National Center for Education Statistics, *Projections of Education Statistics to 1985-86*, U.S. National Center for Education Statistics, H.E.W., Education Division (Washington, D.C.: U.S. Government Printing Office, 1977).

3. Peter M. Blau and O. Dudley Duncan, *The American Occupational Structure* (New York: Wiley, 1967), pp. 434–435.

4. David Riesman, "Educational Reform at Harvard College: Meritocracy and its Adversaries," in S. M. Lipset and D. Riesman, *Education and Politics at Harvard* (New York: McGraw-Hill, 1975).

5. For information on these two survey investigations, see "Technical Report: Carnegie Commission National Surveys of Higher Education," Survey Research Center, (Berkeley: University of California, April 1971), mimeographed; and "Technical Report: 1975 Ladd-Lipset Faculty Study," Social Science Data Center (Storrs: University of Connecticut), mimeographed.

6. Robert W. Hodge, Paul M. Siegel, and Peter H. Rossi, "Occupational Prestige in the United States: 1925-1963," in R. Bendix and S. M. Lipset, eds., *Class, Status and Power* (New York: Free Press, 1966), pp. 322–334.

7. Donald H. Akenson and Lawrence F. Stevens, *The Changing Uses of the Liberal Arts College* (New York: Pageant Press, 1969), pp. 14–27, 86–110.

8. See Robert M. Hauser et al., "Temporal Change in Occupational Mobility: Evidence for Men in the United States," *American Sociological Review*, 40 (June 1975), 280. The authors cite a number of studies to this effect.

9. See *The Big Business Executive 1964: A Study of His Social Educational Background*, a study sponsored by *Scientific American*, conducted by Market

Studies, Inc. of New York City, in collaboration with Dr. Mabel Newcomer. The study as designed to update Mabel Newcomer, *The Big Business Executive— The Factors that Made Him: 1900-1950* (New York: Columbia University Press, 1950). All comparisons in it are with materials in Dr. Newcomer's published work. It should be noted that *employee* in the *Scientific American* study includes only clerical and sales and manual wage worker occupations.

10. Martin Trow and Oliver Fulton, "Research Activity in American Higher Education," in Martin Trow, ed., *Teachers and Students* (New York: McGraw-Hill, 1975), pp. 50-51.

11. Liston Pope, "Religion and the Class Structure," in R. Bendix and S. M. Lipset, eds., *Class, Status and Power* (Glencoe, Ill.: The Free Press, 1953), p. 320.

12. Stephen Steinberg, *The Academic Melting Pot* (New York: McGraw-Hill, 1974), pp. 107-115.

13. S. M. Lipset and Everett Ladd, "Jewish Academics in the United States," *American Jewish Yearbook, 1971*, Vol. 72 (New York: The American Jewish Committee, 1971), p. 92.

14. See Andrew Greeley, *The American Catholic: A Social Portrait* (New York: Basic Books, 1977), pp. 69-89, for a comprehensive analysis of the changed status of Catholics.

15. Thorstein Veblen, "The Intellectual Pre-Eminence of Jews in Modern Europe," in his *Essays in Our Changing Order* (New York: Viking, 1934), pp. 221, 223-224. The essay was first published in 1919.

16. Lipset and Ladd, *op. cit.*, pp. 106-108; see also Harriet Zuckerman, *Scientific Elite: Nobel Laureates in the United States* (New York: Collier Macmillan, 1977), p. 71.

17. Richard B. Freeman, "Discrimination in the Academic Marketplace," in Thomas Sowell, ed., *American Ethnic Groups* (Washington, D.C.: The Urban Institute, 1977) pp. 170, 172.

18. *Ibid.*, pp. 199-200.

19. *Ibid.*, pp. 170.

20. "Women Academic Scientists and Engineers Increase in 1976," *National Science Foundation News*, 1-443, December 20, 1976.

21. Allan M. Cartter and Wayne E. Ruhter, *The Disappearance of Sex Discrimination in First Job Placements of New Ph.D.s* (Los Angeles: Higher Education Research Institute, 1975), p. 25.

22. Patricia Alberg Graham, "Women in Higher Education: An Historical Perspective," *Signs* (Spring 1978).

23. Jessie Bernard, *Academic Women* (University Park, Penn.: The Pennsylvania State University Press, 1964), p. 67.

24. *Ibid*, p. 70.

25. *Ibid.*, p. 67.

26. *Ibid.*, p. 62; see also Mabel Newcomer, *A Century of Higher Education for American Women* (New York: Harper, 1959), p. 204.

27. Bernard, *op. cit.*, pp. 77–78. See also Helen S. Astin, *The Woman Doctorate in America* (New York: Russell Sage Foundation, 1969), pp. 23–25.

28. *Graham,* op cit.

29. Laura Morlock, "Discipline Variations in the Status of Academic Women," in Alice S. Rossi and Ann Calderwood, eds., *Academic Women on the Move* (New York: Russell Sage Foundation, 1973), p. 283 (emphasis by Morlock). For a comprehensive report on earlier studies, see Bernard, *op. cit.*, "Scholars and Scientists: Productivity," Chap. 10, pp. 146–163.

30. *Statistical Abstract of the United States: 1976* (Washington, D.C.: U.S. Bureau of the Census, 1976), p. 147.

31. *Students Enrolled for Advanced Degrees, Fall 1974. Summary Data* (Washington, D.C.: National Center for Education Statistics, U.S. Government Printing Office, 1976), pp. 16–21.

32. P. J. Bickel, E. A. Hammel, J. W. O'Connell, "Sex Bias in Graduate Admissions: Data from Berkeley," *Science*, 187 (February 7, 1975), 403.

33. Alan E. Bayer and Helen S. Astin, "Sex Differentials in the Academic Reward System," *Science*, 187 (May 23, 1975), 796–802; and Michael A. Faia, "Discrimination and Exchange: The Double Burden of the Female Academic," *Pacific Sociological Review*, 20 (January 1977), 3–8.

34. Helen S. Astin and Alan E. Bayer, "Sex Discrimination in Academe," in Rossi and Calderwood, eds., *op. cit.*, p. 333.

35. Allan Cartter, "Faculty Needs and Resources in American Higher Education, *Annals of the American Academy of Political and Social Science*, 404 (November 1972), 85.

36. See Alice S. Rossi, "Summary and Prospects," in Rossi and Calderwood, eds., *op. cit.*, p. 527. A recent study of the position of women on the faculty of medical schools reports interesting results. Women were represented in larger proportions in medical academia in the past than now, since "large numbers of outstanding women were swept into medicine by the tide of the first feminist movement." As of 1975–1976, women comprised 3.5 percent of full professors, 5.2 percent of associate professors and 7.8 percent of assistant professors. Although there has been a sizable increase in the proportion of women graduating from medical school, there "has been no appreciable upward trend" in the proportion on the faculty. "They are clustered in low, characteristically untenured faculty positions, largely in the traditional nurturant specialties [e.g. pediatrics] and primarily in administrative posts that deal exclusively with student and minority affairs." Kathleen Farrell, Marlys Hearst Witte, Miguel Holguin, and Sue Lopez, "Women Physicians in Medical Academia: A National Statistical Survey," *Journal of the American Medical Association*, 21 (June 29, 1979), pp. 2808–2812.

23. THE PROFESSIONAL AND ACADEMIC CONTEXT OF PROFESSIONAL SCHOOLS

*Peter M. Blau, Rebecca Z. Margulies,
and John B. Cullen*

Professional schools exist at the intersection of two institutions, the profession for which they supply training and the university of which they are part. Conditions in a professional school are affected by the nature of the occupation it serves and the character of the university to which it belongs. Schools of engineering differ from medical schools, and Harvard's business school differs from Northwestern's. Although such comparisons of particular types or cases might be of interest, they do not permit one to infer which specific attributes of professions and of universities influence various conditions in professional schools. For this purpose it is necessary to classify both professions and universities by their generic attributes in order to ascertain how these attributes are related to characteristics of professional schools. This paper presents such an analysis of the influences exerted on American professional schools by their professional and academic context.

Generic Attributes

Contextual analysis is an important methodological contribution of Lazarsfeld's. After all, the basic objectives of sociology are to explain social structures and how the external constraints of the structural context affect the conduct of individuals, as Durkheim (1938) emphasized, not how the individuals' own characteristics affect their conduct. But, as sociology developed from a philo-

The authors of this essay are grateful to the National Science Foundation for grant SOC71-03617 which supported the research; to the Russell Sage Foundation for a supplementary grant for the reputation survey; and to Hilary Silver for research assistance.

sophical into an empirical discipline, this dictum of Durkheim's has often been lost sight of, especially in survey research, which has tended to focus on the way individuals are affected by their own background and attitudes, for example, their socioeconomic status or political preferences. Whereas these are socially acquired attributes of individuals, once acquired, their influences on conduct do not represent the external constraints of social conditions. Lazarsfeld pointed out that external social constraints can be analyzed in survey research, by classifying individuals not only by their own characteristics but also by aggregate characteristics of others in their social environment or by global characteristics of that environment (Kendall and Lazarsfeld, 1950: 187–192). This allows one to ascertain how such contextual properties, alone or in combination with individual properties, affect attitudes and conduct (Lazarsfeld, 1959:69–73).

Groups, organizations, and communities constitute the social context of individuals, but these collectivities, too, are embedded in a broader institutional context that influences them. The principles of contextual analysis, originally developed to study influences of the social environment on individuals, can be applied on a higher level to study influences of the institutional context on organizations. Professional schools furnish a particularly interesting case for this, because they are rooted in two distinct social contexts, a profession and a university. The empirical investigation of such contextual influences on professional schools here is based on data about 948 schools in 18 different professions located in 309 academic institutions.

Collectivities have some attributes that characterize only certain types and not others. Factories can be classified by degree of mechanization, but religious congregations cannot. Professions can be characterized by whether their responsibilities involve primarily work with people or with nonhuman objects, but families cannot be. However, there are other generic attributes that apply to all collectivities, whatever their nature, and these are of major theoretical interest. Size is a good illustration. Any collectivity—whether a nuclear family or a nation, a union or a city—can be classified by the number of its members to analyze general implications of variations in size for social life (see Simmel, 1950). Most aggregate properties of collectivities, which are derived from the distributions of individual properties in them, are generic attributes applicable to collectivities of nearly every type, as exemplified by median education, income inequality, or proportion deviants. Formally established and organized collectivities have still other generic attributes, and two of these are singled out for special attention: age and social standing.

A basic ascribed attribute of an organized collectivity is its age, which indicates the length of time during which a distinctive tradition has become institutionalized. A basic achieved attribute of an organized collectivity is its reputation, which indicates its socially acknowledged status in the society generally and among those qualified to judge it specifically. The professions include some that are old and well-established, such as the ministry, medicine, and law, and others that have recently developed, such as public health and library science. Universities similarly vary in the time that has elapsed since they were founded, and so do professional schools. Professions also differ in prestige; physicians and dentists command higher prestige than social workers and musicians. Correspondingly, universities differ in their reputations as academic institutions, and the same is the case for the various schools in a given profession. Hence, both the professional and the academic context of professional schools as well as the schools themselves can be characterized by age, and all three can be characterized by social standing.

Of central concern in the analysis here presented are the implications for conditions in professional schools of these two generic attributes of the three relevant institutions—the age and reputation of the school's profession, of the school's university, and the school itself. The significance of these six factors for financial conditions in professional schools, extent of graduate training, and academic practices are examined. Other contextual influences are also explored, and other relevant attributes of the schools themselves are controlled. But, whereas the six factors of primary concern are included in the analysis of every dependent variable, other independent variables are included only if they exhibit an appreciable direct relationship with a given dependent variable. Aside from the intrinsic interest of other influences, controlling correlated independent variables in the analysis of a dependent variable makes it possible to apply Lazarsfeld's "scheme of elaboration" (Kendall and Lazarsfeld, 1950:147–67) in order to infer which relationships are spurious, which ones reflect an indirect effect mediated by specific intervening variables, and which ones imply a direct effect.

Let us first briefly examine how a professional school's age and reputation are affected by the ages and reputations of its profession and its university. A school's age is substantially correlated with the age of its profession (r = .46) and the age of its university (r = .39), and it is also positively related to the profession's prestige, though not, if these three other factors are controlled, to the university's prestige.[1] In short, old high-status professions have established numerous schools a long time ago. The relative standing of a school among those in its profession is affected by both the university's age (r = .30) and reputation (r = .28), but only a little by its own age (r = .12). There is no reason for the status of a school within a profession to be related to the status of that profession in society, and indeed it is not.[2] Thus, professional schools with high reputations tend to be found in old universities with high reputations.

Research Procedures

The accredited and university-affiliated American professional schools in 18 fields are included in this study: architecture, business, dentistry, education, engineering, forestry, journalism, law, library science, medicine, music, nursing, optometry, pharmacy, public health, social work, theology, and veterinary medicine. Lists of accredited institutions were obtained from the accrediting associations of the various types of professional schools, and institutions that are not university-affiliated or are departments rather than schools were eliminated. The data were collected in 1972 and 1973 through questionnaires mailed to the deans of the 1,250 remaining schools meeting the criteria. When returns from 53 percent of the deans had been received, a shorter questionnaire was sent to a random sample of the nonrespondents to check on response bias, as well as to the other nonrespondents to increase the response rate. Special efforts, including ultimately telephone interviews, succeeded in obtaining information from most deans (106 of 114) in the random sample. Comparison of these answers with those of the original respondents revealed significant differences on few items, largely attributable to slightly altered wording, and none of these items are used in the analysis. Inasmuch as the earlier responses differ little from the later ones, the data from all respondents were combined.

Information is available on 948 professional schools, which represent 76 percent of all American accredited, university-affiliated professional schools in 18 fields. But many variables have some missing data, because the shorter schedule did not include all questions and because deans did not answer every question on their schedule. The data collected in the survey of deans were supplemented in several ways. Information on the professions represented by the schools were obtained from various published sources, as specified in the following paragraphs. The data on universities (with one exception) were coded from the eleventh edition of *American Universities and Colleges* (Furniss, 1973), as was the information on faculty degrees and proportion of graduate students in schools. Finally, the three indicators of social standing—of the profession, of the university, and of the school—are based on three different studies.

The measure of a profession's prestige was taken from the prestige ratings of all detailed occupations (Siegel, 1971) derived in research by Hodge, Siegel, and Rossi, who asked a national sample of the American population (actually, three samples) to judge the "social standing" of occupations on a nine-point scale.[3] The prestige scores of the 18 professions under consideration are shown in Table 1. A profession's prestige is, of course, strongly correlated with the median education (.68) and income (.76) of its practitioners. The measure of university reputation is a dummy variable indicating that at least one of its departments was rated as outstanding in the survey of graduate education by the American Council of Education (Roose and Andersen, 1970; coded from Petrowski et al., 1973).[4]

To obtain a measure of the reputation of professional schools, we conducted a separate survey. In the original questionnaire, deans were asked to name the five best schools in their profession. However, this question was not included in the shorter followup questionnaire, and it was not answered by many of the original respondents. As a result, the response rate was only 36 percent, which undermined our confidence in the scores. Hence, another survey of the 1,250

TABLE 1. Attributes of Professions

	Prestige	Health	Complexity of Work with People
Architecture	70.5	0	0.0
Business	50.6(a)	0	3.0
Dentistry	73.6	1	8.0
Education	61.2(a)	0	6.5
Engineering	64.2(a)	0	3.0
Forestry	53.9	0	0.0
Journalism	52.8(a)	0	2.6
Law	75.7	0	6.9
Library Science	54.6	0	0.1
Medicine	81.5	1	8.0
Music	46.0	0	5.0
Nursing	61.5	1	3.0
Optometry	62.0	1	8.0
Pharmacy	60.7	1	0.0
Public Health	65.8(a)	1	6.1
Social Work	52.4	0	8.0
Theology	69.0	0	8.0
Veterinary Medicine	59.7	1	0.0

(a) Based on weighted average of two or more occupations.

deans was carried out asking them only a single question: Which are the five top schools in your profession? Repeated followups by mail and telephone yielded a response rate of 79 percent, with the schools of all but one profession (public health) being rated by more than half of the deans in the field. The measure of a school's reputation is the proportion of the responding deans of other schools in the same profession who rated it as one of the top five. This measure is highly correlated (.94) with the corresponding measure from the original study, despite the low response rate, which suggests that there is much consensus on the standing of professional schools among deans. In three fields (engineering, medicine, and library science), we have compared our ratings by deans with published ratings of schools by faculty members (Blau and Margulies, 1974-1975), and results are largely parallel.[5] Since the chances of being considered one of the top five schools are naturally much greater in a profession with few than in one with many schools, the number of schools in the various professions is controlled throughout in the analysis.[6]

Most other variables are simple enough to be described when they are first introduced, but a few require brief explication. Health professions have been distinguished from others by a dummy variable, as indicated in Table 1. The extent to which a profession's responsibilities entail complex work with people is based on a score developed by experts in the U.S. Department of Labor (1965:649-655), except that complex work with animals, which that score includes, is here excluded (Table 1). A profession's age in this country is indicated by the number of years since its first American school of higher education was founded. The number of volumes in a university's library divided by its number of students is considered to be an indication of the university's academic investments relative to the scope of its activities.[7] The measure of faculty size must take into account part-time faculty in a study of professional schools, where many faculty members are part-time. Hence, both the university's and the professional school's faculty size are computed by summing the number of full-time and one half the number of part-time faculty members (used in logarithmic transformation).

Regression analysis is used, which makes it possible to examine simultaneously the relationships of a considerable number of independent variables to a dependent variable. The unit of analysis is the professional school, and the five dependent variables studied are attributes of professional schools. The independent variables are attributes of the professional context of schools (which can take 18 values), attributes of their university context (which can take 309 values), and attributes of the schools themselves.[8] The standardized regression coefficient (beta weight) of an independent variable indicates its direct relationship to the dependent variable when the other independent variables are controlled. The difference between the correlation and the beta weight of any two variables can be decomposed to ascertain how much of it is accounted for by each of the other variables controlled in the analysis, indicated by a decomposition coefficient for each of the other variables (for which the symbol d is used).[9] The decomposition coefficients supply clues for explaining the original correlation. But interpreting the clues—as revealing a spurious correlation or indirect effects, for example—depends on assumptions about the causal sequence among variables. This creates problems because many conditions in academic institutions exert mutual influences on each other. Path analysis, which requires strong assumptions about the causal ordering of nearly all variables, is therefore not used.

However, some causal assumptions are implicit in the decision to perform a regression analysis of a dependent variable on certain independent variables, and additional causal assumptions are introduced in interpreting the results. At least weak assumptions about causal sequence are necessary. Attributes of the professional and the academic context of schools are assumed to be antecedent to attributes of the schools themselves. For professions, the two variables characterizing the nature of their responsibilities (health and work with people) and their age are considered to be antecedents of their other characteristics. For universities and for schools, their age is considered to be an antecedent of their other attributes. These inferences are highly plausible. It is more likely that a school is influenced by its social contexts than that it influences them (but there are feedback effects, as we shall see), and the year of founding of an institution cannot be affected by the characteristics it develops, except that the year that an occupation has become institutionalized as a profession can be affected by its nature.

Not all causal assumptions implicit in the research design are unequivocal. To compare the significance of the profession's, the university's, and the school's own standing for conditions and practices in the school, it is necessary to treat the school's reputation as an independent variable. But some of the dependent variables, such as a school's finances and research, contribute to its reputation, though they are probably also affected by it. The proportion of a school's faculty with advanced degrees may also be influenced by some of the dependent variables. The conservative procedure in contextual analysis is to use more rather than fewer controls, which is the procedure adopted in cases of doubt about causal ordering. Of course, the interpretation of results has to take account of such equivocal and reciprocal influences.

A matrix of correlations of all independent variables is presented in the Appendix.[10]

Financial Conditions

Nearly three-quarters of the average professional school's budget came from university funds in the year preceding the survey, but there were great variations among types of schools. Schools of journalism and music depended on university funds for more than nine-tenths of their budget, on the average, schools of medicine and optometry for less than three-tenths. Most of the budget of professional schools from other sources—17 percent of the total on the average—derives from government funds, and a good part of this is undoubtedly in support of research. What conditions enable a professional school to mobilize much outside support for training and research and thereby reduce its financial dependence on the university?

Schools in the health professions are substantially less dependent for economic support on their universities than schools in other professions, as Table 2 (row 2) shows. In terms of the exchange theory of professionalism, the great educational investments needed to acquire professional knowledge and the highly valued contributions of a profession are rewarded by benefits to the profession and its practitioners (Goode, 1969). Contributions to the population's health are highly valued, and society reciprocates by supplying generous support for training and research in the health professions. The readiness of Congress to appropriate funds for cancer research is a dramatic case in point. Much outside support enriches the schools in the health professions (as we shall see) and simultaneously diminishes their dependence on their universities, which illustrates that initial benefits owing to valued contributions often beget further benefits (Merton, 1968).

A profession's age slightly reduces the financial dependence of its schools, and so does a profession's prestige, because both old and high-prestige professions have schools with more faculty members with advanced degrees, and

TABLE 2. Regression Analysis of Financial Dependence

Independent Variable	Beta Weight	Zero-Order Correlation
Profession		
1. Age	−.02(a)	−.10
2. Health	−.28	−.31
3. Number of schools	.02(a)	.19
4. Prestige	−.03(a)	−.18
University		
5. Age	.03(a)	−.24
6. Books/students	−.30	−.38
7. Reputation	−.14	−.25
School		
8. Age	.05(a)	−.15
9. Faculty degrees	−.19	−.24
10. Reputation	−.11	−.32

$R^2 = .31$
$N = 594$
(a) Less than two standard errors.

better qualified faculties apparently help a school mobilize outside resources that make it less dependent on university funds. This conclusion is arrived at by decomposition of the zero-order correlations. Both a profession's age and its prestige have small negative correlations with financial dependence, but the beta weights indicating direct effects are virtually nil in both cases (rows 1 and 4). The correlation of profession's age is largely accounted for by school faculty's degrees ($d = -.07$). The correlation of profession's prestige is partly spurious, owing to the older and less dependent health professions ($d = -.08$), and partly mediated by faculty degrees ($d = -.06$).[11]

The size of a university's library is known to be strongly related to its academic quality (Lazarsfeld and Thielens, 1958:411; Cartter, 1966:114–115; Gross and Grambsch, 1968:56–57). A university's large library relative to its size reflects superior academic investments, which probably further research endeavors directly by furnishing scholarly resources and indirectly by attracting scholarly faculty and students and creating an academic climate conducive to research. This may be the reason for the substantial negative influence of a university's ample library on the financial dependence of its professional schools (row 6): the superior academic conditions in a university improve the likelihood that its schools can mobilize outside funds. A possible alternative reason for this negative relationship is that universities with strong academic commitments reserve more of their funds for the arts and sciences and reduce their contributions to the budgets of professional schools. Which one of these two interpretations is probably valid can be tested, because the former implies that universities with superior libraries have more affluent schools, whereas the latter implies that these universities have less affluent schools. The data show that

TABLE 3. Regression Analysis of Affluence (Budget/Student)

Independent Variable	Beta Weight	Zero-Order Correlation
Profession		
1. Age	−.09	.21
2. Health	.14	.36
3. Number of schools	−.06(a)	−.19
4. Median income	.52	.56
University		
5. Age	−.09	.12
6. Books/student	.18	.24
7. Reputation	.01(a)	.14
School		
8. Age	.04(a)	.23
9. Financial dependence	−.18	−.40
10. Reputation	.04(a)	.19

$R^2 = .45$
$N = 809$
(a) Less than two standard errors.

universities with better libraries have more affluent professional schools (Table 3, row 6), which negates the second interpretation and lends support to the first, that superior academic conditions in a university enhance the abilities of their schools to obtain outside funds.

A long academic tradition of a university diminishes its school's financial dependence because older universities have greater academic investments than younger ones. The entire negative effect of university age on school's financial dependence is indirect (compare two entries in Table 2, row 5), and university's library accounts for most of it ($d = -.17$). A long tradition enables a university to accumulate a large library over the years, and it probably strengthens academic investments and commitments in other ways. A university's superior reputation exerts an independent effect, further reducing the financial dependence of schools, as the beta weight in row 7 indicates. The university's reputation and its library, as two indications of academic conditions and scholarly pursuits in the university, have parallel reinforcing effects on the chances of various schools to mobilize outside funds.

The proportion of a professional school's faculty with doctorates or equivalent professional degrees is negatively related to financial dependence (row 9), and it mediates several other influences that lessen a school's dependence on the university. A profession's age and its reputation reduce the financial dependence of its schools only because both increase the proportions of the faculties with advanced degrees, as we have seen, and a school's own age lessens its dependence for the same reason. The negative correlation between the age and the financial dependence of schools (row 8) is partly spurious, owing to the effects on both of academic conditions indicated by the university library

($d = -.08$), and it partly reflects an indirect effect of age transmitted by faculty degrees ($d = -.07$). Faculty members with superior formal qualifications seem to be attracted to schools with long traditions,[12] and better academic qualifications enable faculties to obtain more outside funds enlarging the school's budget, undoubtedly often in the form of support for research. Independent of all other conditions, the superior reputation of a professional school increases chances to attract outside funds and decreases dependence on the university for financial support (row 10).

The affluence of a professional school, as indicated by its annual budget per student, is adversely affected by its financial dependence on the university. The regression analysis of affluence in Table 3 reveals this (row 9). If schools that receive a smaller share of their budget from their university are more affluent, it implies that most of the differences in affluence among schools are the results of government and other outside funds that supplement those supplied by the university. It seems that university support of schools does not compensate for differences in externally derived funds, so that schools that cannot attract considerable outside funds tend to be poor.

The prestige of a profession is substantially correlated with the affluence of its schools ($r = .35$), but its economic status—defined by median income— exhibits a far stronger correlation with their affluence ($r = .56$). For this reason, the median income of a profession is substituted for its prestige as the indicator of its status in the regression analysis of affluence (Table 3, row 4).[13] Nearly a third of the entire variation in affluence among 809 professional schools is accounted for by the differences in median income among the 18 professions they serve. Most of the influence of the profession's economic status on the affluence of its schools is direct, as the beta weight shows; that is, it is independent of the other conditions that also affect the affluence of schools. Wealthy professionals and their associations can provide more generous financial support to their schools than poorer ones, but these financial contributions can hardly account for the strong impact of a profession's economic status on the affluence of its schools. Superior economic status commands power and prestige. Wealthy professions tend to be well organized in strong associations, which have the resources and power to influence governments and foundations to furnish economic support to their schools. This collective strength of a wealthy profession is reinforced by the aggregate actions of many of its practitioners, whose superior status often puts them into positions where they can sway policies and administrative decisions in ways that are economically advantageous for their profession and its schools. Affluent professional schools can provide better and more advanced training, improving the market position of their graduates and thereby perpetuating the income differences among professions.

Older professions have more affluent schools, but only because they have higher incomes than newer professions (row 1). In other words, older professions have higher median incomes ($r = .49$), and high-income professions have more affluent schools ($b^* = .52$), which produces an indirect effect of profession's age on school's affluence ($d = .25$). As a matter of fact, the beta weight reveals that a profession's age as such, independent of its income and other conditions, exhibits a small inverse relationship with school's affluence. The schools in the health professions are more affluent than others, partly owing to the generally higher incomes in health professions (d = .14), though partly independent of differences in income and other conditions (beta weight, row 2). Training and research in most health professions is expensive, and the high value that society places on health makes its representatives willing to meet these expenses.

A university's academic investments, as reflected in its plentiful library, increase the affluence of its professional schools (row 6). Books per students in a university are more strongly related to the portion of the budget of schools that does not come from the university than to the affluence of schools (compare rows 6 in Tables 2 and 3), which implies that a university's scholarly conditions affect the affluence of its schools largely by affecting the outside funds they obtain.[14] Professional schools benefit financially from university investments in libraries and other research facilities, which improve their chances of mobilizing outside funds for research and training, since many outside grants depend on available facilities.

The better libraries generally found in older universities, together with the conditions associated with better libraries, account for the somewhat greater affluence of the schools of older universities (d = .10). But, when libraries and other conditions are controlled, university age itself is negatively related to school's affluence (row 5). This influence of university's age corresponds to that of profession's age (row 1). A long tradition tends to enable an institution, whether profession or university, to accumulate resources and investments, which create a favorable context that benefits professional schools. The old age of an institution as such, however, independent of the favorable conditions often though not always associated with it, may well represent the dead hand of tradition that constricts the present and stifles initiative, thus having detrimental effects on success in mobilizing resources in professional schools.

The university's reputation exerts no influence on the affluence of its professional schools (row 7), quite possibly because the university's library is a better indication of its quality than the dummy variable measuring reputation. A school's age and its affluence exhibit a spurious correlation (row 8), which is essentially produced by the effects on both of the profession's income (d = .18). The correlation between the reputation and affluence of a school is partly spurious (row 10), because both are influenced by the characteristics of universities reflected in their libraries (d = .08). But a school's reputation also has a slight indirect effect on its affluence, mediated by low financial dependence (d = .06), since its reputation helps attract outside funds that reduce its financial dependence on the university and simultaneously enhance its affluence.

In sum, much of the variation in affluence among professional schools can be explained in terms of their different professional and university contexts, which affect the affluence of schools by creating favorable conditions for obtaining outside resources to supplement the funds that schools receive from their universities. By far the most important determinant of a school's affluence is the high economic status of the profession its serves. Superior academic conditions in the university also improve a professional school's chances of mobilizing outside financial support and thereby its affluence. Whereas the advantageous conditions that usually distinguish older professions and universities from newer ones increase the affluence of their schools, their age as such, independent of these conditions, decreases it, which suggests that the sheer weight of a long tradition of their institutional contexts saps the vitality professional schools need to attract resources.

Advanced Training

No clear line distinguishes professions from other occupations. But there is wide agreement on some attributes that professions possess to a high degree. The most important of these are a body of abstract knowledge and specialized techniques and the lengthy training necessary to acquire them (Carr-Saunders and Wilson, 1933:284; Goode, 1969:276–277; Moore, 1970:53–54). Accordingly, a degree in higher education has become the badge of professional status, and occupations are socially considered to be professions if universities have curricula and schools for training their practitioners (Merton, 1960).[15] Since university programs are a symbol of professionalism, occupations aspiring to professional status put pressures on universities to institute programs and schools for training in their field. The existence or absence of university-based professional schools in a field reflects only in part the need for complex knowledge and skills and in part the success of the strategies of the organizations of aspiring professions.[16]

Some professions, such as medicine and law, require their practitioners to have doctorates (or advanced professional degrees with another designation), and all their schools concentrate on graduate training. Other professions, such as nursing and pharmacy, have lower educational requirements, and their schools train mostly undergraduates. Within most professions, there are great differences among the schools in the proportion of their students who are graduate students.[17] What conditions are associated with the extent of graduate training?

Professionals who work with people receive more advanced training than those who work with things. Table 4 (row 2) shows that the complexity of a profession's responsibility for people is highly related to the proportion of graduate students in their schools. Indeed, some authors consider work with people as clients the ultimate criterion of professionalism, which distinguishes it from other complex work, such as that in science (Hughes, 1958:139–144). People are more highly valued than material objects or data, even in a materialistic society, and only people have interests that need protection from incompetent or greedy practitioners whose complex important services to them they are not qualified to judge themselves. Lengthy training not only improves the

TABLE 4. Regression Analysis of Percent Graduate Students

Independent Variable	Beta Weight	Zero-Order Correlation
Profession		
1. Age	−.11	.21
2. Work with people	.44	.55
3. Number of schools	−.11	−.23
4. Prestige	.32	.42
University		
5. Age	.01(a)	.21
6. Affluence (revenue/student)	.15	.24
7. Percent graduate students	.24	.41
8. Reputation	−.00(a)	.13
School		
9. Age	−.02(a)	.22
10. Affluence (budget/student)	−.07	.32
11. Number of students (log.)	−.24	−.31
12. Faculty degrees	.24	.35
13. Reputation	.09	.23

$R^2 = .66$
$N = 776$
(a) Less than two standard errors.

likelihood of competence but also provides opportunities for socializing future practitioners in professional standards and emphasizing ethical principles designed to protect clients.[18]

A profession's prestige is also strongly related to the proportion of graduate students in its schools (row 4). Of course, a profession's prestige depends greatly on the education of its practitioners ($r = .68$), and much graduate training in the schools of a profession furnishes the superior education on which high professional prestige depends. Here the independent variable is largely the consequence of the dependent one—graduate training is a major source of professional prestige—though one might also think of the high status of a profession as the antecedent that demands advanced training as a means for individuals to enter the profession and for the profession to sustain its high status. The age of a profession is positively correlated with graduate training in its schools primarily because older professions have superior prestige ($d = .19$) and partly because the faculties of their schools have higher degrees ($d = .09$). A profession's age as such, when other conditions are controlled, reduces the extent of advanced training (row 1). Once again we see that the favorable conditions frequently associated with an institution's long tradition and the deadweight of the tradition itself have opposite implications.

Affluent universities, as indicated by revenues per student, have schools with proportionately more graduate students than poor ones (row 6). Prosperous universities can provide more and better resources for graduate training, such as laboratories and scholarships, which probably encourages establishing professional schools that concentrate on graduate training and expands the graduate training of the schools already established. The larger the proportion of graduate students in a university, the larger is their proportion in its professional schools (row 7). Naturally, the proportion of graduate students in the schools of a university affect the total proportion of them in the university. But many graduate students in a university, and the superior climate and facilities for graduate training their presence implies, probably also help in recruiting students to a school's graduate program. The correlation between a university's age and the proportion of graduate students in its schools (row 5) is mostly accounted for by the proportion of graduate students in the university ($d = .09$), as is the correlation between a university's reputation and the proportion of graduate students in its schools (row 8, $d = .09$). Thus, neither the age nor the reputation of a university has a direct effect on the extent of advanced training in its professional schools.

Superior formal qualifications of a school's faculty are positively related to the proportion of its students who do graduate work (row 12). This is another finding undoubtedly involving mutual influences. Instructing graduate students generally requires faculty members to have completed graduate training themselves, and superior academic qualifications of the faculty attract graduate students. The affluence of a school is positively correlated with its proportion of graduate students, but with other conditions controlled the beta weight reveals a slight negative relationship between the two (row 10).[19] The main factors that account for the difference are the profession's prestige ($d = .11$), complex work with people ($d = .10$), the university's proportion of graduate students ($d = .06$), and the school faculty's advanced degrees ($d = .06$). Graduate training is more expensive than undergraduate education, because it entails better paid faculties and a variety of costly facilities. No data on these facilities are available, and their greater prevalence in graduate training must be inferred. But, aside from the high status of the professions served and of conditions assumed to reflect costly training facilities, professional schools appear to spend slightly less money per graduate than per undergraduate student (see the beta weight in row 10).

Large professional schools have proportionately fewer graduate students than small ones (row 11). Most students are undergraduates, which tends to make schools that concentrate on graduate training relatively small. The number of schools in a profession is also negatively related to the proportion of graduate students (row 3), in part directly (beta weight) but in large part indirectly owing to the school's number of students ($d = -.16$), since this number is positively related to the number of schools in the profession and negatively, as we just saw, to the proportion of graduate students in a school. The strong positive correlation between the number of schools in a profession and the number of students in these schools ($r = .66$), in turn, is a consequence of the size of the profession. The size of a profession (based on occupational census data) is positively correlated with both the number of its schools ($r = .59$) and their size (number of students, $r = .46$). That is, large professions have both more and larger schools than small ones. This can be explained in terms of a theorem derived in previous research on organizations (Blau, 1970), which states that, with increasing size, organizations become internally differentiated into an increasing number of sub-units at a decreasing rate.[20] A strict implication of this theorem is that large organizations have, on the average, both more and larger subunits than small ones. The findings indicate that the theorem applies to professions, though they are not formal organizations. As professions grow in size, training for them becomes differentiated among an increasing number of schools, but the rate of increase in number of schools is generally less than the rate of growth of the profession, so that the average size of schools as well as their number is positively related to the size of the profession.

A professional school's age is correlated with graduate training, without having a direct effect on it (row 9). Their correlation is accounted for partly by the profession's prestige ($d = .12$) and partly by school faculty's superior education ($d = .08$). A school's reputation is positively related to its advanced training, even when numerous other conditions are controlled (row 13). This is hardly surprising inasmuch as advanced work is most likely to gain a professional school a good reputation and such a reputation attracts advanced students.

In short, there are numerous mutual influences between advanced training and associated conditions. However, one attribute of the professional context exerts an unequivocal strong influence on graduate training. Professions that provide complex services to people demand more advanced training than those that work primarily with things.

Academic Practices

Two academic practices in professional schools are examined, one pertaining to research, the other to recruitment. In addition to training future practitioners, professional schools carry out research to advance the knowledge in their fields. Table 5 presents the findings about the emphasis on research, whether basic or applied, in professional schools, as reported by their deans.[21]

The age of a profession indirectly affects the research emphasis in its schools (row 1), because old professions have superior prestige ($d = .07$) and their schools have more faculty members with advanced degrees ($d = .07$). A profession's prestige is directly related to the emphasis on research in its schools (row 3). In the long run, the advancement of knowledge resulting from successful research contributes to the status of a profession, but the short-run direction of influence is probably the reverse; that is, high-status professions, such as medicine, law, and dentistry, place most emphasis on research in their schools and are most likely to help support it.

The university context exerts the strongest influence on research in professional schools. A university's affluence increases the emphasis on research in

TABLE 5. Regression Analysis of Research Emphasis

Independent Variable	Beta Weight	Zero-Order Correlation
Profession		
1. Age	−.03(a)	.11
2. Number of schools	.04(a)	−.02
3. Prestige	.14	.20
University		
4. Age	−.01(a)	.18
5. Affluence (revenue/student)	.24	.29
6. Faculty size (log.)	.15	.29
7. Reputation	.13	.29
School		
8. Age	.02(a)	.19
9. Faculty degrees	.17	.28
10. Reputation	.13	.24

$R^2 = .26$
$N = 869$
(a) Less than two standard errors.

its schools (row 5), as does its large faculty size (row 6). Affluent universities can afford costly research facilities, without which research in their schools suffers. An economy of scale makes the research equipment of large universities superior to that of smaller ones with similar revenues per student. For instance, a university must be large as well as affluent to have a cyclotron or a complex computer installation. Besides, disproportionate numbers of large universities are major universities with high reputation, where promotions depend on research (Blau, 1973:105-117). A university's faculty size (log.) and reputation are strongly correlated ($r = .66$), and the direct effect of its size on research in schools is supplemented by an indirect effect mediated by the superior reputation of large universities ($d = .07$). The pressures to publish and academic climates in universities with superior reputations promote an emphasis on research in their schools (row 7). The indirect effect of the age of a university on research in its professional schools (row 4) results from a combination of conditions in older universities—their larger size, greater affluence, higher reputations, and schools with higher reputations (together, $d = .15$).

Research requires advanced training. The larger the proportion of a professional school's faculty with advanced degrees, the greater the emphasis on research (row 9). The age of a professional school increases the significance of its research (row 8) because older schools have more faculty members with advanced degrees than newer ones ($d = .06$), but most of the correlation between school's age and research is spurious. Finally, the superior reputation of a professional school enhances emphasis on research (row 10). Research contributions undoubtedly further the reputations of professional schools, and schools of great reputation probably seek to maintain it by stressing the importance of research.

The general expectation is that faculty recruitment should be governed by universalistic standards of merit. Ideally, personal preferences should not bias recruitment, nor should intellectual predispositions in favor of a certain professional approach, lest students are confined to a narrow view of professional knowledge and techniques and fail to be exposed to the variety of existing theories and practices. Recruiting faculty from other institutions trained in different academic traditions is an important means for maintaining a diversity of perspectives. Schools and departments often develop a predominant approach to the discipline, and this tendency is reinforced by faculty inbreeding, that is, appointing a school's own graduates to its faculty.

Table 6 shows that the larger the number of schools in a profession, the smaller is the proportion of the average school's faculty members who are its own graduates (row 2). It is, of course, plausible that many institutions in a field that supply candidates for faculty positions increase the chances that outside candidates are appointed to any one school's faculty. Few schools limit outside choices, which makes faculty inbreeding more likely. Ben-David (1960) concludes from his cross-national comparison that the diversity among many independent academic institutions greatly contributes to the advancement of knowledge. One reason for this may be that many independent academic institutions increase cognitive diversity not only among them but also within them, owing to more outside recruitment, and such diversity stimulates academic accomplishments.

A profession's superior prestige promotes faculty inbreeding (row 3). One might at first attribute this to the more advanced training the schools of high-prestige professions provide (Table 4, row 4), which makes their own graduates more suitable for faculty appointments than are the graduates of schools of low-prestige professions, most of whom do not have advanced degrees. But this is not an adequate explanation, for the graduates of other

TABLE 6. Regression Analysis of Faculty Inbreeding

Independent Variable	Beta Weight	Zero-Order Correlation
Profession		
1. Age	−.15	.02
2. Number of schools	−.27	−.31
3. Prestige	.21	.17
University		
4. Age	.02(a)	.18
5. Reputation	−.01(a)	.14
School		
6. Age	.16	.19
7. Reputation	.18	.29

$R^2 = .20$
$N = 576$
(a) Less than two standard errors.

schools of high-prestige professions also tend to have advanced degrees that make them suitable for faculty appointments. Apparently, a profession's high prestige creates a bias in its schools to appoint their own graduates to their faculties. The age of a profession is not correlated with faculty inbreeding, yet decomposition reveals that it exerts two opposite influences on inbreeding that cancel each other (Table 6, row 1). A profession's age indirectly increases faculty inbreeding, as a result of the higher prestige of older professions ($d = .11$), but its direct effect indicated by the beta weight is to decrease faculty inbreeding. This is still another instance of the opposite implications that conditions associated with a long tradition and the tradition itself often have.

The age and the reputation of a university affect faculty inbreeding in its schools only indirectly by influencing the characteristics of these schools (rows 4 and 5). Older universities have schools that are older, that have better reputations, and that are in professions with fewer schools, and so do universities with superior reputations. These three conditions account for the greater likelihood of faculty inbreeding in the schools of older universities (together, $d = .15$) and of universities with superior reputations (together, $d = .12$).

The superior reputation of a professional school increases the proportion of its faculty recruited from its own graduates (row 7). A positive relationship between reputation and faculty inbreeding has also been observed in studies of other academic institutions (Berelson, 1960; Gross, 1970).[22] Faculty recruitment solely on the basis of merit would produce such a relationship, since the objectively best candidates for faculty vacancies are likely to include disproportionate numbers of graduates from the top-ranked institutions. According to merit standards, therefore, the proportion of the faculty with degrees from their own school in highly rated schools is expected to be larger than the corresponding proportion in the rated schools ranked below them. But that proportion is not expected to be larger than the proportions of the same school's faculty with degrees from each of the other highly rated schools in the profession. However, faculty inbreeding is so pronounced (15 percent in the average school and much more in highly rated schools) that it is practically impossible for the proportions of a school's faculty who graduated from other schools of no lesser standing to be as great as the proportion who are its own graduates. The greater prevalence of faculty inbreeding in professional schools with superior reputations, though in part attributable to the undoubtedly superior qualifications of their graduates, may well indicate a stronger ingroup bias of these schools. The long tradition of a professional school undoubtedly creates an ingroup bias in favor of appointing its own graduates to its faculty, as indicated by the finding that a school's age, independent of its reputation and the available candidates from other schools, is positively related to faculty inbreeding (row 6).

There are empirical indications that faculty inbreeding is detrimental to scholarly productivity (Hargens and Farr, 1973). To be sure, some faculty inbreeding may be advantageous, because the loyalty of a school's own graduates enables it to recruit better qualified persons than it otherwise could, and some is inevitable, because there are few other schools supplying candidates in a field or because a school's superior quality makes its own graduates the best qualified candidates. But the influence of a school's age and of its profession's prestige on faculty inbreeding can hardly be attributed to anything other than ingroup bias. It appears that the superior prestige of the profession and the long tradition of the school bestow upon the school and its members a superior and secure social standing that is independent of its reputation and their scholarly accomplishments, thereby relieving pressures to conform with merit standards and subjecting faculty recruitment more to ingroup preferences.

Conclusions

The main theme of this paper has been that the characteristics of organizations depend in part on their social context and that these external influences can be studied by applying Lazarsfeld's contextual analysis to organizations. A secondary theme has been that Lazarsfeld's scheme of elaboration can be used in regression analysis to help explain the empirical relationships. We have focused on the implications for professional schools of the ages and the reputations of three institutions—the schools themselves, their university context, and their professional context. The age of a profession indirectly affects its schools' financial conditions, advanced training, and academic practices, and these effects are mediated primarily by the higher status of older professions and secondarily by the better academic qualifications of the faculties of their schools. The age of a university also has indirect consequences for all the conditions in its schools we have examined, mostly because an older university tends to have accumulated academic investments in a superior library and other scholarly facilities. These university resources contribute to research and advanced training in professional schools and improve their chances of mobilizing outside funds that decrease their dependence on the university and increase their affluence. A professional school's own greater age enables it to attract better qualified faculty members and for this reason to train more advanced students, emphasize research more, and obtain more external funds that reduce its dependence on university funds.

Thus, long traditions of the two institutions—the profession and the university—that constitute the major context of professional schools create conditions that have various beneficial consequences for the schools. However, an old tradition also tends to engender rigid adherence to established ways. The deleterious consequences for professional schools of traditionalism in their institutional context become apparent when the long tradition itself and the advantageous conditions usually associated with it are analytically distinguished. Several of the positive indirect effects of an institution's age on its schools are accompanied by, albeit weaker, negative direct effects. For example, both the age of the profession and the age of the university indirectly increase the affluence of their professional schools, but the direct effect of both is to decrease the affluence of these schools, quite possibly because a traditional institutional context stifles initiative in seeking outside support. The old tradition of a professional school itself restricts outside faculty recruitment, another illustration of the confining impact of traditionalism that inhibits mobilizing outside resources for a school.

The superior status of a profession affects its schools greatly, though it is also affected by the conditions in its schools, notably extent of graduate training and of research. A profession's superior prestige is directly related to its school's affluence, amount of graduate training, emphasis on research, and faculty inbreeding, and it is indirectly related to the financial independence of schools from their universities. The superior reputation of a university increases the research emphasis in its professional schools and the proportion of their budgets from external sources, probably in large part because the pressures to engage in research and the chances to obtain outside support are greatest in universities with high reputations. The superior reputation of a professional school increases the emphasis on research, external financial support, and faculty inbreeding, and it is associated with extensive graduate training.

In sum, the professional and academic context of professional schools exerts much influence on conditions and practices in them. Not only the profession's and the university's age and status but also other attributes of these two contexts affect professional schools substantially—in particular the nature of the profession, whether it serves people and whether it contributes to health, and conditions in universities that reflect their academic investments, facilities, and climate. Ironically, though perhaps inevitably, the very conditions in a university that contribute to the welfare of its professional schools make them, at least financially, more independent of the university.

Appendix
Correlation Matrix of Independent Variables

	Profession						University						School					
	Health	People	Age	Income	Prest.	# Sch.	Age	Affl.	Size	Gr St.	Libry.	Reput.	Age	Reput.	F.Deg.	F.Dep.	Affl.	Enrol.
Profession																		
Health	1.0																	
People	-.04	1.0																
Age	.02	.11	1.0															
Income	.27	.17	.49	1.0														
Prestige	.28	.25	.59	.75	1.0													
# Schools	-.40	.09	.05	-.02	.05	1.0												
University																		
Age	.05	.00	.05	.06	.06	-.16	1.0											
Affluence	.03	.02	.05	.00	-.01	-.08	.14	1.0										
Size (lg)	.12	-.06	-.09	.14	.05	-.14	.27	.01	1.0									
% Grad. St.	-.08	-.12	-.06	-.17	-.12	-.15	-.40	-.11	-.32	1.0								
Library	-.01	.05	.11	.02	.06	-.14	.56	.39	.06	-.45	1.0							
Reputation	.08	-.06	-.08	.06	.02	-.17	.40	.07	.67	-.37	.23	1.0						
School																		
Age	.04	.09	.46	.36	.39	.03	.39	.11	.08	-.21	.27	.14	1.0					
Reputation	.12	.01	-.08	-.00	-.02	-.28	.30	.13	.26	-.25	.44	.28	.12	1.0				
Fac. Degrees	-.02	.19	.38	.47	.31	.18	.07	.12	.09	-.10	.14	.07	.35	.07	1.0			
Fin. Depend.	-.31	-.11	-.10	-.20	-.18	.19	-.24	-.07	-.18	.29	-.38	-.26	-.15	-.32	-.24	1.0		
Affluence	.36	.22	.21	.56	.35	-.19	.12	.13	.16	-.25	.24	.14	.23	.19	.25	-.40	1.0	
Enrol. (lg)	-.29	.02	-.07	-.00	-.01	.66	-.12	-.10	.17	.11	-.22	.02	.05	-.07	.09	.17	-.16	1.0
Mean	.24	3.95	128	11076	61	110	104	4753	2.86	.27	77	.58	53	.06	.56	.73	3740	2.81
St. Dev.	.42	2.99	52	5968	9	54	46	1.406	.33	.14	80	.49	31	.15	.28	.29	8170	.44

Notes

1. In the regression analysis of school's age, the beta weights are profession's age, .35; university's age, .36; profession's prestige, .16 ($r = .38$); university's reputation, .01 ($r = .13$).

2. In the regression analysis of school's reputation, the beta weights are profession's age, $-.12$ ($r = .08$); profession's prestige, .01 ($r = -.02$); university's age, .18; university's reputation, .15; school's age, .09; number of schools in the profession, $-.22$ ($r = -.28$). The reason for controlling number of schools is explained in the text.

3. An alternative considered was to use Duncan's (1961) index of the socioeconomic status of occupations, based on their income and education. But a profession's prestige parallels an academic institution's reputation more closely than does the profession's socioeconomic status.

4. The dummy variable yielded more consistent results than the alternative score ("weighted mean") published by Petrowski et al. (1973), probably because the latter is highly skewed for our 309 universities.

5. To be sure, the ranks of all schools are not identical in ratings by deans and by faculty members. A study commissioned by the senate of the University of California (Anonymous, 1977) as a reaction to our earlier report (Blau and Margulies, 1974–1975) shows that their ratings by faculty members of schools of business, education, and law yield several higher rankings of campuses of the University of California than our ratings by deans. Perhaps the University of California's schools are more popular with faculty members than with deans. Perhaps there is a response bias in favor of a study's sponsor, so that their ratings of the schools of the University of California and our ratings of the schools of Columbia University are ranked too high. In any case, despite the disparities in a few top-ranking schools shown in their publication, it seems to us very likely that their and our ratings of all schools are highly correlated, which is all that matters for the use of such ratings in quantitative analysis, as distinguished from their use to make a few invidious comparisons of particular schools.

6. But this variable is only discussed when it exerts a significant direct effect.

7. Originally, the raw number of volumes in the library was used, but its high correlation with faculty size (.73) fails to distinguish the significance of a good library from that of a large university.

8. Seven independent variables are included in every regression analysis: profession's age, number of school, and prestige; university's age and reputation; school's age and reputation. Other independent variables are included only if their standardized regression coefficient exceeds two standard errors. (Of course, the regression analysis was repeated after variables not meeting the criterion were eliminated.) To minimize problems of multicollinearity, independent variables that are correlated .60 or more are generally not included in the same regression analysis, but two exceptions were made for substantive reasons: number of schools and school's enrollment (log.), though correlated .66, are used in Table 4; university's faculty size (log.) and reputation, though correlated .66, are used in Table 5. (Pairwise deletion of missing data is used.)

9. A decomposition coefficient shows how much the correlation between a given independent (x) and dependent (y) variable is produced by one of the control variables (i). It is the product of the correlation of the independent with the control variable (r_{ix}) and the standardized regression coefficient (beta weight) of the control variable indicating its direct effect (b_{yi}^*). Thus, $d = r_{ix}b_{yi}^*$. The sum of all these indirect connections between x and y and the direct effect of x on y ($\Sigma r_{ix}b_{yi}^*$) equals the zero-order correlation (r_{yx}).

10. The correlations between contextual variables in the matrix are only of technical interest and do not represent accurately the correlations between the characteristics of professions or between those of universities, because they are based on the number of schools, not on the number of professions or the number of universities. Each profession and each university is weighted by its number of schools in these correlations. For example, for the eighteen professions under consideration, the correlation between their age and reputation is .49, but the correlation in the matrix for these two contextual variables is .59, which implies that age and reputation are more closely related in larger professions with many schools than in smaller ones with few schools.

11. The regression analysis of percent of school's faculty with advanced degrees (not shown) indicates that profession's age ($b^* = .23; r = .38$) and its prestige ($b^* = .09; r = .31$) have direct effects on the proportion of the faculty with advanced degrees when seven other variables are controlled.

12. The regression analysis mentioned in the preceding footnote shows that school's age has a direct effect on the proportion of its faculty with advanced degrees ($b^* = .20; r = .35$).

13. The strong correlation between profession's median income and prestige (.76) precludes entering both into the regression analysis of affluence. Affluence is the only dependent variable under investigation that is substantially more correlated with median income than with prestige.

14. The stronger beta weight of health profession with percent of school's budget from outside funds than with school's affluence (compare rows 2 in Tables 2 and 3) has corresponding implications.

15. This is the reason for our defining an American profession's age by the year when its first school in this country was founded.

16. Cullen (1978) found that the education required for a particular occupation—the General Educational Development Score of the U.S. Department of Labor (1965)—is strongly but by no means perfectly correlated with the median education in the occupation (.82). His unit of analysis was the detailed occupation, defined by the U.S. Census, and the case base was 267 nonfarm occupations, including the majority of manual as well as nonmanual occupations.

17. Although some types of professional schools have mostly graduate students and some types have few, the assumption is that the general attributes of professions included in the regression analysis largely account for these differences. There are empirical grounds for this assumption. When 17 of the 18 dummy variables representing the 18 particular professions are substituted for the four variables characterizing professions in Table 4 (rows 1–4), the R^2 is .80; in Table 4, the R^2 is .66; for a regression analysis including only the nine independent variables characterizing universities and schools in Table 4 (rows 5–13), the

R^2 is .39. Thus, the attributes of universities and schools alone account for 39 percent of the variation in proportion graduate students among schools; the maximum increment in that variation accountable for by the 18 types is 41 percent (.80–.39); the increment produced by the four general attributes of professions in Table 4 is 27 percent (.66–.39) or two-thirds (.27/.41) of the possible maximum.

18. A five-point score of the extent to which professional ethics is taught in a school (ranging from not at all to required courses) is positively correlated with percent graduate students (.26)

19. The measures of school's affluence and percent graduate students have the same denominator (number of students), which creates a positive mathematical nexus between the two, making the positive correlation possibly larger and the negative beta weight possibly smaller than they would be without this distorting effect. A similar mathematical nexus may make the negative coefficients in row 11 (number of students) larger than they otherwise would be.

20. The data on professional schools and their departments conform to this theorem, as do data on universities and their various subunits (Blau, 1973: 49–57).

21. The measure of research emphasis is the unweighted sum of the two five-point ratings supplied by the deans in answer to the questions about the importance of basic research and of applied research in the school.

22. However, another study reports a curvilinear relationship, with inbreeding being more pronounced in both the highest and the lowest ranking departments than in those with intermediate prestige (Schichor, 1970).

References

ANONYMOUS. 1977. "The Cartter Report on the Leading Schools of Education, Law, and Business," *Change,* 9(January), 44–48.

BEN-DAVID, JOSEPH. 1960. "Scientific Productivity and Academic Organization in Nineteenth Century Medicine," *American Sociological Review,* 25, 830–840.

BERELSON, BERNARD. 1960. *Graduate Education in the United States.* New York: McGraw-Hill.

BLAU, PETER M. 1970. "A Formal Theory of Differentiation in Organizations," *American Sociological Review,* 35, 201–218.

————. 1973. *The Organization of Academic Work.* New York: Wiley.

————, and REBECCA Z. MARGULIES, 1974–1975. "The Reputations of American Professional Schools," *Change,* 6(October), 42–47.

CARR-SAUNDERS, A. M., and P. A. WILSON. 1933. *The Professions.* Oxford: Oxford University Press.

CARTTER, ALLAN. 1966. *An Assessment of Quality in Graduate Education.* Washington: American Council of Education.

CULLEN, JOHN B. 1978. *The Structure of Professionalism.* New York: Petrocelli Books.

DUNCAN, OTIS D. 1961. "A Socioeconomic Index for All Occupations," in A. J. Reiss et al., eds., *Occupations and Social Status,* New York: Free Press, pp. 109–138.

DURKHEIM, EMILE. 1938. *The Rules of Sociological Method.* Chicago: University of Chicago Press.

FURNISS, W. TODD. 1973. *American Universities and Colleges.* Washington, D.C.: American Council of Education.

GOODE, WILLIAM J. 1969. "The Theoretical Limits of Professionalism," in A. Etzioni, ed., *The Semi Professions and their Organization,* New York: Free Press, pp. 266–313.

GROSS, EDWARD, and PAUL V. GRAMBSCH. 1968. *University Goals and Academic Power.* Washington, D.C.: American Council of Education.

GROSS, GEORGE R. 1970. "The Organization Set," *The American Sociologist,* 5, 25–29.

HARGENS, LOWELL L., and GRANT M. FARR. 1973. "An Examination of Recent Hypotheses About Institutional Inbreeding," *American Journal of Sociology,* 78, 1381–1402.

HUGHES, EVERETT C. 1958. *Men and Their Work.* Glencoe, Ill.: Free Press.

KENDALL, PATRICIA L., and PAUL F. LAZARSFELD. 1950. "Problems of Survey Analysis," in R. K. Merton and P. F. Lazarsfeld, eds., *Continuities in Social Research.* Glencoe, Ill.: Free Press, pp. 133–196.

LAZARSFELD, PAUL F. 1959. "Problems in Methodology," in R. K. Merton et al., eds., *Sociology Today.* New York: Basic Books, pp. 39–78.

_____ , and WAGNER THIELENS. 1958. *The Academic Mind.* Glencoe, Ill.: Free Press.

MERTON, ROBERT K. 1960. "Some Thoughts on the Professions in American Society," *Brown University Papers* 37.

_____ . 1968. "The Matthew Effect in Science," *Science,* 159, 55–63.

MOORE, WILBERT E. 1970. *The Professions.* New York: Russell Sage Foundation.

PETROWSKI, WILLIAM R., EVAN L. BROWN, and JOHN A. DUFFY. 1973. "National Universities and the ACE Ratings," *Journal of Higher Education,* 44, 495–513.

ROOSE, KENNETH D., and CHARLES J. ANDERSEN. *A Rating of Graduate Programs.* Washington, D.C.: American Council of Education.

SCHICHOR, DAVID. 1970. "Prestige of Sociology Departments and the Placing of New Ph.Ds," *American Sociologist,* 5, 157–160.

SIEGEL, PAUL M. 1971. "Prestige in the American Occupational Structure." Unpublished Ph.D. dissertation, University of Chicago.

SIMMEL, GEORG. 1950. *The Sociology of Georg Simmel.* Glencoe, Ill.: Free Press.

U.S. DEPARTMENT OF LABOR. 1965. *Dictionary of Occupational Titles.* Washington, D.C.: U.S. Government Printing Office.

THE WRITINGS OF PAUL F. LAZARSFELD: A TOPICAL BIBLIOGRAPHY

Paul M. Neurath

This bibliography of Paul F. Lazarsfeld is divided into two parts. The first, shorter part provides a chronological list of books as well as edited symposia and anthologies. The second part consists of all his writings grouped in nine topical categories:

1. Unemployment
2. Mass Communication
3. Voting and Political Activities
4. Education and Psychology
5. Social Research: Methods and Procedures
6. Social Research: Perspectives and Reflections
7. Mathematical Sociology
   a. Latent Structure Analysis
   b. The Algebra of Dichotomous Systems
8. Market Research
9. Book Reviews and Miscellaneous Writings

Each topical category includes a list of book titles, the full references appearing in Part I, which are followed by chronologically ordered lists of articles and unpublished materials. A few articles are listed under more than one heading.

Book titles marked with an asterisk (*) are collections of articles edited by Lazarsfeld alone or with others. Articles that were reprinted in *Qualitative Analysis* are designated by *QA*, those reprinted in *The Language of Social Research* by *LSR*, and those in *Continuities in the Language of Social Research* by *CLSR*.

The list of unpublished materials is incomplete. Of about 160 unpublished papers found in Lazarsfeld's personal files and in those of the Bureau of Applied Social Research, I have included only those papers central to the development of his work.

The bibliography is based on two earlier compilations: a comprehensive list up to 1968, prepared for the most part by Louise B. Moses and John Reed, and a supplement for the subsequent period prepared principally by Helen Hudouskova. The "Bibliography of the Bureau of Applied Social Research," compiled by Judith S. Barton, has proved to be very useful.

I wish to thank Patricia L. Kendall and Judith S. Barton for their patient and efficient help in assembling the materials, Robert K. Merton and Thomas F. Gieryn for helpful advice about arranging them for this bibliography, and Mary Wilson Miles for preparing an accurate version of this difficult transcript.

Part One: Books and Symposia

1924 *Gemeinschaftserziehung durch Erziehungsgemeinschaften: Bericht über einen Beitrag der Jugendbewegung zur Sozialpadagogik* (with Ludwig Wagner). Leipzig-Wien: Anzengruber Verlag.

1929 *Statistisches Praktikum fur Psychologen und Lehrer.* Jena: Gustav Fischer.

1931 *Jugend und Beruf: Kritik und Materials* (with Beiträgen von C. Bühler, B. ˙Biegeleisen, H. Hetzer and K. Reininger). Jena: Gustav Fischer.

1933 *Die Arbeitslosen von Marienthal: Ein Soziographischer Versuch uber die Wirkungen langdauernder Arbeitslosigkeit* (with Marie Jahoda and Hans Zeisel). Leipzig: S. Hirzel. 1960 Second edition (with a new preface, pp. xi–xxvii). Allensbach und Bonn: Verlag für Demoskopie. 1971 American edition, *Marienthal: The Sociography of an Unemployed Community* (with a "Foreword—Forty Years Later," pp. vii–xvi). Chicago: Aldine-Atherton.

1933 *Der Milchverbrauch in Berlin.* Gutachten der Wirtschaftspsychologischen Forschungsstelle. Milchversorgungsverband Berlin.

1937 *Research Memorandum on the Family in the Depression* (with Samuel A. Stouffer). New York: Social Science Research Council. 1972 Reprint. New York: Arno Press.

1939 **Radio Research and Applied Psychology.* Special issue of the *Journal of Applied Psychology*, 23, 1–219.

1940 *Radio and the Printed Page: An Introduction to the Study of Radio and its Role in the Communication of Ideas.* New York: Duell, Sloan and Pearce. 1971 Reprint. New York: Arno Press.

1940 **Progress in Radio Research.* Special issue of the *Journal of Applied Psychology*, 24, 661–870.

1941 **Radio Research 1941* (edited with Frank Stanton). New York: Duell, Sloan and Pearce.

1944 *The People's Choice: How the Voter Makes up His Mind in a Presidential Campaign* (with Bernard Berelson and Hazel Gaudet). New York: Duell, Sloan and Pearce. 1948 Second edition (with a new preface). New York:

Columbia University Press. 1968 Third edition (with a new preface). New York: Columbia University Press. *Translations:* German, Spanish.

1944 **Radio Research 1942-1943* (edited with Frank Stanton). New York: Duell, Sloan and Pearce.

1946 *The People Look at Radio* (with Harry Field). Chapel Hill: University of North Carolina Press.

1948 *Radio Listening in America: The People Look at Radio—Again* (with Patricia L. Kendall). Englewood Cliffs, N.J.: Prentice-Hall.

1949 **Communications Research 1948-1949* (edited with Frank Stanton). New York: Duell, Sloan and Pearce.

1950 *Measurement and Prediction* (with Samuel A. Stouffer, Louis Guttman, Edward A. Suchman, Shirley A. Star, and John A. Clausen). Vol. IV of *Studies in Social Psychology in World War II*. Princeton, N.J.: Princeton University Press.

1950 **Continuities in Social Research: Studies in the Scope and Method of "The American Soldier"* (edited with Robert K. Merton). New York: The Free Press. 1974 Reprint. New York: Arno Press.

1954 *Voting: A Study of Opinion Formation in a Presidential Campaign* (with Bernard R. Berelson and William N. McPhee). Chicago: University of Chicago Press.

1954 **Mathematical Thinking in the Social Sciences*. New York: The Free Press. 1969 Reprint. New York: Russell and Russell.

1955 *Personal Influence: The Part Played by People in the Flow of Mass Communication* (with Elihu Katz). New York: The Free Press. *Translations:* German, Italian, Japanese.

1955 **The Language of Social Research* (edited with Morris Rosenberg). New York: The Free Press.

1958 *The Academic Mind: Social Scientists in a Time of Crisis* (with Wagner Thielens, Jr.). New York: The Free Press.

1959 *Social Science Research on Business: Product and Potential* (with Robert A. Dahl and Mason Haire). New York: Columbia University Press.

1964 *Organizing Educational Research* (with Sam D. Sieber). Englewood Cliffs, N.J.: Prentice-Hall.

1966-1970 **Methode de la Sociologie*. 3 Vol. Paris: Mouton. Vol. I: *Le Vocabulaire des Sciences Sociales* (edited with Raymond Boudon, 1967). Vol. II: *L'Analyse Empirique de la Causalité* (edited with Raymond Boudon, 1966). Vol. III: *L'analyse des Processus Sociaux* (edited with Francois Chazel and Raymond Boudon, 1970).

1966 **Readings in Mathematical Social Science* (edited with Neil W. Henry). Chicago: Science Research Associates.

1967 *Metodologia e Ricerca Sociologica. Saggi Sociologici* (edited and with an introduction by Vittorio Capecchi). Bologna: Società Editrice il Mulino.

1967 **The Uses of Sociology* (edited with William H. Sewell and Harold L. Wilensky). New York: Basic Books.

1968 *Latent Structure Analysis* (with Neil W. Henry). Boston: Houghton Mifflin.

1968 *Am Puls der Gesellschaft* (edited and with a Foreword by Gertrude Wagner). Wien: Europa Verlag.

1970 *Philosophie des Sciences Sociales* (edited and with an Introduction by Raymond Boudon).

1970 *Qu'est-ce que la Sociologie?* Paris: Editions Galimard.

1972 **Continuities in the Language of Social Research* (with Ann K. Pasanella and Morris Rosenberg). New York: The Free Press.

1972 *Qualitative Analysis: Historical and Critical Essays.* Boston: Allyn and Bacon.

1973 *Main Trends in Sociology.* New York: Harper & Row.

1975 *An Introduction to Applied Sociology* (with Jeffrey G. Reitz and with the collaboration of Ann K. Pasanella). New York: Elsevier.

Part Two: Topical Bibliography

1. Unemployment

Books

1933 *Die Arbeitslosen von Marienthal: Ein Soziographischer Versuch über die Wirkungen langdauernder Arbeitslosigkeit.*

1937 *Research Memorandum on the Family in the Depression.*

Articles

1932 "An Unemployed Village," *Character and Personality*, 1, 147–151.

1935 "Psychological Consequences of Unemployment" (with B. Zawadski), *Journal of Social Psychology*, 6, 224–251.

1938 "The Psychological Effects of Unemployment" (with Philip Eisenberg), *Psychological Bulletin*, 35, 358–390.

1940 "Introduction" and "Description of Discerning," in Mirra Komarovsky, *The Unemployed Man and His Family.* New York: The Dryden Press, pp. ix–xii, 135–156. 1971 Reprint. New York: Octagon Books. 1971 Reprint. New York: Arno Press.

1941 "Who Gets a Job?" (with Hazel Gaudet), *Sociometry*, 4, 64–77.

Unpublished

1936 "Factors Influencing Length of Unemployment as Found in the Occupational Characteristics Survey." 40 pp.

1937 "The Study of Job Hunting." Reported at the Eastern Psychological Association. National Youth Administration (NYA).

1937 "Logical Analysis of Unemployment Indices." Paper presented to the American Sociological Society, Atlantic City. 19 pp.

1937 "Coming of Age in Essex County. An Analysis of 10,000 Interviews with Persons 16–24 Years Old." Office of Essex County Superintendent and University of Newark Research Center. 126 pp.

2. Mass Communication

Books
1939 *Radio Research and Applied Psychology*.

1940 *Radio and the Printed Page: An Introduction to the Study of Radio and Its Role in the Communication of Ideas*.

1940 *Progress in Radio Research*.

1941 *Radio Research 1941*.

1944 *Radio Research 1942-1943*.

1946 *The People Look at Radio*.

1948 *Radio Listening in America: The People Look at Radio—Again*.

1949 *Communications Research 1948-1949*.

1955 *Personal Influence: The Part Played by People in the Flow of Mass Communication*.

1967 *Metodologia e Ricerca Sociologica. Saggi Sociologici*.

1968 *Am Puls der Gesellschaft*.

Articles
1937 "Magazines in 90 Cities—Who Reads What?" (with Rowena Wyant), *Public Opinion Quarterly*, 1, 29–41.

1939 "Radio Research and Applied Psychology," *Journal of Applied Psychology*, 23, 1–7.

1939 "An Index of 'Radio-Mindedness' and Some Applications" (Elias Smith, pseudonym, with Francis Ollry), *Journal of Applied Psychology*, 23, 8–18

1939 "A Difficulty in the Feature-Analysis of a Radio Program" (Elias Smith, pseudonym), *Journal of Applied Psychology*, 23, 57–60.

1940 "Introduction by the Guest Editor," *Journal of Applied Psychology*, 24, 661–665.

1940 "The Use of Mail Questionnaires to Ascertain the Relative Popularity of Network Stations in Family Listening Surveys," *Journal of Applied Psychology*, 24, 802–816.

1941 "Audience Building in Educational Broadcasting," *Journal of Educational Sociology*, 14, 533–541.

1941 "Studying the Effect of Radio," *Transactions of the New York Academy of Sciences, Series II*, 3, 1–4.

1941 "Some Notes on the Relationship Between Radio and the Press," *Journalism Quarterly*, 18, 10–13.

1942 "The Daily Newspaper and Its Competitors," *The Annals of the American Academy of Political and Social Science*, 219, 42–43.

1942 "Are Newspaper Stations Different from Others?" (with Herman S. Hettinger). Testimony and analysis of certain exhibits before the Federal Communications Commission. New York: Newspaper-Radio Committee, 11 pp.

1942 "The Effects of Radio on Public Opinion," in Douglas Waples, ed., *Print, Radio and Film in a Democracy*. Chicago: University of Chicago Press, pp. 66–78.

1942 "What We Really Know About Daytime Serials." Notes for a talk delivered to *The Pulse of New York*, October 21. New York: Columbia Broadcasting System, pp. 3–14.

1943 "Studies in Radio and Film Propaganda" (with Robert K. Merton), *Transactions of the New York Academy of Sciences, Series II*, 6, 58–79.

1944 "The Psychological Analysis of Propaganda" (with Robert K. Merton), in *Proceedings of Writers' Congress Conference* (October 1943). Berkeley and Los Angeles: University of California Press, pp. 362–380.

1945 "Who Influences Whom—It's Same for Politics and Advertising," *Printer's Ink*, June pp. 32–36.

1945 "Research Problems in the Field of Public Relations," *Public Relations Directory and Yearbook*, 1, 93–95.

1945 "The Listener Talks Back" (with Patricia L. Kendall), in *Radio in Health and Education*. New York: Columbia University Press, pp. 48–65.

1945 "Communications Research and International Cooperation" (with Genevieve Knupfer), in Ralph Linton, ed., *The Science of Man in the World Crisis*. New York: Columbia University Press, pp. 465–495.

1945–1946 "Problems and Techniques of Magazine Research" (with Patricia Salter). A series of thirteen articles in *Magazine World*.

1946 "Radio and International Cooperation as a Problem for Psychological Research," *Journal of Consulting Psychology*, 10, 51–56.

1947 "Some Remarks on the Role of Mass Media in So-Called Tolerance Propaganda," *Journal of Social Issues*, Summer, 17–25.

1947 "Audience Research in the Movie Field," *The Annals of the American Academy of Political and Social Science*, 254, 160–168.

1948 "The Role of Criticism in the Management of Mass Media," *Journalism Quarterly*, 25, 115–126. 1972 Reprint in *QA*, pp. 123–138.

1948 "Mass Communication, Popular Taste and Organized Social Action" (with Robert K. Merton), in Lyman Bryson, ed., *Problems in the Communication of Ideas*. New York: Harper & Row, pp. 95–118.

1948 "Communication Research and the Social Psychologist," in Wayne Dennis, ed., *Current Trends in Social Psychology*. Pittsburgh: University of Pittsburgh Press, pp. 218–273.

1949 "Research for Action" (with Helen Dinerman), in *Communications Research 1948–1949*, pp. 73–108.

1949 "Motion Pictures, Radio Programs and Youth," in Frances Henne, Alice Brooks and Ruth Ersted, eds., *Youth Communication and Libraries*. Chicago: American Library Association, pp. 31–45.

1952 "The Prognosis for International Communications Research," *Public Opinion Quarterly*, 16, 481–490.

1953 "Dynamics of Response to Mass Communications: Comparative Study of Meaning and Formation of Public Opinion and Remarks on Projection; Identification as Mechanisms of Response," in Hortense Powdermaker, ed., *Mass Communications Seminar, May 11-13, 1951*. New York: Wenner-Gren Foundation, pp. 55–57, 108–113.

1955 "Why Is So Little Known about the Effects of Television on Children and What Can Be Done?" Testimony before the Kefauver Committee on Juvenile Delinquency. *Public Opinion Quarterly*, 19, 243–251.

1958 "Tendances Actuelles de la Sociologie des Communications et Comportement du Public de la Radiotélévision Américaine," *Cahiers d'Etudes de Radio Télévision*, 23.

1960 "A Researcher Looks at Television," *Public Opinion Quarterly*, 24, 24–31.

1961 "Mass Culture Today." Preface to Norman Jacobs, ed., *Culture for the Millions?* Princeton, N.J.: D. Van Nostrand, pp. ix–xxiii. 1972 Reprint. The Mass Media and the Intellectual Community, in *QA*, pp. 139–145.

1963 "Trends in Broadcasting Research," in Alkinori Katagiri and Koichi Motono, eds., *Studies of Broadcasting*. Tokyo: The Theoretical Research Center of the Radio and TV Culture Research Institute, The Nippon Hoso Kyokai, pp. 49–64.

1963 "Mass Media and Personal Influence," (with Herbert Menzel) in Wilbur Schramm, ed., *The Science of Human Communication*. New York: Basic Books, pp. 1–10.

1963 "Some Reflections on Past and Future Research on Broadcasting." Afterword to Gary Steiner, *The People Look at Television*. New York: Knopf, pp. 409–422.

1965 "Introduction" in "Culture Supérieur et Culture de Masse," Special Issue of *Communications*, 5. Paris, Ecole Pratique des Hautes Etudes, pp. 3–12.

1966 "Communications Research," *Grassroots Editor*, 8, 3–6.

1971 "Introduction" in Bernard Rosenberg and David Manning White, eds., *Mass Culture Revisited*. New York: Van Nostrand Reinhold, pp. vii–ix.

1972 [1954] "Mass Media of Communication in Modern Society," in *QA*, pp. 106–120.

1975 "Zwei Wege der Massenkommunikationsforschung," in Oskar Schatz, ed., *Die Elektronische Revolution*. Graz, Austria: Styria Verlag, pp. 197–222.

Unpublished

1941 "Study of Coverage by American Radio Stations: Notes on the Available Data on Radio Listeners for the Use of Government Officials Concerned with Broadcasting" (with M. Bayne and Edward A. Suchman). Office of Radio Research, Columbia University. 60 pp.

1941 "General Statistical Analysis of Joint Newspaper-Radio Ownership." Office of Radio Research, Columbia University. 35 pp.

1942 "Should She Have Music?" 40 pp.

1942 "The Daytime Serial as a Social, Commercial and Research Problem." 51 pp.

1944 "On the Postwar Future of Radio." 16 pp.

1951 "Methodological Considerations in International Broadcasting Research." Report for the Division of Radio Program Evaluation, International Broadcasting Service, Department of State. 220 pp.

1953 "Report from the Implementation Committee to the Citizens' Group on Television Regarding Plans for a Television Development Center." 62 pp.

3. Voting and Political Activities

Books

1944 *The People's Choice: How the Voter Makes Up His Mind in a Presidential Campaign.*

1954 *Voting: A Study of Opinion Formation in a Presidential Campaign.*

Articles

1939 "The Change of Opinion During a Political Discussion," *Journal of Applied Psychology,* 23, 131–147.

1942 "National Morale, Social Cleavage and Political Allegiance" (with Ruth Durant), *Journalism Quarterly*, 19, 150–158.

1944 "Polls, Propaganda and Politics" (a series of articles, some with co-authors), *The Nation*, 19, August–November.

1944 "The Election Is Over," *Public Opinion Quarterly,* 8, 317–330.

1945 "Woman: A Major Problem for the PAC (Political Action Committee)" (with Bernard Berelson), *Public Opinion Quarterly*, 9, 79–82.

1945 "Prediction of Political Behavior in America" (with Raymond Franzen), *American Sociological Review,* 10, 261–273.

1949 "The Contribution of the Regional Poll to Political Understanding" (with Morris Rosenberg), *Public Opinion Quarterly,* 13, 570–586.

1949 "Should Political Forecasts Be Made?" in Norman C. Meier and Harold W. Saunders, eds., *The Polls and Public Opinion: The Iowa Conference on Attitude and Public Opinion Research.* New York: Henry Holt, 278–286.

1949 "Unsettled Problems of Survey Methodology," in Meier and Saunders, eds., pp. 322–328.

1950 "Votes in the Making," *Scientific American,* 183, 11–13.

1954 "The Psychology of Voting: An Analysis of Political Behavior" (with Seymour M. Lipset, Allen H. Barton, and Juan Linz), in Gardner Lindzey, ed., *Handbook of Social Psychology.* Vol. II. Reading, Mass.: Addison-Wesley, pp. 1124–1175.

1963 "Political Behavior and Public Opinion," in Bernard Berelson, ed., *The Behavioral Sciences Today.* New York: Basic Books, pp. 176–187.

Unpublished
1949 "Religious Voting in New York." Paper delivered at the Institute for Religious and Social Studies. 23 pp.

4. Education and Psychology

Books
1924 *Gemeinschaftserziehung durch Erziehungsgemeinschaften: Bericht über einen Beitrag der Jugendbewegung zur Sozialpädagogik.*
1931 *Jugend und Beruf: Kritik und Material.*
1958 *The Academic Mind: Social Scientists in a Time of Crisis.*
1964 *Organizing Educational Research.*

Articles
1923 "Die Sozialistische Erziehung und das Gemeinschaftsleben der Jugend," *Die Sozialistische Erziehung*, 3, 191–194.
1927 "Marxismus und Individualpsychologie," *Die Sozialistische Erziehung*, 7, 98–101.
1927 "Ergebnis der de Man Debatte," *Arbeit und Wirtschaft*, 5, Heft 16, 684–690.
1927 "Die Berufspläne der Wiener Maturanten," *Mitteilungen aus Statistik und Verwaltung der Stadt Wien*, Jahrgang 1927, 21–25.
1927 "Die Psychologie in Hendrik de Man's Marxkritik," *Der Kampf*, 20, 270–275.
1927 "DINTA (Deutsches Institüt für Technische Arbeitschulung)," *Arbeit und Wirtschaft*, 5, Heft 11, 437–440.
1928 "Die Berufspläne der Wiener Maturanten des Jahres 1928," *Mitteilungen aus Statistik und Verwaltung der Stadt Wien*, Jahrgang 1928, 311–315.
1928 "Zur Normierung Entwicklungspsychologischer Daten," *Zeitschrift fur Psychologie*, 107, 237–253.
1929 "Die Bedeutung der Normalen Verteilungskurve fur die Leistungsmessung," *Psychotechnische Zeitschrift*, 4, 104–107.
1929 "Körperliche und Geistige Erziehung," *Die Quelle*, 79, 803–809.
1929 "Das Weltbild des Jugendlichen" (with Karl Reininger and Marie Jahoda), in Sofie Lazarsfeld, ed., *Technik der Erziehung.* Leipzig: S. Hirzel, pp. 212–237.
1929 "Hinter den Kulissen der Schule," in Sofie Lazarsfeld, ed., pp. 94–104.
1932 "Die Kontingenzmethode in der Psychologie–Zur Erinnerung an Wilhelm Betz," *Zeitschrift für angewandte Psychologie*, 41, 160–166.
1936 "Erhebung bei Jugendlichen über Autorität und Familië" (with Kaethe Liechter), and Max Horkheimer, ed., *Studien uber Autoritat und Familie.* Paris: F. Alcan, pp. 353–415.

1955 [1932] "The Affinity of Occupation and Subject Matter among Adult Education Students" (Elias Smith, pseudonym, with Lotte Radermacher), in *LSR*, 100–106.

1957 "Social Scientists and Recent Threats to Academic Freedom" (with Wagner Thielens, Jr.), *Social Problems*, 5, 244–266.

1959 "Amerikanische Beobachtungen eines Bühler-Schülers," *Zeitschrift für experimentelle und angewandte Psychologie*, 6, 69–76.

1964 "The Admissions Officer: Fulcrum for Academic Leadership–An Elaboration" (with Jane Z. Hauser), *The Journal of the Association of College Admission Counselors*, 10, 3–6.

1964 "The Admissions Officer in the American College: An Occupation under Change" (with Jane Z. Hauser). *Report for the College Entrance Examination Board*. New York: College Entrance Examination Board. 121 pp. (mimeo). Reprint (excerpt). *CLSR*, pp. 58–63.

1965 "The Seminars and Graduate Education," in Frank Tannenbaum, ed., *A Community of Scholars: The University Seminars at Columbia*. New York: Praeger, pp. 74–85.

1966 "Innovation in Higher Education," in *Expanding Horizons of Knowledge About Man*. A Symposium on the Occasion of the Convocation held on March 21 to announce the establishment of the Ferkauf Graduate School of Humanities and Social Sciences of Yeshiva University. New York: Ferkauf School, pp. 12–21.

Unpublished

1931 "Der Einfluss der Interessen auf die Wahrnehmung" (with Robert J. Cone). 93 pp.

1953 Introduction to Bernhard Stern, ed., *Historical Materials on Innovation in Higher Education*, pp. i–vii.

1959 "Report on a Project to Map Out the General Area of Non-Intellectual Factors in the Prediction of College Success." College Entrance Examination Board. 51 pp.

1965 "Innovation in Higher Education" (with Amitai Etzioni). 36 pp.

5. Social Research: Methods and Procedures

Books

1929 *Statistisches Praktikum für Psychologen und Lehrer*.

1933 *Die Arbeitslosen von Marienthal: Ein Soziographischer Versuch über die Wirkungen langdauernder Arbeitslosigkeit*.

1939 **Radio Research and Applied Psychology*.

1940 **Progress in Radio Research*.

1944 *The People's Choice: How the Voter Makes up His Mind in a Presidential Campaign*.

1950 *Continuities in Social Research: Studies in the Scope and Method of "The American Soldier."*

1954 *Voting: A Study of Opinion Formation in a Presidential Campaign.*

1955 *Personal Influence: The Part Played by People in the Flow of Mass Communication.*

1955 *The Language of Social Research.*

1958 *The Academic Mind: Social Scientists in a Time of Crisis.*

1959 *Social Science Research on Business: Product and Potential.*

1966–1970 *Methode de la Sociologie.* (3 volumes)

1967 *Methodologia e Ricerca Sociologica. Saggi Sociologici.*

1972 *Continuities in the Language of Social Research.*

Articles

1929 "Der Anwendungsbereich des Ruppschen Koeffizienten," *Psychotechnische Zeitschrift*, 4, 9–15.

1932 "Die Kontingentzmethode in der Psychologie—Zur Erinnerung an Wilhelm Betz," *Zeitschrift für angewandte Psychologie*, 11, 160–166.

1934 "The Psychological Aspect of Market Research," *Harvard Business Review*, 12, 54–71.

1935 "The Techniques of Market Research from the Standpoint of a Psychologist" (with Arthur Kornhauser). *Institute of Management Series 16.* New York: American Management Association, pp. 3–24. 1955 Reprint. *LSR*, 392–403.

1935 "The Art of Asking Why," *National Marketing Review*, 1, 32–43. 1972 Reprint. *QA*, 183–202.

1936 "Public Attitude Toward Economic Problems," *Market Research*, 5, 13–15.

1936 "The Outlook for Testing Effectiveness in Advertising," *The Management Review*, 25, 3–12.

1937 "The Use of Detailed Interviews in Market Research," *Journal of Marketing*, 2, 3–8.

1937 "Psychological Aspects of Questionnaire Development; Further Consideration of Psychological Aspects; Psychological Techniques of Classification; Psychological Approach in the Development of Conclusions," in Ferdinand C. Wheeler, Louis Bader, and J. George Frederick, eds., *The Technique of Marketing Research.* New York: McGraw-Hill, pp. 62–81, 82–91, 190–213, 267–281.

1937 "The Tactile-Kinaesthetic Perception of Fabrics with Emphasis on Their Relative Pleasantness" (with Rowena Ripin), *Journal of Applied Psychology*, 21, 198–224.

1937 "Some Remarks on the Typological Procedure in Social Research," *Zeitschrift für Sozialforschung*, 6, 119–139.

1938 "The 'Panel' as a New Tool for Measuring Opinion" (with Marjorie Fiske), *Public Opinion Quarterly*, 2, 596–612.

1939 "Interchangeability of Indices in the Measurement of Economic Influences," *Journal of Applied Psychology*, 23, 33–46.

1940 "Do People Know Why They Buy?" (Elias Smith, pseudonym, with Edward A. Suchman), *Journal of Applied Psychology*, 24, 673–684. 1955 Reprint. *LSR*, pp. 404–410.

1940 "The Quantification of Case Studies" (with William S. Robinson), *Journal of Applied Psychology*, 24, 817–825.

1940 "'Panel' Studies," *Public Opinion Quarterly*, 4, 122–128.

1940 "Some Properties of the Trichotomy 'Like, No Opinion, Dislike' and their Psychological Interpretation" (with William S. Robinson), *Sociometry*, 3, 151–178.

1940 "Description of Discerning," in Mirra Komarovsky, *The Unemployed Man and His Family*. New York: The Dryden Press, pp. ix–xii, 135–146. 1971 Reprint. New York: Farrar Straus and Giroux.

1941 "Repeated Interviews as a Tool for Studying Changes in Opinion and their Causes," *American Statistical Association Bulletin*, 2, 3–7.

1941 "Evaluating the Effectiveness of Advertising by Direct Interviews," *Journal of Consulting Psychology*, 5, 170–178.

1942 "The Statistical Analysis of Reasons as Research Operation," *Sociometry*, 5, 29–47.

1944 "The Controversy over Detailed Interviews—An Offer for Negotiation," *Public Opinion Quarterly*, 8, 38–60.

1945 "Mail Questionnaires as a Research Problem" (with Raymond Franzen), *The Journal of Psychology*, 20, 293–310.

1945 "The Validity of Mail Questionnaires in Upper Income Groups: Part I" (with Raymond Franzen), *Time, Inc. Research Report #940*, Oct. 1, 1945. New York: Time, Inc., pp. 1–6.

1945 "The Validity of Mail Questionnaires in Upper Income Groups: Part II" (with Raymond Franzen), *Time, Inc. Research Report #950*, May 15, 1945. New York: Time, Inc., pp. 1–6.

1948 "The Use of Panels in Social Research," *Proceedings of the American Philosophical Society*, 92, 405–410. 1972 Reprint. *CLSR*, pp. 330–337.

1950 "Problems of Survey Analysis" (with Patricia L. Kendall), in *Continuities in Social Research: Studies in the Scope and Method of "The American Soldier,"* pp. 133–196.

1951 "Qualitative Measurement in the Social Sciences: Classification, Typologies and Indices" (with Allen H. Barton), in Daniel Lerner and Harold Lasswell, eds., *The Policy Sciences: Recent Developments in Scope and Method*. Stanford, Calif.: Stanford University Press, pp. 155–193.

1951 "The Panel Study" (with Morris Rosenberg and Wagner Thielens, Jr.), in Marie Jahoda, Morton Deutsch and Stuart W. Cook, eds., *Research Methods in Social Relations*. New York: The Dryden Press, pp. 587–610.

1955 [1945] "The Interchangeability of Socio-Economic Indices" (Elias Smith, pseudonym, with Hortense Horwitz), in *LSR*, pp. 73–77.

1955 [1946] "The Interpretation of Statistical Relations as a Research Operation," in *LSR*, pp. 115-125.

1958 "Who Are the Marketing Leaders?" *Tide*, May 9, pp. 53-57.

1959 "Some Aspects of Human Motivation in Relation to Distribution," in *Boston Conference on Distribution*, pp. 61-64.

1961 [1956] "On the Relation Between Individual and Collective Properties" (with Herbert Menzel), in Amitai Etzioni, ed., *Complex Organizations: A Sociological Reader*. New York: Holt, Rinehart and Winston, pp. 499-516. 1972 Reprint. *CLSR*, pp. 225-236.

1967 "Rémarques sur la Signification Formelle de Deux Indices" (with Raymond Boudon), in *Le Vocabulaire des Sciences Sociales*, pp. 224-228.

1967 "Définition d'Intention et Espace d'Attributs" (with Jean Stoetzel), in *Le Vocabulaire des Sciences Sociales*, pp. 189-193.

1968 "Measurement," in Talcott Parsons, ed., *American Society: Perspectives, Problems, Methods*. New York: Basic Books, pp. 101-114.

1972 [1950] "Development of a Test for Class Consciousness," in *CLSR*, pp. 41-43.

Unpublished

1931 "Umgang mit Zahlen." Vienna: Psychologisches Institut.

1937 "Logical Analysis of Unemployment Indices." Paper delivered to the American Sociological Society, Atlantic City. 19 pp.

1942 "Magazine Reading Before and After Pearl Harbor: Report to the Office of War Information." 22 pp.

1943 "Solution of the Selection of the Best Combination of Dichotomous Arrangements to Distinguish a Categorical Criterion" (with Raymond Franzen). Washington: Civil Aeronautics Administration, Report No. 12, pp. 19-24.

1947 "Experiment with Two Methods of Measuring Magazine Readership" (with Thelma Ehrlich). Bureau of Applied Social Research. 65 pp.

1948 "The Analysis of Communication Content" (with Bernard Berelson). Bureau of Applied Social Research and University of Chicago. 149 pp.

1953 "Dartmouth Seminar on Concepts and Indices." 222 pp.

1954 "Dartmouth Seminar on Social Process." 459 pp.

1954 "The Analysis of Repeated Interviews. Panel Analysis Exemplified through Studies of Voting Decisions." Paper for the Dartmouth Conference on Social Process. 41 pp.

1954 "A Case Study of Methods in Social Science" (with Charles E. Lindblom). 57 pp.

1971 "Measurement in Today's Social Sciences." 27 pp.

6. Social Research: Perspectives and Reflections

Books

1950 *Continuities in Social Research: Studies in the Scope and Method of "The American Solider."

1967 Metodologia e Ricerca Sociologica. Saggi Sociologici.

1967 *The Uses of Sociology.

1968 Am Puls der Gesellschaft.

1970 Philosophie des Sciences Sociales.

1970 Qu'est-ce que la Sociologie?

1972 Qualitative Analysis: Historical and Critical Essays.

1973 Main Trends in Sociology.

1975 An Introduction to Applied Sociology.

Articles

1937 "The Outlook for Testing Effectiveness in Advertising," Management Review, 25, 3–12.

1941 "Remarks on Administrative and Critical Communications Research," Studies in Philosophy and Science, 9, 2–16. 1972 Reprint. QA, pp. 155–167.

1947 "Preface," in Ernest Greenwood, Experimental Sociology: A Study in Method. New York: Kings Crown Press, pp. vii–x.

1947 "Introduction," in Hans Zeisel, Say It With Figures. New York: Harper & Row, pp. ix–xvi.

1948. "What is Sociology?" Oslo: Skrivemaskinstua Universitets Studentkontor, mimeo., 20 pp.

1950 "The Obligations of the 1950 Pollster to the 1984 Historian" (presidential address to the American Association for Public Opinion Research), Public Opinion Quarterly, 14, 618–638. 1972 Reprint. QA, pp. 278–299.

1952 "The Prognosis for International Communications Research," Public Opinion Quarterly, 16, 481–490.

1954 "Friendship as Social Process: A Substantive and Methodological Analysis" (with Robert K. Merton), in Morroe Berger, Theodore Abel, and Charles Page, eds., Freedom and Control in Modern Society. New York: Van Nostrand, pp. 18–66.

1955 "Some Functions of Qualitative Analysis in Social Research" (with Allen H. Barton), Frankfurter Beiträge zur Soziologie, 1, 321–361.

1955 "Foreword," in Herbert Hyman, Survey Design and Analysis. New York: The Free Press, pp. v–xiii.

1955 "A Logical Analysis of the Measurement Problem in the Social Sciences," in Conference Proceedings on Measurement of Management, November 3–4. New York: Society for Advancement of Management, pp. 21–30.

1955 "Communications Problems in Sociology," Report of the Fifth Conference of the Association of Princeton Graduate Alumni, December, pp. 17–25.

1955 "Progress and Fad in Motivation Research," Proceedings of the Third Annual Seminar on Social Science for Industry—Motivation, March. San

Francisco: Stanford Research Institute, pp. 11–23. 1972 Reprint. *QA*, pp. 203–224.

1956 "Comments," on Walter J. Blum and Harry Kalven, Jr., *The Art of Opinion Research. The University of Chicago Law Review*, 24, 65–69.

1957 "Concluding Remarks," in *Mathematical Models of Human Behavior: Proceedings of a Symposium.* Stamford, Conn.: Dunlap and Associates, pp. 97–103.

1957 "Public Opinion and the Classical Tradition," *Public Opinion Quarterly*, 8, 39–53. 1972 Reprint. *QA*, pp. 300–320.

1957 "The Historian and the Pollster," in Mirra Komarovsky, ed., *Common Frontiers of the Social Sciences.* New York: The Free Press, pp. 242–262.

1958 "Evidence and Inference in Social Research," *Daedalus*, 87, 99–130.

1959 "Problems in Methodology," in Robert K. Merton, Leonard Broom, and Leonard S. Cottrell, Jr., eds., *Sociology Today: Problems and Prospects.* New York: Basic Books, pp. 39–78.

1959 "Foreword," in Allen H. Barton, *Studying the Effects of College Education.* New Haven: The Edward W. Hazen Foundation, pp. 5–10.

1959 "Methodological Problems in Empirical Social Research," *Proceedings of the Fourth World Congress in Sociology.* Vol. II. London: International Sociological Association, pp. 225–249.

1959 "Reflections on Business," *American Journal of Sociology*, 65, 1–31. 1972 Reprint. *QA*, pp. 241–244. 1972 Reprint *CLSR*, pp. 111–113.

1959 "Sociological Reflections on Business: Consumers and Managers," in *Social Science Research on Business*, pp. 99–155.

1960 "Foreword," in Rose K. Goldsen, Morris Rosenberg, Robin M. Williams, Jr., and Edward A. Suchman, *What College Students Think.* Princeton, N.J.: D. Van Nostrand, pp. iii–xi.

1961 "Notes on the History of Quantification in Sociology: Trends, Sources and Problems," *Isis*, 52, 277–333.

1961 "Introduction," in Allen H. Barton, *Organizational Measurement and its Bearing on the Study of College Environments.* New York: College Entrance Examination Board, pp. vi–ix.

1961 "Observations on the Organization of Empirical Social Research in the United States" (with Sidney S. Spivack). *International Social Science Council Information* No. 29. Paris: UNESCO, pp. 1–35.

1962 "Introduction," in Samuel A. Stouffer, *Social Research to Test Ideas.* New York: The Free Press, pp. xv–xxxi.

1962 "Philosophy of Science and Empirical Social Research," in Ernest Nagel, Patrick Suppes, and Alfred Tarski, eds., *Logic, Methodology and Philosophy of Science.* Stanford, Calif.: Stanford University Press, pp. 463–473. 1972 Reprint. *QA*, pp. 263–277.

1962 "International Sociology as a Sociological Problem" (with Ruth Leeds), *American Sociological Review*, 27, 732–741. 1972 Reprint. *QA*, pp. 341–360.

1962 "The Sociology of Empirical Social Research" (presidential address, American Sociological Association), *American Sociological Review*, 27, 757–767. 1972 Reprint. *QA*, pp. 321–340.

1962 "The Methodology of Quantitative Social Research" (with Allen H. Barton), in Baidya Nath Varma, ed., *A New Survey of the Social Sciences*. Bombay: Asia Publishing House, pp. 151–169.

1964 "Some Problems of Organized Social Research," in Ozzie G. Simmons, ed., *The Behavioral Sciences: Problems and Prospects*. Boulder, Colo.: Institute of Behavioral Sciences, University of Colorado, pp. 9–19.

1964 "A Note on Empirical Social Research and Interdisciplinary Relationships," *International Social Science Journal*, 16, 529–533.

1965 "Max Weber and Empirical Social Research" (with Anthony R. Oberschall), *American Sociological Review*, 30, 185–199.

1965 "Preface," in Anthony Oberschall, *Empirical Social Research in Germany 1848–1914*. Paris: Mouton and New York: Basic Books, pp. v–viii.

1966 "Preface" and "Concept Formation and Measurement in the Behavioral Sciences: Some Historical Observations," in Gordon J. DiRenzo, ed., *Concepts, Theory and Explanation in the Behavioral Sciences*. New York: Random House, pp. xi–xii, 144–202. 1972 Reprint. *QA*, pp. 5–52.

1967 "Some Recent Trends in United States Methodology and General Sociology," in *First International Conference of the Social Sciences*, September. Bologna, pp. 653–688.

1968 "An Episode in the History of Social Research: A Memoir," in Donald Fleming and Bernard Bailyn, eds., *The Intellectual Migration: Europe and America 1930–1960*. Cambridge: Harvard University Press, pp. 270–337. 1972 Reprint (excerpts). *QA*, pp. 245–259.

1968 "Foreword," in Morris Rosenberg, *The Logic of Survey Analysis*. New York: Basic Books, pp. vii–x.

1968 "Introduction," in Hans Zeisel, *Say It With Figures*. 5th ed. New York: Harper & Row, pp. xiii–xiv.

1968 "Introduction," in Hans Zeisel, *Ditelo con i numeri*. Padova: Marsilio, pp. 15–17.

1968 "The Place of Empirical Social Research on the Map of Contemporary Sociology," in *The Social Sciences: Problems and Orientations*. Paris and The Hague: Mouton/UNESCO, pp. 223–241.

1968 "Adolphe Quetelet" (with David Landau). *International Encyclopedia of the Social Sciences*. New York: Macmillan and Free Press, Vol. XIII, pp. 247–257.

1969 "From Vienna to Columbia," *Columbia Forum* (Summer), 31–36.

1969 "Uber die Brauchbarkeit der Soziologie," in Leopold Rosenmayr and Sigurd Hoellinger, eds., *Soziologie: Forschung in Oesterreich*. Graz: Hermann Boehlau's Nachf., pp. 13–31.

1970 "Toward a Theory of Applied Sociology" (with Jeffrey G. Reitz). A Report for the United States Office of Naval Research. New York: Bureau of Applied Social Research, Columbia University. 78 pp.

1970 "Introduction," in Charles Y. Glock, Gertrude J. Selznick, and Joe L. Spaeth, *The Apathetic Majority*. New York: Harper & Row (Torchbook edition), pp. xiii–xvi.

1970 "Sociology," in *Main Trends of Research in the Social and Human Sciences*. Paris and The Hague: Mouton/UNESCO, pp. 61–165.

1970 "A Sociologist Looks at Historians," in Melvin Small, ed., *Public Opinion and Historians: Interdisciplinary Perspectives*. Symposium at Wayne State University, May 8–9. Detroit: Wayne State University Press, pp. 39–59.

1971 "Accounting and Social Bookkeeping," in Robert R. Sterling and William F. Bentz, eds., *Accounting in Perspective: Contributions to Accounting Thought by Other Disciplines*. Cincinnati: South-Western Publishing, pp. 88–101.

1972 [1950] "A Professional School for Training in Social Research" (with Robert K. Merton), in *QA*, pp. 361–391.

1972 [1958] "Historical Notes on the Empirical Study of Action: An Intellectual Odyssey," in *QA*, pp. 53–105.

1972 "Introduction," in Douglas C. McDonald, *Some Problems in the Organization and Use of Social Research in the U.S. Navy*. Report for the U.S. Office of Naval Research. New York: Bureau of Applied Social Research, Columbia University, pp. i–vii.

1972 "Foreword," in Anthony Oberschall, ed., *The Establishment of Empirical Sociology: Studies in Continuity, Discontinuity and Institutionalization*. New York: Harper & Row, pp. vi–xv.

1973 "Toward a History of Empirical Sociology," in *Methodologie de l'Histoire et des Sciences Humaines. Mélanges en l'Honneur de Fernand Braudel*. Paris. Editions Galimard, pp. 289–301.

1973 "Foreword," in Sam D. Sieber, *Reforming the University: The Role of the Research Center*. New York: Praeger, pp. v–x.

1973 "Introduction," in Jeffrey G. Reitz, *The Gap Between Knowledge and Decision in the Utilization of Social Research*. Report for the U.S. Office of Naval Research. New York: Bureau of Applied Social Research, pp. i–v.

1973 "Introduction: The Use of Social Science in Business Management," in *Views from the Socially Sensitive Seventies*. Seminars presented to the Supplemental Training Program. New York: American Telephone and Telegraph Co., pp. ix–xv.

1973 "Some Problems of Research Organization" (with Douglas McDonald). A Report for the U.S. Office of Naval Research. New York. Bureau of Applied Social Research. Mimeo., 67 pp.

1973 "The Social Sciences and the Smoking Problem," in William L. Dunn Jr., ed., *Smoking Behavior: Motives and Incentives*. Washington, D.C.: V. M. Winston & Sons, pp. 283–286.

1973 "Foreword," in Wolf Heydebrand, *Hospital Bureaucracy: A Comparative Study of Organizations*. New York: Dunellen Publishers, pp. xvii–xxiv.

1973 "Preface," in Ann K. Pasanella and Janice Weinman, *The Road to Recommendations*. Report for the U.S. Office of Naval Research. New York: Bureau of Applied Social Research, Columbia University, pp. i–ii.

1975 "The Policy Science Movement (An Outsider's View)," *Policy Sciences*, 6, 211–222.

1975 "The Uses of Sociology by Presidential Commissions" (with Martin Jaeckel), in Mirra Komarovsky, ed., *Sociology and Public Policy*. New York: Elsevier, pp. 117–142.

1975 "Working with Merton," in Lewis A. Coser, ed., *The Idea of Social Structure: Papers in Honor of Robert K. Merton*. New York: Harcourt Brace Jovanovich, pp. 35–66.

1976 "Preface," in Caroline U. Persell, *Quality, Careers and Training in Educational Research*. New York: General Hall, pp. vii–xi.

1976 "Evaluation of Social Experiments: Commentary," in Clark C. Abt, ed., *The Evaluation of Social Programs*. Beverly Hills, Calif.: Sage, pp. 60–61.

1977 "Some Episodes in the History of Panel Analysis," in Denise Kandel, ed., *Longitudinal Research in Drug Use: Empirical Findings and Methodological Issues*. New York: Wiley, 249–265.

7. Mathematical Sociology

Books

1950 *Measurement and Prediction*.

1954 **Mathematical Thinking in the Social Sciences*.

1967 *Metodologia a Ricerca Sociologica. Saggi Sociologici*.

1967 *Metodologia a Riserca Sociologica. Saggi Sociologici*.

1968 *Latent Structure Analysis*.

7a. Latent Structure Analysis

Articles

1950 "The Logical and Mathematical Foundations of Latent Structure Analysis," in *Measurement and Prediction*, pp. 362–412.

1950 "The Interpretation and Computation of Some Latent Structures," in *Measurement and Prediction*, pp. 413–472.

1951 "A Simple Model for Attitude Tests" (with Peter Rossi), "The General Solution of the Latent Class Case" (with Jack Dudman), in *The Uses of Mathematical Models in the Measurement of Attitudes*. Santa Monica, Calif.: The Rand Corporation. Parts I and II and Chapter 5.

1954 "A Conceptual Introduction to Latent Structure Analysis," in *Mathematical Thinking in the Social Sciences*, pp. 349–397.

1955 "Recent Developments in Latent Structure Analysis," *Sociometry*, 18, 391–403.

1959 "Latent Structure Analysis," in Sigmund Koch, ed., *Psychology: A Study of a Science*, Vol. III. New York: McGraw-Hill, pp. 476–543.

1959 "Latent Structure Analysis," in *Contributions to Scientific Research in Management*. Los Angeles: University of California, Graduate School of Business Administration, pp. 1–8.

1960 "Latent Structure Analysis: Test Theory," in Harold Gulliksen and Samuel Messick, eds., *Psychological Scaling*. New York: Wiley. 1966 Reprint. *Readings in Mathematical Science,* pp. 78–88.

1965 "Latent Structure Analysis," in S. Sternberg et al., eds., *Mathematics and Social Sciences.* Paris and the Hague: Mouton/UNESCO, pp. 37–54.

1965 "The Application of Latent Structure Analysis to Quantitative Ecological Data" (with Neil W. Henry), in F. Massarik and P. Ratoosh, eds. *Mathematical Explorations in Behavioral Science*. Homewood, Ill.: Dorsey Press, pp. 333–348.

1972 [1968] "The Problem of Measuring Turnover," in *CLSR*, pp. 358–362.

Unpublished

1947 "Latent Attribute Analysis." Paper presented to the American Sociological Society, Atlantic City.

1948 "The Concept of Latent Attribute." 18 pp.

1948 "The Qualitative Study of Larger Cross Product Matrices with Positive Entries." 42 pp.

1948 "The Use of Indices in Social Research." 32 pp.

1952 "A System of Scales Derived from a Standard Trace Line Model" (with David G. Hays). 75 pp.

1955 "*An Algebraic Introduction to Latent Structure Analysis.*" 142 pp.

1956 "Some New Results and Problems in Latent Structure Analysis." 49 pp.

1961 "An Extended Solution of the Discrete Class Case." 10 pp.

Note: No dates were found on the following unpublished papers on latent structure analysis. They were probably all written in the 1950s.

"The Problem History of Latent Structure Analysis." 68 pp.

"The Computation of Latent Distance Scales." 14 pp.

"Three Applications of Latent Structure Analysis to Empirical Data" (with Peter Rossi). 55 pp.

"Applications of and Materials for the Study of the Dichotomous Cube" (with Allen H. Barton). 77 pp.

"Some Theories of Structor Algebra." 52 pp.

"The Present State of Latent Structure Analysis." 35 pp.

"The General Discrete Class Case." 34 pp.

7b. The Algebra of Dichotomous Systems

Articles

1955 [1946] "The Interpretation of Statistical Relations as a Research Operation," in *LSR*, pp. 115–125.

1961 "The Algebra of Dichotomous Systems," in Herbert Solomon, ed., *Studies in Item Analysis and Prediction*. Stanford, Calif.: Stanford University Press, pp. 111–157. 1972 Reprint. *CLSR*.

1965 [1961] "Introduction," in Saul Sternberg, V. Capecchi, T. Kloek and C. T. Laenders, eds., *Mathematics and Social Sciences*. Paris and The Hague: Mouton/UNESCO, pp. 11-34.

1965 [1961] "Repeated Observations on Attitude and Behavior Items," in S. Sternberg et al.., eds., pp. 121-142.

1967 Modelli matematici per lo studio dei panels" (Models for Opinion Change) (with Neil Henry), in *Metodologia e Ricerca Sociologica*, pp. 581-592.

1968 "The Analysis of Attribute Data," *International Encyclopedia of the Social Sciences*. New York: Macmillan and The Free Press, Vol. XV, pp. 419-429.

1970 "A Memoir in Honor of Professor Wold," in Tore Dalenius, Georg Karlsson and Sten Malmquist, eds., *Scientists at Work: Festschrift in Honor of Herman Wold*. Uppsala: Almquist and Wicksell, pp. 78-103.

1972 "Regression Analysis with Dichotomous Attributes," *Social Science Research*, 1, 25-34. 1972 Reprint. *CLSR*, 208-214.

1972 "Reply to Comments on Lazarsfeld's 'Regression Analysis with Dichotomous Attributes,'" *Social Science Research*, 1, 425-427.

1972 "Mutual Relations over Time of Two Attributes: A Review and Integration of Various Approaches," in M. Hammer, K. Salzinger and S. Sutton, eds., *Psychopathology: Festschrift in Honor of Josef Zubin*. New York: Wiley, pp. 461-480.

1972 "Algebra of Dichotomies," in Henry A. Selby, ed., *Notes of Lectures on Mathematics in the Behavioral Sciences*. Boston: Mathematical Association of America, pp. 162-196.

1972 [1946] "Mutual Effects of Statistical Variables," in *CLSR*, pp. 41-43.

Unpublished

1957 "Index of Dichotomous Turnover." 4 pp.

1969 "Problems in the Analysis of Mutual Interaction Between Two Variates." Memorandum to the National Broadcasting Corporation, Research Department. 20 pp.

1971 "Linear Systems of Dichotomies." 54 pp.

1971 "The Algebra of Dichotomous Systems." Lecture Notes. 42 pp.

8. Market Research

Articles

1932 "Neue Wege der Marktforschung." *Mitteilungen der Industrie- und Handeskammer zu Berlin*. 4 pp.

1932 "Marktuntersuchungen auf Psychologischer Grundlage," *Mitteilungen der Gesellschaft fuer Organisation*, 127-128.

1934 "The Psychological Aspect of Market Research," *Harvard Business Review*, 34, 54-71.

1935 "The Techniques of Market Research from the Standpoint of a Psychologist" (with Arthur Kornhauser), *Institute of Management Series 16*. New York: American Management Association, pp. 3-24. 1955 Reprint. *LSR*, pp. 342-403.

1935 "The Art of Asking Why," *National Marketing Review*, 1, 32-43. 1972 Reprint. *QA*, pp. 183-202.

1935 "The Factor of Age in Consumption," *Market Research*, 3, 13-16.

1935 "Public Attitude toward Economic Problems," *Market Research*, 5, 13.

1936 "How Cities Differ in their Magazine Reading Habits." *Sales Management*, 38, February 15, 218-220, 262.

1936 "How Magazines Differ—As Shown by City Preferences," *Sales Management*, 38, March 1, 296, 322-325.

1937 [1935] "The Outlook for Testing Effectiveness in Advertising," *The Management Review*, 25, 3-12.

1937 "The Use of Detailed Interviews in Market Research," *Journal of Marketing*, 2, 3-8.

1937 "Psychological Aspects of Questionnaire Development," in Ferdinand C. Wheeler, Louis Bader, and J. George Frederick, eds., *The Technique of Marketing Research*. New York: McGraw-Hill, pp. 62-81, 82-91, 190-213, 267-281.

1937 "The Tactile-Kinaesthetic Perception of Fabrics with Emphasis on Their Relative Pleasantness" (with Rowena Ripin), *Journal of Applied Psychology*, 21, 198-224.

1937 "Purchase of Gasoline and Oil" (with David Craig), *Market Research*, 6.

1940 "Do People Know Why They Buy?" (Elias Smith, pseudonym, with Edward A. Suchman), *Journal of Applied Psychology*, 24, 673-684. 1955 Reprint. *LSR*, pp. 404-410.

1941 "Evaluating the Effectiveness of Advertising by Direct Interviews," *Journal of Consulting Psychology*, 5, 170-178.

1971 "The Mathematical Revolution and the Management of Marketing Communications," in William S. Hale, ed., *16th Annual Conference Proceedings*, Advertising Research Foundation.

Unpublished

1934 "Some Measurement of the Acceptance and Rejection of Rayon by Pittsburgh Women: An Experimental Study of 800 Women" (with David R. Craig). Presented on October 18 to the Rayon Subcommittee of the Committee on Textiles, American Society for Testing Materials. 30 pp.

1935 "A Study of the Psychological Factors Influencing the Drinking of Plain Milk by Adults" (with various co-authors). Report to the Milk Research Council, Inc. by the Psychological Corporation of New York. 71 pp.

1936 "Dislike of Milk Among Young People. Development of a Method to Measure and Analyze this Dislike: A Psychological Study" (with Edward Fisher Brown). Milk Research Council, Inc. and University of Newark Research Center. 63 pp.

1938 "Milk Drinking Habits of Young People: A Psychological Study" (with Edward F. Brown). Milk Research Council, Inc. and University of Newark Research Center. 100 pp.

1942 "An Interpretive Comparison of Readership Data."

9. Book Reviews and Miscellaneous Writings

1925 "Über die Berechnung der Perihelbewegung des Merkur aus der Einsteinschen Gravitationstheorie," (Ph.D. thesis in Mathematics). *Zeitschrift für Physik*, 35, 119–128.

1934 "Die NRA und der Konsument," *Der Oesterreichische Volkswirt*, 26, 479–482.

1945 "The Columbia Office of Radio Research" (with Marjorie Fiske). *The Hollywood Quarterly*, 1, 51–59.

1945 "The Office of Radio Research: A Division of the Bureau of Applied Social Research, Columbia University" (with Marjorie Fiske). *Educational and Psychological Measurement* 5, 351–361. 1946 Reprint. Albert B. Blankenship, ed., *How to Conduct Consumer and Audience Research*. New York: Harper & Row, pp. 137–150.

1948 Review, Leonard W. Doob, *Public Opinion and Propaganda. Public Opinion Quarterly*, 12, 496–498.

1949 "*The American Soldier*: An Expository Review," *Public Opinion Quarterly*, 13, 377–404.

1957 Review, S. M. Lipset, M. Trow, and J. S. Coleman, *Union Democracy*, *Public Opinion Quarterly*, 21, 212–214.

1960 Review, Hans Zeisel, Harry Kalven Jr., and Bernard Buchholz, *Delay in the Court*, *Public Opinion Quarterly*, 24, 694–700.

1963 "Sociological Aspects of Planning" (with Jane Z. Hauser), *International Social Science Council Information*, 2, 82–88.

1964 "Social Sciences Information Services: Progress Report on a Survey" (with Jack Ferguson), *American Behavioral Scientist*, 7, 20–22.

1968 "Preface," in Yvon Bourdet, ed., *Otto Bauer et la Revolution*. Paris: EDI (Etudes et Documentation Internationales), pp. 7–8.

1973 "Motivational Conflicts Engendered by the Ongoing Discussion of Cigarette Smoking" (with Alan S. Meyer and Lucy M. Friedman), in William L. Dunn, Jr., ed., *Smoking Behavior: Motives and Incentives*. Washington, D.C.: W. H. Winston and Sons, pp. 243–254.

Unpublished

1940 "A Study of Giving to the Federation" (with Hans Zeisel). Federation for the Support of Jewish Philanthropic Societies. 68 pp.

1945 "Preface," in Marjorie Fiske, C. Wright Mills et al., *Research Activity in the (New York) Department of Labor*, pp. 1–16.

1949 "The Psychological and Sociological Implications of Economic Planning in Norway" (with Allen H. Barton et al.). Oslo: Skrivemaskinstua, Universitets Studentkontor. 90 pp.

1958 "Social Research in Poland." 22 pp.

1967 "Occupational Problems of Young People." 48 pp.

1974 "An Evaluation of the Pretrial Service Agency of the Vera Institute for Criminal Justice." New York: Vera Institute for Criminal Justice.

PUBLICATIONS ABOUT
PAUL F. LAZARSFELD:
A SELECTED BIBLIOGRAPHY

David L. Sills

It is difficult in April 1979 to assemble a useful bibliography of works about Lazarsfeld, for two reasons. In the first place, only a brief span of time has elapsed since his sudden illness and death in August 1976. At that time, it seemed to his associates that he was still in midcareer. Several intellectual biographies are now in preparation, but it is premature to cite them here.

In the second place, Lazarsfeld's intellectual impact upon his contemporaries and his students throughout his life was immediate: much of his most important work was done in close collaboration with others, and his ideas were for this and other reasons absorbed very quickly into the mainstream of social research— often without reflection, often without attribution. As Raymond Boudon noted, many of Lazarsfeld's ideas have become so familiar that "hardly anyone bothers to attribute their paternity to him" (1976, p. 7). This process has been described by Robert K. Merton as "a pattern of 'obliteration of the source of ideas or findings by their incorporation in currently accepted knowledge'—obliteration by incorporation, or OBI, for short" (cf. Robert K. Merton, *Social Theory and Social Structure*, pp. 27-28, 35-38, in the 1968 edition). The fact that Lazarsfeld's ideas were subjected to the process of OBI will provide a challenge to future intellectual historians and sociologists of science, who will need to trace the assimilation of his ideas into the writings of his contemporaries and successors. However, the contemporary bibliographer is able to find comparatively few published descriptions of the transmission of this influence. Immediate acceptance is a tribute to a scholar, but a source of frustration for a biographer or a bibliographer.

Nevertheless, there is a sufficient number of useful publications for them to be listed here. Together with many of the articles in this *Festschrift*—particularly those by Bernard Bailyn, Charles Y. Glock, Marie Jahoda, Robert K. Merton, Ann K. Pasanella, Hanan C. Selvin, and Hans Zeisel—they will provide the reader with a substantial amount of information about the life and ideas of Lazarsfeld.

Barton (1979), Coleman (1979), and Sills (1979) are attempts by three of Lazarsfeld's students to describe the nature of his impact upon social research. Lipset (1955), Lipset (1979), Morrison (1978), Rosenmayr (1962), and Zeisel (1968) provide illuminating glimpses of different phases of Lazarsfeld's career. Lazarsfeld (1962) and Lazarsfeld (1968) are autobiographies. J. S. Barton (1977) is a bibliography of the Bureau of Applied Social Research that is a useful supplement to the bibliography of Lazarsfeld's writings prepared by Paul Neurath and published in this volume. The only obituaries included—of the many that were published shortly after Lazarsfeld's death—are those that have a special interest. Substantive publications, no matter how directly based they are on Lazarsfeld's work, are not included.

Abrams, Mark 1977 Social Research and Market Research: The Case of Paul Lazarsfeld. *Journal of the Market Research Society* (U.K.) 19, no. 1:12–17. A review of Lazarsfeld's contributions to market research.

Barton, Allen H. 1976 Paul F. Lazarsfeld: 1901–1976. *The Bureau Reporter* 23, no. 1:1–2. An obituary by the director of the Bureau of Applied Social Research, Columbia University, which was founded by Lazarsfeld in 1937.

Barton, Allen H. 1979 Paul Lazarsfeld and the Invention of the University Applied Social Research Institute. Unpublished manuscript. Scheduled for publication by Schenckman in a book edited by Burkart Holzner and Jiri Nehnevajsa, tentatively entitled *Organizing for Social Research.*

Barton, Judith S. (compiler) 1977 Bureau of Applied Social Research, Columbia University: Bibliography From Its Founding in 1937 to Its Closing in 1977. Mimeo. New York: The Bureau. To be published by Clearwater Publishing Company, New York. Based upon the Bureau's files, now located in Lehman Library at the School of International Affairs, Columbia University. The bibliography includes many reports and other publications by Lazarsfeld, and hundreds of reports and publications by his students and associates, many of which were written under his direction or influenced by his ideas. Included is a list of 128 Columbia University doctoral dissertations that were completed during the years 1943–1977, a majority of them by Lazarsfeld's students. The unpublished research reports of the Bureau were published in microfiche by Clearwater Publishing Company in 1979.

Blecha, Paul; Gmoser, Rupert; and Kienzl, Heinz 1976 Paul Lazarsfeld. *Journal für angewandte Sozialforschung* 16, no. 3:1. An obituary.

Boudon, Raymond 1972 An Introduction to Lazarsfeld's Philosophical Papers. Pages 411–427 in Paul F. Lazarsfeld (editor), *Qualitative Analysis: Historical and Critical Essays.* Boston: Allyn & Bacon. By one of Lazarsfeld's leading French collaborators. First published in French in 1970 as the preface to Lazarsfeld's *Philosophie des Sciences Sociales.*

Boudon, Raymond 1976 Un marginal devenu un classique: Paul Lazarsfeld. *Société française de soçiologie, Bulletin* 3, no. 8:5–7. An obituary article that was first published in *Le Monde.*

Capecchi, Vittorio 1978 Paul F. Lazarsfeld: A Link Between American and European Methodology. *Quality and Quantity* 12:239-254. A useful summary of Lazarsfeld's trans-Atlantic activities. Contains a number of errors in the details of his life in the United States.

Coleman, James S. 1972 Paul Lazarsfeld's Work in Survey Research and Mathematical Sociology. Pages 395-409 in Paul F. Lazarsfeld (editor), *Qualitative Analysis: Historical and Critical Essays*. Boston: Allyn & Bacon. By Lazarsfeld's student and leading successor in the field of mathematical sociology.

Coleman, James S. 1978 Lazarsfeld, Paul F. In volume 1, pages 505-507, *International Encyclopedia of Statistics*, William H. Kruskal and Judith M. Tanur (editors). New York: Free Press. A biographical article that emphasizes Lazarsfeld's contributions to mathematical sociology.

Coleman, James S. 1979 Paul F. Lazarsfeld: The Substance and Style of His Work. Unpublished manuscript. Presented at the meetings of the Eastern Sociological Society in New York City in March 1979. Scheduled for publication in a book on eight of the makers of American sociology, edited by Matilda White Riley and Robert K. Merton, *Sociological Traditions From Generation to Generation*, Norwood, New Jersey: Ablex Publishing Corporation

Freund, Michael 1978 Sociography: The Marienthal Story. *Austria Today* 3: 55-57. A discussion of the research that led to the publication in 1933 of *Marienthal*, by Marie Jahoda, Paul F. Lazarsfeld, and Hans Zeisel, including a brief description of plans for a restudy of Marienthal. Includes photographs of Jahoda, Lazarsfeld, and the village of Marienthal.

Girard, Alain 1976 Eloge de Paul F. Lazarsfeld. *Revue française de sociologie* 17, no. 3:379-382. The text of the citation read on the occasion of Lazarsfeld's receiving an honorary doctorate from the Sorbonne in 1972, published as an obituary notice.

Gitlin, Marc 1978 Media Sociology: The Dominant Paradigm. *Theory and Society* 6, no. 2:205-253.

Lazarsfeld, Paul F. 1962 Interviews with Paul F. Lazarsfeld. *Oral History*. A transcript of interviews on file at the office of the Oral History Project, Columbia University. Contains both autobiographical material and comments upon his work and his associates.

Lazarsfeld, Paul F. 1968 An Episode in the History of Social Research: A Memoir. *Perspectives in American History* 2:270-337. An autobiography. This issue of *Perspectives in American History* was also published in 1969 as *The Intellectual Migration: Europe and America, 1930-1960*, Donald Fleming and Bernard Bailyn (editors). Cambridge, Mass.: Harvard University Press.

Lipset, Seymour M. 1955 The Department of Sociology. Chapter 13 in *Columbia University—History of the Faculty of Political Science*. Bicentennial Series. New York: Columbia Univ. Press. Includes details about Lazarsfeld's appointment at Columbia and his establishment of the Bureau of Applied Social Research.

Lipset, Seymour M. 1979 Some Personal Notes for a History of the Department of Sociology of Columbia University. Unpublished manuscript. Chiefly about the experience of being a junior colleague of Lazarsfeld. Scheduled for publication in 1979 by Irvington Publishers in a book edited by Robert B. Smith and Peter K. Manning.

Martinelli, Alberto 1963–1964 Teoria e metodologia nell' opera di Paul Lazarsfeld. Unpublished Ph.D. dissertation, Universita Commerciale L. Bocconi (Italy).

Mills, C. Wright 1972 Abstract Empiricism. Pages 428–440 in Paul F. Lazarsfeld (editor), *Qualitative Analysis: Historical and Critical Essays.* Boston: Allyn & Bacon. A well-known criticism of Lazarsfeld's work. Reprinted in part from Mills' *The Sociological Imagination* (1959).

Morrison, David E. 1976 Paul Lazarsfeld: The Biography of an Institutional Innovator. Unpublished Ph.D. dissertation, University of Leicester (U.K.). Based in part upon personal interviews with Lazarsfeld and his associates. A revised version is being prepared for publication.

Morrison, David E. 1978 Kultur and Culture: The Case of Theodor W. Adorno and Paul F. Lazarsfeld. *Social Research* 45:331–355. An account of Lazarsfeld's complex relationship with a leading member of the Frankfort School who worked at the Princeton Office of Radio Research in the late 1930s, directing research on the audiences of serious music broadcasts.

Oberschall, Anthony 1978 Paul F. Lazarsfeld and the History of Empirical Social Research. *Journal of the History of the Behavioral Sciences* 14:199–206. A review of Lazarsfeld's efforts to locate the European origins of empirical social research.

Pollak, Michael 1979 Paul F. Lazarsfeld: Fondateur d'une multinationale scientifique. *Actes de la recherche en sciences sociales* 25:45–59. Contains descriptions, heavily couched in marketing metaphors, of Lazarsfeld's work both in Vienna and in New York, with an emphasis upon his establishment of trans-Atlantic ties.

Rosenmayr, Leopold 1962 *Geschichte der Jugendforschung in Oesterreich: 1914–1931.* Vienna: Oesterreichische Institute für Jugendkunde. See chapter 5, "Die Systematische Anwendung soziologischer Gesichtspunkte und Methoden in der Jugendforschung: Paul F. Lazarsfeld."

Sills, David L. 1969 Review of Donald Fleming and Bernard Bailyn (editors), *The Intellectual Migration: Europe and America, 1930–1960. Public Opinion Quarterly* 33:510–512. Largely devoted to a review of Lazarsfeld's essay, "An Episode in the History of Social Research: A Memoir."

Sills, David L. 1976 Paul Lazarsfeld . . . "He Taught Us What Sociology Is— or Should Be." *Columbia Today* December: 41–42. The recollections of life with Lazarsfeld at Columbia in the 1950s, by a former student.

Sills, David L. 1979 Lazarsfeld, Paul F. In Volume 18, *International Encyclopedia of the Social Sciences:* Biographical Supplement, David L. Sills (editor). New York: Free Press. A biographical article that reviews Lazarsfeld's life and attempts to assess his importance in the social sciences. Published in a 1979 supplementary volume to the *Encyclopedia.*

Stehr, Nico et al. 1979 *Issues in the Development of Sociological Knowledge.* Edmonton: Univ. of Alberta Press. Contains "Conversations with P. F. Lazarsfeld," a transcript of a long interview with Lazarsfeld conducted several months before his death. First published in German in *Kölner Zeitschrift für Soziologie und Sozialpsychologie* in 1976.

Stoetzel, Jean 1976 Paul F. Lazarsfeld 1901–1976. *International Social Science Journal* 28, no. 4:833–834. An obituary.

Zeisel, Hans 1968 L'école viennoise des recherches de motivation. *Revue française de sociologie* 9, no. 1:3–12. Describes the psychological work of Lazarsfeld's Vienna research center.

Zeisel, Hans. 1969 Der Anfang moderner Sozialforschung in Österreich: Die Wirtschaftspsychologische Forschungsstelle, 1925–1938. Pages 43–46 in Leopold Rosenmayr and Sigurd Höllinger (editors), *Soziologie in Österreich.* Vienna: Verlag Hermann Bohlaus. A history of Lazarsfeld's Vienna research center.

Zeisel, Hans 1976–1977 In Memoriam: Paul F. Lazarsfeld 1901–1976. *Public Opinion Quarterly* 40, no. 4:556–557. An obituary by a life-long friend and colleague.

INDEX

INDEX OF NAMES

Abel, Theodore, 118
Abrams, Mark, 212
Adler, Alfred, 10–11, 232
Adler, Friedrich, 10
Akenson, Donald H., 322, 336
Allison, J., 149, 152
Allport, Gordon W., 245–46, 251, 255–58
Alpert, Harry, 34
Altmann, Franz, 18
Alves, Wayne, 186
Anděl, Jiri, 97
Andersen, Charles J., 342, 362
Anderson, C. D., 145, 152–53
Anderson, T. W., 82–97
Ando, A., 73, 81
Andrews, Frank M., 238, 244
Angell, Robert C., 39, 295
Antin, Mary, 277, 281
Arrow, Kenneth J., 152, 153, 155
Arthur, C. J., 208
Astin, Alexander, 222, 229
Astin, Helen S., 334–35, 338
Atkinson, R. C., 138, 145, 152

Babbie, Earl, 33
Bacon, Francis, 189
Bailyn, Bernard, 9, 16–18, 34, 280
Bakan, David, 242
Barber, Bernard, 186
Bartlett, M. S., 82, 92, 97
Barton, Allen, 45
Barzun, Jacques, 19, 21
Bauer, Otto, 13
Baxter, Richard, 279
Bayer, Alan E., 334–35, 338
Beaver, R. J., 140, 152
Becker, G. M., 148, 152
Becker, Howard, 223, 227, 229
Bell, Daniel, 189

Ben-David, Joseph, 361
Bendix, Reinhard, 64, 336–37
Bennett, Nicholas, 303, 315
Benney, Mark, 212, 215–17, 219,228–29
Benson, Lee, 189–209
Bentzel, Ragnar, 239–40
Berelson, Bernard, 35,, 82, 97, 215, 229–30, 302, 315, 356, 361
Berger, Morroe, 118
Berk, Richard, 186
Berlin, Isaiah, 3, 9
Bernard, Jessie, 337–38
Bernert, Christopher, 232, 238
Berthoff, Rowland, 280
Bickel, P. J., 338
Billingsley, Patrick, 82, 97
Blalock, A. D., 117–18
Blalock, H. M., Jr., 75, 78, 80–81, 117–118, 244
Blau, Peter, 161–62, 170–72, 175, 237, 242, 336, 339–363
Block, H. D., 138, 140, 153
Blumer, Herbert, 247, 258
Bohrnstedt, G. W., 81
Bonjean, C., 247, 259
Borgatta, E. F., 81
Bose, Christine A., 186
Boudon, Raymond, 6–9, 17, 39, 46, 51–64, 117
Bower, G. H., 138, 145, 152
Bower, Robert, 33
Bradley, R. A., 140, 144–45, 153
Braginsky, B. M., 288, 296
Braginsky, D. D., 288, 296
Braida, L. D., 146, 153
Bremner, Robert H., 288, 297
Bridge, James H., 281
Broadbent, D. E., 146, 153
Brody, David, 281

Brooke, Joel I., 42–43, 45–47
Broom, Leonard, 46, 259
Brown, Evan L., 362
Bryson, Lyman, 316
Bühler, Charlotte, 4–5, 10–12
Bühler, Karl, 4, 10–12
Burke, C. J., 140, 144, 153
Burton, Roger V., 258–59
Bush, R. R., 147, 153, 155–57

Calderwood, Ann, 338
Campbell, Angus, 242, 296
Campbell, Donald T., 116–17, 246, 259
Cantril, Hadley, 34
Caplovitz, David, 232
Caplow, Theodore, 229
Cardona, Elizabeth de, 303, 315
Carnap, Rudolf, 4, 11, 13
Carleton, Sir Dudley, 269, 280
Carr-Saunders, A. M., 350, 361
Carter, Lewis F., 244
Carterette, E. C., 156
Cartter, Allan M., 335, 337–38, 346, 361
Catlin, J., 147, 153, 157
Chakrabarti, S. K., 138, 153
Chalmers, W. H., 209
Chipman, J. S., 148, 153
Choules, John Overton, 280
Cibois, P., 64
Clark, Burton R., 223, 229
Clarke, F. R., 145, 153
Clayton, K. N., 117
Cochran, William G., 236, 242
Cohen, Wilbur J., 288, 297
Cole, Donald B., 281
Coleman, James S., 3, 29, 35, 44–45, 47, 98–118, 143, 153, 210, 221, 229, 242
Conway, Alan, 281
Coombs, C. H., 148, 153
Corbin, R., 142, 150, 153
Cottle, Thomas J., 221, 229
Cottrell, Leonard S., 46, 259
Cournand, André, 19
Crashaw, William, 268
Cronbach, Lee J., 46
Crothers, E. J., 138, 145, 152
Cullen, John B., 339–363
Curnow, P. F., 145, 157

Curtis, Alberta, 35

Davis, James A., 242
Davis, Kingsley, 234
Debreu, G., 141, 145, 151, 153
Decker, L., 145, 156
DeGroot, M. H., 148, 152
Demerath, Nicholas Jay III, 234
Deming, William E., 235, 242
Demos, John, 227, 229
Deutsch, Karl, 314–15
Deutscher, Irwin, 247, 250, 256, 259
Diaconis, Persi, 82
Diamond, Sigmund, 263–281
DiRenzo, G., 259
Donne, John, 264
Doreian, Patrick, 45, 47
Drake, Elizabeth, 217
Duberman, Martin, 223, 229
Duffy, John A., 362
Duncan, Otis Dudley, 81, 237, 242, 336, 358, 361
Durkheim, Emile, 8, 23, 52, 56, 62, 63, 233, 242, 288, 339, 361
Durlach, N. I., 146, 153

Easton, Loyd D., 207–8
Edgell, S. E., 145, 153
Egan, J. P., 145, 154
Ehrlich, June Sachar, 212, 219
Eisenberg, Philip, 284, 295–96
Eisler, H., 150, 154
Ekman, Paul, 314, 316
Elderton, Marion, 297
Elliott, Phillip, 302, 315
Elsaesser, Thomas, 34
Engels, Friedrich, 192, 195–96, 198–200, 202–6, 208–9
Engstrand, R. D., 145, 154
Erickson, Charlotte, 281
Erikson, Kai, 8
Estes, W. K., 145
Etzioni, Amitai, 361

Faia, Michael, 334
Fantino, E., 150, 154
Fararo, T. J., 63–64, 138, 143–44, 154, 157

Farr, Grant M., 356, 362
Fay, R., 133
Feuer, Lewis S., 208
Field, Harry, 33
Fisher, Franklin M., 81
Fisher, R. A., 140, 154
Fiske, Marjorie, 35, 212, 231
Fleming, Donald, 9, 34
Freedman, Lawrence Z., 296
Freedman, Ronald, 311, 315
Freeman, Richard B., 328, 337
Freud, Sigmund, 3, 10–11, 232
Frey, Frederick, 300, 302, 311–13, 316
Friedman, M. P., 156
Friedrich, Carl, 210–11
Frisch, Ragnar, 80
Fromm, Erich, 211
Fulton, Oliver, 325, 337
Furniss, W. Todd, 361

Gamson, Zelda, 222, 231
Gans, Herbert, 294
Garrett, Karen, 186
Gaudet, Hazel, 34–35, 82, 97, 230, 284, 295
Geer, Blanche, 223, 227, 229
Geertz, Clifford, 303, 316
Geisler, W. S., 145, 153
Georgescu-Roegen, N., 143, 154
Gerbner, George, 317
Glazer, Nathan, 211, 231, 234, 241
Glock, Charles Y., 23–36, 47, 210, 228–29, 234, 241, 299, 301, 316
Goldberger, A. S., 81
Golding, Peter, 302, 315
Goldsen, Rose K., 35
Goodchilds, J. D., 295
Goode, William J., 345, 350, 361
Goodman, Leo A., 82–83, 89, 92, 97, 116, 118, 119–137
Goodman, Nelson, 247, 255, 259
Goody, Jack, 306, 316–17
Graham, Patricia Alberg, 332, 337–38
Grambsch, Paul V., 346, 362
Grant, Gerald, 220, 224–25, 229
Greeley, Andrew, 337
Green, D. M., 138, 146–47, 156
Greeno, J. G., 145, 149, 154, 156

Gregg, Lee W., 76, 81
Gross, Edward, 346, 362
Gross, George R., 356, 362
Gross, Larry P., 317
Gruen, Victor, 12
Guddat, Kurt H., 207–8
Guilford, J. P., 144, 154
Gulliksen, H., 144, 154
Gumbel, E. J., 140, 154
Gurevitch, Michael, 314, 316
Gusfield, Joseph, 222, 229, 231
Guttman, Louis, 137

Hagstrom, Warren, 240, 242, 244
Halberstam, Aron, 42–43, 46
Halldin, C., 143, 154
Hammel, E. A., 338
Handlin, Oscar, 281
Hansen, Bent, 239, 240
Hargens, Lowell L., 356, 362
Harris, Louis, 228
Harrison, Randall, 314, 316
Hartmann, Heinz, 4
Hartshorne, H., 247, 255, 258–59
Hauser, Philip, 235
Hauser, Robert M., 242, 336
Havemann, Ernest, 35
Head, Sydney W., 315–16
Hegel, G. W., 198–200, 203–4, 206
Hempel, Carl G., 245, 250, 258–59
Henderson, James, 159, 175
Henderson, W. O., 209
Henkel, Ramon, 243
Henry, Neil W., 82, 119, 129, 136–37, 228, 230
Herrnstein, R. J., 150, 154–55
Herzog, Herta, 34
Hevner, K., 144, 155
Hill, R. J., 247, 259
Hirschi, Travis, 235, 237–38, 241, 243
Hodge, M. H., 145, 155
Hodge, Robert W., 336, 342
Hoeffding, W., 153
Hogben, Lancelot, 243
Hohle, R. H., 144, 155
Hollingshead, August B., 178, 186
Holman, E., 140
Holzner, Burkart, 45

Hopkins, J. W., 155
Horney, Karen, 249, 259
Hornik, Robert C., 312, 316
Hughes, Everett C., 210–11, 213, 225, 229, 350, 362
Humman, Norman P., 45, 47
Hunt, Richard N., 208
Hutchins, Robert, 213–14, 218
Hyman, Herbert, 35, 196, 234, 243, 282–298
Hyman, Richard, 208, 210–11

Indow, T., 138, 155
Inkeles, Alex, 311, 316
Innis, Harold A., 314, 316

Jaeckel, Martin, 45, 47
Jahoda, Marie, 3–9, 10, 34, 211, 284–85, 294–95
James, William, 251, 259
Jencks, Christopher, 229
Jones, Maldwyn Allen, 264, 280

Kadane, Joseph B., 80–81
Kanal, L., 147, 155
Karamata, J., 155
Karlin, S., 153, 155
Karlsson, G., 46
Kato, Hidetoshi, 305, 316
Katz, Elihu, 35, 220, 229, 299–316
Keayne, Robert, 270, 280
Kelman, Herbert C., 227, 229
Kendall, Patricia L., 35, 51, 63, 240, 243, 315, 340–41, 362
Kandel, Denise B., 99, 116, 118
King, Bert, 41
Kingsbury, Susan M., 380
Kinsey, Alfred L., 236, 243
Klausner, Samuel, 33
Knight, Max, 15
Koch, S., 259
Kohlberg, Lawrence, 218
Komarovsky, Mirra, 47, 284, 295
Korman, Gerd, 209
Kornhauser, William, 234
Krantz, D. H., 138, 148, 155

Lachman, J., 158
Ladd, Everett, 319–338
Lagneau, J., 64
Lamperti, J., 147, 155
Lander, Bernard, 238–39, 243
Landes, David S., 280
LaPiere, Richard, 247, 250, 256–57, 259
Lasswell, Harold, 211
Lazarsfeld, Paul F., See Subject Index
Lazarsfeld, Robert, 178
Leavy, Stanley A., 296
Lebergott, Stanley, 296
Lécuyer, Bernard, 36
Leggett, John, 293–94
Lerner, Daniel, 34–35, 302, 312–15, 317
Lewis, I. M., 306, 317
Lewis, Richard, 42
Light, Donald, 210
Likert, Rensis, 33
Lipset, Seymour Martin, 29, 35, 64, 220, 234, 241, 319–338
Locke, John, 266
Lombardo, Antonio, 271–72
Lorenz, Konrad, 11
Love, Ruth, 45, 47
Loveland, D. H., 150, 155
Lowenthal, Leo, 212, 230, 234
Luce, R. Duncan, 138–157
Lynd, Helen, 211
Lynd, Robert, 4, 211

Maccoby, Michael, 218
Madow, W., 153
Malmquist, S., 46
Manheimer, Dean, 33
Margulies, Rebecca Z., 339–363
Markovic, Mihailo, 207
Marley, A. A. J., 138, 140, 142, 150, 153, 156
Marschak, J., 138, 140, 148, 152–53, 156
Marshall, T. H., 276, 281
Marx, Karl, 189–209, 226, 232
Mason, Edward, 211
Mattelart, Armand, 303, 305, 317
May, M. A., 247, 255, 258–59
McCarthy, Joseph, 213–17, 219, 226
McCormack, Thelma, 305, 317

McDonald, Douglas, 42–43, 46
McDougall, William, 245, 259
McFadden, D., 140, 143, 156
MacIver, Robert M., 259
McLemore, S. O., 247, 259
McLuhan, Marshall, 317
McMurey, Robert H., 298
McPhee, William N., 35, 215, 229, 315
Mead, George H., 250, 256, 259
Meissner, Werner, 239
Melody, William H., 317
Merivale, Herman, 265–66, 280
Menzel, Herbert, 35, 240, 243
Merton, Robert K., 4, 19–22, 29–31, 37, 43, 45–46, 63, 99, 118, 190, 207–8, 210–12, 220, 226, 228, 230, 239, 243, 250, 259, 312, 316, 345, 350, 362
Meyer, E., 252
Meyersohn, Rolf, 212, 315
Miciak, Michael, 232
Miliband, Ralph, 208
Miller, D. C., 247, 260
Miller, G. A., 146, 156
Miller, Perry, 280
Mills, C. Wright, 3, 6, 35, 211
Mitchell, Robert, 33
Moeller, G., 145, 154
Moore, Wilbert E., 350, 362
Morgan, B. J. T., 145, 156
Morgenstern, Oskar, 13
Morlock, Laura, 333, 338
Morrison, Denton E., 243
Mosel, James N., 306, 317
Mueller, Eva, 293

Nakatani, L. H., 143, 147, 156–57
Namboodiri, N. Kischman, 244
Nasatir, David, 234
Navarick, D., 150, 154
Nehnevajsa, Jiri, 45
Neurath, Otto, 11–13
Neurath, Paul M., 317, 365–387
Newcomb, Theodore, 223, 230
Newcomer, Mabel, 337
Newell, Allen, 81
Nicholls, William L., 33, 234, 241
Nicosia, Francesco M., 229
Nordenstreng, Kaarle, 303, 317

Oberschall, Anthony R., 36, 158–175
O'Connell, J. W., 338
Odum, Howard A., 25, 34
Ogburn, W. F., 294
Olkin, I., 153
Olson, David E., 317
Olson, Mancur, 60, 64

Page, Charles, 118
Pap, Arthur, 245, 248, 260
Park, Robert E., 213, 227
Pasanella, Ann K., 9, 37–47, 243
Pasley, Fred D., 280
Pelz, Donald C., 238, 244
Peterson, William, 241
Petrowski, William R., 342, 359, 362
Pilsworth, Michael, 300, 315
Plant, James S., 297
Polanyi, Karl, 12
Pollack, I., 145, 155, 156
Pool, Ithiel de Sola, 313, 316–17
Pope, Liston, 337
Pory, John, 269, 280
Powell, David, 310, 317
Pye, L. W., 317

Quandt, Richard, 159, 175
Quetelet, Adolphe, 21

Raiffa, Howard, 150, 156
Rao, P. V., 140, 152
Reader, George C., 35, 243
Reginall, John, 34
Reiss, A. J., 361
Reitz, Jeffrey G., 7, 9, 42–43, 46–47
Restle, F., 145–46, 150–51, 156
Richards, Dickinson, 19
Riesman, David, 3, 210–231, 336
Riley, Matilda White, 137
Ringer, Benjamin E., 299, 315, 317
Robinson, John, 247, 260
Robinson, William S., 241, 244
Rogers, Everett M., 302, 311–312, 317
Roose, Kenneth D., 342, 362
Roper, Elmo, 214–15, 227–28
Rosenberg, Morris, 35, 63, 158, 175, 230, 241, 243, 245–60
Rosenbloom, Gerald, 281

Rossi, Alice S., 208, 336, 338
Rossi, Peter H., 29, 33, 35, 176–186, 336, 342
Rousseau, 198, 278
Rowntree, B. Seebohm, 297–98
Ruhter, Wayne E., 337
Rumelhart, D. L., 145, 156
Runciman, W. G., 63
Rundquist, Edward A., 297
Russo, J. E., 148, 157

Sanford, Nevitt, 231
Sattath, S., 151, 156
Saville, John, 208
Schad, Suzanne, 36
Schegloff, Emmanuel, 234
Schichor, David, 362
Schiller, Herbert I., 302, 305
Schramm, Wilbur, 302, 316–17
Schueller, G. K., 315, 317
Sells, Lucy, 329
Selvin, Hanan, 34, 232–244
Selznick, Philip, 234
Senior, Clarence, 35
Sewell, William H., 38, 46, 294
Shaman, Paul, 82
Shapiro, Clara, 228
Shaver, Philip, 247, 260
Shaw, M. E., 247, 260
Sheatsley, Paul, 211
Sheppard, Harold, 294
Shils, Edward, 211
Shipley, E. F., 143, 146, 156–57
Shinar, Dov, 300
Shoemaker, F. Floyd, 317
Sieber, Samuel, 31–32, 36
Siegel, Paul M., 336, 342, 362
Sills, David L., 29, 35, 299, 315, 317, 389–393
Silver, Hilary, 339
Simmel, Georg, 340, 362
Simon, Herbert A., 51, 63, 65–81
Singh, J., 140, 157
Skinner, B. F., 247, 260
Skvoretz, J., 138, 144, 157
Sletto, Raymond F., 297
Smith, Adam, 264–65, 280
Smith, David H., 311, 316

Smith, E. E., 295
Smith, John, 267, 269, 280
Sowell, Thomas, 337
Spivak, Sydney S., 31, 36
Stanton, Frank, 212, 231
Star, Shirley A., 228–29
Steele, J. M., 157
Steinberg, Stephen, 326, 337
Stern, Bernhard J., 213, 231
Sternberg, S., 147, 157
Stevens, Lawrence F., 322, 336
Stouffer, Samuel, 51, 119, 129, 131, 137, 212, 214, 231, 237, 244, 284, 295–97
Strauss, Anselm, 223, 227, 229
Strauss, Richard, 10
Struik, Dirk J., 209
Stycos, J. M., 315
Sullivan, Eugenia, 288, 297
Sun, T. H., 315
Suppes, Patrick, 46, 138, 140, 147, 153, 155–57
Svenning, Lynne, 317

Takeshita, John Y., 315
Tambiah, S. J., 318
Tanur, Judith M., 244
Tawney, R. H., 293, 298
Terry, M. E., 144–45, 153
Thielens, Wagner, Jr., 29, 35, 210, 217–18, 230, 233, 243, 346, 362
Thomas, Brinley, 280
Thompson, W. A., Jr., 140, 157
Thorold, James E., 280
Thurstone, L. L., 140–41, 144, 150, 157
Tilly, Charles, 280
Tippett, L. H. C., 140, 154
Toby, Jackson, 119, 129, 131, 137
Tocqueville, Alexis de, 52, 56, 62–63, 192, 195, 197, 199, 208
Townsend, J. J., 146, 157
Treisman, M., 147, 157
Tresca, Carlo, 274
Trilling, Lionel, 19
Trow, Martin, 29, 35, 220, 231, 234–35, 325, 337
Tukey, J. W., 144, 154
Tversky, A., 138–39, 145–46, 148, 150–51, 155, 156

Tunstall, Jeremy, 303, 318
Tyler, Lyon Gardiner, 280

Varis, Tapio, 303, 317
Veblen, Thorstein, 337
Villiers, P. A. de, 150, 154
Vogelin, Erich, 4

Wagenaar, W. A., 145, 157
Walter, Bruno, 10
Ware, Caroline F., 281
Weber, D. L., 146, 156
Weber, Max, 5, 252, 260
Wedell, E. G., 300, 316
Weinman, Janice, 43, 46
Weiss, Carol, 42–43
Weissman, David, 249, 252, 260
West, Patricia S., 35
Whitehead, Alfred North, 278
Whyte, William F., 231
Wicker, Allen, 256, 260
Wilensky, Harold, 38, 46, 294
Wilson, P. A., 350, 361

Williams, Raymond, 310, 318
Windell, P., 138, 144, 157
Wirth, Louis, 34
Wittgenstein, Ludwig, 11
Wold, Herman, 46, 232, 239, 242, 244
Wolfe, Katherine M., 212, 231
Wright, Charles R., 241, 244
Wright, J. M., 247, 260
Wright, Sewall, 78, 81

Yankelovich, Daniel, 336
Yellott, J. I., 138, 140–41, 145, 157
Young, Donald, 38
Young, P. T., 149, 157

Zawadski, Bohdan, 284, 287–88, 298
Zeisel, Hans, 10–15, 24, 34–35, 284–85, 294–95
Zeisel, Ilse, 14
Zeitlin, Maurice, 234
Zinnes, J. L., 140, 144–45, 153–54, 157
Zuckerman, Harriet, 337

INDEX OF SUBJECTS

Abilities, as dispositions, 246
Academic Freedom Survey, 213–14
Academics, American, 319–38; ethnic background of, 325, 328–29, 330–331; and McCarthyism, 213–20; religious background of, 325–28; socio-economic background of, 320–25; women among, 329, 331–36. *See also* Teacher Apprehension Study.
Acceptance mechanisms, and the choice axiom, 142–43
Accounting scheme, 158
ACLU, 217
Affirmative Action, 320, 329, 335
Aggregate data, and causal analysis, 238–40
"Aggregative variables" (Selvin and Hagstrom), 240
America, as archetypal capitalist society, 202–205
American Association for Public Opinion Research, 33
American Institute of Public Opinion, 212
"Americanism," and immigration, 274–78
American Soldier (Stouffer, *et al.*), 51–56, 62
Analytical philosophy, 11
"Analytic variables" (Lazarsfeld), 240
Animal behavior: motivations of, 11; and the "choice axiom," 149–50
Anomie, 211, 239
Anthropology, 222, 224, 304, 306
Apathy, as a result of unemployment, 5, 294n1
Applied social research, 37–39, 42; Lazarsfeld's lifelong commitment to, 37; Lazarsfeld on its relation to basic research, 38–39. *See also* Utilization.

A priori assumptions: and prior probabilities in Bayesian theory, 71, 80; and estimating equations, 77–78; and the identification problem, 68–69, 71; techniques for determining in research, 72; three principal forms of, 74–75
"Archetypal" societies, 195–96
Areal data, and problems of causal inference, 238–40
"Art of asking why," 9, 28
Asymptotic theory, 89
Atomism, 62
Austrian socialist youth movement: Lazarsfeld's role in, 4, 12–13
"Automatic science" (Simon), 75–79
Autoregressive coefficients, estimation of, 90–91
Autoregressive model, 83, 85–86; relation to Markov chain model, 87, 91–92; tests for, 94–96

Basic research, Lazarsfeld on relation to applied, 38–39. *See also* Utilization.
Bayesian statistical theory, 71, 80
Berkeley Department of Sociology, 234
Bernoulli distributions, 85
Beta learning model, 147
Biform scales, 128
Blacks: in American professoriate, 328–29; and social status ratings, 184
Boyle's Law, 242n8
Bradley-Terry model (BTL), 139, 144–45
Budget constraints, 159–60, 171; and utility functions, 161–66
Bühler Institute (Vienna), 4, 10, 12, 14
Bureau of Applied Social Research, 17, 21–22, 24–26, 36, 39, 42, 210, 211–12, 215, 220, 226, 299, 301; founding

of, 24; Lazarsfeld's role in, 26–32, 212; methodological contributions of, 28–29; as prototype, 33–34; organizational attributes of, 26–30; substantive contributions of, 26–28
Bureau of Social Science Research, 33

Capitalism, 190, 323; conflict in, 196 207; and multiculturalism, 195 96, 200, 202–7
Carnegie Commission on Higher Education, 220, 320, 326
Causal analysis, 51–52, 65–81, 115, 235; and *a priori* assumptions, 68–69, 71; and areal data, 238; and disposition concepts, 252–53; and ecological variables, 237–40; and generating models, 51–52; and the identification problem, 66–69; and interdependent systems, 239–40; and "mechanisms," 66–67, 70–74; misuses of, 75–80; and recursive systems, 239–40; and regression analysis, 344; as technology, 75
Census Bureau, 236
Center for Advanced Study in the Behavioral Sciences, 31, 214
Center for International Studies (MIT), 302
Center for the Social Sciences (Columbia), 22
Center for the Study of Leisure (University of Chicago), 212
Center for the Study of the Acts of Man (University of Pennsylvania), 32
Central limit theorem, 141
Charles's Law, 242n8
Child abuse, vignette analysis used in study of, 185
Child behavior, 5, 12
Chi-Square test, 76, 92, 122
Choice: and empirical analysis of action, 158–59; and vignette analysis, 177. *See also* Microeconomic model *and* Choice axiom.
Choice Axiom, 138–52; applications of, 143; and animal behavior, 149–50; and Beta learning model, 147; and

Constant Ratio Rule (CRR), 145–46; and discard and acceptance mechanisms, 142–43; experimental tests of, 144–50; relation to discriminable dispersion model, 140–41; and response bias model, 146–47; and "simple calculability" and "order independence," 147–48; strengths and weaknesses of, 151–52
Choice-by-elimination model, 148
"Chunk" (Hauser), 235–37
Circular reasoning: in disposition concepts, 248–49; in history of science, 248. *See also* Tautologies.
"Circumstances," and disposition concepts, 244, 250–54; determinacy of, 251–52; specification of, 253–54; types of, 250–51
Citizenship: desire for among American immigrants, 275–78; Hegel's concept of, 198; relation to class loyalties, 276
Civil liberties, 211, 215, 217, 319
Class, 276, 323, 325; compared to cultural groups, 195; compared to "economic interest groups," 194, 201, Marx's concept of, 199, Marx and Hegel's notions of the "universal," 198
Class consciousness: cultural barriers to in capitalism, 202–7; Marx's overestimation of in capitalism, 199–200. *See also* False consciousness *and* Consciousness, Marx's concept of.
Cobb-Douglas utility function, 163–66
Codification, and social inquiry, 28
Collectivities, generic attributes of, 339–41
Colonies, American: and immigration, 263–71
Columbia University, 4, 17, 19, 21–23, 30, 39, 211, 233, 332
Communality, as criterion for distinguishing between groups, 193–94
Communications research, international, 299–318; Lazarsfeld's prognosis for, 299–300, 304, 306–7, 311, 313–14; shifts in, 303. *See also* Media, broadcast.
Comparative statics, 73

Comparative studies: compared to "archetypal" studies, 196
Competition structures: and game theory, 52–60
Concordant condition (Marley), 142–43
Confidentiality, in social research, 215, 222–23
Conflict: Marx's general theory of, 190–92, 198, 200, 206; Marx's middle range theory of, 190, 192–93, 198–99, 206; Marx's theories of, 190–207; a reference group theory of, 190, 192, 196, 198, 207
"Confluence problem," 80n3
Consciousness, Marx's concept of, 196–97. *See also* False consciousness *and* Class consciousness.
Constant ratio rule (CRR), 139, 141, 145–46
Constant utility models, 147–48
Consumer behavior, and the "choice axiom," 143
Content analysis, 25
Contextual analysis, 214, 219, 339–40, 357; applied to professional schools, 340–63
Contextual effects, 242n9, 242n10, 340, 341
Contextual variable, 51, 240, 359n10
Continuous data, 96; and autoregressive processes, 85
Control, types of, 101–2. *See also* Effective control.
Control matrix, 104–6
Control variables, 359
Correlation coefficients, 76, 78–79, 233
Cosmopolitanism, 206; and television in Third World, 312
Cost-benefit analysis, extended to include social costs and benefits, 13
Cultural change, and broadcast media in Third World, 303, 306, 311–13. *See also* Media, broadcast.
Cultural groups, 194–95; and conflict in capitalism, 202–7

Darwinism: compared with Marxism, 191

Decomposition coefficient, 359n9
Deduction, 71, 161, 172–75
Delinquency, Lander's approach to: 238–40
Demand, classical theory of and the "choice axiom," 143
Demand function, 165
Demi-demi scales, 128
Demi-scales, 128
Dependent variable, 72, 78, 86, 235, 238, 241n1, 245, 344, 359n9
Descriptive studies, 28, 234; relation to explanatory studies, 236–37
Developing countries, role of broadcast media in, 299–314
Deviant cases, 223, 226, 228n10
Diminishing marginal utility (in microeconomic theory), 159, 162; and Weber-Fechner law, 116n5
Discard mechanisms, and the choice axiom, 142–43
Discrete data, and Markov chains, 83–85; Lazarsfeld's interest in, 96
Discriminable dispersion model (Thurstone), 138, 144; relation to choice axiom, 140–41
Disposition concepts, 245–58; and "circumstances," 244, 250–54; complexity of, 257–58; criticisms of, 247–54; as intervening variables, 256; Lazarsfeld's contribution to study of, 246–47, 258; passive-driving dimension of, 247, 257; and prediction, 250–54; as tautological, 247–49, 254; uses of, 254–58
Distributive justice income, vignette analysis applied to, 184–85
"Domains of aggregation," 239
Double exponential distributions, 140–41
Drives, as dispositions, 246

"Ecological fallacy," 238
Ecological studies, 237; and causal analysis, 238–40
Econometrics, 239–40, 242n7
Economic determinism, Marx's, 196–97, 200

Economic-interest groups, 194, 201
Economics, 7; and causal analysis, 65;
 and the "choice axiom," 138–39, 143,
 152
ECTA (Everyman's Contingency Table
 Analyzer), 133n1, 134n3
Edgeworth box, 171
Educational attainment, and social status
 ratings, 181–83
Educational opportunities: relation to
 social mobility, 60–62, 319–25
Effective control, in friendships, 101–2;
 estimation of, 102–4, 109–14
Elaboration formula, 28, 233, 241n1,
 357
"Empirical analysis of action" (EAA),
 158–59, 246; compared to
 microeconomic approach, 161;
 limitations of, 159
Empirical social research, 51, 233; roots
 of, 11
Empiricism, blind, 6
"Empty world assumption," 74
"End of ideology," 189
Estimating equations, 76–78
Ethical problems in social research, 39,
 219, 220–26
Ethnicity: and American immigration,
 272–78; of American professoriate,
 325, 328–31; and enmity between
 American immigrants, 273–74; and
 labor discipline, 272–78; and class
 loyalties, 203–4; and social status
 ratings, 182–84
Ethnocentricism, 206
Evolution in Marxism and Darwinism,
 191
Exchange, social: Blau's model of, 171–
 72; and choice, 158–75; compared to
 economic exchange, 162; in a federal
 agency, 161–74
Expected random utility model, 148–49
Experimentation, and specification of
 "mechanisms," 71–72
Explanatory studies, 28, 234; compared
 to descriptive studies, 236–37;
 Lazarsfeld's preference for over
 descriptive, 28
"Explication" (Lazarsfeld), 241n4

Factor analysis, 75–76, 241n5
Faculty inbreeding, 355–57
"False consciousness," 200–204
Family planning, 311
Federal Trade Commission, 225
Feedback loops, 239
Focused Interview, 28
"Forces," in Darwinism and Marxism,
 191
Ford Foundation, 31, 218, 315
Four-way contingency tables, 14, 119
Friendship: and homophily, 99; and
 marijuana use, 102–15

Game theory, 52–60
"Gap," Lazarsfeld's notion of, 38. *See
 also* Translation.
General theory, 190; compared to
 middle-range theory, 190; of conflict in
 Marx, 190–93
Generating models, 51–63, core elements
 of, 60; examples of, 52–62; and game
 theory, 52–60; advantages of, 62–63;
 and Lazarsfeld's work, 52; and
 statistical structures, 52, 62–63
Genetics, and causal analysis, 78
"Global variables" (Lazarsfeld), 240,
 340
Groups, types of, 193–95

Habits, as dispositions, 246
Harvard University, 222, 332
Hegelian thought, in Marx, 195, 197–
 201, 203–4
Higher education, 213, 319; ethical
 problems in study of, 220–26; in
 France, 56–60; growth of in U.S., 319;
 Lazarsfeld's interest in sociology of,
 213; and social mobility, 60–62, 319.
 See also Professional schools *and*
 Academics, American
History: importance for social research,
 263, 278–79
Homogeneity, and Markov chains, 93
Homophily, 99
Household social-status ratings, 179; and
 educational attainment, 181–83; and
 ethnicity, 182–84; and occupational

attainment, 181–83; and vignette analysis, 180–84
"Housestyles," of interviewing, 212–13, 215. *See also* Interviewing.
Hypothesis-testing techniques, 75

"Identification problem," 68–69; and causal analysis, 66–69
Ideology, 189–91, 202, 271–72, 274
Immigration, American, 203–4, 263–81; conservative consequences, 264, 271–78; and ethnicity, 272–78; and labor discipline, 267–78; radical consequences, 263–71; and social mobility, 268–71
Imperialism, 302
Independence models, 119–22, 126, 133n1, 134n3; compared to quasi-independence models, 124–25; restricted, 127. *See also* Quasi-independence models.
Independent variable, 72, 78–79, 235, 238, 241n1, 344, 359n9
Indifference curve, 160, 171
Induction, 71, 79
Inequality: and conflict, 191–92; and higher education, 319–20
Infinite regress, 71
"Insiderism," of small colleges, 226
Institute for Communications Research (Stanford), 302
Institute for Research in Social Behavior (Berkeley), 33
Institute for Social Science (University of North Carolina), 25
Institute for Social Science Research (UCLA), 33
Institute for Survey Research (Temple University), 33
"Integral" variables" (Selvin and Hagstrom), 240
Intention, and outcome: paradoxical relation between, in nineteenth-century American immigration, 264, 271–78; paradoxical relation between in seventeenth-century American immigration, 264–71; relation between, 264–79

Interdependent systems, 239–40
Interdisciplinary research, 7, 32
"Interest" in friendships, 100; estimation of, 104–6
Interest matrix, 104–6; for friendship pairs, 109–13; for non-friendship pairs, 113
Intervening variables, 235, 312; dispositions as, 256
"Interviewer effects," 212, 228n9
Interviewers, 218–19; scorn for, 216, 226n7
Interviewing, 14, 25, 27; dialectical, 217, 221; "house-styles" of, 212–13, 215; non-directive, 221; research program on, 212–13; and Teacher Apprehension Study, 215–20
"Irish question" (Marx), 200–2

Jews, and intellectual achievement, 325–28

Labor discipline, 272–73; and nineteenth-century American immigration, 271–78; and seventeenth-century American immigration, 267–71
Language: of different sciences, 6–7; Karl Bühler's psychological analysis of, 11–12
LaPlace distribution, 152n1
"large sample theory" (Anderson and Goodman), 89
Latent class models, 133
Latent distance models, 133
Latent structure analysis, 9, 98, 125, 178, 241n5
Latent structures, 129–30, 133, 134n7, 135n16, 135n18; and quasi-independence concept, 130; restricted, 130–32, 134n7, 135n14; unrestricted, 134n7
Latent variables, 215
"Lateral" transfer (Lazarsfeld), 43
Laws, scientific: and "mechanisms," 70–71; of qualitative structure, 71

Lazarsfeld, Paul F.: and academic freedom, 226; adjustment to United States, 6, 24; and applied research, 37–39; and Bureau of Applied Social Research, 21–22, 24–32, 36, 39, 42, 210, 212, 214; on "case" and "case history," 226; and causal analysis, 51, 65; collaboration with Robert Lynd, 4; collaboration with Robert Merton, 4, 19, 30–31; commitment to clarity of, 20, 27; on contextual analysis, 214, 339–40; and continuities in social research, 226; contributions to development of research organizations, 23–34; contributions to psychology, 8; contributions to social sciences, 3, 6, 8–9, 19, 22, 23, 226; contributions to study of dispositions, 246–47, 258; contributions to vignette analysis, 177–78; "conversion" to sociology, 20–21; and decision-making processes, 28; and discrete data, 96; on ecological and individual correlations, 241n6–242; and empirical analysis of action, 158–59, 246; on explanatory and descriptive research, 28; and the *Forschungsstelle*, 12–15; as "fox," 3–9; on historical analysis, 263, 278–79; and human motivation, 14; influence of the Bühlers on, 11–12; influence of Friedrich Adler on, 10; influence of Otto Neurath on, 13; influence on David Riesman, 211–12; influence on Herbert Simon, 51; influence on James Coleman, 98; influence on Lee Benson, 207n1; influence on Peter Rossi, 177–78; and interdisciplinary research, 7, 20, 32; involvement in Austrian socialist movement, 4, 12–13; leadership style of, 5, 212, love of coincidences, 16; main areas of investigation, 63; and *Marienthal*, 4–6, 13, 284–89; masquerading as "hedgehog," 3, 6; and mathematics, 4, 10, 20, 253; and methodology, 4–7, 9, 14, 20, 23–25, 28–31, 39, 207n1, 232–40; and model building, 96; in Offenbach's *Beautiful Helène*, 12;

personality of, 16–18, 19, 233; philosophy of research, 25; and planning of Center for Advanced Study in the Behavioral Sciences, 31; political style of, 39–40; as President of the American Sociological Association, 21, 37; professional identity of, 4, 5, 20–21; prognosis for international communications research, 299–300, 304, 306–7, 311, 313–14; proposal for "professional school for training in social research," 30–32; on relation between quantitative and qualitative research, 20; research style of, 4, 23–24, 98, 212; on revolution, 4; and socialism, 226; and sociology of higher education, 213; as teacher, 19, 29, 98; "terminological embarrassment" of, 4, 21; and the unity of the social sciences, 7; in Vienna, 10–15, vitality of, 19, 227n2; work-style of, 5

Least Squares, method of, 66, 86
Legal distinctions, and the formation of social groups, 198–200, 206
Liberalism, as a "disposition" concept, 245–46
Linear operator models, and the choice axiom, 147
Literacy, and broadcast media in Third World, 311–13
Locals and cosmopolitans, 43, 220
Logit analysis, 139
"Luce process," 141–42

Marienthal (Lazarsfeld *et al.*), 4–6, 13, 284–89. *See also* Unemployment.
Marijuana: application of 16-fold table problem to use of, 102–15; research on use of, 99
Market research, in Vienna, 13–14
Markov chains, 82–85, 94; and panel data, 82–83, 89, 93; relation to autoregressive models, 87, 91–92; tests for, 92–94
Marxism, 189–90; compared with Darwinism, 191
Mathematical sociology, 20, 98, 143
Matrix formula, 4

Maximization of utility, 159–162, 164–66, 171

McCarthyism, 213–18, 226. *See also* Teacher Apprehension Study.

"Mechanism" (Simon), 66–67; and *a priori* assumptions, 71–72; defined, 70–71; and experimentation, 71–72; related to ideas of lawfulness and reducibility, 70; specification of, 71–74; and "tangible links," 73–74; and temporal ordering, 72–73

Media, broadcast: and cultural change in developing countries, 303, 306, 311–313; in developing countries, 299–314; effects on modernization, 299, 311–313; and program output in developing countries, 306–11, 313–14; and relationship between Western and Third World cultures, 304–6, 313–14; and Western imperialism, 302

Methodology, 4–6, 20, 23–25, 28–31, 37, 215; Bureau's contribution to, 28–29; and codification, 28; and explication, 241n4; Lazarsfeld and, 4–7, 9, 14, 20, 23–25, 28–31, 39, 207n1, 232–40; qualitative, 20, 207n1, 218–220; quantitative, 4, 20, 207n1

Microeconomic model, 159; application to social interaction, 160–74; compared with empirical analysis of action, 161; outline of, 159–61. *See also* Exchange, social.

Middle-range theory, 190; of conflict in Marx, 190, 192–93, 196, 201, 206; of reference groups and conflict, 190, 192, 196, 198, 207

Model building, PFL's preference for, 96

Mode of production, 191–92; as Marx's basic concept, 192–93, 198, 200

Modernization, and broadcast media, 299, 302–3, 311, 314

Motivations, and social research, 11, 14. *See also* Disposition concepts *and* Purposive action, models of.

Mover-stayer model, 120

Multicultural society: America as, 202–7; capitalism and, 195–97, 200–7; defined, 195–96

Multinomial distributions, and Markov chains, 85, 93

Multivariate analysis, 23, 158

Mutual effects, 98, 114. *See also,* 16-fold table problem.

M-way contingency tables, 119, 125

National Opinion Research Center (NORC), 33, 181, 211–14, 219, 227n7, 228n9, 289–91

National Science Foundation, 45, 331

News media, in Third World, 304

Nobel laureates, religious background of, 327

No-fault divorce, vignette analysis used in study of, 185

Non-study, 237

Normalized coefficients, 78–79

Occupational attainment, and social status ratings, 181–83

Oesterreichische Wirtschaftpsychologische Forschungsstelle, 12–15

Office of Education, 43, 331

Office of Naval Research, 39, 41, 44

Office of Radio Research (Princeton), 24, 26, 29

Operant conditioning, 149

Opinion formation, 27

Order independence, and the "choice axiom," 147–48

"Overinvestment effects," 56–60

Panel analysis, 9, 28; and homophily, 99; and Markov chains, 82–83, 89, 93

Panel surveys, 82, 215

Participant observation, 25

Particularistic values, 119, 129, 130

Passive-driving dimension, of dispositions, 247, 257

Path analysis, 65, 78, 242n7, 344

Path coefficients, 76, 78

Patriotism, among nineteenth-century American immigrants, 274–78

People's Choice, The (Lazarsfeld *et al.*), 82

Personal influence, 212, 220

Personality characteristics, as dispositions, 246

Phlogiston, as disposition concept, 248

Policy, and "uses of sociology," 38, 42. *See also* Utilization.

Policy centers, 40

Policy science, 7

Political participation, effects of broadcast media on, 301, 313

Political science, 7; and causal analysis, 65

Polytomous variables, 125, 129

"Postindustrial society," 189

Poverty, 249n1; as distinct from unemployment, 287–88

Power, in friendships, 101, 106–7; estimation of, 114–15; and "principle of least interest," 113–14. *See also* Control, types of *and* Effective control.

Prediction, and disposition concepts, 250–54

Preference groups, 207

Preference schedules, and choice, 176–77. *See also* Choice.

Prejudice, relation to discrimination, 250

Prestige, 340; of college professors, 181, 322; NORC ratings of occupational, 181; of professional schools, 341–43, 356; of professions, 341–43, 346–48, 355, 358

Princeton University, 23–24, 332

"principle of least interest" (Waller), 113–14

Probit analysis, 140

Product rule, 139, 144

Professional schools, 339–363; effects of professional and university context on, 339, 341, 345–363; factors affecting graduate training in, 350–53; factors affecting research emphasis in, 353 54; factors affecting faculty recruitment to, 353–57; factors affecting financial condition of, 345–50; for social research, 30–32, 45

Professor, relative occupational prestige of, 322

Proletariat, 193–95, 198–201

Property space, 28

Protocol sentences (Carnap), 11

Pseudonyms, use in social research, 222–224, 228n11

"psychic mobility," 312

Psychoanalysis, 10–11

Psychology, 7–8, 11, 138, 143, 152, 245, 247; influence on Lazarsfeld, 10, 12

Puritanism, and the American colonies, 269–71

Purposive action, models of, 98; applied to marijuana use, 102–15; and causal models, 115; as special case of 16-fold table problem, 99–102. *See also* 16-fold table problem.

Qualitative methods, 20, 207n1; relation to quantitative methods, 20, 218–20. *See also* Methodology.

Quantitative methods, 4, 20, 207n1; relation to qualitative methods, 20, 218–20. *See also* Methodology *and* Mathematical sociology.

Quasi-independence models, 120, 122–25, 133, 133n1, 134n3, 134n6, 135n18; compared to independence models, 124–25; parsimony of, 125–28; relation to scaling models, 120, 128, 132; restricted, 127, 134n7; unrestricted, 127. *See also* Independence models.

Radio, 24, 26, 29, 44; in Third World, 301–2, 305, 313. *See also* Media, broadcast.

Random utility model, 140, 150

Rational action, 11, 99, 143, 151–52, 159; and "disposition" concepts, 255–56. *See also* Purposive action, models of.

Reason analysis, 28

Recruitment, to professional schools, 353–57

Recursive systems, and causal analysis, 239–40, 242n8

Reducibility, and "mechanisms," 70

Reference groups, 52, 61–62

Reference group theory, 196–97; anticipation of in *Marienthal*, 285–86; of conflict, 190, 192, 196, 198, 207

Regression analysis, 63, 86, 233, 344; compared to intuitive causal analysis, 63n4

Regression coefficients, 76, 78–79

Relative deprivation, 43, 52, 285–86

Religion, of American academics, 325–27

Research bureau, Lazarsfeld's concept of, 39. *See also* Bureau of Applied Social Research, Lazarsfeld's role in.

Research emphasis, factors affecting in professional schools, 353–54

Resource stock, concept of in microeconomic theory, 159–60

Response bias, 151

Response bias model, 146–47

Revolution, 197, 200–1; Lazarsfeld's aperçu on, 4

"Rising frustrations," and media in Third World, 312

Rockefeller Foundation, 24

Role conflict, 119, 253–54

Russell Sage Foundation, 38, 45

Sampling, 23, 25, 29, 235–36. *See also* "Chunk."

Scalability, and the "choice axiom," 147–48

Scaling models, 120, 125, 133, 136n23; relation to quasi-independence models, 128; as special kinds of latent structures, 120, 128, 132, 135n18

Sex discrimination in academe, 335–36. *See also* Women, in American professoriate.

Shimer College, 225

Significance tests, 240

16-fold table problem, 98; applied to interdependence of friends in marijuana use, 102–15; Lazarsfeld's contribution to, 98; a special case of, 99–102.

Size, effects of its variation on social life, 340, 353

Socialism, 12, 190, 204; Lazarsfeld's life-long nostalgia for, 226

Social mobility, 60–62, 268–71, 302, 319, 322–23

Social psychology, 4, 7–8, 236

Social stratification, 178–79. *See also* Status *and* Class.

Sociologism, 62

Spatial propinquity, as basis for marking off boundaries of mechanisms, 73. *See also* "Tangible links."

Spurious correlations, 14, 51, 235

State, 303; Hegel's view of, 198; Marx's view of, 198

Statistical significance, 767

Statistical structures: explanations of, 51–52; and "generating theory," 52, 62–63

Statistics, abuses of, 76. *See also* "Automatic science."

Status: and social exchange, 161–74; problems in measuring, 178–84; and vignette analysis, 178–84

St. John's University, 225

"Story line," 7

Strength of association, 79

Structural equation estimation, 65

Student uprisings, at Columbia, 39

Substruction, 29, 234–35

Suicide, Durkheim's approach to, 8

Survey research, 23–24, 51, 284, 340. *See also* Teacher Apprehension Study.

Survey Research Center of the University of California (Berkeley), 33

Survey Research Center of the University of Michigan, 33, 228n13, 235

Survey Research Centre of the Chinese University of Hong Kong, 33

Survey Research Laboratory (University of Illinois), 33

Survey Research Laboratory of the University of Hawaii (Honolulu), 33

Survey Research Laboratory of the University of Wisconsin-Extension, 33

"Tangible links," and specification of "mechanisms," 71, 73–74

Target population, 235

Tautologies, disposition concepts as, 248–49

Teacher Apprehension Study, 210, 213–27

Teacher-student relationships, 232; "imitating," 233–37; "following," 237–40; "taking the role," 233

Television, in Third World, 301, 304–12. *See also* Media, broadcast.

Temporal ordering, and specification of "mechanisms," 71–73

"Terminological embarrassment," of Lazarsfeld, 4, 21

Trade unions, and "economism," 201

"Training documents," 29

Training, graduate: Lazarsfeld and, 29–30

Traits, as dispositions, 246

Transition probabilities, estimation of, 88–90

"Translation problem," Lazarsfeld's concept of, 38, 42. *See also* "Gap," Lazarsfeld's notion of.

T-test, 76

"Two-step flow of communication," 312

Typology construction, 226, 237, 241n5

Unemployment, 4–6, 13, 282–98; absolute versus relative rates of, 285–86; as distinct from poverty, 287–88, 293; effects of, 282–94; Lazarsfeld's early work on, 4–6, 13, 284–89; outlook on life as result of, 290–93; survey research on, 289–93

UNESCO, 301

United Auto Workers, 223

Unity of science, 7–8, 13; Lazarsfeld's work and, 7

"Universal class," concept of in Hegel and Marx, 198; proletariat as, 200, 203

Universalistic values, 119, 129–30

University of Chicago, 25, 212–13, 215, 217, 219, 222, 332

University of Newark, Lazarsfeld's early association with, 23–24

University of Oslo, 21

University of Pittsburgh, Lazarsfeld's association with, 17, 19, 44

University of Vienna, 4

Unobtrusive indicators, 222

Urban ecology. *See* Ecological studies.

Uses of Sociology (Lazarsfeld, *et al.,* eds.), 40–42. *See also* Utilization.

"Uses of Sociology," as theme of 1962 ASA convention, 37–38, Lazarsfeld's list of five, 38

Utility: concept of in microeconomic theory, 159–61; maximization of, 159–61; diminishing marginal, 159

Utility function (in microeconomic theory), 159, 161, 171; Cobb-Douglas, 163–66

Utility model, 139

Utilization, of social research, 37–45; case studies of, 43–44; cognitive aspects of, 42; defined, 37

Values, as dispositions, 246

"Vertical" transfer (Lazarsfeld), 43

Vienna: formative influence on Lazarsfeld, 10–15

Vienna Circle, 10–12

Vienna Institute for Advanced Studies, 33–34, 45

Vignette Analysis, 176–86; advantages of, 178–80; applied to criminal justice, 185; of child abuse, 185; of distributive justice income, 184–85; of household social status ratings, 179–84; Lazarsfeld's contribution to, 177–78; of no-fault divorce, 185; unresolved issues of, 185–86

Voice of America, 299

Voting behavior, 82, 158, 211, 235, 246

VPRES, 181

Weber-Fechner Law, 116n5

Weibull distribution, 152n1

Women, in the American professoriate, 329, 331–36. *See also* Academics, American.

ZPRES, 181